JOSEPH E. JOHNSTON: A CIVIL WAR BIOGRAPHY

JOSEPH E. JOHNSTON

Also by CRAIG L. SYMONDS

Navalists and Antinavalists:
The Naval Policy Debate in the United States, 1785–1827

A Battlefield Atlas of the Civil War

A Battlefield Atlas of the American Revolution

Edited by CRAIG L. SYMONDS

Charleston Blockade:
The Journals of John B. Marchand, U.S. Navy, 1861–62

Recollections of a Naval Officer
by William Harwar Parker

A Year on a Monitor and the Destruction of Fort Sumter
by Alvah Hunter

JOSEPH E. JOHNSTON

A Civil War Biography

CRAIG L. SYMONDS

W·W·NORTON & COMPANY
New York   London

The author gratefully acknowledges permission of the following archives and libraries to publish selections from their collections:

U.S. Army Military History Research Collection, Carlisle Barracks, Pennsylvania
Special Collections Department, William R. Perkins Library, Duke University,
    Durham, North Carolina
Western Reserve Historical Society, Cleveland, Ohio
The Henry E. Huntington Library, San Marino, California
The Earl Gregg Swem Library, College of William & Mary, Williamsburg, Virginia
The West Point Museum, U.S. Military Academy, West Point, New York
The Maryland Historical Society Library, Baltimore, Maryland
Southern Historical Collection, Manuscripts Division, University of North Carolina,
    Chapel Hill, North Carolina

Printed in the United States of America.

The text of this book is composed in Caledonia, with the display set in Nubian
Composition by and manufacturing by The Haddon Craftsmen, Inc.
Book design by Jacques Chazaud.

First Edition

Library of Congress Cataloging-in-Publication Data

Symonds, Craig L.
    Joseph E. Johnston : a Civil War biography / Craig L. Symonds.
        p.   cm.
    Includes bibliographical references and index.
    1. Johnston, Joseph E. (Joseph Eggleston), 1807–1891.
    2. Generals—Confederate States of America—Biography.   3. Generals—United States—
Biography.   4.   Confederate   States   of   America.   Army—Biography.
    5. United States—History—Civil War, 1861–1865—Campaigns.   I. Title.
    E467.1.J74S95 1992
    973.7'3'092—dc20
    [B]   91-17899

ISBN 0-393-03058-X

W.W. Norton & Company, Inc., 500 Fifth Avenue, New York, N.Y. 10
W.W. Norton & Company, Ltd., 10 Coptic Street, London WC1A 1PU

1 2 3 4 5 6 7 8 9 0

For Marylou

Contents

Acknowledgments

Like any author, I owe many debts to individuals who provided help, advice, or encouragement.

First nod must go to Barbara Manvel, Barbara Breeden, and the rest of the staff of the Nimitz Library at the U.S. Naval Academy who helped me with my many interlibrary loan requests. I also want to thank Ellen Strong and the staff of the Manuscripts and Rare Books Room at the Earl Gregg Swem Library at the College of William & Mary; Linda McCurdy and the staff of the William R. Perkins Library at Duke University; Marie Capps and Suzanne Christoff of the U.S. Military Academy Library; Frances McClure of the Walter Havinghurst Special Collections at Miami (Ohio) University; Anna K. Sindelar at the Western Reserve Historical Association; Anne Armour of the Jesse Ball duPont Library at the University of the South; Richard Sommers at the U.S. Army Military History Collection at the Army War College in Carlisle, Pennsylvania; and Harriet McLoone at the Henry E. Huntington Library in San Marino, California. Mary M. Ison, Head of the Prints and Photographs Reading Room at the Library of Congress, was very helpful in identifying illustrations. I was the recipient of cheerful and efficient service from the staffs of the Pennsylvania Historical Society in Philadelphia, the New York Public Library, the always-helpful Manuscripts Reading Room staff at the Library of Congress, and the staff of the National Archives.

I was enriched by a day spent with Mr. L. C. Angle, Jr., president of the Washington County Historical Society, for the insight he provided about the early history of Abingdon, Virginia, during a tour of that charming city, and I am indebted to him as well for his help in obtaining photos of both Panecillo and Peter Johnston. Thanks, too, to Polly Boggess, Executive Director of the Crown Gardens & Archives in Dalton, Georgia. I am indebted to Gary Gallagher for allowing me prepublication access to the Porter Alexander manuscript which became *Fighting for the Confederacy,* to Richard M. McMurry for lending me his transcription of the original Thomas B. Mackall Journal, and to Steven Newton of Clarion University for allowing me access to his manuscript on Johnston's campaign on the Yorktown peninsula. Thanks, too, to Joseph S. Johnston for permission to examine family papers, and to Lynn and Anne Krause for the etching of Joe Johnston.

Several Civil War scholars have read portions of the manuscript and offered invaluable advice. James L. Morrison read the chapter on West Point; Larry Daniel looked at the chapters on Vicksburg; Steven Newton read the chapters on the peninsular campaign and Seven Pines; Richard McMurry examined the chapters on the campaign in North Georgia; both Gary Gallagher and Archer Jones read the entire manuscript. This book is much improved by their suggestions, but of course the interpretations, right or wrong, are my own.

My colleagues in the History Department at the Naval Academy have encouraged me and offered helpful advice and thoughtful criticism. In particular, the members of the Works-in-Progress faculty seminar group read portions of the manuscript and made useful suggestions. Working in a community of scholars was both inspiring and fulfilling.

I am again indebted to Bill Clipson for his superb rendering of the twenty maps in the book. Thanks, too, to my editor at Norton, Steve Forman, who continually encouraged me to expand the scope of the narrative and place Joe Johnston in a broader context, and to Ann Adelman who tried to control my tendency to overwrite.

And, finally, I offer my thanks and gratitude to my wife, Marylou, who listened patiently to drafts of the manuscript, travelled with me to archives and battlefields, and to whom this book is dedicated.

Craig L. Symonds
Annapolis, Spring 1991

Maps

JOSEPH E. JOHNSTON

Prologue

Joseph E. Johnston and History

He was the first graduate in the history of the Military Academy at West Point to be promoted to a general's rank in the regular army. He was the most senior U.S. Army officer to resign his commission and "go South" to fight for the Confederacy in 1861. He was the only man to command both of the Confederacy's principal field armies—the Army of Northern Virginia in 1861–62, and the Army of Tennessee in 1864. He won the South's first victory, at Manassas in July 1861, and its last, at Bentonville, North Carolina, in April 1865. Many of his contemporaries considered him to be the greatest southern field commander of the war; others ranked him second—and not by much—only to his West Point classmate Robert E. Lee. Both Ulysses S. Grant and William Tecumseh Sherman considered him the most skillful opponent they faced during the war.

And yet Joseph E. Johnston is strangely absent from the pantheon of Confederate heroes, a pantheon that is dominated by Robert E. Lee and "Stonewall" Jackson, both of whom are frozen in idealized bas-relief along with Jefferson Davis at Stone Mountain, Georgia, east of Atlanta. Lee's memory is sacred at Washington and Lee University, as is Jackson's at V.M.I. Other Confederate heroes include a number of men who served under Johnston and who greatly admired him, men like Jeb Stuart and A. P. Hill, P. G. T. Beauregard and Albert Sidney Johnston (no relation). Many would include even John Bell Hood, whose brash and irresponsible leadership destroyed the army that he inherited from Joe Johnston. All of these men are remembered in monuments and memorials from Fort Hood in Texas to Fort A. P. Hill in Virginia.

For much of the late nineteenth century, Johnston shared in the South's deification of its heroes. Many of the popular group portraits of the postwar years linked Johnston with Robert E. Lee and "Stonewall" Jackson as the unofficial trinity of the South. But after the turn of the century, he was included less frequently. Today, there is but one statue of Joe Johnston in the Old South. It is on the main street of Dalton, Georgia, where he made his headquarters during the winter of 1863–64. He stands there now, staring eastward—looking, a wag would say, for a line of retreat in case the Yankees outflanked his position. During spring break not long ago, students from the local junior college sold T-shirts depicting Johnston's figure in swim trunks and holding a cooler. It is an indignity he would have felt deeply, for his public image was important to him.

Aside from that one statue, and a bust in the Virginia state capitol at Richmond, there are few extant reminders of Johnston's role in the American Civil War. There is no monument to him at his birthplace near Farmville, Virginia, no statue of him to commemorate his victory at Manassas, or at Seven Pines where he fell wounded and had to be carried from the field; there is no memorial at Kennesaw Mountain, at Bentonville, or anywhere else. The explanation is that Americans, North and South, have had trouble understanding who he was and in agreeing about what he did. The public record is clear enough. His long list of campaigns fills up the entries dedicated to him in encyclopedias. But the man himself has been difficult to illuminate. One reason is that he left behind few private letters: a handful to his brothers, a few dozen to his friends, and a score or so to his wife. And even in these he is reserved, as if holding something back or unwilling to reveal his inner self too clearly. When in 1887 a prospective biographer wrote to ask him where he could find information about his life, Johnston wrote back, "I am afraid . . . that the difficulty of finding 'data' will make you drop the enterprize."

Another reason for Johnston's relative obscurity is that his record of performance during the Civil War has provoked wide disagreement. He commanded Confederate armies in four battles—Manassas (1861), Seven Pines (1862), Kennesaw Mountain (1864), and Bentonville (1865). He, at least, counted all four as Confederate victories. But none of them was decisive, and in between he avoided as many battles as he fought. He failed to save Pemberton at Vicksburg in 1863, and he retreated deep into the heart of Georgia in front of Sherman's inexorable advance in 1864. Throughout much of the war, he was troublesome, secretive, and occasionally sullen in his relations with the Confederate president, Jefferson Davis.

As a result, historians are divided in evaluating his contribution to the Confederate war effort. Some have praised him as the South's only true strategic genius, a man who knew better than either Davis or Lee what the Confederacy needed to do to win. That he was not heeded, his champions assert, is the great tragedy of the Confederacy, for it led ultimately and inevitably to the South's defeat. Because Jefferson Davis was the man who did not listen, who instead dismissed Johnston from his command at a crucial point in the war, Johnston's admirers have often concentrated on attacking Davis. Other historians dismiss Johnston as a man who talked a good game and was popular with his troops, but who was simply too timid to fight. Like George McClellan, a close friend from the Old Army, Johnston could organize an army, feed it, inspire it, and maneuver it—but, these critics say, he was a man who could not or would not fight. "Retreatin' Joe," he is called: all bluster and protest, but no fight.

Both sides exaggerate. No single judgment can capture this complex man. To assess him as a soldier, it is necessary to understand him as a man. This book, therefore, is not merely a chronicle of his military campaigns, but a history of his life. As reticent as he was about his private self, he nevertheless left behind fragments of a mosaic that, when filled in with the official accounts, begins to exhibit the outlines of an accomplished, flawed individual.

Several threads run through this narrative. The one great tragedy of Johnston's professional life—and it was crucial—was his feud with President Jefferson Davis. There can be no doubt that their mutual distrust and suspicion was largely responsible for the crisis in command that ensured the collapse of the Confederacy's western campaign in 1864. The president's relations with all of his generals were complicated by the fact that he was a West Point graduate and a genuine hero of the Mexican War, who considered his designation as commander-in-chief to be more than a courtesy. He concerned himself more with detailed military planning than was usual for a head of state. Some field commanders resented this, and a few made their resentment known. But no other general managed to provoke Davis the way Johnston did. From the first summer of the war, when Johnston objected to Davis's ranking him below three other officers, their feud became increasingly personal and engendered a deep mutual distrust that made effective cooperation impossible. As others took sides in the dispute, Johnston became a rallying point for political opponents of the administration. Texas Senator Louis T. Wigfall was Johnston's particular champion in Richmond, and although Wigfall's admiration and affection were genuine, his advocacy of Johnston's cause made Johnston the focus of a political schism in the government.

Johnston's relationship with his West Point classmate Robert E. Lee is another thread in his life's story. "I loved and admired him more than any man in the world," Johnston wrote of his friend. But as their careers diverged, they became rivals, and ultimately there crept into Johnston's references to Lee a note of envy and resentment. Lee took over the command of

Johnston's army after the Battle of Seven Pines, where Johnston was wounded, and built a near-mystical reputation by winning unlikely victories against long odds. In the end, although Johnston was never reconciled with Davis, he did overcome his envy of Lee; during the last months of the war, and in the postwar years, they were again comrades.

Finally, there is Johnston's relationship with his wife Lydia. A partner in all his battles—political and military—Lydia followed him whenever she could, and was his staunch defender against all detractors. Her poor health was a burden for them both, and may have been the reason they never had children. In the postwar years they spent a great deal of time at health spas and springs seeking relief for Lydia's ailments. When she died in 1887, Johnston was left truly alone. He followed her to the grave four years later.

Johnston worried about his place in history. Almost from the moment the war ended, he began to collect the official papers that he believed would demonstrate the correctness of his actions and the unfairness of Davis's treatment of him. Alas, his turgid *Narrative of Military Operations* (1874) did little to succor his reputation as a soldier, and much to expose his weaknesses as a writer. Since then, he has been the subject of three biographies. The first appeared in 1891, the year of his death, and is more an extended eulogy than a biography. The second, published only six years later as part of a series on Confederate commanders, is no more satisfying. Then, in 1956, Gilbert E. Govan and James W. Livingood published a lengthy biography entitled *A Different Valor.* They carefully mined the sources and chronicled the events of Johnston's life, but in the process they became advocates in his feud with Davis, and as a result they spent nearly as much energy denigrating Davis as they did delineating Johnston. As Frank Vandiver wrote in his introduction to the 1959 edition of Johnston's *Narrative,* "They described him, sympathized with him, went with him into battle, and yet failed to understand him." For the student of the Civil War, Joe Johnston remains largely an enigma—idealized by a few, vilified or dismissed by many others, ignored by most.

This book is his story.

PART ONE

CASTLES

IN THE AIR

CHAPTER ONE

West Point

In June 1825, a favorite subject of conversation for many Americans was how John Quincy Adams had "stolen" the recent presidential election from Andrew Jackson. Although Jackson had clearly won the popular vote—the first time that particular statistic was even tabulated—the presence of four candidates in the field meant that no one of them had received a majority of the electoral votes. The election had been thrown into the House of Representatives, which chose Adams by the narrowest of margins. The new president took the oath of office in March, but Jackson and most of his supporters had not yet reconciled themselves to the result, and looked upon Adams's occupation of the White House as a usurpation.

Another popular topic that month was the visit of the Marquis de Lafayette, a hero of two revolutions, who was travelling city-to-city on a triumphal tour of America that had begun the previous year and showed no sign of abating. Lafayette had spent the fall and winter receiving the accolades of Americans from Boston to New Orleans and discussing old times with both John Adams (the elderly father of the new president) and Thomas Jefferson, each man then within a year of his death. By June 1825 Lafayette had completed another swing through the South and was back in New England laying the cornerstone of the University of Vermont.

News of other events occasionally intruded: Bolivia and Peru had won their independence from Spain; the Greeks continued to fight the Turks in a war that had claimed the life of Lord Byron and inspired Eugène Delacroix to paint *The Massacre at Chios,* one of the works that would open the way from romantic to impressionist art.

That same June, eighteen-year-old Joseph Eggleston Johnston boarded a steamboat in New York Harbor for a thirty-five-mile trip up the Hudson River to the United States Military Academy at West Point. It was an occasion unmarked by ceremony; indeed, it is unlikely that any of Johnston's fellow passengers took notice of him at all. There was no reason they should, for there was nothing particularly striking about him. He was of medium height: about five foot seven (though he carried himself with such assurance that he was often described as being taller) and rail thin. Neither were his features extraordinary: he had deep brown eyes, a broad forehead, and he wore his brown hair cropped close. Challenged to come up with a distinguishing characteristic, a casual observer might have offered the opinion that despite his age, this young man wore an expression of profound seriousness. On this day Joe Johnston was on especially serious business, for his journey to West Point as a potential member of the United States Military Academy class of 1829 was clearly the most important event of his life to that moment.

In many ways Joseph E. Johnston had been preparing for West Point all his life. His pedigree was certainly adequate. His grandfather, Peter Johnston, had emigrated to Virginia from Scotland in 1726. Settling near Petersburg, he prospered in the merchant trade. During the Revolution he sided with the Patriot cause, and his eldest son, also named Peter, ran away from home at the age of sixteen to join the rebel army. This younger Peter served in the brigade of "Light Horse Harry" Lee, the daring cavalry leader of the southern campaigns and the father of Robert E. Lee. After the war, this young runaway, now Lieutenant Peter Johnston, married Mary Valentine Wood, the niece of Patrick Henry, and brought her home to the family estate of Longwood in Prince George County near Farmville. The couple's first child, named Martha, died in infancy, but then they were blessed by a succession of healthy babies—all of them boys—the seventh (but not the last) of whom was born on February 3, 1807, and christened Joseph Eggleston in honor of the man who had been Peter's squad commander during the war.

In 1811, Peter Johnston was elected a judge of the General Court and assigned a circuit in central Virginia. But eager, perhaps, for new challenges, he traded circuits with Judge William Brokenbrough and moved his family to Abingdon, a small, genteel community in the mountains of southwest Virginia only half a dozen miles from the Tennessee border and more than three hundred miles from the nearest city. A mile east of town, on a small rise that overlooked the principal road into Abingdon, Peter Johnston and his older sons constructed a two-story log house. It was a modest home at first, and certainly no match for the grand brick houses built in the popular Federalist style along Valley Road where the town's wealthy lived. Later, however, the Johnstons added an extension off the back and a decorative porch on the front, and covered the logs with planking which was then whitewashed to present a much finer appearance. Fireplaces at each end provided heat, while the cooking was done in a small outbuilding. In that home, which Peter rather grandly named Panecillo, Joe Johnston spent his formative years.[1]

Judge Johnston became prominent in Abingdon society. He presided over the meetings of the County Court (where his portrait still hangs in pride of place over the judicial bench), and he was invited to join the board of trustees of the Abingdon Academy, the school where the Johnston boys were educated. Joe admired his patriarchal father and worshipped his gentle and "most virtuous" mother. His oldest brother, John Warfield Johnston, at twenty-one already an adult when the family moved to Abingdon, was more like an uncle than a brother to Joe. For most of his life, in fact, Joe was closer to John's wife, Louisa, who was an older sister to him, a confidante and adviser. Beverly, who was three years older, and Ben, who was eighteen months younger, were the two brothers closest to him in age, and along with his cousin John Preston, were his most frequent playmates.[2]

Abingdon was both a frontier town and a thriving center of nineteenth-century American culture when the Johnstons moved there in 1811. A half century earlier, Daniel Boone had stopped at the site on his first trip across the Blue Ridge and named it Wolf Hill, allegedly because wolves from a nearby den had attacked his dogs. Less than a decade later, building lots were being sold to settlers. In 1776 the settlers built a fort, and two years afterward they gave the town its name. By 1811, when Judge Peter Johnston brought his large and still growing family there (Jane, the only daughter, would be born that November), Abingdon was cosmopolitan enough that the town council felt obliged to order the mayor to establish a citizen's group "to patrol the town of nights" to ensure evening quiet. The three-story brick buildings along Main Street testified to Abingdon's new commercial importance as a stopping point between the eastern seaboard and the trans-Allegheny settlements in Tennessee and Kentucky, and the imposing homes along Valley Road one block to the north gave evidence of the pretensions of Abingdon society. Where only fifty years before Daniel Boone's dogs had contested the ground with the local wolves, the leading families of Abingdon now hosted "levees" on Friday evenings and sought membership in the new Masonic Lodge on the corner of Court and Water Streets.

Young Joe and his brothers grew up amidst the contradictory influences of the Appalachian frontier and Abingdon society. Like other Abingdon boys, they learned to ride, to shoot, and to cope with the rough and tumble life of the frontier where courage and boldness were particularly admired. On a few occasions they even trekked over the mountains into Tennessee, ostensibly under the watchful eye of a family slave, but in fact almost completely on their own. On one such journey, while riding two-to-a-horse behind his cousin John Preston, Joe was thrown and fell awkwardly to the ground, breaking his leg. It was a bad break—the naked bone stuck out prominently through the skin. But Joe retained his coolness: "Hello, boys," he called out. "Come here and look—the confounded bone has come clear through." It was hardly a laughing matter, for if the bone were not set properly he might be crippled for life. With no other option, the boys took turns carrying him on their shoulders to the nearest doctor, miles away. Despite having to be manhandled for hours over rough country trails, Joe never cried out. Such bravado reflected Joe's acceptance of the frontier values of quiet courage and stoicism, and established his local reputation for personal bravery.[3]

In addition to trips into the wilderness, another of Joe's favorite boyhood activities was to reenact the Battle of King's Mountain, the Revolutionary War conflict that had destroyed the forces of Tory leader Major Patrick Ferguson in 1780 and started Cornwallis on the road that would lead him eventually to Yorktown. The Patriot army in that battle had been drawn largely from the nearby Watauga and Nolichuky River settlements, and over the years of retelling the battle had grown to heroic proportions. More than any of his brothers, Joe avidly absorbed these stories; no doubt he spent idle hours exploring the glade south of town where the King's Mountain volunteers had gathered. From a very young age, he came to look upon the great achievements of military leaders as the most important measure of man's triumphs. In recognition of this bent, and perhaps to encourage it, when Joe was only eight years old, his father presented him with the military sword that he had carried in the Revolution, even though six older brothers stood ahead of him in right of inheritance. That sword, and all that the young boy believed it stood for, remained one of Joseph E. Johnston's icons throughout his life.[4]

But life was not all wilderness adventures and war games for Joe and his brothers. Judge Johnston and his wife were strong advocates of formal education, and there was never any question but that their sons would go to school. Joe's early education was conducted at the Abingdon Academy. Established less than a decade before the Johnstons moved to town, the Academy was a typical boys' school in which the master, the Reverend Thomas Erskine Birch, charged from ten to twenty dollars a year to serve (as his advertisement read) "the American Youth who thirst for literacy acquirement." His announcement promised that at the Abingdon Academy, "the muses are about to pour out their treasures from the Pierian Spring in this seminary." The curriculum tended strongly toward the three Rs, but more advanced students (those capable of paying the twenty-dollar tuition) could study "Elocution, Philosophy, Belles Letters, and Astronomy, Bookkeeping, Geography and Navigation &c." Notably absent was any reference to higher mathematics or foreign language. As in most such schools, the goal was as much to inculcate the discipline of learning as to challenge the intellect.[5]

There is no record of Joe Johnston's performance at the Abingdon Academy, but his strong sense of determination probably ensured that his work was satisfactory at least. He was motivated to do well, for he had decided to apply for admission to the United States Military Academy at West Point. His academic preparation was as adequate as most applicants at West Point. In a letter of enquiry about the nominating process for West Point, Judge Johnston informed Secretary of War John C. Calhoun that his son's "literary attainments are . . . at least equal to those of most young gentlemen of his years." More to the point, the judge noted that the prospective candidate was "the son of a father who served in the continental army" and that "no cadet has ever been admitted at the military school from this section of Virginia." Calhoun apparently found such arguments convincing, for he dispatched the nomination a few days before the end of his term as Secretary of War and before he took office as vice president. Joseph received the letter on March 3—the day before Adams and Calhoun were inaugurated—and the next day he responded that he accepted the appointment "cheerfully."[6]

Since the roads to West Point—little more than trails—were impassable by wheeled vehicles, almost all prospective cadets travelled to the Military Academy by steamboat from New York. As his vessel left Manhattan Island behind, Johnston may have marvelled at the technology that could propel a steam vessel upriver at the impressive rate of fifteen miles an hour. Ten miles upstream, the vessel passed between Fort Washington on the east bank and Fort Lee on the west, both of which had been captured by Lord Howe's British army in 1776. Another ten miles to the north, the river broadened to a width of two miles before it passed Stony Point, where "Mad Anthony" Wayne had surprised the British in 1779. Another half dozen miles upriver, the Hudson narrowed again at Verplanck's Point and bent westward around the broad shoulder of Dunderburg Mountain. Just beyond that, probably at about the point where Henry Hudson had decided that this was not the Northwest Passage after all, Johnston espied for the first time the high plain where sat the fort that Benedict Arnold had tried to turn over to the British in 1780, and which Congress in 1802 had designated as the nation's Military Academy.

Since West Point was not yet a regular stop on the Hudson River steamship lines, Johnston disembarked into a small skiff and was rowed ashore to the tiny dock at the foot of the bluff. After he climbed the steeply sloping path, he got his first look at his home for the next four years. The physical setting was positively inspiring: an open plain backed by high hills and crowned by the ruins of old Fort Putnam overlooking the majestic Hudson River. The Academy itself was less impressive. To his left were the ruins of Fort Clinton, to his right the gray stone buildings of the cadet barracks, and stretching out in front of him was the open field that served as campsite and drillfield for the corps.[7].

The idea of a school for the training and education of officers in the American Army dated back to the Revolution. The notion had received further consideration during the military preparations that preceded the Quasi War with France in 1798, but the institution did not receive official sanction until March 1802, when Congress decreed that an Engineering Corps should be established at West Point. For fifteen years the school struggled along with indifferent success, until the arrival of Sylvanus Thayer as Superintendent in 1817. Himself a graduate (class of 1807), Thayer had served in the War of 1812 against the British, and in 1815 he went to France to learn as much as he could from the military system of the great Napoleon. Somewhat frustrated at first because the victorious English and Prussian allies had shut down many of the sites he wanted to visit, Thayer finally had an opportunity to visit the *Ecole Polytechnique*. After two years there he returned to the United States brimming with ideas of how to improve—indeed, virtually revolutionize—military education in the United States. His appointment as Superintendent in 1817 gave him the chance, and by 1825, when Joe Johnston of Virginia received his nomination as a cadet, the new system was fully in place.[8]

The Napoleonic wars had proven, to Thayer's satisfaction at least, that mastery of the art of war meant mastery of the principles of engineering. Fortifications, bridges, and the successful employment of artillery—these were the critical elements of modern warfare, and they required a command of two things: mathematics—because the principles of engineering could not be comprehended otherwise; and French—because, Waterloo notwithstanding, Thayer believed that all the important military texts came from the French. Moreover, Thayer was convinced that the way to ensure the highest standards among students of the military art was to judge and grade the performance of every cadet every day. By pitting them against one another academically, the strongest would rise to the top, and the weakest would be revealed—publicly. At the end of four years of this kind of competition, only the very best would be selected into the prestigious Corps of Engineers, the aristocracy of the U.S. Army. For Johnston and his classmates in the class of 1829, the testing began almost at once.

A total of 105 young men received appointments to the class of 1829, nine of them Virginians. But all of their appointments, including Johnston's, were conditional on passing a preliminary exam. For him as for most others, that first test proved to be largely perfunctory. The cadets were asked to read a few sentences from a history book to ensure that they were literate, and to solve a simple arithmetic problem. Those who successfully completed these tasks assembled at eight in the morning on June 28 in front of the cadet barracks where, while they stood at attention, an officer read off the names of those who had passed. At the sound of his name, Johnston stepped forward and joined eighty-six other cadets as a member of the class of 1829. He took the formal oath along with the rest of his class on July 1, 1825, and stood in line to receive his first uniform issue, which included, among other more mundane items, "1 black leather cap, bell crown, seven inches high with a semi-circular visor of strong leather highly polished; diamond shaped yellow plate, black plume, eight inches long; leather cockade, two and a half inches diameter, with a small yellow eagle; yellow scales to fasten in front, or under the chin." The very next day he put on his new full dress uniform, including the spectacular cap, to participate in a formal parade in honor of Lafayette, who was continuing his seemingly endless tour of the United States.[9]

Johnston's home as a first-year cadet, or plebe, was a tent pitched on the plain. Every June the corps of cadets moved out of the barracks and into a canvas encampment. A virtual tent city sprang up, dubbed "Camp Adams" that summer in honor of the new president. The plebes' summer regiment consisted mostly of close order drill—four and a half hours a day—under the direction of the upperclassmen. Physical "hazing" was officially banned as it was Thayer's philosophy that while direct competition was healthy, personal abuse had no place in the brotherhood of the corps; berating or humiliating the plebes carried the threat of immediate dismissal. There was, however, plenty of marching. Johnston's day began at sunrise, and drill commenced at 5:30 A.M. For three periods a day—from five-thirty to seven in the morning, from noon to one, and again from five to seven in the evening—the plebes marched and countermarched across the plain under the critical eyes of the first class cadets. The most exalted of all the first classmen that summer was the Cadet Adjutant, Albert Sidney Johnston of Louisiana (no relation to Joe), who was tall and imposing in his first classman's uniform with its rows of inverted chevrons.[10]

Besides the drill and the intimidating presence of the first classmen, the plebes also had to contend with the dust, the stifling heat, and the ubiquitous insects. The canvas tents only intensified the heat and screened the cooling breezes, without providing much useful shade or protection from the insects. The plebes' woolen uniforms with their tight collars were particularly uncomfortable in the summer humidity. Cadets had permission to "bathe"— that is, to swim in the Hudson River—but when they became too boisterous in their frolicking, as often happened, such privileges were suspended. Only infrequently did a summer rain squall blow in to halt most of the activities, leaving behind the blessed feeling of cooler air and the fetid aroma of wet wool.[11]

One such storm swept through on the last Sunday in July. Rain thundered down in such torrents that it virtually flooded many of the tents in Camp Adams. The plebes, including Johnston, simply made the best they could of the break in routine, but a few of the more daring upperclassmen sneaked away from camp in an effort to find more secure shelter. Five second-year students, or yearlings, all southerners, found a refuge in Benny Havens's public house about two miles away near Buttermilk Falls. Later to become a West Point landmark, Benny Havens's tavern had been open only a few years in the summer of 1825 and was strictly off limits. The five cadets were sitting at a table enjoying rounds of cider (according to them), or spiritous liquors (according to others), when the tactical officer, Captain Ethan Allen Hitchcock, walked in and caught them red-handed. Hitchcock immediately placed the five cadets under arrest and the next day he filed formal charges. The ensuing court-martial was the talk of the camp for weeks.

The court-martial was convened two days later, and after lengthy testimony all five were found guilty and sentenced to dismissal. Three of them were actually dismissed. One of the others, Samuel Hays of Tennessee, who was Andrew Jackson's nephew and ward, was forgiven, although he later resigned anyway. The last defendant was Jefferson Davis of Mississippi. Davis's sentence was remitted, in part because of his good record, but also because of his soldierly demeanor before the court. During his defense, Davis argued, somewhat legalistically, that the Academy's rule proscribing visits to "any inn, public house, or place where any . . . liquors are sold" had not been properly announced to the corps. The argument was dubious at best, but it served its purpose.[12]

What Johnston thought of Davis's escapade, or his defense, is not recorded, but it is not hard to imagine that he found it all rather distasteful. Johnston's own conduct record is the paper trail of a cadet so well behaved as to be almost invisible. He received not a single demerit that summer, and only seven during the ensuing academic year. Indeed, over the full four years of his life at West Point, the *Register of Cadet Delinquencies* lists only fourteen infractions for Joseph E. Johnston. Other cadets in his class filled several columns with charges: "use of tobacco," "absent from class," "neglect of duty," "disorderly conduct," and so on. None of these charges appears on the mostly blank page dedicated to the misdemeanors of Joseph E. Johnston. The most serious infraction listed there is "absent from parade," a notation which appears twice—once when Johnston was a plebe, once when he was a firstie.[13]

Johnston never joined Davis's circle of friends even though it was composed almost exclusively of southerners, including at least one of Johnston's fellow Virginians in the class of 1829. There is no evidence that Johnston ever even visited Benny Havens's; he simply moved in entirely different circles than Davis. His seriousness of purpose led him to take West Point and its rules of behavior to heart. By contrast, Davis's narrow escape from dismissal that summer did not deter him from further escapades. On a later visit to Benny Havens's, Davis avoided discovery only by diving off the road as a group of officers approached from the other direction. Alas, his plunge in the dark took him over the edge of a cliff and he was so badly injured that he required hospitalization. Johnston may have concluded that it served him right.[14]

At last the long summer of drill came to an end. Cooler breezes off the river announced the onset of autumn and the return of those upperclassmen who had been granted summer furloughs. There were several names at West Point that fall that would later become famous. Johnston noticed the other Virginians in particular: Philip St. George Cooke and William Magruder in the class of 1827, and Hugh Mercer, who would graduate third in the class of 1828.

Classes began in September. As an academic institution, West Point was unique not only in that it was a military school, but in the content of its curriculum. While almost every other college in the nation emphasized the classics—especially Greek and Latin literature—West Point's curriculum reflected Sylvanus Thayer's determination to ignore the classics in order to concentrate on mathematics, engineering, and natural science. First-year cadets studied mathematics and French almost exclusively.

In mathematics, the fourth class cadets—or plebes—were arranged into classes alphabetically, but gradually over the first several weeks they were sorted out by ability into sections of about twenty men each. Johnston found himself relegated to the second section. Instead of receiving his instruction from Lieutenant Dennis Hart Mahan, therefore, he suffered under the tutelage of First Class Cadet Alexander H. Bowman.° Instruction began at 8:00 A.M. Half of the class worked problems at the chalkboard while the rest studied; after an hour and a half, the students changed places for another ninety minutes. Johnston was more dogged than brilliant. The Abingdon Academy, with its emphasis on reading, writing, and simple calculations, had not prepared him for the standard texts, Lacroix's *Algebra* or Legendre's *Geometry*.[15]

Johnston was better at French, which he studied from noon to one and again from two to four. Although he started slowly, he soon learned to love the language, and became quite fluent. He excelled at reading and translating French books on fortification and engineering—the main objective in the course at West Point. Before long he had worked himself up into the first section in French, where he learned from Professor Claudius Berard and read the *Histoire de Gil Blas*, an eighteenth-century romantic novel by Alain-René La Sage, as well as Voltaire's *Histoire de Charles XII*, a biography of the great Swedish commander of the early eighteenth century. Such fare was appealing to Johnston, an apostle of Homer and an avid reader of Scott's romances since his boyhood. Eventually Johnston developed a lifelong fondness for French, especially French history. In his later years his library was dominated by military histories, biographies of French military leaders, and volumes on French military engineering, all well thumbed and often annotated.[16]

Like many others, young Cadet Johnston often felt alone in his first year at the Military Academy. His sense of isolation was reinforced by the impact of a deep personal blow in November, when he learned that his mother had died. The news cast him into deep melancholy. "How is it possible," he wrote in despair, "for me to bear the loss of such a mother, the best, the tenderest, and the most virtuous, with other than the greatest anguish?" Of

---

°Civil War historians have often speculated about the influence that Mahan's views on war had on a generation of West Point cadets. Lieutenant Mahan, however, left West Point for Europe in 1825 and did not return until 1830, after Johnston graduated. Thus Cadet Johnston and the other members of the class of 1829 had no opportunity to be influenced by his strategic theories.

course he had no choice but to continue with the daily drill and regimen of West Point, but the demands of plebe year seemed even more daunting now. In a letter to his sister-in-law Louisa he indulged himself in his melancholy: "Alone, without a single friend to sympathize in my grief, surrounded and almost distracted by the noise and laughter of idle young men far differently situated from myself, my situation is rendered still more miserable by the contrast between their feelings and my own."[17]

For Johnston and the rest of the plebes, the first big academic hurdle was the January examinations. The exams were oral, not written, but that only intensified the fear of the cadets, who faced the members of the examining board in small groups. Thayer and his professors, all of them in full uniform, sat at one large table. Thayer called in the cadets, six at a time, and directed each to a chalkboard where he was assigned individual problems to work, in public, while the examiners watched. As one cadet recited his answer, the other five worked furiously at the chalkboards on their solutions. When they finished with one cadet, the questioners passed on to the next. The process was as demanding of the faculty as of the students. The exams began at eight in the morning and lasted until long after dark, and they went on for three full weeks.[18]

The last to be examined, Johnston and his fellow plebes waited nervously, studying French verbs and working geometry problems. When his turn came—finally—Johnston performed indifferently in mathematics, ranking in the lower half of the class, but he did much better in French, ranking 24th. Overall, Johnston's academic performance in January was adequate but hardly stellar. By the end of the year, however, after the June exams, he had pulled himself up to rank a respectable 27th out of the eighty-five who remained. In conduct, the straitlaced Johnston did better, ranking 26th out of the whole corps of 222, ahead of such luminaries as Albert Sidney Johnston (29th) and considerably ahead of Jefferson Davis, who ranked 156th.[19]

Over time, some of the plebes decided that West Point was not the experience they had anticipated, and they left. Others "washed out" academically over the next three years. Of the nine Virginians who came to West Point in June 1825, only two would graduate with the class. One was Johnston; the other was Robert E. Lee. That these two young men should have become friends was natural enough. Johnston, at least, was acutely aware that their fathers had served together during the Revolution. But even without that connection there was much to draw them together. Both were Virginians, both were intelligent and ambitious, both avoided the kinds of illicit activities that earned demerits, and both were good students, although Lee was clearly the superior of the two. Johnston greatly admired his classmate. Later in life he admitted to a friend that "In youth and early manhood I loved and admired him more than any man in the world." That there was also an element of rivalry between the two was natural. The very nature of Thayer's system encouraged—even required—competition: at drill, in the classroom, on the athletic field. In such competitions Johnston did well, but never as

well as Lee. Although Lee was in every case gracious and seemingly oblivi-
ous to his easy successes, they may have seemed to Johnston living proof of
what many Virginians believed and what Johnston himself may have
feared—the natural supremacy of the Tidewater over the Piedmont. Joe and
Robert were comrades, but they were also rivals.[20]

In academics, Lee outperformed Johnston in both mathematics and
French, and even in conduct. Lee finished his plebe year ranked third in
academics and fifth in conduct. Over the next three years, while Johnston
improved his standing in the class—from 27th as a plebe, to 17th as a year-
ling, and to 13th as a firstie—he could never come close to Lee's record of
achievement. Johnston's was a commendable academic record, envied, no
doubt, by those beneath him in the "Roll of the Cadets." But it was no threat
to Lee, who finished the four years second academically behind the almost-
mystical academic performance of Charles Mason of New York.[21]

During their second year, Lee, Johnston, and the rest of the class of 1829
added drawing to their study of mathematics and French, and the next year
they took up natural philosophy, chemistry, and minerology. By their first
class year, the curriculum was almost exclusively engineering. The engineering course included instruction in the building of roads and runnels, railroad
beds and trestles, and artificial harbors. Johnston did well in engineering, but
he remained strongest in French. He also did well in tactics, the most "military" subject, and he performed adequately in artillery, rhetoric and moral
philosophy, and chemistry and minerology. But he continued to do poorly in
math, and he was nearly hopeless in drawing. Johnston's best grade was in
conduct—a category that encompassed military bearing and behavior, and
that was achieved by avoiding the kind of violations that earned demerits.
Johnston was a good student—certainly better than average—and his steady
improvement over the four years suggests that he was dogged in the pursuit
of his studies.[22]

West Point was not all academics, of course, and its unique mission made
leadership within the corps as important to budding officers as their performance in the classroom. Like all cadets, Johnston had an opportunity to demonstrate his leadership potential by exercising responsibility as an officer in
the corps of cadets. First classmen could aspire to the rank of cadet lieutenant or captain, or even to the most exalted rank of all: Adjutant of the Corps.
Selected second classmen served as cadet sergeants, and a few third classmen, or yearlings, as cadet corporals. Johnston's sterling conduct record
made him a candidate for selection as a cadet officer, and he donned the
chevrons of a cadet sergeant in the First Company in June 1827, at the
beginning of his third summer at the Point. Johnston retained his chevrons
through the ensuing academic year, and at the end of that year he was
promoted to cadet lieutenant in the Third Company. His friend and erst-
while rival Robert E. Lee was named Adjutant.

Lee presided over the corps that summer, and Johnston served as one of the cadet officers who helped run the camp, designated this year as "Camp Brown" in honor of the recently deceased General Jacob Brown, a War of 1812 veteran who had been general-in-chief since 1821. There is no record of Johnston's performance in that assignment, but there is a tantalizing hint that he may not have performed to everyone's satisfaction. When the list of cadet officers for the full academic year was announced at the end of August, Johnston's name was not on it. Lee remained as Adjutant and most of his staff also kept their jobs; all four cadet captains retained their posts; and of the sixteen cadet lieutenants, only two were not reappointed. One was Simon H. Drum, who became a member of the color guard, and the other was Johnston, who received no office at all. Of course there were many other first classmen who did not hold cadet rank that year, but none of them had previously held rank only to have it withdrawn. What Johnston had done to merit such a dubious distinction, or what he thought of it, the official records do not reveal.[23]

It is not inconceivable that Johnston's very seriousness of purpose may have contributed to his fall from grace. Although he never rose above the rank of cadet lieutenant, his earnestness earned him a different rank as a nickname—his classmates called him "the Colonel." This may have been a reflection of their respect for his leadership, but perhaps Johnston's peers also sought to mock him gently for his somber demeanor, for the tag implied fastidiousness and old age. Colonels in the U.S. Army of the 1820s were ancient, dignified souls, and despite his youth, Johnston was a model of restraint and dignity. Colonel Thayer and his staff may have believed that Johnston was taking his cadet rank too seriously and hoped that a year in the ranks would help to cure him.

Another possible explanation is that a medical disability forced him to step down from his responsibilities as a cadet lieutenant. Robert M. Hughes, Johnston's nephew and nineteenth-century biographer, noted that during his cadet years Johnston suffered from "an affection [sic] of the eyes" that rendered him blind at night. And throughout his later life Johnston complained to his correspondents that he could not work at night because of his eyesight. Very likely, Johnston suffered from *retinitis pigmentosa*, a hereditary and degenerative disease that causes night blindness. If this affliction occurred during his first class year, it may be that the Academy staff took that into consideration in making the assignments for the cadet officers in the class of 1829.[24]

Of all the possible explanations, the most unlikely is that Johnston was "broken" in rank for some overt transgression of the rules. There are no court-martial records for Cadet Johnston, nor did he earn a single demerit that summer. Johnston's conduct ranking in the class dropped from eighth to eleventh in his first class year, but that can hardly explain such an ignominious demotion, and many of Johnston's classmates who kept their rank that year rated well below him in both academics and conduct. In any case, the kind of dramatic violation of the rules that might have earned Johnston such a demotion was uncharacteristic of him. At West Point, Johnston applied himself, fulfilled his assignments, and stayed out of trouble. But whatever the explanation, Johnston's failure to hold a cadet rank in his first class year must have been a disappointment. Even if the explanation was completely innocuous, the fact remained that he had to remove the impressive inverted chevrons of a cadet lieutenant and spend his last year in relative anonymity.

Despite that anticlimax, Johnston's four years at West Point were unquestionably a success. He earned few demerits, passed all of his exams comfortably if not brilliantly, and had the opportunity to exercise leadership responsibility, though not in his final year. In June 1829, Johnston at last saw the end of his four-year indenture as a cadet and the prospect of a commission. He was not altogether sure what came next. Indeed, he harbored some doubts that he would stay in the Army. To Louisa he wrote: "Next June you will see with how little profit to himself or probable advantage to any body else, this hopeful brother of yours has spent the last four years. Before that time it will be necessary to decide whether or not I am to remain in the army." But staying in the Army was not really the question at all. The real question, as he admitted to his sister-in-law, was to "choose (that is to say if the choice is left me) between the two departments of service, Infantry & Artillery."[25]

Even without the loss of his chevrons in his final year, Johnston's cadet record was not nearly good enough for him to be selected into the ranks of the prestigious Army Corps of Engineers. Graduating thirteenth out of forty-six, Johnston had no chance to make the Engineers, which accepted only the top two that year—Lee and the brilliant Charles Mason, who graduated first. The other branches of the Army—the artillery, the infantry, and especially the cavalry—were for the also-rans. Although the cavalry promised a certain amount of dash, it was held to be the least desirable branch of service for a graduating cadet. The next best thing to the Engineers was the artillery, and this was Johnston's choice. If the Engineer Corps was the aristocracy of the U.S. Army, the artillery was at least respectable, and a broad step above the infantry or cavalry.

Johnston fulfilled his boyhood ambition to become an officer in the United States Army on July 1, when he graduated along with Mason, Lee, and forty-three other members of the class of 1829. The ceremony was not as elaborate as similar ceremonies in the twentieth century; since West Point was still largely inaccessible except by riverboat, the audience was small. The cadets paraded, were recognized, and received their commissions. With the balance of his back pay and a two-month furlough in his pocket, Johnston boarded the Hudson River steamer for the trip downriver. For only the second time in four years, he was going home.

CHAPTER TWO

Indian
Fighter

All preceding experiments for the improvement of the Indians
have failed. It seems now to be an established fact that they
can not live in contact with a civilized community. . . .

—President Andrew Jackson, 1835

A great deal had changed in the republic while Joe Johnston was at
West Point. Most significantly, three months before Johnston's
graduation, Andrew Jackson took the oath of office as the sixth president of
the United States. Bolstered by his belief that the "virtuous portion of the
people" had redeemed his bitter and controversial defeat of four years
before, but also grief-stricken by the loss of his wife only a month after the
election, Jackson embarked on his presidency determined to return the republic to first principles.[1] Jackson's presidency marked a turning point in the
life of the American nation. He was the first president born and raised on the
frontier; the first to break the Massachusetts-Virginia monopoly on the
White House. While most of his predecessors had looked east to Europe,
Jackson looked west. Moreover, he had an intensely personal view of the
rights and privileges of his office, and was determined to use his powers to
expand and consolidate national authority over the western lands. His determination was the driving force behind the enactment in 1830 of the Indian
Removal Act, which mandated that all Indians living east of the Mississippi
be relocated west of that river. There followed a series of wars against the
western Indians: the Sacs and Foxes in the Northwest; the Choctaws,

Creeks, and Cherokees in the Southeast; and the Seminoles in Florida. In all these wars, young Second Lieutenant Joseph E. Johnston played a part.

At the same time, Jackson's overt nationalism and his expectations of personal loyalty led him into conflict with his own vice president, John C. Calhoun, and helped to fuel a feud that flashed over states' rights in the Nullification Crisis of 1831–32. This dispute with South Carolina foreshadowed future sectional conflict, and was all the more emotional for the rebellion led by the slave Nat Turner in Virginia during the summer of 1831. The Army played a part in these events, too—first in helping allay the terror of Virginians who feared that Nat Turner's rebellion was only the prelude to a general slave uprising, and then as a warning to South Carolinians not to push their nullification theories too far. Each of these national events affected Johnston personally, and provided him with a wide variety of practical lessons about the ambiguous demands of military service.

Johnston's first commissioned service as a second lieutenant of artillery was anticlimactic to his long preparation. There were only four regiments of artillery in the regular army of the 1830s and their principal job was to man the guns of the coastal defense forts. Johnston had known that choosing the artillery over the infantry meant that he was "choosing between the seacoast and western frontier." As a second lieutenant in Company C of the Fourth U.S. Artillery, Johnston's first duty was to serve as part of the garrison of Fort Columbus on Governor's Island in New York Harbor, about a mile off the tip of Manhattan. Johnston and his fellow junior officers took great pride in their tight-fitting blue coatees trimmed in yellow, loose gray wool trousers, and tall leather shakos distinctively designed so that they were wider at the crown than at the brim, and which the soldiers derisively called "tar buckets." At Fort Columbus, the easy access to New York was pleasant, but Johnston's days of duty were so uneventful as to be stultifying; this was not the life of military glory he had imagined as a youth.[9]

Johnston's two-year stay at Fort Columbus ended in the late summer of 1831. That August in Virginia's Southampton County, not far from Johnston's birthplace, a house servant named Nat Turner led a slave revolt that spread from plantation to plantation across the county, leaving sixty whites and scores of blacks dead in its wake. Nat Turner's "rebellion" was every slaveholder's nightmare. In the aftermath, some Virginians argued that slavery itself should be terminated since its existence placed every white Virginian in peril. But the more immediate reaction was a public plea for military protection. In response, Johnston's Company C was one of five sent in the early fall of 1831 to reinforce Fortress Monroe in southwestern Virginia.

Johnston left Fort Columbus in the first week of October and travelled to Virginia by sea. Prone to seasickness, he was relieved when the ship dropped anchor in Hampton Roads, and he was impressed by his first glimpse of Fortress Monroe—at the tip of the peninsula formed by the York and the James Rivers. Begun in 1817, the fort was still under construction when

Johnston arrived in 1831, but even in its unfinished state it was imposing. Fortress Monroe was the largest fortification in the western hemisphere, and one of the largest in the world. Completely surrounded by a moat, it was a gigantic masonry structure that boasted an armament of over four hundred pieces of ordnance. In the three decades before the Civil War, virtually every artillery soldier in the U.S. Army saw service there, in part because it was the host to the Army's Artillery School of Practice.[3]

By the time Johnston arrived in Virginia, the crisis that had led the Army to order him there had entered a new phase. The capture and execution of Nat Turner ended the brief slave uprising, but it did not still the widespread sense of terror. For most Virginians, the Nat Turner rebellion was a disorienting experience. Like most well-to-do Virginia families, the Johnstons of Abingdon were slaveholders, although Joe himself claimed late in life that he had regarded the institution of slavery as a moral and political evil since boyhood. Even so, he was confident in the loyalty of the family servants, one of whom he referred to in letters home as "my friend Sam." Now, however, slaveowners throughout the state confided their unspoken fears to their diaries and looked with new wonder upon the dark faces of their chattels, trying to read meaning into the expressions they saw there. Even the fort commander was not exempt. Lieutenant Colonel Abraham Eustis was so nervous about the prospect of further slave uprisings that on November 13, soon after Johnston arrived, he issued an order banning all Negroes from the fort.[4]

In addition to his informal duty of helping to provide a greater sense of security for the population, Johnston's assigned duty at Fortress Monroe was as a student in the Artillery School of Practice that had been established there in 1824. The first service school of its kind in the country, its purpose was modest enough. According to the Army's commanding general, it was "to guard against the approaches of sloth and imbecility."[5]

Despite this unambitious goal, Johnston's regimen was fairly strict. Reveille sounded at dawn, and he formed up with the garrison as a battalion of infantry. After the morning ceremonies, half of the commissioned officers went off for classroom instruction in the school, while the other half received less formal instruction from the senior officer present. They were allowed a half hour for breakfast between nine and nine-thirty, then fell in again to exercise on infantry and artillery drill until eleven. At eleven-thirty there was a Grand Parade, and at noon all commissioned officers reported to the captain of ordnance for "laboratory instruction." This consisted of "the preparation of ammunition for small arms, viz., casting balls and buckshot, cutting paper, forming the cylinder, filling, choaking, bundling, and packing musket cartridges." According to the 1825 manual, "The officers under instruction are required to make memoranda of the weight and dimensions of balls, quantity of lead, powder, paper and thread required for any given number of cartridges; wastage in manufacturing, quality and size of paper most suitable, etc., etc.,—dimensions of packing boxes of kegs to contain 1000 musket cartridges and their weight when filled, time and number of workmen required to complete any given number, etc., etc." Such activities lasted until three, at which time dinner was served. There was a dress parade at four, and then free time until tattoo at nine.[6]

This crowded regimen still left time for social activities of a sort. Johnston's West Point classmate Robert E. Lee was one of the engineers assigned to the construction work at the giant fort, and at night, after tattoo, Johnston and Lee would "prowl about" the fort to visit other junior officers for late night bull sessions. On other occasions they took the boat across the James River to Norfolk for more formal socializing. Lee reported to a friend that "from occasionally accompanying me over the river, [Johnston] is in some danger of being caught by a pair of black eyes." But when his sister-in-law accused him of being in love, Johnston denied it. "No, sister Louisa," he wrote, "I am not. Never was, more than a philosopher should be." To her he posed as a man of the world: "I am 24—too old to believe in romance and sentimentality & too much a philosopher to be under their influence even if they really existed." But his pose was disingenuous, for he was a sentimentalist at heart and if he did not fall in love, he was frequently infatuated.[7]

Johnston soon had less fanciful and more pressing things on his mind. Spring had barely arrived in 1832 when rumors began to circulate in the fort that the regiment might be called out for active service. In May, Chief Black Hawk of the Sac Indians violated what was patently an unfair treaty by returning across the Mississippi to his tribe's ancestral hunting ground in Illinois. The local militia forces under General Henry Atkinson had trouble locating, much less capturing, the renegade chief and his followers, and an impatient President Jackson ordered General Winfield Scott to raise an army of regulars to go to Illinois, capture Black Hawk, and send him back across the Mississippi.[8]

Scott was the nation's greatest living military hero—Johnston had been only seven years old and still playing at soldier with his brothers and neighbors in Abingdon when Scott won a hero's plaudits and a brevet promotion to the rank of major general during the War of 1812. In response to this new call to battle, Scott summoned nine companies of regular artillery for infantry service. This was a fairly common use of artillery troops; many artillery soldiers spent as much time as foot soldiers as artillerymen. One of the nine companies chosen for the expedition was Johnston's Company C of the Fourth Regiment. He was delighted, for he had grown weary of the routine at Fortress Monroe. "I am heartily tired of this sand bank," he wrote to Louisa. "It is the most villainous abode ever occupied."[9]

Johnston's participation in the Black Hawk War of 1832 was his first expedition against a hostile force, and it taught him in most dramatic fashion that war was not all heroics and glamour. Scott arrived at Fortress Monroe in June to take command of the expedition; on June 28, Johnston's company boarded a transport vessel for the first leg of a thousand-mile trip to the scene of the war. They travelled north by sea to New York, then upriver to

West Point, where virtually the entire graduating class of 1832 joined the expedition. This officer-heavy army then moved on to Albany and along the Erie Canal to Buffalo on Lake Erie. There Scott chartered four lake steamers to carry the entire expedition of about 850 men to Detroit. On this voyage Johnston would not have to worry about the Atlantic rollers that led to his bouts of seasickness, but he would encounter another enemy just as elemental and far more deadly.

About halfway along the coast of Lake Erie, two cases of Asiatic cholera appeared on board the steamer *Sheldon Thompson*. Just where the two soldiers had contracted it is uncertain, but steamships crowded with soldiers made an ideal breeding ground for the pestilence. The disease spread rapidly, and by the time the expedition arrived at Fort Gratiot at the entrance to Lake Huron, it had run rampant through two of the vessels. A witness recalled that "the disease came upon us with fury, and the boat became a moving pestilence, every soldier who was well became a nurse for the sick." A frightening aspect of this illness was that it struck with such suddenness. "Men died in six hours after being in perfect health," one wrote. And a survivor recalled that he had been feeling fine until he was "thrown down on the deck almost as if suddenly shot."[10]

Although a few of the officers came down with the disease, including Johnston's company commander, Captain Patrick H. Galt, it was much more frequent among the rank and file, whose quarters were more cramped and less hygienic. Terrified by this enemy they could neither see nor hear, the soldiers became panicky. On some ships discipline broke down entirely. When one vessel neared the shore at Fort Gratiot, the men sprang over the side and ran blindly into the woods. "Some fled to the fields, some to the woods, while others lay down in the streets, and under cover of the river bank, where most of them died unwept and alone." At Fort Gratiot, those too ill to flee were carried ashore. Of the 850 men who left Buffalo, only about 200 were fit for duty by the time the disease had run its course. Nearly a fourth of all the artillerymen in the expedition (81 of 372) died en route. Johnston apparently did not contract the disease himself, but his men died all around him.[11]

Only two of the four steamers that set out from Buffalo continued the journey: north across broad Lake Huron, then through the narrows at Fort Mackinac into Lake Michigan. Here the disease broke out again. As men died—a near-daily occurrence—they were buried hastily at sea. The disease continued to rage even after the vessels reached Fort Dearborn (Chicago) on July 10. In the clear waters of Lake Michigan, the weighted body bags could be seen from ship's deck as they rocked gently in the current. With the disease raging unchecked until the end of the month, Fort Dearborn became a virtual hospital filled with the dying.[12]

Johnston stayed behind in Chicago as Scott travelled 150 miles ahead of his troops to Galena, arriving at the scene of the war on August 3. For all Scott's haste, one hundred miles to the north General Atkinson and the militia had virtually ended the war the day before by catching up with Black Hawk's band and annihilating it in the Battle of Bad Axe. Scott nevertheless continued on to Fort Crawford (Prairie du Chien), where he took over command of the Army on August 7. Practically his first act was to dismiss the volunteers. The war was over in any case, and like most regulars, Scott had little respect for volunteers, especially idle volunteers. On August 10, he started down the Mississippi on the steamship *Warrior* with General Atkinson and his staff, arriving the next day at Fort Armstrong, where he set up his headquarters. It was probably at Fort Armstrong on the tip of Rock Island in the Mississippi that Johnston caught up with Scott. An unimpressive blockhouse and palisade structure, Fort Armstrong was the site chosen by Scott for the negotiations with the defeated Indians.[13]

Johnston was a witness to those negotiations, which provided a pointed lesson in *realpolitik*. In fact, of course, there was nothing to be negotiated. Black Hawk himself was not even present. He had been taken prisoner by a group of Winnebagos eager for Scott's promised hundred-dollar reward. Lieutenant Jefferson Davis escorted the prisoner to Fort Armstrong, but the cholera had broken out again and so Scott ordered the steamer to go immediately to Jefferson Barracks, Missouri—three hundred miles downriver. As a result, Johnston never got a look at the man whose break for freedom had brought him a thousand miles west. Without their leader, the minor chiefs readily agreed to all the terms presented to them. The final document, signed on September 21, required the Sac and Fox Indians to foreswear all rights to any land east of the Mississippi, and to evacuate a strip of land fifty miles wide on the west bank. Johnston signed the treaty as a formal witness; his signature marked his only active role in the entire campaign.[14]

On November 11, four and half months after starting out, Johnston arrived back at Norfolk on the steamer *Potomac*. His first experience with war had been a sobering one. Although perhaps half of his command had died, he had never faced a human enemy; though he had travelled twice a thousand miles, he had never fired a shot in anger. Johnston's experience in this, his first war, consisted entirely of a long voyage under a cloud of pestilence, and a treaty negotiation that was virtually a *diktat*. It could hardly have appealed to his sense of glory.[15]

Johnston did not even have time to fall back into the routine of the Artillery School before another crisis called him again to special duty. He had planned to request a furlough for a visit to Abingdon, especially after he heard of the accidental death by drowning of his brother Charles in June. This blow made him "doubly anxious" to see those who remained. But it was not to be. This time it was not a battle with Indians that demanded his services but a dispute over tariffs. The high tariffs of 1828 and 1832 were so unpalatable to South Carolinians that they elected delegates to a convention which declared both tariff laws to be null and void within the state. These "nullifiers" based their arguments on a compact theory of government elaborated by Calhoun, but

President Jackson saw nullification as a personal affront to his authority and threatened to use force to ensure compliance with the law. South Carolina responded defiantly, promising to "repel force by force." Defiance was a red flag to Jackson, and he ordered that national forces be sent to Charleston. Once again Johnston's Company C of the Fourth Artillery was among those sent to the scene, and he left two days before Christmas, again braving the Atlantic rollers before arriving in Charleston Harbor.[16]

Johnston's arrival in South Carolina caused him a special difficulty. Although he did not record his own political views on the issue at stake, his family's attitude is apparent from the public positions of two of his brothers. Charles Clement Johnston had represented Virginia in Congress as a states' rights Democrat, and though he thought Jackson's December 1831 State of the Union address "a clear, able state paper," he also wrote to a colleague soon afterward, "All the men of the South who are not 'Bastards' have either denounced the opinions of the President . . . on the all absorbing question of the tariff as you and your friends have done; or doubted as I and mine have done." Another brother, Algernon Sidney Johnston, spent the summer of 1832 writing a volume of political satire modeled on Dante's *Inferno* which he entitled *Memoirs of a Nullifier*. In it he poked fun at all Yankees, condemned the authors of the tariff bill to hell, and raised John C. Calhoun, the father of nullification, to sainthood. At one point in this fanciful novel, the hero calculates that Yankees are made up of:

Cunning	125 parts
Hypocrisy	125 parts
Avarice	125 parts
Falsehood	125 parts
Sneakingness	125 parts
Nameless & Numberless Small Vices	140 parts
Essence of Onions, New England rum, Molasses & Cod fish	235 parts

More seriously, three of Joe's brothers were by then living in Columbia and were members of the South Carolina state militia, which would have constituted "the enemy" in the event that the president decided to force the issue.[17]

Much to Johnston's relief, it never came to a test of military strength. The national crisis was resolved by a compromise engineered in Washington. Congress moderated the high tariff ordinance of 1832 with a new tariff bill, while at the same time affirming the sovereignty of the national government with a so-called Force Bill that authorized the president to use the Army and Navy to enforce the laws. For its part, South Carolina repealed its nullification of the tariff bill, but maintained the principle of state sovereignty by nullifying the Force Bill. Jackson chose to ignore this last defiant gesture, and the crisis passed.

No doubt much relieved, Johnston returned to Fortress Monroe in the spring of 1833 and remained there for nearly six months before being shipped off to confront yet another crisis: keeping the peace on the Alabama frontier between the land-hungry whites and the Creeks. He had dreamed of wintering in Virginia on extended furlough, but instead he found himself ordered to what he considered a useless mission in an unhappy land. It began on December 18, 1833, when his company left Augusta, Georgia, on a three-week march to central Alabama. It was "a miserable march," he wrote his brother Beverly. "Think of riding so long at the rate of 15 miles a day, generally in the rain & thru' the most uninteresting country that has ever been created." He would not have minded the discomfort if he thought that the expedition could do some good. But, in fact, there was no unrest on the frontier that winter. "This part of the country, according to all accounts, has never before known such a state of tranquility," he wrote. Personal sacrifice for a noble cause was honorable, but to endure such travails to no good end was absurd. "Life is short, & I am totally opposed to loss of time, & time can never be more completely lost or misspent than a winter here." He described his circumstances to his brother: "Imagine yourself living in a tent, compelled to employ yourself chiefly in turning round before a fire like meat on a spit to keep warm & consequently unable to pursue any rational occupation & you may form an estimate of the winter I am to pass." In the spring Johnston was finally released from his purgatory when his company was again ordered to return to Fortress Monroe. But by then Johnston was not quite as delighted to leave Alabama as he had expected to be. He had discovered that "delicious moonlight nights" in Alabama were pleasant, especially in the company of one of the "very pretty Indian girls" who, as he told his brother, "could say Na (no) . . . as coquettishly as any flirt of your acquaintance."[18]

He returned to Virginia and took up duty for the summer in Washington, where he worked drafting maps of the Ohio Territory. He lived at Mrs. Ulrich's boardinghouse, sharing meals with cabinet members, congressmen, and, occasionally, his friend Lee, who also dined there. The unhealthful climate of the nation's capital laid Johnston up for much of the summer of 1834 with "a bilious fever," but he was fully recovered the next summer to be available for the most serious of all the antebellum Indian wars, which had erupted in Florida in June of 1835. There, Second Lieutenant Joseph E. Johnston would taste real war for the first time. The nation's war against the Seminoles was particularly nasty, fought in appalling conditions, and marked by bitter personal arguments among the army commanders. It was a disillusioning experience for many young officers, and especially for West Point graduates, Joe Johnston among them.[19]

In the years following the passage of the Indian Removal Act, the U.S. government had conducted negotiations in which the several Indian nations were cajoled, bribed, or threatened into agreeing to relocate. In June 1835, in the midst of stalled negotiations with the chiefs of the Seminole Indians of central and southern Florida, the U.S. Indian agent, Wiley Thompson, committed a gross violation of a pledged truce by having the most intransigent Seminole chief, Osceola, seized and clapped into irons. It was a humiliation the proud young chief never forgot. The next day Osceola affixed his name to a treaty and won his release, but his apparent acquiescence was only a ruse, and that winter, after laying careful plans, the Seminoles struck.

In coordinated assaults miles apart, the Indians ambushed and destroyed an armed column of more than a hundred U.S. soldiers commanded by Major Francis Dade, and also gunned down Wiley Thompson and his dinner guest as they took their evening walk. The so-called Dade massacre made it dramatically clear that the Seminole Indians were determined to fight rather than submit. Although they numbered no more than four thousand in all, the Seminoles relied on the difficult terrain of the unmapped and largely unexplored Florida peninsula to deter their would-be evictors. They retreated into their strongholds in the cypress swamps and defied the U.S. government to move them. In January 1836, Congress accepted the challenge and appropriated the money to conduct a full-scale war.[20]

That January Johnston won what was perhaps the most desirable assignment in the Army from which to advance his own professional prospects—he was appointed to Winfield Scott's staff as an aide-de-camp. The young second lieutenant had barely attracted Scott's notice during the Black Hawk campaign, but now, as a member of Scott's staff, Johnston could not only observe the war firsthand from the highest levels, he would also have an opportunity to win the favor of an influential patron. Johnston's assignment was a high-profile job for a young and ambitious officer, and he was determined to make the most of it.

Johnston left Washington on January 23 and travelled to Columbia, South Carolina, for a brief reunion with some of his brothers before riding on to Augusta and Savannah. There he spent several weeks "employed in correspondence with 4 Governors & divers generals & colonels, not to mention Qr. Masters & commissaries, on all matters pertaining to arming & equipping militia & subduing Indians." Like his boss, Johnston was dubious about the military reliability of the volunteer militia that made up the bulk of the Army. Already they were complaining of the hardships of camp life. "If garrison life exposes the gentlemen to such hardships," he wondered, "what is to be expected from marching thru' the interminable marshes of E. Florida?"[21]

For Johnston, active campaigning in the Second Seminole War began on March 9, 1836, when, along with Scott and the rest of the staff, he set out on a fifty-mile trek from Picolata on the St. Johns River south of St. Augustine to Fort Drane, a frontier outpost in central Florida. Johnston could not have been impressed with Fort Drane. A typical frontier fortification, it consisted of a 12-foot-high stockade fence driven into the sandy soil around a rectangle 150 yards long and 80 yards wide; a small two-story blockhouse at the eastern end boasted a single cannon. From this unlikely headquarters, Scott would direct his grand campaign to crush the Seminole "rebellion" at a single blow.[22]

Scott planned nothing less than a three-pronged offensive into the heart of the Seminole nation, an offensive to be carried out by forces operating from bases hundreds of miles apart and with no means to communicate with one another. Scott's orders required Colonel William Lindsay with 1,250 men to march north and east from Fort Brooke (Tampa) on the Gulf coast to a site about forty miles inland. At the same time, a second force of about 1,400 men under Brigadier General Abraham Eustis would march west from Mosquito Inlet. These two forces were to "communicate" their location to one another by firing an evening and a morning gun each day. Scott's orders called for them to be in place by March 25. In Scott's mind, these two forces would constitute the anvil upon which his troops would deliver the hammer blow. Scott himself would accompany the third and largest column, two thousand men commanded by Brigadier General Duncan L. Clinch, which would march south from Fort Drane, driving the hostiles before them into the arms of Lindsay and Eustis. It was an ambitious plan even for professional soldiers, and completely unrealistic for volunteers. But if Scott's young aide-de-camp had any doubts, he kept them to himself.

From the first, nothing went right. Both Lindsay and Eustis were several days late in arriving at their rendezvous points. When they did arrive, Lindsay's men fired off the required cannons into the Florida silence and then listened carefully for a reply. Nothing. After waiting three days, Lindsay ordered his force back to Fort Brooke. Meanwhile, General Eustis's men were slogging their way across central Florida, but since the terrain was invariably more difficult in fact than it appeared on the maps, they were several days late in arriving. Knowing he was late, unable to contact any other forces, and dangerously low on supplies, Eustis, too, headed for Fort Brooke.

Unaware of any of this, Scott and his entourage, including Johnston, left Fort Drane with Clinch's main force on March 26. The road was a new one and passed over ground so marshy that the men had to cut trees and lay down logs to make the road passable for the wagons. Finally, on the morning of March 28, the army reached the northern bank of the Withlacoochee at Camp Izard. On the other side of the river was the Cove of the Withlacoochee, a large, irregularly shaped inland lake surrounded by heavy forest and dotted with small islands. It was a natural stronghold and the heart of Seminole power. Here on the banks of the Withlacoochee, Johnston experienced his first hostile fire.

Scott allowed his men to rest the night after their difficult march, but at four the next morning, the army began preparations to cross the river. Sharpshooters manned the northern bank to cover the main body, which crossed in flatboats constructed at Fort Drane. Except for occasional harassing fire, the crossing was uncontested. That night, however, the Seminoles reminded Johnston and the rest of the expedition that they were in enemy territory by

Florida During the Second Seminole War, 1836–38

firing several rounds into the camp. The next morning, March 30, the soldiers proceeded upriver in hopes of coming to grips with the main Seminole
force. At midmorning they encountered hostile fire from one of the small
islands that were the dominant feature of the Cove of the Withlacoochee.
Scott ordered the baggage train drawn up in a circle and, leaving three
hundred men behind to protect it, launched an attack. The Seminoles resisted briefly, but overwhelmed by numbers, soon fled. The soldiers pursued
them for four miles to another strongpoint where the Seminoles turned to
fight, but once again they were dislodged. This time the Indians crossed the
river where the army could not follow. Scott let them go. His men were
nearly exhausted from chasing an unseen enemy through difficult terrain,
and they had gone almost twenty-four hours without food. He therefore
ordered the army to fall back onto the baggage train. The campaign in the
Cove of the Withlacoochee was over. The next day, April Fool's Day, after
establishing a camp of observation, Scott and his army set out for Fort
Brooke, where they arrived on April 5.[23]

There was no disguising the fact that the entire campaign had been a
fiasco. Scott himself blamed it on the unreliability of the volunteer soldiers he
had to command, and he did not keep his opinions secret. He announced that
Floridians were too prone to panic at rumors of hostiles on the rampage, and
that the volunteer soldiers were too quick to seek the shelter of fortifications.
Scott believed that only an aggressive campaign conducted by professional
soldiers could achieve victory over the Seminoles. For their part, the volunteers were equally disillusioned by Scott and his entourage of professionals
(including, presumably, the young Lieutenant Johnston), all of whom
seemed to insist on fighting a European-style war amidst the palmetto scrub
of the Florida peninsula.[24]

Like his commanding officer, the general's young aide endured a professional's frustration in directing undisciplined volunteers, and his sense of
loyalty to Scott led him to find excuses for his commander. At the same time,
Johnston also shared in the general disappointment after the fiasco of the
March campaign. The Seminoles had proved themselves a wily, elusive foe,
fighting the kind of war appropriate to the geography and climate while U.S.
forces bulled their way noisily from place to place. Scott's plan had been
overly ambitious in its expectations and timetable. Although there is no evidence that his participation in this campaign led Johnston to draw any specific conclusions about the inherent difficulties of coordinating widely dispersed forces, it is likely that this early strategic lesson stayed with him into
the years when he himself commanded large armies in the field.

For his part, General Scott was now anxious to leave Florida and go to
Alabama, where a Creek uprising promised a better chance of military success with fewer frustrations. Scott received permission from the War Department to leave for Alabama in mid-April, but there was a great deal of uncertainty and maneuvering about who would succeed him in Florida. As a
result, Scott had to stay on in Florida, an unhappy lame duck, until late May.

He filled his time, and kept his staff busy, engaging in small exploratory expeditions. In late April, for example, Johnston accompanied his boss on "a miserable little steamer" (as Scott called it) to explore the St. Johns River.[25]

Scott left Florida for Alabama and the Creek War on May 21, but Johnston did not go with him. Promoted to first lieutenant in July, Johnston served under new commanders in Florida, first under Governor (and acting commander) Richard Keith Call until December, and then General Thomas S. Jesup until the spring. If his service with Scott had been disappointing, his year under Call and Jesup was completely demoralizing. Scott's criticism of the Florida war, plus a bitter personal feud between Scott and Jesup that broke out soon afterward, meant that neither Call nor Jesup was likely to entrust any significant command responsibilities to a former member of Scott's staff. As a result, Johnston found himself an unwelcome supernumerary during the winter campaign of 1836–37. The only evidence of his involvement in active campaigning is a brief mention of his presence at the Battle of Wahoo Swamp on November 21, 1836, where apparently he was once again more of an observer than a participant.[26]

In the spring of 1837, the surrender of several of the important Seminole chiefs convinced Jesup that the war in Florida was drawing to a close, and he made preparations to disband his command. Johnston had not had even one opportunity to command troops in combat. Moreover, his professional prospects had become uncertain. He had not served with Scott long enough to earn that officer's patronage, and he had served only in a minor—indeed almost unnoticed—capacity under Jesup. His promotion to first lieutenant had not brought him any greater responsibilities or opportunities, and the war itself had proved to be a sobering and disillusioning experience. With the end of the war in Florida, there would be dozens of unassigned artillery officers seeking the few career-enhancing positions available in the peacetime Army. Johnston had no intention of competing for one of them; he had other plans. In May, First Lieutenant Joseph E. Johnston submitted his resignation from the U.S. Army, effective on the last day of the month.

Johnston's principal motive for resigning was his impatience with the slow process of promotion. He explained the circumstances to his brother Beverly: "from the rules of our service, of promotion by regiments, many of my juniors who had the luck to be assigned to regiments in which promotion was less slow than in that to which I belonged had got before me on the army list." It is worth noting that Johnston was not alone in his disappointment. Officer resignations from the Army, especially by West Pointers, had begun to increase dramatically in 1835 and reached a peak in 1837, when a total of 117 officers, 99 of them West Point graduates, submitted their resignations. Johnston, in short, was part of a virtual flood of resigning officers that year.[27]

Pay was one reason. In the 1830s a second lieutenant earned less than eight hundred dollars a year at a time when his engineering skills could command three, four, or even five times as much in the civilian world. The *Army and Navy Chronicle* pointed out angrily in 1837 that army pay "bears no proportion to the compensation which can be obtained in civil life." The 1830s were boom years for the contruction of roads, bridges, and especially canals and railroads. Recent graduates of West Point, products of Sylvanus Thayer's intensive engineering curriculum, were the best qualified individuals in the nation to superintend such projects, and it was difficult for them to resist lucrative offers from railroad and canal companies.[28]

A second reason for this flood of resignations was the disillusionment many young officers experienced during the Seminole War. Little of what they had learned at West Point or in their subsequent careers had prepared them for the kind of war they encountered in Florida. Moreover, their superiors from the "Old Army" seemed to spend much of their time and energy bickering with one another or with the government about how to prosecute the war.

Finally there was the recognition that in the mid-1830s, the Jacksonian vision of America exalted the civilian-soldier or militiaman, but remained suspicious of professional officers. Although in 1823 Andrew Jackson had called West Point "the best school in the world," as president he made it clear that as far as he was concerned, Thayer's engineering school was wrongheaded in its emphasis and downright dangerous in its encouragement of an officer elite. Congress, too, joined in the popular condemnation of professional officers—a letter to the *Army and Navy Chronicle* in 1836 spoke openly of "the contempt in which the military service is held by Congress." In short, West Pointers in the 1830s felt underpaid, overqualified, and unappreciated.[29]

On the last day of May 1837, Joe Johnston formally left the U.S. Army. The Army had provided him with superb training, but his experiences as a commissioned officer, first in Illinois, then in Alabama, and finally in Florida, had left him disappointed. Officers whose talents and dedication he considered inferior to his own, men who were junior to him at West Point, were advanced over his head simply because they belonged to the right regiment. He surrendered his commission and returned to Virginia, hoping to make his fortune in civil life as a trained engineer.

CHAPTER THREE

The
Florida Coast

Johnston could not have picked a worse moment to resign his commission. Almost as if a malevolent spirit were watching over him, the very month that he submitted his resignation, New York City banks suspended specie payments—that is, they stopped accepting paper currency in exchange for gold and silver. This action triggered the Panic of 1837, which cast the nation into a deep economic depression from which it did not recover fully until the next decade. The roots of the Panic were widespread and deep. President Jackson's animus against the Bank of the United States, which he called a "hydra of corruption," had led him in 1833 to withdraw government deposits from the B.U.S. and direct new government receipts to the proliferating state banks. These "pet banks" provided almost unlimited opportunities for speculation, printing banknotes without restraint. In the words of Jefferson's Secretary of the Treasury, Albert Gallatin, Jackson's policies opened American society to a "shameless scramble for public money" and a "wild mania for speculation."[1] But the speculation—and the willingness of states to incur heavy debt—fueled a dramatic increase in construction projects during the 1830s, the kinds of projects that created high-paying jobs for West Point-trained engineers. There is little doubt that in addition to his disappointment over the slow, and to him unfair, promotion process in the Army, Johnston's resignation was motivated by his expectation that he could find ready and lucrative employment in one of these projects.

In a belated attempt to quash speculation in western land, Jackson issued his "specie circular" in July 1836. It directed the government to accept only gold or silver in payment for land, a policy that brought the state banks up short and caused a severe contraction of credit. The failure of a major New Orleans cotton firm in April 1837 fed the increasing anxiety, and when New York banks suspended specie payments in May, the economy collapsed. Entrepreneurs with plans for new construction projects suspended or cancelled them.[2]

Johnston arrived back in Virginia during the first panic-filled days after the announcement by the New York banks. Although six months earlier he could have written his own ticket, by June 1837 he was simply one of hundreds of unemployed engineers. He learned almost at once that the project which he had anticipated would make his fortune had been cancelled because of "the money pressure." Johnston consoled himself with a visit to the Fairfax home of Smith Lee, Robert's older brother, a visit which he reported "was worth resigning for." Indeed, the splendid few days he had there almost made him forget his financial woes. "This is a delightful part of the country," he wrote euphorically to Beverly, who was a close friend of the eldest Lee brother, Carter Lee. "Noble bowls of punch & apple toddy & glorious bottles of champagn [sic] which prepared me so admirably to appreciate the little divinities in pettycoats. I rode home sadly singing my heart's in the highlands."[3]

Despite this pleasant interlude, Johnston had to find employment—and soon. With the economy in depression, he turned again to the federal government, which in uncertain times was at least a sure paymaster. Johnston applied for a job in the Topographical Bureau in Washington, where he resolved to remain at least "until something better appears." He may have anticipated that his new job would consist mostly of drafting maps in an office; instead, it led him back to Florida. In the late summer he was assigned as the surveyor and engineer in an expedition under the command of Navy Lieutenant Levin M. Powell. Powell's assignment was to explore and survey the 450-mile stretch of coastline from St. Augustine to Key West, and select sites for new fortifications. Because hostilities with the Seminoles had broken out again, the civilian Johnston found himself right back in the middle of the war.[4]

Often overlooked as a dimension of the Seminole War is its connection to slavery and racism. One of the Seminoles' "crimes" was that they harbored runaway slaves from the plantations of Georgia, Florida, and Alabama. In 1796 the Creek Indian chiefs had agreed to return all such runaways, and U.S. government agents decided that the Seminoles, too, should be bound by that agreement. Scott's orders had forbidden him to agree to any peace so long as one white man's slave remained in Indian hands. Moreover, a few of the escaped slaves rose to positions of leadership among the Seminoles and became effective military leaders. Southerners were terrified by the presence of armed blacks so near the plantations of Georgia and Alabama—one reason why so many southerners volunteered to fight in the Seminole War. Many volunteers saw themselves as the protectors of white civilization from a barbarous race of mixed-breed savages.[5]

Under these circumstances, it is worth noting that the expedition Johnston joined as a civilian topographical engineer in the fall of 1837 was a polyglot body not only of sailors and soldiers, but blacks and whites. Powell's command consisted mostly of U.S. Navy sailors as well as soldiers, a total of about 120 men altogether. The Navy had been accepting free black enlistees for years, and many of the sailors attached to the expedition were black. One observer noted that Lieutenant Powell's force, "When drawn up in a line . . . presented a curious blending of black and white, like the keys of a piano forte." Powell, the expedition's commander, was a career naval officer who had spent the previous year chasing Seminoles in southern Florida. The senior army officer, First Lieutenant Henry Fowler of the artillery, was also an experienced Indian fighter.[6]

A second party of soldiers, which was to follow Powell's "pioneers" and construct forts at designated sites, was commanded by Lieutenant John Bankhead Magruder. Johnston and Magruder were old friends. A handsome young man with a broad forehead and flashing eyes, Magruder had graduated from West Point in the class of 1830, a year behind Johnston, and as a fellow Virginian had been one of Johnston's regular companions. Oddly enough, though he had more professional military training and experience than anyone else in the expedition, Johnston was the only "civilian."

In mid-December 1837, Powell's motley assemblage of "soldiers and sailors, white men and black," piled into thirty-three small boats at St. Augustine and headed south along the Florida coast. Sixty miles on, they passed through Mosquito Inlet into the quiet waters of Mosquito Lagoon. Twenty-five miles farther south, they put ashore onto a narrow spit of land separating Mosquito Lagoon from the head of the so-called Indian River, which was not a river at all but a saline lagoon that "emptied" into the Atlantic ninety miles to the south at Fort Pierce. Here, on a sand spit where they could portage their boats from one body of water to another, they set up camp. One observer described the site, dubbed "Camp Haulover," as "one unbroken expanse of scrubb-saw-palmetto from two to four feet high, and entirely bare of trees." Magruder's three companies of regulars, travelling separately, had arrived first, and Johnston and Magruder had an opportunity to compare notes while the men spent several days hauling the boats and equipment across the narrow sand spit.[7]

On Christmas Day the men of both expeditions shared a holiday dinner on the sand amid the scrub palms. Although the sky swarmed with "unnumberable flocks of ducks," their feast consisted mainly of "gopher soup and whiskey toddy"—probably more of the latter. Then the men sprawled on the sand and Johnston listened along with the others as two of his friends and fellow officers, John Magruder and Lieutenant William H. French—one a future Confederate general, the other a future Union general—played the guitar and sang together under the Florida night sky.[8]

Despite the festivities, Powell had the expedition up and under way early the next morning. Johnston probably had an easier time of it than his friend Magruder, who had a well-earned reputation as an enthusiastic drinker. The men of the expedition broke camp and headed south down the Indian River past "thickly wooded shores wrapt in silence and solitude." On the evening of December 27, they pulled in to set up camp on the western shore and were startled when they flushed a group of Seminoles who had been concealed in the foliage along the bank. The Indians fled quickly into the interior before a pursuit could be organized, but later that night, Powell sent men out in the boats to look for telltale fires that would betray the presence of an Indian campsite. Finding none, the expedition pushed on, arriving the next day at Indian River Inlet. They again set up camp and awaited the arrival of supplies from St. Augustine. Lieutenant Magruder's group joined them there on the last day of the year for another impromptu celebration.[9]

On January 6, Powell, Johnston, and the rest of the expedition headed south again, exploring the mouth of the St. Lucie River, where they skirmished with a small group of Seminoles who fled inland. A week later, they entered the waters of the Jupiter River, or as the Seminoles called it, the Locha Hatchee. The party landed "at the head of a little bay on the south side," and marched inland "through a flat country and open pine woods." Soon they came to a clearing where a domesticated herd of both cattle and horses was being tended by a lone Indian woman. After some forceful questioning, she agreed to guide them to the Seminole camp, and Lieutenant Powell determined at once to attack it. Assaulting Seminole campsites was hardly the primary mission of the expedition, but Powell had been frustrated during an earlier campaign by his failure to come to grips with the elusive enemy, and he did not want to let this opportunity pass. He detailed two dozen men to stay behind and watch the boats, and led the rest—about fifty-five sailors and twenty-five soldiers—into the interior. As the civilian topographical engineer, Johnston could have stayed behind, but he was as eager as Powell for a chance to get into a fight.

Powell pushed his men rapidly up the trail, determined that his quarry would not escape him this time. After about six miles, the path intersected "a very large and much used Indian Trail, about parallel to the coast." That trail led them "within sight of a large camp from which the warriors hastened to meet us." Eager to come to grips with the enemy, Powell ordered an immediate attack. But the response from the ranks was less than enthusiastic. The fifty-five or so sailors who made up two thirds of the American expedition were recruits who only recently had been detailed to active service. Johnston was both disgusted and alarmed to find that these recruits "couldn't be induced to use their arms, but stood helpless before the enemy." Both Powell and Johnston urged them to attack before the Seminoles recovered from their surprise; instead, they halted in front of a small stream and refused to cross. Powell tried to engineer a double envelopment of the Indians' position, but the Seminoles' fire was steady and accurate, and seemed to concentrate particularly on the officers. Midshipman Horace Harrison, leading one wing of the attack, fell at the first fire, wounded in the shoulder. Midshipman William P. McArthur also fell wounded, and the naval surgeon, Dr. Leitner, was shot dead. Johnston heard and felt dozens of rifle balls pass near him—three struck the trunk of a small tree next to him, and he later claimed to have counted no less than thirty bullet holes in his clothing, including two in his cap. One bullet creased his scalp. Although it left a scar that he bore for the rest of his life, it did not put him out of the fight.[10]

The Seminoles soon organized a counterattack. With the naval recruits beginning to fall back in near panic, the twenty-five or so regular soldiers of the expedition came up. Johnston later recalled that "I placed them in ambuscade hoping to check the advancing Indians by their fire and encourage our retreating poltroons." This tactic slowed the enemy advance, but as two dozen had been killed or wounded and night was coming on, Lieutenant Powell ordered a retreat to the boats. Even retreat would be difficult now. The recruits had seen several of their officers fall wounded. At the order to retreat, they turned and fled back down the path without a backward glance. Only the two dozen soldiers remained to constitute a rear guard and prevent a rout. Johnston stayed with the soldiers, retreating slowly, firing steadily. He recalled that "the little rearguard, less than thirty, disputed every yard of ground."[11]

Early in the retreat, Lieutenant Fowler was wounded, first in the wrist and then in the thigh. He told Johnston to leave him behind and take command of the rear guard, but Johnston ordered two "very vigorous Mulatto men" to pick up the wounded lieutenant and carry him to the boats. Exuding the steady manner that had earned him the nickname "the Colonel" at the Point, Johnston took command, holding the rear guard together during the long retreat. For five hours they fended off the attacking Seminoles, who knew the terrain and fired from ambush. A contemporary later testified that Johnston's "coolness, courage, and judgement" won the admiration of everyone in the party. Johnston was the last one to reach the landing site, and the last to board the boats. So eager was he to ensure that every member of the party was accounted for that he was almost left behind. Since Dr. Leitner had been one of the fatalities, it was necessary to return to the camp at Indian River Inlet to get treatment for the wounded. "By the help of sails and a fair wind," Johnston wrote, "we reached Ft. Pierce near Indian River Inlet, about 8 o c[lock] next morning." Johnston concluded that "we escaped by God's help."[12]

Of the eighty soldiers and sailors who had taken part in the battle, five had been killed—their bodies left behind on the battlefield—and twenty-two wounded, including Johnston.[13] Indian casualties were uncertain; Powell later guessed the number of enemy killed to be eight. All in all it was an ignominious defeat, a product of Powell's foolish decision to order a precipitate attack on an unknown force over unfamiliar ground. His decision, no doubt, was motivated in part by his scorn for the fighting capabilities of the Seminoles, a scorn he learned to repent.

Johnston's commendable conduct in the battle and subsequent retreat won him high accolades. It was his first experience leading men in combat, and he proved himself to be not only personally brave, but also able to exercise effective command over others at a crucial moment. Indeed, his command presence had saved the expedition from almost certain disaster. Equally important to his professional future, he was prominently mentioned in Powell's formal report to Commodore Dallas, which was subsequently printed in the *Army and Navy Chronicle*: ". . . to the steady courage and conduct of this officer," Powell wrote of Johnston, "we are mainly indebted for the comparative security in which we returned to our boats."[14] Johnston was gratified by the professional notice, and wiser for having learned two valuable military lessons: never underestimate your enemy, and know what is in front of you before you attack.

Powell was eager for revenge, but that would be the task of General Jesup, who conducted a punitive campaign in the area and won the Battle of Lochahatchie on January 24. Powell's mixed group of soldiers and sailors was reinforced by the addition of another company of regulars commanded by newly commissioned Second Lieutenant Robert McLane, while Magruder succeeded the wounded Lieutenant Fowler. Their orders remained unchanged: continue to explore the southern coast of Florida and map appropriate sites for new fortifications.

They headed south from Fort Pierce to the mouth of the New River, the site of Fort Lauderdale, and then south again into Biscayne Bay. During the 1836 campaign, Powell had established a campsite on the southern bank of the Miami River that he had dubbed "Fort Dallas" after the commodore of the West Indian Squadron. When Powell brought his new command there in February 1838, he instructed Johnston to survey the site and supervise construction of a blockhouse to serve as a citadel for the fort. This may have been the first "permanent" structure erected at the site of the future city of Miami, although a year later it was burned by the Indians and Fort Dallas became, once again, merely a tented campsite rather than a fortress.[15]

In March, Powell's group at Fort Dallas received orders to scout the perimeter of the Everglades for evidence of a party of Seminoles that had withdrawn into the security of that trackless swamp. The Seminoles believed they were secure in this sanctuary that no white man had yet explored. Lieutenant Colonel James Bankhead, in command at Fort Lauderdale, decided that scouting this new frontier was exactly the kind of job for a surveying party such as Powell's, and as a result Johnston became one of the first white men to enter the mysterious Florida Everglades. When the expedition discovered what was apparently a navigable "trail" through the sawgrass, Powell reported its existence to Colonel Bankhead, who then ordered Powell's group to act as the vanguard of a major expedition to attack the Seminoles in their sanctuary.

A recent drought made the glades more shallow than usual that March. In many places the water was only a foot or two deep, and the men of the expedition, including Johnston, had to climb out of the boats and manhandle them forward "with infinite labor," pushing or dragging them through the ooze. Occasionally someone would step unexpectedly into a deep pool and come up sputtering. Nevertheless, the men plodded on "without a murmur," according to Bankhead's subsequent report, tripping over invisible roots, bruising themselves on cypress knees, and cutting their shoulders and thighs on the sawgrass.[16]

Finally, late in the afternoon, they came to an "island" of dry ground amidst the swamp where the Seminoles had made their camp. Bankhead sent in a flag of truce, but the Indians fired on it, so the colonel deployed his forces for an attack. He assigned Powell's force to assault that part of the island where the water was deepest and where the boats could come closest. When the Indians reacted to this feint, Bankhead with seven companies of regulars and two hundred Tennessee volunteers would storm the island from the other side.

The first part of the plan worked well enough. Powell's force of soldiers and sailors—and one civilian topographical engineer—rowed up close to the island; when the Indians rushed to repel the approaching boats, they were met by the blast of a four-pounder cannon mounted in one of the vessels. But before Bankhead could spring the trap, the Seminoles recognized their vulnerability, as well as the odds against them, and fled the island, abandoning a large store of valuable supplies. It was not a decisive victory, but it did demonstrate clearly that the Seminoles were no longer inviolate in their sanctuary.[17]

The campaign into the Everglades was Johnston's last combat service of the Second Seminole War. Powell's "pioneer" force returned to Fort Dallas and then proceeded down the east coast of Florida all the way to Key West where, somewhat the worse for wear, the survivors of the expedition arrived in April. There the expedition broke up. Powell and the navy officers headed for Pensacola and duty with the West Indies Squadron. The army officers returned to St. Augustine and points north.[18] Powell was not altogether happy with what they had accomplished; he had hoped to destroy the Seminoles completely. But measured against the original orders, the expedition had to be rated a success. This was especially so for Johnston. In five months, he had explored and surveyed over 450 miles of the Florida coast from St. Augustine to Key West; he had selected the sites for several forts and helped supervise their construction; he had fought in two battles with the Indians and provided evidence of both his bravery in combat and his leadership; and he had been mentioned favorably in dispatches. He had seen more combat during his year as a civilian than in his seven years as an artillery officer. Not incidentally, he had demonstrated his ability to fulfill the duties of a topographical engineering officer. All in all, it was much more satisfying a professional experience than his year of nondescript service under Governor Call and General Jesup.

The war in Florida sputtered on for several more years. One by one, small bands of Seminoles gave themselves up for passage to the trans-Mississippi West. Others stayed and fought, but in ever-diminishing numbers. In 1842, one authority estimated that there were only about three hundred Seminoles left in the state.[19] Joseph E. Johnston was not yet finished with the Seminole War; he would return again in 1842 to serve in an administrative capacity as Assistant Adjutant General. But in April 1838 he left the ugly war behind him and returned to Washington. Three months later he reentered the Army as a first lieutenant in the newly formed Corps of Topographical Engineers, and that same month he was breveted to captain for his gallantry in the battle at Jupiter Inlet and his service in the Everglades expedition.

Johnston's brief civilian career had convinced him that his proper destiny was in the military after all. His work as a topographical engineer had smoothed the way for his appointment in the new branch of service, but it had cost him, too. Of the ten officers appointed to his rank in the new Corps, all had been junior to him before his resignation. Whereas Johnston was from the West Point class of '29, the other first lieutenants were from the classes of '31, '32, and '33, and one was from the class of '36. Worse, one of Johnston's classmates, who had graduated just five places ahead of him in the class of '29, received a commission as a captain effective the same day as Johnston's commission as first lieutenant. It would be another decade before Johnston achieved the permanent (as opposed to brevet) rank of captain.

CHAPTER FOUR

Lydia

When he left Florida in the spring of 1838, Joseph E. Johnston was thirty-one years old—near middle age by nineteenth-century standards. Despite his disappointing experiences in Illinois, Alabama, and Florida, his year as a civilian engineer had confirmed his early conviction that he was destined for a military career. The scarcity of business opportunities in the civilian world—still suffering the effects of the Panic—and the prospect of service in the new Topographical Engineer Corps, made an army career appear more promising in 1838 than it had a year before. Then, too, Johnston was by nature a man who enjoyed the camaraderie of the Army. He had grown up with six older brothers, and he had gone to a school that encouraged, almost demanded, comradeship. Johnston had developed special bonds of friendship with many of his fellow officers. The Army was his family.

But it was not his only family. Throughout the 1830s his letters manifested a strong interest in the activities of relatives and friends in Abingdon. He chided his brothers when they did not respond to his letters, and he begged for gossip of the activities of his extended family. "I have heard none of you since the summer," he wrote to Beverly from Alabama. "Do give me some intelligence." Knowing that the family had gathered at Abingdon for the Christmas holidays, he told Beverly to "Give them my love & tell them I'd give my left hand to be able to express it in proper person."[1]

His hunger for news, and his homesickness, was sharpened during the 1830s as members of his family died or moved away from Abingdon. His father died in December 1831, after twenty-one years on the Circuit Court bench and only two years after he had remarried. Johnston went home to Abingdon for the funeral early in 1832, returning to Fort Monroe in time to participate in the Black Hawk War. Only six months later, he learned that his older brother Charles and his wife had both drowned while crossing the Potomac River from Alexandria to Washington, leaving behind two orphaned children. In 1837, tragedy struck again when death claimed Joe's oldest brother, John Warfield Johnston. Other members of the family left Abingdon to seek opportunities elsewhere. Two of Joe's brothers and his cousin John Preston all moved to Columbia, South Carolina, and another brother left to set up a Female Seminary in Boutetourt Springs near Roanoke. With both his parents and two of his brothers dead, and three brothers having moved away, Abingdon did not feel like home any more. Even the family slaves at Panecillo were sold to pay outstanding debts. When Joe learned of it, he was distressed. He wrote to Beverly, who was acting as the executor of the family estate, to express his disapproval: "I am very sorry that Sam has been sold, unless you have bought him, which I hope is the case." Although Panecillo remained the family home until it was sold in the 1870s, after 1838 it was to Columbia and not Abingdon that Joe travelled during his infrequent visits "home."[2]

If his roots in Abingdon were tearing loose, Joe Johnston did not relinquish his commitment to family. Charles's death in 1832 had made orphans of his two children: Eliza, called Lizzie, and Preston. The court appointed Beverly Johnston as guardian, although Eliza eventually moved in with her maternal aunt and uncle, the John B. Floyds. Twelve-year-old Preston was adopted by his host of uncles, and Joe offered himself as a surrogate father. He asked young Preston "to regard me as not a formal old uncle, but as a brother, and to let your intercourse with me be free and unrestrained, as if we were of the same age." But Joe felt at least as paternal as he did fraternal toward Preston, writing him at one point that his feelings were both "fatherly & brotherly." He took a father's pride in Preston's achievements, and suffered a father's pain at his failures. "Nothing in my own professional prospects ever gave me such satisfaction as I derive from your position," he told his young ward. Later he encouraged Preston to apply to West Point, and acted as Preston's adviser and professional mentor throughout his army career. His letters were full of both affection and encouragement: "Your father's son has no right to be a common boy," he wrote, "or common man either. Never forget that." To Beverly he confided that "the little fellow's love is well worth having—no one has a nobler, purer, heart nor warmer affections. The more I see of him the fonder I am of him."[3]

Surrogate parenthood was rewarding, but at thirty-one, Johnston was a prime candidate for marriage and a family of his own. His friend Robert Lee had been married for eight years and was already the father of three. As for his own prospects, he claimed to have none. Several years earlier he had written his sister-in-law that he had never been in love, but it may be more accurate to say that he was in love all the time. He teased Beverly for his bachelorhood, but excused his own because, as he said, it resulted from very different propensities: "You are a bachelor because insensible to such charms as furnish my life with its little share of happiness," he wrote. "While I on the contrary am so vastly susceptible as to face the influence of every female fascination between the St. Lawrence & the Gulf of Mexico, the Missi[ssippi] & the Atlantic. So many attractions operating in different directions neutralize each other of course, & they can't operate together you know, because polygamy is contrary to the statute." On another occasion he confessed that he was "occasionally throwing my heart" at pretty girls "these spring evenings." During the few days he spent at Smith Lee's home in Fairfax between his resignation from the Army and joining the Powell expedition, he was enthralled by "the little divinities in pettycoats." In short, Johnston's infatuations were frequent but not lasting.[4]

As lightly as he treated the subject of his romantic attachments, Johnston was genuinely attracted to the idea of family—after all, he had grown up as one of nine children, and his doting affection for Preston was paternal in instinct. But despite his numerous flirtations, there is no evidence that Johnston had any serious or lasting relationships before the winter of 1840. One reason—typically for him—was pragmatic. With his first lieutenant's pay of $750 a year, Johnston could not afford to support a wife. When he went home to Panecillo for his father's funeral, his sister-in-law Louisa asked him about his matrimonial prospects. His response was to reach into his pocket and produce from it a quarter of a dollar, his entire fortune at the moment. His poverty, as he saw it, was conclusive: since supporting a wife required at least moderate wealth, he was disqualified.[5]

Another practical reason why Johnston remained single was that like most army officers of his generation, he was frequently off on expeditions where few white women lived. At Fort Mitchell in Alabama, there were only the "very pretty Indian girls" who, however beautiful, were not matrimonial prospects to Johnston. In Florida, there was no polite society on the edge of the wilderness. It was already becoming an old joke at West Point in the 1830s that cadets were expected to marry their roommate's sister—and, in fact, many did. One reason was that the relatively closed circle of army officers in the first half of the nineteenth century provided few opportunities for social intercourse. In addition, officers' sisters (who were often officers' daughters as well) understood and accepted the often demanding obligations of army life. In the end, Johnston did not marry his roommate's sister, but he did marry the sister of a fellow officer.

After leaving Florida in the spring of 1838 as a first lieutenant in the newly created Topographical Engineering Corps, Johnston served on a series of expeditions to the western frontier. He was charged first with command of a project to improve the navigation of the Black River in New York near Sackett's Harbor on Lake Ontario. He then spent the winter in South Florida, where he was frustrated by the absence of efficient military command as the Seminole War sputtered on. He found the state of military affairs there "disgusting in the extreme" because as he saw it the Army was being used up to no good end by "minute diversion."[6] He was relieved, therefore, to be ordered back to Washington, where he arrived in mid-March. After a few weeks rest, Johnston received orders to serve as one of three officers assigned to survey the U.S.-Canadian border in the newly admitted state of Michigan.

Johnston had planned to stop at West Point to visit Preston—now in his second year—on his way north, but somewhere between Philadelphia and New York his surveying instruments "escaped" him and his pursuit of them kept him from seeing Preston, which distressed him. Nevertheless, both he and his instruments arrived safely in Detroit in July. The last time Johnston had been in the far Northwest, he had come in a ship filled with the dead and dying. He was much more impressed by the country this time. "Your Uncle Edward would find abundant sport among the trout & whitefish," he wrote to Preston. "But one so deficient in capacity as myself will be obliged to mind his own business."[7]

That business was to survey the international boundary, and more particularly to locate and recommend sites for the construction of military fortifications. Canadians had rebelled against British rule in 1837, and by 1840 Canada was in a state of near anarchy. Americans provided aid as well as sympathy to the insurgents, and military incursions by both sides had taken place across the international border. At the same time, the United States was engaged in a diplomatic quarrel with Britain concerning the right of British ships to stop and search slavers off the coast of West Africa. Long the leader in the international movement against the slave trade, Britain found its efforts frustrated by the American insistence that ships flying the Stars and Stripes were not subject to inspection by warships of the Royal Navy. American officials reminded the British that the two nations had fought a war over that issue in 1812. The British found these sensibilities a bit precious, and pointed out that the slave trade was, after all, a violation of American as well as British law. There followed a period of tense relations between the two countries, and it was during this time that Johnston and his two colleagues were charged to survey the country between Lake Huron and Lake Superior north of the Straits of Mackinac.

The other two officers on the survey were Captain Augustus Canfield and Second Lieutenant Robert McLane. Johnston had known both men in Florida. Canfield had served with Johnston on Scott's staff in the 1837 campaign, and McLane had replaced the wounded Lieutenant Fowler in Po-

well's expedition after the skirmish at Jupiter Inlet. Johnston got along well
with them both, but he became particularly close to McLane, one of several
young protégés he adopted during his career. Theirs was an unlikely friendship. McLane, who was ten years younger than Johnston, was as outwardly
demonstrative and mercurial in his personality as Johnston was dignified and
reserved. Whereas Johnston took hold of an idea and pursued it in a thoughtful, determined way, McLane changed his mind frequently, often losing
interest before completing the task at hand. McLane's own brother concluded that "Robert is a vacillating white man. He wants half a dozen things
at once and don't know which to take hold of first." McLane had chafed at
the discipline of West Point, and twice tried to quit, only to be talked out of it
by no less a personage than Andrew Jackson himself.[8]

The president took a personal interest because the McLane family was
one of the most prominent in the country. Robert's father, Louis McLane,
was then president of the Baltimore & Ohio Railroad and one of the nation's
leading statesmen. He had served in both the House and Senate for a dozen
years, as Minister to England (where young Robert had attended the birth-
night ball for Princess Victoria), and finally as Secretary of the Treasury and
then Secretary of State under Andrew Jackson. He was mentioned frequently as a possible presidential candidate and was a personal friend of
Jackson, who, though now in retirement, was still a dominating influence in
national politics.[9]

Johnston, Canfield, and McLane conducted their survey work in the summer months, selecting sites for defensive works at appropriate points along
the St. Mary's River. During the winter they retired to Washington to draw
their maps. Joe wrote to Preston to express his regret that he would not be
able to make a visit, and also to squelch a family rumor that some unnamed
young lady had rejected his suit and instead had married a naval officer.
"Tell Lizzie," he wrote, "that nobody has yet been furnished with an opportunity to commit what she esteems the folly of rejecting me." He referred to
a popular song of the day, the title of which was "I Don't Propose." Johnston
wrote this letter in November; in December, Robert McLane invited him
home for the Christmas holidays. With most of his family now gone from
Abingdon and scattered across the country, Johnston found the offer a welcome one, and he accepted.[10]

The home to which Johnston accompanied Robert McLane that Christmas
of 1840 was Bohemia—a two-story brick mansion on Maryland's eastern
shore. Approached by water, it crowned a gentle rise on the south bank of
the Bohemia River, which flowed into the eastern shore of the Chesapeake
Bay. The land sloping up from the private dock was cultivated with formal
gardens in the English style, now dormant, and huge oaks that shaded and
framed the house. As he walked up to the north facade, Johnston must have
been impressed by the grandeur and gentility. Inside the house, probably in
the large drawing room, Johnston met Robert's illustrious but somewhat
irritable father, his invalid mother Kitty, and his four brothers and three

sisters, including eighteen-year-old Lydia Mulligan Sims McLane, whom everyone called Lid.[11]

Like her brother Robert, Lydia McLane had grown up in a world of gentility on Maryland's eastern shore. She, too, had been at court for Victoria's birthday parties in 1829 and 1830 (Lydia, another sister, and their father had required seven servants in their London home). Early photographs show a young woman with dark hair and eyes, a long straight nose, a strong chin, and a firm mouth softened by a mischievous half smile. She struck most observers as handsome rather than pretty. But if not a great beauty, Lydia showed a genuinely sweet disposition.[12] She did not share her brother's flamboyant personality. In the patriarchal McLane family, the men were bluff and boisterous, the women quiet and reserved. Lydia took after her mother, Kitty, who, weakened by ill heath, was as agreeable as her husband was irascible.

Robert no doubt introduced his guest as a military hero. Seated perhaps in Bohemia's small sitting room on furniture newly covered in gray linen, with his feet resting on a carpet recently bought in New York, Johnston may have been amused as Robert dramatically recalled his friend's heroic exploits in Florida. In his memoirs, Robert recalled that Johnston had saved Powell's expedition from virtual annihilation in Florida: "but for the courage and skill of Johnston," he wrote, "he [Powell] would have been utterly destroyed." With the fire crackling and the family drawn about to listen, Bob would have embellished the tale to impress his brothers and sisters with the drama of the event: "Johnston took command of the soldiers of Fowler's Company," Bob wrote, "and covered Powell's retreat to his boats. Fowler and Harrison were carried off the field by two stalwart negroes, and Johnston held a position to cover the boats on the river, in the last of which he found refuge himself."[13] Such a tale would have established Johnston's credentials with the family. How could it fail to impress the eighteen-year-old Lydia, who had made her debut in Baltimore society only a few months earlier? As for Captain Johnston, who fell half in love with every pretty young woman he met, he was no less susceptible on this occasion.

After the holidays, Johnston and Robert McLane returned to Washington to work on the detailed maps of their summer surveys. But they did not go back to the Canadian border in the spring. Instead, Johnston was sent south to Texas to survey the Sabine River on the Texas-Louisiana border, and both McLane and Canfield received orders to travel to Holland and Italy, where they were to inspect fortifications that might be appropriate for use on the Mississippi. Johnston's connection with Bohemia was temporarily severed.[14]

But there is some evidence that Johnston continued to visit the McLanes. After spending the winter of 1841 in Texas, and the following fall surveying Sackett's Harbor in New York, he returned to Washington for the winter of 1842 and worked again at the Topographical Bureau where, as before, his job was to render the maps of his summer surveys. He bought a new wardrobe for himself that fall, including a cashmere vest and a merino scarf, and in February he plunked down thirty-four dollars, a huge sum on his income, for a new frock coat. His concern for sartorial perfection may be evidence that he was making trips out to Bohemia during his stay in Washington.[15]

Even if he did not visit, it is likely that he at least maintained a correspondence with Lydia McLane. Although there are few surviving letters from this period—most that existed were almost certainly destroyed by Johnston himself before his death—there are some hints of a continuing relationship in his other correspondence. One such hint is in a letter Johnston wrote to Preston in May 1842, a year and a half after he first met Lydia. Preston had written him to complain that his other uncles did not write frequently—a sign, as he saw it, that they didn't "care a curse" for him. Johnston replied tenderly that Preston should not feel their neglect too deeply—these uncles did not write to him either, or to each other. "I write to you more than to all my brothers," he told Preston. So, "don't think yourself so little loved. For myself, there is nothing (except my sweetheart) that I love more than you & if you could see her, Pres, you couldn't be mortified at being put in the 2d place."[16]

While Lydia's brother Robert was in Europe ostensibly studying European fortifications, he also fell in love—dramatically of course—with Georgine Urquhart, whom he married almost at once, in August 1841. But Johnston's romance with Lydia did not lead to immediate matrimony. Two considerations stayed him. The first was his lack of money. He was not significantly better off in 1842 than he had been in 1831, when he produced his solitary quarter as evidence of his unreadiness for marriage. In May 1839, he wrote Preston to apologize that he could not send him any money for he had none to send. The second reason for delay was Lydia's age. She was only eighteen when they met in 1840; Johnston was then thirty-three. Although such an age discrepancy was not uncommon between married couples in the antebellum South, Johnston's sensitivity to Lydia's youth may have prolonged their courtship.[17]

In the fall of 1842 Johnston returned again to Florida, where he served for six months as the Assistant Adjutant General on the staff of the commanding general, William A. Worth. Unlike his predecessors, Worth resolved to bring the intermittent war against the Seminoles to an end by abandoning attempts to track down war parties in the wilderness and focusing instead on the destruction of Indian towns and fields. He announced that henceforth the Army would campaign year round. Cruel as it was, the strategy was effective, and the Seminoles gradually capitulated and accepted peace. Johnston became a great admirer of Worth, who had been the commandant at West Point during Johnston's first three years there. Known as "Haughty Bill" in those days for his dignified demeanor, Worth may have struck Johnston as a kindred spirit. Johnston reported to Preston that "Genl Worth is my earliest admiration as a military man & has always shown the kindest disposition for me, & then, Pres, his family is such a one as nobody else can boast of. These things together make the position of Adjt Genl more agreeable in his staff than that of any other general."[18]

Throughout the 1840s—as throughout his professional career—Johnston's ambition never faltered. He continued to hope that his hard work and dedicated service would yet bring him recognition and promotion. His old friend Lee, who knew his heart well, wrote a friend that "Joe Johnston is playing Adjt. Genl. in Florida to his heart's content. His plan is good, he is working for promotion. I hope he will succeed."[19]

At the same time, while Johnston continued to think of Lydia as his "sweetheart," others teased him about his family reputation as a lady's man. When he went to Savannah for a short visit in the winter of 1842–43, Preston wrote to accuse him that he had left the simmering war in Florida for a romantic interlude. Johnston denied it. "No, no, Pres," he replied, "women are pleasant and attractive creatures, beyond denial, when one has nothing else to think of, or to excite him, but those who believe such a story know me little. There are not—never were—women enough in the world to allure me from the chance of one hostile shot."[20] No doubt some of the bravado of this comment may be attibuted to Johnston's eagerness to set a good professional example for his young ward, who was scheduled to graduate from West Point that spring.

Johnston returned to Washington in the spring but he was unable to attend Preston's graduation. He did, however, send some advice, urging Preston to choose the infantry over the artillery, because opportunities for promotion were much better in the infantry. The advice was a poignant confession that he had chosen badly himself—not only in selecting the artillery upon his own graduation, but in joining the Topographical Engineers when he reentered the Army in 1838. Neither branch promised speedy promotion, and Johnston ruefully watched his peers from West Point gain higher rank largely by virtue of their attachment to regiments in which promotion was accelerated by rapid turnover.[21]

Back in Washington, Johnston again had the opportunity to make regular visits to Bohemia. His campaign progressed satisfactorily, and a year later Joe and Lydia were engaged. Lydia's aunt and namesake Lydia Sims died in August 1844, and her will made Lydia McLane her primary heir. Did this enable Johnston to propose marriage? Poverty was no longer a barrier, and neither was age—Lydia was now twenty-three, Johnston thirty-eight.

On July 10, 1845, Joseph E. Johnston and Lydia McLane were married by the Reverend Dr. William E. Wyatt at St. Paul's Episcopal Church on the corner of Charles and Saratoga Streets in Baltimore. Old Louis McLane, once again Minister to England, heartily approved the match. Johnston was a southerner, a gentleman, a soldier, and a friend of Robert's. Indeed, of all McLane's sons-in-law, Joe Johnston was the one who pleased him most. The news of the marriage came as a surprise to many; Canfield, who had served with both Johnston and McLane on the Canadian border surveys, sent his congratulations, but also expressed his "surprize" at Johnston's abandonment of his bachelorhood.[22]

For the rest of his years, the most important individual in Joe Johnston's life was his wife Lydia. As distant as he often seemed to others, as formal and precise as he was to strangers, Lydia was the one person with whom he shared all his private hopes and terrors. Theirs was a relationship that grew slowly and ripened fully over many years. Their correspondence brimmed with affection, even passion. The publicly restrained Johnston concluded his letters to his wife with, "Good night my love, my life, my soul." Lydia's sweetness was a perfect counterpoint to her husband's occasional irritability. One contemporary rightly commented that Lydia "supplied many of the qualities in which he was so lacking," and that she "did more to keep him out of hot water and smooth over the rough places . . . than anybody else in the world."[23]

The greatest disappointment of their long marriage was that they had no children. Johnston's loving letters to Preston suggest that he would have delighted in fatherhood. And Lydia, perhaps wistfully, often referred to her husband as her "only baby," lavishing her attention on him. He reciprocated. Lydia's frequent illness was a constant concern, necessitating regular visits to Hot Springs and other spas in pursuit of relief. Twenty years later, when her illness began to age her beyond her years, she worried that her husband would no longer find her attractive. From his command tent in the field, he wrote to reassure her: "Do you really think that what you describe would affect your appearance to me? Do you not know that I see your face with my heart, & that it is as lovely to me now—that it gives me as much happiness to look at it—as it did when you were eighteen?"[24]

For several months after his marriage, Johnston continued to serve as a surveyor and a topographer for the Army. He worked with Andrew A. Humphreys on the coastal survey in 1845–46. Humphreys was an 1831 graduate of West Point who found more joy and stimulation in solving engineering problems than in soldiering. Not so Johnston. Surveying was rewarding enough, but despite the comfort he found in marriage, his professional ambition did not wane. He continued to long for "the chance of one hostile shot" in honorable battle. He watched the agitation in Texas carefully, wondering if that might brew up into a full-scale war with Mexico, a war that would provide him with an opportunity to achieve both glory and promotion. To his gratification, it did.

CHAPTER FIVE

War
in Mexico

On the morning of April 25, 1846, Major General Zachary Taylor, commanding U.S. forces on the Rio Grande in support of American territorial claims in Texas, sent Captain Seth Thornton and two squadrons of dragoons to investigate a report that Mexican forces had crossed to the north bank of the river. Since both the United States and Mexico claimed the area between the Rio Grande and the Nueces as national territory, the Mexicans insisted that they had as much right to send patrols across the river as Americans did to camp there. Indeed, the Mexicans considered Taylor's army an invading force, and for several months observers on both sides had assumed that the outbreak of hostilities was only a matter of time. On April 25, the time had come. Thornton's dragoons rode into a Mexican ambush, losing eleven killed and six wounded in the brief fight, while the rest, about eighty men, were taken prisoner. News of the destruction of Thornton's patrol reached Washington two weeks later, on May 9. President James K. Polk, who had been elected a year and a half before on a platform of national expansion, had just dismissed a cabinet meeting, but he called it back into session to present it with this new information. The cabinet unanimously recommended that Polk ask Congress for a declaration of war.[1]

In his war address, Polk declared that Mexico was responsible for the outbreak of hostilities; American blood, he said, had been shed on American soil. Members of the opposition Whig Party asked pointedly if the soil had been established conclusively as "American," and wondered aloud what Taylor's army was doing there anyway if not to provoke a war. Northern Whigs in particular suspected that the war was deliberately contrived by the president in order to expand the national territory where slavery might prosper. But they could not deny support to American forces already engaged, and on May 13, Congress passed the war bill. Most Americans responded to the call to arms with enthusiasm.

Joseph E. Johnston was as enthusiastic as anyone. Although he had campaigned against the Sac and Fox Indians in Wisconsin, against the Creeks in Alabama, and the Seminoles in Florida, he yearned for a war against a European-style enemy; an enemy that wore uniforms, an enemy with artillery and cavalry, an enemy that organized its army into regiments and brigades, and that, to many European observers, had at least a reasonable chance of winning. Here, at last, was an opportunity for personal glory, professional recognition, and a chance to face hostile bullets for his country. Much more so than his Indian war experience, the Mexican War provided Johnston with his first important lessons about modern warfare, and as a member of the staff of the commanding general, he would have ample opportunity to learn.

Historians have frequently noted that the United States' war with Mexico served as a training ground for Civil War commanders. Besides Johnston, future Confederate leaders including Lee, Beauregard, "Stonewall" Jackson, and Jefferson Davis first made their military reputations in Mexico. Future Union commanders, too, received their first trial by fire in this war. Their experiences helped mold their views on both strategy and tactics; helped accustom them to the perils of leading volunteer troops into battle; and introduced them to the kind of political dissension that marked both wars. Not incidentally, this war also introduced them to each other. As the topographical engineer on Scott's personal staff, Johnston became part of a distinguished group. His classmate and friend Robert E. Lee was another staff officer, as was Captain Pierre Gustave Toutant Beauregard from Louisiana, and young Lieutenant George B. McClellan from Pennsylvania. Another Pennsylvanian, Lieutenant George G. Meade, joined the staff in Mexico.

The initial front of the war was on the Rio Grande, where Taylor's army crossed the river and advanced to fight and win the battles of Palo Alto, Resaca de la Palma, and Monterey between May 1846 and February 1847. None was a model of military art; for the most part Taylor simply relied on the superior morale and fighting ability of his troops and turned them loose against the enemy. Nevertheless, those victories made Taylor a national hero, and Johnston, still in Washington, may have begun to worry that he might miss out on the war altogether. But Polk had determined to send an

expedition to Vera Cruz on the Gulf coast and carry the war to the very heart
of Mexico. This would give Johnston his chance.

Polk had discussed such an expedition with his cabinet as early as August.
In October, Winfield Scott presented a plan to capture Vera Cruz by investing it from the landward side, and by November, Polk had committed himself to it. Having made the decision to relocate the scene of the war, Polk's
next problem was deciding who would command. Scott was the logical candidate, but Polk resisted the idea. The president's principal objection was that
Scott was a Whig—as was Taylor—and either man would become a likely
presidential candidate if he emerged from the war as the conqueror of Mexico. The only other possible candidate was the aging Edmund P. Gaines, who
was eccentric and unreliable. Polk had no alternative but to give Scott the
command. In November, therefore, Secretary of War William L. Marcy sent
Scott his orders and the general began planning the campaign in earnest.[2]

A major general since 1814, Scott was by far the most senior military figure
in the republic. A man of undoubted military ability and imposing size—he
was six feet four and a quarter and well over 250 pounds—his weakness was
a tendency to take affront, often where none was intended, and to react out
of pique. Scott embarked on his campaign believing that he had the full
confidence of the president. His orders read, in part, "It is not proposed to
control your operations by definite and positive instructions, but you are left
to prosecute them as your judgment . . . shall dictate." But while these orders
implied the administration's confidence in Scott, it was also clear that full
responsibility for any disasters would rest squarely on the general's shoulders.[3]

Evidence that Polk was being less than candid with Scott reached the
general in New Orleans on the first leg of his trip to Mexico, when friends
reported that Polk had asked Congress to revive the rank of lieutenant general (last held by George Washington) with the intention of offering it, and
command of the expedition, to Senator Thomas Hart Benton, who was a
Democrat. Scott was hurt and angered; he later wrote that "a grosser abuse
of human confidence is nowhere recorded," and called Polk's behavior "bun-
gling treachery" and a "vile intrigue." In the end the scheme came to nothing, but Scott was unforgiving. "I had then discovered," Scott later wrote,
"that . . . instead of a friend in the President, I had, in him, an enemy more to
be dreaded than Santa Anna and all his hosts." As a member of Scott's staff,
Johnston could not have failed to note the discord between the general and
his commander-in-chief.[4]

Prone as he was to seasickness, Johnston suffered horribly on the trip south
from New Orleans. He shared a cabin on the wooden steamer *Massachusetts* with Lee, whose ability to go about his business unaffected by the
movement of the vessel only added to Johnston's discomfort. Finally, just
before Christmas, the ship put in at the mouth of the Rio Grande. Scott had
expected to meet there with General Taylor to discuss the campaign, but

Scott's message had been delayed and no meeting took place. Scott issued orders to Taylor to send a portion of his troops overland to Tampico on the Gulf coast, and on February 15, 1847, he and his staff headed south to join the scores of vessels anchored off Lobos, about halfway down the coast to Vera Cruz. Two weeks later this armada headed south again, arriving off Vera Cruz itself on March 5.

Johnston's first glimpse of Vera Cruz was overwhelmed by the vision of hundreds of vessels—steam warships, troop transports, old three-decked ships-of-the-line, small packet steamers—crowding the anchorage. This largest maritime expedition in American history virtually covered the surface of the water with ships of various shapes and sizes. Another imposing sight was the castle of San Juan de Ulloa, the offshore masonry fortress that guarded Vera Cruz. Stoutly built and armed with heavy-caliber guns, it kept the American armada at a respectful distance. Beyond the fort, hugging the coastline, was the city itself: Vera Cruz—the City of the True Cross—where the Spanish conqueror Cortes had come ashore more than three hundred years before.

Johnston got a much closer view of the city the next day when he and the rest of Scott's staff joined Navy Commodore David Connor aboard the *Petrita,* a small navy steamer, for an examination of the proposed landing site. They headed southward to inspect the beach near Sacrificios Island, and then turned north for a run past Vera Cruz. Johnston was seasick again, but he forgot his discomfort when the gunners at San Juan de Ulloa opened fire. The shell splashes bracketed the little vessel, and Connor immediately ordered the helm over to take the *Petrita* out of range. Johnston thought Connor was foolish to steam so insolently within range of the Mexican heavy guns. The Mexicans fired eleven shots, but they all fell harmlessly into the sea.[5]

By now Johnston was anxious to get his feet onto solid ground. So was Scott, and on March 9 the landing took place. The troops were loaded into whale boats rowed by sailors, and departed in a line-abreast formation to hit the beach simultaneously. "It was a glorious sight," remarked Johnston's friend and fellow Virginian, Dabney Maury, who kept a diary during the expedition. "The fifty great barges kept in line till near the shore," then grounded in the shallow surf. The American soldiers ran up the beach to the crest of a small hill, where they planted the American flag. The Mexicans did not resist the landing. A single piece of enemy artillery barked defiance, but the Mexican gunners then rode out of range and out of sight. By nightfall the bulk of the American Army of some ten thousand men was ashore. Scott had his foothold.[6]

Johnston, Scott, and the rest of the staff went ashore the next day (March 10), the hard part of the campaign still ahead. Vera Cruz was a walled city, well fortified and garrisoned. Despite the eagerness of many of his subordinates who wanted to attack at once, Scott issued orders to invest the city and begin a siege. The prospect of a lengthy siege was somewhat daunting. The

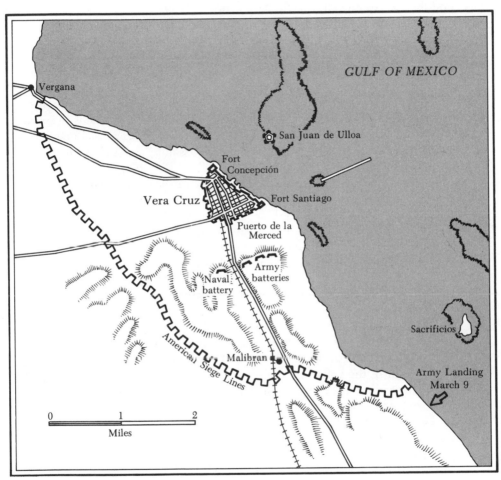

The Siege of Vera Cruz

daytime weather was hot, the nights cold, and there was no real shelter for the troops. Food was scarce and poor. But the worst plague of all was the fleas. The sandy soil was filled with millions of sand fleas that tormented the men day and night. "I have never seen anything like those Vera Cruz fleas," Dabney Maury recalled. "If one were to stand ten minutes in the sand, the fleas would fall upon him in hundreds." McClellan and Beauregard were so desperate to escape the torment that they smeared grease on their faces and tied themselves into bags while they slept.[7]

Over the several days following the landing, during nearly constant storms, Scott directed an advance westward and northward to surround the city. By the 14th they occupied a semicircle some seven miles in length, completely investing the city from the landward side. A week later the gun emplacements were completed, and Scott decided to give the Mexicans a chance to surrender before opening fire. He drafted a flowery invitation to the Mexican governor, Juan Morales, stating that he was "anxious to spare the beautiful city of Vera Cruz from the imminent hazard of demolition [and] the inevitable horrors of a triumphant assault." Scott chose Johnston to carry the invitation to the city.[8]

At two o'clock in the afternoon on March 22, bearing a white flag and accompanied by an army bugler, Johnston rode out from the American lines toward the Puerto de la Merced, the southern gate to the city. The Mexicans received him politely and courteously asked him to wait while Governor Morales composed a response. That done, Johnston recrossed to his own lines with the governor's equally polite, but firm, negative. The whole episode could have come directly from a Walter Scott novel, and it must have appealed to Johnston's romantic sense of chivalry.

The American batteries opened fire on March 24. The heavy American guns, including a battery of naval guns hauled into position by great effort, made short work of the Mexican fortifications. Governor Morales escaped by boat on the night of the 25th, and the next morning the Mexicans hung a white flag out over the ruined walls of the city. The surrender of the fortress of San Juan de Ulloa along with the city was particularly important, for with its heavy walls and large-caliber guns, the fort could have resisted American siege efforts for some time. Both Johnston and Lee were among those chosen to participate in the surrender ceremony. Their friend and fellow Virginian Dabney Maury could barely contain himself: "In rich uniforms, superbly mounted, they [Lee and Johnston] were the most soldierly, as they were the ablest, men in the army," he wrote. In his report on the capture of the city, Scott included Johnston's name along with Lee's and those of the other engineers on his staff. The citation must have been gratifying, but so far Johnston had not had much chance to test his mettle in battle.[9]

Scott's decision to take Vera Cruz by old-fashioned siege tactics had not been popular with his brigade commanders, who had wanted to storm the city. By sticking to his decision, Scott had saved hundreds, perhaps thousands, of American lives. The capture of Vera Cruz set a pattern for the campaign: Scott's desire to preserve American lives led him to avoid direct assaults whenever possible.

Now, however, Scott was eager to leave the coast behind, for it was already April, and with the hot weather came yellow fever. He wanted to get his army off the coastal plain and into the cooler, healthier air of the mountains before summer. On April 8, he ordered the division of Brigadier General David E. Twiggs to march inland. Johnston was in the vanguard. Scott believed that in addition to designing and constructing siege lines, his engineers should act as scouts for the army. Johnston found the countryside largely barren. "Dense thickets of thorn, cactus, and bramble covered the hill sides and valleys, and were the only vegetation," wrote a fellow officer. Riding ahead of the main force, Johnston in his halting Spanish questioned the Mexicans he encountered. He learned that Santa Anna, the Mexican president and commander-in-chief, had established himself at a ranch known as Cerro Gordo some thirty-five miles inland, where the national road began to wind up into the Sierra Madre.[10]

Santa Anna had picked a well-protected spot. At the village of Plan de Rio, the national road crossed a small stream and then wound westward and upward through a narrow defile to the plateau where the Rancho Cerro Gordo was situated. Santa Anna's guns completely commanded the highway, from a position on the right of the road atop three separate bluffs: His right flank rested securely on the river, and he relied on the roughness of the terrain to protect his left. Apprised by Johnston of the enemy's presence, Twiggs imprudently decided to attack at once. He ordered Johnston and Lieutenant Zealous Tower to reconnoiter the Mexican position. They pushed forward toward the Mexican batteries and discovered the strength of the enemy position in a particularly dramatic way: the Mexican gunners on the heights opened fire on the impertinent American scouts, and Johnston fell to the ground severely wounded by grapeshot. He had to be carried back to the village of Plan del Rio.[11]

Johnston spent two weeks in Plan del Rio at the American "hospital"—a house with interior walls constructed of reeds. Meantime Twiggs decided to postpone his frontal attack, convinced by his brigade commanders and by General Robert Patterson to wait until the rest of the army had caught up. When Scott arrived, he dispatched Lee to find a way around Santa Anna's position. Lee reconnoitered the Mexican left, where Santa Anna believed he was safe, and found a pathway to the enemy rear. Scott sent his forces to turn the enemy strongpoint, which they succeeded in doing at the Battle of Cerro Gordo on April 18. Although outnumbered, the American forces thoroughly routed their foe.[12]

Recuperating in the American camp, Johnston chafed at his immobility while the battle raged elsewhere. He chafed, too, at some of the company he was forced to keep. A man of impeccable integrity, Johnston found his rest disturbed and his sensibilities offended by John P. Denby, a wounded volun-

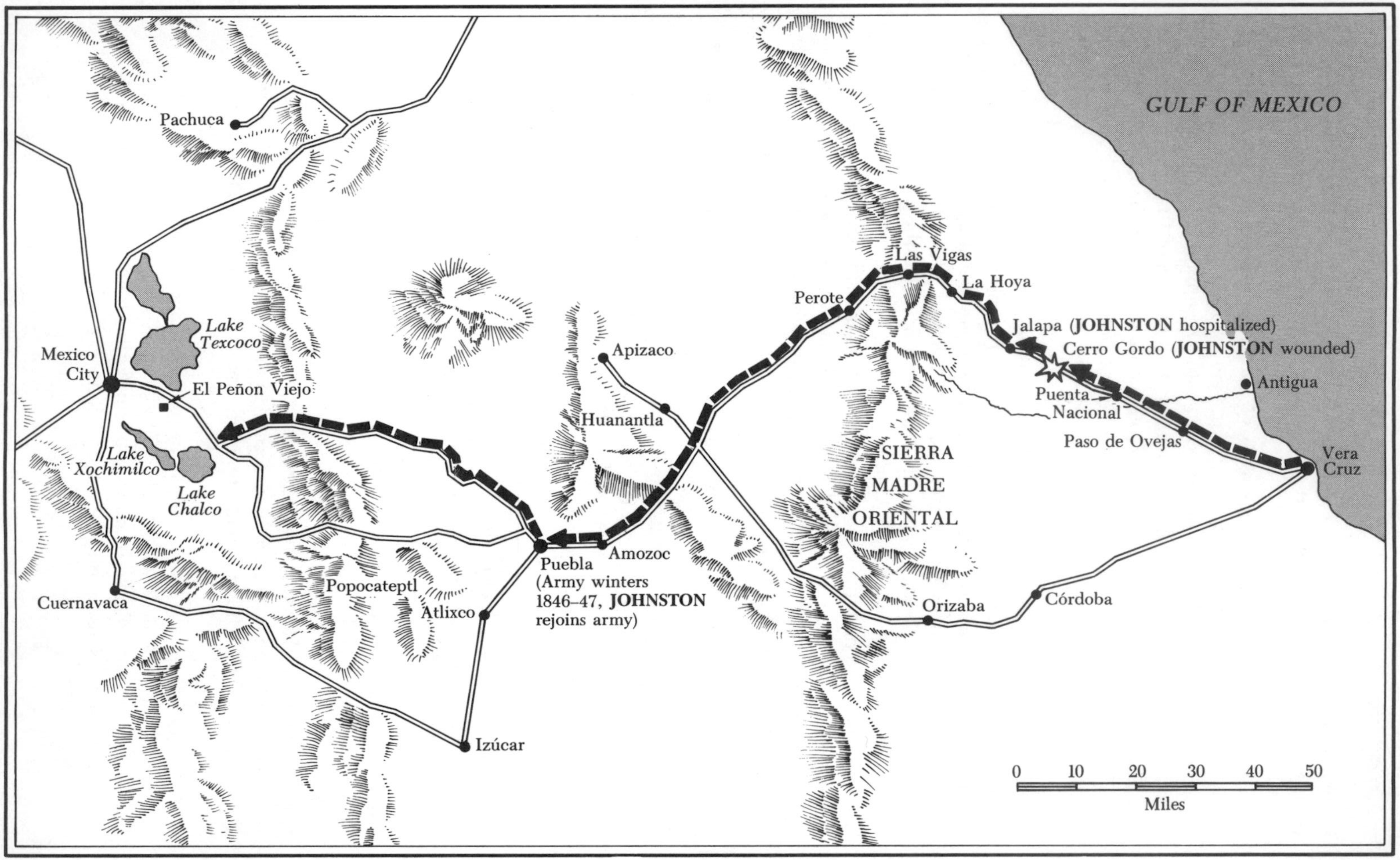

The Road to Mexico City

GULF OF MEXICO

Vera Cruz

Antigua

Jalapa (JOHNSTON hospitalized)
Cerro Gordo (JOHNSTON wounded)
Puenta Nacional
Paso de Ovejas

La Hoya

Las Vigas

Córdoba

Perote

SIERRA MADRE ORIENTAL

Orizaba

Apizaco

Huamantla

Amozoc

Puebla
(Army winters 1846–47, JOHNSTON rejoins army)

Atlixco

Izúcar

Popocatepetl

Pachuca

Lake Texcoco

El Peñon Viejo

Lake Chalco

Mexico City

Lake Xochimilco

Cuernavaca

Miles
0   10   20   30   40   50

teer officer, who, according to Dabney Maury, carried on "a stream of coarse wit, to the great disgust of Joe Johnston, who endured it in silence." Johnston held his tongue until the day Denby ordered his servant to go out and steal the kid from a passing flock of goats. Unable to endure Denby's offensive behavior any longer, Johnston burst out: "If you dare to do that, I'll have you court-martialed and cashiered or shot!" Johnston was cheered by a surprise visit from his brother-in-law Allan McLane, a midshipman on board the *Potomac* off Vera Cruz. Hearing of the battle at Cerro Gordo, and of Johnston's wounds, McLane wangled a pass from his captain to look in on Lydia's husband.[13]

Johnston was badly hurt, but his wounds were not life-threatening, and, in fact, they proved to be a distinct professional advantage, for in recognition of his bravery during the advance, and his courage during the reconnaissance, he was breveted to lieutenant colonel effective April 12, the day he was wounded. Although his double promotion meant that he had to leave Scott's staff, he was slotted for a more senior command position in one of the new regiments being formed back in the States. On April 19, the day after Cerro Gordo, Secretary of War Marcy announced the formation of eight new regiments of volunteers to serve for the duration of the war. Until they arrived, Johnston would spend his days in recuperation.

After the victory at Cerro Gordo, the American Army marched westward to Jalapa, "a lovely little town on the slope of the mountains, looking toward the sea." Ten days later, Johnston and the rest of the wounded were moved there as well, borne up into the mountains by litter bearers. The cool air at 4,680 feet was a relief after the heat of the road from Vera Cruz. One officer described Jalapa as "the prettiest town I have seen, surrounded by the finest country with the most delicious climate in the world." While recovering there, Johnston enjoyed daily visits from his nephew Preston, who was serving in the First Artillery under Johnston's old compatriot from the Florida campaign, John B. Magruder.[14]

During the Army's stay in Jalapa, General Scott received another slight from the administration. To add to the sense of betrayal he had felt in New Orleans when he learned of Polk's scheming to replace him, Scott now felt aggrieved by the arrival of Nicolas P. Trist, a chief clerk in the State Department and Secretary of State James Buchanan's personal representative, whose orders were to negotiate a treaty of peace. Scott interpreted Trist's arrival in camp as a sign that Polk did not trust him to make the terms himself. It is degrading, Scott asserted, "that the commander of this army shall defer to the chief clerk of the Department of State. . . ." Scott talked openly of "working with Polk's halter around my neck." Trist made things worse by treating Scott with a studied discourteousness that elicited a like response from the general. Scott could not send Trist back, but he barely tolerated the envoy's presence and warned him not to overstep his place or risk facing "the contempt and scorn you merit at my hands."[15] Feeling what he, at least, perceived as a "total want of support and sympathy on the part of the War Department," Scott asked Polk to relieve him. When the president received this petulant request, his first response was to accommodate his miffed general and accept his resignation. Secretary Marcy had to talk him out of it. By July, Scott and Trist had patched things up, but their quarrel was common knowledge in the American camp and provided any who cared to observe some further lessons on the difficulties of civil-military harmony.[16]

While Johnston recuperated in Jalapa, the bulk of the Army—Trist included—moved on to Puebla, nearly a hundred miles further inland and several thousand feet higher in elevation. But Scott could go no farther without reinforcements. The one-year terms of his volunteer soldiers had expired, and in May, Scott sent home ten regiments of men who had fulfilled their terms of service. With their departure, and the absence of the 1,000 sick and wounded he had left behind, Scott had only 5,820 troops left to deal with an army estimated to number over 20,000. He therefore waited in Puebla for the arrival of the new regiments.[17]

The reinforcements began to arrive at Vera Cruz in June, and the first elements straggled into Jalapa after the hot, dusty march from the coast on June 16. The Americans at Jalapa were incorporated into the new units. Johnston's assignment was as second-in-command, under Colonel Timothy P. Andrews, of a new regiment of volunteers known as the "voltigeurs"—a French term meaning light infantry or riflemen. Comprising men from Maryland, Virginia, Pennsylvania, Georgia, and Kentucky, Johnston's new unit was brigaded with the 11th and 14th Infantry regiments under the command of Major General George P. Cadwalader, a volunteer officer himself. The voltigeurs, along with the rest of Cadwalader's brigade, started out along the winding mountain road for Puebla. Mexican guerrillas threatened, but the size of the American column discouraged them. Cadwalader nevertheless stopped his column at Perote on the eastern slope of the Sierra Madre to wait for help. They were joined by Major General Gideon Pillow with two thousand more troops, and this combined force marched to Puebla, arriving on August 8.[18]

The arrival of this column, and the appearance a few days later of a regiment under Brigadier General Franklin Pierce, gave Scott about twelve thousand effectives, which he organized into four divisions under Worth, Twiggs, Pillow, and John A. Quitman. As part of Cadwalader's brigade, Johnston's voltigeurs belonged to Pillow's command. Pillow was Polk's friend and former law partner, and he owed his command position to that relationship. Not particularly effective in command, Pillow provided Johnston another example, if one were needed, that politically appointed generals could have feet of clay.

Thus reinforced, Scott embarked upon the next phase of the campaign. Knowing he could not keep up communications with Vera Cruz, he abandoned his supply line and, on August 7, plunged westward toward Mexico City. In his report, Scott declared that he threw away the scabbard and went forward with the naked blade. As the American Army marched out of Puebla with flags unfurled and bands playing, Scott rode past the cheering ranks. Here was a martial scene to make Johnston's pulse pound.[19]

In the second week of August the American soldiers descended snakelike from the mountains into the great basin of Mexico. In front of them the valley spread out as if in a painting, the great lakes glinting in the sun, with the city itself just visible in the distance. The direct approach to the city—from the west—would require the invading army to fight its way past El Peñon Viejo, a high fortification where Santa Anna had placed the bulk of his forces. Instead, however, the Army's scouts found a passable road that circled around Lakes Chalco and Xochimilco to approach the city from the south. The road was narrow, flanked by the lakes on one side and the mountains on the other, but it was not defended, and Scott at once chose it.[20]

The southern approach to Mexico City was no uncontested march. A strong Mexican force under General Nicolas Bravo occupied the village of San Antonio west of Xochimilco, blocking the road to the capital. Bravo's forces were protected on both their flanks: to the east was Xochimilco, and to the west was a trackless lava bed, called the Pedregal, so rough that it looked like "a raging sea that had been turned instantly to stone."[21] There seemed no alternative to a frontal assault. But once again Scott discovered another way, sending out Lee, who found a narrow path that led westward across the Pedregal. Scott then sent elements of Pillow's division under Brigadier General Persifer Smith to improve it for artillery. Johnston's voltigeurs, along with the rest of the division, set to work with pick and shovel to make the path passable.

When they emerged from the Pedregal, the Americans discovered that General Don Gabriel Valencia with five to seven thousand Mexican soldiers had occupied a commanding bluff only about one thousand yards to the southwest, near the town of Contreras. Worse yet, as Smith's soldiers filed out of the lava field they could see another large Mexican force crowning the hills about a mile to the north. It was Santa Anna himself, with the main body of the Mexican army, perhaps twelve thousand men. The Americans were trapped between two superior enemy forces, with mountains to their front and the Pedregal to their rear. They had marched into a trap from which there was no escape. But Smith was not thinking of escape: he sent General Bennet Riley's brigade to San Geronimo to cut off Valencia's retreat, and laid plans for an attack. Beauregard, Pillow's staff engineer, was appalled, and tried to persuade Johnston to join him in an attempt to change the general's mind. Johnston declined—either he approved of the attack, or he considered it inappropriate for a brevet lieutenant colonel to challenge the plans of his general. It turned out that Beauregard's protestations were unnecessary, for Smith, unable to get his attack organized before late afternoon, decided to postpone it until the next morning. He sent Cadwalader's brigade off to follow Riley's force to San Geronimo, from which he would launch an attack at dawn.[22]

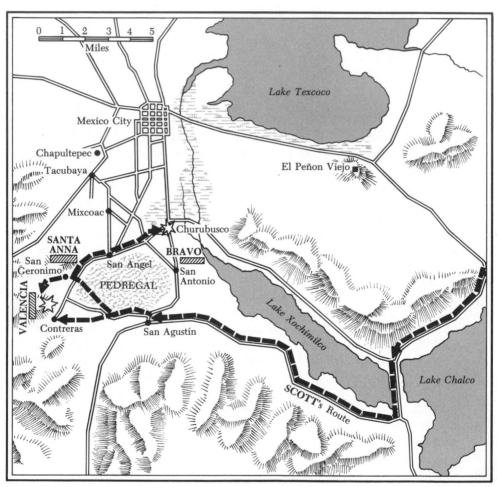

The Battles of Contreras and Churubusco, August 19–20, 1847

Johnston and his voltigeurs clambered down a ravine, crossed the road to San Angel, and marched up a narrow valley to the little village of San Geronimo. Here they were on Valencia's flank, but fully exposed to the fire of his batteries. Throughout the rest of the afternoon, the voltigeurs encountered heavy fire from the Mexican artillery. For more than three hours, the Mexican gunners shelled them with twenty-two pieces of heavy artillery; with no field guns of their own, the Americans could not respond. Along with the rest of Cadwalader's brigade, Johnston's voltigeurs hugged the earth and awaited the order to advance.[23]

As the sun set, the Mexican fire slackened, but then the rain began to fall. With no shelter or food, outnumbered and virtually surrounded, the Americans huddled in their bivouac awaiting the dawn. While the troops slept, the inexhaustible Captain Lee recrossed the Pedregal to inform Scott of Smith's plan to attack Valencia's position at dawn, and to request that Scott launch a simultaneous attack from the other side. Scott ordered Twiggs to gather together what forces he could in order to comply. Lee immediately volunteered to join him.[24]

General Smith awoke the men at San Geronimo at 2:30 A.M. Lieutenant Tower, with whom Johnston had investigated the Mexican position at Cerro Gordo, had found a path leading to the rear of Valencia's position, and Smith was determined to have his division in place for a dawn assault. Because most of the voltigeurs were new troops, undisciplined to army life, many of them had to be hunted up and awakened with the toe of a boot. It was pitch dark, the rain still falling. There was much slipping and whispered cursing as the men made their way out of the town along a narrow valley path to the rear of Valencia's position.[25]

At six o'clock, the Americans attacked. The Mexicans had spent the night celebrating their pounding of the enemy the afternoon before, and they had failed to establish any defenses in their rear. The Americans swept over them in a single rush. Johnston and the voltigeurs, on the American right flank, joined with the rest of Cadwalader's brigade as it swept over the crest of the hill. At almost the same time, Twiggs attacked from the east. Mexican resistance collapsed. Valencia's men fled into the surrounding hills in compete disorder, their general in the forefront of the stampede. Santa Anna had already given up his position behind San Angel, so that the American victory gave them control of the road north to the capital. The whole assault lasted barely a quarter of an hour. Scott claimed in his official report: "I doubt whether a more brilliant or decisive victory . . . is to be found on record."[26]

Americans from the two pincers met amid the abandoned Mexican trenches to exchange mutual congratulations. Johnston spied his friend Lee and offered his own felicitations. But Johnston's elation at this easy military success soon turned to ashes. With a solemn expression, Lee took Johnston's hand and told him that the night before, while manning his guns, Preston had been hit by a Mexican artillery shell. He had died during the night. Lee could not restrain his own tears as he watched his friend's face register the pain. He was astonished at the way Johnston's "frame was shrunk and shivered with agony." Johnston was completely overcome with grief. Preston was the son he never had, "a bright joyous young fellow, full of hope and courage." "I loved him more than my own heart," Johnston protested in a letter to Beverly five days later. "I have never before known the full bitterness of grief. Nobody else could love him as I have done. He was the pride of my heart—the companion of my manhood—& I looked to him for stay & comfort in declining years. I cannot tell you the bitterness of this event."[27] Johnston's grief did not fade. He could not bring himself to write to his niece Lizzie, Preston's sister, for several months. When he did, it was less to comfort her than to bemoan his own loss. "It will be long before I am fit to be a comforter," he wrote to her. "He had taken too firm a hold of my heart, for the time that has elapsed . . . to have softened in any degree the sense of bereavement in me." "Oh," he cried, "no one who had not Pres to love knows how one man may love another."[28]

The war would not wait for Johnston's grief. With the road to Mexico City opened, Scott pressed the Army to pursue the fleeing Mexicans. The voltigeurs and the rest of Cadwalader's brigade marched north past San Angel to Coyoacan and toward Churubusco, where Santa Anna and General Bravo were making a stand. Three American divisions closed in on them. Worth's division marched up from the south through the abandoned Mexican lines at San Antonio; Twigg's division approached from the west; and Pillow's division, with Cadwalader's brigade and the voltigeurs, swung off the road to attack from the southwest. The key to the Mexican position was the convent of San Mateo, which the Mexicans had turned into a fortress. Along with the rest of Twigg's division, Johnston and his men charged toward this strongpoint through fields of tall corn. The rows of corn hampered their visibility, and the irrigation ditches made it difficult to maintain an alignment with Worth's division on their right. The Mexicans fought more furiously than they had at any point in the campaign so far, but finally they were driven from their positions and so thoroughly defeated that the citizens of Mexico City feared the gringos would soon be sacking the city.[29]

In the aftermath of the battle, the Mexican foreign minister, Francisco Pacheco, sent a letter to Trist that was a reply, finally, to the letter Trist had brought with him from Secretary Buchanan. Hoping that Pacheco's letter might presage the opening of negotiations, Scott proposed an armistice. It was a controversial decision. The road to Mexico City ran straight as a die from Churubusco to the capital five miles away. But Scott knew that a peace on American terms—not a complete conquest—was the national goal. The destruction of Santa Anna and the seizure of the capital would bring down the government, making it more difficult to find anyone with whom a peace agreement could be concluded. There was, of course, the chance that Santa Anna would take advantage of the armistice to pull his scattered, discouraged forces together for another defense of the city, but it was a chance Scott felt he had to take. In fact, the talks led nowhere. Santa Anna could not come to terms with the invaders and still hold power.

After the collapse of the armistice, Scott assigned Worth's division the job of seizing Molino del Rey, an old foundry where, rumor had it, the Mexicans were melting down church bells to make guns. The Molino was a large, oblong building that formed the southwestern wall of an even larger compound housing the Mexican military academy, high on the bluff of Chapultepec. To ensure success in the assault, Scott reinforced Worth's division with Cadwalader's brigade.[30]

Worth attacked at daylight on September 8, 1847. He gave the site a brief artillery preparation and launched a frontal bayonet attack, holding the voltigeurs regiment in reserve. The Mexican defenders repulsed the initial American attack. As the American forces fell back, Mexican cavalry on the American left flank threatened to ride down the retreating troops. Cadwalader ordered the voltigeurs to turn and block this threat. The raw troops executed the maneuver flawlessly, and the line of light infantry and supporting artillery repelled the Mexican thrust. Two companies of the voltigeurs actually crossed a ravine to pursue the retreating enemy, capturing scores of prisoners. Having met that challenge, the voltigeurs were next called from the American left and sent into the thick of the fight on the American right. They battered in a gate at the southern end of the building and fought room to room until finally the Mexicans gave up, fleeing to the greater safety of Chapultepec.[31]

Johnston had admired Worth during the time he spent on his staff in Florida, but the hasty assault at Molino del Rey had led to 116 American battle deaths and 665 wounded. The Army's reaction was split. Some officers thought Worth's conduct little short of murder and said so, although others defended him, blaming Scott, whose armistice had provided the Mexicans time to prepare their defenses. Scott and Worth stopped speaking to each other. Johnston's own conduct during this battle was exemplary. Cadwalader specifically mentioned him in his report to Worth as one of ten officers who had performed gallantly.[32]

With the capture of the Molino, Scott's only remaining strategic decision was which route to use in his final approach to the city. There were no good options. Built on an island in a lakebed, Mexico City could be approached only along one of several causeways over marshy land. In a lengthy meeting with his staff, Scott decided that the Army would attack from the southwest, which made it necessary to assault the towering eminence of the citadel of Chapultepec. This time he assigned the job to Gideon Pillow's division.

Chapultepec was a daunting obstacle. Sitting on a high plateau 150 to 200 feet above the plain, its masonry walls rose another 15 to 20 feet above that. Around the base of the plateau another imposing wall enclosed the grounds; it stood fifteen feet high and had only one entrance, a gate on the southern face. Through that one gate, a road wound its way up the hillside to the citadel.[33] The assault would provide Johnston with his first independent command, for Pillow divided the voltigeurs into two battalions of four com-

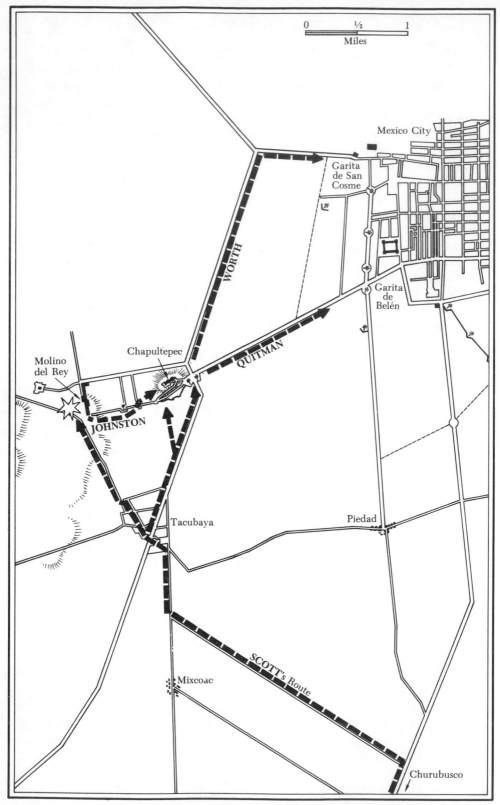

Molino del Rey, Chapultepec, and the Assault on Mexico City

panies each. Colonel Andrews would command one half and Johnston the other. Johnston's four companies were assigned the crucial role of leading the assault and seizing the gate in the southern wall. They were then to move into the inner court and hold a line of departure halfway up the plateau. The assaulting party, carrying scaling ladders, would pass through them to assail the walls of the fortress itself. A lull in the American cannonade would be Johnston's signal to attack.[34]

At daylight on September 13, the U.S. guns opened fire and did not stop until 7:30 P.M. After a brief pause they began again. Johnston led his battalion along the outside of the southern wall to the main gate. His men charged the Mexican guard at the redoubt and forced their way through, seizing the road up to the citadel. Here they linked up with the other battalion of voltigeurs under Andrews, and with Pierce's brigade. The voltigeurs advanced to their assigned positions, took cover, and began sniping at the parapets.[35]

The Americans were now inside the outer wall, but they were no more than halfway up the plateau, which was itself topped by the stone citadel that towered above them. Scott's plan had called for the storming party to pass through this line and place ladders up against the walls of the fort. But a delay in bringing the ladders forward meant that while they clung precariously to the base of the bluff, the voltigeurs were subjected to a continuous fire from the Mexican defenders.

Although a member of the headquarters staff, Beauregard had not wanted to miss out on the climactic action of the campaign and had joined in the assault as a volunteer. He reported in his memoirs that "the gallant Colonel Johnston" encouraged his men forward "against as terrible a fire as I had yet seen!" This steady fire poured down from the walls of the citadel. To Beauregard's eye, "the top of the parapet was one continued sheet of flame." Far from being discouraged, however, he thought it was "as grand and sublime a scene as I have yet witnessed." He was especially impressed by the steadiness of Johnston's voltigeurs. "I never saw new troops behave as well as this voltigeur battalion under such trying circumstances and they did infinite credit to their officers," he wrote.[36]

Even the best troops could be daunted by the towering mass of Chapultepec, however. Pinned down under the walls of the citadel, the voltigeurs huddled among brush and boulders for over a quarter of an hour, answering as best they could the fire from the heights. The Mexican fire was inaccurate, mainly because the defenders, in order not to expose themselves, held their muskets out over the walls, shooting blindly. Still, the sheer mass of fire was terrifying, and to bolster the morale of the men, Beauregard called over to Johnston during a lull: "Colonel," he shouted, "what will you bet on this shot?" Johnston immediately caught the spirit of the question and called back: "Drinks in the City of Mexico." Beauregard thereupon fired, and whether or not his bullet found its mark, he called back to Johnston: "You have lost, you will have to pay it."[37]

By now the storming party under Captain Samuel Mackenzie had finally formed up at the foot of the hill with its ladders. But when the men reached the line held by the voltigeurs, they hesitated. Mackenzie had to urge them on. As Johnston added his voice to Mackenzie's, the voltigeurs joined in the assault on the citadel. They charged forward, placed the scaling ladders against the walls, climbed to the parapet, and fought the defenders hand-to-hand. A soldier from Johnston's battalion was the first to clamber over the walls; soon the blue flag of the voltigeurs' regiment, riddled with holes, flew from the parapet. From atop the ramparts of Chapultepec, Johnston could see the whole Valley of Mexico: the surrounding mountains, the silvery lakes, and less than two miles away, the capital city itself. It was both literally and figuratively the peak of the campaign. He had led the charge of his own troops in the decisive engagement of the war. The enemy's capital lay at his feet. For his part in this assault, Johnston would receive another brevet to the rank of colonel.[38]

Major General Quitman gathered together the heterogeneous elements of the units that had taken part in the assault on Chapultepec to lead them in a headlong pursuit up the causeway toward the Garita de Belén, at the southwest corner of the city. They charged all the way to the gate, where Johnston's classmate Simon Drum was killed before they fell back. As part of Cadwalader's brigade, Johnston and his voltigeurs joined Worth's division in an attack on the Garita de San Cosme at the western entrance to the city. After a brief resistance there, the Mexican defenders fled; by six o'clock, Worth's men were in the city. The city fathers had seen enough. They did not want to endure prolonged street fighting with its consequent civilian casualties and destruction to property. They begged Santa Anna to yield, and the general abandoned the city.

Johnston's participation in the American entry into the city of Mexico was a triumph to match his dreams of military glory. Although the American Army was ragtag to Mexican eyes, it had duplicated the feat of Cortes. And if the odds were not as long, this time the defenders had been equipped with all the modern weapons of war. An army of ten to twelve thousand, cut off from its base, had conquered an empire by skill and by bravery. Johnston had been in the thick of it from the start, and though severely wounded, he had not missed out on the climax of the campaign. "Joe Johnston is fat, ruddy, & hearty," Lee wrote to a mutual friend. "I think a little lead, properly taken, is good for a man."[39]

With the fall of Mexico City, the war was all but over. Santa Anna managed to gather yet another army and continued to constitute a threat to American outposts like Jalapa, but the serious campaigning had ended. During the winter months that followed, Johnston served with the occupation forces in Tacubaya and Toluca, west of Mexico City. For a few brief weeks he acted as commander of the district, presiding over various courts-martial in an effort to maintain order. His room commanded a beautiful view of the Valley of Mexico and the snow-capped mountains that surrounded it. At night the inevitable fleas made sleep difficult, but on the whole it was a pleasant winter. With the exception of occasional visits from fellow officers, there was little to do. The months of quiet gave him a chance to digest the lessons of the campaign.[40]

Johnston could not help but admire Scott's generalship. Professionals in Europe as renowned as the Duke of Wellington had predicted his destruction, yet Scott had fought his way inland, defeating natural and man-made obstacles and an army twice the size of his own. Even Wellington was impressed: "He is the greatest living soldier," said the man who had defeated Napoleon at Waterloo. Scott had achieved his victory by eschewing frontal assaults in favor of siege tactics and battles of maneuver, though when frontal assaults were necessary, as at Chapultepec, the Army had proved equal to the task.[41]

Johnston had also learned scorn for the interference of politicians and amateurs. It would not be hard for him to conclude that Polk's duplicity in working behind Scott's back to replace him with a politically compatible commander, Trist's "interference" (as Scott saw it) in the negotiations that ended the war, and the appointment of Polk's law partner as a division commander were all part of the same phenomenon: political meddling with the conduct of a military campaign.

Johnston learned respect, however, for the prowess of the American fightingman. His own heroism at Cerro Gordo, Contreras, and Chapultepec was notable, but so too was that of most of the Army. He had less respect for the enemy. In 1856 he wrote a friend, "I hope it may never be my lot to fight troops much better than El Senor Mexicano. There is no comfort like that of going into battle with the certainty of winning."[42]

For Johnston, the great tragedy of the war was Preston's death in the Battle of Contreras. In his heart at least, Johnston had adopted Preston as his son. It was not merely the conceit of a doting uncle that the entire Army mourned Preston's loss: "Regretted by all grades in the army—from the soldier to the commander in chief." Johnston arranged to have Preston's remains returned to Baltimore. "I couldn't bear that a Mexican foot should tread over them," he wrote to Lizzie. Johnston never fully recovered from the loss. More than forty years later, and only a few weeks before his own death, he reminded a visitor how clever and winning Preston had been. "When Lee came to tell me of Preston's death," the old general recalled, "he wept as he took my hand." Johnston ended his war in Mexico bathed in military glory, but plunged into deep personal sorrow.[43]

CHAPTER SIX

The 1850s: Pathfinder, Peacekeeper, Filibusterer

Johnston had gone off to war in 1846 as a captain of Topographical Engineers; he returned in 1848 as a brevet colonel of volunteers, having advanced further in two years of war than in twenty years of peace. His delight in professional success was muted by the personal tragedy of Preston's death, but he returned from the war with excellent prospects, full of dreams about the future—his own and the country's. The peace settlement brought vast new western lands into the national domain: as a soldier and topographical engineer, Johnston saw it for what it was, a western empire to be explored, mapped, and developed. In his most fanciful moments he envisioned an even larger empire—stretching below the Rio Grande and embracing the Gulf of Mexico. For all his practicality, Johnston was a romantic, both personally and in his sense of nationalism, and the decade of the 1850s provided him with many opportunities to conjure up visions of grandeur. Few of his visions would be fulfilled, but as he wrote to a friend at the decade's end: "I can't help building castles in the air."[1]

During the 1850s, the national consciousness was dominated by the question of what would become of the new lands gained from Mexico. The Treaty of Guadaloupe-Hidalgo required Mexico to surrender not only all its claims to Texas north of the Rio Grande, but also a vast territory of more than half a million square miles stretching to the Pacific, in return for which the United States paid Mexico $15 million. The most sensitive question about these new territories was what legal limits, if any, would be placed on the status of slavery. Pennsylvania Congressman David Wilmot's proposal that slavery be banned in the new lands triggered a frenzy of debate and excitement that lasted throughout the decade. Southerners saw Wilmot's proviso as an attempt to exclude them from lands won, in part at least, by their efforts, and to place slavery in a condition where it could neither thrive economically nor protect itself politically. Northerners concluded that the South's determination to allow slavery into the new territories was evidence that the slavocracy planned to extend its influence throughout the country.[2]

This national debate would eventually touch all Americans, but in the 1850s it infringed on Johnston particularly in three ways: as chief topographical engineer in Texas, he participated in the question of routing a transcontinental railroad through the Mexican Cession to California; as second-in-command of the First Cavalry Regiment in Kansas in 1856 and 1857, he was intimately involved in the tragedy of "bleeding Kansas"; and as a romantic nationalist, he would play a role in the filibustering schemes of the late 1850s. Johnston was not particularly political, but the sectional question was so dominant in the 1850s that no one could remain untouched.

The dream of a transcontinental railroad was already decades old when the war with Mexico ended. Virtually everyone favored such a project; senators North and South pushed hard to promote routes that would benefit their own regions. Stephen Douglas of Illinois was the foremost advocate of a northern route, with an eastern terminus in Chicago; Thomas Hart Benton and David Atchison of Missouri championed a central route, starting at St. Louis; Sam Houston and Thomas Rusk of Texas campaigned for a southern route across Texas, from Vicksburg to El Paso. Memphis, too, had its advocates; in October 1849, a convention in that city endorsed a southern route across Texas provided that Memphis, and not Vicksburg, became the hub.

The southern route also had a strong ally in Colonel James J. Abert, commandant of the Topographical Corps of Engineers and therefore Johnston's boss. "A stern, upright man, a bluff soldier of the old school," Abert was a strong advocate of a trans-Texas railroad. The viability of this route soon became an obsession, and on his own initiative he ordered several expeditions to map possible routes westward from San Antonio. Since Johnston was the senior topographical engineer in the state, it became his responsibility to conduct or supervise those expeditions.[3] In January 1849, Congress approved an appropriation of $50,000 for railroad surveys in Nebraska, California, New Mexico, and Texas; and in June, Abert ordered Johnston to survey the route from San Antonio to El Paso. The very fact that Abert dispatched Johnston suggests that he sought to invest the subsequent report with as much prestige as possible.[4]

Johnston responded by organizing two expeditions, the first under Lieutenant Francis T. Bryan, whom he ordered to explore a northern route, and a much larger one to trace a more southerly route, which he would command himself. He detailed a company of infantry and twenty civilian laborers to help construct a road, and set out from San Antonio on June 13 in the summer heat. He led his party due west, skirting the Balcones Escarpment, then tracked generally northwest, fording the Pecos south of Horse Head Crossing. Turning west again across the Stockton Plateau, he more or less followed the route of modern Interstate 10 to the Davis Mountains, which forced him to swing south again, then west to the Rio Grande and along its northern bank to El Paso. Johnston reported that "The road is generally excellent, with abundance of grass and fuel." He stayed in the El Paso area for a month, conducting local explorations of the Sacramento Mountains and accumulating supplies. The return trip began on October 11. They had intended to take the northern route, but winter came early, in mid-October, forcing the party to swing south for the sake of the mules. Johnston was back in San Antonio on November 23.[5]

Though he fully supported Abert's goal of a southern railroad to California, as a military man Johnston was at least as interested in providing efficient transport to the western forts as he was in blazing the way for a transcontinental railroad. His reports included lengthy paragraphs on the arming of the troops—he preferred Colt revolvers to sabers—and on "the disturbed condition of the frontier." He also believed that supply routes might best be maintained not by a railroad, but by opening the Colorado and Rio Grande Rivers to steam navigation. The idea of a transcontinental railroad never fired his mind the way it did Abert's.[6]

Nevertheless, Johnston became deeply involved in a railroad scheme of his own during the winter of 1851–52. A group of eastern businessmen who hoped to build a railroad across West Texas offered to hire him to conduct the survey work. Johnston saw no difficulty in accepting their offer; he even wrote Abert to solicit technical details about railroad construction, explaining that he had been engaged by "a chartered company" to make examinations for a railroad "in my leisure time this winter." He asked a series of technical questions: the cost and weight of railroad iron, the manner of laying rails, the width of cuts, the optimum slope for grades, even "the ordinary cost of a locomotive" and passenger cars.[7]

No doubt Johnston believed he was performing a public service, though the entrepreneurial nature of the enterprise was obvious. At a time when the national government was giving away public land to railroad companies for little more than vague promises to construct a railroad at some future date, the distinction between private enterprise and public service was blurred. There is some evidence that Johnston might have expected to serve as president of the new company—years later he referred to himself as the former chief executive of the San Antonio & Rio Grande Railroad. But just as Abert's dream of a government-sponsored railroad across Texas fell victim to the political schisms in Congress, Johnston's affiliation with private railroad entrepreneurs lasted only a single winter, then collapsed amid the growing sectional conflict.[8]

In the fall of 1852, Johnston requested and was granted a year's extended leave from the Army. He spent most of that year in Baltimore, returning to active duty in the fall of 1853. For the next two years he served as the supervisor of river improvements in the West, with overall responsibility for projects designed to facilitate navigation on the Mississippi, Arkansas, Illinois, and Ohio Rivers. Most of his correspondence dealt with account books and tours of inspection to various sites: the harbor at Dubuque, the rapids at Des Moines, the snags in the Arkansas River. The civilian snag boat captains were particularly frustrating, for they were not subject to his "command," often declined to accept his instructions, and just as frequently asked for higher pay. In Johnston's view, they were simply not professional. In the spring of 1854, he fell seriously ill and spent most of April and May sweating out a fever in Little Rock. Not until June did he feel well enough to continue his round of inspection tours to Dubuque, Keokuk, and Louisville, with intermittent trips home to Baltimore. All in all it was unsatisfying work, and he used the excuse of ill health to ask Abert for reassignment to Washington.[9]

Johnston really wanted to get out of the Topographical Corps and into a regular line regiment where promotion was faster. He complained to his brother Edward that "In the Topl. corps there is no promotion, a thing I desire more than any man in the army."[10] The authorized strength of the Corps allowed only one man to be a full colonel in the "Topogs"—and that man was Colonel Abert. Unless Abert died, retired, or transferred to another service, no one else could hope to advance beyond lieutenant colonel.

Then, too, Johnston preferred service with soldiers in the field to working with surveying instruments. He disliked commanding from an office, and looked with disdain upon those who did, telling Edward, "I prefer serving with troops on such a frontier as this." Johnston was more interested in the accoutrements of his soldiers than the details of his surveys. He even equipped his men as for frontier service, ordering them to put away their sabers, don broad-brimmed western hats, and stick a revolver in their belts.[11]

Johnston's dream was the command of a regiment, something he would never have as long as he remained in the Topographical Engineers. Almost immediately after the end of the Mexican War, rumors had begun to circulate in the officer corps that Congress intended to create new regiments for service in the Mexican Cession. Johnston seized on this rumor as an opportunity to achieve both promotion and command. Scott, he believed, would be willing to support his application. Although he thought it unseemly to solicit promotion for himself, he was convinced that his competitors would have no such qualms. That being the case, he feared that his peers would claim all the best spots in the new regiments.[12]

As it turned out, the rumors in 1851 were premature; but two years later, when Franklin Pierce became president and appointed Jefferson Davis as his Secretary of War, Davis convinced Congress that additional regiments were necessary. Congress in response authorized the creation of four new regiments—the Ninth and Tenth Infantry, and the First and Second Cavalry. Immediately, officers began to jockey for preferment. Appeals to Scott were not likely to do Johnston any good now, for Scott and Davis were not on good terms. Indeed, Scott resented Davis's assertive management of the War Department and moved his headquarters to New York to distance himself from the Secretary. Johnston therefore asked Major General Cadwalader, now retired to a law practice in Philadelphia, to put in a word on his behalf. Cadwalader wrote the Adjutant General, praising the "valuable and efficient services rendered by Colonel Johnston" in Mexico, and urging his selection in the strongest terms.[13]

But there were only four command billets, and dozens of deserving officers. When orders to the new regiments were posted in March 1855, Johnston was listed as a lieutenant colonel of cavalry and appointed second-in-command of the First Cavalry Regiment, to be stationed at Fort Leavenworth. Johnston was disappointed but after examining the list of selections, he decided that Davis had based his choice exclusively on longevity of service, and that therefore a lieutenant colonelcy was all he could expect.[14] The two men who did receive command appointments to the cavalry regiments were Colonel Edwin Vose Sumner, already white-haired and a veteran of long service, and Albert Sidney Johnston, who had been Adjutant of the Corps at West Point when Joe Johnston was a plebe. Sumner got the First Cavalry and thus became Johnston's immediate superior; A. S. Johnston got the Second Cavalry Regiment, with Joe's old friend Robert E. Lee as his second-in-command. Once again Johnston and Lee had parallel assignments.

Johnston's new commanding officer had earned the nickname "Bull" in the Army, for his powerful frame, and because during the Battle of Cerro Gordo a musket ball had glanced off his skull. He was a strict disciplinarian—his enemies called him a martinet—and thoroughly unpopular in all of his commands with the officers under him. In the time-honored vein of younger officers who are convinced that their commanders are over the hill, Johnston complained of Sumner's tradition-bound methods. To a fellow officer, he wrote: "You have yet to learn how ignorant a man can keep himself who relies, for knowledge, upon *experience* & yet never observes or remembers." Johnston also resented having to defer to Sumner, complaining: "The best opinions an officer of [this] regiment can cultivate are (that is to say for his own comfort) that he is utterly ignorant professionally & that his colonel is not—the last most difficult."[15]

According to Johnston, Sumner's idea of authority was to ensure that the post looked good, that the troops made a good show on parade, and that all reports were filed on time. "The old infantry notion exists here," Johnston wrote to a friend, "that to make a decent appearance on dress parade is the only object of instruction." Johnston complained that "There has been no practice of any sort with arms (except that the arms of the guard are discharged at a mast every morning) & very little in riding other than in riding to water." He thought it absurd that there was no standardization within the cavalry for management of horses and arms. Sumner simply imposed whatever system he had grown used to in his former service, and continued it out of habit and inertia. Johnston believed that the War Department should establish precise regulations for training in the new branch of service, particularly requiring officers to train their charges in horsemanship and the use of arms. "We want a system of instruction the decent observance of which will teach our men to ride & use arms on horseback, which can't be said of the present one." His concern extended to the horses as well as the men: "We want, too, regulations for stable service to protect horses from the effects of the ignorance or indifference of Sen[io]r officers to their welfare."[16]

The First Cavalry was initially assigned to conduct an expedition to pacify the Sioux in the Wyoming Territory. Under Sumner's command, the regiment started out from Fort Leavenworth for Fort Laramie in late September 1855. After several hard weeks on the road, word reached the column that the crisis had passed. Sumner ordered the regiment to turn around and march back. The men arrived at Fort Leavenworth on November 5 much the worse for wear, having lost seventy horses on the trail and worn out most of the rest. Johnston estimated that the expedition set the regiment back at least three months.[17]

This useless march only confirmed Johnston's frustration at his inability to reform what he saw as deficiencies in the regiment. Although he had lobbied hard for the job, after a year as second-in-command he was cursing his fate. "I regret very much my assignment to this regiment," he wrote in March 1856. The sole satisfactions he derived from his posting at Fort Leavenworth were that Lydia was there to welcome him home every night, and the pleasure of his friendships with several of the younger officers. Johnston relied heavily on two young captains in the First Cavalry Regiment who became special friends: Delos B. Sacket of New York, and George B. McClellan of Pennsylvania. To McClellan he wrote, "You and Sacket preserve me from despair."[18]

As in the relationship with Preston, Johnston adopted the twenty-eight-year-old Captain McClellan as a protégé, developing a genuine affection for him. McClellan had graduated from West Point in 1846, just in time for orders to the war in Mexico where, like Johnston, he had won two brevet promotions. Clearly McClellan was a rising star in the Army, and when he was later temporarily detached from the regiment to go to Europe as an official observer in the Crimean War, Johnston remained a faithful correspondent. Even after McClellan's resignation from the Army to head up the troubled Illinois Central Railroad, they continued to write and visit one another. It was to McClellan that Johnston reported gossip from the regiment, vented his frustration at Sumner's latest blunder, and offered ideas for the improvement of the service.[19]

Both men were committed to improving the Army—especially the cavalry accoutrements such as saddles, sabers, and pistols. Johnston became an enthusiastic advocate of the more comfortable "McClellan saddle," which was eventually adopted by the Army; he argued repeatedly for the use of gutta percha rather than India rubber in scabbards, and he was eager to get his hands on new models of revolvers for testing on the frontier. The two shared ideas about the design of barracks buildings. Johnston was particularly interested in the cavalry barracks he had seen in Mexico, where the horses were stabled directly under the living quarters—rather like an urban firehouse. And they shared a commitment to improving the training program. But their correspondence, and presumably their personal relationship, was also full of the usual affectionate banter associated with barracks life. Johnston teased McClellan about his amorous adventures with a mysterious "Sardinian woman," and McClellan responded that he assumed an efficient command would issue women along with horses. Johnston replied: "Sacket is charmed with your notion of assimilating allowances of women & horses & flatters himself that his chances of applying those principles are pretty fair as there is a suspicion prevailing that we shall be sent to Utah next summer." Lydia shared in her husband's friendship with Captain McClellan; most of Johnston's letters ended with the note that "Mrs. J. sends her love."[20]

Johnston first heard rumors of McClellan's resignation from the Army in the fall of 1856. Then in December he saw the published orders, and was vastly disappointed. "Nothing since the 14th of Aug '47 [the day Preston died] has grieved me so much," he wrote. "It has overturned many castles-in-the-air." There was no one now with whom he could discuss things: "On the subject of professional daily talks, reading, fencing, marches, and coffee talks, chases of Buffalo, wolves & Indians, there is no one left in the regiment or army to take your place." Then, sadly, "I wish I was young enough to resign too."[21]

Indeed, Johnston did think about resigning. He asked McClellan repeatedly if he knew of any profitable business ventures open to a man of his education and experience. Johnston had no income except for his army pay, and though it was respectable now that he was a lieutenant colonel, he was still not a wealthy man. At the same time, he was cautious. Once when McClellan suggested a possible opportunity, Johnston responded that he could not ask for a leave of absence for a temporary job, however profitable. "For something likely to lead to another thing handsomer & permanent," he wrote, "I might & probably would. . . ." Lacking such guarantees, he would stay in the Army.[22]

In the last days of 1855, Johnston wrote McClellan that "we now have a little speck of war in the Kansas horizon."[23] That "little speck" was the first breath of the gale that would sweep away his generation. Two years earlier,

Stephen Douglas had introduced a bill to organize the Kansas and Nebraska Territories as part of his effort to establish a transcontinental railroad from Chicago to San Francisco. The immediate effect of his proposal was to revive the slavery issue that had been temporarily quieted by the Compromise of 1850. In exchange for southern support of his bill, Douglas added a provision that voided the Missouri Compromise of 1820, which had banned slavery north of the 36° 30' line. Convinced that slavery could not survive in such a hostile climate, Douglas stipulated that each territory would determine its status—free or slave—by vote, that is, by popular sovereignty. His bill opened a Pandora's Box. Slaveholders from Missouri and the rest of the slaveholding South were determined that Kansas (at least) should become a slave state. Many northerners were just as determined that it should not. On the national level, the issue gave birth to the Republican Party. In Kansas, advocates of both sides flocked into the territory to save the state for their cause. Moderates who were perfectly willing to let slavery survive unmolested in the South did not want to see it expand into the West.

The stage was set for violent confrontation the very month that the First Cavalry Regiment was organized at Fort Leavenworth. In March 1855, the first territorial elections were marked by widespread fraud as so-called border ruffians from Missouri crossed over to Kansas to vote for the pro-slave ticket. Ironically, these illegal voters probably did their cause more harm than good. The pro-slave candidates might very well have won a majority in a fair election, but the obvious fraudulence of the polling tainted their victory. Although the total voting population numbered only 2,905, some 6,307 votes were cast. The territorial governor, Andrew H. Reeder, called for re-votes in some districts; but despairing of victory, the free state voters stayed home. Pro-slavery forces were jubilant. Within a few months, the majority in the legislature had compelled the few free state delegates to resign, and had begun to adopt a set of restrictive slave laws that were even more assertive than those of South Carolina or Mississippi: reading an anti-slavery tract was now punishable by imprisonment, and questioning the virtue of slavery punishable by confiscation of property.[24]

Calling these "the bogus laws," free state forces responded with defiance. They announced plans to meet in Topeka in July to write a free state constitution, and armed squads of free state volunteers began drilling in Lawrence. For their part, the pro-slavery forces called for a convention of their own, inviting the new territorial governor, Wilson Shannon, to preside. Shannon accepted the invitation; in his remarks he denounced the actions of the free staters as not only illegal but treasonable.

Despite all this posturing, the situation might have stopped short of bloodshed but for a seemingly innocuous event. On November 21, 1855, Franklin Coleman, who was pro-slave, shot and killed Charles Dow, a free state man, in an argument over land claims. Since the local sheriff showed no evidence of making an arrest, a mob of Dow's friends threatened to lynch Coleman. Claiming that he had acted in self-defense, Coleman placed himself under the governor's protection. Shannon called out the militia, and an armed mob of about fifteen hundred men gathered on the banks of the Waruska River, determined to see that "justice" was served. About the same number of free state men gathered in Lawrence, equally eager for their own version of justice. Frightened by what he had wrought, Governor Shannon wired President Pierce asking for authority to call out Federal troops, at the same time sending a rider to Colonel Sumner at Fort Leavenworth asking him to take the field.[25]

Johnston was repulsed by the whole charade. Peacekeeping between groups of unruly and bloodthirsty civilians was the most distasteful military service he could imagine, and he believed that Governor Shannon's intemperance was at least partly responsible. As he wrote to McClellan: "The gov[vernor of Kansas] has called on Col. Sumner for help, after doing what he could to set the two parties together by the ears & has probably made the same application to the pres[iden]t." Sumner, however, declined to respond without orders from Washington. For once Johnston agreed with his commander.[26]

Although Shannon managed to avoid bloodshed in this so-called Waruska War, he did no more than postpone it. On May 21, 1856, the situation took a sharp turn for the worse when border ruffians from Missouri rode into the free state stronghold of Lawrence and put it to the torch. That raid prompted John Brown, a fanatical opponent of slavery, to conduct a series of grisly murders along the banks of the Potawatomie River. Together, these two events triggered a summer of violence that gave the territory the moniker "Bleeding Kansas."

With orders to keep the peace without taking sides, the Army, and particularly the First Cavalry, was caught in the middle. For the rest of the summer, as violence raged, units of the First Cavalry Regiment raced around the territory trying to keep the two sides apart. Because the Pierce administration took the line that the legitimate government was represented by Shannon and the pro-slave legislature, free state settlers looked upon the Army as "an army of subjugation." Pierce ordered that the free state Topeka convention should not be allowed to meet, as planned, on July 4. That morning, therefore, Sumner led two hundred troopers into the celebrations in Topeka. Making a great show of unlimbering his artillery and preparing for battle, he politely informed the convention that it would not be allowed to meet. Lacking a quorum in any case, its leaders acceded. Sumner had accomplished his mission without bloodshed. But Republican forces in Congress were angered by Sumner's interference, and they got their revenge four days later by refusing to pass the army appropriation bill as long as U.S. forces were being used to suppress free-soil men in Kansas. The Pierce administration denied any such intention, and made Sumner the scapegoat. He was removed from command and replaced by Major General Persifer Smith. Mollified, Congress relented and passed the appropriations bill.[27]

Sumner felt betrayed. Johnston reported to McClellan that Sumner "left his post in high dudgeon . . . regarding himself as ill-used by an ungrateful administration." Johnston was not sorry to see him go, particularly since he greatly admired Persifer Smith, with whom he had served in both Mexico and Texas. Indeed, Johnston and Smith were soon messing together. Partly because Smith refused to respond to Governor Shannon's pleas for help, there were no more confrontations in the field for the First Cavalry that summer. Yet the regiment was often in the field, deployed across the territory. In August, Johnston wrote to McClellan, "The regiment is still scattered, 2 companies here [Fort Leavenworth], one at Fort Kearney, & 7 keeping Kansas in subjugation to the governor."[28]

In the fall, Johnston was freed from his unpleasant duty in Kansas and ordered to Jefferson Barracks, Missouri, just south of St. Louis to preside over the depot for new recruits. He took the first available boat downstream. "I thank providence (& General Smith)," he wrote, "for my escape from this d—d civile bellum. Soldiers were never on more disgusting service." Lydia, who had spent the summer back East with her father and sisters, returned and despite bouts of continuing ill health, set to work turning their temporary billet at Jefferson Barracks into a home. " 'The Madam' has exhausted the pleasures of fixing up," Johnston told McClellan, "& I am in hourly fear of taking up of carpets & moving of furniture."[29]

His new command was not an impressive one: Johnston presided over a few "dilapidated storehouses which are empty & two wooden stables (empty tambien) on their last legs." His duties were primarily administrative. His eyes continued to bother him, especially at night when he could not do any paperwork or reading. He wrote McClellan to ask him "confidentially" to buy him "a pair of the best & cheapest *young* spectacles," though he feared his request would elicit "impertinent allusions" about his age from his younger colleague.[30]

In the spring of 1857, after a particularly bitter winter, Johnston returned to Kansas, not as part of the peacekeeping force this time, but in his former capacity as explorer and topographical engineer. On March 25, 1856, Congress had enacted a bill to survey the southern boundary of Kansas as a preliminary step to statehood. Legally designated as the 37th parallel, the line was "to be surveyed and distinctly marked." The survey had been postponed because of the bloodshed of the ensuing summer and fall, but by the following spring the civil war in Kansas had abated. On April 25, 1857, the new Secretary of War, John B. Floyd, who as Lizzie Preston's adopted father was a kind of cousin-by-adoption, appointed Johnston to command the survey party.[31]

The Plains Indians remained a threat, so Johnston's party was a large one. He commanded four "reasonably full companies" of the First Cavalry, plus two companies of the Sixth Infantry under Captain Richard B. Garnett. The party was accompanied by over 100 wagons, each drawn by 6 mules, and a herd of 150 oxen. Johnston was concerned, however, because the vast majority of his troopers were untested recruits. While in Washington he had urged Floyd not to detail raw recruits for frontier service. Floyd had "promised that it should never be done," yet within a few weeks of Johnston's return to Fort Leavenworth, three hundred recruits arrived from Carlisle Barracks and now constituted the bulk of his expedition. Johnston ruefully described the situation to McClellan: "Fully 120 boobies who never straddled a horse, starting on an expedition of near two thousand miles with a chance of getting into an occasional skirmish with the best horsemen in the world."[32]

Cold weather in May meant little grass for the horses and a delay of the start. Finally, on May 16, Johnston assembled the entire party at Westport on the south bank of the Missouri, read them the orders for the summer's campaign, and started southward. Somewhere in southeast Kansas, the expedition waited another week for the "scientists," J. H. Clarke and Hugh Campbell, the astronomers; and J. E. Weyss, the surveyor, to arrive. Having established the precise location of the southeast corner of Kansas and erected an appropriate monument, the whole party started west, stopping every mile to mark the boundary line with a conical mound topped by a wooden stake. They had some trouble crossing the Neosho River on June 10–13, and even more crossing the Arkansas on July 2, which was finally achieved by constructing boats.[33]

During the first five weeks of the expedition they had no contact with Indians. Tongue-in-cheek, Johnston wondered if the Indians failed to appear because their instruments were too imperfect to allow them to find the 37th parallel. Finally, on July 8, "a party of 30 to 40 Osage Indians of the band of Big Head & Black Dog paid us a visit while we were pitching our tents." The Indians wore "a piece of cotton cloth tied about their loins" and "an abundance of rings, partly on their fingers, partly on their arms, and partly through their ears." Johnston gave them "a little hard bread & sugar," but the Indians asked for more; they were especially eager for coffee and tobacco. When Johnston told them that he had no tobacco to spare, the Osages remarked (as Johnston noted wryly in his journal) that men who travelled in the West without extra tobacco to give away were "very improvident."[34]

These Indians were friendly enough, in part out of respect for the size of Johnston's party. But a few days later, two stray Kiowas tracked the last wagon in the train, and when the rest of the wagons passed over the crest of a small rise, they attacked with fierce suddenness. They shot the driver, leaped onto the backs of two of the mules, and drove off, "one riding on each side of the mules till they were far enough to have time to cut off the harness and travel in a more convenient manner." Johnston sent a party in pursuit: they found the wagon ransacked and the wagon master dead.[35]

Of necessity Johnston's route meandered north and south of the 37th parallel as close as the terrain would allow. One soldier wrote home to his parents that there was nothing west of the Missouri "but buffalo, grass, and gravel." Although the country itself was uninteresting, Johnston was pleased to be on the move. "There is something in marching & continued change of scene very much to my taste," he told McClellan.[36] As usual Johnston dressed for the climate and conditions, spurning the formal uniform of the parade ground and donning the broad-brimmed hat of the frontier. One soldier recalled that in terms of dress, "there is no distinction between officer and private." Johnston was also on easy terms with the men, a practice he regularly affected in command. A soldier wrote home to his parents that "I never hesitate to speak just as freely and frankly to our colonel as I might to one of our sergeants.....".[37]

Johnston found the company he was forced to keep less to his taste. He could bear the tedium, he wrote to McClellan, if only there were "at least one in the party whose temper or whose tastes make him agreeable to me." Alas, "there is no such person in this party." The worst part was his enforced companionship with a congressman who imposed himself on the expedition. "Such an impudent bore never before came out of Yankeedom," Johnston complained. "Of course I had him in my tent, not to do things by halves he brought a nephew with him."[38]

On September 10, Johnston and his command reached the southwest corner of the territory at 102° 10' longitude and set the cornerstone, 462 miles, 1,001 feet from the Missouri border. Despite all the provisions they had carried with them, they were now out of supplies and had to await the arrival of a relief wagon train from Fort Leavenworth. Hearing rumors that a large band of hostile Indians planned to attack the train, Johnston on September 7 ordered a forced march eastward to meet it at Cimarron Springs. After a short rest, the whole expedition started back on September 20. On the return trip, they encountered a band of about twenty Kiowas. Since two Kiowas had murdered the wagon driver on the westward trip, Johnston told the Kiowa chief he would hold his nation responsible until the tribe turned over the culprits. The conversation then turned to happier subjects. In his private journal, Johnston recorded that the chief was "so grieved to see us going, that he thought nothing but whiskey could revive his drooping spirits."[39]

Johnston reached Fort Leavenworth on November 15, 1857. The violence in Kansas had quieted, though a political settlement was not yet in sight. Increasingly, Johnston's own attention turned away from the Kansas plains to a new scheme, involving affairs in Mexico. Of all his "castles in the air," this was his most ambitious and most enigmatic. Almost from the moment the war with Mexico had ended in 1848, some Americans had expressed disappointment that more territory had not been gained in the peace treaty. Polk himself had been disappointed that Nicolas Trist had obtained so little in the peace negotiations, for the president had seriously contemplated the annexation of all Mexico. But Whig opposition to the war, and the fact that Trist's treaty granted the United States everything it had gone to war to achieve, forced him to send the treaty to the Senate. Nevertheless, Americans, and especially southerners, continued to look hungrily at Mexico.

The most flamboyant of these expansionists was William Walker, a curious and diminutive adventurer, who raised an "army" of a hundred or so followers in southern California and sailed off to Baja California in 1853, declaring himself president of the Republic of Sonora and Baja California. Walker and his followers, mostly brigands, did not last long and had to escape back to U.S. territory on foot, where Walker was promptly arrested. Later he would establish a short-lived "republic" in Nicaragua. Johnston did not think much of Walker's adventurism. "The Walker filibustering is not to my mind," he wrote to McClellan. "I regard him as a mere robber with robbers for associates." Nevertheless, Johnston himself soon became involved in a plot to add Mexican territory to the United States. He saw his own motives as higher and purer than Walker's: "To justify a gentleman in joining such an enterprize, he must have a right to believe that those who conduct it are actuated by a love of human liberty or high ambition. I am as ready for such a one now as I was at five & twenty." It is worth noting that Johnston ranked "high ambition" on a scale with "human liberty."[40]

James Buchanan's election to the presidency in 1856 on a platform of nationalism and expansionism opened a new chapter in American relations with Mexico. Buchanan had a long record of support for expansion into Latin America. In 1854 he had been one of the principals in the announcement of the Ostend Manifesto, which declared that Cuba was properly part of the United States, and that if Spain did not agree to sell it, the nation would be justified in seizing it. Moreover, the situation in Mexico at the time of Buchanan's inauguration invited schemes of national expansion. The country in political shambles, unable to control its own border or pay its foreign debts. Americans were particularly concerned that European powers would use the excuse of unpaid debts to intervene in Mexico.[41]

In 1854, liberal reformers in Mexico had rebelled against Santa Anna, forcing him to flee the country. The rebels took over, wrote a constitution, and elected Ignacio Comonfort as their president. Comonfort, however, soon tired of democracy, dissolved Congress, suspended the constitution, and ruled as a dictator, whereupon the liberal element set up a rival government in Vera Cruz with Benito Juarez as president. By 1858, Mexico had two governments, which Americans referred to as the "conservative" (Comonfort) and the "liberal" (Juarez) government. Buchanan tried first to deal with Comonfort. He instructed the American minister to offer up to $15 million for the purchase of Baja California, Sonora, and Chihuahua. Comonfort rejected the offer as insulting, and publicly pledged that he would not sell off national land for American dollars. Comonfort's successor, Felix Zuloaga, was even tougher: he enacted a tax on the property of rich foreigners— including Americans. Buchanan decided that more vigorous measures were necessary. Texas Senator Sam Houston's motion to establish a Senate committee to report on establishing a U.S. protectorate over Mexico prompted Buchanan to open negotiations with the other Mexican government—that of Benito Juarez at Vera Cruz.[42]

Buchanan's December 1858 message to Congress stopped just short of calling for a declaration of war. Claiming that Mexico had been reduced "to a condition of almost helpless anarchy and imbecility," the president insisted that "abundant cause now undoubtedly exists for a resort to hostilities." However, he pinned his hopes on the liberal government in Vera Cruz: "should the constitutional party prevail," he declared, "there is reason to hope." Regardless of who was in power in Mexico, it was up to the United States to end the violence on the border, where "anarchy and violence prevails" and "life and property [is] wholly insecure." His solution was a blatant land grab: "I can imagine no possible remedy for these evils . . . but for the government of the United States to assume a temporary protectorate over the northern portions of Chihuahua and Sonora, and to establish military posts within the same—and this I earnestly recommend to Congress." In theory, the United States would hold these lands in pledge for unpaid debts; but it was clear that Buchanan was more interested in land than money. In practice, Buchanan's policy was to offer the Juarez government official recognition in exchange for a promise to sell the northern provinces to the United States.[43]

Throughout 1858–59, Johnston, McClellan, and several other officers corresponded about the possibilities for personal glory, national expansion, or both. The details of their scheme are uncertain, but it is clear that they envisioned some action by a volunteer American army on behalf of the "Constitutional" forces under Juarez, either to bring all of Mexico under U.S. dominion, or to establish an independent republic in northern Mexico. In the spring of 1858, McClellan wrote Johnston to solicit his approval of such a scheme. Johnston was cautious. "I agree with everything you say," he replied, "except as to ease of raising money. That & govt opposition constitutes in my opinion the difficulty of the enterprise. If you see how to overcome them, make me easy by telling me." Their prospects seemed to improve dramatically after Buchanan's belligerent address in December, but Johnston soon concluded that Old Buck was more talk than action. "It isn't worth while to talk of Mexican affairs as connected with this govt," he wrote McClellan. "Old Fogyism is in the ascendant." Only a few months later it seemed that their best opportunity was at hand, for in the last week of March 1859 Buchanan named Johnston's own brother-in-law, Robert McLane, as Minister to Mexico. McLane was authorized to recognize any government in Mexico that he thought was legitimate—that is, any government willing to accept U.S. proposals. Armed with these instructions, McLane sailed from Washington for Vera Cruz in March. Joe Johnston went with him.[44]

Officially, Johnston's orders were to inspect possible military routes across Mexico; but that, he knew, "was merely an excuse." His actual assignment was to aid his brother-in-law in his effort to conclude an agreement with the Juarez government. There was, Johnston now wrote to McClellan, a "faint hope of founding a Spanish castle upon the basis of last year."[45] McLane,

Johnston, and the rest of the American delegation landed at Vera Cruz on April 1. Four days later, McLane recognized the Juarez government as the legal government of Mexico, an announcement greeted by "great ringing of bells & firing of guns." But the Mexican people had still to recognize their government, and most Mexicans considered the price Juarez would have to pay for U.S. support too high. Even as the celebration continued in Vera Cruz, Johnston doubted that it would lead to anything. "I am convinced that there is no chance for anything like our schemes of last year," he wrote McClellan. "The leaders, both civil & military, are too jealous of us to adopt any such course. They had rather run the risk of being overthrown by the opposition party of their countrymen, than that of being supported in the control of their own party by us." Indeed, as Johnston predicted, Juarez's unwillingness to be a U.S. puppet marked the end of American adventurism in Mexico. Johnston knew it. To McClellan he wrote: "Our Castles in the air, my dear Mc, are blown away. You'll have to consent to become a rich civilian instead of a member of a small but select party of Maintainers of human liberty."[46]

Johnston stayed on in Vera Cruz for another three weeks, leaving in late April. Although Juarez still controlled Vera Cruz, his army had been repulsed from the gates of Mexico City. Johnston speculated that "an offensive & defensive alliance sealed with some cessions of territory for which we may pay a few millions" might save the situation. But it was out of his hands. He and McLane boarded the steamer *Alabama* for the return to trip to Washington in May. "I am going back to Washington in the hope that some better scheme may be gotten up for my employment in that country," he told McClellan.[47] By this time he had pretty much given up hope. From Washington he wrote that "I am still making use of Mexican affairs, not thinking them worth a real thought. I have been hoping to learn here the intentions of the administration, but three or four interviews with the people in question have not enlightened me much." Johnston concluded that "things will probably remain as they are."[48]

McLane returned to Vera Cruz in November—without Johnston—to negotiate the McLane-Ocampo Treaty, which was so obviously a sell-out to the Norte Americanos that even many of Juarez's most ardent supporters began to turn against him. Soldiers in his own army denounced the treaty as a surrender of sovereignty and called Juarez a traitor to Mexico. Buchanan submitted the treaty to the Senate, but Republican senators were skeptical, seeing this ploy as yet another southern effort to expand the area into which slavery might be extended. They defeated it.[49]

Johnston's own infatuation with filibustering did not derive from an ambition to extend slavery. His disgust with the activities of the pro-slavery governor of Kansas was evidence that he had little sympathy with schemes to create a slave empire. He believed that extending American sovereignty over the Rio Grande would bring the blessings of a superior civilization to Mexico. At the same time, an American crusade in Mexico was an adventure—a chance for glory, his own and his nation's.

Denied his crusade, Johnston's professional prospects appeared much more mundane in the spring of 1859. He tried to get orders to conduct an inspection tour of European fortifications, but the War Department had other ideas; in June, he was ordered to New Mexico as acting Inspector General. "I shall, in all probability, be employed in inspecting for the next four or five months," he sighed to McClellan.[50] He did not stop dreaming, however. As late as December 1860, he wrote McClellan a remarkable letter—remarkable because it was dated December 3, after Abraham Lincoln had been elected president, and after South Carolina had already announced plans for a convention to discuss secession from the Union:

> I have been pining to see you, to talk with you about the future. I cant help building castles in the air, as you have perhaps observed & wanted you to help me. The present times afford fine opportunities for that amusement, of which I have been availing myself to the full. These structures generally rise in a Southern Confederacy extending its area southward.

Six months later Johnston and McClellan would be in arms against one another. Johnston probably did not appreciate the full irony of the last line of his letter: "Interesting times these for gentlemen of leisure."[51]

CHAPTER SEVEN

Promotion and Resignation

In 1851, Johnston had written his brother Edward that he desired promotion "more than any man in the army."[1] Johnston was certainly ambitious—driven not just by a natural desire to succeed in his profession but also by a real financial need, for he had no independent source of income. Still, his assertion to Edward was significant, because professional ambition was a marked characteristic of virtually all regular army officers in the 1850s. Most of them found their ambitions frustrated. Johnston's friend Lee complained of the "small progress" he had made professionally, and wondered whether his lack of single-minded commitment was responsible.[2] Others, like McClellan, resigned from the service to seek greater financial rewards in business; some quit simply out of boredom. Johnston did not resign, though he considered it more than once. Instead, he doggedly pursued his professional prospects within the Army, and in particular he sought to obtain official confirmation of the brevet promotion to colonel he had won at Chapultepec. For more than a decade, Johnston was unable to convince the War Department of the justice of his claim. Then, in the first year of the new decade, he received two promotions, one hard upon the heels of the other: first his claim to a colonelcy was confirmed by a friendly Secretary of War;

within weeks, he was promoted again, to become the first graduate in the fifty-eight-year history of West Point to pin on the stars of a brigadier general in the regular army. Johnston barely had time to celebrate his twin promotions before the accelerating spiral of national events confronted him with the greatest crisis—and opportunity—of his life.

Throughout the decade of the 1850s, while he served in Texas, in Kansas, and elsewhere, Johnston had borne the rank of lieutenant colonel. All that time, he believed that he was actually entitled to the next highest rank. The War Department disagreed. The dispute hinged on differing interpretations of the two brevet promotions he had won in Mexico. A brevet promotion was awarded for noble services performed in battle. The officer wore the insignia of his new rank and carried the title as well, though it was generally considered temporary, and often he did not receive the pay of the higher rank. In previous wars, officers would revert to their substantive rank upon the conclusion of hostilities. But after the war with Mexico, Congress, in an expansive mood, passed a law that officers of the regular army who had won brevets in temporary regiments should "have the benefit of any promotion" when they returned to their regular regiments.[3]

This was wonderful news for Johnston, who had won two brevets in Mexico: he had been made a brevet lieutenant colonel at Cerro Gordo, skipping over the rank of major altogether, then he had won another brevet after his heroics at Chapultepec. Johnston calculated that the second brevet made him a colonel. But the War Department asserted that since he had entered the war as a captain, Johnston's two brevet promotions had made him first a major, then a lieutenant colonel. As a result, when the *Register of Officers* in the Army was published, Johnston was listed as a brevet lieutenant colonel. On March 13, 1849, Johnston appealed his case for a colonelcy. A week later Secretary of War William L. Marcy denied his petition, declaring that his decision was final. The Senate confirmed Marcy's decision.[4]

Johnston was disappointed, but unreconciled, continuing to believe that the War Department's interpretation of the case was incorrect and that a more sympathetic Secretary might reverse the decision. Six years later, on July 11, 1855, he appealed his case again, this time to Secretary of War Jefferson Davis. Johnston may have hoped that a fellow graduate of West Point and a fellow veteran of the war would take a different view of the case. He didn't. Deciding that the case had already been determined by his predecessors, Davis refused even to reopen it. Johnston noted that he had served as a lieutenant colonel at Chapultepec and had afterward been awarded another brevet promotion. Did not that make him a colonel? Davis responded with the remarkable declaration that Johnston had not actually been a lieutenant colonel during the campaign for Mexico City. All the official documents of the war, including Johnston's orders and the *Register of Officers*, had designated Johnston a lieutenant colonel after Cerro Gordo. Yet Davis argued that Johnston had not actually become a lieutenant colonel until after Chapultepec. Absurd as this seemed, there was no appeal as long as Davis remained Secretary of War. Davis's decision was the first overt disagreement between the two men. Years later, Johnston would look back and see it as an omen.[5]

Johnston's prospects improved considerably in March 1857 when James Buchanan became president and appointed John B. Floyd as his Secretary of War. Floyd was an Abingdon native, the legal guardian of Lizzie Johnston, and the brother-in-law of John Warfield Johnston, Joe's nephew. Here, surely, was a sympathetic audience for Johnston's petition. Johnston therefore appealed his case once again. A report compiled for Floyd in the spring of 1858 reiterated Davis's position that "This case is settled by the previous decision." In essence, the report argued that only the Senate could confirm promotions, and that the Senate's action in Johnston's case (back in 1849) had settled the matter. Nevertheless, Secretary Floyd rejected the report and overturned the previous decisions, ruling in Johnston's favor.[6]

Floyd's reasoning, developed in a ten-page handwritten document, was somewhat tortured. He began by asserting that "This case can hardly be said to have been decided in any sense which would stamp the decision with the character of finality"—an astonishing claim made on the tenuous grounds that the decisions of previous Secretaries referred only to their refusals to list Johnston in the army *Register* as a colonel, and not to his *legal right* to that rank. Floyd argued that since Johnston had received a brevet to colonel, only his resignation or dismissal from the service could revoke his promotion. No action by a Secretary of War or by Congress, he said, could "affect his legal right to the brevet commission of Colonel which he held in his pocket at the time, guaranteed to him in strict conformity to the laws of the land." The decision of his predecessors to deny him that rank was "simply a mistake." Floyd concluded that "no other sentiments but those of respect and admiration can be entertained for an officer who has distinguished himself in every campaign with which he has been connected since he entered the service, and who has shed his blood freely upon the battlefield."[7]

Finally confirmed as a colonel, Johnston believed that he had been vindicated. But much of the Army saw it differently. After all, a whole succession of Secretaries had denied Johnston's claim, and the Senate had never acted to reverse its original decision. Some officers whispered that Johnston's promotion was the result of special treatment. Colonels Edmund B. Alexander and Philip St. George Cooke protested Johnston's promotion to Davis, now a U.S. senator, in a formal petition. Even Lee, always reluctant to assume anything uncharitable about anyone, believed that Johnston had obtained his promotion by favoritism, and wondered how he could accept his new rank knowing that it did not represent the will of Congress. "I think it must be evident to him," Lee wrote his brother Custis, "that it never was the intention of Congress to advance him to the position assigned him by the Sec'y."[8]

Less than three months later, in May 1860, Colonel and Mrs. Joseph E.

Johnston travelled to New York to attend McClellan's wedding to Ellen Marcy. Upon their return to Washington, they learned that General Thomas S. Jesup, who had been Johnston's commander in Florida in the 1830s and who had been serving as Quartermaster General of the Army for years, had died on June 10. His death left the office vacant. It was not a glamorous post, but it carried with it automatic promotion to the rank of brigadier general in the regular army. It was Winfield Scott's responsibility as Commander of the Army to designate a successor. Instead of naming one individual, Scott nominated four, any of whom, he said, could do the job. His list was a distinguished one: Robert E. Lee and Joe Johnston, plus Albert Sidney Johnston and Charles F. Smith. Charged to pick one, Secretary Floyd chose Joe Johnston.[9]

For Johnston, this was another giant professional step. His competitors for the job were all distinguished officers with long records of achievement. But Johnston's selection, following hard on the heels of his disputed promotion to colonel, raised more questions within the Army about favoritism. There can be little doubt that Floyd's decision was motivated at least in part by his own relationship to the younger of the two Johnstons, whose service record he had recently reviewed. That is not to say that Johnston did not deserve the appointment. Floyd chose Joe Johnston as Quartermaster General because he knew him better than the other nominees, because he admired his record, and because he believed that Johnston would do a good job. Johnston was not the first to benefit from having friends in high places. He, at least, did not believe that his appointment was tainted in any way.

On June 28, 1860, Joseph E. Johnston became Quartermaster General of the Army, with the rank of brigadier general. One attractive aspect of his new job was that he would be headquartered permanently in Washington, where he and Lydia could have a real home. In the fall of 1860 Washington was an unprepossessing city. "A city of magnificent distances," it was called, more as a jibe at its vast empty spaces than in tribute to its grandeur. Many of its streets were unpaved, and Henry Adams complained that the capital was a "rude colony," consisting of "unfinished Greek temples for workrooms, and sloughs for roads." Even Johnston was dismissive. "I find the town in no respects comparable to San Antonio," he wrote to a colleague who had served with him in Texas. The Johnstons moved into a rented house on H Street, not far from the War Department. Every day Johnston walked to his office in the large brick War Department Building near the White House, and every evening he walked home again. It was the closest thing to a normal domestic life he had had in fifteen years of marriage. Lee wrote to congratulate Johnston on his appointment, but also to tease him: "Please present my Cordial Congratulations to Mrs. J & say that I fear now that she will have you Constantly with her, she will never want to see me again."[10]

Johnston's principal responsibility was to manage the supplies and accounts for the Army. As Quartermaster General he administered a budget of over $7 million. The biggest budget items were the transportation of troops and supplies ($1.9 million), forage for horses ($1.5 million), and subsistence for the troops ($575,000). It is interesting that the Army spent more on forage for the horses than food for the men—though this probably would not have surprised the men in the ranks. In his official report for 1860, Johnston boasted that during his tenure, "The various supplies required for the Army were furnished promptly, as well as transportation for those supplies and the troops." But he had to report that he had run up a significant deficit, due to "unforeseen expenditures" arising from the outbreak of Indian hostilities in the West. "The suppression of these Indian hostilities was not provided for in the appropriation for this year," he explained. He also blamed the accounting procedures in the far western departments, maintaining that "the military expenditures in these distant departments cannot be controlled here." To save money and reduce the deficit, he recommended closing some of the western forts that were no longer needed; and in November 1860, he asked for a temporary appropriation to tide the Department over until the end of the fiscal year.[11]

As Quartermaster General Johnston was not an unqualified success. The characteristics that made him an effective troop commander in the field did not serve him well in his carpeted office in the War Department. A personable and compassionate commander, whose great strengths were the ability to win and keep the loyalty of subordinates and a willingness to put himself in the front of the battle, Johnston found the daily routine of continuous paperwork unfulfilling.[12] Still, the frustrations of office work were offset by the pleasures of a regular home life. After all his years on the frontier, Johnston felt he deserved a few comforts. It was worth a day of paper shuffling in the office to come home in the evening and let Lydia pamper him. He wrote to McClellan, now returned from his honeymoon, to advise him not to work too hard at his railroad business: "I never yield my personal rights to Company or government. Do not you [do so] either. Reasonable relaxation is a privilege very dear to me & highly beneficial. . . . Let me recommend it."[13]

Lydia, too, enjoyed life in Washington. Her health had improved, and while her husband worked in the War Department, she explored the social opportunities of the nation's capital. The Johnstons fit easily into the circle of prominent southern senators who gave Washington whatever social pretensions it had: the Slidells of Louisiana, the Toombeses of Georgia, the Jefferson Davises of Mississippi. Along with "a well-known wit," Matilda Emory, the wife of Lieutenant Colonel William H. Emory in the Third Cavalry, Varina Davis was Lydia's closest friend and nearly constant companion. The diarist Mary Chestnut reported that "Mrs. Davis, Mrs. Emory, and Mrs. Johnston were always together, inseparable friends, and the trio were pointed out to me as the cleverest women in the U.S." Years later she added: "Now that I know them all well, I think the world was right in its estimate of them." Another mutual acquaintance confided in her diary that "I see a great deal of Mrs. Johnston, our conversations ranging from grave to gay, from lively to severe, in the most impartial manner. She is altogether the most agreeable woman I have ever met."[14]

But the Johnstons' tenure in Washington was destined to be a short one. Even during the first idyllic days in the fall of 1860 it was impossible to ignore the national crisis triggered by the election of Abraham Lincoln in November, and the secession of South Carolina in December. The capital was abuzz with rumors of what the new president might do. The president-elect was offering no hints and keeping his own counsel, but Lincoln's known antipathy toward slavery led many southerners to conclude that he was certain to devise national policies harmful to the South. Even if Lincoln proved tolerant of the South's "Peculiar Institution," the very fact that he had been elected as a sectional candidate without southern support was a signal that the North had gained control of the national government. Then, too, for many southerners, mere tolerance was not enough; radical "fire-eaters" demanded a national government that was openly supportive of slavery, and of its extension into the West. These southerners were unwilling to wait. South Carolina's secession from the Union in December made the crisis more serious than any in the nation's history.

Johnston continued his daily walks to the War Department and tried to maintain a professional, non-political posture. Nevertheless, for Johnston, as for most Americans, the crisis was personal as well as national. He believed that the advocates of secession were foolish to assume that all the slave states would cooperate in a southern Confederacy. "I often tried to convince them," he later wrote, "that the division of the country would give the slaves of the border Southern States so near and safe a refuge that those states would soon cease to have slaves and be compelled . . . to abandon the Confederacy." Johnston had never been a defender of slavery in any case, though he admitted that he had no solution to the problem, for he did not see how emancipated Negroes could be tolerated either.[15]

As Quartermaster General, Johnston's dilemma was a professional one. He presided over the nation's storehouse of war material, and as the likelihood of civil war grew, he found himself in an increasingly delicate position. Southern by birth, Union by profession, he sought to meet all his obligations honorably—but determining what those obligations were was often difficult. The fact that Johnston's boss, Secretary of War Floyd, was also a Virginian made it even more difficult. Unlike Johnston, Floyd had no qualms about slavery or the importance of defending it. Indeed, as a patron, Floyd proved to be something of an embarrassment. Not only did he show doubtful loyalty to the government he served, he was so casual in his recordkeeping that before the year was out he would be the object of a congressional investigation.

In November, Georgia Governor Joseph E. Brown wrote to Floyd to ask if the Secretary would send him samples of U.S. Army equipment. Brown made no secret of the purpose of such a request: it was to obtain "samples or patterns" that could be copied in mass production. He asked for knapsacks, cartridge boxes, belts, holsters, and Colt revolvers. Floyd passed the buck to Johnston. Ingenuously, he asked if the Quartermaster General could supply the governor of Georgia. Johnston replied that the requested items could be sent without inconvenience, but he did not send the revolvers, and he submitted Brown an invoice: "Two knapsacks, $5.56; two haversacks, 78 cents; and two canteens and straps, 92 cents." Within two weeks Floyd had to resign his office under a cloud of accusations about financial improprieties. He left to become an active campaigner for secession in Virginia. But Johnston did not resign; instead, he continued to walk a tightrope, balancing the demands of his sense of duty and his professional responsibilities to the nation.[16]

The crisis caused Johnston a great deal of personal anguish. Those who visited him in his office found him distracted; one person said he had to speak to Johnston several times before he could be jolted from his private thoughts to acknowledge the visitor's presence. Others found him pacing, his head bent deep in thought, and decided not to interrupt him. Johnston was not a proponent of slavery, and he doubted that secession was a legal right guaranteed by the Constitution, but he did believe in the right of revolution as a natural consequence of the principle of free government proclaimed by Jefferson in the Declaration of Independence. Every government, Johnston believed, was "founded on the consent of the governed, and . . . every community strong enough to establish and maintain its independence has a right to assert it." Secession was not merely a philosophical question for Johnston. For all his agonizing, one thing was clear from the outset: his strongest loyalty was to Virginia, and he would serve his state in any way that he could. If Virginia remained in the Union, so would Johnston; if she left, Johnston would leave with her.[17]

Winfield Scott tried to convince him to stay in the Union no matter what Virginia did. The old general even tried to enlist Lydia in his campaign. "Get him to stay with us," Scott told her. "We will never disturb him in any way." Lydia knew instinctively that was impossible. "My husband cannot stay in an army which is about to invade his native country." she replied. "Then let him leave our army," Scott said, "but do not let him join theirs." But that too was impossible. Lydia realized that her husband would never be able to sit idly by while the great issue of his generation was decided; he was a soldier, he had always been a soldier, and he had no other way to support himself and his family. "This is all very fine," she said, "but how is Joe Johnston to live? He has no private fortune. And no profession, or no profession but that of arms." Scott had no reply. From the beginning of the crisis it was clear that if Virginia left, so would Joe Johnston, and that he would fight for her. Everything depended, therefore, on Virginia.[18]

In the first week of February 1861, the citizens of Virginia went to the polls to select delegates to a state convention that would determine whether Virginia would secede or remain in the Union. Johnston was able to keep close track of the deliberations, for his oldest living brother Peter was one of those elected as a delegate. Peter Johnston was a conservative, opposed to secession—in fact, one of the leaders of the conservative forces. He reported to Joe that he had been "counting noses," and that he did not think the secessionists could win a majority, though they tried every tactic they could, including intimidation, to win their point: "Every device is resorted to—every appliance is used—every outside pressure is brought to bear, that the seceders can *invent:* amongst others, *mobs* are gathered and paraded along the streets, in one of which on Friday evening the proposition was made to turn the convention neck & heels out of doors. But I have no fear that our conservative majority will be, or can be, moved. The country has seen no body of men more calm and *firm.*" Indeed, for the first month of the Virginia Convention, the conservatives and moderates were in clear control. The secessionist Richmond *Examiner* complained that the body was made up of "old fogies" who were out of touch with the opinions of the people.[19]

Soon after the convention met, Peter was appointed to the crucial Federal Relations Committee of twenty-one members that would recommend to the convention what action, if any, the state should take in the crisis. Meanwhile the convention listened to public speeches. On February 19, Joe's cousin and boyhood friend John S. Preston, now living in South Carolina, spoke defending South Carolina's decision to secede without waiting to see what the new Lincoln administration would do. He made a strong appeal to Virginia's pride in his peroration, reporting that upon leaving South Carolina, he had promised "that before the spring grass grows long enough to weave a chaplet of triumph, they will hear the stately tramp as a mighty host of men—a sound as if the armies of destiny were afloat—and they will see floating above that host a banner whose whole history is one blaze of glory, and not one blot of shame . . . and on that banner will be written the unsullied name of Virginia."[20]

Despite Preston's speech, and the continued pressure of the secessionist minority, Peter reported to Joe that most delegates were willing to give the Lincoln administration a chance. The crucial issue was coercion. The conservative majority would fall apart if Lincoln attempted to compel the southern states to remain in the Union by force of arms. But the new president's inaugural address on March 4 did not offer the olive branch that conservatives in Virginia had expected. The response of the secessionist Richmond *Enquirer* was gleeful: "Civil War must now come," it exulted. "Sectional war, declared by Mr. Lincoln, awaits only the signal gun. . . . No action of our Convention can now maintain the peace. *She must fight!*"[21]

The Federal Relations Committee made its crucial report on March 9. Although it upheld the right of secession "for just cause," it also expressed a "hope" that the Union would be preserved. Instead of advocating immediate secession, the committee called for a national convention to discuss ways to protect the rights of the South. It also warned the North that hostilities against the southern Confederacy would be considered an "unfriendly act against Virginia." The convention applauded both the tone and the content of the committee report. The next day, Peter wrote to Joe that "I do not think there is any probability of the passage of an ordinance of secession now." He advised his brother "that there is no reason now for your resignation—so hold on, and wait the course of events, *without saying what you may hereafter do.*" That same week Johnston received an unsolicited letter from Pope Walker, acting Secretary of War in the Confederate government at Montgomery, offering him a commission as a brigadier general in the Confederate service. Johnston did not bother to answer it—at least not yet.[22]

The last hope of conservatives in Virginia was that Lincoln would find some way to solve the Fort Sumter crisis short of conflict. When it became evident in early April that Lincoln intended to send reinforcements to the fort in Charleston Harbor, many of the moderates shifted to the secessionist camp. Johnston's hometown newspaper, the Abingdon *Democrat*, reported that "Union fever" was "gradually but surely dying out." News of the firing on Fort Sumter on April 12 created a sensation in the convention, and Lincoln's announcement of a call for volunteers to put down the resistance to government authority was the death knell of conservative hopes. They made one last effort to avert secession: Peter Johnston supported the motion to convene a conference of all the border states to discuss a united response. When that failed (79–64), he gave up hope of avoiding a final break. On April 17, he cast his vote with the majority to secede.[23]

News of Virginia's decision reached Washington two days later, on Friday, April 19. Joe Johnston knew at once what he had to do, but he put it off through the weekend. His reluctance to abandon the Union was genuine, yet so was his conviction that he had no real choice but to go with his state. On Monday morning, April 22, 1861, Johnston walked to the War Department as usual, but this time he carried in his pocket a letter of resignation. In the outer office of Simon Cameron, Lincoln's Secretary of War, he encountered Samuel Cooper, the Adjutant General; he asked Cooper to go in with him to see the Secretary. The meeting was highly charged, and it was a struggle for Johnston to hold his emotions in check. "I must go with the South," he said bluntly. He volunteered that his action seemed "ungrateful," even to him. "I owe all that I am to the government of the United States," he told the Secretary. "It has educated me and clothed me with honor. To leave the service is a hard necessity, but I must go." He left the Secretary's office quickly, his head bowed to hide his tears. In the outer office, back in control of himself, Johnston asked Cooper to write out the government's acknowledgment immediately so that he would be freed from his professional obligations. Then he went to tell Lydia.[24]

Lydia was staying in a room in the Mansion House in Alexandria on the day that her husband resigned. They had already moved out of their H Street home, though they left behind all their personal belongings, including Joe's professional books and the mementoes of three decades of military life.

The parlor of the Mansion House was crowded with excited men and women, all chattering about the dissolution of the Union and the coming war. Uniformed officers of the Army and the Navy were much in evidence. The mood was festive, but Lydia was more depressed than excited. A friend noted that "Mrs. Johnston is sick and in low spirits; she feels the parting from old friends and, I imagine, does not look upon the future with a very bright eye, though she is too politic to say so; but we sometimes instinctively feel what others think." Finding the crowded lobby intolerable, Lydia retreated to her room, which "was a relief after the noisy parlor, . . ."[25]

The Johnstons left Alexandria for Richmond by train the next day. Johnston took with him only his side arms and his father's Revolutionary War sword. The trip South was somber rather than celebratory. Counting his years at West Point, Johnston had served thirty-five years in the United States Army. He left it now with no joy, but with a strong sense of foreboding. As if to symbolize his reluctance, though the distance was barely a hundred miles, the trip took the better part of two days, for the rails were crowded with people moving in both directions, and there were frequent minor accidents along the way. Finally on Thursday, April 25, the Johnstons arrived in Richmond. Even before taking a room, Johnston went to see Governor John Letcher to offer his services to Virginia. Letcher was not surprised to see him. Lee had arrived in Richmond four days earlier, and Letcher had already named him a major general and endowed him with command of all Virginia State troops. Now, on Lee's advice, Letcher offered Johnston the same rank and the command of state forces in and around Richmond. Johnston accepted at once.[26]

He set to work to try to bring some military order out of the chaos of arriving volunteers. Johnston's magnetic personality and martial bearing made a strong impression on recruits and officers alike, and his fame as the highest-ranking officer in the U.S. Army to resign and come South endowed him with the prestige necessary to prod others into action. He put the troops to work drilling, and fired off enquiries about uniforms, blankets, tents, and other military equipage, especially the number and quality of shoulder arms in the state's armories. The endless demands and frantic pace of the work distracted him from his melancholy.

After less than two weeks, however, the Virginia Convention decided that the state required only one major general, and that it should be Lee. Letcher offered Johnston a brigadier general's commission, but it had become clear that with Virginia's adherence to the Confederacy, the Confederate government residing in Montgomery, rather than the state government, would conduct the coming war for southern independence. Johnston therefore accepted instead a brigadier general's commission in the Confederate service. In the first week of May, he and Lydia left Richmond for Montgomery. As one of Lydia's friends put it, "If one must be in a revolution . . . the center is more desirable than the circumference."[27]

Compared to the frenzy in Washington and Richmond, Montgomery in

May 1861 was positively pastoral, allowing Johnston a calmer look at the crisis. He engaged in long, thoughtful discussions with Jefferson Davis, who was now provisional president of the Confederacy; with Pope Walker of Alabama, the acting Secretary of War; and with Samuel Cooper, who had left his job as Adjutant General of the U.S. Army to take up the same duties for the Confederate army. Johnston expressed his desire for service in Virginia, preferably in a field command. The administration obliged him with orders to go to Harpers Ferry and take command of the forces there. It took him nearly a week to make arrangements for Lydia, and to gather a staff. Then, on May 22, he bade Lydia farewell, boarding a train for Virginia and the war.[28]

PART TWO

THE WAR IN

VIRGINIA

CHAPTER EIGHT

First Command

Joseph E. Johnston was fifty-four years old when he boarded the train in Montgomery for Virginia and his first command as a Confederate general. In thirty-five years as a professional soldier, his hair had grayed and receded from his broad forehead; his Van Dyke beard had turned nearly white. But the effects of age only added to the personal dignity and self-assurance that so impressed people when they first met him. An unmistakable quality of disciplined composure set him apart from his peers, leading his contemporaries to conclude that here, surely, was a man in whom the new nation could repose its trust. Johnston had been a soldier for more than three decades and fought in two wars, yet he had never commanded in battle a body of men larger than the four companies of voltigeurs he had led at Chapultepec. Now he was headed for the command of an army as large as Scott's in Mexico, larger than Washington's at Yorktown. Was he prepared? Like virtually every other general officer on both sides of the Civil War, Johnston would learn that peacetime service was not necessarily the best preparation for high command. A willingness to obey orders and demonstrate personal bravery was no longer enough; a vital element of senior responsibility was the moral courage to make hard decisions. In his new assignment, Johnston would discover the particular loneliness of high command.

Johnston travelled to Harpers Ferry with a staff of four men, two of whom would play major roles in his new command, and indeed throughout the war. Colonel Edmund Kirby Smith of Florida and the West Point class of 1845, acted as Johnston's chief of staff. Only thirty-six years old, with a full dark beard and deepset dark eyes, Kirby Smith was already a dynamic troop leader and absolutely committed to the Confederate cause. He would earn a hero's plaudits at First Manassas, and much later the distinction of being the last Confederate commander to surrender his army at the end of the war. Johnston's chief engineering officer was Major William Henry Chase Whiting, usually identified in reports by his initials as W. H. C. Whiting, and known to his friends as Chase. A classmate of Kirby Smith's at West Point, he was something of an intellectual, graduating first in his class with the highest scholastic record ever attained by a cadet in the history of West Point. Yet Whiting, though unarguably brilliant, was an indifferent troop leader and intolerant of those he considered less intellectually gifted than himself. He got along well enough with Johnston, but was unable to hide his disdain for many others—a weakness that would keep him from achieving promotion to high command.[1]

Johnston and his party journeyed to Harpers Ferry directly from Montgomery, without stopping in Richmond. Davis had directed him to travel via Lynchburg in order to take charge of whatever reinforcements might be waiting for him there. But when they reached Lynchburg, not only were there no troops waiting, none were expected. Otherwise unimportant, this episode illuminates the haphazard nature of Confederate mobilization in 1861. Disappointed, Johnston and his staff reboarded the train and travelled on to Harpers Ferry.[2]

En route, Johnston contemplated his new assignment. It was not the best available in Virginia. That honor had gone to Pierre Gustave Toutant Beauregard, the hero of Fort Sumter, who was rewarded for a dubious victory with command of the principal field army of the Confederacy in and about Manassas Junction. But Johnston's assignment was surely the next best. Three factors made Harpers Ferry particularly important. First, it was the site of the U.S. Armory. More than a weapons warehouse, the Armory at Harpers Ferry was also a factory for the manufacture of small arms, especially the so-called Harpers Ferry rifle, a .54-caliber rifled musket that was standard issue on both sides at the beginning of the war. In the decade before the war, the Harpers Ferry Armory had produced over 25,000 such weapons. Because the Confederacy had almost no other munitions industries within its territory, the facility was virtually priceless. Second, Harpers Ferry was located at the confluence of the northward-flowing Shenandoah River and the southward-flowing Potomac. Here the conjoined rivers cut through the Blue Ridge Mountains to form a natural pass for the Chesapeake & Ohio Canal along the northern bank of the Potomac, and for the Baltimore & Ohio

Railroad, which crossed the Potomac at Harpers Ferry, joining the Winchester & Potomac Railroad. The easy access to transportation had been a primary reason for locating the national Armory in such an isolated site, where presumably it would be safe from foreign invaders. Third, Harpers Ferry was the doorway to the Shenandoah Valley—the granary of Virginia, and one of the most fertile regions in the Confederacy. Its hard, dry roads were natural invasion routes for both sides. Davis had impressed upon Johnston at Montgomery his conviction that Harpers Ferry was "a natural fortress" that controlled access to the "Valley of Virginia."[3] These factors, taken together, made Harpers Ferry second only to Richmond itself as a strategic site in the eastern theatre.

Johnston's train pulled into Harpers Ferry a little after noon on May 23. The army he found waiting for him consisted of nine regiments—six from Virginia, two from Mississippi, and one from Alabama. In addition there were a few unregimented companies from Maryland and Kentucky, four companies of artillery, and one regiment of cavalry—a total of some 5,200 men. Command was being exercised by the senior colonel, Thomas J. Jackson (West Point, '46), until recently a mathematics and physics professor at the Virginia Military Institute. Shortly after his arrival, Johnston met briefly with Jackson and showed him the order from Davis assigning him to the command of Harpers Ferry and the troops defending it. Jackson read the order without comment, but the next day when Johnston asked him to copy and distribute it to the troops, he politely refused. Jackson explained that he held his commission from the state of Virginia, not the Confederate government at Montgomery, and he was unwilling to surrender his command without authorization from Governor Letcher. Rather than confront Jackson personally, Johnston sent Whiting to see him and point out that his orders were signed "by order of General Lee," who represented Letcher. Whiting was probably not the best person for the job. His tendency toward abruptness certainly extended to Jackson, whose intellectual efforts were marked more by determination than brilliance. But in this case Whiting managed to convince Jackson of the legality of the order. Johnston had learned, however, what many others would soon know: that Jackson was a stickler for precise orders and absolutely incapable of being intimidated.[4]

Johnston was favorably impressed by the caliber of the officers in his new command. Despite the early misunderstanding, he readily appreciated the uncompromising dedication of the dour Colonel Jackson, and he was also pleased by the professionalism of the commander of the 13th Virginia, Colonel Ambrose Powell (A.P.) Hill (West Point, '47), who affected checkered shirts and a floppy hat in lieu of the regulation gray tunic and képi. He was even more pleased by the lively twenty-eight-year-old commander of the cavalry regiment, Colonel James E. B. Stuart (West Point, '54), whom his friends called Beauty for his rather homely countenance. Johnston's faith in Stuart would grow during his command in the Valley and he would consistently urge Stuart's promotion to his own superiors at Richmond.[5]

Johnston was appalled by the condition of the army itself. Although Colonel Jackson had established a demanding drill schedule, the soldiers in the ranks were still raw troops, undisciplined to army life in general and camp life in particular. Some had come to camp with neither arms nor ammunition. Johnston was shocked to learn that his entire command had only about twelve to fifteen rounds of ammunition per man, hardly enough for a sharp skirmish. Finally, on any given day, as much as 40 percent of the entire army was on the sick list, mostly from measles and mumps. New units arrived periodically, often unexpectedly, tending to undermine what little progress toward discipline had been effected.[6]

All of this was grounds for legitimate concern. Even more worrying was Johnston's conviction that the particular geography of Harpers Ferry made it a virtual trap for a defending army. Two days after his arrival, Johnston conducted a personal reconnaissance of the area accompanied by Chase Whiting. What he saw appalled him. Harpers Ferry is a beautiful spot— Thomas Jefferson wrote that the view from above Harpers Ferry was worth a trip across the Atlantic. Nestled in the fork of the two rivers, the village of Harpers Ferry and the Armory buildings were dominated by a trio of high hills. Bolivar Heights immediately behind the village to the west was the lowest, rising gradually to a height of about 200 feet above river level. Directly south of Harpers Ferry, across the rushing Shenandoah, was Loudoun Heights, a peak that towered 954 feet above the river and so dominated Harpers Ferry itself that in the early morning hours it cast a shadow over the town. Maryland Heights, across the Potomac to the northeast, was the third imposing precipice, whose nearest peak rose 840 feet above the river. Harpers Ferry controlled the rail and water traffic between Baltimore-Washington and the West, but Harpers Ferry was in turn controlled by the mountains that surrounded it. After his reconnaissance, Johnston wrote to his superiors in Richmond: "I regard Harper's Ferry as untenable by us at present against a strong enemy."[7]

If the tactical situation was grim, the strategic circumstances were just as bad, for Johnston's position could be turned, or outflanked, by an enemy army crossing the Potomac north or south of Harpers Ferry. The Potomac was fordable at more than a dozen places within a day's march, and once across the river, it was a mere matter of marching for an enemy force to take possession of the railroad to Winchester. Under those circumstances, even a defending army that commanded the heights would be trapped at Harpers Ferry, for there was no other avenue of escape to the south. If Johnston spread out his forces to cover every possible river crossing, he would disperse his strength; if he concentrated them at Harpers Ferry, he could easily be outflanked. He chose a reasonable compromise, distributing his forces to cover as many river crossings as possible without dissipating his strength. One unit he placed as far away as Williamsport, thirty miles upstream, and another at Point of Rocks, twelve miles downstream. He put 350 men on Maryland Heights, across the river on enemy territory, and the rest on or

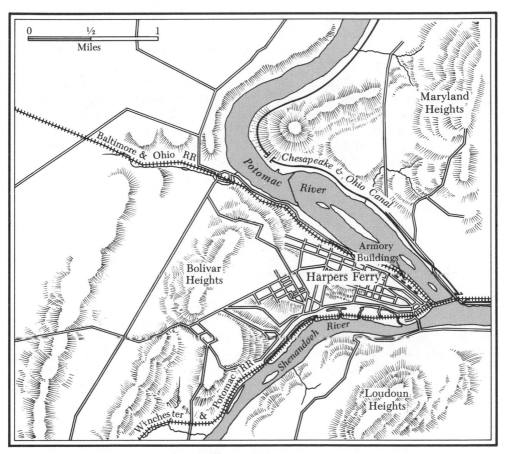

Harpers Ferry

near Bolivar Heights behind Harpers Ferry. These dispositions were reasonable considering the circumstances, but Johnston felt very uneasy and did not hesitate to advise Richmond of his concern.[8]

He needed a clear sense of what the government expected of him in his new command. In his conversations with Davis in Montgomery, Johnston had received the impression that the government conceived of his force not as a field army but as the garrison of a vital fortress. After his reconnaissance of Harpers Ferry, however, Johnston became convinced that any attempt to defend this "fortress" would mean the loss of both the Armory and the army. Harpers Ferry was not so valuable that it justified risking the army's safety. Since Lee had been directed by the War Department to exercise control over all Confederate forces in Virginia until further orders, Johnston addressed his concerns to him.

Lee was inspecting Beauregard's army at Manassas when Johnston's letter reached Richmond, but upon his return he wrote a soothing reply, assuring Johnston that the government placed "great reliance" on his discretion and good judgment. A follow-up telegram was a little more specific. After informing Johnston that more reinforcements were on their way, Lee expressed the hope that "With this reinforcement . . . you may probably hold your position and prevent passage of the Potomac by hostile troops until further troops can reach you."[9]

Were those positive orders? What did Lee mean by "further troops"? From what Johnston had seen of the undisciplined, ill-equipped, and often unruly recruits who had been coming into camp since his arrival, such reinforcements were unlikely to render his position any more secure. Would the arrival of yet another green regiment, unarmed and untrained, constitute "further reinforcements" and obligate him to stay in this untenable cul-de-sac? Lee's telegram, in short, did not give Johnston the kind of answer he wanted. Once again Johnston wrote to Lee to complain that no "instructions" had been sent to him. At the same time he made it clear that his own preference was to evacuate Harpers Ferry: "You say that 'the abandonment of Harper's Ferry would be depressing to the cause of the South,' " quoting Lee's own words to him. "Would not the loss of five or six thousand men be more so?" With a hint of desperation, he added: "I beg you, therefore, let me understand my position."[10]

Lee took Johnston's letter to Davis, and they discussed it at length. The president appreciated the precariousness of Johnston's position, but was reluctant to issue positive orders to abandon such a valuable site. Afterward, Lee wrote Johnston that "The President places great value upon our retention of the command of the Shenandoah Valley and the position at Harpers Ferry." But, he added, "Precise instructions cannot be given you. . . ." Again, Johnston was asked to exercise his discretion: "being informed of the object of the campaign," Lee wrote, "you will be able to regulate its conduct to the best advantage."[11]

Johnston's frustration was evident in his letters to Richmond. He complained about the lack of reinforcements, the scarcity of ammunition, and the undisciplined nature of the reinforcements that did arrive. While justified by actual circumstances, the complaints masked his real concern at having to remain in an indefensible position at Harpers Ferry in the first place. Convinced that his situation was dangerous, even reckless, Johnston did not want to begin his service as a general officer by abandoning the post assigned to him. He may also have believed that if he evacuated Harpers Ferry without positive orders, he would become the target of official and unofficial criticism.[12]

For the first time in his life, Johnston confronted the ambiguities of high command. In fact, he had the authority to withdraw from Harpers Ferry any time he felt that circumstances required it; that much was implicit in his discretionary orders. Worrying daily about his position, Johnston felt that honor would not allow him to withdraw until the last possible moment. What he wanted was for the Richmond authorities, persuaded by his reports, to order him to pull back. They would not do so.

In mid-June, events forced Johnston's hand. On June 10, the commander of the Union forces in western Pennsylvania, Brigadier General Robert Patterson, the aged veteran of the War of 1812, advanced from Chambersburg, Pennsylvania, to Hagerstown, Maryland, only six miles from the Potomac at Williamsport. Once across the river, Patterson would be as close to the railroad at Winchester as Johnston. A Hagerstown newspaper published a list of the twenty-four regiments in Patterson's army, giving Johnston a pretty good idea of the size of the force: simple arithmetic revealed that Patterson had about eighteen thousand men, approximately three times as many as Johnston.[13] Three days later, on June 13, forces under the command of his old friend George McClellan, now a Union major general, raided the town of Romney, Virginia, some forty-three miles to the west. Johnston sent A. P. Hill with two regiments to counter this thrust, but the pattern was ominous. Johnston saw Patterson's move as the first step of an offensive directed at him, and McClellan's as an effort to cut off his line of retreat into the Valley. Convinced that the crisis had come, Johnston decided to evacuate Harpers Ferry.

June 13 was the date scheduled for moving the army's baggage, but Johnston discovered that his men, though largely ill-equipped, were burdened with mountains of unnecessary baggage; nearly every man had brought along a trunk full of personal effects. The result threatened to immobilize the army. Meanwhile Johnston issued the orders to destroy the Armory and demolish the railroad bridges.

At four o'clock in the morning on June 14, a massive explosion shook the girders of the iron bridge across the Potomac. Majestically, the bridge collapsed into the shallow river. The spur trestle of the Winchester & Potomac was kept open for another day to aid in the evacuation, then it too was destroyed. The machinery that could not be moved from the Armory was wrecked and the buildings set afire. Since the massive railroad engines of the

B&O were too heavy for the rails of the Winchester & Potomac, enthusiastic rebel soldiers manhandled them off the rails and into the river. Coal cars, fully loaded, were dumped and set afire; a local resident noted that they were still burning a month later. Long afterward, Johnston's critics charged that he had not done enough to save the rolling stock of the B&O Railroad for the Confederacy. Johnston's own view, recorded in his *Narrative,* was that "Nothing worth removing was left."[14]

Finally, on June 15, the army itself began to move. It made only about eight miles that day, camping just beyond Charlestown on the road to Winchester. That night Johnston received a message that suggested he had acted just in time: Patterson was across the river and moving in force on Martinsburg. Eager to prove that his withdrawal was the appropriate strategy rather than an improvident decampment, Johnston immediately cancelled the next day's march south and directed instead that the army march westward, across country, to block Patterson's advance on Winchester, which Johnston believed was the real gateway to the Shenandoah.

On June 16, Johnston deployed his seven thousand men on some high ground just north of Bunker Hill, Virginia, in full expectation that he would have to defend the town against Patterson's continued advance. But around noon his scouts brought the intelligence that the Federals had reversed direction and recrossed the river. Lacking an explanation for this curious and enigmatic behavior, Johnston continued his own movement toward Winchester. There he contemplated the meaning of Patterson's sudden advance and equally sudden withdrawal. But he also had time to contemplate the significance of a letter he had received from Samuel Cooper during the march from Harpers Ferry. On the 15th, as he was preparing to march across country to block Patterson's advance, a courier rode up to hand Johnston a letter from Cooper dated June 13 that authorized him to abandon Harpers Ferry if necessary.[15] Johnston may have been relieved to receive authorization, but the tone of Cooper's letter implied rebuke:

> As the movements of the enemy could not be foreseen, so it was impossible to give you specific directions. . . .
> As you seem to desire, however, that the responsibility of your retirement should be assumed here, and as no reluctance is felt to bear any burden which the public interests require, you will consider yourself authorized, whenever the position of the enemy shall convince you that he is about to turn your position . . . to destroy everything at Harpers Ferry . . . and retire . . . towards Winchester."[16]

Like most southern officers of his generation, Johnston was particularly sensitive to official criticism, and he felt compelled to answer. That same night from the army's bivouac at Bunker Hill, halfway between Martinsburg and Winchester, he defended himself: "I am confident that nothing in my correspondence with my military superiors makes me obnoxious to the charge of desiring that the responsibility of my official acts should be borne by any other person than myself." No doubt Johnston wrote his protest in a spirit of righteous innocence, but if he was thoroughly righteous, he was not altogether innocent. The tone of his lengthy correspondence with Richmond since May had pleaded for orders that would absolve him of the responsibility for ordering a retreat. Cooper might have cited Johnston's own words to that effect, but by now he was only interested in smoothing over the rift. "If the instructions seemed to you specific," Cooper wrote back, "be assured it was only intended to respond to the desire manifested in the letter communicated by you, and . . . the fullest reliance was placed in your zeal and discretion, and you are expected to act as circumstances may require. . . ."[17]

There is little doubt that Johnston's anguished decision to evacuate Harpers Ferry was sound. The site was indeed indefensible without control of the mountains around it, and Johnston's force was simply too small to control the high ground. Nevertheless, he had irritated his superiors by demonstrating an apparent reluctance to assume the full burden of command, and he provided the first hint of a sensitivity to criticism that would later become prominent.

At Winchester, Johnston felt that he could congratulate himself on a timely escape and on foiling the enemy offensive. Now he could concentrate on the reorganization and training of the army. He began to style his force "the Army of the Shenandoah," and to think of it as a field army rather than a garrison force. With a strength of nearly nine thousand, Johnston reorganized his force into four brigades (a fifth was added a few weeks later). As the senior colonel, Jackson received command of the first brigade—the future "Stonewall" Brigade—composed of four regiments of Virginia infantry. Barnard Bee, Texas-born but commissioned by South Carolina, commanded the second brigade. Bee had graduated from West Point in the class of 1845 and, like Johnston, he had been breveted twice for gallantry in Mexico. His brigade was made up of two Mississippi regiments, one from Alabama and one from Tennessee. The third brigade was put under Arnold Elzey, another West Pointer. Elzey was a Marylander, and his promotion was in part motivated by the hope that it might encourage other Marylanders to join the southern cause. Francis S. Bartow commanded the fourth brigade. A Georgia planter and Yale graduate, Bartow had been serving as a congressman in the Confederate Congress, but resigned to accept a colonel's commission. His brigade was made up of three Georgia regiments and a battalion from Kentucky. A. P. Hill, who no doubt deserved a brigade command, was passed over largely because Richmond wanted to defuse the charge that Virginians were dominating too many of the high command positions. Jeb Stuart remained in command of the cavalry. In mid-July, Jackson, Bee, and Kirby Smith were all promoted to brigadier general, and Johnston organized a fifth brigade for his chief of staff.

Johnston continued to bombard Richmond with requests for support. Food and forage were plentiful at Winchester, but he needed more cavalry, more artillery, and especially more ammunition. To be sure, Johnston's force was not fully equipped. But then neither were any of the Confederate field forces in 1861. Unable to provide what Johnston needed, Davis could send him only encouraging letters. On July 13, he wrote a long and sympathetic note in which he promised to make every effort to send more reinforcements as soon as he could, and concluded: "I need not assure you that my confidence and interest in you both as an officer and as a friend cause me to turn constantly to your position with deepest solicitude."[18]

Davis, of course, had more than one army to worry about. Throughout June and July he was receiving letters from his other field commanders, especially Beauregard at Manassas who, like Johnston, pleaded for more support. Indeed, on July 9, both Beauregard and Johnston fired off telegrams to Richmond in which each man claimed that the enemy was upon him in overwhelming numbers and preparing to attack.[19] Both reports proved to be premature, but the episode illustrates the problem Davis faced in trying to respond to pleas from his field generals. In addition, Davis was the recipient of unsolicited and unrealistic proposals from Beauregard for grand strategic plans that, on paper at least, led inevitably to the defeat of the enemy. In the second week of July, Beauregard forwarded one such plan to Davis that called for Johnston to bring twenty thousand men from the Valley and join Beauregard at Manassas for a joint offensive against the 35,000-man army of Federal Major General Irvin McDowell. In Beauregard's imagination, McDowell's army would be divided into two wings, and the Confederates would drive between these wings and destroy the Federals. Then, assuming that Patterson had thoughtfully remained stationary in the Valley, Johnston, reinforced with ten thousand of Beauregard's men, would return to the Valley to defeat him. Beauregard was so enthusiastic about this plan he sent a copy of it to Johnston. Johnston, of course, had only about half the twenty thousand men Beauregard ascribed to him, and in any case he already faced a numerically superior army.[20]

Indeed, the enemy's forbearance so far seemed to be all that protected the Army of the Shenandoah from being overwhelmed. After his brief foray south of the Potomac in mid-June, Robert Patterson had fallen back north of the river, where he remained quiet for about two weeks. Johnston sent Stuart's cavalry to patrol the fords across the river and keep an eye on the Federals, and on July 1, Stuart sent word that Patterson's regiments were once again crossing the river. Johnston responded by posting Jackson's brigade of infantry to support Stuart and to feel out the enemy strength. The result was a sharp skirmish with the Federal advance guard at Falling Waters on July 2. After inflicting some losses on the Federals, Jackson fell back in accordance with Johnston's orders. Convinced that Patterson was finally beginning his long-expected offensive, Johnston ordered the Army of the Shenandoah to advance to Jackson's support. At Darkesville, three miles north of Winchester, Johnston had Whiting lay out defense lines for the expected fight. Although Patterson still had clear numerical superiority (about 3:2), Johnston held a strong position and he was committed to defending Winchester.[21]

For four days, Johnston and his Army of the Shenandoah waited at Darkesville for an attack. Then Johnston ordered the army to return to Winchester. The campaign slipped into a pattern of Federal feint and Confederate response. Johnston's own anxiety and frustration with this situation was shared by the men in the ranks. "We confronted Patterson for days," one Virginian wrote, "marching from point to point . . . until we were all disgusted and began to feel the Yankees would not fight."[22]

The Yankees were not there to fight. Johnston did not know that Patterson's intention was not to defeat him but to distract him. The Federal plan, put together in Washington by Johnston's old commander Winfield Scott, was for Patterson to act aggressively in the lower Valley, thus holding Johnston in place while McDowell marched against Beauregard. The Federals had numerical superiority in both theatres; the only thing that could stop them was a combination of the two Confederate armies. Although Johnston ignored Beauregard's proposals for a grand offensive, he agreed that a concentration of forces was the key to success. Each man therefore pledged himself to come to the aid of the other in case of an attack. Patterson was only modestly aggressive, yet his actions were convincing to Johnston, who still expected to be attacked at Winchester.[23]

After another week of waiting, Stuart reported on July 15 that the Federal army was again in motion. This time Patterson advanced ten miles from Martinsburg to Bunker Hill, halfway to Winchester, where, once again, he halted. The Union forces probed cautiously toward Smithfield on July 17, leading Johnston to suspect, finally, that Patterson "was merely holding us in check while General Beauregard should be attacked at Manassas. . . ."[24]

At one hour past midnight on the morning of July 18, Johnston was still awake and worrying about the meaning of Patterson's movements when Chase Whiting handed him a telegram from Cooper. The first words set off alarms in his head: "General Beauregard is attacked. To strike the enemy a decisive blow a junction of all your effective force will be needed. If practicable, make the movement, sending your sick and baggage to Culpeper Court-House either by railroad or by Warrenton. In all arrangements exercise your discretion." Here at last were unequivocal orders; Johnston was to use his "discretion" only in the "arrangements." It was an unmistakable call to battle. Johnston replied immediately to this fateful summons: "We shall move toward General Beauregard tomorrow."[25]

CHAPTER NINE

Manassas

In the first summer of the war, the Battle of First Manassas (or Bull Run)°
struck the public mind, North and South, as a conflict of Homeric proportions. Two mighty armies, each bearing the hopes of a nation, collided in
the northern Virginia countryside where Jackson stood like a stone wall and
the Federal army was put to flight. The results of First Manassas shattered
the hopes of a short war in the North, and set off exuberant if premature
celebrations in the South. In fact, measured either in terms of casualties or of
strategic significance, First Manassas was little more than a skirmish in the
long history of the American Civil War, and the performance of the Confederate army, far from being a model of military art, was a comedy of confusion
in which accident and exhaustion played a larger role than command leadership. Directing his first major battle, Johnston found himself reacting to circumstances and responding to Union initiatives rather than exercising effective control. Even victory was not completely satisfying, for Johnston was

°Throughout the war, the Confederates tended to name battles after the nearest
community (Manassas), while the Federals chose the nearest geographical feature,
especially rivers (Bull Run).

unable to organize a pursuit, and in the aftermath of the battle the public came to believe that most of the credit belonged not to the quiet and dignified Johnston, but to the flamboyant and dynamic P. G. T. Beauregard, a perception that rankled with Johnston so much that he felt compelled to defend himself.

From the moment that Johnston read Cooper's telegram in the pre-dawn hours of July 18, he determined to take his whole force with him to Manassas. Cooper had ordered Johnston to send his sick and wounded to Culpeper, but Johnston was authorized to use his discretion. He resolved instead to leave the seventeen hundred sick and wounded men at Winchester, largely because the wheeled transportation necessary to carry them to Culpeper would slow the movement of the army to Manassas. He did not fear for their safety in Winchester, because he was convinced that once Patterson learned that Johnston's army had slipped away, he would be forced to "follow the movement to Manassas Junction."[1]

Even as he issued orders to rouse the army, Johnston had to confront the problem of how to disengage from the Valley without inviting the attention of the Federal army under Robert Patterson. If Patterson learned that Johnston was evacuating, he might be tempted to strike while the Confederates were on the march. Johnston's options were either to attempt to defeat Patterson in battle and throw him back over the Potomac, or to try to escape the Valley without Patterson's notice. Of course if Beauregard were already under attack, a battle was out of the question, for even if Johnston won a decisive victory over Patterson, the delay would prevent him from getting his troops to Manassas in time to succor Beauregard. A quiet escape, then, was essential. In this, as always, Johnston counted heavily on Jeb Stuart's cavalry to screen his movements. Stuart's morning report for nine o'clock indicated that the Federal army had not moved from its encampment. Johnston decided that he could safely make his move.[2]

The troops had been shaken awake before dawn and ordered to strike their tents. A great deal of speculation, much of it alarmingly accurate, filtered through the army. Johnston wondered what, if anything, to tell the men. Ordinarily he would have told them nothing; in his view, a soldier should be expected to do his duty without asking for explanations from his officers. But a considerable number of these soldiers—including all of the militia—were natives of the Valley, and there had been rumors in camp that some of them would be reluctant to leave their homes undefended while Patterson remained threateningly at Smithfield. Moreover, if Beauregard were even now under attack, speed was critical, and the troops might be inspired to greater efforts if they knew just how critical. Johnston decided that the troops should be told of their destination and the consequent need for speed. A soldier in the thirtieth Virginia recalled that after the men heard that they were marching to battle, they felt "new life" and "marched with light hearts."[3]

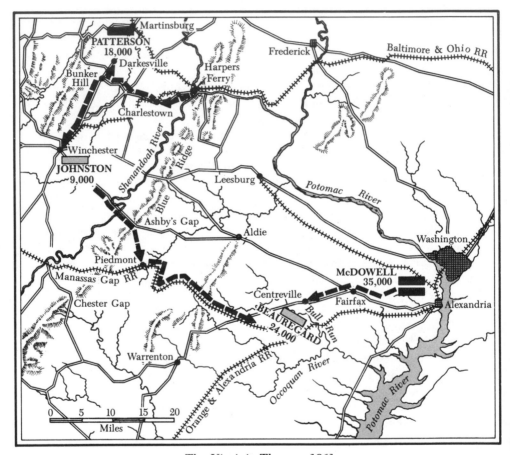

The Virginia Theatre, 1861

For all their enthusiasm, the troops moved with frustrating slowness. Jackson's brigade stepped out smartly enough at noon, but behind them the long line of infantry and wagons advanced accordion-like: men bumped up against those in front, waited in place, then hurried forward as the line again lurched into motion. "The weather was intensely hot," one soldier recalled, "and the roads dusty. . . ." Accustomed to "the steady gait of regular soldiers," Johnston found the slow pace of his army agonizing. Although it was more than fifty miles to Manassas, he had hoped to cover the distance in twenty-four hours; but before many hours had passed, Johnston realized such a march was beyond his troops. He sent Whiting ahead to the nearest station of the Manassas Gap Railroad at Piedmont to determine if sufficient numbers of railroad cars were available to carry some of the army. Whiting returned with good news: there were two trains at Piedmont ready to carry Johnston's troops to Manassas. Johnston immediately ordered Jackson's brigade to turn southward to the railroad. The artillery and cavalry would continue by wagon road.[4]

Jackson's men arrived at Piedmont at six in the morning on July 19, but the promised freight cars were not there, so the men sat down to breakfast. The cars arrived at eight, and Jackson's men clambered aboard for the thirty-four-mile ride to Manassas Junction. Two more regiments entrained at about three o'clock that afternoon, then there were no more cars available; the bulk of Johnston's army simply waited. Enough cars returned from Manassas by late evening to allow two more regiments to entrain before midnight, but the engineers were nowhere to be found and the rest of the army bivouacked for another night at Piedmont. Johnston fumed. He was convinced that the engineers had gone home to sleep rather than work through the night. Forty-eight hours had now passed since he had received the telegram from Cooper, and Johnston had sent only six of his sixteen regiments—perhaps 3,500 men—to Beauregard at Manassas. Would they be in time? Would he be in time?[5]

Some of Johnston's concern was eased when Colonel Alexander Chisolm arrived in camp after a hard ride from Manassas. Chisolm reported that the battle had not yet been joined, but he also brought a characteristically visionary communication from Beauregard, advising Johnston to advance toward Manassas via Aldie, a dozen miles to the north, so as to strike McDowell's advancing army in the flank. Johnston immediately dismissed this suggestion as impractical. But perhaps the letter prompted him to wonder who would be in command once the two armies did join ranks. Only President Davis could answer; Johnston dispatched a telegram to the president asking specifically who would command the combined armies.[6]

After another all-night vigil, Johnston embarked for Manassas the next morning, Saturday, July 20, at about eight o'clock, along with two regiments of Barnard Bee's brigade. He left Kirby Smith behind at Piedmont with orders to expedite the loading of the rest of the troops as soon as possible. Now finally on his way to Manassas, Johnston found the train ride nearly as frustrating as the waiting. The heavily burdened engine moved at a mere ten miles an hour, pulling into Manassas Junction after noon. But the depot was still in Confederate hands; McDowell had not yet attacked. He was in time after all.

Johnston went immediately to Beauregard's headquarters. The question of their relative rank was answered by the arrival of a telegram from President Davis. "You are a general in the Confederate Army," Davis replied, "possessed of the power attaching to that rank." A subsequent reference in the same telegram to "Brigadier-General Beauregard" made it clear that Johnston was senior. There were now eight regiments of Johnston's Army of the Shenandoah at Manassas, but five times as many troops from Beauregard's Army of the Potomac, and Beauregard was more familiar with the terrain, having commanded there since June 1. Although gratified to learn that he was the senior commander, Johnston believed that to supersede Beauregard now, solely on the basis of seniority, would be professionally discourteous. From the start, therefore, Johnston determined to allow Beauregard great leeway in the forthcoming battle.[7]

Johnston examined Beauregard's position with intense interest, but did not have time to study it in the kind of detail he would have liked. The position was "too extensive," he later wrote, "and the ground, much of it, too broken, thickly wooded, and intricate, to be studied to any purpose in the brief space of time at my disposal." And time, he believed, was crucial. Still convinced that Patterson would bring his army to Manassas as soon as he realized that Johnston had given him the slip, Johnston was desperate to conclude things with McDowell before Patterson arrived. Surely by now Patterson had discovered his absence and was even at that moment marching with all haste from the Valley. "Battle being inevitable," Johnston wrote, "it was certainly our part to bring it on before the arrival of our enemies." Delay, he felt, "was dangerous."[8]

For this reason he immediately agreed with Beauregard's suggestion to attack. Beauregard produced a map—though it did not detail any terrain or forestation, only roads and streams—and showed him how the combined Confederate army could take advantage of the network of roads that converged upon Centreville, where the Federal army was located, to attack from several directions at once. The plan required coordinating raw troops over a complicated road network, yet Johnston accepted it "without hesitation," and because he was exhausted from having been up three nights in a row, he directed Beauregard to have his staff prepare the necessary orders. He was going to take a nap. He walked to a nearby grove of trees, fell to the ground, and was asleep almost instantly.[9]

Except for brief catnaps, he had not slept for more than seventy-two hours; still Johnston was awake before dawn the next day. At 4:30 A.M. an aide from Beauregard was at his side with the written orders for the day's battle. Johnston read through them quickly and was struck immediately by the fact that the orders were so vague as to be positively confusing. The first section ordered Benjamin S. Ewell's brigade to "place itself in position of attack upon Centreville or to move . . . according to circumstances." D. R. Jones's brigade was to be "held in readiness . . . according to circumstances," and to act "according to the nature of the country and attack." Such orders were unclear even to Johnston, who had heard Beauregard describe his plan the night before. Twenty years later, he declared that this attack, if executed, "in all probability would have been defeated." But though he clearly had the authority to overrule Beauregard, he was reluctant to do so. In any case, it was too late to rewrite the orders now, for time was of the essence. Indeed, the battle had already been joined. From the north, the sound of a Federal cannonade proved that the enemy was on the move. At the bottom of the document, therefore, Johnston wrote: "The plan of attack given by Brigadier-General Beauregard in the above order is approved, and will be executed accordingly."[10]

The orders were never delivered. Only General James Longstreet, commanding the nearest brigade, received a copy, and by that time they had been rendered meaningless by events. It was just as well. Beauregard's plan almost certainly would have thrown the southern army into such chaos that McDowell could have destroyed it piecemeal.[11] Instead, as daylight broadened, the continued sound of firing to the north convinced Johnston and a reluctant Beauregard that the enemy was attempting to seize the initiative on the Confederate left.

Beauregard did not easily give up the idea of conducting an offensive of his own across Bull Run Creek. If the Federals were moving to the north, he argued, so much the better. He could still cross Bull Run and strike them in the flank. He dispatched new orders to the various brigade commanders along Bull Run, ordering them to ascertain the strength of the enemy forces in their front. At about eight o'clock, Beauregard, Johnston, and their escorts left headquarters and started out on the road toward Lewis Ford. As the group approached an open clearing, a local resident warned the generals that the enemy had a battery sighted on the clearing. Johnston ordered the staff members and escorts "to scatter in the timber" while he and Beauregard dismounted and walked alone to the top of a nearby hill. By now "the firing on the left had increased & the rattle of musketry could be heard in the brief intervals." It was a crucial moment in Johnston's military career. Beauregard continued to insist that the firing on the left was a feint. Johnston, however, remembered that Winfield Scott had planned this campaign, and he recalled Scott's fondness for turning movements in Mexico. He began to suspect that the noise of the battle to the north was yet another example of Scott's favorite maneuver.[12]

In fact, the Confederate troops to the north were being very roughly handled, for the Federal "feint" was a full-fledged assault by two complete divisions. The Federal attack at dawn on the stone bridge had been designed to draw attention away from an even broader flanking movement further north. In the pre-dawn darkness, the divisions of Major Generals David

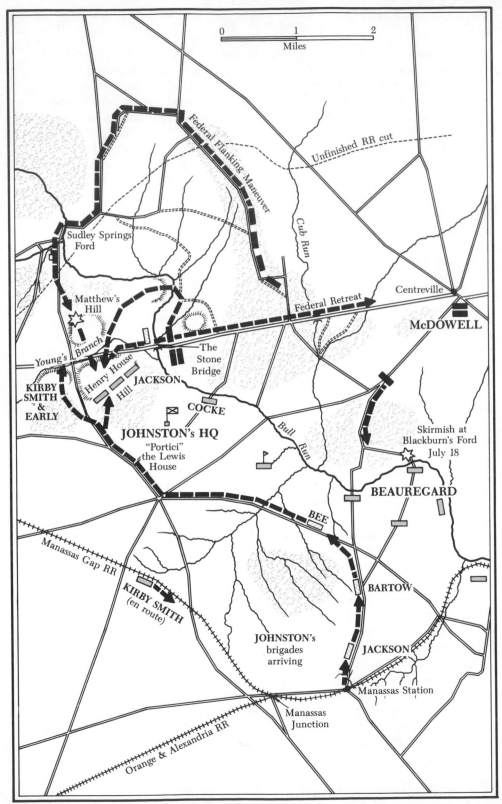

The Battle of Manassas, July 21, 1861

Hunter and Samuel Heintzelman had crossed Bull Run at Sudley Springs Ford and were now falling on the exposed Confederate left flank. While Johnston and Beauregard stood atop Lookout Hill searching "for evidence of General McDowell's design," the two regiments of Colonel Nathan G. "Shanks" Evans were assaulted by forces five times their number. At nine o'clock, concerned by the mounting sound of battle to the north, Johnston turned to Beauregard to urge that the brigades of Bee and Jackson—Johnston's own troops from the Army of the Shenandoah—be sent there. Beauregard complied, and also sent Wade Hampton's South Carolina "Legion" recently arrived from Richmond.[13]

The two generals waited atop Lookout Hill for another two hours. Johnston grew increasingly restless. Despite his repeated sugggestions that the battle was being fought to the north, Beauregard continued to insist that the main enemy attack would still be against the center, and that he would then launch a counteroffensive of his own across Bull Run. At eleven o'clock, Confederate scouts reported that the Federals across the river were felling trees, evidence that they were planning to act on the defensive, not massing for an attack. A few minutes later the noise of the battle to the north grew even louder. Unable to stand it any longer, Johnston abruptly announced, "The battle is there. I am going." He strode down off the hill to his horse, mounted, and curtly ordered his staff: "Mount and Follow!" Without another word he set off at a gallop. Beauregard, convinced at last that his grand attack was not going to take place, went with him. The staffs of both generals followed in their wake, some thirty or forty of them, the whole lot "a calihooting" according to one witness. Passing Sandy Pendleton's battery of guns, Johnston stopped his horse to inquire: "Whose battery is that?" Told that it was Pendleton's, he ordered: "Tell him to go in a gallop to the left to where the firing is heaviest." Then he spurred his own horse back into a gallop and pressed on.[14]

The two generals rode up onto the broad uneven plateau of Henry House Hill at about 12:30 P.M. There they encountered a stirring if somewhat alarming sight. Jackson's brigade held the center of a makeshift Confederate line facing northwest in a shallow fold of the hill. To Jackson's left were the remnants of Bee's shattered brigade, and to their front the lead elements of two full Federal divisions were advancing. Obviously, the first thing to be done was bolster the Confederate line. To Jackson's right and a few hundred yards to the rear, Johnston noticed a large group of disciplined soldiers who apparently lacked a commander. It was the Fourth Alabama Regiment that Johnston had accompanied on the train from Piedmont only the day before. All of their field grade officers had been killed, and the senior captain was searching the field for his missing brother. Johnston rode up and addressed the color bearer, laying his hand on the staff. "Sergeant, hand me your flag! I will lead you. Follow me." The sergeant, Robert Sinclair, was reluctant to give up his flag. Still holding onto the staff, he said: "General, don't take my colors from me. Tell me where to carry them & I will place them there."

Johnston then let go the staff and personally led the regiment onto the field, placing it on Jackson's right.[15]

Almost immediately, Brigadier General Barnard Bee rode up to Johnston with an anguished expression on his face. He dropped the reins of his horse and "in a voice tremulous with emotion & tears streaming down his cheeks," said, "General, my command is scattered and I am alone." Instinctively, Johnston sought to comfort him. "I know it was not your fault, Genl. Bee," he replied. "But don't despair, the day is not lost yet." Johnston directed Bee's attention to another group of men resting along a fence nearby and asked him who they were. "They are So. Carolinians," Bee answered. "Rally them," Johnston commanded, "and lead them back into the fight." Bee rode off to obey. Spurring them back into the fight, he urged them to follow the example of Jackson's Virginians, who were standing, he said, like a stone wall.[16]

By all accounts the arrival of Johnston and Beauregard on the field was a tonic to the embattled Confederates. Heavily outnumbered, they had been driven from their initial positions on Matthew's Hill and across Young's Branch, and they still faced a much larger enemy force that showed no evidence of halting its attack. Beauregard now suggested that since Johnston was the senior officer and had responsibility for the whole battlefield, command of the troops on Henry House Hill properly belonged to the second-in-command—himself. Although undoubtedly self-serving, the suggestion did have a certain merit. The commander of the combined armies should not tie himself up in directing small tactical movements at the point of contact, and the collapse of Beauregard's scheme for the day's battle suggested that perhaps Johnston had better devote himself to trying to bring order out of the existing chaos. Johnston accepted Beauregard's suggestion. Quitting Henry House Hill, he withdrew a mile to the rear to Portici, the home of Francis W. Lewis, where he established his headquarters.

The Lewis House stood alongside the road that ran up to Henry House Hill from Manassas Junction and the nearby fords. From there, Johnston dispatched couriers to hurry reinforcements forward as fast as possible. Scraping together whatever forces he could, including fragments of units battered in the morning fight, Johnston re-formed them, assigned members of his staff to command them, and sent them back into battle. He rode personally to General Philip St. George Cock's command, the closest to the battlefield, and ordered it into the fight. But Cocke insisted that there were still large numbers of Federals to his front across Bull Run, and that abandoning his position would turn the Confederate right. Johnston left him where he was for the time being.[17]

Meanwhile, the battle on Henry House Hill raged back and forth. From two until four in the afternoon, the heat, the smoke, and the psychological tension of unrelieved combat tested the mettle of individual soldiers on both sides. Bee fell mortally wounded; but Beauregard rode up and down the line, shouting encouragement to the troops. Indeed, encouragement was all he could offer, for little generalship was needed here. It was an uncomplicated pitched battle.

From the Lewis House, Johnston tried to judge the progress of the fight by the changing sounds of battle as he orchestrated the movement of reinforcements. At two o'clock, a young staff officer arrived from Manassas to report that a strong Federal force had seized the railroad junction there and was moving up the road against the Confederate rear. If true, such information meant ruin, and the report caused Johnston a few bad moments. But it was not Yankees who had arrived at Manassas, it was Johnston's own chief of staff, Edmund Kirby Smith, with the last four regiments of the Army of the Shenandoah. At about three-thirty, Kirby Smith rode into the yard at Portici in advance of his forces and asked Johnston for orders. "Take them to the front," Johnston said immediately. "It is our left that is driven back: but the ground is new to me, and I cannot direct you exactly." He urged Smith to use his judgment when he arrived on the battlefield: "Go to where the fire is hottest."[18]

Smith suggested that Johnston should personally direct the troops to the battlefield. Johnston agreed, and guided the column to the Confederate left. Even as the troops deployed, Kirby Smith fell wounded from his horse. A witness recalled that "He fell in the most spectacular way, the reins falling from his grasp, he reeled in the saddle, threw out his arms and fell to the ground. . . ."[19] Smith was carried to the rear, and Brigadier General Arnold Elzey, the Marylander, took command, "gallantly" assaulting the Federal right flank. Having marched all night and fought all day, the men in blue finally began to yield. Then, only a few minutes later, the brigade of Colonel Jubal Early arrived on the field. Johnston ordered it, too, to move to the left. Screened by Elzey's brigade, Early's men extended the Confederate line even further and in so doing overlapped the Federal right. Launching his attack against the exposed Federal flank, Early's relatively fresh troops swept the Federals from their path, and seeing the enemy falter, Beauregard sent the rest of the line forward. It was too much all at once. The Federals broke. As Johnston reported it: "The right of the Federal army fled in wild confusion from the field toward Sudley Ford, while the centre and left marched off hastily by the turnpike toward Centreville."[20]

It was not Confederate strategy that had won the day, nor superior tactics, nor even personal bravery—the men on both sides of Henry House Hill had proved their bravery beyond doubt. Elzey and Early arrived on the field just when the Federals, exhausted by an all-night flanking march and a long stand-up fight in the July sun, had spent themselves. The Confederate reinforcements were at the right place at the right time to precipitate a rout. The right place was due to Johnston; the right time was simply a matter of good fortune. Years later Johnston admitted candidly: "Instead of taking the initiative and operating in front of our line, we were compelled to fight on the defensive more than a mile in rear of that line, and at right angles to it, on a field selected by Bee,—with no other plans than those suggested by the changing events of battle." [21]

Now that the Federal line was broken and the bluecoats were in retreat, it was time to follow up on the victory. Beauregard arrived at Portici flushed with excitement, and Johnston ordered him to conduct a direct pursuit while he himself organized a converging attack across Bull Run. Johnston sent orders to M. L. Bonham and James Longstreet for their infantry brigades to cross Bull Run and block the Federal retreat along the turnpike. But he did not go personally to ensure that his orders were executed. After crossing the stream, Bonham reported that there were Federal troops in strength in his front and he returned to the south bank. Longstreet also crossed Bull Run, but then Chase Whiting, worried that Patterson's force or some other fresh column of Federals might yet appear to turn the tide, took it upon himself to order Longstreet back to the southern bank. Johnston himself rode first to Henry House Hill, where he ordered C. W. Squires's artillery to open fire on the stone bridge over Bull Run. After only a few rounds, Jackson ordered Squires to hold his fire and save his ammunition, but Johnston rode back and told him to resume. The confusion of orders was characteristic of the moment. Although the Federals had broken, the Confederates were in no condition to pursue. The only effective pursuit was mounted by the ever reliable J. E. B. Stuart, who took his troopers up the road toward Sudley Ford whence the Federals had come, and by two squadrons of the 30th Virginia Cavalry under Colonel R. C. W. Radford, who harassed the fugitives escaping up the turnpike. [22]

At twilight, President Jefferson Davis, unable to stay away from the battlefield, rode into the yard at Portici after a long train ride from Richmond. Johnston, who had returned to his headquarters, came out to meet him. "How has the battle gone?" the president asked anxiously. Johnston was happy to be able to tell him that the enemy was defeated and fleeing the field. Elated, Davis rode off to investigate, no doubt wishing that he could lead the pursuit personally. Johnston stayed at Portici and continued his efforts to organize a pursuit. Finally, some sixteen hours after the battle started at the Stone Bridge, Johnston left his headquarters and rode slowly back in the darkness to Manassas. En route he encountered the president and Beauregard. The three men rode together to Beauregard's headquarters, arriving at about ten o'clock. [23]

After exchanging mutual congratulations, Davis asked what measures Johnston had taken to pursue the defeated enemy. Johnston summarized the efforts he had made that afternoon and evening, and assured the president that he would continue the next day. But as reports arrived of mass confusion among the retreating Federals, Colonel Thomas Jordan, Beauregard's adjutant, suggested that perhaps Davis would like to dictate orders for an immediate pursuit. Davis did so. Then someone recalled that the officer who had sent the news of Federal confusion had a reputation for eccentric behavior;

perhaps his message was not wholly trustworthy. Davis changed the orders
to require a reconnaissance in force at dawn. Before he left that night, Davis
decided that word of this victory must be sent to Richmond as soon as possible. He composed a brief telegram that was both dramatic and to the point:
"We have won a glorious though dear-bought victory. Night closed on the
enemy in full flight and closely pursued."[24]

The Battle of Manassas was Joseph E. Johnston's first great military triumph
as an army commander. Sweet as it was to be able to tell Jefferson Davis that
the army had triumphed, Johnston's personal victory was incomplete. His
ambiguous role as commander of the combined armies was underscored by
Beauregard's grandstanding behavior atop Henry House Hill—behavior
that one historian has likened to that of "a dime novel general." In the heady
aftermath of the battle, Beauregard's reputation as the hero of Fort Sumter
and his colorful personality lent support to the popular belief that it was he,
not Johnston, who deserved the laurels. Southern newspapers extolled him
in print, popular songs likened him to Napoleon; he was even mentioned as a
candidate for president. Johnston could hardly avoid a certain amount of
jealousy, and eventually he became quite touchy on the question. "The battle was made by me," he later wrote. "Bee's and Jackson's brigades were
transferred to the left by me. I decided that the battle was to be there, and
directed the measures necessary to maintain it. . . ." Indeed, if it can be said
that anyone directed the Confederate army at First Manassas, Johnston
certainly deserves the credit. While Beauregard was rushing up and down
the line on Henry House Hill shouting encouragement to the troops, Johnston was orchestrating the arrival of the reinforcements that eventually won
the day.[25]

The second factor that dampened Johnston's mood was the criticism directed his way because no effective pursuit had followed the victory. If Johnston was, as he claimed, in command of the combined Confederate army,
then the failure to pursue rested, officially at least, with him. As it happened,
it was pouring with rain by dawn the day after the battle, and the reconnaissance that Johnston sent out found only a few stragglers on the road. Years
later, men would argue about whether the Confederacy had missed an opportunity to end the war at Manassas by failing to destroy the Federal army.
The reports of Federal confusion and disorganization had been entirely accurate. A damaged wagon on the bridge over Cub Run had blocked the road,
sending the fleeing Federals roaming the countryside where they lost cohe-
sion and discipline. Troops straggled back toward the nation's capital in
small groups, arriving, in most cases, well after dark. Never again in the war
would a Federal army fall apart so completely after a battle. Once the initial
glow of victory had begun to fade, southerners wondered why such an opportunity had been allowed to slip away. Davis claimed that he had specifically urged a rigorous pursuit on both Johnston and Beauregard during their
evening discussions, and he blamed both generals for their failure to harvest

the fruits of the victory that had been won by the men on Henry House Hill. Defending himself against such charges, Johnston claimed that Davis gave "gave no instructions" about a pursuit that night and, indeed, that Davis "was satisfied with the victory as it was."[26]

The memories of both men were colored by two circumstances. First, the belief that First Manassas was a lost opportunity was accentuated during the war as the fortunes of the Confederacy declined, so that after the war it seemed more necessary to find some place to lodge the blame for that lost opportunity. Second, as the relationship between Davis and Johnston soured in the coming months and years, each man tended increasingly to blame the other for past failures. An unbecoming quarrel ensured. After Davis's post-war biographer implied that Davis's presence on the battlefield had helped to turn the tide at First Manassas, Johnston responded rather uncharitably that Davis "arrived upon the field after the last armed enemy had left it, when none were within cannon shot, or south of Bull Run, when the victory was 'complete' as well as 'assured,' and no opportunity left for the influence of 'his name and bearing.' "[27]

In fact, speculation about a Confederate pursuit and an end to the war is entirely fantastic. The victory had exhausted the conquerors as much as it had the conquered. Colonel A. C. Cummings of the 33rd Virginia later testi- fied that "I could not have collected together as many as twenty men to have united in pursuit, so complete was the disorganization after the victory." Johnston himself believed that "our army was more disorganized by victory than that of the United States by defeat. . . ." Lacking sufficient cavalry, he simply did not have the forces necessary to organize an effective pursuit. "It is well known," Johnston later argued, "that infantry unencumbered by baggage trains, can easily escape pursuing infantry." The southern army could not have pursued the Federals into the streets of Washington. The exhausted state of the volunteer soldiers made it unlikely that they could have held to the road for more than an hour or two, and even had they managed to do so, they were "raw troops," unfit for "assailing entrench- ments" like those around Washington. Finally, the Confederate army lacked the necessary supplies, food, and ammunition to sustain such an advance. In short, all the speculation about what might have resulted from a pursuit is exactly that: speculation. Johnston's final conclusion remains the most sensi- ble: "The victory was as complete as one gained in an open country by infantry and artillery can be."[28]

In the euphoric mood of the night of July 21, there was little thought of lost opportunities or placing blame. The victory had been won, the enemy was in flight, and southern arms had been vindicated. First Manassas was the South's first victory. Across the Confederacy, southerners celebrated this triumph of arms and boasted that the war was all but over. In fact it had barely begun.

CHAPTER TEN

Genesis
of a Feud

In the six months after the victory at Manassas, Johnston's army in north-ern Virginia fought no battles and hardly moved from its campsites—first at Fairfax Court House, then at Centreville. And yet those months were in many ways the most critical of Johnston's entire professional career, for they witnessed the outbreak of a bitter personal feud between Johnston and his superiors: first with President Jefferson Davis, and then with Davis's closest political associate, Secretary of War Judah P. Benjamin. Johnston's falling out with Davis was particularly important, for it permanently soured relations between the president and his field general. As the quarrel grew and deepened, it came to have a profound impact on the course of the war. Johnston's feud with Jefferson Davis was the decisive event of his life, and the genesis of the controversy that would surround him until the day he died.

Despite their different views about whose fault it was that the Federal army had been allowed to "escape" after Manassas, Johnston's relations with Davis remained cordial in the first several weeks after the battle. His confi-dential reports to the president were characterized by openness and a sense of partnership. When he reported that many of the volunteer troops had turned to souvenir hunting after the battle at Manassas, undermining the discipline and efficiency of the army for several days, he noted that "This confession is to yourself—it has been made to no one else." If he had a suggestion for Davis, he couched it with great deference, and in all his correspondence to the president he subscribed himself: "Respectfully & truly, Your friend & obt sevt."[1]

As Johnston directed a cautious advance north to Fairfax Court House in the week after Manassas, weaknesses in the army's organization and equipage became more apparent. Increasingly, his dispatches to Davis were filled with references to these difficulties. His forces were too weak, he had too few cavalry, too little artillery, insufficient ammunition, and no reliable supply system. Johnston's complaints were justified, and Davis responded with promises that he would do his best, though he gently reminded his general that there were other armies in the field. Significantly, in light of subsequent events, Davis subscribed his letter: "Your friend."[2]

The open break between Johnston and his commander-in-chief occurred in the second week of September 1861, although in retrospect it is possible to glimpse elements of the gathering storm as early as midsummer. Before the Battle of First Manassas, Johnston had assured himself, by direct communication with Davis, that he held the rank of full general in the Confederate army and that, as such, he outranked Beauregard. A few days after Manassas, Johnston went out of his way to make the point that he did not consider himself within the command structure in Virginia presided over by his old West Point classmate, Robert E. Lee. For weeks Johnston had been receiving letters from Lee on formal stationery headed: "Headquarters of the Virginia Forces." But someone on Lee's staff carefully—and Johnston thought pointedly—lined out the word "Virginia," so that the heading implied that the orders came from the headquarters of all Confederate forces in the field. Johnston complained to Cooper that he could not accept or obey such orders, "because they are illegal." The orders themselves were for the most part purely routine, certainly not intended to intrude on Johnston's perquisites as army commander. But Johnston was touchy on the question of rank, particularly where Lee was concerned. Orders to his army, Johnston claimed, should come only from Cooper who, as Adjutant General, spoke for the president. When his old friend Dabney Maury showed up with orders from Lee assigning him to Johnston's staff, Johnston exploded. As always, the anger soon passed, and he made it a point to explain his reaction to Maury. He "put his arm over my shoulder," Maury recalled, "spoke to me very affectionately . . ., but he could not recognize Lee's right to order officers to his army for 'I rank Genl. Lee.'" That night Johnston wrote Cooper to protest. "I had already selected Major Rhett for the position in question," he complained, "and can admit the power of no officer of the Army to annul my order . . . being myself the ranking General of the Confederate Army." Johnston won few friends in Richmond with his assertive tone. At the bottom of the letter, Davis scribbled the word: "Insubordinate."[3]

Johnston was sensitive to questions of rank and status. When Major General Isaac Trimble, a visitor to headquarters, addressed him as "Mr. Johnston," Johnston at first gently corrected him. But Trimble was uncontrite. "Pshaw," he said, "this is only militia rank." Johnston stiffened and afterwards was cool to his visitor. Throughout his professional career Johnston had made careful calculations about the impact of particular decisions on his career prospects. The opportunities of war did not change that. He was fully aware, for example, that the Confederate Congress had passed two laws back in March which declared, first, that there should be five officers of the grade of brigadier general in the Confederate army, and second, that "the relative rank of officers of each grade shall be determined by their former commissions in the U.S. Army." In other words, whoever was senior in the Old Army would continue to be senior in Confederate service. Ten days later, Congress passed a third act that raised the top rank to full general while retaining the same stipulations about seniority within that rank. Since Johnston was one of the five original appointees to the rank of brigadier general, and since he was the most senior officer of the Old Army to resign and accept a Confederate commission, he calculated, reasonably enough, that he would be ranked first overall in the new Confederate service.[4]

On August 31, five months after these laws were passed, and five weeks after the Battle of Manassas, Davis sent the names of the five individuals to be named as full generals in the Confederate army to the Senate for formal confirmation. Johnston's name was among them, to be sure, but Davis sent the names to the Senate in order of seniority based on their graduating class from West Point and their standing within that class. Thus in Davis's list, Samuel Cooper (class of 1815) came first, followed by Albert Sidney Johnston (class of 1826), then Robert E. Lee, who had graduated second in the class of 1829, then Johnston, who had graduated thirteenth in that same class, and finally Beauregard, who had graduated in 1838. Davis later explained his ranking by claiming that since Lee and Johnston, among others, had entered state service before accepting commissions in the Confederate army, the congressional legislation did not apply to them. Still later, he claimed that Johnston's commission as a brigadier general in the Old Army was a staff rank and therefore did not count. Whatever his real reasons, he chose to interpret the legislation in his own way.[5]

The news struck Johnston like a slap in the face. He perhaps could have tolerated being ranked fourth, except that he already believed statutory authority had decreed him first. In his view, therefore, Davis's list of nominations amounted to a summary demotion. Characteristically, Johnston took immediate offense, for in his value system, public censure was far worse than private failure. As Bertram Wyatt-Brown has pointed out, the antebellum code of primal honor "made the opinion of others inseparable from inner worth." For Johnston, official approval served as the mirror that allowed him to assess his own value. Thus Davis's list of general officers, with its implied public rebuke, touched him to the quick. It was not just Johnston's professional reputation that was at stake, it was his public honor.[6]

Almost immediately Johnston sat down to vent his wounded sensibilities in a long, rambling, and emotional letter to the president. He began by expressing his "surprise and mortification," then hurled down the gauntlet in a challenging phrase: "I now and here declare my claim, that notwithstanding these nominations by the President and their confirmation by Congress, I still rightfully hold the rank of first general in the Armies of the Southern Confederacy." He painstakingly outlined the legislation that, as he saw it, granted him legal seniority, then offered his conclusion that the proper order of seniority should be: J. E. Johnston, Cooper, A. S. Johnston, Lee, and finally Beauregard. Since the order of seniority was unchanged with the single exception of Johnston's place in it, he was forced to conclude that "this is a blow aimed at me only." Davis's list of appointments, Johnston maintained, was tantamount to his being broken in rank. Surely it would be perceived by the public as evidence of the government's disapproval of his performance, perhaps even of his loyalty. Such an interpretation led him to offer an impassioned defense of himself as a soldier and a patriot. Johnston's wounded dignity urged him into fatuous verbiage he should never have committed to paper:

> It [the ranking] seeks to tarnish my fair fame as a soldier and a man, earned by more than thirty years of laborious and perilous service. I had but this, the scars of many wounds, all honestly taken in my front and in the front of battle, and my father's Revolutionary sword. It was delivered to me from his venerated hand, without a stain of dishonor. Its blade is still unblemished as when it passed from his hand to mine. I drew it in the war, not for rank or fame, but to defend the sacred soil, the homes and hearths, the women and children; aye, and the men of my mother Virginia, my native South.[7]

All in all, it was an ill-judged and foolish letter. After writing it, Johnston placed it in a bottom drawer and left it there for two days. But upon rereading it on September 12, he decided that it said exactly what he felt—and he sent it. It was the single worst decision of his professional career.

Johnston's momentary lapse of self-control may be forgiven. But his decision to send the letter—unchanged—betrayed how deeply he was hurt, for the letter was self-indulgent and deliberately confrontational. Johnston never repented of his decision, nor did he ever cease to argue the rightness of his case. Instead, he brooded about it for the rest of the war—indeed, for the rest of his life. His enemies said he sulked. Twelve years later, long after the war was over, Johnston again took up the issue in his autobiographical *Narrative*, referring to Davis's list of nominees as "altogether illegal, and contrary to all the laws enacted to regulate the rank of the class of officers concerned." And in 1887, when the editors of *Century* magazine asked him to write a piece on the First Battle of Bull Run (Manassas) for their "Battles and Leaders" series, Johnston began his article by invoking Davis's "illegal act . . . by which I was greatly wronged," even though that "act" played no role in the battle he was asked to describe.[8]

An angered President Davis took Johnston's letter of protest with him to a cabinet meeting on September 16 and railed to his advisers about its "intemperate" tone. He also read them his brief reply: "I have just received and read your letter of the 12th instant. Its language is, as you say, unusual; its arguments and statements utterly one sided, and its insinuations as unfounded as they are unbecoming."[9] Officially, that was the end of it. Johnston did not threaten to resign, as many other southern officers might well have done. If indeed it was a question of honor—of public reputation—Johnston's reaction was remarkably restrained; evidently duty and responsibility were stronger than wounded pride. Instead, he resumed the role of military stoic. But underneath he remained deeply hurt. He internalized his disappointment, allowing the memory of that wound to embitter him for the rest of his life.

Davis and Johnston never again corresponded with one another about this issue, nor did they speak of it when they met. But it was always there. Johnston never forgave Davis for the ranking, and Davis never forgave Johnston for his outburst. The seeds of a lifelong feud would flourish in the ensuing years until that feud defined their whole attitude toward one another. During the war, men and women would take sides in the dispute until the bitterness of it permeated the inner circles of the Confederate government. Lydia Johnston and Varina Davis became seconds in the duel. Previously close, they now formed rival salons where they indulged in catty remarks about one another, remarks that were soon passed on to members of the rival circle. Eventually the feud was felt in Congress as well, where Davis's political opponents cited his poor treatment of Johnston as evidence of Davis's unfitness for office. Such accusations, of course, did nothing to mend the breach. Even in their last years, both men remained unrepentant and unforgiving; they died unreconciled.

Johnston and Davis did not meet face to face until two weeks after their exchange of letters, and then it was not to discuss questions of seniority but of army strategy. But the question of their mutual enmity lurked in the background. The two men would never again be able to exchange full and frank ideas about strategy, logistics, or any other subject. Nor would either man subscribe any of his letters to the other "Your friend."

When they did meet, it was at Johnston's initiative. In late September he wrote to the newly appointed acting Secretary of War, Judah P. Benjamin, to report the disposition of his troops in and about Fairfax, and to ask for guidance about the army's next move. That army, renamed the Army of the Potomac, had grown substantially since July, now numbering nearly forty thousand men of all arms. Beauregard commanded the First Corps of nearly 24,000 men, and Johnston designated Major General Gustavus Woodson Smith to command the smaller Second Corps—essentially his own old Army of the Shenandoah. Smith was an 1842 graduate of West Point, a veteran of the Mexican War, and Johnston's friend and protégé. Prominent in the campaigns of the first year of the war thanks largely to Johnston's sponsorship, he would later be passed over by Lee and fade into obscurity until his resignation from the army in February 1863.[10]

Despite its increased strength, Johnston reported to Benjamin that his army was not sufficiently strong to mount an offensive across the Potomac without reinforcements. At the same time, he was reluctant to order the army to pull back from Fairfax if reinforcements could be expected. Fairfax was an appropriate site from which to launch an offensive, though as a defensive site it shared some of the basic geographical weaknesses that Johnston had noted at Harpers Ferry. The eastward bend of the Potomac River, only fifteen miles away, and the converging road network from the fords across the river, "made it easy for the Federal army to turn either of our flanks. . . ." In his letter, therefore, Johnston asked if either Benjamin or Davis could visit the army at Fairfax Court House to discuss future strategy. Even before he received a response, Johnston ordered the forces manning the outposts along the Potomac to fall back. During a heavy rainstorm on September 28, the army abandoned the range of hills overlooking the Potomac Valley.[11]

Davis arrived toward evening a few days later. Significantly, perhaps, he went first to Beauregard's headquarters, where Johnston later joined them. At about eight o'clock the next evening, Davis, Johnston, Beauregard, and G. W. Smith sat down to a formal conference. The three generals at once put forward a proposal to launch a fall offensive across the Potomac, though all three also insisted that such a move was impossible without significant reinforcements. Davis inclined toward an offensive; like the generals, he believed that delay would only work to the advantage of the Federals. But he seemed surprised to learn that despite all the reinforcements he had forwarded to Johnston, the effective strength of the Confederate army was still less than forty thousand, and that not all of those troops were sufficiently trained or healthy to take the field. What kind of reinforcement would it take, Davis asked, to enable the army "to cross the Potomac, cut off the communications of the enemy with their fortified capital, and carry the war into their country?" Smith thought that a total of fifty thousand good men could do it; both Johnston and Beauregard thought that too optimistic, and said that sixty thousand would be needed. Where were they to come from, Davis asked. Johnston had an answer: He suggested that reinforcements could be found by stripping Georgia and the Carolinas of all available troops and sending them to Virginia. After all, he argued, the Carolinas could be conquered only if Virginia fell, and if the army in Virginia triumphed, the Carolinas would be safe. Likewise, Federal forces in Kentucky could not remain there if McClellan were defeated in Maryland. In short, Johnston argued, "Success here . . . saves everything; defeat here loses all."[12]

Davis was as interested in a fall offensive as any of the generals, but he saw at once that he could not promise the kind of army concentration that Johnston and his wing commanders declared to be necessary. There were, after all, political as well as military implications in such a decision. "The whole country was demanding protection," he told them, and he could not denude the rest of the Confederacy of troops for the benefit of Virginia. Besides, the Confederacy did not even have sufficient weapons to arm all those who volunteered. Davis had hoped that shipments of arms from Europe might go to the new recruits, but those shipments had not arrived; without them, Davis could not supply even raw recruits as reinforcements. The idea that he could strip the rest of the Confederacy of its protection to reinforce one army he rejected as politically impossible as well as militarily unsound.[13]

Johnston did not press him. He later claimed that he did not believe it was his place to express an opinion about forces outside the area of his own command. But Johnston may have been relieved by Davis's decision, for it lifted the burden of responsibility from his own shoulders. Johnston's loyal protégé G. W. Smith wrote the "official" account of this meeting. His memorandum, dated October 1, 1861, but actually written the following January, casts Davis as the obstacle to a fall offensive: the generals had proposed an offensive, and Davis had rejected it. Almost certainly Smith wrote the account largely to protect himself—and Johnston—from accusations that they had failed to take advantage of an offensive opportunity. Davis's own account of the meeting, also composed much later, was that the generals had indicated a need for such huge reinforcements as to make any fall offensive impossible. In any case, Johnston was now satisfied that he had no option left but to pull the army back from its exposed position at Fairfax, and return to the more strategically significant and more easily defensible site of Centreville.[14]

The army moved back to Centreville on October 19. Johnston first established his headquarters in a field tent, but later moved into a hotel in Centreville. A large central foyer housed the combined staffs of Johnston and G. W. Smith, and the generals established their offices in adjacent rooms. Johnston's personal staff consisted of his two young aides—Jimmy Washington and Wade Hampton, Jr.—and L. Q. C. Lamar, a Mississippian whose self-appointed role was to try to smooth over the differences between Johnston and Davis. The two generals' staffs shared administrative duties as well as office space, and even messed together.

Another regular member of the headquarters mess that winter was Johnston's brother Beverly, still a bachelor at age fifty-seven, and a man who, according to one of the younger staff officers, had grown "very choleric and disputatious, too fond of his toddy." Beverly proved to be something of an embarrassment. When he had too much to drink, he had a habit of contradicting his younger brother on virtually any subject. The staff found this great sport, and occasionally deliberately introduced topics at dinner in order to provoke the old bachelor. On one occasion, Beverly, who stood about five foot seven but weighed over two hundred pounds, insisted upon riding one of his brother's favorite horses in a jumping contest. At the first barrier, horse and rider went down "most disastrously," and General Johnston could not hide his displeasure. On this, as on so many other occasions, Johnston's temper flared and his perceptible fury soon brought the contest to an end. As always, his anger passed just as quickly, and harmony was restored.[15]

Before the troops had settled into their new bivouac, Johnston found himself involved in yet another confrontation with the Davis administration, this time with acting Secretary of War Judah P. Benjamin. One of the more intriguing personalities in the Confederate government, Benjamin was a brilliant but driven administrator who had served as U.S. senator from Louisiana, and then as Attorney General of the Confederacy after secession. Once it became clear that the job of Secretary of War was too much for Davis's original appointee, Pope Walker of Alabama, Davis shifted Benjamin to that position. It was an unfortunate choice. Benjamin had no experience or familiarity with the military, and that fact, combined with his intense loyalty to Davis, made him primarily a conduit for Davis's ideas rather than a full partner in the development of military plans and policy. Benjamin's most recent biographer, Eli N. Evans, notes that "he brought none of his own preconceptions to the task . . . no way to sift and weigh the president's demands and balance their reasonableness. . . ." Benjamin simply adopted Davis's opinions as his own and relied upon his legal skills to implement them. So close were they that when Davis fell ill, as he frequently did, it was Benjamin who exercised the duties of the presidency. Given the nature of that special relationship, Johnston's difficulties with the Secretary of War became an extension of his feud with the president.[16]

While still at Fairfax, Johnston wrote to Benjamin to ask if the War Department intended to contract out the construction of huts for the troops. Benjamin responded that the whole question of winter quarters was "a purely military question, which must be decided by yourself as commander-in-chief of the Army of the Potomac." Nevertheless, the Secretary did dispatch two civilian contractors, James Hunter and John P. Hale, who, according to Benjamin's letter, had "devised a scheme" to construct huts for the army that would be ready by December.[17]

The two men arrived at Johnston's headquarters to explain their plan. By the time they left, Johnston believed they had reached a "clear understanding" that the contractors would have ten sawmills in operation by the end of the month, cutting planks for the huts. Hunter told Johnston they would begin work in ten days. But later that day while both contractors waited in Beauregard's headquarters, they spoke to an unidentified major who maintained that the soldiers could build their own huts. Taking this as a decision, without speaking to anyone else, they left the army encampment and returned to Richmond. Johnston believed that a "scheme" to provide winter quarters sponsored by the War Department was under way; Benjamin believed that Johnston was taking care of it on his own. In fact, no one was doing anything.[18]

The early November weather was particularly harsh in northern Virginia that year. The temperature dropped to below freezing at night, and there was snow on the western mountains. Strong winds knocked over Johnston's field tent, forcing him to work on his lap. He was concerned that he had heard nothing from the two civilian contractors since September. "I have not heard of the Man who was to saw lumber for us," he wrote to Beauregard. "He told me he would commence in ten days. You saw him afterwards, did he hold different language then?" Beauregard was also unsure, and so Johnston wrote to Benjamin.[19]

The Secretary wrote back to express "the greatest surprise and regret" at Johnston's misunderstanding of the situation: "I had not the remotest idea that you expected any aid from Mr. Hunter or from this Department in relation to the winter quarters for the troops, nor can I conceive on what basis you entertained such expectation." Benjamin noted that when Hunter returned to Richmond, he "represented that you declined his services. . . . Mr. Hunter has long since gone home. . . ." Benjamin also expressed his disappointment: "I find it impossible to account for your long delay, and your failure to exhibit any sign of uneasiness" when the workmen did not appear. Words like "delay" and "failure" were red flags to Johnston who felt that, once again, his personal reputation was being challenged. This time, however, he bit his tongue and remained silent.[20]

The resolution of this mini-crisis was not completely satisfactory. Johnston had to order the troops to fend for themselves. A veteran recalled that "Some of us built huts of logs while others spent the winter in tents and were comparatively comfortable." For his part, Benjamin merely reported that he was "gratified" that Johnston had managed to obtain winter quarters "without the assistance of the Department."[21]

A more serious confrontation between Johnston and the Secretary of War concerned Johnston's response to Davis's plan to reorganize the Confederate army. The original bill authorizing the president to accept regiments from the states and to appoint officers to command them had also urged that there should be a just apportionment of officers among the states. Davis took this to mean that, whenever possible, regiments from the same states should be brigaded together and placed under the command of a general officer from that same state, at least, that was his own ambition. In the first month of the war, regiments had been thrown together arbitrarily as they arrived in order to meet the crisis of the moment. Now that it was clear there would be no fall offensive, and with the army preparing to move into winter quarters, Davis thought it was time to reorganize to meet this goal. The president calculated, no doubt correctly, that both morale and recruiting could be improved by creating state brigades, and when possible, divisions. After all, "states' rights" was one of the battle cries of the Confederate armies. Presumably the soldiers would fight better under their own state flags, and under the command of officers from their own state.

Davis first brought up this issue at the meeting with Johnston and Beauregard at Fairfax on October 1, and he pursued it in follow-up letters later that month. Benjamin urged Johnston to make the changes in order "to gratify the natural State pride of the men. . . ." A few days later, Davis himself wrote G. W. Smith to ask directly: "How have you progressed in the solution of the problem I left—the organization of the troops, with reference to the States and terms of service?" As if anticipating his commander's objections, Davis noted pointedly that "The authority to organize regiments into brigades and the latter into divisions is by law conferred only on the President. . . ."[22]

Johnston did not think the reorganization scheme was a very good idea, and in any case he did not believe it was pressing. He was convinced that a complete reorganization of the army while in the field would jeopardize its security, and he also believed that Davis and Benjamin's orders left him sufficient discretion to postpone such a reorganization until a time of his choosing. He did not refuse to order the changes, he simply postponed them. To Beauregard he wrote: "I think . . . it is not practicable to make the entire reorganization now. We can not move the Mississippi regiments from Leesburg and send others to that point at present without risk of harm."[23]

Throughout the winter, Johnston stalled. It was foolish of him because it served mainly to diminish even further Davis's confidence in him. When pressed, he responded that the president's reorganization order was not possible given the proximity of the enemy. But with the armies on both sides now in winter quarters, and with the Union commander, Johnston's old friend George B. McClellan, showing no sign of aggression, Davis and Benjamin reasonably wondered if Johnston would ever consider it safe enough. Even Johnston later admitted that the Yankee army made "no demonstrations" that winter. Davis's patience began to wear thin. Speaking for the president, Benjamin wrote to Johnston in the second week of December to lecture him: "Fully two months have elapsed since the President's verbal expression of his desires that the will of the Congress on this subject should be obeyed. Six weeks or more have elapsed since orders were formally issued from this Department. . . ." In particular, the president was irritated that regiments from his own home state of Mississippi were scattered into brigades and divisions throughout the army, "as far apart," Benjamin noted, "as it is possible to scatter them. . . ."[24]

Even this strong note had no effect. Johnston wrote to explain, yet again, that it was not safe to undertake a complete reorganization of the army except by slow and gradual steps. In all likelihood, Johnston would never have found the time opportune to carry out the kind of changes that Davis envisioned. He simply did not believe that the potential benefits outweighed the risks, and as army commander he thought he was in the best position to assess those risks. Nevertheless, he was in an awkward position. At Harpers Ferry and elsewhere he had insisted on specific instructions; now he found himself with such specifics and was reluctant to carry them out. His senior subordinates, especially G. W. Smith and his former chief of staff Chase Whiting, supported Johnston's position. Whiting even wrote to Benjamin himself. His letter has not survived, but it is easy to imagine its tone, given Whiting's personality. Both Benjamin and Davis found the letter insubordinate, and responded by instructing Johnston to relieve Whiting of his command and send him to the Valley to act as Stonewall Jackson's engineering officer. This was clearly a rebuke not only of Whiting but of Johnston also. Benjamin's covering letter to Johnston was harsh: "The President requests me to say that he trusts you will hereafter decline to forward to him communications of your subordinates having so obvious a tendency to excite a mutinous and disorganizing spirit in the Army."[25]

Johnston must have felt a twinge of guilt. He readily appreciated that Whiting had written Benjamin at least in part because he knew Johnston believed the administration's reorganization scheme to be foolish. It is not inconceivable that Johnston had even encouraged Whiting to complain. Now Whiting was to be sacrificed. "I beg to be allowed to intercede in this case," Johnston replied on New Year's Day, 1862, "partly because this officer's services as brigadier-general are very important to this army, and partly because I also share in the wrong." Benjamin's response was cursory: "The President . . . declines making any change in his former order relative to Major Whiting." Eventually further pleas from Johnston and an apology from Whiting led Benjamin and Davis to relent; but the episode left further resentment on both sides.[26]

If Benjamin found Johnston uncooperative, Johnston found Benjamin intolerably meddlesome. The president was eager to secure long-term enlistments from veterans; to that end he encouraged Benjamin to authorize liberal furloughs and individual transfers as incentives for reenlistment. The Confederate Congress had passed a Furlough and Bounty Act in December, and in a New Year's Day general order, the Secretary offered sixty day furloughs to anyone who would reenlist for three years, as well as authorizing both recruits and veterans to organize themselves into new units and elect new officers. It was not an unreasonable idea—the Confederacy would need all the men it could get for the spring campaign, and the time to grant furloughs was surely in midwinter with both armies in camp. But Benjamin did not consult or even inform Johnston of the program. On January 18, 1862, Johnston wrote the Secretary to complain that he had not received a copy of the order, and to ask for clarification. Benjamin's response urged Johnston to "go to extreme verge of prudence" in granting furloughs. "The rest I must leave to your own judgment." Two weeks later he advised Johnston to "take some risk of reducing your force now, in order to secure your trained soldiers for the rest of the war." But Benjamin did not stop at giving advice. He authorized recruiters to move among the troops offering pre-signed furloughs, or interservice transfers to the cavalry or artillery, to any infantryman who would sign on for a longer term.[27]

Johnston felt he could not ignore such direct interference. As far as he was concerned, Benjamin's issuing of furloughs was only a symptom of a much more serious problem: Richmond's meddling in the organization and administration of the army. Such interference, he was convinced, bred inefficiency and "confusion" among the officers, and led to "demoralization" in the ranks. Simple put, he objected to Benjamin's "giving orders to the army in matters of military detail which should come only from the commanding officer present." He protested to Benjamin, citing several particularly irritating offenses. "The matters mentioned are purely military, and I respectfully submit should be left under the control of military officers." Johnston concluded that "The discipline of the army cannot be maintained under such circumstances."[28]

Benjamin ignored his complaint, so Johnston took his objections directly to Davis. On March 1, he wrote the president to protest that "Orders of the War Department are received daily granting leaves of absence and furloughs and detailing soldiers for service away from their companies based upon applications made directly to the honorable Secretary of War, without the knowledge of commanding officers and in violation of the Army Regulations. . . ." Johnston argued that "The course of the Secretary of War has not only impaired discipline, but deprived me of the influence of the army, without which there can be little hope of success. I have respectfully remonstrated with the honorable Secretary, but without securing his notice."[29]

Appeals to Davis, of course, were unlikely to have any effect. It was virtually certain that Davis would back his Secretary in this argument, but Johnston should in any case have been able to calculate that his protests would be taken personally by the president, for the government's military policies did not originate with Benjamin but with Davis himself. Three days later, the president replied that he had checked with the Secretary of War, and that Benjamin had assured him he had not signed any furloughs for Johnston's army in over a month. Davis suggested that Johnston conduct an investigation to see if the furloughs he had mentioned were spurious. That, of course, was hardly the point. Johnston's objection was not based on a specific furlough, spurious or no, but on the whole manner of army administration. But Davis was not finished. He added that Benjamin had at least as many criticisms of Johnston as Johnston did of Benjamin. In a clear reference to Johnston's refusal to reorganize the army, Davis noted that the Secretary of War "has complained that his orders are not executed, and I regret that he was able to present to me so many instances to justify that complaint, which were in nowise the invasion of your prerogative as a commander in the field." Davis's letter was distinctly cool. Back in August the president had subscribed his letters: "Your friend." This one ended: "Very truly yours."[30]

Johnston was not the only officer who suffered from Benjamin's interference. Before he left for the West, Beauregard had found time to expostulate in a letter to Davis about "that functionary at his desk, who deems it a fair time . . . to debate about the prerogative of his office . . . and to write lectures on the law while the enemy is mustering on our front. . . ." And Stonewall

Jackson, whose sense of personal honor was as sensitive as anyone's, also found Benjamin to be an irritant. Throughout the winter, Jackson had exchanged correspondence with Brigadier General William W. Loring, who commanded three Confederate brigades at Romney. Loring's men did not like their exposed position and believed that their assignment to Romney was intended as a punishment for their indifferent performance in the fall campaign. Loring repeatedly asked Jackson for orders to fall back to Winchester, where the rest of Jackson's army was encamped. He even implied that unless Jackson were more reasonable, the men would probably refuse to reenlist. Such threats carried absolutely no weight with Jackson, who rejected Loring's complaints out of hand. In January, Loring finally wrote directly to Secretary Benjamin to emphasize the precariousness of his position at Romney and to suggest that his forces might be cut off. Benjamin treated the letter as if it were intelligence of the most vital nature. Without consulting either Jackson or Johnston, he peremptorily instructed Jackson to "order him [Loring] back to Winchester immediately."[31]

Jackson obeyed the order, but whereas Johnston had managed to swallow his pride when offended by the administration, Stonewall Jackson would not. He sent off a formal letter to the Secretary, via Johnston, asking to be immediately relieved. "With such interference in my command," Jackson wrote, "I cannot expect to be of much service in the field, and accordingly respectfully request to be ordered to report for duty to the superintendent of the Virginia Military Institute at Lexington. . . . Should this application not be granted, I respectfully request that the President will accept my resignation from the Army." Johnston received this letter on February 3—his fifty-fifth birthday—but he did not immediately forward it to Richmond. He was probably not surprised by Benjamin's interference—it was the kind of behavior he had come to expect from the Secretary of War. But he certainly did not want to lose Jackson's services in the Valley. He therefore decided to hold onto the letter until he had a chance to smooth things out. Meanwhile, he wrote to Jackson begging him to reconsider: "Let us dispassionately reason with the Government on this subject of command, and if we fail to influence its practice, then ask to be relieved. . . ."[32] Whether Johnston would in fact have agreed to resign with Jackson is moot. In addition to Johnston's own protest to Richmond, Virginia Governor John Letcher lambasted Benjamin in his office until the Secretary agreed to recant. Mollified, Jackson withdrew his resignation.

By now, Johnston had developed a healthy disgust for almost anything that emanated from Benjamin's office. As Johnston saw it, Benjamin was a lawyer and a hair-splitter, more interested in winning an argument or finding fault than in getting the job done. Benjamin's absolute devotion to Davis, whose frequent illnesses made him the de facto president on more than a few occasions, gave him inordinate power. Though Johnston would not openly assail the president, he felt little restraint in attacking Benjamin, and occasionally he even became abusive. To Lydia, he predicted that "If that miserable little Jew is retained in his place our country will never be able to defend itself."[33]

This growing animosity took place in a political environment that was sure to make Davis touchy about criticism of his administration, especially from a popular general. The rest of the country was becoming impatient with the lack of military progress. Davis's honeymoon with Congress over, the president was now the target of widespread criticism in the government and in the press. The Richmond *Whig* was particularly virulent, charging him with manifest incompetence. Johnston became a useful cat's paw for Davis's critics, and Johnston's frustration with Benjamin led him to be indiscreet. In February, Johnston remarked within the hearing of several witnesses that Davis must have been placed in office by the Yankees "to perplex and annoy them."[34]

After Davis was inaugurated on February 18 as the "permanent" president of the Confederacy, his cabinet appointments also had to be made permanent, subject to the confirmation of the Senate. Benjamin was already the target of opposition senators who believed that he had withheld guns and ammunition from the defenders of Roanoke Island (North Carolina), which capitulated to the Yankees on February 8. Following his visit to Davis on February 20, Johnston attended a dinner party in Richmond where the other guests included twenty or so members of Congress. One of them turned to Johnston to ask "whether he thought it even possible that the Confederate cause could succeed with Mr. Benjamin as war minister." Johnston thought about it for a minute, no doubt weighing his answer, then responded "emphatically" in the negative.[35] On March 4, while Congress debated a resolution of no confidence in Benjamin, Johnston's views were cited as evidence of Benjamin's unfitness for office.

Davis capitulated, withdrawing Benjamin's name and nominating George W. Randolph as Secretary of War. At the same time, Davis nominated Benjamin as Secretary of State, in which capacity he would remain one of Davis's closest advisers. Johnston was nevertheless delighted with the change. Randolph's appointment, he later wrote, "enabled the military officers to reestablish the discipline of the army." Probably he felt that he had won the battle of wills with the administration. In the long run, however, it was Johnston who was the loser, for following so close on the heels of his intemperate letter to Davis about his own seniority in the army, his nearly constant bickering with Benjamin, and his impolitic public statements, Johnston's intransigence confirmed Davis's growing conviction that he was not a man in whom the president could repose unalloyed trust.[36]

The estrangement between Johnston and Davis was disastrous for the Confederate cause. The mutual lack of trust and confidence led each man to be less than fully forthcoming with the other, to the extent that the South suffered from what amounted to a divided command. Despite Johnston's nominal command of all troops in northern Virginia, Davis began to issue orders directly to detached elements of those troops without consulting or even notifying Johnston. For his part, Johnston was tight-lipped with Davis, sending infrequent reports and keeping his own counsel about his plans. Effective coordination of strategy became impossible, fueling the mutual distrust that had grown up over the winter. Only the tact of Robert E. Lee, who acted as intermediary, prevented the feud from growing into an open break. It did not augur well for the spring campaign.

CHAPTER ELEVEN

The Peninsula

Despite his feud with the administration in Richmond, among the general population it was an article of faith that Joseph E. Johnston possessed the best military mind in the Confederate army. The victory at Manassas had added luster to the distinction of being the most senior officer in the Old Army to go South. The British journalist William Howard Russell reflected the consensus of popular opinion North as well as South when he noted in his journal in the fall of 1861 that "Johnston is their best strategist."[1] That popular assumption, however, had not yet been tested. At Harpers Ferry, Johnston had been an organizer; at Manassas, he had reacted to events; during the fall and winter, in the midst of his quarrels with Davis and Benjamin, he had been an administrator. Now in command of the Confederacy's principal field army, and with a reorganized and well-supplied Federal army poised for an invasion, Johnston's popular reputation for strategic genius would be tested.

The essence of Johnston's strategic vision can be stated in a single phrase: concentration of force. The previous October, he had argued that all Confederate forces in the eastern theatre should be brought together into a single army, capable of assuming the offensive and striking into the North to seek a decisive battle. Since then he had continued to sponsor that strategy. Confederate troops in the Carolinas and Georgia were being wasted, he insisted. The North's superiority of numbers meant that the Confederacy could not afford to parcel out its strength trying to defend everywhere, nor could it afford to wait passively for the North to turn its superior manpower and industrial potential into battlefield dominance. He therefore argued that troops from the Carolinas and elsewhere should be sent to Virginia, where the issue would be decided. In Richmond, however, Davis had come to appreciate that such a view was politically impossible. As the head of a government whose battle cry was "states' rights," he knew that such a strategy would be unacceptable to the Deep South states. Then, too, the Confederacy lacked the armaments and supplies even to equip those volunteers who did come to Virginia. Davis insisted that a policy of concentration was both politically and logistically impossible. Johnston therefore accepted what he saw as the only available option, which was to adopt a defensive role and attempt to defeat the Federal army when it again invaded Confederate soil. Johnston disapproved of the strategy, but he perforce accepted it. From his perspective, he bore a double burden: he confronted a vastly superior enemy army, and was undermined by an unsympathetic, frequently hostile, administration. He was, in his own mind, a martyr to Davis's lack of vision.

In March 1862 the lengthening days and the distant music of the geese returning north signalled the end of winter to the men in Johnston's army. One recalled that "The buds began to swell, the dogwood to blossom, and the wild onions, which the men gathered by the bushel and ate, began to shed their pungent odor. . . ." The return of spring also marked the beginning of the campaign season. Even more than the clash at Manassas the previous summer, the spring campaign would decide the immediate fate of the Confederacy. Across the Potomac, Johnston's old friend George McClellan commanded a growing Federal army. Passive during the winter months, with warmer weather that army would almost certainly be on the move soon, striking southward toward the Confederate capital at Richmond only a hundred miles away. This time it would be no amateur army that came marching into Virginia, overconfident and ripe for destruction; McClellan's force of more than 100,000 men was as polished and professional as a winter's hard work could make it.[2]

Johnston's own army had successfully survived the winter, but it had not grown substantially—indeed, it was no larger in March 1862 than it had been at Manassas eight months earlier. Johnston reported the presence of an aggregate total of 36,267 men at Centreville. In addition, Major General Theophilus Holmes commanded six thousand men at Aquia Creek, and Stonewall Jackson another five thousand in the Shenandoah Valley, both forces under Johnston's nominal command. But even if all those forces could be brought together, they would still number less than half of McClellan's powerful and well-supplied Federal army. There were simply not enough

Confederate soldiers in Virginia to match the Federal juggernaut. Moreover, April 14 would mark the anniversary of Fort Sumter, and the majority of the soldiers in Johnston's army had enlisted for a single year. Many of them would eventually reenlist for the duration, but Johnston could not be sure of the numbers; it was not impossible that a substantial portion of the Confederate army would simply go home just as the real fighting was about to begin. For a few anxious days Johnston feared that the South Carolina troops might depart en masse. Even those who did reenlist (with the encouragement of a hefty bonus) insisted on reorganizing and electing new officers, and Johnston knew that such a shake-up would reduce their effectiveness at least temporarily.[3]

One change that Johnston much regretted was the departure of the flamboyant Beauregard. After Manassas, Johnston had organized the combined Confederate army into two wings, or corps, roughly approximating the two armies that had come together at Manassas in July: Beauregard's former command became the First Corps, and Johnston's old Army of the Shenandoah the Second Corps, which Johnston turned over to his friend Gustavus Smith. Davis and Benjamin, however, had conceived of Beauregard not as a corps commander but as a kind of vice commander of the whole army, with no specific troop command. In October 1861, Benjamin answered Beauregard's query about his status by telling him that "You are second in command of the whole, and not first in command of half the army." Because it involved no specific troop command, such a role did not appeal to Beauregard, who requested a transfer. In January 1862, Davis gratified him by ordering him to an assignment in the West—one that would lead him in a few months to the bloody battlefield of Shiloh. Davis was not unhappy to send Beauregard West; he had been displeased by Beauregard's official report on Manassas, in which Beauregard had assumed credit for the victory and implied that the president was responsible for the failure to pursue.[4]

Johnston now reorganized the army into three divisions. Smith's 12,000-man "wing" became the First Division, and Johnston split Beauregard's former command into two more divisions, one commanded by Major General James Longstreet, the other by Major General Daniel Harvey (D. H.) Hill. Both men were natives of South Carolina and had graduated together from West Point in the class of 1842. In all other respects, however, they were virtual opposites. Longstreet was physically massive: large and powerfully built, with a high forehead and a full bushy beard. Hill was small and fine-boned, with lank blond hair and pale blue eyes. Each man's appearance belied his inner nature. Longstreet's principal battlefield characteristic was caution. Thoughtful and deliberate, he would later be accused of being too cautious at critical moments. At meetings and conferences, he tended to keep his own counsel and refuse to be drawn. Hill, on the other hand, spoke his mind freely, and on the battlefield he was often overly bold, even reckless, willing to hurl his men—and himself—into battle without thorough consideration. He was loved by the men in the ranks, but he lacked Longstreet's tact, and had an unfortunate tendency to criticize others, which led him into occasional disputes with fellow officers, including superiors. These two men, if properly directed, could provide the stability and the daring needed for success; but Johnston would have to choose their roles with some care.[5]

Satisfied with the new organization, Johnston was less pleased about his advanced position at Centreville. The army was supplied by the single line of the Orange & Alexandria Railroad—a road so crowded and overworked that by February it required thirty-six hours for trains to cover the sixty-one miles from Gordonsville to Manassas.[6] Although Centreville covered the vital junction with the Manassas Gap Railroad, it was not otherwise particularly well suited to the defensive. As long as Johnston thought it possible that Davis might provide the reinforcements for an offensive, he was willing to accept the precariousness of his position at Centreville; but if his role were to be limited to the defensive, the site offered neither natural barriers nor advantages. As McClellan's Federal army across the Potomac continued to strengthen throughout January and February, Johnston became increasingly concerned about his exposed position. He believed it would be prudent to pull the army back behind the protection of the Rappahannock River. The Federals outnumbered him by as much as three to one; they were also particularly dominant in the long arm—artillery. Fearing that the Federals would pounce upon him if McClellan discovered his true weakness, Johnston tried to deceive his old friend by erecting elaborate fortifications north of Centreville and arming them with so-called Quaker guns—logs trimmed and painted to resemble large-caliber artillery. The ruse worked largely because McClellan was cautious by nature and did not want to confront the rebel army directly if he could find a better way.

Eventually McClellan would overcome his caution, and the two armies would come to grips. But where? McClellan might decide simply to march overland toward Centreville and the fords across Bull Run, as McDowell had attempted to do. Or he could take advantage of Union naval superiority to bypass the line of Bull Run and move all or part of his army by sea to some port on the lower Rappahannock, or even to Fortress Monroe at the tip of the peninsula formed by the York and James Rivers. Johnston thought it most likely that McClellan would attempt to outflank the Confederate position at Centreville by crossing the Potomac downstream from Washington at Dumfries or Aquia Creek. From there it was but a short march to Fredericksburg and the railroad to Richmond.[7]

Jefferson Davis took the oath of office as the first (and, as it would prove, only) "permanent" president of the Confederacy on February 18, 1862. The official inauguration would take place four days later. In between, Davis summoned Johnston to Richmond for a conference. Johnston arrived by train early in the morning on February 19 and presented himself at Davis's office at 10:00 A.M. The cabinet was already in session and Davis invited Johnston

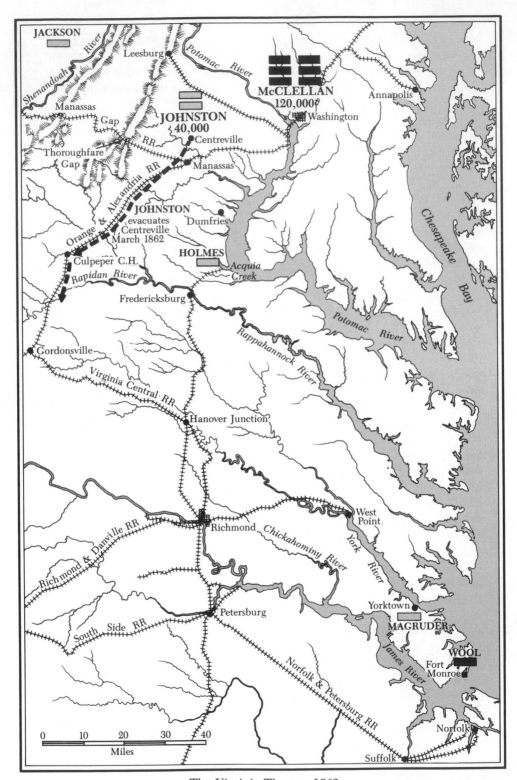

The Virginia Theatre, 1862

to join the discussion. Davis held cabinet meetings frequently—too frequently, some thought. He conferred with each cabinet member almost daily, yet still scheduled full-scale cabinet meetings two or three times a week for discussions that invariably lasted three to five hours or even longer, and just as often ended without reaching a decision. According to Navy Secretary Stephen R. Mallory, Davis had an "uncontrollable tendency to digression" that derived from his desire to know every detail of every department, especially in military matters. To use the modern euphemism, Davis was a micro-manager.[8]

At the meeting on February 19, most of the cabinet members sat, watched, and listened while Davis spent hours questioning Johnston about the situation of the army and its future. Davis had accepted the idea that an attempt to defend everywhere was doomed to failure, and that to hold Richmond it would be necessary to pull the army back closer to the capital. Johnston certainly agreed, but he suggested waiting until spring before moving in order to avoid hardship on the troops. Even then, he noted, it would be difficult to move the heavy siege guns along the Potomac. Typically, a long, technical discussion ensued about how to remove those guns—hardly a concern of the entire cabinet. The meeting lasted more than seven hours, ending "near sunset." Despite these lengthy discussions, Davis and Johnston emerged from the meeting with different conceptions of what had been decided. It was neither the first nor the last time they would leave a conversation with opposing views of the outcome. On this occasion, Johnston believed that it had been agreed "that the army was to fall back as soon as practicable." Davis was equally certain that it had been decided to hold on until a withdrawal became absolutely necessary. Although Davis agreed that the timing of the withdrawal had to be a matter of circumstances, best left to Johnston's discretion, apparently the president assumed that it was not imminent. As always, Benjamin had participated only to second Davis's views. That night at a dinner party in Richmond, Johnston made his impolitic public denial that the Confederacy could win the war with Benjamin as Secretary of War.[9]

Johnston returned to Centreville satisfied that Davis had approved a withdrawal, and that the timing was left entirely to his discretion. En route to Manassas, however, an acquaintance approached him to ask if it were true that the cabinet had debated an evacuation of Centreville the day before. Johnston was distressed by the lack of security, and he asked the friend where he had heard such a rumor. The answer was even more distressing: from the wife of a cabinet member. Johnston began to think that he should pull the army back before the rumors also reached McClellan's ear, and he also silently vowed never again to trust Davis and his advisers with military secrets. When two weeks later, on March 5, J.E.B. Stuart's cavalry patrols reported a significant increase in Federal activity across the river, Johnston concluded that the long-awaited Federal offensive was about to get under way, and he issued the necessary evacuation orders. After two days the army began to fall back in the direction of Culpeper Court House. The evacuation was completed on the 9th, and the army crossed the Rappahannock on March 11. At last the barrier of a major river lay between the Confederate army and the Federals. Johnston notified Davis of his new position, dating his report March 13 from Rappahannock Station.[10]

Davis was not pleased. The president had continued to hope that despite all that had been said at Richmond, somehow he could come up with the reinforcements that would enable Johnston to assume the offensive. He had written twice to Johnston claiming that reinforcements were on their way and hinting that Johnston's army could be increased up to as many as a hundred thousand. Johnston did not inform Richmond of the precise date of his withdrawal for fear of security leaks. Thus Davis was both surprised and disappointed by Johnston's news, and wrote to complain of his "precipitate retreat." Moreover, as in the weeks following his evacuation of Harpers Ferry, there were complaints that Johnston had abandoned valuable military supplies. This time his withdrawal had forced the abandonment of a meat-packing plant at Thoroughfare Gap and the destruction of a million pounds of cured meat, as well as the loss of the heavy guns along the Potomac. Although Johnston mourned the loss of both the meat and the guns, he felt no personal responsibility for either. He had protested the construction of the meat-packing plant at such an advanced site, and he had given Richmond plenty of earlier notice of his intentions.[11]

Davis did not see it that way. His disillusionment with Johnston had been growing for some time. Even before acknowledging Johnston's withdrawal from Centreville, he had moved to restrict the general's authority. On March 13, the president endowed Lee with the conduct of "the military operations of the armies of the Confederacy" under the president's direction. For the rest of the spring campaign, Davis and Lee would direct the movements of Confederate forces in Virginia, including those of Jackson in the Valley and Holmes at Aquia Creek, both officially assigned to Johnston's command. Worse, they would issue their orders without consulting or even notifying Johnston, who continued to assume that Jackson and Holmes were still under his command.[12]

The day after Johnston abandoned Centreville, the Federals marched in to take possession of the town and the important nearby railroad junction of Manassas. There they discovered the "Quaker guns," and other evidence that the Confederate camp had housed not the hundred thousand men McClellan had insisted were there, but probably less than half that number. As for the valuable stores that Johnston supposedly left behind, McClellan reported that the rebels left "many wagons, some caissons, clothing, ammunition, personal baggage, &c." but that "the country [was] entirely stripped of forage and provisions. . . ."[13]

On March 18, continued Federal activity convinced Johnston to take the next step and move the left wing of his army to the south bank of the Rapidan. Johnston set up his headquarters at the home of Mr. Sidney Jones, about a mile east of the railroad bridge over the Rapidan, and only a few hundred yards south of the river. A staff officer later recalled the nearly constant diet of "Jowl and spinach" served there. Johnston's new position was the best defensive line in northern Virginia. For much of the war, the line of the Rappahannock-Rapidan would be the de facto military boundary between North and South. The two rivers offered a protective barrier that curved in a gentle arc to provide the defenders with interior lines of communication. Over the next two years, Federal commanders would cross that barrier at their peril.[14]

A week after the withdrawal, Davis and Lee visited Johnston's army in its new locale, which even Davis had to admit was "a position possessing great natural advantages." They rode together to Fredericksburg and discussed the general strategic situation in Virginia, which was complicated by several factors. First, neither Johnston, nor Davis, nor anyone else knew for sure what McClellan planned to do in Virginia. But more importantly, Lee and Johnston had fundamentally different views of the Confederacy's strategic imperatives. Whereas Johnston believed in concentration of force, even if he had to give ground to achieve it, Lee wanted to meet the enemy as far from the strategic center as possible. Three days after Davis endowed him with overall command, Lee wrote to one officer that "It is not the plan of the Government to abandon any country that can be held."[15]

This disagreement had immediate repercussions, for a second Federal army under Major General Ambrose Burnside had appeared off the coast of North Carolina and was threatening Roanoke Island and the city of New Bern. Johnston considered this a relatively unimportant sideshow, but Davis and Lee were concerned about all Federal initiatives, and the president wanted Johnston to dispatch Longstreet's division to North Carolina. Johnston protested, not only because this would be yet another dispersion of forces, but because he needed Longstreet personally. G. W. Smith had fallen seriously ill and his division was being led by the relatively inexperienced D. R. Jones. If Longstreet left, Johnston would have only one experienced division commander. Davis agreed that Johnston could instead send Holmes's two brigades from Fredericksburg.[16]

The uncertainty about Federal intentions deepened the next day. At dawn on March 24, while Davis and Lee were returning from their visit to Johnston's army, Confederates manning the lines in and about Norfolk were startled by the appearance of more than twenty steamers off Old Point Comfort, where Federal troops commanded by the aged veteran of the War of 1812 John E. Wool had occupied Fortress Monroe since the onset of hostilities. Throughout the morning the ships discharged blue-coated infantry. One witness noted that "The force is immense—entirely out of my power to estimate." From Norfolk, Benjamin Huger telegraphed the news to Richmond. Later, John Magruder at Yorktown confirmed the information and called for reinforcements of "at least 10,000." Was this the beginning of the long-awaited Federal offensive?[17]

The news reached Davis and Lee at Gordonsville. Concerned, but still uncertain whether this was the main Federal effort, they tried to hedge their bets by ordering Johnston "to organize a part of your troops to hold your present line, and to prepare the remainder to move" to Richmond. Lee wrote that "nothing less than 20,000 or 30,000 men will be sufficient. . . ." Johnston remained convinced that such dispersal of forces was a serious mistake, and suggested that if the major effort were to be made near Richmond, he should take the whole army there. But Davis and Lee were not yet ready to put all their eggs in any one basket. Instead, Lee (apparently after consulting Davis) wrote ordering Johnston to send only about ten thousand. Johnston did as he was told, but he continued to warn that "We cannot win without concentration."[18]

With the dispatch of these reinforcements, Johnston's army on the Rappahannock dwindled to only about 23,000 while Magruder's on the peninsula grew to 31,000. Johnston believed that such dispositions threw away the advantage of interior lines. Instead of using that advantage to concentrate Confederate forces against first one and then the other of the Federal armies, Davis and Lee apparently intended to contest the issue at both places simultaneously. As a result, neither Confederate army was sufficiently strong to be confident of success. Johnston argued as before that all of the available Confederate forces should be concentrated against the principal threat, and that was at Richmond. Northern Virginia could be recovered later. For his part, Davis could not bear the idea of giving up any territory to the enemy, even temporarily. On March 28, he authorized Lee to write Johnston that if he thought the enemy on his front posed no immediate threat, he could begin to move his own army to Richmond. Then, only a few hours later, Davis had second thoughts. Spies had brought information that the Federal forces north of the Rappahannock were present in strength and that if Johnston withdrew, they might seize control of the Virginia Central Railroad and sever communications with the Valley. Under such circumstances, Lee could only urge Johnston to use his judgment.[19]

On April 4, all doubt about Federal intentions vanished when the Federal host at Fort Monroe sallied out of Point Comfort and began to advance cautiously up the peninsula. Lee telegraphed Johnston urgently that "the movement of the troops directed from your line must immediately be made to this place [i.e., Richmond]." Five days later, news from another of Davis's spies convinced him that McClellan was on the peninsula personally, and that this was indeed the main Federal effort. He ordered Johnston to bring his whole army except for a small observation force. Johnston left Major General Richard S. Ewell with about eight thousand men to hold the line of the Rappahannock and took the train to Richmond.[20]

At the Confederate White House, Davis informed Johnston that he would command the forces on the peninsula opposing McClellan. Johnston left almost immediately to make a personal inspection of the lines. He was not impressed. The works that Magruder had begun at Yorktown were well laid out behind the Warwick River, but they were still incomplete and, in Johnston's opinion, not capable of standing up to a regular assault. The defenders were short of virtually everything necessary to a successful defense, especially artillery ammunition. Moreover, as Johnston had suspected, the entire position could be flanked by Federal gunboats or by Federal seizure of the weak Confederate batteries at Gloucester Point across the York River. By the time he had finished his inspection, Johnston was convinced that rather than face the Federal juggernaut on the peninsula, the Confederate army should withdraw out of reach of the Federal gunboats, concentrate all its forces in front of Richmond, and fight the battle that would decide not only the campaign, but possibly the war. Once again he suggested that Confederate forces in the Carolinas and Georgia should be committed to the campaign. If such a transfer rendered those areas temporarily insecure, that was a small price to pay for ultimate victory.[21]

Johnston cut his inspection short, hurrying back to Richmond to lay his proposal before Davis. In essence it was no different from proposals he had made a dozen times since October, and he knew that Davis would be skeptical. He therefore invited both G. W. Smith and James Longstreet to the conference. Smith, he knew, was a staunch supporter of the principle of concentration. For his part, Davis asked Lee and the new Secretary of War, George Wythe Randolph, to attend. The conference began at 11:00 A.M. on April 14. Johnston described what he had seen on the peninsula in discouraging terms. The lines were incomplete, he reported, and in any case the position could be turned by the Federal navy operating on the York River. Moreover, the line was too extended and Magruder's men were exhausted from their efforts. He offered a written proposal drafted by Smith which was virtually the same as the plan that he had presented in October: concentrate Confederate forces in front of Richmond.

Both Lee and Randolph expressed serious reservations about such a plan. Randolph, who had some naval experience, did not want to surrender Norfolk; its yards and docks, he noted, were irreplaceable. And Lee, who had recently commanded in South Carolina, said that it was not possible to withdraw forces from the Carolinas, for it would mean the immediate loss of both Savannah and Charleston. Besides, Lee thought the peninsula was a fine place to fight: it narrowed the fighting front and thus reduced the Federal advantage of numbers, making it a kind of Thermopylae. Johnston countered by arguing that a victory over McClellan on the peninsula could not be decisive; it would only delay the enemy, not defeat him. As long as McClellan was within supporting distance of the Federal navy, he could not be destroyed. If Johnston had counted on Longstreet for support in this argument, he was disappointed. The brooding, dark-eyed general sat quietly and did not commit himself either way.

The conference lasted all day. The men broke for dinner at six, then reconvened at Davis's house on Clay Street at seven. There the discussion continued until one in the morning, though Smith, pleading illness, left early.

With Longstreet maintaining his stolid silence and Smith absent, the discussion gradually turned against Johnston's proposal. Finally Davis announced himself in favor of Lee's suggestion to confront McClellan on the peninsula, and ordered Johnston to take command of the army on the Yorktown line.[22]

Johnston was disappointed, but he remained convinced that time and circumstances would vindicate his view of things. He had no intention of waiting at Yorktown until McClellan's siege guns and the Federal navy pounded him into submission. Sooner or later—probably sooner—the Confederate army would have to fall back out of reach of the Union gunboats and fight a decisive battle with McClellan's army. Johnston did not hesitate to declare his view openly. To Cooper, he reported his determination "to hold the position as long as it could be done without exposing our troops to the fire of the powerful artillery," but presumably no longer.[23]

Johnston led the army as it paraded through the streets of Richmond en route to the peninsula. He was greeted by the populace as a savior. Citizens threw their hats in the air and "cheered themselves hoarse." To fifteen-year-old John Wise, "the sight of General Johnston, riding at the head of his staff through the streets of Richmond, followed by the heroes of Manassas, made every drop of blood in my body tingle." As always, Johnston cut an impressive figure. Wise remembered the event in some detail:

> He sat his mount as if he had been a part of her, a little bay mare that looked as if she had been specially built to carry him. They were perfectly matched in size, and her step was as proud as his bearing. His uniform, from cap to spur, her housings, from head-stall to shab rack, were in exact conformity to army regulations. The adulation paid him evidently pleased him. So also did it please the bay filly, whose crested neck, tossing head, cocked tail, and caracoling step made her seem conscious that she was bearing a Caesar and his fortunes.[24]

With the addition of Magruder's force, comprising a fourth division, the men under Johnston's command now numbered some 55,000 "effectives," and may have reached a total of as many as 70,000—by far the largest army the Confederacy had yet assembled, but still less than two thirds the strength of the Federal army it faced. Johnston assigned Magruder's division to the right wing, on a line from Lee's Mill on the Warwick River to Skiff Creek. Here the Confederate flank was protected by the dominating presence of the ironclad C.S.S. *Virginia*. Longstreet's division occupied the center of the line, dug in behind the Warwick River. And D. H. Hill's division occupied Yorktown itself, employing some of the same works that Cornwallis's men had constructed eighty years earlier. Smith's division constituted the reserve.[25]

Technically, Huger's ten thousand men at Norfolk and Ewell's eight thousand men at Fredericksburg were also within Johnston's command responsibility. Even Jackson's forces in the Shenandoah Valley stil belonged, officially at least, to Johnston's command. But throughout April and into May, Lee

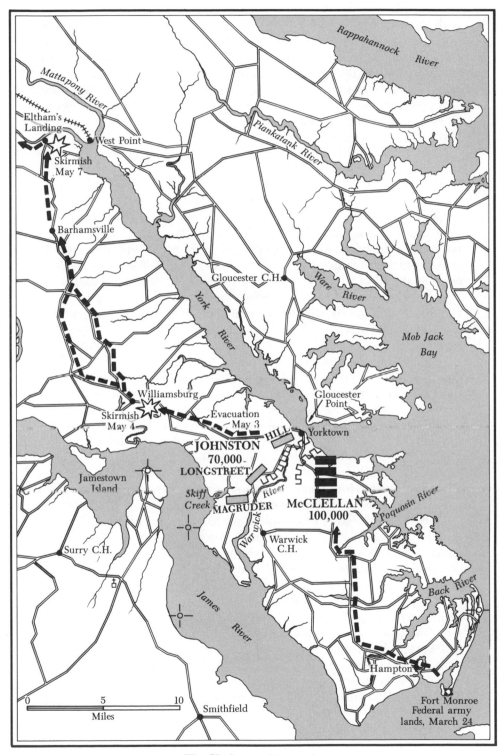

The Yorktown Peninsula

with Davis's authority took over de facto command of these forces by sending directives to them without notifying Johnston. Indeed, he accepted and
responded to letters that were addressed to Johnston without informing
Johnston of either the letters or his actions. For his part, Johnston was not as
fully forthcoming in his infrequent reports to Davis as he might have been.
One authority has counted fourteen letters that Johnston sent to either Lee
or Randolph during the sixteen days he defended Yorktown; nevertheless
Davis was frustrated by the lack of detailed information.[26]

When Johnston did write, it was often to argue yet again for a concentration of force in front of Richmond. McClellan had upward of a hundred
thousand men on the peninsula, he wrote, with more continuing to arrive. In
addition, another Federal army commanded by Irvin McDowell, the man
whom Johnston's armies had routed at Manassas, was just north of Fredericksburg with perhaps another forty thousand. If those two armies combined
north of Richmond, no force the Confederates could assemble could possibly
stand up to them. As Johnston read the situation, the Confederacy needed to
concentrate all of its forces—his own, Huger's, Ewell's, even Jackson's if
possible, along with whatever reinforcements could be garnered from the
Carolinas—and defeat McClellan's army before McDowell arrived. Every
day that passed was crucial, for it brought McDowell and McClellan closer
together.[27]

Lee, too, believed that it was essential to keep the two Federal forces
apart, but he believed that McDowell could be lured away by diversions in
the Valley and in northern Virginia. In this hope, he had ordered Ewell's
force at Fredericksburg to march to Jackson's support in the Shenandoah
Valley. This nearly trebled the size of Jackson's army, but it also meant that
the only force between McDowell and Richmond was a single brigade of
some 2,500 men under Brigadier General Charles W. Field. If McDowell
failed to take the bait offered by Jackson's maneuvers, he could march virtually unhindered to Richmond. Risky as it was, Lee's strategic view predomi-
nated in Richmond because Lee had Davis's ear and Johnston did not.

Johnston continued to contemplate an early withdrawal from Yorktown.
As far as he was concerned, the army's presence there was never anything
but temporary, and he made this clear in repeated reports back to Richmond.
On April 24, he wrote to Lee to ask him to have a few days provisions ready
in wagons "in the event of our being compelled to fall back from this place."
On April 27, he wrote again to report that the army's movement was imminent; and two days later, he reported that "We must abandon the Peninsula
soon." Since a day or two more or less could not really matter, and since the
wet weather had made the roads bad, he announced that "I shall therefore
move as soon as can be done conveniently. . . ." On April 30, the first shells
from McClellan's siege guns exploded among the wharves at Yorktown, and
Johnston decided that he could wait no longer. The next day, May 1, he
announced to his staff that he would evacuate the Yorktown line immediately. Despite all of Johnston's previous reports, Davis responded to this

news by claiming that "Your announcement to-day that you will withdraw to-morrow takes us by surprise. . . ." Johnston defended his decision in an emotional telegram: "I determined to retire because we can do nothing here. . . . The enemy will give us no chance to win. We *must* lose. By delay we may insure the loss of Richmond too. I have explained this to General Lee."[28]

The decision was some relief for Johnston, but the disengagement would not be easy. McClellan's engineers had been sapping forward near York-town, and the two armies were almost in physical contact. Surely the Federals would note the Confederate evacuation and might be encouraged to attack while it was still under way. Precise timing, stealth, and a little luck would be needed. There were a thousand details to arrange. The sick and wounded had to be evacuated first, then the supplies and ammunition trains, followed by the heavy guns, and finally the infantry. The order and route of the march had to be detailed so as not to clog the muddy roads. To D. H. Hill, Johnston confided that "I am continually finding something in the way never mentioned to me before." First, there were simply not enough wheeled vehicles to carry all of the sick and wounded; he had to appeal to the Confederate navy to supply a gunboat to take off the sick. Although Lee had reminded him that "The safety of all your ammunition is of the highest importance," the lack of transport forced Johnston to suggest to Hill: "Any powder you don't shoot away had better be thrown away." There were not even enough horses to haul away the heavy guns, most of which had to be abandoned.[29]

There was a great deal of confusion among Johnston's subordinates. The recent reorganization of the army consequent to the election of new officers was partly to blame. Another problem was that a few officers simply did not appreciate the need for both speed and secrecy. Although Johnston had instructed his division commanders to put their wagons on the road at first light on May 2, Hill either misunderstood or else decided that a few hours more or less didn't really matter, and instead issued orders for his wagons to start at sunset. Not only would that impede the march of Hill's infantry, but those wagons would be using the road Johnston had assigned to Whiting's division. Whiting, too, was confused. Johnston had ordered him to put his wagons on the road as soon as Hill's had passed, then follow with the infantry. But if Hill's wagons did not start until sunset, Whiting's wagons might not get away at all. The basic problem was that although Johnston had issued orders to each division commander assigning his particular responsibilities, he did not provide any of them with a clear understanding of the overall plan. Thus division commanders made modifications without understanding that they might throw off the whole schedule. As a result, Johnston and his overworked staff had to run around fixing things.[30]

Despite all these problems, the evacuation began on schedule during the night of May 2. Confederate cavalry kept the fires burning in the rebel camps, and the infantry marched away to the east, toward Richmond. Johnston did not learn until years later how narrow his escape was. McClellan's artillerists had twenty-eight more heavy guns ready to open fire on May 4; the Confederates escaped by a matter of hours a bombardment that might have kept them pinned in their lines. As at Centreville, Johnston had stolen a march on his old friend.

The roads were as bad as Johnston had feared. Hill reported that "Our Revolutionary sires did not suffer more at Valley Forge than did our army at Yorktown and in the retreat from it. Notwithstanding the rain, mud, cold, hunger, watching, and fatigue I never heard a murmur or witnessed a single act of insubordination." There was a great deal of straggling. Tired and cold men simply sat down alongside the roads to wait for the Yankees. Others tossed away their muskets and crawled off to conceal themselves in the brush.[31]

The main body of the army came up to Williamsburg that night and fell into the designated campsites. Morale was low. A month lying besieged in a trench, then a retreat through cold rain on muddy roads without sufficient food, tried the spirit of even the most patriotic Confederate soldier. Johnston took a room in town, along with his aide Jimmy Washington and the army's chief ordnance officer Major Porter Alexander. They discussed the retreat and the probability of having to fend off Federal cavalry probes. That led to a review of cavalry tactics and the use of the saber. Glad to focus for a moment on tactics rather than strategy, Johnston entered the discussion with enthusiasm. He had already stripped off his uniform tunic, then he picked up a saber to illustrate a particular technique. Captain Alexander later recalled that though he had seen many of the most famous and powerful cavalrymen of the age, he had "never seen a sabre whistle & sing like that one."[32]

The next morning, Stuart reported to Johnston that the Federals were pursuing, but apparently not in earnest. As always, the wagons and guns pulled out first to fight their way through the treacly mud. It was so deep in places that drivers joked about their wagons disappearing altogether. Johnston rode out along the road northwest of town to check on progress, and soon came across a gun crew struggling with a twelve-pound Napoleon stuck up to its axle. Johnston received the salute from the discouraged lieutenant in charge.

"Well, Lieutenant," Johnston remarked, "you seem to be in trouble."

"Yes, sir," the unhappy lieutenant replied, "and I am afraid we shall have to abandon this gun."

"Oh, no," Johnston said jovially. "I reckon not! Let me see what I can do."

With that, Johnston dismounted, and in the words of the astonished lieutenant, he "waded out in the mire, seized one of the wheel spokes, covered as it was with mud, and called out, 'Now, boys, altogether!' The effect was magical, and the next moment the gun jumped clear of the mud hole." Johnston had salvaged one of the army's guns and demonstrated that he was willing to pull his weight alongside his soldiers. Almost certainly, he did it quite deliberately. He cultivated the affection and loyalty of the men in the ranks, knowing that episodes like this one helped to boost the confidence those men had in the high command. The lieutenant later wrote that after this incident, "our battery used to swear by 'Old Joe.' "[33]

While most of the army was "escaping" to the west, Longstreet's division was deploying two miles to the east in the hope of halting the Federal pursuit. The Battle of Williamsburg was a confused melee. The Federal division of Major General Joseph Hooker flung itself headlong against Longstreet's line, met resistance, and pulled back. Longstreet was not seriously pressed, but on his left another Federal major general, Winfield Scott Hancock, found a weak spot and threatened to turn the whole position. Because the division's ammunition reserves were in wagons headed for Richmond, the only way to obtain more, once his men had fired off the cartridges in their pouches, was to call upon Hill for support. True to his pugnacious spirit, Hill countermarched his whole division and came in on Longstreet's left. Thus a rear guard action turned into what was nearly a full-scale battle.

At about three-thirty in the afternoon, Johnston and his staff cantered up to where the phlegmatic Longstreet sat his horse observing the action. Longstreet offered him command of the field, but Johnston refused it, telling Longstreet to carry on. A severely wounded Confederate soldier came walking toward them from the battlefront. The blood was running freely from his head and Johnston spoke to him with concern in his voice: "My man, I hope you are not badly hurt." Wiping the blood from his eyes, the soldier answered gamely but irreverently: "No, General, damn 'em. They all shoot too high."[34]

Over on the left, Hill's division bolstered the rebel line despite an unsuccessful assault against Hancock that cost several hundred Confederate lives. The inability of the Federal high command to organize an effective pursuit was as important to Confederate survival in this battle as any decision made by Longstreet or Johnston. Still, it was a gratifying victory. Longstreet's men took four hundred prisoners and several guns. Longstreet later wrote diplomatically that Johnston's "occasional valuable suggestion, was enough to ensure success." The next morning Johnston returned Longstreet's compliment by issuing a general order to the troops praising the success of Longstreet's men.[35]

But Johnston had little time to enjoy this small victory. That same afternoon, he directed Hill and Longstreet to follow the rest of the army on the road to Richmond. Transformed into bogs by 25,000 pairs of feet and hundreds of wagons, the roads were now barely passable. Many of the Confederate soldiers simply gave up. Hill reported that his men were "Cold, tired, hungry, and jaded, many seemed indifferent alike to life or capture. . . ." Several thousand of them threw away their arms and "straggled off to Richmond, either to procure food or to escape the perils of battle."[36]

Johnston halted the army at Barhamsville, a tiny crossroads village five miles south of West Point at the head of the York River. From there he sent Davis the first communication since his evacuation of Yorktown, though he had sent regular messages to Lee, who had presumably kept Davis informed. Davis was frustrated by the lack of specific and detailed information, and silently blamed Johnston for his lack of candor. Alas, the president was no more candid himself. While Johnston argued for a concentration of force outside Richmond, Lee, with Davis's approval, was orchestrating a more complex strategy, sending orders to Ewell at Fredericksburg and to Jackson in the Valley in the hope of preventing a junction between McDowell and McClellan. Johnston was aware of Jackson's potential value as a decoy, but Lee did not inform Johnston of his plans or actions. The result was that Johnston never had an accurate picture of the location and strength of the forces beyond those under his immediate command.[37]

Occasionally Johnston's frustration led to outbursts of temper. The most spectacular took place on the afternoon of May 7. Johnston had been concerned all along that McClellan would gain control of the York River and use it to outflank his position on the peninsula. He felt that he had stolen a march on McClellan by evacuating Yorktown when he did, and now he was ready to resist any Federal assault from the York River landing. On May 6, the Federals did land several brigades there—Johnston estimated the force at three to five thousand. To Johnston, this was both a threat and an opportunity. He ordered Smith to send a brigade to "feel the enemy" and then fall back, "avoiding an engagement and drawing them from under the protection of the gunboats." Smith assigned the task to John Bell Hood. Not for the last time in his career, Hood proved overzealous in the execution of his orders. His brigade charged into the Federals, driving them back to the riverbank. Hood's men had the better of the brief skirmish, but the Federal force remained secure under the guns of the Federal fleet.[38]

Hood was delighted. Johnston, however, was "greatly annoyed." "What would your Texans have done," Johnston asked him, "if I had ordered them to charge and drive back the enemy?" Hood, not the least bit chagrined, replied: "I suppose, General, they would have driven them into the river, and tried to swim out and capture the gunboats." Johnston believed that Hood's impetuosity had ruined an opportunity to inflict an important check on the enemy, but he was loath to dampen such enthusiasm. "With a smile," he told Hood: "Teach your Texans that the first duty of a soldier is literally to obey orders."[39]

In fact, the general was more disappointed and frustrated than he showed. Shortly afterward, he suddenly strode to his horse, mounted, and galloped off at such a furious pace that members of his staff thought he was trying to leave them behind. Porter Alexander recalled that Johnston was "in a terrible temper" and set off "at full speed or as near it as could possibly be made through the mud & around all the wagons, guns, ambulances &c. which encumbered the road." Alexander decided that he would not let the general outpace him, so he too dug in his spurs and recklessly followed. Alexander described what happened next:

At one place we got into a long sort of lane—[a] road with fence on each side—& just ahead of us went an ambulance. As Gen. J. neared it, at a full gallop, he took the left side of the road to pass it. But the ambulance driver could hear the approaching splashing without being able to see, as the ambulance curtains were all down & wishing to give more room for the rapid riders to pass, he also at the same moment swerved out to the left, heading the general off & pocketing him in a fence corner where he had to rein up his horse so suddenly that he almost went over its head.

Johnston lost complete control of himself. "I don't think I ever saw any one fly into such a fury in my life," Alexander wrote.

"God damn you!" Johnston shouted at the ambulance driver. "What do you mean?" Then, spotting Alexander, he demanded: "Give me a pistol & let me kill this infernal blankety blank!" Alexander had to pretend not to have a pistol in order to save the life of the driver, who was "scared almost into a jabbering idiot." Finally, the driver whipped his team back into the center of the lane, unpinning the furious commander. Johnston spurred again into a gallop and did not stop until he got to his quarters soon after dark.[40]

Whatever personal demon was driving Johnston that day, it was gone by next morning, and Johnston was once again the dignified commander of the army. As one of his staff officers noted, "his passion, which was sometimes of unseemly violence, was always as quickly followed by regret and acknowledgement so hearty and full that one could never harbor resentment against as true and right-minded a gentleman as ever lived." But Johnston could not allow himself many such tantrums, for the fate of the Confederacy was in his hands.[41]

The army had now drawn back to the open ground between the Pamunkey and Chickahominy Rivers beyond the reach of the Union navy. Supplies began to reach the army from Richmond, and morale in the ranks improved. Johnston believed that here he could reasonably contest the issue with McClellan. From his headquarters at New Kent Courthouse, Johnston took up his pen to argue once again for a concentration of force: "It is necessary to unite all our forces now," he wrote to Lee. "If the President will direct the concentration of all the troops of North Carolina and Eastern Virginia, we may be able to hold Middle Virginia at least." As far as he was concerned, the other options had already been played out. His was the only chance the Confederacy had left. "A concentration of all our available forces may enable us to fight successfully. Let us try." His tone left no doubt of his view that unless the government took his advice—and soon—the game was up.[42]

The next day Johnston received a letter from Davis, written the day before, and the first since the campaign had begun. But the subject was an old one: rather than respond to Johnston's plea for army concentration, Davis instead urged the reorganization of the army by states. Johnston was astonished, and vented his frustration in a letter to Lydia: "I got yesterday one of the President's letters such as are written to *gentlemen* only by persons who can not be held to personal accountability. I can not understand the heart or principles of a man who can find leizure [sic.] in times like these to write four pages of scolding to one whom he ought, for the public interest, to try to be on good terms with."[43]

In fact, Johnston had made some progress toward organizing the army by state units. Many of the army's twenty-two brigades were composed entirely of regiments from a single state. The brigades of A. P. Hill and George Pickett, both in Longstreet's division, were composed exclusively of Virginia regiments; those of R. H. Anderson and J. B. Kershaw were composed of troops from South Carolina; and R. A. Toombs's brigade exclusively of Georgians. In other brigades, regiments from a single state were predominant: Hood's "Texas Brigade" included one orphan regiment from Georgia. But there were a few brigades like Chase Whiting's, which contained one regiment from Alabama, two from Mississippi, one from North Carolina, and a battery from Virginia. James J. Pettigrew's contained one regiment each from Arkansas, Georgia, North Carolina, and Virginia. What disturbed Davis most was that the regiments from the president's home state of Mississippi were scattered throughout the army. However guilty Johnston may have been in delaying the reorganization of Mississippi regiments, he believed that this was neither the time nor place to bring the issue up again.[44]

On May 14, Davis and Lee rode out to Johnston's headquarters for a long but "inconclusive" conversation that lasted "late in the night"—so late, in fact, that Davis and Lee stayed overnight. Davis asked Johnston what plans he had, and Johnston replied that since he lacked sufficient force to assume the offensive, he intended to await McClellan's attack where he was and hope that circumstances or Federal mistakes would provide him an opportunity to counterattack.[45]

The president and his chief of staff had barely left when Johnston received news of an assault by Federal gunboats on the Confederate works at Drewry's Bluff. When Huger had evacuated Norfolk in consequence of Johnston's withdrawal from Yorktown, the Confederates had been forced to scuttle the C.S.S. *Virginia*. That effectively surrendered control of the James River to the Union navy, and on May 15 Federal gunboats steamed upriver to assault Drewry's Bluff, thirty miles behind Johnston's position and only seven miles below Richmond. The Confederate gunners at Drewry's Bluff managed to hold off the Yankee gunboats, but Johnston began to fear that the Union navy might seize Richmond by the back door while he defended the front porch. "I should feel no anxiety for Richmond if it were well away from navigable water," he wrote to Lydia. "But troops can not fight against iron-clad gun boats." Fearing a naval end run, he pulled the army back yet again, crossing the rain-swollen Chickahominy on May 16.[46]

Johnston had backed himself up to the very outskirts of Richmond. The enemy was within seven miles of the Confederate capital; Federal soldiers in their camps could hear the bells in Richmond chime the hours. The army's morale was at its nadir—men feigned illness or simply walked away from their posts. The administration was making efforts to bring troops from other parts of the country—especially from the Carolinas—but it might be too late. The crisis was at hand.[47]

CHAPTER TWELVE

Seven Pines

Seven miles east of Richmond, where the stage road to Williamsburg crossed the Nine Mile Road, seven loblolly pine trees stood like a row of sentinels over the intersection—the landmark that gave the crossroads its name. There, on the last day of May 1862, Confederate soldiers of D. H. Hill's division charged into the Federal division of Silas Casey to initiate Johnston's long-awaited attack on McClellan's army. The Battle of Seven Pines, which the Yankees named the Battle of Fair Oaks after the nearby railroad station, was the first large-scale battle that Johnston planned and executed. For him personally, it was the climax of the spring campaign: he had finally turned to give battle after his long retreat. But before the day was over he would be carried from the field on a litter, so badly wounded that he would have to relinquish command of the army.

At their meeting on May 15, Johnston had told Davis that he hoped circumstances or Federal mistakes would provide him with the opportunity to strike McClellan a telling blow. A week later, Johnston learned that such an opportunity was at hand: Stuart's scouts reported that a part of McClellan's army was crossing the Chickahominy River at Bottom's Bridge. These Federals, from Major General Erasmus Keyes's IVth Corps, advanced slowly and tentatively along the Williamsburg Road toward Richmond, followed by Samuel Heintzelman's IIIrd Corps a half dozen miles behind. On the 24th, these Yankees skirmished with Robert Hatton's Tennessee Brigade three miles from Seven Pines; the next day, they began digging in near the crossroads.[1]

But McClellan apparently had no intention of moving the rest of his army to the south bank, for that same week Federal cavalry drove the Confederates out of Mechanicsville ten miles north and west of Seven Pines on the opposite side of the Chickahominy. McClellan had split his army into two unequal groups, sending nearly 36,000 men in two corps south of the river and keeping between 70,000 and 80,000 to the north. The rainstorms that had made Johnston's retreating soldiers so uncomfortable all month had swollen the banks of the Chickahominy, rendering several of the fords and bridges nearly impassable, so that Keyes's and Heintzelman's forces were cut off from the main body. McClellan, normally so cautious, felt it necessary to divide his forces because although the direct approaches to Richmond were south of the river, he needed to keep his right wing well to the north in order to link up with McDowell's 40,000-man corps which he hoped and expected would arrive any day from Fredericksburg.

From his headquarters on the Nine Mile Road about three miles outside Richmond, Johnston studied the scouting reports. Ideally, he should concentrate the bulk of his army against the two isolated Federal corps, the destruction of which would go a long way toward evening up the odds between the two armies, and might convince McClellan to give up his advance altogether. But the greater danger threatened from the north. McDowell's corps, on its way from Fredericksburg, was as large as both of the Federal corps south of the Chickahominy. If McDowell succeeded in linking up with McClellan north of the river while the bulk of Johnston's forces were engaged to the south, Richmond would be theirs for the taking.

As if to underscore the point, McClellan on May 27 extended his right flank to seize the small village of Hanover Court House, ten miles north of Mechanicsville on the road to Fredericksburg. The Confederate defenders—a lone brigade commanded by Brigadier General L. O'Bryan Branch— were hopelessly outnumbered. After a brief struggle, they fled the field, leaving behind several hundred prisoners. On the same day, Confederate cavalry brought news that McDowell's force was on the move and had already advanced as far as Guiney's Station, ten miles south of Fredericksburg and barely thirty miles north of Fitz John Porter's new position at Hanover Court House. These two events, apparently part of a coordinated Federal effort to achieve the concentration that could overwhelm the Confederate defenders, forced Johnston's hand. He now decided that it was essential to throw McClellan's northern wing back from Hanover Court House. "I thought it absolutely necessary under such circumstances," he later wrote, "to attack McClellan before the junction [of the two Federal armies]." He sent instructions to his division commanders "to hold their troops ready to move."[2]

Johnston selected his trusted second-in-command, Major General G. W.

Smith, to lead the assault. Designating him a "wing commander," Johnston gave Smith command of three divisions, two of which were hastily improvised. In addition to his own division (temporarily under Whiting), Smith also would command a new division under newly promoted Major General A. P. Hill, and two brigades of Magruder's division that were given over to the command of D. R. Jones. These three divisions would attack Fritz Porter's Vth Corps along the line of Beaver Dam Creek near Mechanicsville. If successful, they would drive Porter eastward, uncovering the New Bridge, so that the divisions of "Prince John" Magruder and Benjamin Huger could cross the Chickahominy and attack from the south. D. H. Hill's division would constitute the reserve.[3]

By any objective measure, Johnston's decision to attack McClellan's right wing was a risky, almost desperate, gamble. His dispositions would send three Confederate divisions (perhaps 18,000 men) against Porter's one Federal corps, but that one corps was of equal size and occupied a position of great natural strength. Smith himself noted later that although he believed his three divisions could carry the works of the enemy, "it would be a bloody business." Moreover, Porter was within easy supporting distance of two more Federal corps, perhaps another forty thousand men. Finally, Johnston failed to communicate the overall arrangements to all of his division commanders. Smith, for example, said later that he "did not know, in any detail, what General Johnston intended to do with the rest of his forces. . . ." This was particularly unfortunate because Johnston's plan called for the coordination of units that were both out of sight of one another and divided by the rain-swollen Chickahominy River. Somewhat optimistically, Johnston hoped that "The bridges and fords of the little river would furnish sufficient means of communication. . . ." Johnston was aware of the problems, but he believed that the imminent arrival of McDowell made such risk taking necessary.[4]

On the afternoon of May 28, new intelligence reports from Stuart's active cavalry patrols changed the whole strategic picture. McDowell's men had stopped, turned around, and were marching back toward Fredericksburg! Whatever the cause of this incredible decision, it was a godsend for Johnston, and more so for A. P. Hill's men, who were even then marching into position before Beaver Dam Creek. At sunset, when Smith and Longstreet came to Johnston's headquarters to receive their final orders for the battle the following morning, Johnston was relieved to tell them that the attack was now unnecessary. In fact, McDowell's march southward to Guiney's Station had not been part of a move to link up with McClellan—he had been merely exercising his troops. Indeed, McDowell had already been ordered to dispatch part of his forces to the Shenandoah Valley in response to Stonewall Jackson's maneuvers. Lee's high-risk strategy there was paying off.

Longstreet immediately suggested that Smith's "wing" should hold on the defensive and that the morning attack should be directed instead against the Federals at Seven Pines. Johnston agreed, but he wanted to ensure that the blow, when it fell, would be decisive. Rather than attack the next morning, he directed Smith to recall A. P. Hill's division to the south bank of the Chickahominy and Longstreet to send an armed reconnaissance in the direction of Seven Pines. Unfortunately, Johnston did not bother to inform Davis either that the attack for the 29th had been postponed, or that he was considering a different plan. When Davis decided to ride out to observe the battle, he found only confusion as the army reoriented itself in preparation for the new plan of attack. Johnston later maintained that "I did not consult the president . . . because it seemed to me that to do so would be to transfer my responsibilities to his shoulders. I could not consult him without adopting the course he might advise, so that to ask his advice would have been, in my opinion, to ask him to command for me." This latter-day justification does not explain why he did not at least *inform* the president, only a half dozen miles away, that his plans had changed. Nor does the obvious fact that Johnston was busy provide an adequate explanation. Perhaps he kept silent because he wanted his next dispatch to contain news of a victory. Perhaps, too, Johnston had come to distrust and dislike Davis so much that he simply avoided communication with him.[5]

On May 30 Brigadier General Samuel Garland, who had been promoted to his new rank just that week, led his men out the Williamsburg Road toward Seven Pines. Two miles west of the crossroads, Garland's men encountered "a strong body" of Federal troops dug into a series of entrenchments protected by felled trees. This information reached Johnston a few hours later. He immediately began to dictate the orders that would bring on the Battle of Seven Pines.[6]

Johnston's plan was simplicity itself: he would use the road network outside Richmond to concentrate twenty-one Confederate brigades against Keyes's lone Federal corps. (Heintzelman's III Corps was a half dozen miles further east.) First, soon after dawn on May 31, the brigade of Robert E. Rodes would take a position on the Charles City Road near the Federal left flank. It would halt there, in a position of observation until the arrival of Benjamin Huger's three brigades (approximately 5,000 men), marching from Richmond. Then, while Huger's men held the right flank secure, Rodes's brigade would tramp cross-country to the Williamsburg Road to join D. H. Hill's reinforced division (approximately 11,000 men) in a direct assault against the Federals at Seven Pines. Meanwhile, Longstreet would lead eleven more brigades (approximately 13,800 men) along the Nine Mile Road to Old Tavern, where that road intersected the New Bridge Road. There they would halt until they heard the sound of Hill's attack to the south, at which time Longstreet's men would pitch into Keyes's right flank. Thus the battle would erupt from south to north across the Federal front. As second-in-command of the army, the privilege of leading the attack properly belonged to G. W. Smith; but since Smith's division was holding down the northern end of the Confederate line, Johnston instead gave the command to Longstreet.[7]

The plan was straightforward, but it did require Johnston to bring to-

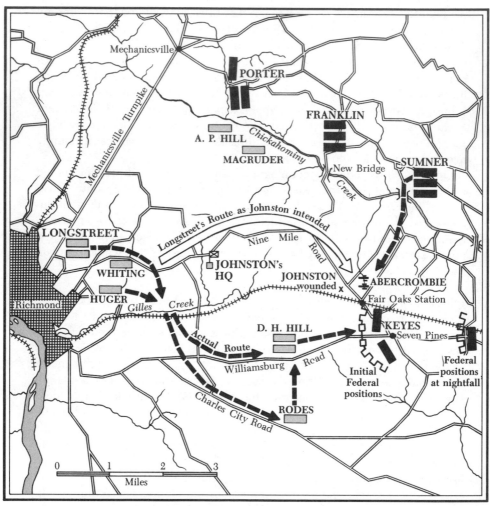

The Battle of Seven Pines, May 31, 1862

gether Huger, Hill, and Longstreet in converging columns on different roads, and have them arrive more or less simultaneously at the same place. Such a maneuver mandated clear orders, an efficient staff, and cooperative subordinates. The day's events would prove that Johnston lacked all three. The result was a poorly managed battle, in which the Confederates succeeded in driving Keyes's corps back a few miles, but utterly failed to inflict the kind of defeat that might have disrupted McClellan's advance. Johnston had 55,000 men at his disposal to deal with an isolated corps of 15,000 Federals, yet he never succeeded in getting more than 14,000 of his men into the battle. Although his orders called for the concentration of twenty-one brigades against the enemy, only nine became heavily engaged.[8]

The afternoon before the fight, Johnston dispatched written orders to Hill, Huger, and G. W. Smith, but since Longstreet was nearby, Johnston gave him verbal instructions. Longstreet's role was crucial: as he was to command the actual assault, Johnston spent several hours in conversation with him to be certain that he understood his assignment. E. P. Alexander, who was present during their conversation, later wrote that "it is hard to imagine how any serious misunderstanding of such a simple movement could have taken place in a conversation prolonged for hours. . . ." But obviously it did. Since there is no written record, it is impossible to determine whether the fault lay primarily in Johnston's instructions or in Longstreet's inability to translate those instructions into action. In any case, the result bore very little resemblance to the original plan.[9]

If Johnston's verbal instructions to Longstreet can be judged by his written orders to the other division commanders, it is fair to conclude that they were not a model of clarity. Johnston believed in allowing his division commanders the opportunity to exercise initiative, but in this case that desire led him to write vague orders that unquestionably contributed to the subsequent confusion. Smith and Whiting were told only that "we will fall upon the enemy in front of Major-General Hill . . . early in the morning," and that their troops should "be ready to move." If he sent written orders to Hill, they did not survive. At least Hill was in no doubt about what he was to do—he wrote his subordinates at 4:45 A.M.: "We are ordered to attack the enemy this morning."[10]

To Huger, Johnston wrote that his division should concentrate on the Charles City Road, describing it as "the second large one [road] diverging to the right." After that, Huger was to "Be ready, if an action should be begun on your left, to fall upon the enemy's left flank." What Johnston did *not* explain was that Huger's arrival on the Charles City Road was to be the trigger for the entire attack. In fact, he did not tell Huger what any of the other division commanders would be doing. As in the evacuation of Yorktown, and his planning for the cancelled battle of the 29th, Johnston made sure that each major general knew his part, but he never explained how that part fit into the overall scheme. Huger could be forgiven if he wondered whether Johnston *expected* "an action" to begin on his left, or if his three brigades were being placed there purely as a contingency.[11]

Perhaps aware of his vagueness, Johnston dispatched another message to Huger the next day. "I fear that in my note of last evening . . . I was too positive on the subject of your attacking the enemy's left flank," he wrote. "As our main force will be on your left, it will be necessary for your progress to the front to conform at first to that of General Hill." Huger now knew that Hill would be on his left, presumably on the Williamsburg Road, and that his own movements were to conform to Hill's. He was not specifically ordered to do anything but occupy the road. Nowhere in these orders did Johnston specify that Huger was to inaugurate the battle or that the movements of others all depended on him. Finally, James Longstreet, the man charged with commanding the assault, was not mentioned in either of Johnston's messages. Huger could reasonably conclude that he would continue to receive his orders directly from Johnston.[12]

The evening before the attack, the camps of both armies were again swept by torrential rains. The rain began in the afternoon, and by nightfall it was coming down in sheets. The men in the ranks were miserable, but Johnston saw a positive side, for such a rain would cause the Chickahominy to overflow its banks and make the river even more of a barrier between the two wings of the Federal army, increasing the isolation of Keyes's fifteen thousand men. Keyes himself later recalled that it was "a storm the like of which I cannot remember. Torrents of rain drenched the earth, the thunderbolts rolled and fell without intermission, and the heavens flashed with a perpetual blaze of lightning." More laconically, one of Johnston's aides wrote simply: "It was the worst night I ever saw." Major Alexander estimated that three inches of rain fell in just the first two hours of the storm. The immediate effect was to turn the roads, once again, into quagmires. "The face of the country was literally flooded," Smith wrote. "At daylight on the 31st the Chickahominy was booming, passable only at the bridges. . . ." While this effectively isolated Keyes, as Johnston had hoped, it also made the going very tough for the attackers.[13]

Johnston was up before dawn on the 31st. The rain had stopped, though the skies were still threatening. G. W. Smith showed up a few minutes later and the two generals fell into a discussion of the day's plan. As he chatted with Smith, it must have occurred to Johnston that the next twelve hours would decide the fate of the campaign; and perhaps the war. Smith later recalled that "General Johnston was then not only hopeful, but elated." If all was going well, most of the Confederate army would already be on the move, marching by different roads to close the trap on the isolated Federals.[14]

In fact, all was far from well. Chase Whiting, marching his three brigades toward the Nine Mile Road, found his path blocked by Longstreet's men. Whiting immediately sent a message to Johnston that Longstreet was blocking his way, and he suggested that Johnston send a staff officer to clear the road. This message reached Johnston a little after 6:00 A.M. On the face of it, it presented no difficulty. Johnston assumed that Longstreet's men were marching ahead of Whiting on the Nine Mile Road and advancing more or less on schedule. He ordered an aide to inform Whiting not to worry, that "Longstreet will precede you," and settled down to wait for further reports. But Longstreet's men were not marching eastward ahead of Whiting, they were headed *south* across Whiting's front. Johnston, still at his headquarters, continued to assume that all troop movements were proceeding as planned.[15]

No further word came from the various columns until about eight o'clock, when Whiting himself showed up at headquarters to report to Smith, who was Whiting's immediate superior, that Longstreet's men were still blocking his path. Smith ordered Captain Robert F. Beckham to ride out on the Nine Mile Road and look for Longstreet. Beckham rode eastward along the empty road for several miles until he concluded that neither Longstreet nor his division were on it. This disquieting news arrived at headquarters at nine o'clock. Johnston was reluctant to believe it. Longstreet had to be there— Beckham simply hadn't ridden far enough. Johnston turned to Jimmy Washington, his loyal aide, and ordered him to ride out along the Nine Mile Road and not to stop until he found Longstreet. Jimmy rode eastward "at full speed" until he was challenged by Federal pickets, who gleefully took him prisoner. By eleven o'clock, Johnston was seriously worried. To no one in particular he muttered aloud that he wished all the troops were back in camp. Where was Longstreet?[16]

Where indeed? While Johnston paced about his headquarters, Longstreet was engaged in his second great error of the morning. En route south, Longstreet's men found their way barred by the rain-swollen Gilles Creek. The water was no more than waist-deep, but the lead regiment stopped the whole column in order to build an improvised bridge consisting of a wagon anchored in midstream with planks leading from it to each bank. At this point Huger's division marched up. Because they had arrived first, Longstreet's men claimed precedence, and Huger's men stood by leaning on their arms waiting while the men of Longstreet's division completed the bridge and began to cross on the planks. The hours slipped by while fourteen thousand men walked single file over the improvised bridge. Only then did someone realize that Huger's division was supposed to precede Longstreet's into battle, and so Longstreet's men turned off the road to stand on their arms and wait while Huger's division marched past. This ridiculous charade might have been prevented if either of the division commanders had been present. But Longstreet and Huger were several miles away in a farmhouse arguing over who had seniority. Longstreet claimed that Johnston had placed him in command of the right wing; Huger, however, had received no notice of that fact and he was a stickler for detail. Finally Huger accepted Longstreet's word, and by eleven o'clock the matter was cleared up. But more valuable hours had been lost.[17]

Johnston remained five miles away on the Confederate left. Indeed, Johnston's greatest mistake in the battle may have been his assumption that after their long conversation, Longstreet had things well in hand, and that he could safely leave the right wing in his care. He explained later that he wanted to be in a position to observe any Federal efforts to bring reinforcements across the Chickahominy. But Smith was second-in-command of the army and should have been able to handle that assignment himself. It was Longstreet, charged with the initial and main assault, who needed guidance. Even Johnston's own artillery staff officer, E. P. Alexander, later wrote that "It would have been much wiser to have first visited the right and seen his battle started."[18]

At eleven o'clock, while Huger's division was playing leapfrog with Longstreet's men on the Williamsburg Road and Johnston was wishing that all the troops were back in camp, D. H. Hill was losing his patience. He had alerted Robert Rodes at six-thirty that morning to be ready to move "at a moment's notice." But with the delay at Gilles Creek, Huger's column did not arrive on the Charles City Road to relieve Rodes until after ten-thirty. Even then the men of Rodes's brigade had to struggle across a flooded countryside to reach Hill's position near the Williamsburg Road. By this time, Hill was fairly bursting with impatience. At one o'clock, although only the first regiment of Rodes's brigade had reached him, Hill decided that he could wait no longer, and he ordered the signal gun to be fired sending his division in to the attack.[19]

Even without the concentration Johnston had planned, the initial phase of Hill's attack went surprisingly well. His three brigades drove in the enemy pickets and advanced over the soggy ground to the Federal main line. There, Silas Casey's Federal division resisted briefly before it broke and fled. Hill's men pursued with enthusiasm, shrieking the "rebel yell." But behind this first Federal defense line were two others, and behind Casey were three more Yankee divisions. Despite their initial success, Hill's men were soon slowed, then stopped by increasingly heavy Federal fire. This should have been the moment for Longstreet's eleven brigades to hit the Yankees in their weakened right flank. The sound of Hill's attack, after all, was supposed to be the signal for Longstreet's assault along the Nine Mile Road. But Longstreet was not on the Nine Mile Road. The extent of Longstreet's missed opportunity is suggested by the experience of three regiments of Hill's division commanded by Colonel Micah Jenkins that fought their way north to the Nine Mile Road, then turned back to advance along that road toward the enemy right. Jenkins's three regiments pierced the disorganized Federal flank like a spear thrust. Indeed, they soon found themselves more than a mile behind enemy lines; but, unsupported, they had to fight their way back. Such an attack by Longstreet's entire division rather than three regiments would almost certainly have proved decisive. Keyes himself later reported: "If Johnston had attacked us there an hour or two earlier . . . I could have made but a feeble defense. . . ." Instead, when Hill sent to Longstreet for

support, the "wing commander" could do no more than send first one brigade and then another (those of R. H. Anderson and James L. Kemper) to
join in the frontal assault at Seven Pines.[20]

Longstreet's direction of the battle on the right wing that day demonstrated that he had no clear understanding of the concept of the battle plan
or even the principle of concentration at the vital point. An example of his
confusion was the series of orders he sent to Major General Cadmus Wilcox.
As the Confederates approached the scene that morning, Longstreet ordered Wilcox to take three brigades off onto the Charles City Road behind
Huger's three brigades. Then, once the battle was under way, he recognized
that a flanking movement would drive the Federals out of their position at
Seven Pines, and he ordered Wilcox to march past Huger's men, take the
lead, and seek out the Federal left. Then he apparently changed his mind
again, ordering Wilcox to return to the Williamsburg Road and join the fight
there. The result of all these orders was that Wilcox's men never got into the
fight at all. Only five of an available thirteen brigades under Longstreet's
command saw any action that day.[21]

By early afternoon it was clear to Johnston that his planned concentration
was not going to take place. Although upset by Longstreet's behavior, his
subsequent actions suggest that Johnston was also feeling responsible for the
confusion. He confessed as much to Smith as they paced about the headquarters. Still, Longstreet and Hill between them might yet be able to rout Keyes,
and Johnston himself could lead Whiting's three brigades against the Federal right. Before he could do that he had to know if the battle at Seven Pines
had begun, or even if it would take place at all. As fate would have it, an
"acoustic shadow"—a rare atmospheric phenomenon that acted as a barrier
to sound—kept the noise of the fighting at Seven Pines from his ears. He
could hear the low-voiced rumble of artillery, but not the higher-pitched
rattle of musketry, and no messages had come from either Hill or Longstreet
announcing the onset of battle. By two-thirty, anxiety at headquarters "was
extreme." Finally Johnston sent off Major Jasper Whiting, Smith's chief of
staff, to look for Longstreet and find out what was going on.[22]

A half hour later, Lee walked into headquarters. He had ridden out from
Richmond out of curiosity—his own and the president's. Johnston could not
satisfy even his own curiosity about the course of the battle, much less that of
others. Lee suggested that he had heard the sound of musketry to the south,
but Johnston shook his head. It was only artillery, he said. The waiting
continued—except that now Johnston's classmate and rival stood witness to
the unraveling of his battle plan. At four o'clock, Jasper Whiting returned
with a message from Longstreet. The battle was indeed under way, and had
been for several hours. Longstreet declared that the enemy was in retreat
but that he needed reinforcements "to keep the drive going"; with astonishing effrontery, he complained of Johnston's "slowness." Ignoring the implied
criticism, Johnston was relieved to have some hard information at last. In his

mind, he saw the field at once: Longstreet and Hill would be arranged in an eastward-facing arc north and south of the Williamsburg Road. All Johnston had to do was bring Whiting's three brigades into the battle on Longstreet's left to extend the Confederate line and overlap the Federal right.[23]

Johnston's grasp of the situation was very nearly correct. Indeed, had he moved forward an hour earlier, he might yet have snatched victory from confusion. But the information came too late and it was not entirely accurate. In fact, Longstreet's undermanned drive had completely stalled, and the Federals had rallied. Instead of a disorganized flank, Whiting's men would be moving forward against troops who were entirely ready for them. But at least now Johnston had something he could do personally. He took command of Whiting's men and ordered an advance.

At that moment President Jefferson Davis rode into the yard at Johnston's headquarters.

Davis was probably the last person on earth that Johnston wanted to see just then. First of all, Johnston would have to explain why he had not informed the president of the impending battle, what had happened that morning, and where all the troops were now—and none of that would be easy. Second, Johnston was now finally about to embark on the maneuver that he hoped would save the day. He simply had no time for Davis and his detailed questions. He solved the problem by pretending not to see Davis and hurrying off. Perhaps Johnston did not mean to be publicly disrespectful to the president; he was after all in the midst of fighting a battle. But Davis saw him leave and drew his own conclusions.[24]

From south to north, the three brigades that Johnston now led into battle were those of John Bell Hood, Evander M. Law (in temporary command of Whiting's brigade), and James J. Pettigrew. Johnston directed Hood to take his brigade off into the woods on the right. Somewhere in that direction, presumably, lay Longstreet's imperiled left flank. Hood had disappointed Johnston in the skirmish at Eltham's Landing by being too aggressive, but aggressiveness was just what was wanted now. In effect, Johnston's order took Hood's men virtually out of the battle, for Longstreet's left was not where Johnston believed it to be. It would have been hard for anyone, including Longstreet himself, to know where Longstreet's left flank was at that time, for the battle around Seven Pines had disintegrated into a series of small unit actions. As a result, Hood's men blundered around in the soggy woods for an hour before finding their way back to the Nine Mile Road.[25]

The central brigade—Whiting's nominal command, but headed now by Evander Law since Whiting was acting as division commander—proceeded straight ahead on the Nine Mile Road, which curved south to Fair Oaks Station, then crossed the Richmond & York River Railroad. Johnston went with them. As he neared the crossing, he could see Federal soldiers off to the left, on the road that led to the Grapevine Bridge over the Chickahominy. These Yankee soldiers consisted of three regiments under Brigadier General

John Abercrombie and a battery of four guns. Sitting astride their horses on the Nine Mile Road, Johnston and Whiting discussed the situation. Johnston assumed that the Federal soldiers were in the process of retreating from Seven Pines, and he ordered Whiting to push on across the railroad. He was in a hurry to hit the Federal right flank which, according to Longstreet's note, was being hard pressed by Longstreet and Hill's continued attack. But Whiting saw that an advance southward along the road would leave these Federals in his flank and rear, and he protested. Johnston discounted the threat; after all, the enemy was on the run. "Oh! General Whiting," he said, "you are too cautious."[26]

Chastened, Whiting sent his troops toward the crossing, where they were hit almost immediately by artillery fire from the Federal battery. The tactically correct response was counter battery fire from Confederate artillery. But the Confederates had no artillery on this part of the field. Instead, all Whiting could do was order his infantry to charge the Federal guns. The troops responded with enthusiasm, but their attack was repulsed. Even before Whiting's men could catch their breath from this first effort, an unidentified Confederate officer, more enthusiastic than thoughtful, galloped up and ordered them once again to charge the battery. Again the men responded, but with no better result than before. Now the decisive importance of the loss of all those hours since noon became evident as Federal reinforcements from the north side of the Chickahominy began to fall in alongside Abercrombie. Although the men of Whiting's brigade tried several more times, they could not move the Federal line. Lacking any artillery of their own, the Confederate advance was stymied.

The third Confederate brigade under James J. Pettigrew had no better luck. With Smith's two brigades in close support, Pettigrew came into the fight on Whiting's left, north of the Nine Mile Road, and ran into General Sedgwick's division of Sumner's corps, which had also just crossed the Chickahominy. Here, too, Federal artillery was decisive. Lieutenant Edmund Kirby, son of a former army commander who was the namesake of Edmund Kirby Smith, commanded a six-gun battery that dominated the field. Pettigrew himself was so severely wounded that he believed he was dying and ordered his staff to abandon him. (Eventually the Federals took him prisoner and he was later exchanged, living long enough to take part in Pickett's charge at Gettysburg.) As elsewhere on the field, the Confederate attack sputtered into a series of small, uncoordinated, and unsuccessful assaults. Indeed, with Federal reinforcements continuing to flow across from the north bank of the Chickahominy, it seemed possible that they would soon go over onto the offensive.[27]

Finally, at six o'clock, Johnston admitted to himself that his three brigades (plus the two under G. W. Smith) were engaged with more than the single Federal brigade he had believed was present. Realizing that the fight could not be concluded in the little daylight that was left, he issued orders for the troops to sleep upon their arms and renew the fight the next day—though by then, surely, the chance of surprising an isolated Federal corps would be long past. Johnston issued these orders from astride his horse as he watched the battle from atop a small rise behind Fair Oaks with two members of his staff. Shot was flying thick and fast, and Johnston noticed that a young colonel on his staff was bobbing and weaving as bullets zipped by. With a bemused smile, Johnston turned to him and said, "Colonel, there is no use dodging; when you hear them they have passed." Almost at that moment, Johnston was jolted by a musket ball in his shoulder. It was not a serious wound, and he did not even bother to dismount, but then an artillery shell burst nearby and fragments struck him in the chest and thigh. He fell heavily from his horse—some witnesses thought he had been killed outright. Drury Armistead, one of Johnston's young couriers, raised him from the ground and carried him about a quarter mile back, out of the line of fire. His staff gathered round and ordered a litter on which they carried him from the field, still conscious but in great pain. The litter bearers slipped frequently on the muddy ground, making him cry out.[28]

As Johnston was borne to the rear, President Davis rode up, dismounted, and bent over the litter with genuine concern. Johnston opened his eyes, smiled, and reached out to take the president's proferred hand. Could he do anything, Davis asked, all his differences with Johnston temporarily forgotten. Johnston shook his head, saying he did not know how seriously he was hurt, though he "feared a fragment of shell had injured his spine." Davis sent the litter bearers on their way and rode off to see what was happening with the battle. Johnston remained conscious enough to be concerned about his pistols and sword—especially his sword. "That sword," he said aloud, "was the one worn by my father in the Revolutionary war, and I would not lose it for ten thousand dollars; will not someone please go back and get it and the pistols for me." Armistead immediately ran off to find and return his precious possessions to the general. Johnston was so pleased he gave the young man one of the pistols.[29]

After Johnston was borne away, the fighting at Fair Oaks sputtered on until nightfall. Although no one knew it at the time, the battle was already over. As next in command, G. W. Smith tried to renew the fight the following morning, but with little success; that afternoon, Robert E. Lee, who assumed command of the army at Davis's request, decided that there was nothing more to be gained and ordered the army to fall back to its positions outside Richmond. At a cost of more than six thousand casualties, the Confederates had moved the Federal army back a mile or so from its initial position. The Battle of Seven Pines was over. So, too, was Johnston's command in Virginia.

Curious as this battle was for all its mistakes, misunderstandings, and lost opportunities, the aftermath was even more curious. By rights Johnston should have been furious with Longstreet, whose misunderstanding of his orders had so utterly wrecked his plan. But Johnston never said a word against Longstreet, either in his formal reports written some weeks later after he had partly recuperated from his wound, or in private. Instead, he praised Longstreet effusively and allowed that officer to lay all the responsibility for the day's failures on Benjamin Huger. In his official report, Longstreet claimed: "I have reason to believe that the affair would have been a complete success had the troops upon the right [Huger] been put in position within eight hours of the proper time."[30]

Such a claim is hard to credit except as a deliberate distortion of events. If Huger's men had been late in arriving on the Charles City Road it was because Longstreet's troops had cut them off at Gilles Creek, and even then Huger's three brigades had arrived in position ahead of Longstreet. Huger was no more than a convenient scapegoat. Indeed, Huger's sins of omission that day fade alongside Longstreet's sins of commission. Longstreet's initial error in advancing on the "wrong" road not only made Huger late, disrupting the coordination of the battle; it also ensured that thirteen brigades—thirty thousand men, the bulk of the Confederate army—would advance toward the enemy along a single road. G. W. Smith wrote that the "movements of Longstreet's division" were "in very marked contrast with General Johnston's intention," and E. P. Alexander concluded that Longstreet's complete misunderstanding of his orders "utterly wrecked and ruined Johnston's excellent and simple plan."[31]

Why, then, did Johnston allow Longstreet to get away with his absurd report, and why did he agree to lay the blame on Huger? Part of the reason is that Johnston probably felt he was protecting Longstreet. In addition, Johnston knew that he was himself partially, perhaps even fully, responsible for the misunderstanding that had sent Longstreet down the wrong road. A month after the battle, Johnston admitted to Smith that Longstreet's "misunderstanding . . . may be my fault." In war, of course, it is the commanding general who bears responsibility for how the parts fit together. Knowing that, Johnston adopted the public position that he had intended Longstreet to use the Williamsburg Road all along, and allowed Longstreet to assert that it was Huger with his lateness and his passivity who had disrupted the arrangements. He believed that to accuse Longstreet of misunderstanding his orders would reflect as badly on the author of those orders as on the recipient. Simply put, Johnston did not want anyone to know that he had been unable to make his orders clear to Longstreet.[32]

Johnston even went so far as to ask Gustavus Smith to change his official report by omitting all references to Longstreet's movements. He acknowledged to Smith that his draft report contained references to "subjects which I never intended to make generally known," specifically "the misunderstanding between Longstreet and myself in regard to the direction of his division. . . ." He did not feel any difficulty in asking Smith to remove the offending passages, for, as he asserted, "these matters concern Longstreet and myself alone." At the same time, Johnston publicly praised Longstreet for his "skill, vigor, and decision" during the battle and endorsed Longstreet's criticism of Huger. Even in his *Narrative*, written more than twenty years later, Johnston blamed the Confederate disappointment at Seven Pines on Huger's men, who were too used to garrison life, he said, to perform effectively in battle.[33]

Huger received a copy of Longstreet's report on August 10, some ten weeks after the battle. He immediately fired off a letter to Longstreet asking him "to correct the errors he has made." Longstreet did not respond. Huger then took his case to Johnston, who was convalescing in Richmond at the home of Texas Senator Louis T. Wigfall. "As you have endorsed his erroneous statements," Huger wrote, "I must hold you responsible, and desire to know from you if you have any reason to believe an answer will be made by General Longstreet." Huger also wrote to President Davis requesting that formal charges be brought against him so that he could clear himself in a court-martial. Quite rightly, he complained to Davis that "the plan of attack was not communicated to him," and that he was "kept in ignorance of the troops he was to act with."[34]

Understandably, Johnston was not anxious to reopen the question. "I have no disposition to prefer charges against Major-General Huger," he wrote to Randolph. After all, Huger's objections were to Longstreet's report, therefore only Longstreet could settle the matter. Davis told Randolph to wait to see if Longstreet's reply satisfied Huger, and if not, then to allow a court of inquiry.[35] But Huger never got his day in court, and Davis let the matter drop. As for Huger, he served without particular distinction during the Seven Days Battles in July and was relieved from active command by Lee on July 12.

Johnston's battlefield wound probably saved him from having to face a more rigorous public investigation of his own conduct of the battle—an investigation that would have hurt him in the area where he was most sensitive: his public reputation. Instead, sympathy for Johnston's physical condition and concern about the fate of Richmond under the untested leadership of the new army commander, Robert E. Lee, suppressed any investigation in the immediate aftermath of the battle. The Battle of Seven Pines went down in Confederate lore as a victory—an incomplete victory to be sure, but a victory nonetheless. It was not. Johnston had bungled a splendid opportunity. He had failed to communicate his plans adequately to his subordinates; he had failed to keep track of the developing battle; and after he had taken charge personally of the battle on the left, he had led his men into a hornet's nest. Worse than all these errors, in the coming weeks and months he would falsify his written report to shield a favored subordinate. G. W. Smith's final verdict was that "There is but little to commend General Johnston's practical management of the army, May 31; and the same may be said in regard to the accounts he has given on these events."[36]

Despite his subsequent efforts to put the best possible face on his conduct of the battle, Johnston's disappointment must have brought him a mental discomfort equal to his physical pain as the litter bearers loaded him into a horse-drawn ambulance for the bumpy ride to Richmond.

CHAPTER THIRTEEN

Louis T. Wigfall

The ambulance that carried Johnston from the battlefield at Seven Pines brought him, after seemingly endless jostling and rocking, to a private home on the corner of 28th and Broad Streets in Richmond. His stretcher was gingerly manhandled up the front steps and deposited in the parlor, where Johnston could be attended by the physicians. Fortunately the musket ball that struck his shoulder had missed the bone, for otherwise the doctors would almost certainly have decided to amputate. Johnston's shrapnel wounds were more serious, causing him a good deal of pain. Several of his ribs were broken, and the doctors feared the onset of pleurisy. They bound him up and prescribed the usual nineteenth-century therapy of bleeding, blisterings, and "depletions of the system." It soon became clear that Johnston's wounds were not fatal and that he would recover fully, though it might be months before he could again take the field. Unhappily, he resigned himself to a long recuperation. Lydia moved into the house to be near her husband and to add her ministrations to those of the attending physicians.[1]

He was out of the war for nearly six months. While Johnston recuperated in Richmond, Lee took vigorous command of the army, launching a series of offensives—known subsequently as the Seven Days Battles—that broke

McClellan's will and drove the Union army from the gates of Richmond south to the banks of the James River. Lee achieved this miracle by bringing "Stonewall" Jackson's army from the Valley, thus securing the concentration of force that Johnston had pleaded for from the outset of the campaign. Then, following close upon the heels of his victories outside Richmond, Lee took the army north, crushing a second Union army under John Pope near the old battlefield at Manassas. In the fall he struck north again, crossing the Potomac into Maryland. All that time Johnston remained an invalid in Richmond. It became clear, even to him, that his old friend Lee had made the army his own, and that it was unlikely Johnston would be restored to his former command. Indeed, his simmering feud with Davis made it problematical that he would get *any* command, for Johnston's slow recuperation in Richmond embroiled him in the politics of the Confederacy's capital. His presence in Richmond made him a focus of the social and political activity of that city, bringing him new connections with powerful, sometimes dangerous men.

He was soon able to sit in a chair, and even to work on his official report of the battle that had nearly taken his life. By June 12, Johnston had access to Longstreet's report, with its accusations of Huger's tardiness; that report was in front of him while he worked on his own, which he submitted on June 24. Then, only a few days later, he received a copy of G. W. Smith's report, which specifically mentioned Longstreet's mistake in taking the wrong road to the battlefield. Having already submitted his own report, Johnston wrote to Smith asking him to strike out the references to Longstreet. Johnston's report heaped praise on both Hill and Longstreet. Although it did not specifically condemn Huger, its endorsement of Longstreet carried an implied criticism. Johnston concluded by asserting that Seven Pines had been a Confederate victory since "The troops of Longstreet and Hill passed the night of the 31st on the ground which they had won." For the rest of his life, Johnston thought of the Battle of Seven Pines as a lost opportunity. He would have heartily endorsed the view of D. H. Hill, whose men bore the brunt of the fight, and who wrote privately to his wife that "Genl. Johnston was wounded & Genl. Lee did not order a pursuit. We will never have such another opportunity."[2]

Even during the first weeks of his period of recovery, visitors began to arrive to pay their respects. Generals, politicians, and the merely curious stopped by to wish Johnston a speedy recovery. Others sent their solicitations by mail. Lee wrote pleadingly to Lydia: "You must soon cure him." The day Johnston sent his report to the War Department, Senator and Mrs. Louis T. Wigfall stopped by the house on Broad Street to pay their respects. Johnston was still heavily bandaged, and out of delicacy, Charlotte Wigfall remained in the carriage while the Senator went inside. Ever the thoughtful hostess, Lydia went out to sit with her. Inside the house, Johnston asked Wigfall of news from the front where McClellan's army, only a half dozen miles away, still threatened. Wigfall was a good source of information, for he had volunteered his services as an aide to Longstreet. And there was some good news: Jeb Stuart had conducted a cavalry raid on the peninsula in which his horsemen had ridden completely around the Yankee army. But the mood in the city remained somber. Lee had the army digging entrenchments, and it seemed that Richmond was about to be subjected to a siege. The grumble of Federal artillery could be heard plainly in the streets of Richmond; even as they talked, Johnston and Wigfall could hear heavy firing in the distance.[3]

But the very next morning—June 25—circumstances changed dramatically when the Confederate army, now under Lee's command, attacked McClellan's forces north of the Chickahominy at Mechanicsville. In secrecy and haste, Lee had summoned Jackson's army from the Valley and outlined a coordinated assault on McClellan's right wing. Although the results were less than hoped for, the aggressiveness of the attack caused McClellan to pull his right wing back to Gaines' Mill, where Lee attacked him again. For seven days Lee assailed the Yankee host. None of the battles was a clear Confederate victory, yet together they broke McClellan's spirit, leading him to seek a new base on the banks of the James River where his forces huddled under the protection of the Federal gunboats.

The price had been high, almost unbearably so. More than twenty thousand Confederate soldiers had fallen in the fighting, nearly five thousand of them at Malvern Hill in a bold but foolish display of gallantry. For more than a week, ambulances and wagons carried the carnage into the city. The fifty hospitals filled up at once, churches and hotel lobbies were converted into temporary shelters for the wounded, and Richmond itself became an open-air hospital. It was hard to know which was more horrible: the bodies of the dead stacked like cordwood in the streets, or the piles of severed limbs outside the hospitals. Patriotic Confederates consoled themselves by remarking that all great victories came with a price, and that Federal losses were surely much greater. Actually, the Federals had lost four thousand fewer men. Still, McClellan had been driven back, and the city would not be so endangered again until 1864.

After the Seven Days Battles, Wigfall's visits to Johnston became more frequent. The senator was a great source of military information, and Johnston's views as a professional soldier were valuable to Wigfall as well. Lydia and Charlotte soon became fast friends. Before long the two couples had agreed that the Johnstons should move into the Wigfall home. For Johnston, it was a fateful decision. The senator would prove to be a good and loyal friend, but he was also one of the most outspoken of Davis's political opponents. By pitching his tent in the enemy's camp, so to speak, Johnston fueled Davis's suspicions that he was not to be trusted.

Forty-six years old in 1862, Louis T. Wigfall was one of the Senate's most colorful personalities. Physically imposing, he had flashing black eyes, thick dark hair combed away from a broad forehead, prominent eyebrows, and a luxuriant beard. William H. Russell, the correspondent for *The Times* of London, described his appearance as "not to be forgotten":

> If you look . . . into the eye of the Bengal tiger, in Regent's Park . . . you will form some notion of the expression I mean. It was flashing, fierce, yet calm—with a well of fire burning behind and spouting through it, an eye pitiless in anger which now and then sought to conceal its expression beneath half-closed lid, and then burst out with an angry glare, as if disdaining concealment.[4]

Originally from South Carolina, Wigfall had earned a reputation there for heavy drinking, frequent brawling, and extravagant gambling. His excesses eventually led to bankruptcy, and in 1848 he moved to Texas, where such behavior was considered more colorful than antisocial. In 1859 his fellow Texans elected him to the U.S. Senate, where he at once became deeply involved in the secessionist movement, for Wigfall was a "proslavery fanatic" and an early and vociferous advocate of southern independence.[5]

During the Fort Sumter crisis, the bellicose Wigfall went to Charleston to be at the very center of things. In the midst of the bombardment, he had himself rowed out to the fort to ask the Federal commander if he had struck his flag. Afterward, he served on Jefferson Davis's personal staff during the government's brief tenure in Montgomery. A hint of future difficulties in their relationship was suggested by a falling out between Varina Davis and Charlotte Wigfall in May. Nevertheless, Wigfall remained on Davis's staff and travelled with him in the president's car to Richmond when the government moved there at the end of the month.

In the anxious months before the Battle of First Manassas, Wigfall left Davis's staff to accept a colonel's commission and the command of a Texas regiment. Later, Davis promoted him to brigadier general and the command of a brigade where he served, officially at least, under Johnston. But Wigfall's military service was brief, for in February 1862 his constituents in Texas again elected him to the Senate—this time to the Confederate Senate, though he ever afterward retained the title of general.

Wigfall and Davis had disagreed on some issues prior to his election to the Senate, but in the fall of 1862 while the Johnstons and Wigfalls were sharing a home, Wigfall broke openly with the president. The cause of the break was a bill that Wigfall introduced to allow army commanders to appoint their own staff officers, each of whom would bear the rank of brigadier general even though the nomination of generals was traditionally a presidential prerogative. It is virtually certain that Wigfall discussed this legislation with Johnston beforehand, and it is even possible that Johnston suggested it. But after Wigfall's bill passed both houses of Congress, Davis vetoed it. Both Davis and Wigfall took the issue personally, and their disagreement marked the beginning of a lengthy political feud.

Wigfall soon became one of the leaders of a small but vocal opposition to

President Davis's management of the war, men who were convinced that Davis was narrow-minded in his prosecution of the war, that he played favorites in his appointments, and that he was unwilling to do what was necessary to win. Because there were no political parties in the Confederacy, opposition to government policy took on the aspect of personal opposition to the president himself. As far as Davis was concerned, this was nothing more nor less than treason. Davis therefore branded Wigfall, and all who associated with him, as simply disloyal. Johnston's presence in the Wigfall household confirmed Davis's conviction that Johnston was untrustworthy.

The Johnston-Wigfall partnership was a strange alliance and an even stranger friendship. Although Wigfall had mellowed in middle age, his flamboyance, his intemperance, and his bellicosity were attributes altogether absent in Johnston, and disparaged by him in others. About all the two men had in common was a shared antipathy for Jefferson Davis. But opposition to Davis made allies of stranger bedfellows than Wigfall and Johnston. For months, Senators Henry S. Foote of Tennessee and William Lowndes Yancey of Alabama had been bitter personal and political opponents—Foote had been pro-Unionist before the war and Yancey was the fiercest of fire-eaters. In the fall of 1862, however, they were reconciled by the intervention of mutual friends. Such a reconciliation was possible largely because of their shared opposition to Davis. Yancey had called the Confederate president "conceited, wrong-headed, wranglesome, and obstinate," and the hot-tempered Foote had attacked virtually every initiative Davis brought to the Senate. They also had in common a shared admiration for Joseph E. Johnston; indeed, what they may have liked most about Johnston was the well-known fact that Davis despised him.[6]

To celebrate their formal reconciliation, the friends of Foote and Yancey organized a breakfast in November in their honor. Johnston was invited, and since he had almost fully recovered, he decided to attend. Yancey and Foote were in a splendid mood, offering toasts and jests. Johnston, for the most part, was his usual reserved self. The breakfast lasted for two hours, fueled by champagne that had been run through the blockade. Finally, near noon, Yancey rose, and with a sign to Johnston that he was to remain seated, informed the others that "This toast is to be drunk standing." Chairs scraped as the guests rose, and Yancey announced: "Gentlemen, let us drink to the health of the only man who can save the Confederacy—General Joseph E. Johnston!" Amidst the "hear hears," the glasses were emptied. Then it was Johnston's turn. "Gravely," according to one witness, he rose from his seat. "Mr. Yancey," he said, "the man you describe is now in the field, in the person of General Robert E. Lee. I will drink to his health." Not to be outdone in courtesy, Yancey responded: "Your modesty is only equalled by your valor!"[7]

Johnston's presence at this anti-administration celebration was further evidence that he had become not only a political issue but a political player. Davis's opponents exalted Johnston's "military genius" largely because they knew that his views were contrary to those of the president. For his part, Johnston cannot have been so naive as to doubt the political significance of his sharing a home with the Wigfalls, or his presence at a breakfast honoring two of Davis's bitterest opponents. Since Davis equated loyalty to the administration with loyalty to "the Cause," it was certain that he would conclude that Johnston was nothing more nor less than an enemy—and as dangerous as any Yankee.

Whatever its political cost, the Johnstons' new living arrangement with the Wigfalls was comfortable enough. The combined household consisted of seven people: the Wigfalls, their two daughters, the Johnstons, and the general's aide Major A. D. Banks, a former Cincinnati newspaperman and open opponent of Davis. Johnston chafed somewhat at his forced inactivity, yet life was not unpleasant. The enemy had been driven from the gates of the city and optimism was running high. One of the Wigfall girls recalled the summer and fall of 1862 fondly, remembering that "The house stood back from the street with a large garden in front . . . fragrant with the aromatic scent of that sweetest of all flowers, the white chrysanthemum, which grew in great profusion in the old fashioned borders." By late summer, Johnston was no longer confined to his cot. He was able to move about, but he was not yet ready to resume command, even if one had been available for him, so he received visitors and played the role of armchair general.[8]

The presence of the Wigfall girls created a pleasant domestic environment. Lydia in particular enjoyed being part of a family. With her gentle disposition, Lydia was very popular with the girls, and soon became their special confidante. She grew particularly close to Louise, the older of the two whom everyone called Luly. Luly wrote to her brother Halsey, who was serving with the army, that "Mrs. Johnston is a sweet lovely person." (Two years later, when the Wigfalls travelled to Texas to touch base with their constituents, the daughters chose to stay with Lydia in Georgia rather than accompany their parents.)[9]

Lydia's subsequent correspondence with Charlotte reflected the intimacy of their friendship. Months later, when the war prospects had turned dark again, Lydia wrote to her friend, "I seem always to turn to you when I am in trouble or heartsick . . . ," and in another letter she acknowledged openly, "I love you dear Mrs. Wigfall." She also sided with Charlotte in her "bitter feud" (as Mrs. Roger A. Pryor called it) with Varina Davis, and they shared private catty remarks with one another about the shortcomings of the first lady of the Confederacy. "By the way," Lydia wrote to Charlotte a few months later, "I have some funny things to tell you when I see you. Have you heard of any of the executive finery being of *pastel?*" Unsure of her sources, she cautioned Charlotte not to breathe a word of this "unless you heard it also. . . ."[10]

The relationship between their husbands was likewise grounded in a mutual dislike of the occupants of the Confederate White House. Wigfall's overtures may have been motivated from the first by his perception that

Johnston would be a useful political ally against the Confederate president. Almost certainly Wigfall's encouragement led Johnston to commit public indiscretions that irreparably damaged his credibility with the chief executive. At the same time, Johnston considered Wigfall a friend as well as an ally. In a dark moment of his own, he wrote plaintively to Wigfall that "there is no one in civil life except yourself who has upon me the claim of friendship. . . ." And after the war, annotating some of his wartime letters for his memoirs, he jotted at the bottom of one sent to him by Wigfall: "A distinguished C.S. Senator and my devoted friend." Throughout the autumn of 1862, as the Johnstons and the Wigfalls shared a home and a table as well as daily views about the progress of the war, the two men developed a sense of partnership that was grounded in their shared conviction that the policies of Jefferson Davis threatened the very life of the Confederacy.[11]

With Johnston recovering rapidly, with good news from the front, and with solicitous visitors at the door, the time passed pleasantly enough. There was the irritant of food shortages in the wartime capital of the Confederacy, and the accompanying economic inflation. By 1862, the population of Richmond had swollen to three times its prewar size as soldiers, government officials, and opportunists flocked into the city. At the same time, the stiffening blockade cut the flow of imports to a trickle. There were shortages of housing, food, soap, and most everything necessary to sustain a comfortable life. But though "food was an endless topic of conversation," the high prices did not dampen the social bustle at the Wigfall home. Dinner parties were held whenever the goods of blockade runners found their way to Richmond. Important people from all over the Confederacy—and even from Europe— called at the little house on Grace Street. Prince Polignac came to dine; a British member of Parliament called to pay his respects; the "fighting Bishop" Major General Leonidas Polk called, as did General and Mrs. Arnold Elzey, the general bearing a wound from the battles outside Richmond. Indeed, the guest list rivaled that of the Confederate White House, and the socially aware in Richmond considered the two circles to be competing salons.[12]

Johnston followed the accounts of the military campaigns closely in the newspapers; no doubt he engaged in long discussions about them with Wigfall and their frequent guests. In September, the papers reported that Lee had crossed the Potomac into Maryland, hoping to attract new volunteers and to put pressure on the Lincoln government. At about the same time, two Confederate armies, one of them under the command of Johnston's old chief of staff, Edmund Kirby Smith, had invaded Kentucky and were making a bid to reestablish Confederate political authority there. If Johnston could not participate directly in these campaigns, he might have been gratified that his very name continued to cause concern in Washington. Several Federal officers relayed reports of Johnston's presence in the field with a large army, placing him at Winchester one day, at Gordonsville the next, and at Culpeper a few weeks later.[13]

In late September came reports of Lee's check on the banks of the Antietam near Sharpsburg in Maryland, followed almost immediately by news of Lincoln's announcement of the emancipation of the slaves in the Confederacy. Johnston was cheered by accounts of Jeb Stuart's second ride around McClellan's army in October, then depressed by news of the retreat of Confederate armies from Kentucky. In the first week of November, he learned that McClellan had been sacked by President Lincoln and replaced by Ambrose Burnside.[14]

Winter came swiftly to Richmond in 1862—snow began falling as early as November 9. As the weather got cooler, Johnston grew stronger. That month he began taking daily horseback rides around the city and talking seriously about resuming service in the field. He declined an invitation to recuperate at a plantation outside the city because he believed that by staying in Richmond he would be able to influence his orders back to active duty. Wigfall thought Johnston was pushing his recovery too fast and that the rigors of a campaign might prove too much for him. Nevertheless, on November 12, Johnston reported to Secretary of War Randolph as fit for duty.[15]

The question was: duty where? Even Johnston knew better than to hope that he might be restored to command of the army in Virginia. Irrevocably that had become Lee's army. But Johnston's recuperation in November 1862 coincided with the burgeoning of a crisis in command in the western theatre. No less than four separate, independent Confederate armies were operating west of the Appalachian Mountains:

—Braxton Bragg commanded the principal field army in the West, currently located in Tennessee after its retreat from Kentucky;

—Lieutenant General John C. Pemberton commanded a somewhat smaller army in Mississippi, with special responsibility for the citadel of Vicksburg;

—Johnston's former chief of staff, Edmund Kirby Smith, commanded a small independent force in East Tennessee; and

—Major General Theophilus Holmes commanded the forces in Arkansas, west of the Mississippi.

The ill wisdom of relying too much on voluntary cooperation between commanders who were nominally independent of one another had become obvious during the invasion of Kentucky in the fall of 1862. The armies of Bragg and Kirby Smith had not cooperated effectively, and the two generals had quarreled so bitterly that Kirby Smith declared he would have nothing more to do with Bragg. Even the corps commanders in Bragg's own army had become disgusted with his leadership—so much so that they launched a semi-public campaign to have him removed. The long retreat from Kentucky had depressed the men in the ranks and the public squabbling of their officers was doing little to restore it. Meanwhile, a large Federal army under Major General Ulysses S. Grant threatened Pemberton's army in Mississippi, and Holmes claimed to have his hands full in Arkansas. It was obvious that something had to be done to coordinate the movements of the four Confederate armies.[16]

There was no doubt who the logical candidate for such a job must be. Besides the desk-bound Samuel Cooper, there were only three men in the Confederacy who outranked Bragg: Lee, Beauregard, and Johnston. Lee could not be spared from Virginia, and Davis hated Beauregard more than he hated Johnston. In late October, Davis called Bragg to Richmond for a conference during which Bragg himself suggested that Johnston should be ordered West to coordinate the Confederate armies.[17]

When Johnston reported for duty on November 12, therefore, Secretary of War Randolph told him at once that he would be given command of all the area between the Appalachians and the Mississippi. Pleased though he was by such an important command, Johnston soon concluded that the concept was flawed. He argued that the invading Federal army in Mississippi was united under a single commander who had authority on both sides of the river, but his own command authority did not extend to Holmes's army in Arkansas. "I thought," he wrote later, that "as the Federal troops invading the Valley of the Mississippi were united under one commander, our armies for its defense should also be united. . . ." He believed that the most logical organization of Confederate forces would be to create *two* western departments—combining the trans-Mississippi army of Theophilus Holmes in Arkansas with that of John C. Pemberton in Mississippi into one, and the armies of Bragg and Kirby Smith in the other. In that way, Holmes and Pemberton could move troops back and forth across the river to reinforce one another at need while the forces in Tennessee operated independently. What he did *not* believe possible was to link Pemberton's army in Mississippi to Bragg's in eastern Tennessee, because the distance between them was simply too great for mutual support.[18]

After thinking over these problems, Johnston went to see Randolph the next day to urge him to consider a reorganization of the western command structure. As Johnston began to explain his idea, Randolph smiled and reached into his desk for a letter, asking Johnston to listen to "a few lines on the subject." He then read Johnston a letter he had already sent to General Holmes advising him to cross the Mississippi and join forces with General Pemberton. Then Randolph read out another letter: "a note from the President directing him to countermand his instructions. . . ." It was Davis, not Randolph, who had designed the western command structure, and Davis did not wish to change it.[19]

This disagreement over the command organization in the West would remain a point of contention between the president and his field general for the rest of the war. It did nothing to moderate the ill feeling between them. On November 15, Secretary of War Randolph, submitted his resignation, in part because of his disagreement with Davis about the western command structure. Wigfall went to see Davis to discuss a replacement. During their long conversation, the senator suggested several possible candidates. Wigfall's first choice was James A. Seddon of Virginia, though he also said that Johnston would be an excellent choice. Later, however, Wigfall learned that Davis had decided to appoint Seddon even before their meeting took place, and that he had already announced the appointment to several others. The fact that Davis never mentioned this to Wigfall throughout their conference, the senator took as a deliberate snub.[20]

Johnston left Richmond for Tennessee on November 24, accompanied by Lydia and a staff of eight, headed by Colonel Benjamin S. Ewell, a former president of the College of William & Mary. Senator and Mrs. Wigfall accompanied the party for the first thirty miles of the trip, leaving the train at Amelia Springs after an emotional farewell. Johnston and his entourage were delayed en route by no less than three railroad accidents. It was an indication of how precarious the southern railroad system had become—a fact that would make the coordination of armies in the West even more difficult than it appeared on the map.[21]

Johnston was glad to be back in the war, but he had serious reservations about the nature of his assignment. The differences between president and general about the command structure remained unresolved, and resentment lingered on both sides. As a soldier, Johnston's highest ambition was to command an army in the field but on this assignment he would have no specific field command. He was sorry, too, to be leaving Virginia. Still, any command was better than none. Lydia was not so sure. She wondered if her husband was strong enough for field duty, and she determined stay by him and do her best to keep him from attempting too much. Louise Wigfall was also saddened by the Johnstons' departure. "I am really very sorry," she wrote her brother. She would miss Lydia particularly.[22]

Johnston's six months in Richmond had served to heal his body, but they had embroiled him irrevocably in the political turmoil that characterized wartime Richmond. The support of Wigfall and his friends could not compensate for the damage to Johnston's relationship with Davis. Henceforth, the Confederate president would never be able to have complete faith in Johnston's reports or his advice; Johnston would never completely trust Davis's motives. These circumstances doomed Johnston's command in the West before it began.

PART THREE

THE WAR IN

THE WEST

CHAPTER FOURTEEN

Command in the West

Johnston assumed his duties as commander of the Department of the West with a strong sense of uneasiness. From Chattanooga, he wrote plaintively to Wigfall that "Nobody ever assumed a command under more unfavorable circumstances."[1] Three factors would conspire to limit his effectiveness as commander in the West. The most obvious challenge was the geographical immensity of his Department. His orders placed him in command of all Confederate forces from the Appalachians to the Mississippi, from Kentucky to the Gulf of Mexico—more than 180,000 square miles. Within that vast region were two major Confederate armies: Braxton Bragg's Army of Tennessee and John C. Pemberton's Army of Mississippi, plus Kirby Smith's small army at Knoxville. As Davis envisioned it, Johnston's role would be to shuttle forces back and forth from Bragg to Pemberton to protect whatever part of his command was threatened. Davis was determined to defend the Confederacy everywhere, and his insistence that troops could be moved back and forth at will between Tennessee and Mississippi was his way of avoiding having to choose between the two. But to Johnston, such a scenario was unlikely at best. The vast distances between these two armies and the single line of railroad that snaked south from

Chattanooga through Atlanta to Mobile, and then north and west to Mississippi, made timely transfers between the two armies problematical. More familiar with the strategic and tactical situation in Virginia, Davis simply underestimated the increased friction of transfers between Tennessee and Mississippi.

Another inherent difficulty with Johnston's assignment—one that caused him great personal anguish—was the ambiguity of his command authority. Davis and Cooper assumed that Johnston would exercise personal command over either western army whenever he was present. But Johnston's sense of decorum, as well as his sense of justice, would not allow him to supersede an army commander every time he arrived in camp. He believed that to do so would be not only personally and professionally demeaning to the army commander, it would also require him to assume the day-to-day management of an army without having the day-to-day knowledge of its inner workings. Johnston's role in either army would be more like that of a visitor: at best an adviser, at worst a supernumerary. Worse yet, Davis's command system required the army commanders to send their reports directly to Richmond rather than through Johnston, who was their nominal commander. Johnston was therefore left in the dark about the activities of the armies in the West, and often found out about changed plans or new initiatives only after the fact. His orders granted him supreme command, yet Johnston saw at once that he actually commanded nothing at all. He was endowed with great responsibility but very little authority, and eventually he began to wonder if this ambiguity was not intentional, if Davis had not set him up for certain failure.

Serious as both of these problems were, Johnston would in the end be bested by an even more serious flaw in the western command, for the two men who led the principal field armies in the West—Braxton Bragg and John C. Pemberton—were arguably the two worst Confederate field commanders of the war. Both members of the West Point class of 1837, each had inherent weaknesses of personality or vision that fated him to failure. Their failures would be Johnston's failure as well.

Braxton Bragg had the looks of an officer, with his prominent brow, intense dark eyes, and short, bristling beard. He had compiled an enviable record in Mexico, where he commanded an artillery battery, then retired as a lieutenant colonel in 1856 to become a planter in Louisiana. Joining the southern Cause when war broke out in 1861, he received rapid promotion to full general, and in the fall of 1862 when he launched an invasion into Kentucky, his praise was on everyone's lips. After the collapse of the invasion, however, the subsequent retreat made Bragg a target of criticism not only from southern newspapers but from his fellow officers and the men in the ranks. Bragg responded at first by lapsing into melancholy, then he decided to fight back. By December 1862, when Johnston arrived in the West, Bragg was engaged in a bitter feud with his own corps commanders, one that brought out the very worst in Bragg, for his greatest weaknesses—and he had many—were weaknesses of character. He was touchy and self-righteous, indecisive and impatient, rigid and unimaginative. Bragg's own chief of staff described his commander's personal characteristics as "repulsive."

Bragg, however, was sustained in his feud by the knowledge that President Davis remained a loyal supporter. Davis's affection may have originated from their common service in Mexico—Davis had praised Bragg's service in his official report of the Battle of Buena Vista—but was also a product of the fact that however intemperate he was with others, Bragg was always polite and self-effacing in his dealings with the president. Relying on Davis's firm support, Bragg spent most of his time during Johnston's tenure of command in the West engaged in a private war with his own subordinates.

Bragg's army, now called the Army of Tennessee, numbered about forty-thousand men. When Johnston arrived in Chattanooga in December, it was encamped near Murfreesboro ninety miles to the northwest. Indeed, Bragg's decision to bivouac the army at Murfreesboro raised more doubts about his leadership, for it was a bold, if not reckless, move. His army was much smaller than that of his opponent, Federal Major General William S. Rosecrans, and Bragg's choice of Murfreesboro put his inferior army nearer to the Federal supply base at Nashville than to his own base at Chattanooga.[2]

Three hundred miles to the west as the crow flies—more than six hundred miles by the only available railroad—Lieutenant General John C. Pemberton also faced an opponent superior in both numbers and ability in Major General Ulysses S. Grant. Grant's army at Grand Junction, Tennessee, numbered about 40,000, a force nearly twice as large as Pemberton's Army of Mississippi, which could boast perhaps 22,000 men. Then in his late forties, Pemberton was somewhat bookish-looking, with light hair, dark eyes closely set, and a thin, straight nose. Born in Philadelphia, he had married a Virginia woman and in 1861 had sided with the South. That spring he had served briefly as a member of Johnston's staff at Harpers Ferry. Subsequently he commanded the defenses of Charleston, South Carolina, as a major general, then, in October 1862, Davis sent him West to command the Army of Mississippi, promoting him soon afterward to lieutenant general. Although he had achieved rapid promotion, his northern birth, and the fact that two of his brothers fought for the Union, made him suspect in the minds of some, and whispered rumors about his devotion to the South circulated in the ranks. Aware of these suspicions, Pemberton became obsessed with proving his commitment to the Cause. That fixation led him to assume dogmatic positions that limited his tactical flexibility. Finally, Pemberton too was a particular favorite of Davis, and the Confederate president considered criticism of either Bragg or Pemberton to be a veiled attack upon himself.[3]

The third Confederate army in the West was that of Lieutenant General Theophilus H. Holmes, who commanded the trans-Mississippi Department in Arkansas outside Johnston's nominal authority. Holmes had commanded a brigade under Johnston at First Manassas, and a division under Lee during the Seven Days campaign. Promoted to lieutenant general, he was placed in

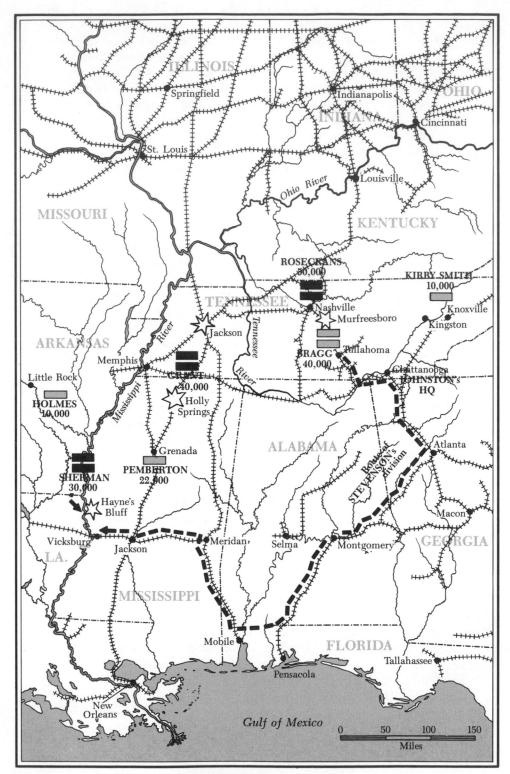

The Western Theatre, 1863

command in the trans-Mississippi West. Geographically, Holmes's army was closer to Pemberton than Bragg's, even though the Mississippi River divided them. Throughout his tenure as commander of the Department, Johnston would urge that the forces of Holmes and Pemberton should be considered as an operational unit, leaving Bragg's Army of Tennessee free to maneuver independently. He would never succeed in convincing the administration to accept this.[4]

Once arrived in Chattanooga, Johnston barely had time to get his bearings before he had to deal with a crisis. When he awoke on the morning of December 4, his first day at Chattanooga, he was handed a telegram from Cooper informing him that Pemberton was under attack by Grant's superior army and was falling back into central Mississippi. Cooper noted that Holmes had been asked (though not ordered) to send reinforcements from Arkansas, but that they might not get there in time. Could Johnston send reinforcements from Bragg's army? Here was the first test of Davis's theatre command concept.

Johnston responded that Holmes's troops were better placed for the job. "General Holmes' troops can re-enforce sooner than General Bragg's," he wired. "Urge him again to press his troops forward." Meanwhile he also fired off a curt telegram to Pemberton: "Urge General Holmes to quick movement. I am without the necessary information. Give it." To Cooper, Johnston wrote that any reinforcements from Bragg to Pemberton "would, by any route, require at least a month." In any case, he added, reducing Bragg's force was undesirable, for Bragg was already outnumbered in Tennessee.[5]

In fact, Holmes had fewer troops than either Johnston or Davis supposed, and they were so dispersed as to make the timely reinforcement of Pemberton unlikely. His army, which numbered between ten and twelve thousand, was scattered all over Arkansas and faced an active threat from a Yankee army in Missouri. Even if he were willing to abandon the state temporarily, as Johnston advised, the distance to Vicksburg (three hundred miles) meant that it would take perhaps three weeks to get there. In a letter to Cooper, Holmes explained his dilemma: "If I withdraw the infantry as directed there will be nothing to prevent the enemy's coming to Little Rock. The whole valley of the Arkansas will be stampeded, and the political party which has constantly cried out that the country is deserted by the Government will pave the way to dangerous disloyalty and disgust" (a reference well calculated to strike home in Richmond). Then Holmes added the last blow: ". . . besides this, I could not reach Vicksburg in less than thirty days." This information forced the administration to reconsider. Whereas only a few days earlier Cooper had urged Holmes to send aid to Pemberton, he now wired Holmes to "exercise your judgment in the matter." Effectively this meant that Pemberton would receive no aid from Holmes.[6]

That left only Bragg's Army of Tennessee at Murfreesboro. After sending his telegrams to Pemberton and Cooper, Johnston entrained for a visit to Murfreesboro to take a look at Bragg's army. He stayed there a week and was generally impressed by the progress that Bragg had made in restoring morale. Things were not nearly as grim, it seemed to him, as they had appeared from Richmond. He returned to Chattanooga—where Lydia had set up house—much buoyed.[7]

Waiting for him was President Davis. Tired of reading reports from the West, Davis had determined to come and see for himself. He arrived in Chattanooga simultaneously with the happy news of Lee's victory over Burnside at Fredericksburg. Johnston was pleased by the news, but he was also a bit jealous. When he learned that Burnside had launched wave after wave of frontal attacks against Lee's elevated and fortified position, he was both amazed and envious. "What luck some people have," he confided to Wigfall. "Nobody will ever come to attack me in such a place."[8]

Johnston offered Davis the hospitality of his home and headquarters in Chattanooga, but the president declined, saying he did not want to impose. Johnston told Davis that conditions were much improved in Bragg's army, but he also repeated his conviction that Bragg should not be expected to supply Pemberton with reinforcements. Pemberton, he insisted, should be reinforced from across the Mississippi, and not from Tennessee. Davis responded that he had given Holmes discretionary orders to cross the river only if he felt certain of the safety of Arkansas. Since Pemberton was clearly in need of reinforcements, and since Holmes could not be counted on to supply them, manifestly they would have to come from Bragg. Davis was on his way to Murfreesboro to inspect Bragg's army for himself and invited Johnston to accompany him.[9]

At Murfreesboro, Davis was as impressed as Johnston had been by the apparent soundness of Bragg's command; and after Bragg assured him that the Federals at Nashville were likely to remain passive, he concluded that Major General Carter Stevenson's division, reinforced to ten thousand men, should immediately be dispatched to Mississippi. Johnston feared that the long journey from Tennessee to Mississippi made it likely issues would come to a head in both theatres before Stevenson's division could complete the move. But Davis insisted, and Johnston saw to it that the necessary orders were written. The decision wrecked Johnston's hopes for the coming campaign. To Wigfall he wrote: "This has blown away some tall castles-in-the-air. I have been dreaming of crushing Grant with Holmes and Pemberton's troops, sending the former into Missouri, and with the latter, Bragg, & Kirby Smith, marching to the Ohio."[10]

After returning to Chattanooga, Johnston and Davis left again almost immediately for Vicksburg to inspect the other principal army in Johnston's command theatre. Lydia remained behind in Chattanooga. She worried about her husband travelling so much when he had not yet completely recovered from his wounds, and she believed that he was being set up to be used as a scapegoat by the administration. To Charlotte she claimed that her husband was being "shabbily used" by "the great commander in chief."[11]

Meanwhile the men of Carter Stevenson's division prepared to embark for their move to Mississippi; the first of them entrained the next day. Their departure would leave Bragg with a total of just under 35,000, including cavalry. Even though Rosecrans's Yankee army at Nashville was larger by at least a third, the Federals seemed content to remain passive, and just then the more pressing crisis appeared to be in Davis's home state of Mississippi. But even as Johnston and Davis travelled south to Atlanta on the first leg of the long journey to Mississippi, Rosecrans's Federal army in Nashville lurched into motion, prodded to action by President Lincoln, who was losing patience with field commanders who found excuses for not taking the offensive. Almost at once the telegraph line between Murfreesboro and Chattanooga was cut. Johnston would not learn until after it was over that one of the two armies in his Department was about to engage in a full-scale battle.[12]

At Vicksburg, Davis and Johnston inspected Pemberton's army, then journeyed north to inspect the defenses at Grenada, before returning to Jackson where Davis offered a public address on Christmas Day. Before the president went back to Richmond, Johnston took it upon himself, once again, to try to convince him that he ought to reorganize the departments in the West. "I firmly believe," he wrote in a memo to Davis, "that our true system of warfare would be to concentrate the forces of the two departments on this side of the Mississippi [Holmes and Pemberton], beat the enemy here, and then reconquer the country beyond it. . . ." Bragg's forces were simply too far away for convenient reinforcement, he argued, and to withdraw any more from Bragg would mean giving up Tennessee.[13]

Johnston's strategic conception was to oppose the invading Federals with an active field army of at least forty thousand. To create that active army, he proposed bringing Kirby Smith's nine thousand-man corps from Tennessee, and Holmes's entire army from Arkansas. He argued that these forces, combined with the 21,000 under Pemberton, would create an army large enough to contest with the Federals on more or less even terms. To opt for static defense of any position surrendered mobility and initiative to the enemy. The garrisons at Vicksburg and elsewhere, he argued, should be no larger than the minimum necessary to hold the position "until succored by the active army." The difficulty, of course, was that Johnston had no authority over Confederate forces west of the Mississippi. He could only request that Davis or Cooper order Holmes to comply.[14]

Another fundamental problem beyond Johnston's control was that Pemberton had a completely different strategic vision. Even without Holmes's forces, Johnston might have assembled a field army in excess of forty thousand men by combining the garrisons at Vicksburg, Port Hudson, and Grenada. But Pemberton did not see it that way. To him Vicksburg was "the vital point," and he could not conceive of a strategy that called for a field army to maneuver independently of the city. Throughout the last week of the year, Pemberton continually called on Johnston for reinforcements. "I want all the troops I can get," he wired from Vicksburg. Johnston explained that "It is necessary to send to Vicksburg just the troops you want [need], not all we have. Can you not estimate the number necessary?" Pemberton missed the point: "I mean that . . . all the troops ordered to reinforce me will be absolutely necessary to ensure the safety of Vicksburg . . . ," he replied.[15]

On December 27–28, Federal forces under Major General William T. Sherman assaulted Haynes Bluff, north of Vicksburg, and were bloodily repulsed. Two of Carter Stevenson's brigades had arrived from Murfreesboro in time to participate in the defense, but the rest of the division, including all of its wagons and artillery, was strung out on the roads across Mississippi and Alabama. Sherman's repulse was a triumph for the Confederacy, and for Pemberton, but it did not eliminate the threat to Vicksburg. Instead, the crisis was resolved suddenly and fortuitously by two other events. The same day that Sherman attacked the bluffs, Johnston learned that a week earlier, on December 20, Confederate Major General Earl Van Dorn had led 3,500 cavalrymen into Holly Springs, Mississippi, on Grant's line of communications. The fifteen hundred Federal defenders surrendered almost immediately, and Van Dorn's troopers proceeded to despoil the huge Federal supply dump, carrying off all they could and setting fire to the rest. Almost simultaneously, about eighty miles to the north Nathan Bedford Forrest had duplicated Van Dorn's feat at Jackson, Tennessee. The strategic impact of these raids was enormous: with his supply lines cut, Grant began to fall back out of Mississippi. Although Johnston did not know it, Grant's decision to pull back was also motivated by his concern over the command situation in the Union army: as long as Grant was in central Mississippi, Major General John A. McClernand—a politically appointed general of untested ability— held command of Union forces on the river. Grant's skepticism about McClernand's capacity to command, as well as the raids by Van Dorn and Forrest, led him to abandon his line of advance in central Mississippi and return to the river. Even the Federals in front of Vicksburg boarded transports and retreated upriver.

Then only days later came even more spectacular news: back in Tennessee, Braxton Bragg had preempted Rosecrans's imminent attack at Murfreesboro by launching one of his own, breaking the enemy right wing and punishing the Federals severely. Johnston was delighted by the news. He telegraphed Bragg to press the enemy force, which he assumed was in retreat.[16]

Suddenly the strategic picture was much brighter, and Johnston ordered Van Dorn to prepare for "another cavalry dash." There was other good news that same week. On January 6, Lydia arrived in Jackson. Johnston thought she looked extremely well and hoped that the mild climate of Mississippi would boost her spirits. His own spirits, however, were soon depressed by news which arrived that same day indicating that Bragg's "victory" was not as complete as his earlier reports had suggested. The Federals in Tennessee were not in retreat at all, and in fact Rosecrans had repulsed a second Confederate attack on January 2. Soon thereafter, Bragg himself had retreated, falling back to the line of the Duck River north of Chattanooga. Johnston telegraphed Davis: "I regret his falling back so far."[17]

The strategic situation was now exactly reversed. Pemberton was apparently secure, and Bragg was calling for reinforcements. Was Johnston expected to draw troops from Pemberton and send them to Bragg? Johnston found such a strategy absurd. He did not believe that troops could be shuttled back and forth between the two armies. The Confederacy would always be reacting to Federal initiatives, and always one step behind. "We cannot foresee attack long enough beforehand to be able to re-enforce the threatened army from either of the others," he wrote to Davis. Another option was to unite the two armies, but Johnston did not think that was practicable, either. "The armies of Bragg and Pemberton have different objects," he wrote to Wigfall. "They cannot be united without abandoning one of them." While agreeing that it was of "utmost importance" to get reinforcements to Bragg, Johnston did not believe that Pemberton's force could supply them. "My own position does not improve on acquaintance," he wrote to Wigfall in frustration. "It is little, if any, better than being laid on the shelf." So impossible did he consider his predicament that he twice asked Davis to relieve him of command. Davis declined.[18]

As it turned out, because Rosecrans did not pursue Bragg after the Battle of Murfreesboro (or Stones River), the Army of Tennessee made it through the rest of the winter without reinforcements. Soon Bragg began to assert that he should be congratulated for having survived a battle with an enemy army that he estimated to have been twice as large as his own. He also began to complain that the withdrawal of Stevenson's division almost literally on the eve of battle had cost him an important victory. "The unfortunate withdrawal of my troops when they were not absolutely necessary elsewhere, has saved Rosecrans from destruction," he reported to Johnston. "Five thousand fresh troops, as a reserve on the first day's battle, would have finished the glorious work."[19]

This was certainly putting the best face on it. It is unlikely, given the way Bragg used the troops he had, that an additional five or even ten thousand men would have made any difference. Bragg survived at Murfreesboro more by the skill of his corps commanders and the hard fighting of his troops than by his direction of the battle. He discarded whatever chance of victory he had by mismanaging his reserves. Instead of exploiting his morning success against the Federal right, he repeatedly dispatched piecemeal attacks against the hinge of the Federal line, a strongpoint known as the Round Forest. Then, on January 2, he foolishly assaulted another Federal strongpoint for no clear purpose, suffering terrible losses. Federal casualties in the two days of battle had not been as great as Bragg had reported; Confederate losses were equally heavy and more irreplaceable. Finally, Bragg's retreat, though it may have saved the army from subsequent destruction, nullified

any strategic value to the "victory" he claimed. Still, it was true that ten
thousand men had been removed from his army on the eve of battle, and that
fact underscored Johnston's objections to the command organization.

The Battle of Murfreesboro and Bragg's subsequent retreat reignited the
anti-Bragg movement inside the army. Two of Bragg's corps commanders,
Leonidas Polk and William J. Hardee, disgusted by Bragg's handling of their
men, renewed their calls for him to be replaced. Bragg solicited a vote of
confidence from his senior officers, but to his surprise and disgust their response was largely negative. Disturbed by news of unrest in the army, Davis
telegraphed Johnston to quit Mississippi, return to Tennessee, and report on
the condition of Bragg's army, and particularly on Bragg's capacity to continue to command it. Davis insisted that his own confidence in Bragg was
unshaken, but noted that if Bragg lacked the support of the army, it might be
necessary to replace him anyway.[20]

Davis's orders placed Johnston—in his own view, at least—in a delicate
situation. Johnston considered Bragg's command assignment far more desirable than his own. If he recommended to Davis that Bragg be dismissed,
Johnston would presumably succeed to the command himself. He wanted
the job, but given his concept of personal honor, it was unthinkable that he
would submit a report that might result in his own elevation at the expense
of another. Officers, he believed, should be appointed because of their manifest virtues, not by climbing over the backs of others. Johnston's value system
was such that his report was a foregone conclusion.

Even in the 1850s, when Johnston, by his own admission, had desired
promotion "more than any man in the army," he had been unwilling to seek
it by putting himself forward. In Johnston's ethical universe, one achieved
greatness through great acts, or because others naturally deferred to one's
leadership. Although he had aggressively and unflaggingly sought confirmation of his promotion to colonel in the 1850s, he did not consider that self-
promotional because he was laying claim to a position he had already fairly
won in battle. In protecting Longstreet from criticism by endorsing that
officer's report on the Battle of Seven Pines in 1862, Johnston committed an
injustice to Huger, but once again Johnston did not consider his actions to be
dishonorable. Honor, after all, involved more than simple justice. Now Johnston was being asked by Davis and Seddon to report to Richmond on the
competence of Braxton Bragg, with the obvious implication that if he were
critical it would result in his own elevation to command. Even if justice
demanded that Johnston comply, honor would not allow it. Neither Grant
nor Sherman would have hesitated; yet the prospect caused Johnston great
difficulty.

At Chattanooga, it was evident that the army did indeed lack confidence in
Bragg. Polk and Hardee were frank in their advocacy of Bragg's dismissal.
One of Hardee's division commanders, Frank Cheatham, was so completely
disillusioned he told Tennessee Governor Harris that "he would never go

into battle under General Bragg again." Even Bragg's own chief of staff, when asked for an opinion, responded that "under existing circumstances the general interests required that Gen Bragg should ask to be relieved." Yet Johnston concluded that Bragg should be sustained. To Davis, he wrote: "I am glad to find that your confidence in General Bragg is unshaken. My own is confirmed by his recent operations, which, in my opinion, evince great vigor and skill. It would be very unfortunate to remove him at this juncture, when he has just earned, if not won, the gratitude of the country." Apparently Johnston's professed admiration was genuine, for he was just as effusive in his private letters, telling Wigfall: "More effective fighting is not to be found in the history of modern battles." Perhaps he saw in Bragg's conduct of the Battle of Murfreesboro an analogy with his own performance at Seven Pines: Bragg had seized the initiative from a much larger opponent, inflicted heavy losses on the enemy, and his army held the field at the end of the battle.[21]

Johnston was so insistent about Bragg's achievements in part because he believed that his own situation made a critical report impossible. The more others suggested that he ought to assume the command himself, the more he praised Bragg's performance. When Secretary of War Seddon wrote Johnston a long and friendly letter asking him to consider staying with the Army of Tennessee, assuming personal command and employing Bragg as a kind of chief of staff, Johnston replied that such a thing was inconceivable. And when Davis suggested a similar solution, Johnston replied that "the part I have borne in this investigation would render it inconsistent with my personal honor to occupy that position."[22]

His friend Wigfall understood the dilemma. Appreciating Johnston's delicate sense of honor, Wigfall suspected that he really wanted the command, but that he would have to be ordered to take it over his own objections and, to public appearance at least, against his will. "If the appointment to that command by the department without your seeking it would be agreeable to you," Wigfall wrote Johnston in February, "let me know by telegraph & it shall be made." Realizing that even this admission might be too much for his sensitive friend, Wigfall added: "Telegraph me simply—'You are right' or 'You understand me' or some equivalent expression & I'll understand you and act accordingly."[23]

Johnston's reply was dated March 4, and he explained the problem in terms that suggested Wigfall did indeed understand him: "To remove the officer [Bragg] and put me in his place, & upon my investigation and report, would not look well & would certainly expose me, injure me." Polk, too, understood him. The "fighting Bishop" was as eager as anyone for Johnston's appointment to command. He urged Davis to remove Bragg by making him Inspector General, thus clearing the way "for assigning General Johnston to the command of this army, a measure which would give universal satisfaction to the officers and men." Polk reported that Johnston felt "a delicacy . . . in touching the case of a man whose command he might succeed in the event of his being removed." Despite Johnston's official reports, Polk wrote, "the case would be more properly stated by saying that he does not wish to be, or seem to be, the cause of his removal." Like Davis, Polk thought Johnston a bit too delicate on the subject, even "morbid."[24]

In short, Johnston wanted command of the Army of Tennessee and he wanted it badly, but would not say so officially or publicly. He would have to be ordered to take it over his own objections; in his view, there was no other way he could assume the assignment honorably. Perhaps the clearest expression of this is in Lydia's letters to Charlotte Wigfall. Even while her husband sang Bragg's praises to all who would listen, Lydia wrote to her closest friend: "I wish the President could be persuaded to give him Bragg's army . . . he is so sensitive about superseding our officers that I do but [fear that] he will not take either of those armies unless ordered to do so."[25]

Davis, too, faced a dilemma. He agreed with all of Johnston's glowing assessments of Bragg's qualities as a commander—though he and Johnston were about the only ones in the Confederacy who still professed to have confidence in Bragg—and he liked Bragg personally. But Davis feared that because Bragg lacked the support of the army, he might have to be replaced anyway, and he had dispatched Johnston to Chattanooga to make the final decision. Johnston's letters of praise for Bragg were therefore welcome news, but the president grew impatient with Johnston's sense of delicacy. Either Bragg should be sustained in recognition of his competence or he should be relieved because he lacked support. In either case, Davis did not feel that Johnston's sense of delicacy had anything to do with it. He told Johnston flatly that "I do not think that your personal honor is involved." Seddon, too, found Johnston's protestations cloying, urging him to disregard "considerations of scrupulous delicacy" and "make the sacrifice of your honorable delicacy to the importance of the occasion and the greatness of our cause." Of course, if Davis and Seddon really wanted Johnston to replace Bragg, all they had to do was order him to do it. Instead, they urged him to assume the position on his own authority as commander of the Department.[26]

Wigfall and his allies in the Senate had expected that the groundswell against Bragg would force Davis to remove that unpopular officer and make room for Johnston. But when Johnston refused to join in the criticism, and instead heaped praise on Bragg, it enabled Davis to retain Bragg in command. In the midst of Senate debates about the conduct of the war, the president's supporters flourished copies of Johnston's letter praising Bragg. Wigfall complained of this to Johnston; he claimed that Johnston had let down his Richmond friends, who were trying to secure him the command. Johnston rejected such an argument. While expressing great affection for Wigfall and gratitude for his support, he noted accurately that "The friends who have been irritated by my expression of such opinions are less my friends, I take it, than the president's enemies." Johnston stuck to his defense of Bragg despite repeated urging by Wigfall and others to reconsider.[27]

Such self-denial was all the more difficult because Johnston found himself with little to do. In January 1863, he wrote Wigfall: "You perceive how little occupation I can find," and a month later he reported that "I have been very busy for some time looking for something to do. . . . I am virtually laid upon the shelf." By March, nothing had changed: "For more than three months I have been doing next to nothing." Johnston did not exaggerate. His official letters dealt with such trivial matters as the availability of salt for curing meat, the shipment of corn on the Mobile & Ohio Railroad, and the procurement of horseshoe nails for Van Dorn's cavalry. These administrative minutiae left him with plenty of time on his hands. He all but begged Wigfall to find him something better, vowing, "If you can help me out of my present place I shall love you more than ever."[28] At least Lydia was there to comfort him, though both of them suffered from "an uncomfortable frame of mind" wondering when a shift in the tide of battle would send them to a new post. Lydia was stoic: "I am not sorry to go any where to be a little nearer him," she wrote to Charlotte.[29]

What Johnston wanted most of all was his old command in Virginia. He even suggested to Wigfall that he and Lee ought to exchange commands. "I am told that the president & secretary of war think that they have given me the highest military position in the Confederacy," he wrote. "If they so regard it, might not our highest military officer to occupy it? It seems to me that principle would bring Lee here. I might then, with great propriety, be replaced in my old command." This longing fed his latent jealousy of his old friend and rival, a jealousy that became more pronounced through the spring and summer. Johnston's comment about Lee's "luck" in being assaulted by Burnside at Fredericksburg was perhaps an early manifestation of his growing envy. By April, Robert Garlick Hill Kean, head of the Bureau of War, could confide to his diary that Johnston was "eaten up with morbid jealousy of Lee." And the perceptive and outspoken Mary Chesnut, who kept up with the progress of the Davis-Johnston feud through her husband's White House connections, hypothesized in June 1864 that "The quarrel between Joe Johnston and Mr. Davis is that General Lee outranks Joe Johnston. Hence these sulks." Johnston recognized that removing a commander as successful as Lee was impossible; but even if he could not command the army in Virginia, he preferred the command of an army, any army, to a departmental command. "I should much prefer the *command* of fifty men," he wrote to Wigfall.[30]

For Johnston, the key to the Confederacy's difficulties (and his own) in the western theatre remained the faulty organization of the western command structure. It was obvious to him that the Valley of the Mississippi constituted a single command theatre, within which a commander could coordinate the movements of Confederate armies on both sides of the river. The Army of Tennessee, then, would be free to maneuver independently with no responsibility for Mississippi. Although he never succeeded in convincing Davis to change the command system, he did achieve almost the same thing when Edmund Kirby Smith was appointed to replace Holmes in command of the trans-Mississippi West. Because Kirby Smith was an old friend of Johnston's, and still loyal to that friendship, he pledged himself to respond to Johnston's suggestions as if they were orders, and worked to cooperate with the Army of Mississippi. In Richmond, Kirby Smith told Wigfall on the day he left that he would regard any "suggestion" from Johnston as an order. Wigfall therefore reported to Johnston that "practically the Army of the Mississippi would be one and under your command." Once again Wigfall urged Johnston to assume command of one of the two western armies, saying he could keep Bragg on as a chief of staff if he desired, though he advised against it. "For the sake of your country do not impair your usefulness," he wrote. "Let Bragg go."[31]

Johnston could not be moved. Neither Davis, nor Seddon, nor Polk, nor Wigfall could convince him to remove Bragg on his own authority. Finally, Davis took matters into his own hands. On March 9, he ordered Bragg to report to Richmond for consultation. Johnston was to command the Army of Tennessee in Bragg's absence. But when Johnston arrived at Tullahoma on March 19, Bragg informed him that Mrs. Bragg was seriously ill with typhoid fever and he did not want to leave her side. Instantly sympathetic, Johnston told Bragg to postpone his departure and stay with his sick wife. Technically, Johnston assumed command of the army, but he did so without fanfare and even without officially promulgating the order to the army.[32]

Ironically, Bragg was anything but grateful for Johnston's unstinting support. The fact that Johnston commanded the kind of respect and popular support that Bragg could not made him jealous; that Johnston was gracious and supportive somehow only made it harder to bear. Finally, Bragg bitterly resented Johnston's presence in Tullahoma, looking over his shoulder, however benevolently.

On March 23, Colonel William Preston Johnston, the son of the late Albert Sidney Johnston who had died of his wounds at Shiloh, arrived at Tullahoma to investigate on behalf of the president the condition of the army and the state of the command. The young colonel was not an unbiased observer. He had personal ties to several of the officers in the army by virtue of their friendship with his late father. Polk in particular had been close to Albert Sidney Johnston, and now Polk spent several days convincing Davis's emissary that Bragg had to go and that Joe Johnston should be appointed to his place. But Bragg, too, had been a friend of A. S. Johnston, and the young colonel could not quite bring himself to recommend Bragg's removal. For his part, Joe Johnston was happy to have an opportunity to make his points directly to someone with the president's ear. He reiterated his opinion that his own command encompassed two armies that could not cooperate together, and he noted that because Bragg and Pemberton sent their reports directly to Richmond, he was denied the intelligence to make sound decisions about the movement of their armies in any case. Unfortunately, Colonel Johnston's final report was a vague document in which he reported in detail on the physical condition of the army, but remained largely mute on the command issue.[33]

In the first week of April, Bragg's wife recovered from her illness, thus supposedly freeing Bragg to abide by his suspended order to go to Richmond. But at almost the same time Johnston himself took to his cot, suffering from incompletely healed wounds, exacerbated now by his frequent travels. He reported to Davis on April 10 that he was too weak to assume field command and that therefore Bragg's continued presence with the army was essential. He took the opportunity to iterate—again—his objections to the command system. "Our disadvantage in this warfare," he wrote, "is that the enemy can transfer an army from Mississippi to Nashville before we can learn that it is in motion. While an equal body of our troops could not make the same movement (the corresponding one rather) in less than six weeks."[34]

Throughout April—a month when the plans for the spring campaign should have been reaching completion—Johnston exercised only nominal command from his sickbed, and Bragg remained with the Army of Tennessee, even though the army disliked him and anticipated his early removal. There was no firm guiding hand at the helm. Worse yet, the feud between Bragg on the one hand, and Polk and Hardee on the other, threatened to split the army in two. Bragg tried to force his two corps commanders to recant their criticism of him by implicating them in the errors of the Kentucky campaign of 1862. They responded by gathering evidence in the event of a court-martial. Meanwhile April turned to May, the army remained immobile in Tullahoma, and Johnston remained trapped on his sickbed frustrated by the curious circumstances of his "command."

Johnston's five months as commander of the Department of the West provided some of the most difficult moments of his military career. The American Civil War marked a watershed from eighteenth-century warfare to twentieth-century warfare, and like virtually every other Confederate officer of his generation—including Lee—Johnston's strategic notions were linked to the past. His greatest shortcoming as a Department commander was that his strategic views were inextricably tied to the idea that a general's job was to command an army in the field. From the time of his service in the Indian wars, Johnston had been a hands-on commander; his greatest asset was his personal magnetism in leading troops. He was ill-suited to coordinating armies from a desk in a map room.

Johnston's determination to maintain an honorable relationship with the army commanders who served, nominally at least, under him was a second inhibiting factor. That concern, combined with his very fine sense of personal honor, rendered him less than effective in exercising command responsibility. Such niceties did not inhibit men like Grant and Sherman—the new generation of warriors.

Finally, Johnston was stubborn in his repeated criticisms of the command structure in the West. Having made his case for a different structure and lost, he would not let go. His continued pleas for change were interpreted in Richmond as excuses, and his fine sense of delicacy in refusing to supersede Bragg as false pride. His own sense of isolation and frustration affected both his attitude and the tone of his official correspondence.

But the failures and lost opportunities of those five months cannot be ascribed solely or even largely to Johnston's shortcomings, for Davis's command organization was indeed flawed. The Confederate president's vision of the kind of shuttlecock reinforcement system that he hoped would keep the Yankees at bay was based on two misconceptions. The first was that it would be possible to make timely transfers of troops from one army to another in the West. This assumption was a product of Davis's familiarity with the strategic situation in Virginia, where Lee could bring Stonewall Jackson from the Valley, or send Longstreet to North Carolina by using the advantage of interior lines of communication. Such movements were far more difficult in the West, where the distances were much greater and the railroads less reliable. Jackson's troops had covered the 120 miles from the Shenandoah Valley to Richmond virtually overnight; Stevenson's men took more than a month to travel the 600 miles from Murfreesboro to Vicksburg.

Davis's second assumption was that the Federals would mount only one offensive at a time. Instead, Rosecrans's attack on Bragg at Murfreesboro took place simultaneously with Grant's forward movement in northern Mississippi. Thus the bulk of Stevenson's division was en route between the two armies when each faced its crisis in late December. Despite Johnston's protests that Pemberton and Bragg could not be mutually supporting, Davis refused to alter his organizational structure. Instead, he assumed that Johnston's protests were a combination of political hostility and reluctance to assume responsibility.

Finally, Johnston's frustrations resulted from the fact that Davis simply did not trust him to exercise real command in the West. The Confederate president tried to keep effective control in his own hands by requiring his army commanders to send their reports directly to Richmond rather than via the Department commander. If that were not bad enough, Davis (through Seddon or Cooper) frequently sent orders directly to the army commanders without consulting or even notifying Johnston.

In any event, Johnston's purgatory in Tennessee was nearing an end. By mid-April, a new push by Grant against Vicksburg led Seddon, at Davis's direction, to send Johnston new orders. Knowing Johnston's abhorrence of vague instructions, Seddon was blunt: "Proceed at once to Mississippi and take chief command of the forces, giving to those in the field, as far as practicable, the encouragement and benefit of your personal direction. Arrange to take for temporary service with you, or to be followed without delay, 3,000 good troops."

In Davis's original concept of the western command, the decision of when to go or not to go from one state to another was left entirely to Johnston;

what reinforcements to send, or how many, was also left to him. This time, the War Department told him simply: Take three thousand troops and go. Significantly, instead of the usual "With high esteem," Seddon now subscribed himself with a curt: "Acknowledge receipt." Johnston's response betrayed another unflattering characteristic, that of the martyr: "Your dispatch of this morning received. I shall go immediately although unfit for field service. . . ."[35]

CHAPTER FIFTEEN

Vicksburg

The peculiar geography of Vicksburg—set high atop a line of bluffs on the east bank of the Mississippi River—made it the single most important strategic site in the western theatre. The Mississippi flowed past the foot of those bluffs in a leisurely hairpin turn that required vessels travelling north or south to pass directly beneath the city, negotiate the tight bend, and then to steam away again, all the while under the scrutiny of Confederate gunners. Those bluffs also made Vicksburg virtually unassailable in any conventional attack from the river. Sherman had tried to storm Haynes Bluff north of the city in December 1862, and had been bloodily repulsed.

In addition to its commanding tactical position, Vicksburg was also the key link in the Confederacy's tenuous logistic chain from Texas to Virginia. Goods from the trans-Mississippi West were carried by the Shreveport & Vicksburg Railroad to De Soto on the west bank opposite Vicksburg, ferried across the river on barges, then reloaded onto railroad cars for transport to Jackson, to Mobile, and eventually to Richmond. The value of the goods actually shipped from Texas to Richmond was modest, but the connection itself was priceless, for Vicksburg was the psychological buckle holding together the two parts of the Confederacy: the Old South of the cotton belt and the Tidewater, and the Southwest of Texas and Arkansas. In the spring of 1863, Vicksburg, Mississippi, and Port Hudson, Louisiana, 150 miles to the south, were the last secure Confederate bastions on the river. Since Port Hudson could not stand alone, the fall of Vicksburg would sunder the Confederacy in two and surrender command of the river to the Yankees. Its fall would be an economic, military, and political disaster of the first order for the South. Nevertheless, even as Johnston hurried toward Mississippi in the second week of May, Vicksburg's fall was already a virtual certainty.

Johnston received Seddon's telegram ordering him to "proceed at once to Mississippi" on May 9. By that date the situation in Mississippi was already desperate. For months, Federal forces under Grant and Sherman had sought a way to assault Vicksburg. After the failure of Sherman's attack at Haynes Bluff and Grant's simultaneous retreat from northern Mississippi, the tactical situation remained quiescent through the winter. But in early April, while Johnston lay on his sickbed in Tullahoma, Grant had embarked on his third and eventually successful campaign.

He began by sending David Dixon Porter's gunboats and transports past Vicksburg and its batteries in a daring nighttime dash on April 16. Once south of the city, in nominally Confederate waters, the naval vessels and transports ferried Grant's troops over to the western shore at Bruinsburg, where they landed on April 30. Abandoning his lines of communication, Grant then struck out north and east to Port Gibson, which he seized after a short fight on May 1. Meanwhile, Pemberton had expended much of his energy and scattered his reserves in attempting to chase down a force of Federal cavalry under Brigadier General Benjamin Grierson that had started out from West Tennessee at about the same time and rampaged the length of Mississippi before riding into Federal lines at Baton Rouge two weeks later on May 2. By May 9, when Johnston got up from his sickbed to go to Mississippi, Grant's army was closing in on Raymond, where it fought another sharp skirmish with two Confederate brigades on May 12.

Johnston arrived at Jackson the next night. En route, he had heard from John Pemberton that the Federal army was moving "in heavy force" toward Edward's Station, where Pemberton's own army was located. Even as Johnston stepped off the train in Jackson, the city was filling up with the survivors of the two Confederate brigades that had been mauled in the fight at Raymond the day before. Johnston conferred with their commanders, Brigadier Generals John Gregg and W. H. T. Walker, who told him that a force of some 25,000 men under Sherman occupied Clinton only ten miles to the west, blocking the road to Edward's Station and Vicksburg. Johnston immediately wired the bad news to Seddon: "I arrived this evening, finding the enemy's force between this place and General Pemberton, cutting off communication. I am too late."[1]

But perhaps not. Since Pemberton had reported that Grant's main force was moving against Edward's Station, Johnston assumed (or, as he put it

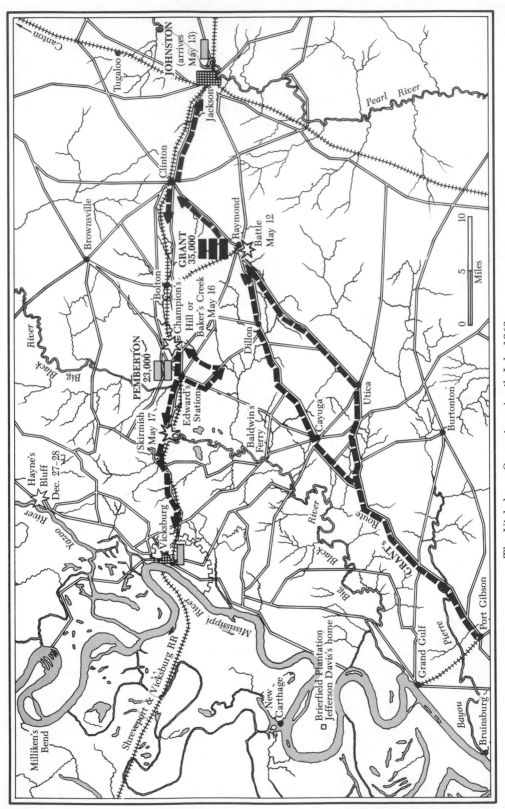

The Vicksburg Campaign, April–July 1863

later, "inferred") that Sherman's corps was separated from the main body. With only six thousand men under his own command (the remnants of Gregg's and Walker's brigades), Johnston could not fight his way through Sherman to join Pemberton, but Pemberton might conceivably be able to fight his way east to join Johnston. From the outset of the campaign, Johnston's primary goal was to combine forces against the invader. Pemberton still commanded some 23,000 men in a field army of his own, plus a garrison of 8,000 in Vicksburg. This army, combined with Johnston's six thousand in Jackson, and five thousand more expected to arrive during the night, would give the Confederates local superiority. That same night, therefore, Johnston ordered Pemberton to attack Sherman from the west: "If practicable, come up in his rear at once. To beat such a detachment would be of immense value. The troops here could cooperate. All the troops you can quickly assemble should be brought. Time is all-important." Johnston instructed his staff to prepare three copies of the order and to send it by three different couriers to ensure that the message got through.[2]

Pemberton received Johnston's message early the next morning, but he was more distressed than pleased. First of all, he considered the enemy force at Clinton too strong. As he read Johnston's message, he turned to an aide and remarked: "Such a movement will be suicidal." Even more disturbing was Johnston's willingness to abandon Vicksburg in order to concentrate on a single corps of the enemy army. Pemberton considered Vicksburg not just his base of operations but the prize for which the armies were contending. To him, Vicksburg was of "paramount importance"; he later wrote that "under no circumstances could I abandon my communications with it."[3]

Pemberton's commitment to Vicksburg was influenced by circumstances peculiar to him. Whispered comments about his northern background circulated even in the ranks of his own army. Pemberton was determined to behave in such a way as to prove beyond any doubt that the suspicions of his loyalty were groundless. He knew what Davis expected of him: to hold Vicksburg at all costs. The president had said as much in official and private letters. Mississippi was the president's home state; Brierfield, Davis's plantation, was only a few miles to the south. For Davis, the fall of Vicksburg would be not only a political and military disaster, but a personal blow as well. On May 7, Davis had wired Pemberton orders to hold both Vicksburg and Port Hudson. The next day, Pemberton wired Major General Franklin Gardner at Port Hudson to hold that city "to the last." He could ask no less of himself. Therefore, when Pemberton received Johnston's urgent instructions to attack the Federals at Clinton, he was deeply troubled. Clinton was more than thirty miles from Vicksburg; even if Pemberton and Johnston won a victory there, Vicksburg would be laid bare to the rest of Grant's army. On the other hand, Johnston was Pemberton's superior officer, and Pemberton would not disobey orders lightly.[4]

Despite his apprehensions, Pemberton immediately wrote Johnston that he would move toward Clinton "at once" with sixteen thousand men, though in fact he did not plan to move until the next morning. The more he thought about it, the more certain he became that such a move was a bad idea. In addition, he may have felt a rising resentment against Johnston for arriving so late upon the scene and handing out peremptory orders. Since he did not have the opportunity to argue his case personally, Pemberton did what he considered the next best thing: he called a council of war. He read Johnston's letter to his generals, and asked for their views. A majority expressed support for the attack. But his two senior division commanders, W. W. Loring and Carter Stevenson, suggested that it might be wiser to attack Grant's supply lines and thereby force the enemy to retreat without confronting his army directly. Seeing a possible compromise, Pemberton accepted it. That afternoon, May 14, he dispatched a courier to inform Johnston that he was going to march south rather than east. It was a bad compromise, for the reality was that Grant was not dependent on his supply lines, and Pemberton's subsequent movement south served mainly to separate him even further from Johnston, making a junction of Confederate forces more difficult.[5]

Unaware of Pemberton's change of heart, Johnston set up his headquarters in the Bowman House Hotel in Jackson and spent most of the night of May 13 placing his small army in a defensive position facing west. It rained all night—a hard, driving spring rain—and it was still raining the next morning at 11:00 A.M. when the Federals attacked. They advanced quickly, driving in the Confederate pickets and completely routing a small advance force two miles west of the city. But the attack bogged down when it hit the main Confederate entrenchments around the city itself. Rather than assault these formidable defenses, Grant began extending his flanks north and south to overlap the Confederate lines.[6]

Johnston had no intention of waiting until he was surrounded. He ordered the Confederate artillerists to keep up a continuous fire on the enemy, and pulled the infantry out of line, sending it northward up the road toward Canton. Eventually the gunners—state troops and therefore expendable—were surrounded and captured, along with seventeen of their guns, but their bold stand allowed the Confederate main body to escape. Grant did not pursue. Instead, he occupied Jackson and slept that night in the same bed in the Bowman House Hotel that Johnston had occupied the night before, though no doubt he slept better.[7]

Johnston wrote to notify Pemberton that he had evacuated Jackson, and to ask if Pemberton could now cut the Federals in Jackson off from their Mississippi River base. He assumed that Pemberton's army was on the move heading east toward Clinton, and that a unification of Confederate forces was still possible, but the fluidity of the situation made specific planning difficult and Johnston was vague about how a junction could be effected. He suggested that the two brigades of approaching reinforcements—five thousand men under Generals States Rights Gist and Samuel Maxey—might join Pemberton's force, but he did not say where or when this might take place. He also noted that he was "anxious to see a force assembled that may be able to inflict a heavy blow upon the enemy," but he did not provide specific instructions as to how this might be achieved. Indeed, the only clear element of Johnston's message was that somehow a concentration of the scattered Confederate forces was essential. All hopes for a Confederate concentration evaporated only minutes later when a courier rode up to Johnston on the road a few miles north of Tugaloo to hand him Pemberton's message that he had decided to march south rather than east.[8]

Johnston was first surprised, then angered, that Pemberton had chosen to disregard his orders. The more he thought about it, the angrier he got. However inspecific he may have been in his written orders, the one certainty that dominated his thinking was his conviction that the only chance the Confederates had in this campaign was to combine forces against the enemy. Now the two Confederate armies were marching in opposite directions! At once Johnston dictated another letter to Pemberton that was anything but vague: "Our being compelled to leave Jackson makes your plan impracticable. The only mode by which we can unite is by your moving directly to Clinton. . . ." Since a large portion of the Federal army was already at Jackson, Johnston knew that he was ordering Pemberton into harm's way, but to his mind it was less hazardous than continuing to march away from each other.[9]

Pemberton received this letter at six-thirty on the morning of May 16. His army had covered only about six miles southward, for the troops had encountered bad roads and a bridge that had been washed away by the heavy rains. This time Pemberton decided to comply; he turned his columns around and started north. But by now it was too late, for while Pemberton had been slogging south, Grant moved to interpose his army between the two Confederate forces. One of the three couriers to whom Johnston's staff had entrusted his urgent message on the night of the 13th was a Union spy, who delivered his copy of the order directly to the headquarters of Major General James B. McPherson, who passed it on to Grant. Recognizing the importance of keeping the two rebel armies separated, Grant ordered McPherson's corps to Bolton to block any move southward that Johnston might make, and concentrated the rest of his army for an attack on Pemberton. Ordering the destruction of the railroad bridge over the Pearl River, he abandoned Jackson and headed west. As Pemberton moved north in response to Johnston's peremptory orders, Grant's main force caught him and inflicted a devastating defeat at the Battle of Baker's Creek (or as the Federals called it, Champion's Hill). The remnants of Pemberton's force were driven back to the banks of the Big Black River, less than ten miles from Vicksburg, though one division—Loring's—retreated south and by a circuitous route eventually managed to join Johnston. Now that Grant had successfully separated the two armies, Pemberton wrote Johnston: "I respectfully await your instructions."[10]

Johnston's grand strategy for the relief of Vicksburg was based on the fundamental assumption that Pemberton's army was more valuable to the Confederacy than the city itself. He argued repeatedly that geographical sites, if lost, could be retaken later, but that an army lost was lost forever. His principal goal from the beginning was to save Pemberton's army from destruction. Even before he left Tennessee, he had warned Pemberton that if the Yankees crossed to the east bank of the Mississippi, he should concentrate his army and defeat them in open battle, though it meant the temporary evacuation of Vicksburg. "Success will give back what was abandoned to win it," he wrote. The worst possible outcome was that the Federal forces would surround Vicksburg with Pemberton's army inside the city. From his new camp on the road from Edward's Station to Livingston, he now warned Pemberton: "If . . . you are invested in Vicksburg, you must ultimately surrender. Under such circumstances, instead of losing both troops and place, we must, if possible, save the troops. If it is not too late, evacuate Vicksburg and its dependencies, and march to the northeast."[11]

But when Pemberton received these instructions, he was shocked. "The evacuation of Vicksburg!" he exclaimed later in his official report. "It meant the loss of the valuable stores and munitions of war collected for its defense; the fall of Port Hudson; the surrender of the Mississippi River, and the severance of the Confederacy." He could not bring himself to do it. He called another council of his generals, and after lengthy discussion, convinced them that the abandonment of Vicksburg was unacceptable. Instead, he would fall back into the prepared defenses around the city and hope that time, circumstances, and Joe Johnston would somehow conspire to rescue him. He informed Johnston that "I have decided to hold Vicksburg as long as is possible, with the firm hope that the Government may yet be able to assist me. . . . I still conceive it to be the most important point in the Confederacy."[12]

Perhaps so. But Pemberton's army was also important to the Confederacy—and virtually irreplaceable. If Pemberton had been willing to follow Johnston's order, he might even then have saved his army. Grant himself later wrote that "Pemberton might indeed have made a night march to the Big Black, crossed the bridge there, and by moving north on the west side, have eluded us, and finally returned to Johnston. But this would have given us Vicksburg. It would have been his proper move, however, and the one Johnston would have made had he been in Pemberton's place."[13]

Johnston might well have castigated Pemberton for twice ignoring his orders and allowing himself to become so completely cut off from the aid he was seeking. Instead, he wrote: "I am trying to gather a force which may relieve you. Hold out." The problem now was to raise a force large enough to break the Federal siege.[14] Over the next several days, Johnston's small force was augmented by troops drawn from throughout the Confederacy: from Bragg in Tennessee, from Beauregard in South Carolina, and from the garrisons at Mobile and Port Hudson. Johnston even wrote Kirby Smith in Arkansas to ask if he could provide any aid. There was one other source of additional manpower—Lee's Army of Northern Virginia. After its dramatic victory at Chancellorsville on May 2, and with the recall of Longstreet's corps from North Carolina, surely it was secure enough to detach a division or two to the West. But Lee had other plans. Arguing that an invasion of the North would do more for the Cause than sending reinforcements to the relief of Vicksburg, Lee began planning the campaign that would take him to Gettysburg.

Slowly—too slowly—other units began to appear. Brigades from Charleston and Tennessee arrived on May 20 and 21, and another on the 23rd. Invariably they came in smaller numbers than promised. By now the actual size of veteran brigades was often only a fraction of the advertised strength; Beauregard reported that he had dispatched 10,000 men to Mississippi, yet the units he sent contained only 6,500. Johnston fired off telegrams to Richmond urging speed. "They come too slowly," he wired to Cooper on May 25. That night he wired again: "Do urge them forward."[15]

By the first week of June, he commanded an army of nearly 23,000 men. But by then Federal reinforcements had raised Grant's strength to 77,000, and the Federals occupied the interior position between Johnston and Pemberton. Grant organized his forces into two "armies," each of which was larger than Johnston's. The larger of the two—43,000 men under his own command—surrounded the Vicksburg defenses to ensure that Pemberton remained well trapped. The other—34,000 men under Sherman—faced east behind the Big Black River to prevent any interference by Johnston. With only 23,000 men of his own, Johnston could not drive the Federals off or even fight his way in, had that been his object. Johnston's arrival in Vicksburg with reinforcements was exactly what Pemberton expected. "My men are in good spirits," he wrote, "awaiting your arrival." Davis, too, expected Johnston to fight his way into the city. "Make a junction," he wired to Johnston, "and carry in munitions." Grant could hardly have hoped for anything better. When a Federal staff officer suggested that Johnston might try to fight his way into the city, Grant replied: "If Johnston tries to cut his way in, we will let him do it, and then see that he don't get out."[16]

For the soldiers and citizens trapped in Vicksburg, the prospect of Johnston's arrival with a rescuing army became the one great hope. Pemberton had announced from the outset of the siege that help was on the way. On the very day that Pemberton decided to fall back into the city, a Vicksburg dentist confided to his diary: "The enemy have a line entirely around us, leaving no outlets. Our only hope now is that we can hold out until Johnston arrives. . . ."[17]

Sustaining that hope was difficult. Soldiers and civilians alike discovered the particular horror of life in a besieged city. After the failure of Grant's initial assault on May 19, the Federal commander began a steady bombardment of Vicksburg that continued even at night. The incessant pounding frayed the nerves and tried the courage of the most stouthearted. The soldiers dug deep into their trenches and hugged the earth during the worst of it; the civilians moved into caves along the riverbank and parceled out their ever-dwindling stock of foodstuffs. The chickens and hogs in the town disappeared almost at once; the horses and mules went next, and finally the dogs and cats. A desperate few were reduced to eating rats and wallpaper. One thought sustained them: Johnston was coming!

The townspeople seized upon that hope. Johnston's very name became a talisman. "We are looking anxiously for *Joe Johnston*," one citizen wrote, the underscoring expressing the mystical qualities attached to his name and powers. Rumor numbered Johnston's force at fifty or sixty thousand; some claimed a hundred thousand. At first they thought that he might arrive almost at once. One soldier recalled that when the troops filed into their entrenchments after their retreat into the city, "we were exhorted to hold the place for only twelve hours longer, being assured that General Johnston would join us by that time, at the head of a heavy force." But Johnston did not come. Not in twelve hours, not in twelve days. And hope began to fade. "We were repeatedly informed that he was coming," one citizen wrote in his journal. "This was repeated so often and the men were so often disappointed that they naturally became despondent."[18]

At Jackson, Johnston was still trying to pull together an army large enough to dislodge Sherman and Grant in order to allow Pemberton an opportunity to evacuate the city and save his army. Johnston had no real hope of raising the siege; rather than fight his way in, his object was to provide Pemberton with an opportunity to fight his way out. On May 29, he wrote Pemberton: "I am too weak to save Vicksburg. Can do no more than attempt to save you and your garrison." But he also warned that "It will be impossible to extricate you unless you co-operate and we make mutually supporting movements."[19]

Saving Pemberton's army would be difficult now. In the first place, Vicksburg was so tightly sealed off by the Federals that effective communication with Pemberton was impossible. Messages had to be floated into the city at night, carried by daring volunteers who clung to debris in the river. Often a week or more passed between the date a letter was dispatched and when it was received. Pemberton did not get Johnston's May 19 letter until the 29th. The second problem was Johnston's own numerical inferiority; by June, his army was less than a third the size of the armies he was expected to dislodge. He wired Davis: "We cannot break the investment without an army. . . . Tell me if additional troops can be furnished." Davis responded that he was "making every effort to aid you." But he also reminded Johnston that delay was dangerous. "We have withheld nothing which it was practicable to give," he wired. "We cannot hope for numerical equality, and time will probably increase the disparity." In other words, Davis suggested that Johnston should not wait for more reinforcements, but do the best he could with what he had. Of course there was a fine line between boldness and foolishness. Pemberton himself wrote Johnston that "I do not think you should move with less than 30,000 or 35,000. . . ." Johnston appealed to Davis one more time. He reported the size of his own army at 23,000 and that of the enemy at 60,000 to 80,000, noting: "The odds against us will be very great. Can you not add 7,000?"[20]

Davis was surprised. He thought Johnston had an army of at least thirty thousand, and when he checked with Seddon, the Secretary of War confirmed it. Davis therefore wired Johnston: "The Secretary of War reports . . . your whole force to be 34,000 exclusive of militia." Johnston responded that "The Secretary of War is greatly mistaken. . . ." and sent an itemized return showing his total manpower to be 24,100 men as of June 1. Davis had to accept Johnston's word for it, though the tone of his correspondence suggests that he suspected Johnston was minimizing his numbers in order to justify his inaction. The president told Seddon to ask Johnston why he didn't simply order more troops to himself from Bragg's army in Tennessee.[21]

Johnston in turn was surprised, for he did not think he had authority over Bragg's army, assuming that his orders to Mississippi had superseded his orders as commander of the Department of the West. He immediately wired Seddon to clarify his position, and Seddon replied that, yes, Johnston remained the commander of the whole Department as well as commander of a field army in Mississippi. Although this news now made it possible for Johnston to summon reinforcements, it did not solve his problem, for in effect he was being asked to make a decision he considered to be essentially a political one: whether to strip Tennessee of its forces in order to save Mississippi. "To take from Bragg a force which would make this army fit to oppose Grant," he told Seddon, "would involve yielding Tennessee. It is for the Government to decide between this State and Tennessee."[22]

Far from solving the Vicksburg crisis, this new information provoked a long exchange of telegrams between Davis and Johnston that did little credit to the president or his general:

> JOHNSTON: I considered the order directing me to command here as limiting my authority to this department.
>
> DAVIS: I do not find in my letterbook any communication to you containing the expression which you again attribute to me. . . . Give date of dispatch or letter.
>
> JOHNSTON: I much regret the carelessness of my reply. . . . I refer to the words "we have withheld nothing which it was practicable to give" in your telegram of May 28. . . .
>
> DAVIS: After full examination of all the correspondence between you and myself and the War Office, including the dispatches referred to in your telegram . . . I am still at a loss to account for your strange error. . . .
>
> JOHNSTON: I considered my assignment to the immediate command in Mississippi as giving me a new position and limiting my authority to this department. The orders of the War Department transferring three separate bodies of troops from General Bragg's army to this, two of them without my knowledge and all of them without consulting me, would have confirmed me had I doubted. . . . I regret very much that an impression which seemed to me to be natural should be regarded by you as a strange error.[23]

It was a silly quarrel. Johnston wanted to explain how reasonable it was for him to have drawn the conclusions that he did. But Davis didn't want explanations or justifications, he wanted Johnston to acknowledge his error.

Johnston's continued stubbornness finally compelled Davis to sit down and write a fifteen-page letter that was virtually a lecture, full of specific citations from official orders, in order to prove that Johnston's misunderstanding was completely unreasonable. One of the few rational voices in this flurry of telegraphic exchanges was Seddon's, who urged tactfully to Johnston: "You must rely on what you have . . . but I venture the suggestion that to relieve Vicksburg speedy action is essential."[24]

Indeed, the enemy noose was tightening about the city. On June 25, the Federals detonated a mine beneath the Vicksburg defenses, and a week later they exploded another. The food supplies inside the city were virtually exhausted, and the morale of soldier and citizen alike was collapsing under the continuing bombardment. By mid-June Johnston had already reported to the government that there was no hope. "I consider saving Vicksburg hopeless," he wrote to Seddon. But the government was not willing to give up. "Vicksburg must not be lost without a desperate struggle," Seddon replied. "If better resources do not offer, you must attack."[25]

Johnston remained adamant. He considered an attack on Grant's numerically superior and entrenched army to be out of the question. "There are such odds against us here as Napoleon never won against," he wrote to a friend. "The only imaginable hope is in the perpetration by Grant of some extravagant blunder and there is no grounds for such hope." Johnston did hope briefly that with the help of a diversion created by Kirby Smith's army in Arkansas, Pemberton might be able to escape across the river to the west. In response to Johnston's urging, Smith sent General Richard Taylor, son of the former president, with three thousand men to attack Federal forces on the west bank of the river at Milliken's Bend above Vicksburg. They drove in some pickets but did not press the issue, mainly because they lacked the numerical strength to make a permanent lodgement. Taylor sent his aide Colonel Elgee across the river to discuss cooperation with Johnston. After a long conversation, Elgee returned to report to Taylor: "I regret to inform you that he [Johnston] considers the situation of Vicksburg eminently critical. Grant is being heavily reinforced by Burnside's corps. This, added to his strength of position, renders the condition of Vicksburg, in General Johnston's opinion, almost hopeless." By the end of June it was clear that Kirby Smith's army could not help and that no more reinforcements would be forthcoming. Barring a miracle, Vicksburg's surrender was only a matter of time, perhaps only a matter of days.[26]

On June 25, Johnston received a letter from Lydia, who was spending an anxious summer in Columbia, South Carolina. She expressed the fear that somehow the public would blame him for the inevitable fall of Vicksburg. Johnston wrote back at once to ease her anxiety, providing a glimpse into his heart during those trying days. "My love," he wrote, "I grieve to find that you suffer." But as far as his public reputation was concerned,

Don't be uneasy on that subject. If I do my best with insufficient means it will soon be understood that those means are insufficient, & the judgement which will be passed by the southern press should Vicksburg fall [will be] reversed. Remember how this southern country condemned me for leaving Harper's Ferry, & how afterwards extolled me for it.

One who discharges his duty manfully & unselfishly will always be respected, altho' he may not be thought a great man, & I assure you that to be the object of popular clamour is no wish of mine. The respect of the respectable I do desire; its admiration would be pleasant too. But that of the crowd which is measured by success alone, I care for as little as for the withered leaves of last autumn. I am serving the country unselfishly & wish it to believe so, but care little for any higher estimation. I hope, darling, that you will be as indifferent, or rather that you will be as confident as I in the ultimate justice of the people to those who fight for them. There is no ground for your unhappiness, take my word for it. I have not the slightest for myself. . . .[27]

The time had come for desperate measures. Pemberton had written that his provisions would enable him to hold out no later than July 10; if Johnston did not move by then, starvation would force him to capitulate. On July 3, Johnston instructed Pemberton that it was time for him to abandon his hope of saving Vicksburg and try instead to save the army. He himself would attack Sherman's lines on July 7 in an effort to create enough of a diversion to allow the Vicksburg defenders to escape. "Our firing will show you where we are engaged," he wrote. "If Vicksburg cannot be saved, the garrison must." The prospects for success were not good: Sherman's men in their entrenchments behind the Big Black River were nearly as impregnable to a direct attack as were Pemberton's men in Vicksburg. Charles A. Dana, Secretary of War Stanton's personal representative to Grant's army, reported to Washington that "Johnston must move up mainly by the Benton or Jackson Road . . . the greater part of the road winds along very narrow and precipitous ridges, heavily wooded, where a column cannot deploy, and where the advance can be easily checked. . . ." Still, it was the only option left. On July 5, Johnston issued orders "to cross the Big Black and attack Grant's line." The army began advancing westward behind a cloud of skirmishers. Two days later, with his forces astride the Big Black River sixteen miles east of Vicksburg, Johnston learned that on July 4 Pemberton's starving soldiers had marched out of Vicksburg and stacked arms in surrender.[28]

Pemberton had never received Johnston's letter of July 3. On that very day, he had polled his brigade commanders about the wisdom of continuing resistance. His officers had responded that their men were too worn out to attempt an escape, and that capitulation was the only recourse. That same afternoon, Pemberton opened negotiations with Grant for a surrender of the city, and on July 4 his army marched out to stack arms.

When Johnston learned that Vicksburg had capitulated, he immediately wired the news to Richmond and began to fall back toward Jackson, for with Pemberton's surrender, Grant's entire force was now freed to deal with Johnston. He reached Jackson on July 9, and reported that the enemy was closing in on him from two sides. Despite his inferiority of numbers, he was confident that he could inflict a costly repulse by fighting from entrenchments. It had not rained for weeks, and during his retreat Johnston had ordered his troops to foul the few wells in the area. He calculated that the shortage of water would deny Grant and Sherman the luxury of conducting a siege, forcing them to attempt a frontal assault. On July 10, he addressed the troops formally—a rare occurrence for him—and gave what one wag called "a longer speech than he has ever been known to make," meaning that he talked for several minutes. He spoke of patriotism, sacrifice, and ultimate victory.[29]

Johnston's men held the Federal host at bay for most of a week, while Johnston sent cavalry patrols to attack the enemy lines of communication. But fate worked against him as the skies opened and heavy rains fell on besieged and besieger alike. The Federals spread out their oilcloth blankets and collected their heaven-sent water ration. Soon afterward, Grant brought up his artillery and prepared to shell the city into submission. A newspaper correspondent reported that "The streets were deserted by all, save here and there a courier, dashing along at full speed, or a straggling citizen, or a negro carrying some article of value to the rear. . . ." Meanwhile, "crash upon crash from exploding shells was heard upon every side." Recognizing the impossibility of holding the city against siege tactics and heavy artillery, Johnston abandoned the Mississippi state capital for the second time on July 16. Although this was more bad news as far as Richmond was concerned, there is no doubt that had he stayed, he would have sacrificed his army as well. The Federals did not pursue Johnston's retreating men. Exhausted themselves, they occupied Jackson and let him go.[30]

Who was responsible for the fall of Vicksburg? Davis blamed Johnston for failing to come to Pemberton's rescue. Johnston blamed Pemberton for allowing himself to be trapped inside the city, although he also reserved some of the blame for Davis, whom he held responsible for the unworkable command system in the West. The real architect of the surrender, of course, was Ulysses S. Grant, whose command of the river, numerical superiority, and iron determination made Vicksburg's fall a reality.

A better question is: Who was responsible for the loss of Pemberton's army? For that, Pemberton is the only candidate. Pemberton's decision to retreat into the city and defy a Federal siege ensured that when Vicksburg did fall, the Federals would capture both the city and the army that defended it. For the Confederates, this was the great tragedy of the campaign—not only the loss of Vicksburg, but also the loss of Pemberton's army, which removed 26,000 Confederate troops from the strategic chessboard.

Johnston had seen it from the outset. On May 17, only four days after he arrived in Mississippi, and two days before Pemberton fell back into his entrenchments around the city, Johnston had cautioned him: "If . . . you are invested in Vicksburg, you must ultimately surrender." As early as January—six months before the capitulation—Johnston had warned Davis that "Should Grant join Sherman at Vicksburg it would be very embarrassing. . . . We could not break the investment . . . but it would be necessary to try."[31] Once Grant's forces were across the Mississippi, the Confederacy's best hope was to ensure the survival of Pemberton's field army. The Federals would still have captured Vicksburg, but it is at least possible that with their combined armies (which eventually totalled 51,000 men) Johnston and Pemberton might have made it difficult for them to stay there. Instead, Pemberton allowed himself to be penned up inside the city. From that moment, his surrender was only a matter of time.

Not everyone, however, considered Pemberton the villain in this drama. In the midst of the siege, Davis wrote to Lee: "All the accounts we have of Pemberton's conduct fully sustain the good opinion heretofore entertained of him." And if Pemberton was the victim, then Johnston had to be cast as the villain. Davis believed that the turning point in the campaign was Johnston's decision to stop in Jackson when he first arrived in the theatre instead of going straight on to Vicksburg. Johnston "halted there," Davis later wrote, "and opened correspondence with General Pemberton, from which confusion and consequent disasters resulted. . . ." Davis was also disappointed by Johnston's failure to rebuild the burned railroad bridge over the Pearl River at Jackson. Though Johnston did order it rebuilt, the work lagged, and as a result Federal cavalry burned hundreds of freight cars and dozens of engines trapped north of Jackson. But most of all Davis blamed Johnston for failing to fight his way into Vicksburg. A few days after its fall, Josiah Gorgas, Confederate chief of ordnance, suggested to Davis that Vicksburg had fallen for want of provisions. Davis spat back: "Yes, from want of provisions inside, and a general outside who wouldn't fight."[32]

Pemberton, too, blamed Johnston for the fall of Vicksburg and for the loss of his army. As he saw it, not only did Johnston remain outside the city making no serious attempt to fight his way in, but he had been primarily responsible for all the errors of the campaign. Pemberton later argued that Johnston's order on May 13 to attack the Federals at Clinton had upset all his plans. Of course, Pemberton had not obeyed those orders, but they had prompted him to quit his prepared defenses and move south seeking Grant's nonexistent supply lines. When Pemberton received Johnston's second order to join forces north of Jackson, he was too far south to effect a junction, but he dutifully turned his army around and headed north. While on the march, he was caught and defeated at Baker's Creek (Champion's Hill). After that, he believed, he had no real option but to fall back into the city. In Pemberton's version of events, Johnston came late into the theatre, upset all of Pemberton's careful planning, and then did nothing to rescue him.[33]

In late July, John Pemberton reported to Johnston's army after being paroled by Grant. Johnston was sitting outside his headquarters tent on a hill near Morton, Mississippi, when he noticed "a tall, handsome, dignified figure" coming up the hill toward him. Johnston recognized Pemberton and jumped to his feet to greet him. He extended his hand, saying, "Well, Jack old boy, I am certainly glad to see you."

Then the smile on Johnston's face faded and he slowly lowered his hand, for Pemberton instead saluted "punctiliously." With a deadpan expression, he recited his prepared comment: "General Johnston, according to the terms of parole prescribed by General Grant, I was directed to report to you, sir!"

Both men stood motionless facing each other, saying nothing. Finally, Pemberton saluted again, turned on his heel, and walked down the hill. They never met again.[34]

CHAPTER SIXTEEN

The Paper War

July 1863 was a bitter month for the Confederacy. Johnston's telegram announcing Vicksburg's surrender arrived in Richmond the same week as the shattering news of Lee's defeat at Gettysburg. The triumphant end of the war had seemed tantalizingly close in May after Lee's victory at Chancellorsville, yet the high hopes of the spring had evaporated in the heat of midsummer. "Yesterday we rode on the pinnacle of success," one Confederate official wrote in his diary, "today absolute ruin seems to be our portion." Another wrote simply: "God help this unhappy country." Even Davis's determined optimism temporarily deserted him: "We are now in the darkest hour of our political existence," he wrote.[1]

July was a bitter month for Johnston, too. From Jackson he fell back to Morton, Mississippi, thirty-five miles to the east, where his small 23,000-man army was all that stood between 80,000 Federals and the heart of the Confederacy's prime resource base. That same week Davis removed him as commander of the Department of the West, creating an independent command for Bragg and reducing Johnston's area of responsibility to Mississippi and southern Alabama plus a small portion of western Tennessee. Davis would have preferred to dismiss Johnston from the army altogether. He laid

the groundwork for such a move by promoting Daniel Harvey Hill to lieutenant general and sending him to Bragg to act as a corps commander. That
made it possible to transfer Lieutenant General William Hardee from Bragg
to command the army in Mississippi, and Hardee assumed command there
when Johnston travelled to Mobile to inspect its defenses in August. But
Davis hesitated to dismiss Johnston outright, for Johnston remained a very
popular officer—more popular in much of the country than Davis himself—
and, of course, Wigfall and his allies in the Confederate Congress would
have protested vehemently. Instead, Davis compromised by restricting Johnston's area of command.[2]

Then, six days later, in Mobile, Colonel Frank Schaller handed Johnston a
fifteen-page letter in the president's own hand that he had brought from
Richmond. It was Davis's final word in their quarrel about whether the
orders that had sent Johnston to Mississippi had superseded his original
orders to departmental command. Davis's letter was a cool and studied dissertation, thirty-four paragraphs long (Johnston numbered them for his
reply), studded with quotations from their official correspondence. Davis
claimed that he wrote this letter "that there may be no possible room for
future mistake in this matter. . . ." Of course since he had already rescinded
Johnston's command authority in the West, the whole issue was moot. Nevertheless, Davis began by quoting Johnston's original orders from the previous November, then laboriously reiterated all their correspondence since.
He concluded that "no justification whatever is perceived for your abandonment of your duties as commanding general. . . ."[3]

How was Johnston to respond to such a letter? His best course, no doubt,
would have been to acknowledge a misunderstanding and to pledge himself
to more frequent correspondence in the future. This might have mollified
Davis and ended the dispute right there. But it was not in Johnston's character. Indeed, he would have considered such a retreat dishonorable, for the
president's letter did not stop with detailing Johnston's misunderstanding of
orders, it charged him with abandoning his duties, terminology that Johnston
could not ignore. Johnston did not worry that anyone would take such
charges seriously, but he was hurt by them nonetheless. To Wigfall he
wrote: "I wish I could show you this letter—full of assertions the incorrect-
ness of which I can't show without trouble."[4]

Lydia was more outraged than her husband. She characterized Davis's
letter as one "only a coward or a woman would write," and she implored her
husband to resign immediately. He tried to quiet her anger. Calmly, "as
cheerful as if Jeff had thrown rose leaves at him instead of nettles and
thorns," he told his wife that "No indignity from Davis could drive him from
the service." Lydia explained her husband's view of the dispute to Charlotte
Wigfall: "He is not serving him [Davis], but a people who have never had
any thing but kind wishes." Still, Lydia feared that Davis was out to ruin her
husband, and she had told him so as early as November, when he first
accepted command in the West. "I said then," she wrote to Charlotte, "he

hates you & he has power & he will ruin you, & [he gave] the same old reply: 'He could. I don't care. My country.' "⁵

In his careful reply to Davis's letter, Johnston asked the president to reconsider whether his "misapprehension of the order" was "a serious military offense," for he claimed that it did not affect his conduct of the campaign. "Your excellency charges me with the abandonment of my duties as commanding general of a geographical district. I respectfully deny the commission of such a military crime." While directing the army in Mississippi, he wrote, he could not have exercised responsible command in Tennessee. Of course he might have ordered Bragg to send more reinforcements, but to do so would have meant the abandonment of Tennessee, and that was a policy question best addressed by the government, not by a soldier in the field. Johnston denied that his efforts to explain the source of his misunderstanding, or as he put it, "to extenuate my misapprehension of the honorable Secretary's telegram," made him guilty of the implied charges in Davis's letter. To a friend he wrote: "I took great pleasure in setting him right, for which doubtless he is Christianly thankful."⁶

This exchange of letters rekindled the feud between president and general that had simmered all through the spring. More importantly, it initiated a political crisis in Richmond, for Davis's enemies in Congress, led by Wigfall, espoused Johnston's cause as a useful weapon with which to assail the president. They introduced and passed a congressional resolution to publish the correspondence between Davis and Johnston, hoping to expose the president's poor management of the campaign and to embarrass the administration. Throughout the summer and fall, the personal feud was transformed into a political issue that threatened to tear the Confederacy apart. The dispute became a protracted guerrilla war of private letters, official reports, newspaper editorials, and backstage political intrigue that gathered momentum until it was national in scope and dominated political disputes in Richmond. Johnston would have denied that he was engaged in a political battle with the president. He would have explained that he was only defending his professional honor against an unjustified attack. Nevertheless, his willingness to accept the aid of Davis's foes made him a political player, whether he would admit it or not.⁷

The fight burst into the open in early August, when Pemberton submitted his official report on the Vicksburg campaign directly to Cooper and Davis, bypassing Johnston, his nominal commander. Johnston should have anticipated that Pemberton's report would not be kind. In addition to Pemberton's studied coolness at their last meeting, Johnston had been warned by Wigfall to expect no justice from that quarter. "Let me warn you against Pemberton," Wigfall wrote from Richmond. "The moment he was whipped at Edward's station (Baker's Creek) he wrote to the President that he had made the fight against his own judgment & under positive orders from you." Reminding Johnston that his decision to shield Bragg had produced unhappy results, Wigfall begged him not to shield Pemberton in the same way:

"Bragg may be worthy of your friendship. Pemberton is not. . . ."[8]

It was not a complete surprise, therefore, that Pemberton's official report placed full responsibility for the fall of Vicksburg on Johnston. Nearly a hundred pages long, the report was a detailed dissertation in which Pemberton attempted to justify every move he had made in the campaign. With tortured logic, he constructed a scenario in which Johnston's order of May 13 to attack the Federals at Clinton emerged as the crucial mistake of the campaign. Although he had believed Johnston's order to be foolish, Pemberton wrote, he had nevertheless dutifully prepared to move, but not in the direction Johnston had ordered: "I took measures for an advance movement at once; not, it is true, directly toward Clinton, but in the only direction which, from my knowledge of the circumstances surrounding me, I thought offered a possibility of success." Pemberton attributed his subsequent defeat to this movement southward, which he saw as Johnston's fault. He concluded that "the advance movement of the army from Edward's Depot on the afternoon of May 15 was made against my judgment, in opposition to my previously expressed intentions, and to the subversion of my matured plans."[9]

In Richmond, Davis studied Pemberton's lengthy report carefully, sending out periodically for copies of the official correspondence for comparison. At length, he found Pemberton's explanation entirely credible, mainly because he was predisposed to assume the worst about Johnston. Davis kept the contents of the report a secret until he had had a chance to digest it. Wigfall tried "several times" to get his hands on a copy, but failed. Eventually, portions found their way into print in the Richmond *Sentinel*. Beyond a doubt, Davis or one of his aides deliberately leaked the report. The *Sentinel* was the only Richmond daily still consistently friendly to the administration. From the day that news of Vicksburg's surrender arrived in Richmond, the *Sentinel* had pointed an editorial finger accusingly at Johnston: "The people are asking, and the world will ask, where was General Johnston, and what part did he perform in this grand tragedy. In answer it will be said that with an army larger than won the first battle of Manassas, he made not a motion, he struck not a blow, for the relief of Vicksburg. For nearly seven weeks he sat down in sound of the conflict, and he fired not a gun . . . he has done no more than to sit by and see Vicksburg fall, and send us the news."[10]

To combat this version of events, Wigfall made liberal use of Johnston's private letters and reports, circulating them among sympathetic colleagues. "I showed your letter to [Thomas J.] Semmes of Louisiana, [Henry C.] Barnett of Kentucky & others who were friends of yours, who promised to see that justice was done to you," Wigfall reported from Richmond. He also sought to win over Secretary of War Seddon, reporting that the Secretary was at first "evidently disposed to throw the whole blame on you." Seddon asserted that Davis had ordered Johnston to attack Grant's lines *even if he did not believe it could be done successfully,* and that Johnston had simply refused to obey orders. Wigfall retorted that if that were true, then Davis "should fall on his knees & thank God that [Johnston] had saved the blood of thousands in which he [Davis] had wickedly intended to immerse his hands in order to cover up the disaster which had been brought upon the country by his own big headedness & perverseness. . . ." Wigfall noted pointedly that Johnston "had friends who would stand by" him, and warned Seddon that if the administration attempted to make Johnston a scapegoat, "I intended to be heard & on the floor of the Senate from which place I could be heard throughout the Confederacy." He maintained that after the war Johnston's papers would be published, and "the wisdom of [Johnston's] views and the stupidity of Davis [would] be exposed." Of course, such threats did little to heal the breach.[11]

In addition to defending Johnston in the halls of Congress and the War Department, Wigfall sought to promote his point of view in the Richmond papers. If the *Sentinel* wanted to publish the administration version of events, there were three papers in Richmond willing to publish a contrary view. The *Whig and Public Advertiser* had foreborne criticizing the president during the first year and a half of the war, but by 1863 its editors had become increasingly caustic. Even the reputable *Enquirer*, the most respectable and restrained of the Richmond dailies, had begun to express doubts. But it was the *Examiner*, under the editorial leadership of the misanthropic John Moncure Daniel, that led the charge against the president. By 1863, Daniel was taking advantage of every opportunity to attack the Davis administration. Through July and into August, the *Examiner* printed a number of articles excoriating Pemberton (and, by implication, Davis) for the debacle in the West. "Taking a view of the whole campaign," Daniel wrote, "we can only come to the conclusion that General Pemberton was outgeneraled in the most glaring manner by General Grant." As for Johnston, "his brave little army was expected to work miracles and accomplish impossibilities; and because it did not, he, General Johnston, has been roundly censured by the *quasi* Presidential organ at Richmond." Johnston was grateful for the public support and expressed his gratitude to Wigfall, whom he assumed had written the articles. Wigfall denied authorship, but he remained the architect of the campaign.[12]

Not surprisingly, Davis and his supporters found the attacks of unfriendly newspapers infuriating. To all concerned it was clear that the editorial wars were less about Pemberton or Johnston than Davis and his management of the war. The *Sentinel* offered an analogy that may have originated with Davis himself: "Suppose that in Gen. Lee's army every brigade had its printing press. Suppose that these were directed by men who, from whatever cause, were hostile to Gen. Lee, or thought very little of him. Suppose that every morning they scattered their publications through the army. . . ?" The attacks on Davis, the *Sentinel* declared, were "but the reckless indulgence of prejudice and of a spirit *determined* to find fault, unless indeed it is laboring to prepare and incite the people to murder and revolution."[13]

The newspaper war was not confined to the capital. By now the whole country was divided into pro- and anti-administration camps, and support for Joseph E. Johnston had become one of the ways newspapers and individuals declared their opposition to the president. In late summer, several western newspapers published a letter written by Johnston's medical officer, Dr. D. W. Yandell, to Hardee's medical officer. Yandell's letter contained a summary of the Vicksburg campaign which praised Johnston and emphasized Pemberton's refusal to obey orders. Moreover, this letter—some five thousand words long—contained detailed information that could only have come from official papers; could only have come, in fact, from Johnston's headquarters. Davis suspected immediately that the letter was part of a deliberate campaign. Without proof, however, he could only write to Johnston demanding that he take "proper action" to punish Yandell for surreptitiously obtaining and disseminating official documents. Johnston wrote back that Yandell had not acquired the official letters "surreptitiously," as Davis charged, but that crowded conditions in the army had required the doctor to live in Johnston's headquarters tent during the campaign, and Yandell had been a witness when Johnston dictated the letters. Davis was not entirely satisfied. At the bottom of Johnston's letter, he wrote: "This shows that the information was not obtained surreptitiously, but does not affect the question of improper use."[14]

As a soldier, Johnston did not put his faith in Wigfall's politics or the *Examiner*'s editorials for vindication. As far as he was concerned, the proper forum to resolve the issue was a formal court of inquiry, composed of fellow soldiers who could examine all the correspondence with a professional and objective eye. He fully expected that such a tribunal would vindicate his conduct of the campaign in Mississippi, even though he suspected that the court would be "packed" by Davis allies determined "to find something in my conduct which may furnish ground for a harsh paragraph. . . ." He was confirmed in these suspicions by a letter from Confederate Congressman Robert Augustus Toombs, a former brigade commander and now an avowed enemy of Davis, who warned him that he had much to fear from such a court, especially if he were not present to defend himself. Toombs's letter was marked "Private Confidential." It informed Johnston that a friend in Richmond, who was "in all things to be trusted," had asked Toombs to warn Johnston "that it was extremely important" for him to be present at the Court of Inquiry. Toombs wrote that this friend "did not give his reasons", but the implication was unmistakable: Davis and his cronies were planning a drumhead court-martial that would pin all the blame for the loss of Vicksburg on Johnston. A few days later, Johnston received a formal summons, and he left at once for Atlanta to defend himself. But when he arrived, he discovered that the Court had been "indefinitely suspended." To Wigfall he suggested that "the administration has thought better of the court of inquiry & determined that it shall not meet again. This will be a serious injury to me for I have been attacked vehemently by this administration itself." Wigfall maintained that he was "not surprised to hear that the court was adjourned." Davis, he said, did not want the public to learn that it had been his idea to send ten thousand troops away from Bragg on the eve of Murfrees-boro.[15]

Denied his day in court, Johnston saw little alternative but to respond to Pemberton's charges directly in a revised report on the campaign. Dated November 1 from Meridian, Mississippi, Johnston's amended report set out to refute Pemberton's arguments one by one, though he devoted most of his effort to refuting Pemberton's assertion that his defeat at Champion's Hill had been Johnston's fault. To be sure, Johnston had ordered Pemberton to move, but he had ordered him to move *east*. Pemberton had ignored that order and marched off to the *south*. Johnston marvelled at the "new military principle that, when an officer disobeys a positive order of his superior, that superior becomes responsible for any measure his subordinate may choose to substitute for that ordered. . . ." He stated categorically that Pemberton himself was the individual most responsible for the defeat. "General Pemberton's belief that Vicksburg was his base rendered his ruin inevitable. . . . His disasters were due not merely to his entangling himself with the advancing columns of a superior and unobserved enemy, but to his evident determination to be besieged in Vicksburg, instead of maneuvering to prevent a siege."

Johnston found it difficult to attack a fellow officer. Pemberton had been a friend in the Old Army; he had served briefly on Johnston's own staff in Virginia. Now Johnston felt compelled to discredit him, but it was not easy for him. "In this report I have been compelled to enter into many details and to make some animadversions upon the conduct of General Pemberton," he wrote. "The one was no pleasant task; the other a most painful duty. Both have been forced upon me by the official report of General Pemberton, made to the War Department instead of to me, to whom it was due." Because they had been circulated in the press, Pemberton's claims had forced Johnston to offer this new report, "to show that in his short campaign General Pemberton made not a single movement in obedience to my orders and regarded none of my instructions. . . ." Perhaps to ensure that his report had the widest possible circulation, Johnston sent a copy of it to Wigfall. Of course, this also made him vulnerable to charges that he was playing politics, for Johnston had to expect that Wigfall would make it available to his anti-administration colleagues, which, indeed, he did.[16]

By now the breach between Johnston and Davis was unbridgeable, although officially their relations remained stiffly cordial. In mid-September Johnston received Davis's reply to his letter of August 8, in which Johnston had denied committing "a serious military offense." Davis's letter was intended to bring the quarrel to a close: "I now cheerfully accept your admission of your 'misapprehension' . . . the mistake made by you . . . being now admitted, it is not necessary to dwell on these extraneous subjects." Johnston described this letter as "the coolest piece of impudence I have ever read." But Davis's coolness was for his official correspondence only; in private he was less restrained. Wigfall reported from Richmond: "I did not see Davis but heard that he was blind as an adder with rage & ready to bite himself." That fall, Mary Chesnut, whose husband was on Davis's staff, confided to her diary that "the president detests Joe Johnston for all the trouble he has given him. And General Joe returns the compliment with compound interest. His hatred of Jeff Davis amounts to a religion. With him it colors all things."[17]

The prolonged dispute contributed little to the Confederate cause. Perhaps if Johnston had swallowed hard and accepted Davis's pedantic letter about abandoning his duties back in July, that might have been the end of it. But had Johnston been capable of doing that, he would also have been capable of writing the daily letters full of detailed information and respectful solicitations that would have convinced Davis from the start that Johnston was a reliable lieutenant. Those who got a long best with Davis were men who were willing to subordinate their own views and personalities to the president—men like Benjamin, Bragg, and Pemberton. Even Robert E. Lee became skilled in drafting the detailed, earnest letters that assuaged Davis's jealousy and suspicion.[18] Johnston could not do it. He would have considered such behavior an abandonment of his professional responsibility. So he kept his own counsel, made his own decisions, and stood ready to bear the consequences. In effect, Johnston's concept of professional responsibility clashed with Davis's commitment to micro-management.

Still, this clash of personalities might not have been fatal but for Johnston's alliance with Wigfall. Johnston turned to Wigfall because he knew he would find a sympathetic audience. But he was not so naive as to fail to perceive that he was, in effect, supplying his friend with political ammunition for his war with the administration. Wigfall wrote him plainly in June, even before the fall of Vicksburg, to advise him to keep copies of all his papers and "send me copies to be used when & as I see fit." Wigfall made no secret of his motives. He sought to wrest control of the government from Davis, whose "bad judgement & bad temper" would ruin the country. "We have fear for the future," he wrote to Johnston, "unless he can be controlled." In accepting Wigfall's support, and sending him copies of official letters, Johnston stepped beyond the bounds of military professionalism—even by nineteenth-century standards.[19]

Throughout the summer and early fall of 1863, as the political feud festered in Richmond, Johnston found little else to keep him occupied in his reduced command. The Yankee army under Grant and Sherman had not pursued him into Mississippi; instead, the enemy evacuated Jackson, returned to the river, and withdrew northward. Only the "Sherman monuments"—charred brick chimneys to show where houses once stood—served as reminders of their passing. The vortex of the war moved away from Mississippi, and Johnston's Department became a backwater. Soon he was beset by calls for reinforcements from elsewhere in the Confederacy—from the garrisons of

JOSEPH E. JOHNSTON in the uniform of a Confederate full general. This was the most widely circulated photograph of Johnston, the source for countless wartime and postwar etchings and composite portraits. *(Library of Congress)*

JUDGE PETER JOHNSTON, Joe's father, as he appears in the official portrait that still hangs above the county judicial bench in the Washington Country Courthouse, Abingdon, Virginia. Peter Johnston served in the Legion of Light Horse Harry Lee during the Revolution, and afterward for twenty years as Circuit Court judge in Washington County. (*Washington County Historical Society*)

PANECILLO, the Johnston family home in Abingdon, where Joe grew up. This photo, taken many years after the home had passed its prime, does little justice to the original edifice. The house no longer stands. (*Courtesy L. C. Angle, Jr.*)

THE UNITED STATES MILITARY ACADEMY AT WEST POINT as it appeared in 1828, when Johnston was a cadet. The cadet barracks surround the plain, which constituted both campground and drill field; old Fort Putnam crowns the hill to the upper right. *(Painting by W. G. Wall, Courtesy of the West Point Museum Collections, United States Military Academy, West Point, New York)*

COLONEL SYLVANUS THAYER, Superintendent of the Military Academy during Johnston's years there, and architect of the West Point system. *(Painting by Robert Weir, Courtesy of the West Point Museum Collections, United States Military Academy, West Point, New York)*

LIEUTENANT COLONEL JOSEPH E. JOHN-
STON at the time of the Mexican War. Already balding in his thirties, Johnston was
sufficiently vain about his appearance to
brush his hair forward over the crown.
This etching is based on a photograph.
(Library of Congress)

THE ASSAULT ON CHA-
PULTEPEC , September
12, 1847, depicted in
two artists' concep-
tions. In the upper
drawing, Johnston's
voltigeurs scramble up
the slope to the walls of
the citadel; in the bot-
tom painting, the main
assault force is poised
for attack, scaling lad-
ders at the ready. *(Both
National Archives)*

THE DESTRUCTION OF THE RAILROAD BRIDGE OVER THE POTOMAC at Harpers Ferry, depicted in an artist's sketch printed in *Harper's Weekly* (July 1861). In his first important command as a Confederate general, Johnston agonized over his decision to withdraw from Harpers Ferry. Even then, critics complained that he left much useful material behind. *(National Archives)*

THE CONFEDERATE LINES AT CENTREVILLE IN 1862 sported so-called Quaker guns—logs shaped and painted to resemble cannon, in an effort to convince the Federals of false strength. Johnston withdrew from Centreville in mid-March 1862, falling back behind the Rappahannock. *(Library of Congress)*

JEFFERSON DAVIS as Secretary of War in the 1850s. Davis returned from Mexico a war hero, and was appointed to fill the Senate term of the recently deceased Jesse Spreight. In 1853, Franklin Pierce appointed him Secretary of War, in which capacity he refused to confirm Johnston's brevet promotion to colonel. *(Library of Congress)*

JUDAH P. BENJAMIN, Davis's closest political adviser and staunchest ally. Benjamin served Davis as Confederate Secretary of War in 1861–62, and was an intolerable irritant to Johnston. When the Senate refused to confirm Benjamin as Secretary of War in March 1862, Davis outfoxed his political critics by making him Secretary of State. Loyal to the end, Benjamin was the only cabinet member who agreed with Davis that the war should be continued after Appomattox. *(Library of Congress)*

JOHNSTON'S AIDE JIMMY WASHINGTON, posing with his West Point classmate George Armstrong Custer behind Federal lines on the day of the Battle of Seven Pines (May 31, 1862). To find out what had happened to Longstreet's column, Johnston ordered Washington to ride out along the Nine Mile Road. Jimmy rode eastward until he was captured by Federal pickets. Behind Federal lines, he encountered Custer, who insisted that they pose together for this photograph. *(Library of Congress)*

LOUIS T. WIGFALL, Confederate senator from Texas, and Johnston's staunchest supporter. William H. Russell, *The Times* (London) correspondent, thought Wigfall's gaze unforgettable: "an eye pitiless in anger which now and then sought to conceal its expression beneath half-closed lid, and then burst out again with an angry glare, as if disdaining concealment." *(Library of Congress)*

CONFEDERATE COMMANDERS
IN THE WEST

JOHN C. PEMBERTON, defender of Vicksburg, was Philadelphia-born but loyal to the South. Promoted rapidly to lieutenant general, he was determined to hold Vicksburg in 1863. Johnston urged Pemberton to abandon the city in order to save his army. Pemberton refused, yet he blamed Johnston for upsetting his plans to defend the city. In the end, he lost both. *(National Archives)*

BRAXTON BRAGG, while in command of the Army of Tennessee in 1862–63, feuded with most of his subordinates and managed to alienate almost everyone except Jefferson Davis and Joseph E. Johnston. Johnston stood by him despite his unpopularity, but when Johnston himself was in command of the army in 1864, Bragg helped orchestrate his dismissal. Ironically, Bragg finished the war back under Johnston's command, leading a corps at the Battle of Bentonville. *(Library of Congress)*

CORPS COMMANDERS IN THE ARMY OF TENNESSE

WILLIAM J. HARDEE, "Old Reliable," was the most senior of Johnston's corps commanders in the Army of Tennessee. He had commanded the army briefly in the last weeks of 1863, and fully expected to be Johnston's strong right arm during the 1864 campaign. *(National Archives)*

JOSEPH WHEELER was the army's cavalry commander. Young, dashing, but irresponsible, Wheeler disliked the routine activities of patrol and reconnaissance, preferring dramatic cavalry assaults such as the one he executed at Varnell's Station in late May 1864. *(Library of Congress)*

JOHN BELL HOOD instead became Johnston's closest confidant during the long campaign from Dalton to the Chattahoochee. Unknown to Johnston, Hood was writing letters to Davis and to Bragg (by then Davis's military adviser) criticizing Johnston's conduct of the campaign. *(Library of Congress)*

LEONIDAS POLK, Episcopalian Bishop of Louisiana, who became a Confederate lieutenant general. Well liked by Johnston and Davis, he was an indifferent troop commander. His death atop Pine Mountain on June 14, 1864, was important largely for its effect on Confederate morale. *(National Archives)*

FEDERAL MAJOR GENERAL WILLIAM
T. SHERMAN called Johnston "my
special opponent." With the single
exception of his ill-advised assault
at Kennesaw Mountain, Sherman
executed a nearly flawless campaign
in Georgia: keeping Johnston off
balance, swinging around his
flanks, and maintaining a critical logistic support line back to his base
in Tennessee. One of the new breed
of modern generals, Sherman's
fierceness and determination are evident in this photograph. *(National Archives)*

THE GREAT SNOWBALL FIGHT at Dalton in March 1864 gave the soldiers a chance to work
off some energy, and demonstrated the improvement of troop morale after the defeat at
Missionary Ridge the previous season. *(Sketch by Alfred Waud, Library of Congress)*

THE BATTLE OF RESACA, May 15–16, 1864, is depicted as a meeting engagement in this drawing by Alfred Waud; that is, the Confederates had no time to dig in before having to stand against Sherman's arriving troops. (From *Century* magazine, 1887)

PHOTOGRAPH OF THE RESACA BATTLEFIELD after the battle, showing that the Confederate soldiers scratched lines out of the soil over the course of the two-day battle. *(National Archives)*

FALLING BACK OVER THE ETOWAH RIVER, the Confederate army dug in near Allatoona Pass. This photo from the Confederate lines shows the railroad bridge over the Etowah that was rebuilt by the Federals after the Confederates burned it. *(National Archives)*

THE ROUGH TERRAIN AROUND NEW HOPE CHURCH made the alignment of units difficult, and the series of battles there reminded some of a "Big Indian fight." This photograph of a portion of the Confederate lines omits one major element: the mud that was the product of almost constant rain. *(Library of Congress)*

A FANCIFUL DEPICTION of the Battle of Kennesaw Mountain (June 27, 1864) that shows an Alplike mountain on the wrong side of the Confederate lines, and rank upon rank of impeccably uniformed Confederate soldiers. The only accurate element is the close range of the action, which resulted in heavy casualties. *(Library of Congress)*

THE VIEW FROM CONFEDERATE LINES on Kennesaw Mountain emphasizes their commanding position. *(Library of Congress)*

THE ORIGINAL TELEGRAM handed to Johnston relieving him of command on July 17, 1864. The text reads: "Lt Gen J B Hood has been Commissioned to the Temporary rank of General under the late law of Congress. I am directed by the Secy of War to inform you that as you have failed to arrest the advance of the Enemy to the vicinity of Atlanta, far in the interior of Georgia and express no confidence that you can defeat or repel him, you are hereby relieved from the Command of the Army & Dept of Tenn which you will immediately turn over to Genl Hood— S Cooper, A & I Genl." *(Huntington Library)*

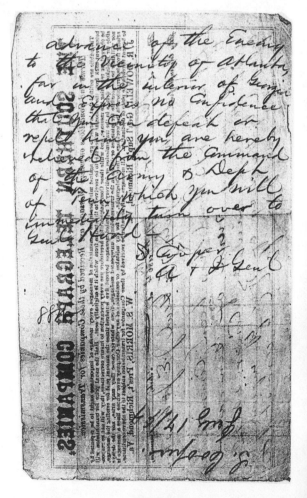

THE HOME OF JAMES BENNETT was the site of the meeting between Johnston and Sherman in April 1865 that led to the surrender of the Confederacy's last major army. Johnston tried to "make one job of it" by including all Confederate troops in the surrender and suggesting a political solution. When that was rejected by the U.S. government, Johnston instead surrendered his own army. Davis never forgave Johnston for capitulating while still commanding an army in the field. *(Library of Congress)*

JOSEPH E. JOHNSTON as a successful businessman and congressman in the 1870s. *(Library of Congress)*

JOHNSTON AND LEE discuss old times in Savannah in 1870, only a few months before Lee's death. *(Library of Congress)*

Charleston, Savannah, and Mobile, and particularly from Bragg in Tennessee, where Rosecrans had become active once again.

Tennessee presented the gravest immediate danger. Even during the siege of Vicksburg, Rosecrans had begun to increase the pressure on Bragg's army at Tullahoma. Braxton Bragg was no more popular within the army in July than he had been in April, and his performance in the face of this new threat did little to boost the confidence of his subordinates. He deployed his cavalry poorly so that his understanding of enemy movements was vague, he issued unclear and confusing orders to his corps commanders, and he seemed to spend most of his time looking for ways to discredit his detractors inside the army rather than finding an effective means to defeat the enemy.

When Rosecrans advanced southward in June, Bragg fell back to Chattanooga, arriving there on July 4, the day of Vicksburg's capitulation. Immediately he called for reinforcements. His first suggestion was that Johnston should bring his entire army to Chattanooga, join forces with Bragg, and together they would drive Rosecrans out of the state. Johnston was willing enough, but Bragg backed down when he learned that Johnston had only about eighteen thousand men, not enough, he thought, to ensure success.[20]

In the first week of August, Johnston dispatched a brigade to Savannah in response to a request from Samuel Cooper. It is typical of Johnston's way of doing business that although he complied with this request immediately, he did not bother to report his compliance to Richmond. As a result, Cooper sent him a second telegram instructing him to "answer immediately." Later that month, Bragg, too, asked Johnston to send him reinforcements. He wrote that he was under threat of imminent attack from both Rosecrans and Burnside, and he begged Johnston to send whatever support he could. Johnston was willing to help, but since Bragg was no longer in his Department, he checked first with Cooper to make sure that he was authorized to send troops across departmental boundaries. Once Cooper assured him that he could do so, Johnston sent Bragg two of his four divisions (those of John C. Breckinridge and W. H. T. Walker), a total of about nine thousand infantry—virtually half of his effective force. He notified Bragg that the troops were on their way, but warned him that due to the wretched condition of the railroad it might take five days or more for them to arrive. He also noted that "This is a loan to be promptly returned." A week later Bragg asked for more help. Johnston had no more troops he could properly spare, but because Bragg had claimed that the safety of Atlanta was at stake, he sent another two brigades, about 2,600 men.[21]

It is consistent with Johnston's long-standing commitment to the principle of concentration that he was willing to denude his own Department to reinforce Bragg. The deductions left him with two small infantry divisions (one of which had only two brigades) and Stephen D. Lee's cavalry, a total of perhaps ten thousand men. This was little enough to ensure the safety of his Department, yet he later told Bragg that if he expected a battle, he would "send every infantry soldier I have." The infantry Johnston had left he needed not only to shield Mississippi and Alabama from Federal probes, but to serve as a ready reserve for the defense of Mobile, Alabama, which now became Johnston's primary responsibility.[22]

After the fall of New Orleans in April 1862, Mobile had become the chief Confederate port on the Gulf coast. The city was well protected by a series of forts and a small naval flotilla, but the defenders had to combat serious morale problems as much as the enemy. The general depression that settled over the South after the twin defeats of Gettysburg and Vicksburg was particularly evident at Mobile. Johnston's old Mexican War friend Dabney Maury, who was in command at Mobile, advised Johnston that Alabama troops should not be allowed to serve at Mobile because the temptation to desert was too great. In addition, inflation was eating away at the money supply, and some merchants were refusing to accept Confederate dollars. Profiteers and speculators bought up cotton at depressed prices, then sold it to the highest bidders, including Yankees, accepting payment only in gold. A former judge wrote Johnston from Mobile that "hundreds of persons . . . are openly engaged in this unlawful traffic with the enemy." Instead of resisting them out of patriotism, local troops charged a fee to ignore it. Bands of deserters roamed the countryside, levying contributions on the citizens. With his "army" reduced to five brigades, about all Johnston could do was encourage Maury to keep the garrison at Mobile busy building fortifications, and maintain a ready reserve within a day's train ride of the city in case of a Federal attack.[23]

Meanwhile, in Tennessee Bragg's fears of a Federal offensive proved justified. In late August, Rosecrans began advancing southward, crossing the Tennessee River west of Chattanooga on August 29. A week later, Bragg evacuated the city and retired some twenty-two miles south to Lafayette, Georgia. Believing that his enemy was in flight, Rosecrans flung his three corps in pursuit. By the second week of September the Federal army was spread out over a wide front in North Georgia, vulnerable to a well-timed counterstroke. The wherewithal to deliver such a stroke was in fact now available to Bragg. In addition to the twelve thousand men sent by Johnston, nine thousand men under Simon Bolivar Buckner arrived from East Tennessee. Then in mid-September the first elements of two divisions ordered to the West by Davis from Robert E. Lee's Army of Northern Virginia began to appear. This last reinforcement represented a major concession by Lee, who sent his most famous corps commander, James Longstreet, and two full divisions—those of John Bell Hood and Lafayette McLaws, veterans of the Peach Orchard and Little Round Top. All in all, by September 15, Bragg could field an army of some sixty thousand men. Bragg, however, had trouble coordinating the movements of his various corps commanders, and he vacillated for several crucial days before issuing the orders that brought on the Battle of Chickamauga.

History ranks Chickamauga as the one great Confederate victory in the West. To be sure, the Federal army was roughly handled, and the victorious

Confederates camped on the field of battle. But the tactical victory yielded little strategically thanks largely to the firm stand of Major General George H. Thomas (known ever after as "the Rock of Chickamauga"), who prevented a Federal rout. The Federal army remained intact, and it continued to hold Chattanooga. Bragg followed up the retreating Federals, but he lacked the strength to drive the enemy from the city, so he dug in on the high ground to the south and declared Chattanooga under siege.

Johnston was pleased by Bragg's victory. He ordered Maury to proclaim the news to the defenders of Mobile to boost their morale, and he wrote Bragg a congratulatory telegram. Still, given his recent reinforcements, Johnston had expected Bragg to win a great victory, and he was not hugely impressed by what had been achieved.[24] Bragg's "siege" was precarious at best, for the Federal army inside Chattanooga was nearly as large as his own. Once again, Bragg called upon Johnston for reinforcements, but now Johnston had none to spare. He did, however, offer to use his cavalry in an effort to cut the Federal supply lines into Chattanooga.

In theory, there were over nine thousand cavalry in Johnston's Department, but these numbers were hugely inflated. Most of the cavalry were partisans who operated on a part-time basis, going home when there was no imminent action. In addition, Stephen D. Lee, Johnston's cavalry commander, who was distantly related to Robert E. Lee, reported that his troopers were poorly armed, had very limited ammunition, and almost no military discipline. Nevertheless, Johnston ordered Lee to take 2,500 men into Middle Tennessee "to break the railroads in rear of Rosecrans' army," giving special attention to the bridges over the Duck and Elk Rivers. He also sent Brigadier General James R. Chalmers to raid the Memphis & Charleston Railroad. To Bragg, he wrote: "I see no other mode in which I can help you. . . . I will do all I can; only suggest."[25]

These raiders might have done serious damage to the Federal supply network in Tennessee. Johnston never forgot that it was Van Dorn's raid on Holly Springs that had led to Grant's withdrawal from northern Mississippi the year before. But when Lee arrived in Tennessee, he discovered that Bragg had sent General Joseph Wheeler's cavalry into the same area for the same purpose, and Wheeler was not particularly interested in cooperating. Worse, Wheeler was being pursued by seven thousand Federal cavalry whose presence in Middle Tennessee required Lee's troopers to spend more time eluding the Yankees than destroying railroads. Finally, with Lee up in Tennessee, the Federals sent their own cavalry probes into Mississippi. A Yankee force under John A. Logan raided Canton, Brownsville, and Clinton in early October, "burning in every direction." Johnston sent his tiny cavalry reserve to intercept Logan, but there was not much more than he could do. "I had not enough horses for my little force," he explained to Longstreet.[26]

Things did not go well for Bragg at Chattanooga. Davis had hoped that the animosity against Bragg would die down once Hardee was transferred to Johnston's command in Mississippi. But Bragg continued to antagonize his other two corps commanders, D. H. Hill and Leonidas Polk, and soon he was feuding with both Buckner and Longstreet as well. Complaints from Bragg's corps commanders led Davis to send his trusted aide James Chesnut on a tour of the western theatre. Chesnut found the hostility toward Bragg as strong as ever; he also reported that "every honest man he saw out west thought well of Joe Johnston." Almost without exception the senior officers in Bragg's army thought that Bragg should be dismissed and command of the army given to Johnston. Determined to resist such a step, Davis decided to come West to see for himself.[27]

The president arrived in Atlanta in the second week of October; from there, he travelled north to Marietta to confer with Bragg. As evidence of just how out of touch he was with sentiment in the Army of Tennessee, Davis brought John Pemberton along with him. He was hoping to convince Bragg to take Pemberton on as a corps commander. Cooper hinted broadly to Bragg that Pemberton "possesses the confidence of the Executive . . . and is believed to have been unjustly assailed." But as much as Bragg wanted to please the president, he knew that the army would not stand for it. Pemberton even talked with Bragg's chief of staff, W. W. Mackall, about getting command of a division. Mackall told him bluntly "there was not a division in this army that would be willing to receive him." Finally, Pemberton settled for a job as a lieutenant colonel of artillery, where he stayed until the end of the war.[28]

Davis met with Bragg on October 9, and he presided over a general conference of the army's senior officers—including Bragg—that night. After a short discussion of the military situation, Longstreet openly raised the issue of Bragg's competence. He asserted that Bragg had handled the army poorly, that he had thrown away a chance for victory after Chickamauga, and he called for Bragg's removal. The other corps commanders, speaking in turn, generally supported Longstreet's view. But Davis had already determined to sustain Bragg. Before he left Bragg's headquarters, he issued a public statement praising Bragg, and privately he assured the army commander that he had the full confidence of the administration. Mackall, who had by now resigned as Bragg's chief of staff, reported the results of the conference to Johnston.[29]

Bragg's behavior over the next month confirmed suspicions that Davis had also privately authorized him to purge the army of his enemies. Bragg began by relieving D. H. Hill, whom he now singled out as the scapegoat for the lost opportunities of Chickamauga. Then Bragg transferred Polk to Johnston in Mississippi, essentially trading him for Hardee, whom he now decided was not so bad after all. Finally, he dramatically reduced the size and scope of Buckner's command while reorganizing the army. None of these decisions helped strengthen the army, which was still engaged in its siege of the Federals in Chattanooga. But Bragg's most tragic blunder was his handling of James Longstreet.

Longstreet had come West with some expectation of being asked to exercise supreme command. He thought little of Bragg and did not keep his opinions a secret. Bragg reciprocated, and by October he found Longstreet's presence nearly intolerable. By mutual agreement, these two decided that Longstreet should operate independently in eastern Tennessee, where he would be outside Bragg's command authority. In early November, therefore, Longstreet took fifteen thousand men eastward toward Knoxville. This was a particularly foolish dispersion of force, for it left Bragg with only about 36,-000 men to besiege a Federal army that had grown to nearly 80,000.

While Bragg embarked on his vendetta against his detractors, Davis travelled on to Meridian to confer with Johnston. He arrived on October 20; immediately, he and Johnston left for an inspection tour through Mississippi and Alabama, stopping at Jackson on the 21st, at Mobile on the 23rd, and at Montgomery on the 24th. There is little surviving evidence of what the two men discussed during their three days together, but it is certain that the conversations were rigidly formal.[30]

After Davis departed for Richmond, Johnston returned to his headquarters in Meridian, where he remained throughout the fall and early winter. Lydia joined him around November 1 and set up housekeeping. It was a remarkably calm existence. They occupied "a little cabin" outside the town, which Lydia made into a home. She even managed to receive a shipment of new clothes that had been smuggled through the blockade, and wrote Charlotte that it included "a box from Paris filled with the most delicious *under* garments of all sorts." As for Johnston, he told Wigfall that he had "been having a very quiet time since July. Almost a peace establishment." If he was disappointed that the war had passed him by, he was stoic about it. "This is the sort of command I expect to have during the remainder of the war," he said resignedly. "The temper exhibited toward me makes it very unlikely that I shall ever again occupy an important position."[31] He was wrong, for the rush of events outside Chattanooga in late October and early November so thoroughly discredited Bragg that once again Johnston began to be talked of as his replacement.

In late October, the Federals succeeded in opening up a precarious supply line—the Cracker Line, they called it—into Chattanooga. That meant that the Federals could not be starved into surrender as Pemberton had been at Vicksburg. Worse yet, it meant additional reinforcements for the "besieged" Federals, commanded now by Grant and Sherman. Whereas Bragg's numerical strength had dropped to 36,000 with Longstreet's departure on November 5, the Federal army now numbered upwards of 80,000 or 90,000. On November 24, a division under Major General Joe Hooker seized Lookout Mountain on the Confederate left, thus effectively breaking the siege. But the real disaster came the next day, when Sherman attacked the Confederate right and George Thomas's men assailed the center of the rebel line on Missionary Ridge. The demoralized Confederates offered only a weak resistance before fleeing. The whole army soon gave way to shameful flight. Bragg was at a loss. "The disastrous panic is inexplicable," he wrote to Johnston.[32]

After the debacle of Lookout Mountain and Missionary Ridge, even Bragg knew that he could no longer hold onto command of the Army of Tennessee. He submitted his resignation on November 28. Davis, too, faced reality and accepted it. He appointed William Hardee, the senior corps commander, to succeed him. But Hardee made it clear at once that he would take the job only on a temporary basis. He desired—and fully expected—that Davis would soon appoint Johnston as the permanent commander. Polk, too, commented that "General Joe Johnston is the person to whom you should offer that command." Davis resisted. Desperately, he sought alternatives. Only four men had sufficient rank: Cooper, who at sixty-six would never again command in the field; Lee, who could not be spared from Virginia; Beauregard and Johnston. Davis distrusted Beauregard even more than Johnston. In the end he had no alternative. As Mackall told Johnston: "I never did believe Mr. D would give you your place as long as he can help it, but he can't. The army wants you . . . he will be forced to yield."[33]

At the crucial cabinet meeting in December where the issue was decided, Seddon formally proposed Johnston as Bragg's replacement. Benjamin argued against it on the grounds that Johnston was too defensively minded and had not proven himself a capable leader. Davis, too, expressed his doubts. But Davis's problem was a lack of alternatives. Time after time the discussion returned to Johnston, who eventually emerged as the only viable candidate. Finally, with enormous reluctance, Davis dropped his opposition and bowed to the inevitable. The universal pressure from the army, from Congress, from the press, and from the general population forced him nominate Johnston. In a terse telegram, Davis ordered Johnston to turn the Army of Mississippi over to Polk and proceed to Dalton.[34]

Wigfall was triumphant: "Davis has at last been forced to do you justice and I trust in fact that you will not again decline the offer." Johnston had no intention of declining. As he wrote to Wigfall, he had never declined a position that Davis had offered him. He had refrained from relieving Bragg in the spring, but as a professional soldier he would undertake any assignment Davis might order him to take. "The president is, by the constitution, the judge of the Military Merit of the officers. I shall, therefore, while the war lasts, serve to the best of my ability, wherever he may place me." Johnston did not share Wigfall's sense of triumph; he felt no vindication or victory at his appointment, for he knew with what reluctance Davis had sent him his orders. He spent another few days in Mississippi to brief Polk and to turn over his command, then he boarded a train for Georgia. Lydia stayed behind. "I cannot say which feeling is strongest," she wrote to Charlotte, "regret that . . . we are separated again . . . or pleasure that the acclaim of his friends have [sic] untied his hands & he may yet do his country some good in its hour of need."[35]

His greatest opportunity, and his greatest trial, were still ahead.

CHAPTER SEVENTEEN

The Army of Tennessee

Two days after Christmas, 1863, Joseph E. Johnston announced to the Army of Tennessee that he was its new commander. That same day he conducted an informal review of his new command by riding through the camps. One soldier, looking up from the ranks, later described what he saw:

> Fancy, if you please, a man about fifty years old, rather small of stature, but firmly and compactly built, an open and honest countenance, and a keen but restless black eye, that seemed to read your very inmost thoughts. In his dress he was a perfect dandy. He ever wore the very finest clothes that could be obtained, carrying out in every point the dress and paraphernalia of the soldier. . . . His hat was decorated with a star and feather, his coat with every star and embellishment, and he wore a bright new sash, big gauntlets, and silver spurs. He was the very picture of a general.[1]

By all accounts Johnston's arrival in Dalton elicited near-unanimous approval from the men in the ranks. They cheered him heartily and Johnston responded, as one officer recalled, "by darting out on his bright bay horse in front of the line & lifting his hat, not merely off his head, but down to his stirrup." For many, perhaps, the news that Bragg was not going to return was as cheering as the intelligence that Johnston was to replace him. But for most, Johnston's reputation, his imposing presence, and especially his manifest concern for his men generated genuine enthusiasm. From the very beginning, Johnston set a completely different tone in the army. The troops learned quickly that their well-being was the new commander's first priority; he was, as one put it, a "feeding general."[2]

From his earliest days as a professional officer, Johnston had made the care and feeding of his men his highest priority. In Dalton, he started by ordering that two days rations be issued to the troops at once. In place of the ancient beef, so rancid and slippery that the men called it, accurately, "blue beef," he ordered the commissary to distribute the small reserves of bacon and sugar, and he announced that tobacco and whiskey would be issued twice a week. Of course, without a dramatically improved supply system, this gesture would have been a very temporary solution, for he would have had to fall back on the detested "blue beef" within a matter of days. So his first administrative efforts were aimed at improving the flow of goods and supplies to the army. In addition, he ordered new uniforms, tents, and especially shoes, for much of the army was barefoot. He offered universal, unconditional amnesty to those who were absent without leave, and ordered that the men who had remained be granted furloughs—one third of the army at a time—until every soldier had had a chance to go home. Soldiers drew furloughs by lot, and the lucky ones if they wished could sell or give their draw to a family man. The system was universally popular. One officer maintained that "these furloughs were the most charming stroke in the management of soldiers that was ever tried."[3]

The impact of all this on the army's morale was dramatic. "A new era had dawned," one recalled. "He was loved, respected, admired; yea, almost worshipped by the troops. I do not believe there was a soldier in his army but would gladly have died for him." Another soldier wrote more succinctly that "we knew we had a Gen that would take care of his men."[4]

The reaction of the officers was more muted. Under Bragg's command they had learned to suspect the motives of the army commander, and had grown surly and suspicious. Although most were happy enough to be rid of Bragg, Johnston would have to prove himself before they would offer complete loyalty.

The senior corps commander was William Joseph Hardee, now forty-eight years old, who had written the U.S. Army's principal book on light infantry tactics. Unimaginative but dependable, he had earned the nickname of "Old Reliable." Johnston had complete confidence in Hardee. Hardee, for his part, was not quite so sure about Johnston. Before Johnston's arrival Hardee had exercised interim command, and although he had declined command of the army when Davis offered it to him, he had expected that Johnston would consult with him regularly. When it became clear that Johnston intended to keep his own counsel, Hardee was hurt and resentful. But he had other things on his mind. On January 13, two weeks after Johnston's arrival, Hardee married twenty-eight-year-old Mary Lewis; he spent the next two weeks on a honeymoon in Mobile and Savannah.[5]

The other corps commander was Thomas C. Hindman, one of the few corps commanders of the war who was not a West Point graduate. Only thirty-five years old, his principal virtue was that he was a native Tennessean in the Army of Tennessee. A major general, he held a command that properly belonged to a lieutenant general, and Johnston repeatedly asked Richmond to send him an officer of appropriate rank. Eventually Davis sent John Bell Hood, once that officer had recovered from the wound he had received at Chickamauga. Johnston expressed genuine delight at Hood's appointment, but his arrival in February 1864 would bring its own complications.

Among the division commanders, at least two were particularly noteworthy, both of them in Hardee's corps. Benjamin Franklin Cheatham, another Tennessean, was a proven combat leader and a veteran of all the western battles since Shiloh. Bragg had accused him of being drunk during the Battle of Murfreesboro; not only was Cheatham's name left off the list of commended officers in Bragg's official report, but Bragg also had blamed him unofficially for the heavy casualties. Jealous, perhaps, of Cheatham's popularity with his troops, Bragg had completely reorganized Cheatham's division only a month before Johnston's arrival, stripping it of most of the Tennessee regiments, which he scattered throughout the army. The troops resented this as much as Cheatham did, and their already low morale was dampened even further.[6]

Patrick R. Cleburne, another of Hardee's notable division commanders, was a native Irishman and a veteran of the British army, who had enlisted in Confederate service as a private in 1861. Elected a captain, he rose gradually to major general's rank by proving himself in battle. Cleburne was without doubt one of the most effective division commanders in the army. But he would earn notoriety in the coming months for his suggestion that the Confederacy should offer slaves their freedom in exchange for military service. Such a plan, he argued, would help solve the Confederacy's manpower problems while at the same time securing recognition by the powers of Europe. Not surprisingly, his proposal brought a storm of criticism from the army as well as the government; in the end it came to nothing, though for many months it remained a volatile issue.[7]

The commander of the army's cavalry arm was twenty-seven-year-old Joseph Wheeler who, like J. E. B. Stuart, his counterpart in the eastern theatre, wore a full dark beard to conceal his youth. One of the few men in the army who was disappointed by Bragg's departure, since Bragg had secured his promotion to major general only four years out of West Point, Wheeler had yet to justify Bragg's faith in him. He had a tendency to interpret orders rather loosely and to act unpredictably in independent command. He resented Johnston's presence in the army simply because Johnston had replaced Bragg. That resentment would color his behavior and even his official reports. In the ensuing campaign, Wheeler would consistently under-estimate Federal strength and frequently treat Johnston's orders as suggestions.[8]

If many of the officers considered Johnston to be on probation, Johnston was just as reserved in his assessment of them. He was certainly aware of the infighting that had characterized the army under Bragg, and he suspected that army politics would continue to be a problem. He wrote to Wigfall that if he were president, he would "distribute the generals of this army over the Confederacy." Since that option was not available to him, he set out instead to put his own stamp on the command.[9]

He began by reorganizing his staff. He retained the services of Ben Ewell, whose fluid pen and calm manner had proven so valuable. But as his chief of staff he appointed Brigadier General William Whann Mackall. A Marylander by birth, Mackall had been a West Point classmate of Bragg's and had served as that officer's chief of staff since April 1863. Mackall was a gifted administrator, who had served Bragg efficiently until after the Battle of Chickamauga, when he had resigned—ostensibly to take command of a brigade in the Army of Mississippi, but at least in part out of disgust at Bragg's management of the campaign. Mackall and Johnston were old friends. They had served together in Mexico, and Johnston had asked Davis to make Mackall a major general back in 1861. Mackall had anticipated Johnston's eventual appointment to command; now he agreed to return to his former role. Johnston would find him an invaluable aide.[10]

Other organizational changes proved more difficult. The army was divided into two infantry corps and a cavalry brigade, but Johnston believed that an army of three corps would be more efficient in battle, and he requested permission from Davis to reorganize accordingly. Unfortunately, he undermined his request by ignoring the political realities that governed Davis's decision making. He asked the president to order Chase Whiting from North Carolina to command the third corps; and when Davis declined, he asked for Mansfield Lovell. Both Whiting and Lovell were associated in Davis's mind with the political opposition, and neither was acceptable to him. The result was that Johnston was told he would have to make do with two corps.[11]

He was able to make other adjustments by restoring specific units to the command of their original officers, many of whom had been demoted by Bragg as part of his vendetta against those who had opposed him. In particular, Johnston restored the original composition of Frank Cheatham's division. Cheatham and his men were delighted: after the formal announcement, the entire division marched out of camp, its band playing at the head of the column, to Johnston's headquarters. There the men called for the army commander to come out. When Johnston appeared, Cheatham threw an arm around his shoulder and patted him on his balding pate. "Boys," he called out to the men of his division, "This is old Joe!" The men cheered themselves hoarse. A slow blush on his cheek, Johnston suffered the familiarity because of his fondness for Cheatham and the obvious enthusiasm of the men.[12]

As usual, Johnston was less successful in winning the support and confidence of his superiors in Richmond. Davis was unimpressed by Johnston's efforts to ensure that the men were well fed. "To consult the soldiers as to what they would eat was to play the part of a tavern keeper rather than that of a general," he later wrote to a friend. In addition, there was Johnston's continued association, through Wigfall, with the political opposition in the Confederate capital. Every time Wigfall rose to his feet in the Senate to defend Joe Johnston, it was obvious that his real purpose was to embarrass Jeff Davis. Since Davis drew no meaningful distinction between political opposition and disloyalty, the president concluded that, however well loved Johnston was by the army, he was not a reliable field commander. He remained suspicious of Johnston's reports and skeptical of his suggestions.[13]

Johnston was equally suspicious. He knew that Davis had been reluctant to appoint him to command the Army of Tennessee, and he suspected that the president secretly hoped he would fail. A staff officer in Alexander P. Stewart's division later described an episode that illustrates Johnston's uneasy relationship with the president. Writing to Stewart after the war, Colonel J. C. Thompson recalled:

> One day when you [Stewart] had gone to the front about Tunnel Hill, Gen. Johnston came to your Hd Qrs, and in your absence informed me that he had received a telegram from Richmond asking whom he wished to have promoted and assigned to Moore's brigade. . . . The Gen. told me that he believed Col. [James T.] Holtzclaw was Gen. Stewart's choice, but had concluded to come out and satisfy himself about it. I assured him that he was not mistaken, and on leaving he remarked that he would immediately answer requesting Col. Holtzclaw's promotion. After several days an order was received direct from Richmond, informing you that Col. Baker (a stranger) had been promoted and assigned to the command of Moore's brigade, and the next day Col. Baker reported. This was my first practical acquaintance with the terms on which Gen. Johnston had to deal with the authorities in control of the government.[14]

Eventually, Johnston grew wary of suggesting any promotions, fearing that his recommendation would provoke an automatic rejection from Richmond.

The president had very high (Johnston would have said unreasonable) expectations for the winter campaign. On the day of his arrival in Dalton, Johnston found a letter of "instructions" from Secretary of War Seddon waiting for him. And on New Year's Eve, he received a similar letter from Davis. Both communications made it clear that the government expected nothing less than an immediate offensive to regain Middle Tennessee. Davis's expectations were in part the product of his tendency to wishful thinking, but he had also received glowing reports from Hardee about the army's condition on the eve of Johnston's arrival at Dalton. In an effort, perhaps, to score one last point in his feud with Bragg, as well as to put his own brief term of command in the best possible light, Hardee reported to Davis on Christmas Eve that under his care the army had recovered fully from its recent defeats and was in excellent condition.[15]

Thus Johnston found himself reading a letter from Davis that was in effect a status report on his own army. His puzzlement grew as he read. Davis informed Johnston that his artillery was adequate and "well supplied with horses and equipments," that "the troops were tolerably provided with clothing," and quoted Hardee's report that "The army is in good spirits, the artillery reorganized and equipped, and we are now ready to fight." The president made it clear that he expected Johnston "to commence active operations against the enemy." Johnston's formal instructions from Seddon were less pointed, but repeated the expectation that he would soon "assume the offensive."[16]

Johnston found such expectations astonishing. He immediately wrote Seddon that the army, far from being "in condition to resume the offensive," was "deficient in numbers, arms, subsistence stores, and field transportation." Moreover, it "had not entirely recovered its confidence." He claimed to appreciate Davis's motives: "Your excellency well impresses upon me the importance of recovering the territory we have lost. I feel it deeply; but difficulties appear to me in the way." Davis, reading this letter in Richmond, might be forgiven for concluding that with Johnston there were always "difficulties" in the way.[17]

Johnston itemized the army's shortfalls. Aside from the obvious fact that the Federal army a dozen miles to the north at Ringgold significantly outnumbered his own, Johnston identified four fundamental weaknesses in the Army of Tennessee that he believed made it incapable of an immediate offensive. The first, and most important, was the lack of adequate transportation. The army was encamped in the hills of North Georgia, dependent for continued sustenance on the single track of the Western & Atlantic Railroad from Atlanta. Any offensive movement would necessarily entail abandoning that supply line, crossing the Tennessee River, and marching through hilly country that had been stripped of supplies by the hard campaigning of the previous season. The army would need hundreds of wagons to carry its own supplies, and more importantly, thousands of draft animals. Even if the horses and mules could be found to haul the wagons, there was nothing for those animals to eat. There was no natural forage in midwinter, and the railroad from Atlanta could not transport enough provisions for the soldiers, much less the tons of fodder necessary for a thousand additional draft animals.

The problem of transportation affected the artillery as well. Although Davis had assured Johnston that the artillery was "well supplied with horses and equipments," Johnston found the exact opposite to be true. The problem was twofold. First, there were simply not enough horses. Those that were available were, in Johnston's words, "so feeble that in the event of a battle we could not hope to maneuver our batteries, nor in case of reverse to save the guns." The second problem was that the guns themselves were of uncertain value. The Army of Tennessee boasted a total of only 113 artillery pieces, a hundred fewer than Lee's comparably sized Army of Northern

Virginia, and 141 fewer than Sherman's three armies. Fully a third of those guns were either small six-pounders, with a range so short as to make them useless, or twelve-pounder howitzers, effective enough in rough terrain, but not in a full-scale battle. Indeed, such weapons were worse than useless, for they tied up teams of horses and artillerists that might otherwise be put to good use. Johnston also believed that the artillery needed stronger leadership. He had no experienced officer commanding a battery larger than twelve guns, and he repeatedly requested that Davis send him Porter Alexander, who had served with him on the peninsula and was now Lee's artillery officer.[18]

A third problem was the inefficiency of the supply line from Atlanta and the general shortage of essential equipment. Besides food, the infantry was desperately short of shoulder arms, bayonets, and shoes. Six thousand men were without muskets, and more than half lacked bayonets, an instrument that every Civil War commander considered essential for an offensive. Shoes were simply not to be had. After his first inspection Johnston noted that "the number of bare feet was painful to see." He went to work at once trying to remedy these problems, even offering to have the men make their own shoes if the Quartermaster's Office would send him the raw leather. Under the best of circumstances, however, he estimated that it would be months before the army was ready for offensive operations.[19]

Finally, there was the whole issue of the army's morale. The fighting edge necessary to carry out a successful advance could not be restored simply by reorganizing the command structure and issuing a few extra rations. Time was needed for both men and officers to develop confidence in themselves and in their new commander. For all these reasons, Johnston believed that an offensive during the winter was not only unwise but absolutely out of the question. "We cannot hope soon to assume the offensive from this position," he wrote to Davis two weeks after assuming command. In fact, "we are in danger of being forced back from it by the want of food and forage, espe cially the latter." Two weeks later he repeated this assessment: "The more I consider the subject the less it appears to me practicable to assume the offensive. . . ." It must have seemed to Davis that the more Johnston considered anything, the less promising it seemed. Johnston, too, was aware of how it must look. "I regret to make a report to Your Excellency so much less favorable than that which you received before my arrival," he wrote. "As it is necessary that you should know the truth I will not apologize for writing it."[20]

Johnston's own strategic view was established during his first few days in command: he would hold the high ground in front of Dalton, repel the enemy's attack there, then launch a counteroffensive that would carry him into Middle Tennessee. Dalton was not the site he would have chosen to make a defensive stand—the series of ridges to the east provided too much opportunity for the Federals to execute a flanking maneuver. He would have preferred to fall back behind the protection of the Oostanaula River, fifteen miles to the south. But that would have been Centreville all over again, and this time the whole country was watching. For the sake of public morale, therefore, he determined to keep the army at Dalton. He did not believe an enemy offensive was imminent in any case, for he knew that the Federals would first have to develop Chattanooga as a base. He half suspected that the Federals would fortify Chattanooga and move their operations to Virginia for the spring. He even wrote to Wigfall that if Virginia were overrun, he would be welcome at Dalton.[21]

In the meantime, Johnston set to work to eliminate the deficiencies in his own army. His first efforts were directed toward ensuring a steady flow of supplies so that he could meet the soldiers' raised expectations. These endeavors pitted him against government bureaucracy at every level. He wrote to the irascible and independent-minded governor of Georgia, Joseph E. Brown, that "The railroad from Atlanta does not supply our needs." Johnston also wrote to L. B. Northrop, the Commissary General, about the quantity and quality of the supplies; and he wrote to A. R. Lawton, the Quartermaster General, about the shortages of bayonets, shoes, and other items. None of the three was willing to admit any shortcomings. Brown informed Johnston that he had checked with the supervisor of the railroad, who insisted that Johnston was simply "misinformed." Northrop—a Davis "pet," according to Wigfall—responded testily that Johnston exhibited "a heedless disregard of the facts of the case," and blamed all the shortages on Johnston himself, even suggesting to Davis that Johnston's "judgement in such matters is of doubtful value." Lawton asserted that Johnston's army was "better served than any other in the Confederacy," and pointed out that Bragg had never complained about supplies.[22]

Wherever the fault lay, the supply of food was a serious and growing problem for the Army of Tennessee. Johnston could avoid issuing the hated "blue beef" only if the flow improved dramatically. Prices had risen so high that even the officers, who by law were not eligible to draw rations, could not afford to feed themselves. One hundred and fifteen officers from Breckinridge's division petitioned the government to allow them to draw rations, and Johnston noted in his endorsement that "at the present prices of provisions the pay of company officers is worth less than privates." He warned Davis that unless the supply system was improved, the army would have to fall back.[23]

By February 1864, Johnston had made some progress in solving the worst of the problems. He arranged to have beef cattle driven to Dalton and slaughtered there, instead of being butchered in Atlanta and shipped salted in barrels. Officers were authorized to draw rations. Johnston told Governor Brown with "great satisfaction" that "the daily receipts of provision and fodder from Atlanta are now fully equal to the consumption." But though the army was now well fed, the stockpiling of supplies for an invasion of Tennessee was another matter altogether. On February 8 Johnston issued a status report on the Army of Tennessee which emphasized the army's weaknesses.

This memorandum was addressed to his own aide-de-camp, so it is possible that Johnston determined to establish a documentary record that could later be used to justify his decision not to take the offensive.[24]

The next goal was to raise troop morale. Believing that a slovenly army was part of the problem, Johnston sought to reestablish discipline and order in the ranks. He drew up a detailed general order mandating reveille at dawn, breakfast at sunrise, and three hours of drill per day, as well as a dress parade at sunset. He insisted that soldiers walking guard duty take their responsibilities seriously, requiring positive identification of all individuals. In mid-March, one soldier even arrested the commanding general himself. "He took it good-humoredly," the soldier wrote home, "while little colonels and majors become very indignant and wrathy under such circumstances." Johnston was also very particular about inspection. He decreed that at all inspections "the quarters are to be in perfect order, knapsacks properly packed, and bedding neatly folded," reminding his officers pointedly that "The test of their fidelity is in the condition of the troops which they command. Men well disciplined, well instructed, and well cared for point out the honest officer and true patriot."[25]

Putting the orders on paper was easy, but Johnston found that old habits died hard. Then, too, the weather was appalling. He confessed to Wigfall that "It is always either too wet to make men stand in the mud or too cold to make them take arms in their hands & so two weeks have passed." Nevertheless, the troops soon learned that "old Joe was a strict disciplinarian." The men of William Bate's Tennessee Brigade demonstrated their enthusiasm by reenlisting—en masse—for the duration of the war. Other units followed suit, and by February Johnston no longer had to worry that his army would melt away with expiring enlistments.[26]

That same February the Federals showed signs of launching an offensive of their own. Sherman's 35,000-man army in Mississippi, which had been quiet since December, ventured out from Vicksburg toward Jackson, which was occupied by a single Confederate brigade. To Davis in Richmond it seemed likely that this column was part of a grand design to capture Mobile. Polk's small Army of Mississippi was hopelessly inadequate to counter such a move; so Polk called on Johnston for support.

A glance at the map showed that Confederate forces were generally poorly located for mutual support in this crisis. Johnston's army of about 42,000 in North Georgia held the center of the Confederacy's defensive position. James Longstreet, whose feud with Bragg had taken him and about sixteen thousand men off to East Tennessee, was engaged in an unproductive siege of Knoxville, 150 miles to the northeast. There Longstreet was effectively isolated by both distance and terrain from Johnston's army at Dalton or Confederate forces in Virginia. In fact, Longstreet had begun to appreciate that he was in a backwater, and had already written to Lee asking if he could return to Virginia. Meanwhile, Polk's Army of Mississippi con-

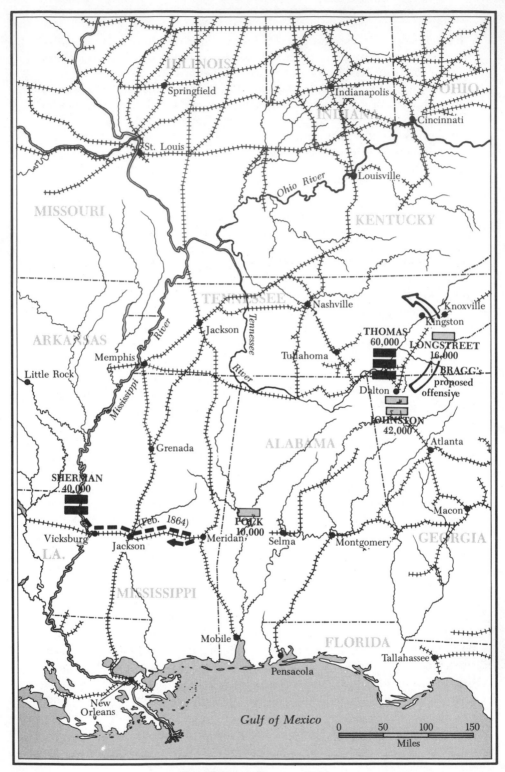

The Western Theatre, 1864

sisted of fewer than ten thousand infantry and cavalry, and faced superior enemy forces in every direction. On February 5, Sherman's army occupied Jackson, and by February 14 it was in Meridian. In Richmond, Davis grew increasingly restive, dispatching a series of telegrams to Johnston to ask if he could detach enough troops "for temporary service" to drive the Yankees back.[27]

Johnston was reluctant to do so. He believed that the Confederate cavalry already in Mississippi would halt the Federal probe, and he explained to Davis that if he sent significant reinforcements to Polk, the Federals at Ringgold would smash through the weakened army at Dalton and "seize Atlanta before our return." By February 17, Davis had stood it as long as he could, and he ordered Johnston to dispatch Hardee's corps to Mississippi in spite of his concerns. Johnston complied. Before Hardee's troops could complete the journey, however, the strategic picture changed abruptly. On February 21, Sherman's army in Mississippi turned around and headed back toward Vicksburg, and the very next day Johnston's cavalry patrols brought word that George Thomas's army at Ringgold was advancing southward. Johnston immediately ordered Hardee's divisions to reverse course and return to Dalton. His telegram to Hardee betrayed his urgency: "The enemy is advancing; is now in force at Tunnel Hill. Lose no time."[28]

Most of Hardee's men were still on the road back when, on February 24, a swarm of Federal skirmishers appeared in front of the Confederate lines near Tunnel Hill. They drove in the cavalry pickets, and from the heights of Rocky Face Ridge, the Confederate infantry looked down into a valley "full of blue coats." Johnston went to the front personally, making sure that the defenders in their rifle pits could see him walking calmly along the line. The fighting that day consisted of tentative probes by both sides, some sharpshooting, and ranging artillery fire. But the next day Federal columns threatened to turn the Confederate right flank in Crow Valley, north of Dalton. Later that night Johnston reported to Davis: "We have been skirmishing most of the day . . . easily holding our ground." The Federals were still there the next morning, but after dark on the 27th they retired, and Johnston concluded that it had been only a reconnaissance.[29]

After this mini-crisis in February, the military situation calmed. Johnston suspected that the Federals were waiting for the return of troops who were on furlough. But he was glad to wait, for he knew that a large number of the Federal enlistments expired in the spring, and he hoped that many of the Union veterans would refuse to reenlist. He was also very pleased by the progress of his own army. "I think that I may say that this army is much improved since December," he wrote to Wigfall. "The men are very healthy & contented & I think full of confidence."[30]

Examples of the improved morale were all around him. Through March and April he exercised the men in mock battles, and they also occasionally engaged in gigantic impromptu snowball fights. On March 22, after a snowfall of five inches, the Army of Tennessee squared off for what may have been the largest snowball fight in history. At first regiments and brigades challenged one another, charging back and forth in military formations with the officers exercising tactical command. Before long the two sides mingled and it turned into a gigantic free-for-all—privates assumed command and officers hurled snowballs from the ranks. Afterward, one veteran recalled, "the soldiers were wet, cold, and uncomfortable."[31]

Manpower remained a serious problem. Except for the return of a few thousand soldiers who had been absent without leave, Johnston's army was no larger in the spring than it had been in January. His own official returns indicated an "aggregate" total of between 55,000 and 60,000 men, with an "effective" strength of about 42,000—the difference consisting of those who were assigned to non-combatant duty or who appeared on the sick list. Johnston estimated the size of the Federal army at Ringgold, a dozen miles to the northwest, at about 80,000. He still hoped that either Longstreet or Polk, or both, would be sent to Dalton to join him; failing that, he faced the likelihood of confronting an enemy that was either a third or even double his own strength, depending on how one counted. He had asked Davis to send reinforcements from elsewhere in the Confederacy, but the president was unwilling to do so without some assurance that they would be employed in activity more productive than snowball fights. Lee reported to Davis that the Federals were taking advantage of Johnston's idleness in the West to send troops from Tennessee to Virginia, and he suggested that only an offensive by Johnston could prevent further transfers. Davis therefore decided that unless Johnston could guarantee an immediate offensive, he would send no reinforcements to Dalton.[32]

One of the ways Johnston hoped to reduce his numerical inferiority was by bringing the nearly ten thousand men who were employed in various support functions into the front lines as soldiers. This could be accomplished, he believed, by turning the support jobs over to slaves. He first broached this proposal to Davis only a few days after taking command, suggesting that blacks could be employed as "company cooks, pioneers, and laborers for engineer service." If this were done, he estimated, it could "add 25 per cent to the fighting force of our armies." Johnston also wrote to Wigfall to ask him to "devise and pass a law to enable us to hold slaves or other negroes with armies." As far as Johnston could see, "There is no other mode by which this army can be recruited before spring."[33]

Bold as his proposal seemed to some, others were willing to go even further. The Irishman Patrick Cleburne believed that slaves themselves could be armed and turned into soldiers. At a general officers' meeting on the night of January 4, he formally proposed such a move. But his suggestion was immediately attacked by other officers present, especially Major General W. H. T. Walker, who remarked that this was not only a foolish idea but, as far as he was concerned, treason. He announced that he was going to inform Richmond of this abolitionist conspiracy and report the names of any officers who spoke in favor of it. Johnston saw at once that the proposal could tear the army apart before he had a chance to heal the wounds left by his predecessor. He stepped into the argument, telling Cleburne that his proposal went too far and ordering Walker not to forward an account of the meeting to the War Department. Although Walker did not write to the War Department, he did notify Davis. The president was as concerned as Johnston about the effect of such a proposal on the army and the country, and he ordered Johnston to squelch the whole issue. Johnston was quite happy to do so.[34]

Johnston's efforts did yield some improvements. Soldiers previously detailed as teamsters and cooks became riflemen, and a general order declared that soldiers "shall not again be detailed as teamsters under any circumstances." These reforms marginally increased its front-line strength, yet the Army of Tennessee remained less than two thirds the size of the Federal army that confronted it. In March, Johnston reported to Wigfall that the army's morale was good, but also that "I wish we had fifteen or twenty thousand more."[35]

Davis continued to prod Johnston to make a move, and by March he had enlisted Braxton Bragg in his campaign. Unwilling as ever to abandon a loyal ally, and unable to find an appropriate field command for his friend, Davis appointed Bragg as his military adviser, charging him "with the conduct of military operations in the armies of the Confederacy." Sitting at Davis's elbow in the Confederate White House, Bragg acted as Davis's executive officer, translating the president's strategic concepts into operational orders. Bragg was not about to take issue with the president. In his new capacity he did nothing to disabuse Davis of his conviction that a firm hand was all that was needed to reclaim Tennessee.[36]

Almost at once Bragg began to write Johnston in no uncertain terms that the government expected him to launch an immediate offensive. He was dismissive of Johnston's excuses and skeptical of his reports. The startling dissonance between Hardee's optimistic report of December and Johnston's gloomy letters of January led Bragg to suggest that "there must be some error on your part." Of course, if anyone knew the condition of the army at Dalton, it was Bragg, but he had allowed himself to be seduced by the optimistic view from Richmond. Bragg now wrote that whatever the defects in the army, Johnston was to remedy them at once and prepare for an offensive campaign. "The enemy is not prepared for us," he insisted, "and if we can strike him a blow before he recovers success is almost certain." If it seemed to Davis that Johnston always saw difficulties in the way, Johnston would have been justified in concluding that success always seemed certain from Richmond.[37]

In the second week of March, Colonel John B. Sale arrived at Dalton with a "confidential" letter from Bragg containing a far more detailed set of instructions, which showed just how completely Bragg had accepted Davis's strategic vision. Five months earlier, when he had been in command himself, Bragg had protested to Richmond that the Army of Tennessee was too small to undertake an invasion. Specifically, he had argued that the army had "inadequate means of transportation" and was especially lacking in artillery horses.[38] Now, he ordered Johnston to do exactly what he had declared impossible in October. Further, he presented the idea in such positive terms as to imply that an invasion would be easy. Johnston was to move "as soon as your means and force can be collected" one hundred miles to the north, up the line of the Tennessee & Georgia Railroad to a crossing of the Tennessee River at Kingston, as far from Dalton in one direction as Atlanta was in the other. This was boldness carried to recklessness, for it would leave the Federal army at Ringgold on Johnston's left flank and rear, and in a position to cut the Confederate army off from its base at Atlanta. (see map on page 258)

Once in Kingston, Johnston should cross the river and link up with Longstreet. The combined rebel armies would pose such a threat that the Federals would be forced to offer battle. Should they refuse, Johnston was then to take the combined armies "across the mountains from Kingston to Sparta," which Bragg declared to be "a very practicable and easy route," into Middle Tennessee. Bragg dealt with the problem of supplies by claiming that once in Middle Tennessee, the army would be "entirely self-sustaining." He did not suggest how the men would be fed or supplied while making the march, nor how they were to survive if they experienced a reversal. "If by a rapid movement . . . you can precipitate your main force upon Nashville, ·and capture that place before the enemy can fall back . . . you place him in a very precarious position," he concluded.[39]

To Johnston, such strategy was completely unrealistic. It seemed obvious to him that it was his own army that would be placed in a "precarious position" by so foolhardy a venture. Johnston outlined his objections in a lengthy discussion with Colonel Sale. He reiterated his conviction that if his own army and Longstreet's were to be combined—which he thought a very good idea—the only way to accomplish it was to bring Longstreet to Dalton rather than uncover Atlanta by sending Johnston to Knoxville. Most important, the army lacked the basic equipment necessary to conduct an offensive, and obtaining it was not simply a matter of determination. He repeated these views in a letter to Bragg: "You direct me to take measures to procure artillery horses as soon as possible. I have been doing so since January, but . . . I am confined to . . . the northwestern part of Georgia and the mountains of Alabama, long since stripped of everything necessary to an army." It might be possible for the soldiers to live off the land once they reached Middle Tennessee, but what would they eat while crossing the mountains? Johnston estimated that, at a minimum, the army needed "food for man and beast for at least ten days." Even if the men could survive temporarily without food, the horses could not. Until the grass grew long enough to allow the draft animals to forage for themselves, the army could not move. Finally, even if the logistical problems could be mastered, a move northward to Kingston from Dalton would leave a superior Federal army on his flank and rear, and closer by a hundred miles to Atlanta. Should the Federals choose not to follow him northward, they could march unopposed south to Atlanta.[40]

Johnston would not waver from his strategic vision that the best plan of action was to concentrate the army in North Georgia by combining the forces of Polk and Longstreet with his own. There they would await a Federal offensive, defeat it, and then launch a counterattack, pursuing the defeated Federals into Tennessee. Richmond received Johnston's suggestions as simply more evidence that he was unwilling to take the offensive. Bragg passed Johnston's letters on to the president, who wrote at the bottom of one: "Returned to Genl. Bragg after being read with disappointment. J.D." Stories of Johnston's timorousness were soon making the rounds in Richmond, and eventually they found their way back to Dalton. "I learn that it is given out that it has been proposed to me to take the offensive with a large army & that I refused," Johnston wrote to Wigfall. "Don't believe any such story. . . . The truth is that in proposing the offensive, a plan of operations was suggested which I regard as impracticable. My saying so was treated in a telegram from Genl. Bragg as a refusal to do anything but stand still."[41]

Johnston's efforts to convince Richmond of the wisdom of his strategic vision were undermined still further by his newest corps commander, John Bell Hood. Hood had arrived in Dalton on February 24 to assume command of T. C. Hindman's corps, with Hindman reverting to the command of a division. Johnston was delighted. He wrote Wigfall that Hood's arrival provided him the greatest comfort he had had since he had assumed command. Unfortunately, Hood brought with him a set of complex motives that would complicate even further the already volatile chemistry of the Army of Tennessee.[42]

Hood had spent the winter in Richmond recovering from the wound he had received at Chickamauga, and renewing his courtship of Sally Buchanan Preston, known to everyone in Richmond as Buck. A dashing young officer when he first set eyes on Buck Preston in 1862, Hood was immediately smitten, but she was less so. Since then he had lost the use of an arm at Gettysburg and a leg at Chickamauga, and had aged far beyond his thirty-three years. By the winter of 1863–64, Hood's pursuit of Sally Preston had become something of an embarrassment in Richmond society. His application for a corps command in 1864 may have been motivated by his determination to impress her. When he told Sally in January that he was soon to go West to command a corps, he announced dramatically: "When I am gone, it is all over. I will not come back." Sally then agreed to an informal engagement, but she insisted that it remain secret. A week later, at a Richmond dinner party, Hood was within earshot when Sally exclaimed to her neighbor: "Absurd! Engaged to that man! Never! For what do you take me?" From the start of the 1864 campaign, Hood was seeking a chance to prove himself in the eyes of Richmond society, and particularly in the eyes of Buck Preston.[43]

In addition, Hood spent much of the winter attempting to ingratiate himself with the chief executive. He invited Varina Davis to become his confidante and adviser in his campaign to win Buck's heart, and he played up to her husband as well. He took carriage rides with the president and sat with him in church. During a discussion in which Davis complained about his commanders in the West, Hood exclaimed: "Mr. President, why don't you come and lead us yourself? I would follow you to the death!" Hood knew well that Davis would like nothing better than to take the field. Like Bragg, Hood was willing to tell Davis what he wanted to hear.[44]

Before he left Richmond for Dalton, Hood agreed to send Davis confidential reports on the condition of the Army of Tennessee. Soon after his arrival he sent the first of what would become a series of private letters in which he emphasized his own enthusiasm for an offensive. Hood later justified his actions by arguing that he wanted to encourage Davis to send reinforcements to the Army of Tennessee so that it *could* take the offensive. But the self-aggrandizing tone of the letters is unmistakable. "We should march to the front as soon as possible," Hood wrote in the first. As for the army's condition, "The addition of a few horses for our artillery will place this army in fine condition. . . . It is well clothed, well fed, and the transportation is excellent." He numbered the army at "60,000 or 70,000 men," although that figure included Longstreet's 15,000 men at Knoxville. He painted visions of advancing to the Ohio and proclaimed: "I never before felt that we had it so thoroughly in our power." This first letter concluded by informing Davis that Hood's own health was never so good, and by offering a prayer that Davis "may be spared to our country." In subsequent letters, Hood implicitly criticized his commanding officer. "How unfortunate for our country it is for the Generals in the field to fail to cooperate with the authorities of the Government," he wrote in April. And in an obvious effort to distance himself from Johnston's objections to an offensive, he added: "You know how anxious I have been to advance." To Seddon he described himself as "an earnest friend of the President"; a week later he wrote Bragg that "From the recent acts of the President I appreciate his greatness even more than before."[45]

Unprofessional as it was for Hood to send these letters, it was equally unprofessional for Davis, Bragg, and Seddon to accept them without notifying Johnston of their contents, or even informing Johnston that Hood was writing to them. Hood did not set out to denigrate Johnston; there is evidence that at first he genuinely admired his commander, but he was trapped by his compulsion for promotion. Hood played the eager soldier restrained by the petty fears of an aging superior who was unwilling or unable to take the reins of command firmly in hand, claiming, "I have done all in my power to induce General Johnston to accept the proposition you made to move forward. He will not consent. . . . I regret this exceedingly, as my heart was fixed upon our going to the front and regaining Tennessee and Kentucky."[46]

Years after the war, when he finally saw the letters, Johnston concluded that in addition to violating military protocol, they were a deliberate slander. Hood knew that Johnston's plans included a counteroffensive, especially if Longstreet's troops joined him at Dalton. Johnston himself indicated repeatedly in his correspondence to both Davis and Bragg that he did not oppose the *idea* of an offensive, only the timing and details of the Davis-Bragg proposal. In Richmond, however, Hood's letters were a welcome change from Johnston's excuses and explanations. Hood was unconditional in his advocacy of an offensive, and the obvious eagerness in his letters contrasted strongly with the more lugubrious, if more realistic, assessments in Johnston's correspondence. Only two days after Davis received a letter from Hood that envisioned the imminent destruction of all Federal forces south of the Ohio, he received one from Johnston which reported that if Sherman brought his forces from Mississippi to join Thomas at Chattanooga—which was likely enough—he would need reinforcements merely to hold onto his present position.[47]

But Johnston, too, had friends in high places, though they were not the kind of advocates who were likely to ingratiate him with the chief executive. Throughout the winter and spring, Wigfall continued to promote Johnston in the Confederate capital, telling him in March: "No man ever had stronger or better friends than you have." Wigfall was still laboring to correct the public record of Johnston's tenure of command in Mississippi. The *Sentinel* had published selections from Pemberton's official correspondence, and Johnston felt aggrieved to be so publicly targeted for abuse. To his brother Beverly, Johnston wrote, "I consider it absolutely necessary to my reputation that the correspondence in question should be fairly published." Unwilling to be Pemberton's scapegoat, he insisted that "There is certainly no reason why I should be a martyr." Beverly passed the letter on to Wigfall, who promised to do his best to set the record straight.[48]

But as always, the Texas senator was motivated as much by animosity toward Davis as his friendship for Johnston. Wigfall's vendetta against Davis had become consuming. "The safety of the country requires that he should be taught that he has no monopoly of bad temper," Wigfall wrote to Johnston, "that if he puts himself out to disoblige others, others will disoblige him." When Johnston objected that that disobliging Davis was not the main point, Wigfall offered a lesson in politics. "Not having been in Richmond for more than a year, you are not likely to know the state of affairs there. Davis's bad judgment of men & bad temper together will ruin the country unless he is controlled."[49]

For his part, Davis suspected that Johnston was exaggerating his army's weaknesses as an excuse not to advance. To find out, he ordered Bragg to send envoys to Dalton to report on the true condition of things there. The first to arrive was William Nelson Pendleton, Johnston's former chief of artillery and a man he considered a friend. Pendleton arrived in Dalton on March 12 and, after paying his respects, began his job at once. He found the artillery "less stong than desirable," especially the six-pounders, which he described as perfectly useless for battle. The animals were quite thin from lack of forage, and many of them were weak, but he did not think they were in any worse shape than those of the Army of Northern Virginia. He estimated that the addition of five hundred animals would make the guns capable of effective service. The difficulty, of course, was that five hundred fresh horses were simply not to be had. The officers he found to be "earnest, capable, experienced, and efficient." The bottom line was that "with the improvements indicated . . . the artillery of the Army of Tennessee will prove satisfactorily efficient. . . ." As read in Richmond, Pendleton's report was inconclusive. The report of the other envoy, Lieutenant Colonel Arthur Cole, was more forthright and substantiated most of Johnston's assertions. He reported that Johnston needed as many as *three thousand* additional draft animals, and that so many animals were simply not available in the West. Curiously, neither Pendleton's nor Cole's report had any impact on Davis, who continued to believe that the primary obstacle to a western offensive was Johnston himself.[50]

Johnston felt the need to defend his viewpoint more forcefully than he could by letters. He therefore sent an envoy of his own to Richmond to explain to Davis that he did, indeed, plan to undertake a forward movement as soon as the deficiencies in the army were remedied. The man he sent was Ben Ewell, his former chief of staff. Ewell arrived in Richmond on April 12, and he went first to see Bragg. Bragg listened sympathetically, but he made it clear to Ewell that when he visited Davis the next day he should be prepared to state "categorically" whether Johnston, if supplied with fifteen thousand reinforcements, was prepared to assume the offensive. Unsure himself of how his boss would answer this question, Ewell telegraphed him that day. Johnston hedged his answer. His ability to assume the offensive, he wired back, depended on the strength of the relative forces in northern Georgia. In any event, "It will be a month or six weeks before we can expect the necessary transportation."[51]

This was hardly the "categorical" response Bragg had demanded, but Ewell decided that its spirit matched the administration's objectives, and so "after a careful consideration" he decided that he could answer in the affirmative to Bragg's question. The next day when Ewell met with the president, their discussion was cordial. Davis listened with "apparent interest" as Ewell outlined Johnston's views of the strategic situation. The president then expressed his "disappointment" in Johnston's lack of aggressiveness, stating that Johnston's passivity in the West had allowed the Federals to seize the initiative elsewhere. He blamed Johnston for the growing strength of the Federal army in Virginia. Had Johnston advanced into Tennessee in February or March, Davis insisted, it would have prevented the Federal buildup that now threatened to overwhelm Lee. Although he was polite, Davis told Ewell frankly that pressures elsewhere in the Confederacy made it impossible to promise any significant reinforcements for Johnston's army.[52]

That same night in Dalton, Johnston received a second visit from Pendleton, who had been sent back to press Davis's argument that the Yankees were transferring forces from Tennessee to Virginia and that it was therefore essential for Johnston to initiate an offensive against the weakened western army to prevent further transfers. But this whole assessment was completely false. Despite Lee's reports to Davis, the Federals were *not* sending forces from Tennessee to Virginia. The buildup in Virginia was being matched by a similar buildup in Tennessee. Instead of sending reinforcements to Virginia, Sherman had brought the bulk of his forces from Mississippi to join Thomas near Ringgold, and Ambrose Burnside had come west with the IXth Corps, increasing the size of the Federal army in and around Chattanooga and Ringgold to more than a hundred thousand. When Pendleton presented Davis's argument, Johnston was able to provide him with conclusive evidence that virtually all of the forces that Lee claimed had been sent to Virginia were still in Tennessee. Even Wheeler, anxious as he was to support Bragg's view of things, testified that those units were still in the West. Pendleton reported back to Davis that Sherman's army was "evidently greater than has been supposed."[53]

The appropriate countermove to the Federal buildup, Johnston believed, was to bring Polk's infantry from Mississippi and Longstreet's army from East Tennessee. But Longstreet was already on his way back to Virginia, where Lee anticipated an offensive by General George G. Meade, and Polk remained in Mississippi. Johnston reported to Wigfall that the Federals at Ringgold could drive him back from Dalton whenever they chose to do so. But he could not convince Richmond of his peril. Despite Pendleton's report, Davis and Lee continued to believe that the Federals were transferring forces from Johnston's front to Virginia, where the main blow would fall. Davis simply discounted the ability of the Federals to mount two major offensives simultaneously. Because Grant was preparing an offensive in Virginia, Davis assumed that Sherman must be vulnerable in the West, and he dismissed Johnston's reports as just more excuses.[54]

By mid-April, the Army of Tennessee was still at Dalton. Johnston had won his strategic argument with Richmond simply by refusing to launch an offensive during the winter months. His stubbornness, however, had cost him a great deal in terms of the trust and support of the government. He did not have the reinforcements he would need to launch a counteroffensive when the time came, nor even to defend his position in northern Georgia. Virtually everyone in camp knew that with the arrival of warmer weather, Sherman's three armies would be on the move. Johnston ordered Wheeler's cavalry to step up its patrols and to keep the advanced pickets well up to the front of the enemy's line. A chaplain in Hood's corps confided to his diary: "We are doubtless on the eve of important events."[55]

On April 19, Johnston held a grand review of the army. With the infantry and artillery all drawn up together, it made a spectacular sight. The men were better clothed, better shod, better fed, and more confident than when Johnston had arrived in December four months before. The officers had not ceased their internal squabbling, but at least they were again on speaking terms. This was a tough, confident army. Johnston cantered down the line, stopping at each brigade to receive the salute of its commander. Then he took his position opposite the center, and the army passed in review. It was a chilly day and the wind whipped at their clothing, but Lydia and several other officer's wives watched as forty thousand men paraded past. The swords swept upward, then dropped again in formal salute as the officers rendered honors to their commander. Astride his mount, impeccably dressed as always, Johnston returned their salute. Although still deficient in transportation and artillery, and significantly outnumbered by its prospective foe, the Army of Tennessee was nevertheless a splendid instrument of war, ready for the supreme test. That test was now only a few days away.[56]

CHAPTER EIGHTEEN

Dalton and Resaca

F or the rest of his life, and for a hundred years thereafter, Joseph E. Johnston would be judged primarily on his conduct of the campaign in northern Georgia during the spring and summer of 1864. Twentieth-century historians continue to argue the merits of the case. His defenders assert that "Few campaigns of the war saw an army kept so well in hand, so precisely controlled, so adroitly maneuvered, as Joe Johnston's defense of northwest Georgia. . . ." His critics, both at the time and subsequently, saw it differently. They charge that like his old friend George McClellan, Johnston knew how to manage an army, and he certainly had a talent for commanding the loyalty of his men, but that he could not—or would not—fight. "A lifetime in the army's bureaucracy had taught him that . . . the way to avoid mistakes was to avoid risks," one critic concludes. "For an army commander, this meant avoiding battle—if he did not fight, he could not lose."[1]

In particular, Johnston's critics contrast his campaign in northern Georgia with Lee's campaign in Virginia during the same period. The comparison is not inappropriate. Both campaigns began the same week, almost the same day, and in each case a numerically superior Federal army drove a Confederate army back one hundred miles to its urban base. The principal difference was that the campaign in Virginia was significantly bloodier. Both armies in Virginia suffered horrible losses. Confederate losses are difficult to establish with precision, but it is likely that Lee's army suffered no fewer than forty thousand men killed and wounded in the three-month campaign. At the same time, that army probably inflicted an astonishing sixty thousand casualties on the enemy. Such numbers testify to the courage of the enlisted men on both sides. But they testify also to Lee's skill as a tactician, and to the bull-headed determination of Grant, whose headlong assaults at Spotsylvania in May, and at Cold Harbor in July, resulted in unprecedented carnage. One might have thought that such casualties would force Grant to rethink his tactics; Grant however was a pragmatist, who had calculated that he could lose three men to every two of the enemy and still maintain numerical superiority. It was a cruel calculus, but in the end it proved valid.

By contrast, the opposing armies in the West suffered significantly fewer casualties. Although the men in the ranks were no less courageous, Johnston's Army of Tennessee lost only about ten thousand men killed and wounded while inflicting about twice that number of casualties on the enemy. These much smaller numbers—less than a third of the combined losses in Virginia during the same period—were partly due to Johnston's adroit maneuvering, but mainly they were the result of Sherman's determination to avoid frontal assaults. Rather than force his way *through* Johnston's prepared defenses, he sought to find ways *around* them. As a result, Johnston grudgingly but steadily surrendered much of northern Georgia as he and Sherman maneuvered around one another in a deadly minuet.[2]

Ironically, Johnston's minimal casualties during the campaign provided critics with the opportunity to assert that he was not doing all he could to hold back the invader. The long lists of dead and wounded from the Army of Northern Virginia left no doubt in anyone's mind that Lee was doing all that was possible. Could the same be said of Johnston? Many in the South equated long casualty lists with the will to win. After Johnston's evacuation of Dalton, one parlor-room critic commented: "We want a hardened fellow who does not value men's lives. . . ." If that was what was wanted, then Johnston was not the man for the job. Johnston recognized that the Confederacy's most vital resource was not its land, nor even its cities, but the manpower invested in its armies. He saw clearly that while land could be retaken, lives could never be reclaimed. If Pemberton's army had been more important to him than Vicksburg, then surely the Army of Tennessee was more important than Dalton, or Resaca, or any other North Georgia town— more important, even, than Atlanta if it should come to that. "I therefore thought it our policy to stand on the defensive," he wrote later, "to spare the blood of our soldiers by fighting under cover habitually, and to attack only when bad position or division of the enemy's forces might give us advantages. . . ." Johnston crafted a strategy that was both passive and reactive, and therefore unlikely to engender much enthusiasm, especially in Richmond.[3]

   To Davis, the idea of surrendering territory, even temporarily, was unpalatable. It was contrary to his nature; further, he knew that when Federal troops occupied an area, they severed the fragile cords that bound the territory and its people to the Confederacy. In particular, it disrupted the relationship of master and slave. Once told they were free by occupying Yankee soldiers, few slaves willingly reshouldered the burden of bondage, even if the Confederate army later recaptured the area. Federal occupation, in short, ruined an area for slavery and the way of life it supported. Such concerns played no role in Johnston's strategic calculations. In the first place, he was less politically sensitive than Davis. More important, for him the preservation of slavery was not a strategic imperative. Although he came from a slaveholding family, Joe Johnston had never owned slaves himself, and he often referred to the institution as a "curse." Thus on political, social, and economic, as well as military grounds, Johnston and Davis held radically divergent strategic views. Because their personal feud meant that they did not communicate effectively, the stage was set for disappointment before the first shot was even fired.[4]

   In May 1864, Johnston lived and worked in a two-story wooden frame house near the center of Dalton where he made his headquarters. A medium-sized town—not quite a city—Dalton was laid out on a grid near the western edge of the broad valley of the Connasauga River, virtually in the shadow of Rocky Face Ridge. The dozen miles that separated Dalton from the growing Federal army to the north were dominated by a series of narrow ridges, interspersed by a series of equally narrow valleys. From the air, if either commander could have viewed it that way, the terrain in North Georgia resembled nothing so much as a washboard. Immediately to the west of Dalton was Rocky Face Ridge, which constituted Johnston's main line of defense. The landmark Rocky Face rose like a knife edge out of the North Georgia forest, notched by Mill Creek Gap where the Western & Atlantic Railroad ran along the edge of the small creek that gave the gap its name, before passing through Dalton to points south. This pine-covered ridge extended for several miles to the south, where it merged into Chattoogata Ridge; to the north it was much less imposing, tumbling into foothills after only a few miles. To the west, beyond Rocky Face Ridge, was Tunnel Hill— so named because the railroad from Dalton to Chattanooga passed through a tunnel in the ridge—where Johnston placed his cavalry pickets. Another ten miles further west was Taylor's Ridge, the most dominant of the three, which ran all the way from Tennessee into Alabama, cutting across the northwest corner of Georgia. Other ridges marched away westward, rank upon rank, to Missionary Ridge and Lookout Mountain near Chattanooga.
   Nestled in one of several gaps in Taylor's Ridge was Ringgold, the Federal headquarters and the starting point for Sherman's campaign. There Major General William Tecumseh Sherman commanded not one army, but three, each of them named in the Federal tradition after a river. George H.

Thomas, "the Rock of Chickamauga," commanded the Army of the Cumberland, sixty thousand strong, as large by itself as Johnston's Army of Tennessee. James B. McPherson commanded another 25,000 men in the Army of the Tennessee,° and John M. Schofield commanded the smallest of these Federal armies, the Army of the Ohio, actually an enlarged corps, which numbered about fourteen thousand. All told, the Federals could field nearly one hundred thousand men, more than double the effective strength of Johnston's force at Dalton. While Johnston drilled his army to a fighting edge, Sherman was completing preparations for what he expected would be the decisive campaign of the war. He had been instructed by Ulysses S. Grant, recently elevated to the rank of lieutenant general and placed in overall command of the Union armies, "to move against Johnston's army, to break it up and get into the interior of the enemy's country as far as you can. . . ."[5]

The Federal grand strategy for the spring of 1864 was not complicated. Grant, accompanying George G. Meade's Army of the Potomac, would assail Lee's army in northern Virginia, and Sherman, with his three armies, would go after Johnston. The simultaneous application of pressure in both theatres would prevent the outnumbered Confederates from shuttling reinforcements between East and West. More so than at any other time, Confederate fortunes rested on the shoulders of two men: West Point classmates Robert E. Lee and Joseph E. Johnston.

Johnston was not deceived by the illusion of security suggested by the terrain. The ridges athwart Sherman's line of advance were certainly barriers to any direct attack, but they were also fences behind which the Federals could maneuver beyond the sight of rebel cavalry patrols. Johnston fully expected that Sherman would take advantage of the terrain to screen his movements while he executed some kind of flanking maneuver. But where? In February 1864, Thomas had moved two divisions around the north end of Rocky Face Ridge into Crow Valley. Johnston still thought that was the most likely enemy route; it was the one he would have chosen himself had he been in Sherman's place, for the open Connasauga Valley offered the Federals the best opportunity to take advantage of their numerical superiority. He also believed that Sherman might choose to outflank him to the west and south, by sending one of his three armies down the Tennessee River to Gunter's Landing to march overland from there to Rome, Georgia. A third possibility was that Sherman would use the series of ridges and valleys in North Georgia to screen a movement across the Confederate front. Such a maneuver would enable the Yankees to debouch from one of a half dozen possible gaps in the ridgeline to threaten Johnston's communications with his base at Atlanta.[6]

Johnston's uncertainty about Federal intentions was largely a product of

°Often the source of confusion, McPherson's Army of the Tennessee was named for the river; Johnston's Army of Tennessee, for the state.

the weakness of his cavalry—the eyes of the army. On paper, Joseph Wheeler's cavalry consisted of some 10,000 troopers organized into three divisions; its actual strength was under 2,400, and rather than three divisions, Wheeler could field only three brigades. The army did not lack for men willing to serve in the cavalry. Several veteran infantry units had petitioned the government to transfer to the cavalry en masse, but Johnston believed that turning trained infantry into green cavalry was a bad bargain. He suspected that most such requests were a product of the infantryman's belief that life in the cavalry was easier. After all, the soldiers asked one another, who ever saw a dead cavalryman? A more fundamental cause of Johnston's cavalry problems was the shortage of horses. The horses of Wheeler's command were underfed, overworked, and so weak that Johnston had had to send many of them to the Etowah River Valley to recover. There were simply not enough horses left to enable Wheeler to keep a close watch on enemy movements.[7]

Another problem was Wheeler himself. The young cavalry commander was as eager as anyone in the army for a battle, but he was perhaps more interested in crossing sabers with Union cavalry than in conducting routine patrols. Johnston was direct in his requests for information. During the first week of May, he pestered Wheeler daily with telegrams directing him to keep an eye on the various gaps through the ridgelines. Yet Wheeler kept most of his cavalry concentrated north of Dalton, near Varnell's Station, in anticipation of a fight with his Yankee counterpart. One member of Johnston's staff noted with disgust in his private diary that "Not a thing has been ascertained by Wheeler's cav.—inactive." Unwilling to relieve his cavalry commander on the eve of a decisive campaign, and desperate for intelligence, Johnston recalled Brigadier General William T. Martin's cavalry from the Valley of the Etowah and sent it to patrol the territory north of the Oostanaula from Resaca to Rome. Other patrols were posted in the gaps on Taylor's Ridge and on the railroad north of Varnell's Station. But all of these patrols failed to provide the information Johnston needed most: an overall picture of the location and strength of the enemy forces. Instead, Johnston had to piece together isolated scraps of information in the hope that they would form a recognizable pattern.[8]

What he did know was that the Federals were repairing the railroads from Chattanooga to Ringgold, and that they were at work on the road from Chattanooga to Cleveland north of Dalton in East Tennessee. The Federal infantry was also on the move: enemy units were spilling out of Ringgold Gap toward the Confederate center at Tunnel Hill, and south out of Cleveland toward Johnston's right flank in Crow Valley. Patrols reported that Oliver O. Howard's corps was at Red Clay, on the Tennessee-Georgia border, and that advanced units of the enemy had driven in Confederate pickets south of Varnell's Station only nine miles to the north. These reports suggested that the Federals were mounting a two-pronged assault from the west and north. Johnston arrayed his defenses accordingly, placing three of his seven divisions on Rocky Face Ridge facing westward: Stewart held the gap at Mill Creek, flanked by Bate and Cheatham, with Cleburne in reserve. Stevenson and Hindman's divisions held an east-west line across Crow Valley, with Walker's division in reserve. As a safety measure, Johnston ordered the 1,400-man brigade of James Cantey, on its way from Rome, to halt in Resaca and await developments.[9]

The weakness in these dispositions was that they left the southernmost gaps in Rocky Face Ridge almost undefended. Two skeleton Arkansas regiments—perhaps 250 men—occupied Dug Gap, six miles south of Mill Creek Gap; Snake Creek Gap, another twelve miles further south, was left unguarded altogether except for Martin's cavalry patrols. Johnston's excuse for this neglect of his left was that he could not defend everywhere without dispersing his forces. Then, too, his arrangements were a product of his conviction that the enemy was more likely to assail his right flank in Crow Valley.[10]

Johnston also wired Bragg to ask for reinforcements. Bragg and Davis had withheld reinforcements from Johnston's army throughout the winter, dangling the hope of them in front of him as a reward to be bestowed if he undertook an advance. But Johnston had not advanced, and Richmond was no more inclined to send reinforcements to him now than in January. Davis—and therefore Bragg as well—believed that Sherman's maneuvers were a decoy, and that Grant's offensive in Virginia was the real threat. A year earlier, Johnston had written perceptively that "The near danger appears to be much greater than the distant one. The govt. sees with Lee's eyes." Even so, Bragg (through Cooper) authorized Polk to take one division "and any other available force at your command" to Rome. Polk then wired Johnston that he was bringing ten thousand infantry and four thousand cavalry—virtually his whole force—to join the Army of Tennessee. Johnston was grateful, and probably relieved, to hear that the Episcopal bishop-turned-general was on his way. Bragg was less pleased, and he worried that Polk would leave Mississippi and Alabama unprotected; but he did not interfere with Polk's decision. Polk's arrival in Georgia would give Johnston a third corps, significantly reducing his numerical inferiority to Sherman. Moreover, Polk's movement would guard Johnston's vulnerable left flank.[11]

On May 2, Johnston notified the wives of officers on the headquarters staff that they would have to leave Dalton, and he said goodbye to Lydia, who took the train to Atlanta. Three days later Federal skirmishers drove in the Confederate pickets before Tunnel Hill, and two days after that, blue-coated infantry pushed the advanced Confederate units back to Mill Creek Gap in Rocky Face Ridge. At the same time, two Federal corps in Crow Valley advanced southward from Varnell's Station to link up with the forces at Tunnel Hill. The Federal attack that day was vigorous but not serious. Much of the long-range skirmishing was dominated by the sharpshooters on both sides: the Federals with their Spencer rifles, and the Confederates with their

Whitworths, each capable of dropping an enemy soldier at a mile or more.

In front of Rocky Face Ridge, the well-positioned defenders were not seriously pressed. One veteran recalled that their volleys caused "a terrible conspluterment" among the blue ranks. Their long preparation had enabled them to establish interlocking fields of fire that kept the attackers pinned down. In front of Mill Creek Gap, Stewart's division had constructed dams with sluice gates across Mill Creek. When the Federals attacked, the Confederates closed the gates and flooded the valley, forcing the attackers to advance across a narrow field commanded by rebel artillery. As a result, the Federals were somewhat tentative in their assault.[12]

In the midst of all this, Johnston received reports that Yankees had been spotted in the vicinity of Villanow, a dozen miles to the southwest, well beyond his left flank. At least one division of McPherson's army was "between La Fayette and Lee and Gordon's Mills," with the rest presumed to be not far behind. This column might be headed for Rome, or Sherman might have sent McPherson on an end run around the Confederate left to threaten Johnston's communications with Atlanta. Johnston responded to the reports by wiring Polk to "hasten concentration of his troops at Rome," and ordering Cantey at Resaca to "keep close observation on all routes leading from La Fayette." That was all he could spare for his vulnerable left. The threat might or might not be real. What Johnston knew for certain was that a substantial army, one considerably larger than his own, confronted him at Dalton. There was no mistaking the immediacy of that threat, for the movements of Sherman's blue-coated troops could be seen clearly by the defenders atop Rocky Face Ridge.[13]

The fighting in front of Dalton became more serious the next day. That afternoon, an entire Federal corps under "Fighting Joe" Hooker assaulted Dug Gap at the southern end of Johnston's line, where the two small Arkansas regiments and some dismounted cavalry guarded the pass. Johnston sent two brigades from Cleburne's division to bolster the defense, and accepted Hardee's offer to take command there personally. The two brigades marched toward the danger point at the quick-step. The last part of their march was an uphill struggle in the afternoon heat, and for a tense hour or two it was not clear that they would arrive in time. But about an hour before sundown, the first of these reserves reached the pass, and with nightfall Hooker's men withdrew.[14]

Another piece of the strategic puzzle was provided when Hood reported that the men of Stewart's division at Mill Creek Gap had spotted the dust of a Federal wagon train moving westward. Was this an indication of a flanking movement? Hood noted that the train was "not very large," and suggested only that "cavalry should watch our left." Instead, of course, Wheeler's cavalry was concentrated on the *right* in Crow Valley while their commander looked for an opportunity to launch a massed charge at the enemy. Stewart privately expressed his view that Sherman was trying to outflank their defense lines by sending a force to seize Resaca. Johnston thought this

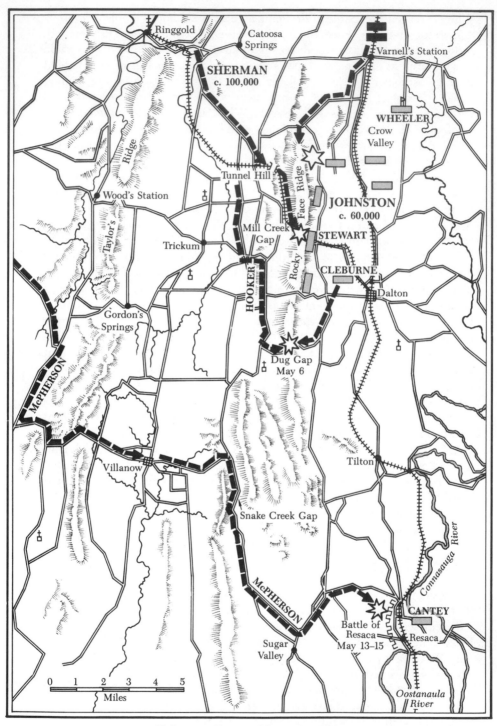

Dalton to Resaca, May 4–16, 1864

was at least possible. He informed Cleburne that he would have to hold Dug Gap unassisted, and he directed two regiments coming up from Atlanta to halt in Resaca to bolster Cantey's force there.[15]

By nightfall on May 8, Johnston's lines were still intact, but he was uncertain where the next blow would fall. The Yankees had assailed Mill Creek Gap in the center of his line, they had attacked Dug Gap on his left flank, and they continued to threaten the right flank in Crow Valley. Johnston's field commanders reported no evidence of a Yankee disengagement in front of Dalton, though there were hints that other enemy forces were on the move behind the front. Hooker's corps was still in plain view across the valley in front of Cleburne, and Hood reported that the enemy was massing in front of Signal Station. Johnston had to consider the possibility that Hooker's attack at Dug Gap was a feint designed to draw attention away from the northern flank in Crow Valley.[16]

During these first few days of the campaign, Johnston's understanding of Federal movements was limited to what he could see from the heights of Rocky Face Ridge. What he desperately needed was knowledge of the disposition of the enemy units he could not see. In the pre-dawn hours of May 9, Johnston sent off Colonel J. W. Grigsby's cavalry brigade, which had participated in the defense of Dug Gap, to investigate Snake Creek Gap. This should have been Wheeler's job, but Wheeler that same morning had requested permission to conduct an independent raid into the rear of the Federal army—a raid similar to those that had made Jeb Stuart famous in the East. Johnston turned him down, ordering him instead to find out "whether the force that can be seen from the different points of Rocky Face Ridge is his whole army." But Wheeler had no opportunity to do so, for that afternoon he found the fight he had been seeking. Near Varnell's Station, his troopers engaged a division of Union cavalry and captured over a hundred prisoners and an enemy standard. It made splendid reading in the official reports, yet the cost was high, for Wheeler's hour of glory meant that Johnston had to rely for information on what he could find out for himself. That afternoon he had to ask Cleburne if he could still see Federals in front of Dug Gap or if they were making a move to the left. Meanwhile the news from Grigsby was that an enemy column had passed through Snake Creek Gap and was still advancing. Johnston sent Cantey another brigade—that of Alfred J. Vaughn—and emphasized to him "the importance of the bridges you guard and the absolute necessity of their being held." If Cantey was heavily attacked, he should hold on in the knowledge that Johnston would come to his aid at once; if not, then Cantey should be prepared to move northward himself.[17]

Johnston spent much of the day on May 9 on the right flank, where he still expected the principal Federal attack to develop. Instead, the Yankees hammered away at the angle of the Confederate line where Hardee's and Hood's corps met. The Federals launched five separate attacks against the rebel line on Rocky Face Ridge but, as on the previous day, they made no gains and suffered substantial losses. Johnston was gratified with the day's successes. When he returned to his headquarters in Dalton that night at about nine, however, he learned that twenty thousand enemy troops had emerged from Snake Creek Gap that afternoon to fall upon the Confederate defenders at Resaca. Screened by the mountains, McPherson had brought his entire army in a round-about march to cut Johnston off from his base. Johnston wrote later that he did not fear for the safety of his communications, yet his reaction at the time suggests that he was seriously alarmed, as well he should have been. He ordered Hood to take the train to Resaca at once, with no less than three full divisions (those of Hindman, Cleburne, and Walker) to follow him as swiftly as possible.[18]

It was ten hours before Johnston heard from Hood. Finally, at eight o'clock the next morning, Hood wired the news that Resaca was "all right," and he urged Johnston to "Hold on to Dalton." Hood had arrived at Resaca to find McPherson withdrawing back into the mountains. McPherson had expected to find Resaca virtually undefended. When instead he encountered Cantey's two reinforced brigades dug in behind prepared fortifications, he was altogether taken aback and decided to withdraw to Snake Creek Gap to await further orders. Historians have generally attributed this to McPherson's timorousness, largely because Sherman, who was hugely disappointed, later wrote that McPherson "could have walked into Resaca." But that is unlikely. The two reinforced brigades, more than four thousand men, that Johnston had directed to Resaca were well placed, and McPherson calculated that a frontal assault risked a repulse at the end of a long and uncertain line of communications. His other option was to occupy the railroad between Dalton and Resaca and await support. But that would have placed him directly between two enemy forces: Johnston could have sent a full army corps against him from the north to act as the hammer on Cantey's anvil. After thinking over the possibilities, McPherson determined instead to withdraw into the mountains, and the opportunity was lost.[19]

Johnston might have been relieved to hear of McPherson's withdrawal, but he also had to wonder whether McPherson's tentative assault meant that his maneuver was only a feint, designed to pull the Confederates out of their defensive position at Dalton. He was still reluctant to abandon his conviction that Crow Valley was the likely scene of the main Federal effort. Heavy skirmishing continued along Rocky Face Ridge all morning, and that afternoon Hardee reinforced Johnston's suspicions when he reported that he expected a Federal turning effort in Crow Valley. Hood asked Johnston by telegraph if he should halt his troops where they were—halfway between Dalton and Resaca—or march them back to Dalton. It was a good question. Johnston decided to leave two divisions at Tilton until the strategic picture clarified.[20]

The situation was fraught with both danger and opportunity. On the one hand, enemy armies threatened from two directions. On the other, Johnston's forces held the interior position, and he had a railroad to shuttle troops back and forth while Sherman had to march on exterior lines across difficult terrain. On the other hand, Sherman's numerical superiority enabled him to field superior forces at both places simultaneously; even with McPherson's entire army of twenty thousand or more at Resaca, Sherman could still put eighty thousand in the field at Dalton. The question Johnston struggled with was which of the two was to be the main Federal effort.

The ideal solution would be for Polk's two divisions from Mississippi to arrive at Resaca in time to parry the Federal thrust there, so that Johnston did not have to commit Hood's corps. Indeed, the first elements of Polk's army—part of a division under the command of Major General William W. Loring—arrived that night, May 10, and Johnston later recorded that their arrival "prevented any immediate apprehension for the place." But the rest of Polk's army was still en route at eight o'clock the next morning when McPherson renewed his advance, this time with reinforcements and seriousness of purpose. Through Mackall, Johnston ordered Loring to assume command at Resaca until Polk arrived. Meanwhile, he and his staff arranged for two hundred railroad cars, the bulk of the rolling stock in Georgia, to carry the rest of Polk's army from Rome. He followed this up with a personal telegram to Polk to emphasize the importance of haste: "Send all the troops you can to Resaca with dispatch. Go in person. The enemy are close upon it." Polk reported at 1:30 P.M. that he would go on the next train. At the same time, Johnston rotated the axis of his defenses at Dalton, with Cheatham taking over the defense at Dug Gap while Cleburne marched southward. But he was not yet willing to abandon Dalton altogether.[21]

Polk arrived in Resaca that afternoon, and in the evening he and Hood took the train north to Dalton, where they met with Johnston in his headquarters. Johnston listened to their reports and decided that, for now at least, Hood and his divisions should remain where they were while Polk returned to Resaca. The meeting broke up a little before midnight, and the two corps commanders left. Before Polk reboarded the train, however, he stopped at Hood's headquarters, where he reverted temporarily to his role as an Episcopal bishop to baptize Hood, using water obtained from a horse trough.[22]

By now Johnston suspected that the growing Federal strength at Resaca indicated that it—not Dalton—was to be the site of the enemy's principal effort. It was hard to credit. He still thought that a Federal move into Crow Valley was Sherman's best opportunity. Nevertheless, the evidence of a Federal buildup west of Resaca was increasingly conclusive, and Johnston determined to move his army there. The timing would be crucial, for substantial Federal forces remained in front of Rocky Face Ridge. If he left too soon, he would have a pursuing Federal army behind him as he moved south to confront the attack at Resaca. Johnston needed precise information about the size and composition of the Federal force at both Dalton and Resaca. Wheeler's troopers investigated the enemy's strength near Dalton, and Martin's cavalry surveyed the roads west of Resaca. Twice on May 12 Johnston wired Polk to ask about enemy strength. "Have you received any information from General Martin," he asked, "require it at once." Finally, Polk responded with the key piece of the puzzle: three Union corps were opposite Resaca, Polk reported; even more important, perhaps conclusive, prisoners had reported that "Sherman is at Snake Creek Gap." Wherever Sherman was, the Federal main effort would be. Johnston met with Wheeler that night and ordered him to conduct a sweep north of Dalton to ensure that the enemy had indeed abandoned his lines there. Meanwhile, he issued orders for the rest of the army to march to Resaca. He himself left that night by train, sharing a ride with Hood as far as Tilton.[23]

There is no evidence that Johnston considered ignoring Sherman's maneuver and embarking on an advance of his own to cut Sherman off from Chattanooga, nor is there evidence that any of his subordinates suggested it to him, Hood included. Years later, Stewart's aide-de-camp wrote that he and Stewart had discussed the idea, but apparently no one brought it up at headquarters. Since December, Johnston had claimed that his long-range plan was to repulse a Federal attack at Dalton and then counterattack into Tennessee. But the skirmishing along Rocky Face Ridge had only bloodied the nose of the Federal army; it had not inflicted the kind of blow that would allow the Confederates to regain the initiative. Moreover, all of Johnston's plans for an offensive were premised on receiving substantial reinforcements. Polk's Army of Mississippi certainly constituted substantial reinforcements, but Polk was at Resaca. Johnston could not leave him there unsupported and strike northward. For now, at least, Sherman had gained the initiative. Clearly, the immediate need was for Johnston to hurry south to block Sherman's move and look for another opportunity.

The same evening that Johnston left Dalton for Resaca, he received a message from Richmond that Lee had won a "victory" over Grant at the crossroads of Spotsylvania Court House in Virginia. Johnston ordered that the message be read to the troops to boost their morale. Ironically, Johnston's movement to Resaca that very night was the western counterpart to Lee's move to Spotsylvania. Grant had tried to steal a march around Lee in the Wilderness in the same way that Sherman was trying to steal a march on Johnston. In each case, the Confederates interposed themselves at the crucial crossroads in sufficient strength to force the Federals to resort to a frontal assault. From Richmond, however, Lee's maneuver looked like a victory; Johnston's looked like a retreat.[24]

In the early morning hours of May 13, the Army of Tennessee conducted the first of what would become a series of night marches. "There was no excitement," one veteran of Hardee's corps recalled, "we were moving along as if on review." En route they passed Johnston, who had arrived ahead of them and was now mounted on his bay horse. "We passed old Joe and his staff," this soldier recounted. "He has on a light or mole colored hat, with a black feather in it. He is listening to the firing going on at the front. One little cheer, and the very ground seems to shake with cheers. Old Joe smiles as blandly as a modest maid, raises his hat in acknowledgement, makes a polite bow, and rides toward the firing."[25]

The Army of Tennessee took a position in front of Resaca at midmorning. It arrived with no time to spare. Johnston later recalled that while the Confederates were occupying the ground he had selected, "the Federal army was forming in front of them." He placed his forces in a defensive posture behind Camp Creek, which paralleled the railroad about a mile to the west. Polk's two divisions held the extreme left, near where Camp Creek flowed into the Oostanaula; Hardee's corps held the center; and Hood's corps held the right, which bent westward across the railroad to anchor its right on the Connasauga. As at Dalton, Johnston's lines faced west and north in a defensive arc, but now Johnston found himself with his back to a major river where a Federal breakthrough might be ruinous. He would have preferred to defend from behind the Oostanaula, but Sherman had left him little choice. One Confederate soldier wrote in his diary: "I consider Gen. Johnston the best General in the Confederacy, not even excepting Robt. E. Lee, but this is one time that old Sherman came near over-reaching him. I will always consider it a mere chance if he gets well away from Resaca."[26]

The Federals attacked with the same fierceness that had carried them over the top of Missionary Ridge, and the Confederate defenders resisted just as fiercely. The Federals did not concentrate on a single point, but assaulted all along the line, as if hunting for a weak spot. To many, the fighting blended into one long battle. A veteran of Cleburne's corps wrote that "for two days the firing was incessant, the Yankees assaulting the works several times." Another, more impressionistically, recorded that "The air is full of deadly missiles. We can see the two lines meet, and hear the deadly crash of battle; we can see the blaze of smoke and fire. The earth trembles." Even where the enemy was repulsed, he did not retreat, but lay down five hundred yards away and continued to snipe at the Confederate line of infantry. There was no respite. To steady the troops, William Hardee walked along the line amid the "storm of bullets," ignoring the shouts from his soldiers to get down.[27]

The fire died out with nightfall, but it welled up again in the morning light of May 14. This time the Federals concentrated their efforts against the hinge of the Confederate defenses, where Hardee's and Hood's corps met. There, near a small white house surrounded by an apple orchard, outnumbered Confederates repulsed three separate attacks between ten in the morning and two in the afternoon. At the same time, Wheeler's scouts, now finally providing the kind of information that Johnston needed, reported that Sherman's own left flank was in the air. Seeing an opportunity to regain the initiative, Johnston ordered Hood to prepare an attack. He drew four brigades from Hardee's front to strengthen the assault, and took up a position on a little hill near the center. He was there, mounted on his "bright bay horse" and gesturing with his sword, when the men of the First Tennessee marched past. It was a tableau long remembered by at least one soldier, who thought, "He looked like the pictures you see hung upon the walls."[28]

At six o'clock, the men of Stewart's and Stevenson's divisions charged forward, wheeling westward like a swinging door, with Stevenson's men as the hinge. The attack caught the Federals by surprise, and the bluecoats broke and fled, throwing off their knapsacks as they ran. Stevenson's men leaped after them through the broken woods, screaming the rebel yell. Their headlong pursuit was halted by an impertinent Federal battery that stubbornly held its ground. Rounds of cannister at close range cut huge gaps in the rebel line, and Stevenson's men fell back to re-form. A single Federal battery could not have stood unsupported for long, but the lead elements of Hooker's corps arrived to secure the guns and halt the Confederate advance.

To their right, the men of Stewart's division overlapped the Federal right and encountered only token resistance; they could barely catch up with the retreating Federals. A staff officer recalled that the Yankees "fled without firing a gun." Stewart's men pursued them until dark, then camped on the ground they had captured. All night they could hear the sounds of enemy axmen felling trees to construct defensive lines in anticipation of having to repel another attack the next day.[29]

After dark, Johnston sought out Hood so that they could lay plans for continuing the attack. They talked together in a cut of the railroad, and personally questioned two Federal prisoners. The success of the afternoon's assault and the apparent vulnerability of the Federal left suggested that even greater things could be achieved the next day. Johnston hoped that Hood's reinforced corps could "defeat the left of the Federal army, while its right was held in check by the remaining third of ours, protected by intrenchments." He therefore directed Hood to renew the attack at dawn, promising that he would provide support from Hardee's corps. "Let the troops understand it," he ordered. His mood was optimistic, even euphoric. A renewed attack on the Federal left might turn the enemy's position, and Sherman was at the end of a precarious supply line. A defeat could send him reeling back into the mountains of North Georgia.[30]

Johnston's mood sustained him as he rode back from the right flank well after nightfall. Then a courier rode up with news that changed his plans as well as his mood: Martin's cavalry patrols had discovered Federal forces crossing the Oostanaula River at Lay's Ferry, five miles downstream (westward) from Resaca. The Federals had rafted over on pontoon boats and driven off the Confederate pickets. Johnston cancelled Hood's orders to attack, and sent Walker's division south with orders to drive the Federals back across the river. But there was other disquieting news that night. Just before dark, Federal troops seized a piece of high ground on the Confederate left east of Camp Creek. Polk's men tried several times to retake it, but failed. The Federals were bringing up artillery, and from this new position they would be able to shell the railroad bridge over the Oostanaula. Johnston ordered his engineers to assemble a pontoon bridge out of range of the Federal artillery to maintain his communications southward.[31]

Skirmishing all along the line began again the next morning as soon as it was light enough to see. Johnston rode first to Polk's front on the extreme left to examine the Federal gains there for himself. Satisfied that the situation had stabilized, he then rode off to the right, where he hoped to renew the attack that had shown so much promise the day before. During the night, Hood had ordered the construction of a small redoubt in front of Hindman's position, where it could enfilade a Federal counterattack. Into it he put four guns of Captain Max Van Den Corput's Georgia battery. But the fort was still unfinished when the Federals attacked. At eleven came the sound of "very heavy musketry and artillery," and at noon the enemy charged out of the woods in a determined attack. The Federal infantrymen overwhelmed Hood's little fort, though it was too close to the Confederate main line for them to hold it. They tried to haul off the guns, but Confederate sharpshooters made that impossible. The Federals withdrew, and the fort and its four guns stood there, abandoned, between the two enemy armies for the rest of the afternoon.[32]

Johnston had ridden to Hood's front at the first sound of the Federal attack. They were discussing the tactical situation a little after noon when a courier from Walker arrived with the welcome news that the report of Federals crossing the Oostanaula was false. Walker reported that he had encountered no Federal infantry south of the river. Johnston could concentrate on the situation in front of him. He now ordered Hood to renew the attack, and suggested that Stewart should advance to strike the attacking Federals in the flank. But only hours later, before Stewart could obey those orders, Johnston heard again from Walker: there were Federals south of the river after all! Martin's initial report had been correct, but the Federals had withdrawn with Walker's arrival. Now they were back across the river in force, and Walker had been unable to drive them back. For the second time, Johnston cancelled orders for an attack and began instead to plan a withdrawal. Unfortunately for Stewart's men, the cancellation order never reached them. At four o'clock in the afternoon they attacked unsupported, and were broken by a "terrible fire" from Hooker's corps, which was poised to launch an attack of its own.[33]

Only an hour after Stewart's ill-fated attack, Confederate wagons began to roll south out of Resaca, crossing the Oostanaula on the new pontoon bridge. After dark, Johnston summoned the corps and division commanders to explain to them the need to withdraw. The enemy was across the river with two divisions; "We could not send a force sufficient to beat the force in our rear and at the same time hold [our] present position." That night, the Army of Tennessee evacuated Resaca and crossed to the south bank of the Oostanaula. Johnston had performed this maneuver before—at Centreville, at Yorktown, and at Dalton—and he knew what he was about. He was aided by the weather: it was a cloudy night and visibility was limited. While the wagons and guns rolled south, Confederate pickets kept up a steady fire on enemy lines. Then, about midnight, the infantry pulled out of line and marched southward. Hardee's and Polk's corps used the railroad bridge; Hood's men crossed on the new pontoon bridge. The railroad bridge was burned, and troops of the rear guard took up the pontoon bridge and loaded it onto wagons for future use. The Battle of Resaca was over.[34]

There is little doubt that Johnston had no choice but to retire from Resaca once the Federal army had secured a lodgment on the south bank of the Oostanaula. But once again he had to surrender the initiative to Sherman. Throughout the spring campaign, Johnston's greatest handicap was that Sherman's margin of superiority allowed him to pin down the Army of Tennessee with three fourths of his force and still have enough troops to probe for an undefended flank. At both Dalton and Resaca, Sherman froze Johnston's army with an aggressive attack, while he sent a force to outflank him to the west and south. In effect, he jabbed with his left and threw a right hook. In each case Johnston parried the jab, and blocked the hook. But both times he had to surrender territory to do so.

Johnston conducted the retreat from Resaca in good order, without the loss of any men or equipment—except for the four guns still in the abandoned fort in front of Hood's former position. For all that, Johnston's defense of Resaca was not a victory. He had met Sherman's flanking movement, only to be flanked again. On the other hand, it was not a defeat, either. The loss of four guns was unfortunate but not important. The casualties were more significant: Johnston's army lost more than 500 killed and 3,200 wounded, with another 1,400 missing.[35] Johnston was confident that he had inflicted far heavier casualties on the enemy which, combined with Federal losses in front of Dalton, must surely have weakened Sherman's armies significantly. Moreover, Sherman had been drawn away from his base and was now operating at the end of a lengthy, vulnerable supply line. Finally, Johnston's junction with Polk added a third corps to his army, which now boasted as many as seventy thousand, including cavalry. Johnston found all these to be reasons for optimism, despite the two retreats. Perhaps south of the Oostanaula he would have the opportunity to strike a telling counterblow.

The authorities in Richmond saw little to encourage optimism in Johnston's retrograde movements. Davis noted that although Johnston reported light losses, he gave up large chunks of territory. The Confederate president contrasted Johnston's brief stand at Resaca with Lee's prolonged defense of Spotsylvania. Whereas Davis wrote Lee to offer his "grateful thanks for the glorious deeds you have done," to Johnston he expressed only "disappointment." In large part, of course, the contrast was due as much to the difference between Grant and Sherman as between Lee and Johnston. Grant was so determined to fight his way through Lee's lines at Spotsylvania that at one point he wired Lincoln that he intended "to fight it out on this line if it takes all summer." Not so Sherman. Two days were enough for him. Grant lost fifteen thousand men over two weeks trying to punch through Confederate defenses at Spotsylvania, whereas Sherman began almost at once to look for a way around Resaca. Nevertheless, to Davis it seemed that Johnston was not doing enough to halt Sherman's advance. In the middle of the Battle of Resaca, he sent Johnston a telegram asserting that Grant was about to be reinforced from Sherman's army and ordering Johnston to let Richmond know when it happened. This was almost too much. Johnston wired back: "We are in the presence of the whole force of the enemy assembled from Tennessee and North Alabama. I think he cannot reinforce Grant without my knowledge (nor do I think he will), as my whole line is engaged in skirmishing. Yesterday he made several assaults that were repulsed."[36]

Johnston's conduct of the campaign had not been without error. He had left Snake Creek Gap undefended, and he had been slow to react to McPherson's flanking movement once it became evident. Partly this was due to the weakness of Wheeler's cavalry, both in numbers and leadership. But partly, too, it was a product of Johnston's reluctance to discard the idea that Sherman's main effort would come through Crow Valley on his right flank. Still, Johnston's foresight in placing two brigades at Resaca, and in reinforcing them, helped convince McPherson not to press his advantage, and Johnston's own move to Resaca was prompt and timely. Finally, at both Dalton and Resaca, Johnston engineered successful escapes. Yet Johnston knew as well as anyone that successful escapes did not win campaigns. Twice Sherman had flanked him out of good positions. The cost had been light, and Johnston was satisfied that Sherman's forces had suffered far more than his own. But no retreat, however timely, ever won a campaign. Eventually, Johnston would have to turn on his foe and inflict a mortal wound.

CHAPTER NINETEEN

Shield and Sword

Johnston's escape southward across the Oostanaula did not bring him or his army any respite, for his opponent was not one to linger over his successes. Sherman's troops poured over the river probing—always probing—for a way around the Confederate flank. For the next two weeks, Johnston successfully maneuvered his army to deny Sherman such an opportunity—to refuse his flank, as the military expression went, blocking Sherman's probes and shielding the critical railroad south to Atlanta. Johnston's great handicap in this *pas de deux* was his numerical inferiority, although the extent of that handicap was then, and remains today, a subject of some dispute. In his official reports, Johnston distinguished between the "effective strength" of his army (which he reported in June as 60,564) and the "aggregate present" (which included the sick and non-combatants, and which totalled 82,413). Naturally, Johnston's defenders consistently cited the smaller number to emphasize his disadvantage to Sherman's force of more than a hundred thousand; just as consistently, his critics cited the larger number to support their argument that Johnston was behaving timidly.

In either case, Sherman's superior numbers allowed him to pin down Johnston's army with three fourths of his own, and use the remaining fourth to probe for a flank, or better yet, to threaten the vital Western & Atlantic Railroad from Atlanta on which Johnston was dependent for support. So Johnston was always reacting to Sherman's initiatives rather than making Sherman react to his. Sooner or later, however, Johnston believed that the Federal commander would make a mistake and give him an opportunity to deliver a telling counterattack. If he could concentrate a significant portion of his own army against one of Sherman's probes, isolate it and destroy it, he would effectively even the odds at a single stroke. Such a defeat deep in enemy territory would be catastrophic for Sherman, so far from his base, and might even force him to withdraw from Georgia. Then, but only then, Johnston could launch his much-anticipated and long-delayed offensive.

While he waited for Sherman to make that mistake, Johnston promoted a corollary strategy: attacking Sherman's supply lines. The further south the two armies moved, the further the Yankees were drawn from their base at Chattanooga. As Johnston saw it, this placed Sherman in a dilemma. Either he would have to leave his supply lines vulnerable to Confederate cavalry raids, or he would have to station so many detachments behind him to protect his communications that his front-line strength would be diminished. Either way, as the two armies moved southward, Johnston would become stronger while Sherman became weaker. Johnston would give ground slowly, grudgingly, making Sherman pay in blood for every mile and watching for an opening; meanwhile, Sherman would be moving southward away from his source of supply, becoming increasingly vulnerable to cavalry raids. In this strategic plan, Hardee's corps would be the shield that would blunt Sherman's advance; Nathan Bedford Forrest's cavalry would harry the Federal supply lines; and when the time was ripe, Hood's corps would be the sword that delivered the counterstroke. Each man would play a role for which he was particularly suited. In the ensuing campaign, however, though the shield proved strong enough, the sword never struck. For the rest of their lives, Johnston and Hood would argue about whose fault it was.

It was still light late on the afternoon of May 16 when Johnston and his staff arrived at Calhoun, Georgia. He set up his headquarters in the Curtin House, and notified Davis by telegraph of his evacuation of Resaca. For now, at least, though the army's situation was serious, it was not desperate. Hardee's corps was serving as the rear guard, fending off the Federal pursuit, while the rest of the army went into bivouac just south of town—Hood's corps on the road south to Adairsville, and Polk's on the road to Rome— blocking both roads. Before morning, Johnston would have to choose between the two. It was already too late to defend the line of the Oostanaula; Federal forces were even now pouring across the river, and a bold spy who had spent the night behind enemy lines had overheard the Federals boasting that they were on their way to cut Johnston off from the railroad. Calhoun offered no special advantages for a defensive stand, and since the roads southward forked, Johnston would have to choose between falling back on

Rome in western Georgia, or continuing due south along the line of the railroad to Adairsville. It was an unhappy choice, but not a hard one— Rome's ironworks were important, but the railroad was vital. That day, therefore, Johnston issued orders for another night march south. Because the move uncovered the road to Rome, that city would have to be evacuated to the enemy—more grist for Johnston's critics in Richmond.[1]

Johnston set out on his second successive night ride in the early morning hours of May 17. This time, instead of reacting to a flanking move by Sherman, he was moving toward what he hoped would be a trap for the Federal army. Ten miles to the south, just north of Adairsville. Johnston planned to make his stand. His engineers assured him that the valley there was narrow enough to allow the Army of Tennessee to present a continuous front to the enemy and rely on the hills to protect both its flanks. But when Johnston arrived at Adairsville just before daylight, he found that the valley was wider, and the hills less forboding, than he had expected. The terrain at Adairsville, he thought, was not significantly better for a fight than that at Calhoun.[2]

He might have to fight anyway. Wheeler reported that the enemy was pressing hard, and as his infantrymen arrived, Johnston immediately deployed them into battle formation just north of town. Almost instinctively, they began to dig in. Skirmishers in front of the battle line were soon exchanging rounds with the Federal advance guard through a steady rain. Cheatham's division bore the brunt of the Federal probe and was soon fully engaged; one soldier recalled that there was "Some hot fighting on our front." The Federals did not press the issue, however, for Sherman was apparently unwilling to commit to a full-scale battle until his army was concentrated.[3]

At about six o'clock that evening, Johnston met with his corps commanders in his headquarters tent. In addition to the sound of the firing from the front, they could hear the muffled growl of artillery coming from the west, which Johnston understood when he was handed a telegram informing him that the enemy was at Rome "in force" and shelling the town. In one sense this was good news. If Sherman had sent substantial forces to seize Rome, he had reduced the strength of his main body by that much. Moreover, while Sherman was dispersing his forces, Johnston continued to be reinforced—Polk's cavalry division of some 3,700 troopers had joined the army that very day. Could the army make a stand at Adairsville?

Hardee thought so. He argued that Adairsville was as good a place as any to turn and make a fight. Johnston later claimed that Hood disagreed, arguing instead that the army should get behind the protection of the Etowah River, another dozen miles to the south. In any event, Johnston decided on a middle course. Although he agreed with Hood that the terrain at Adairsville was not ideal, he still hoped to offer Sherman a fight somewhere north of the Etowah River. All four generals bent over the map, which they studied with some care. From Adairsville, the roads south branched once again. The

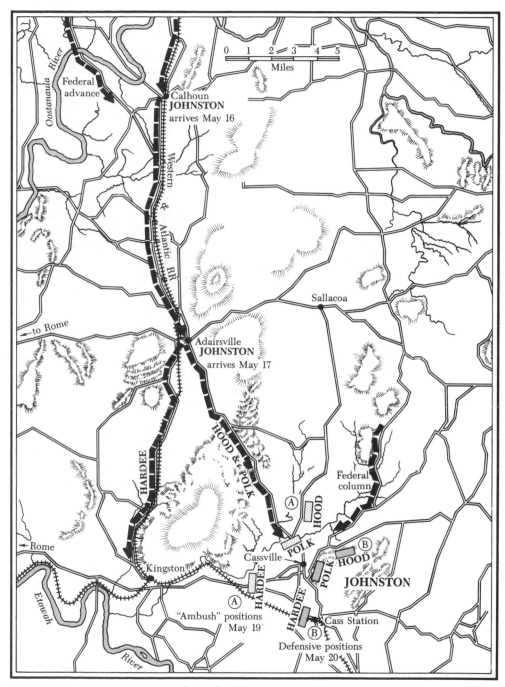

Cassville, May 16–20, 1864

railroad itself, that slender but precious link with Atlanta, led due south to Kingston and a junction with the railroad from Rome. From there it turned sharply eastward, passing through Cass Station six miles to the east. Another route south from Adairsville cut the angle of the railroad and led directly to Cassville.° This road was more difficult, winding across high and largely barren country, but it was also much shorter.[4]

Johnston traced the road to Cassville with his finger and closely questioned the staff topographer and mapmaker, Lieutenant A. H. Buchanan, about the surrounding terrain. The germ of an idea formed in his mind, and he became increasingly animated. The more he thought about it, the better he liked it. He would send Hardee with all of the army's wagons due south to Kingston, along the straight, flat road paralleling the railroad. Since Hardee had been acting as rear guard for the army since Resaca, Sherman would conclude that the entire Confederate army had gone that way. Then, when Hardee reached Kingston, he would turn east, face about, and block the road between Kingston and Cassville. Meanwhile, Hood and Polk would march over the winding road directly to Cassville. Sherman, almost certainly, would divide his forces in pursuit. He would send the bulk of his army after Hardee, but at least part of his forces would take the road for Cassville. Since the Cassville Road vectored away from the railroad at a 30-degree angle, with inhospitable terrain between, the two Federal wings would be effectively isolated from one another. While these separated Federal units marched away from each another, Johnston would unite the Army of Tennessee at Cassville to ambush whatever elements of the Federal force were unlucky enough to be assigned to the Cassville Road. After explaining his plan to his corps commanders, Johnston issued the necessary orders to put the scheme into motion.[5]

Before the generals left Johnston's headquarters tent, there was one more piece of business. Polk produced a letter that Lydia had written to him the week before from Atlanta, asking him to perform "a good deed." Lydia told the former Episcopal bishop that her husband had never been baptized; "it is the dearest wish of my heart that he should be & that you should perform the ceremony." Johnston readily agreed to Polk's suggestion that the ceremony take place immediately. So Polk donned the trappings of his former office and performed the rites of baptism on his commanding general. It was "a deeply solemn scene," Polk wrote to his own wife: by the flickering light of candles, with Hardee and Hood standing witness, Johnston knelt to receive the sacrament. Then he rose, cleansed of his sins, and went to work to implement his plans for battle.[6]

That night the soldiers of the Army of Tennessee once again loaded the wagons and shouldered their packs for a night march. Despite three such

---

°The residents had recently changed the name of their town to Manassas in honor of the July 1861 victory. I have used the original name of the town throughout to avoid confusion.

consecutive marches—all southward, away from the enemy—the troops felt no alarm or disappointment. The diaries and letters of the men in the ranks bespoke undiminished confidence in their general. In each case, the army's movements were conducted in proper order, with no sense of panic or emergency, and with no loss of supplies or equipment. There was little straggling. A Yankee soldier recorded in his diary: "We used to capture stragglers all the time while Bragg was in command but got very few since Johnston has had command."[7]

Johnston himself left Adairsville at 4:00 A.M. on May 18 and rode out on the Cassville Road, past the marching columns of troops from Hood's and Polk's corps. He reached Cassville at seven-thirty, setting up his headquarters in the town. The army arrived piecemeal throughout the morning, and immediately went into bivouac. A staff officer noted that the soldiers had "a good rest" at Cassville. Meanwhile, Johnston received the welcome news from Wheeler that the enemy was behaving exactly as he had anticipated. Thomas's Army of the Cumberland, the largest of Sherman's three armies, was following Hardee along the line of the railroad; but other forces, later identified as Schofield's small Army of the Ohio and Hooker's XXth Corps, were advancing along the Cassville Road. Sherman had taken the bait. Just as Sherman had anticipated trapping Johnston at Resaca, now Johnston eagerly envisioned trapping and destroying a portion of Sherman's army at Cassville.[8]

There was some bad news, too. At Cassville, Johnston learned that Forrest's cavalry raid into Tennessee, which he had hoped would cut Sherman's lifeline to his base, had been suspended because of Federal demonstrations from Memphis. But the news could not ruin Johnston's mood, for events in Georgia were unfolding exactly as he had planned. That afternoon when Johnston met again with his corps commanders, the mood at headquarters was optimistic. The generals' spirits rose even higher when a telegram arrived from Virginia claiming that Lee had inflicted no fewer than 15,000 casualties on Grant's army in the fight for Spotsylvania. The news prompted Johnston to remark to his corps commanders that the "Confederacy was as fixed an institution as England or France."[9]

In planning his ambush at Cassville, Johnston reserved the crucial role for Hood's corps. Hood's enthusiasm for the offensive was his salient characteristic as a commander; his body bore the scars of his impetuosity at Gettysburg and Chickamauga. It was only fitting that he now be assigned the responsibility of delivering the blow that would send Sherman reeling from Georgia. Johnston set the stage by placing Polk's corps directly athwart the road from Adairsville, facing north. Hood's corps was to move by a secondary country road, taking up a position to Polk's right and slightly in advance. In his mind's eye, Johnston could see it clearly: As the unsuspecting Federals moved south, they would encounter Polk's corps and deploy to contest the road. At that moment, Hood's corps would smash into their left flank. One whole wing of the Federal army would be destroyed. It was a well-conceived plan and, for once, the enemy seemed to be unaware of the waiting trap.[10]

At dawn on the 19th, Johnston issued a general order to the troops, announcing the impending battle. Its tone reflected the confidence he felt in the outcome. "Soldiers of the Army of Tennessee," it began, "you have displayed the highest quality of the soldier—firmness in combat, patience under toil. By your courage and skill you have repulsed every assault of the enemy. . . . You will now turn and march to meet his advancing columns. Fully confiding in the conduct of the officers, the courage of the soldiers, I lead you to battle."[11]

Johnston then rode out with his staff to examine the terrain, and to be certain that Polk and Hood were just where he wanted them. After satisfying himself that they were properly placed, he returned to his headquarters. It was full daylight now and the Federals could be expected at any moment; Hardee reported that he was beginning to feel pressure on his front. At ten o'clock, Johnston concluded that the quarry was well into the bag and that it was time for Hood to spring the trap. He dispatched Mackall to urge Hood to advance and "make quick work" of it. After Mackall rode off, Johnston passed an anxious half hour waiting and listening for the sound of the attack. Finally, at 10:20, there it was: the sound of skirmishing in the distance! But only a few minutes later, a courier rode up with a message from Mackall: enemy forces were on the Canton Road behind Hood's right flank. Instead of attacking, Hood had fallen back. Astonished and perplexed, Johnston exclaimed, "It can't be!" and called for a map to understand what that news meant to his plan. The Canton Road was considerably south and east of Hood's position; if the report was true, then Hood was certainly in a bad spot. But it seemed so improbable. How could there be Federals on that road? Where had they come from? Johnston was inclined to dismiss the report as preposterous.[12]

What had happened was this: Hood had started his men forward at about ten o'clock, even before Mackall had arrived to prompt him. But they had advanced only a mile or two when Hood received a report that a second column of Federal troops, in unknown strength, was off to his right. If he advanced as Johnston had ordered, this column would be in his rear; even now it was on his flank. Hood sent a staff officer galloping toward Johnston's headquarters with the news, but at the same time he halted the advance and ordered his men to fall back into a defensive position south of the Canton Road. He was in the midst of executing this movement when Mackall reined up in front of him with Johnston's message to "make quick work" of it. Hood informed Mackall of the existence of the column of Federals "on both the Canton and Spring Place Road." Mackall was shocked; he had not seen the Federal column himself, and eventually he became skeptical that it had ever existed. His cousin Thomas Mackall wrote in his journal that night that the "Report of column on Canton road [was] not afterwards confirmed." Was it there at all?[13]

In his official report to President Davis the next day, Johnston claimed that

Hood had been spooked by a "false report," and that by the time the mistake was discovered, "it was too late to resume the movement." Even ten years later in his *Narrative*, Johnston claimed that "the report upon which General Hood acted was manifestly untrue." But Johnston's unwillingness to believe Hood's report was primarily a measure of his own disappointment. Having staked so much on a successful battle at Cassville to salvage the campaign, he was crushed that it had not come off as planned. Despite Johnston's skepticism, the Federals *were* there. The blue-coated soldiers on the Canton Road belonged to Dan Butterfield's brigade, which had become separated from the main body and was floundering along on unfamiliar back roads. In a word, they were lost, and their appearance at such a propitious moment was simply a matter of chance.[14]

But even if there were Federals on the Canton Road, were they enough of a threat to justify Hood's decision to cancel the attack and fall back? Johnston did not think so. He argued that Hood should have attacked anyway; at the very least he should have investigated the mystery column more fully before withdrawing. Johnston was convinced that in spite of Hood's record of aggressiveness, in this case he proved too ready to yield his advantage. In any event, by the time Johnston learned of it, Hood had already fallen back and the opportunity for an ambush was lost. With great reluctance Johnston cancelled the attack. The sword of the army had been drawn, but it did not strike.[15]

Bitterly disappointed, Johnston fell back on his secondary strategy: that of assuming a strong position and inviting Sherman to attack. His engineers had identified a ridge south and east of Cassville where the army could make a stand. Johnston and Mackall rode out to it, hastily sketched a new line of defense, and issued orders for the troops to occupy the ridge. The army fell back through the town of Cassville and up onto the ridge during the afternoon. Johnston was pleased with the new position and later called it "the best that I saw occupied during the war." He was not alone in this estimate. A staff officer from Stewart's division thought the army's position at Cassville was "the strongest position I ever saw. . . ." Such postwar recollections, however, were influenced by what happened next, for although the placement of the army south of Cassville was strong, it had one weak link.[16]

The ridge on which Johnston now posted his three corps ran roughly north-south. Hardee's corps occupied the left, or southernmost, portion of the line, straddling the railroad; Polk's corps held the center; and Hood's the right. While the troops were digging in, Johnston rode along the line accompanied by his chief of artillery, Brigadier General Francis A. Shoup. At the point where Polk's right met Hood's left, the line jutted out to accommodate the Mississippi battery of Captain James A. Hoskins before running on to the north. Shoup pointed out the salient to Johnston and commented that it could be enfiladed by Federal artillery across the valley. Moreover, the lack of vegetation on that part of the ridge made it particularly exposed. Johnston looked it over and dismissed Shoup's concerns. First of all, he argued, the

Federal guns were too far away to be a serious danger; and in any case, the troops on that part of the line could always withdraw to the reverse slope during the shelling and then reoccupy the line when the Yankee infantry attacked. He suggested that the men build traverses to protect themselves if the Federal artillery fire became heavy.[17]

But it was not that simple. Although the Confederate line ran roughly north-south, the Federal line across the valley curved in a gentle arc so that the exposed portion of the rebel line was subject to a crossfire. That night, the vulnerability of Hoskins's battery became apparent when the Federals opened an artillery barrage that concentrated on the exposed salient. Hood, whose corps occupied the right flank, believed the Federal bombardment proved that the position was untenable; after discussing it at length with Polk, he convinced the bishop-general to go with him that night and present the case to Johnston.

Hood's mood was exactly the opposite of Johnston's, who remarked that evening to the Confederate governor of Tennessee, Isham Harris, that he would be "ready for and happy to receive the enemy next day." After inspecting the line and conversing with Mackall, Johnston rode back to his headquarters well after dark, where he found supper ready. He also found Polk's staff aide, Colonel William D. Gale, who tendered the invitation from Hood and Polk to come to Polk's headquarters and discuss the army's plans. Johnston accepted and asked Major General Samuel French to go with him. After dinner, Johnston and French rode over to Polk's headquarters, where they arrived at about eight o'clock. Hood and Polk were waiting for them. To Johnston's astonishment, Hood announced that he and Polk now believed the army's position was untenable. Johnston objected: the army was in a commanding position with clear lines of fire. But Hood was insistent. He argued that the weakness of the salient made the whole position indefensible, and that Polk's line could not be held for as long as forty-five minutes against a determined attack; his own corps, he said, could hold but little longer. Johnston debated with Hood for more than two hours. General French recalled that "Johnston insisted on fighting." But eventually Hood wore him down.[18]

What finally convinced Johnston to give way was his conclusion that he could not insist on a defense of the ridge in the face of concerted opposition from the two corps commanders whose forces would bear the brunt of the fighting. Their lack of confidence would surely communicate itself to the troops and make their dire predictions a reality. Johnston therefore agreed that the army would evacuate the ridge and fall back to the south bank of the Etowah that night. Then, around ten o'clock, Hardee walked into the room. His corps was on the extreme left of the Confederate position and had no weak salients on its front. He was as surprised as Johnston had been to hear Hood and Polk repeat their objections. But his protests were useless. At two o'clock in the morning, Mackall issued the orders for the army to withdraw.

Unlike previous evacuations, which had been executed with precision and timeliness, this one was marked by confusion and muttered imprecations in the ranks. It was evident to the troops that the retreat was a last-minute decampment and not part of a strategic plan. That morning their commander had issued a stirring call to battle; now they were in retreat again, heading south. They were at first surprised, then disappointed, and finally disspirited. For the first time in the spring campaign, there was significant straggling. Johnston, too, was despondent. "I have been very unfortunate for the past two weeks," he wrote to Lydia. "Events beyond my control have prevented my attacking the enemy." He confessed that he was "very much disappointed to do so little with so fine an army. . . ."[19]

Johnston arrived at Cartersville, five miles south of Cassville, at a little after four o'clock in the morning, but the army straggled out behind him for miles, and the river crossings were still more than two miles ahead. It was a warm Georgia night and the roads were dusty. Confusion reigned: the wagon trains had become mixed together, clogging the roads and bridges, especially the bridges. Not until well after daylight were the wagons safely across the river. Then Johnston ordered Wheeler to take up the pontoon bridges and burn the wagon bridge. In his enthusiasm, Wheeler also burned the railroad bridge, which Johnston had hoped to salvage for a future offensive.[20]

The army finally settled into bivouac around the small town of Allatoona, five miles south of the river, on Saturday, May 21. There the Allatoona Mountains allowed Johnston to take up a strong position in a narrow defile, where the army was relatively secure from any direct attack. They were driven off by a few rounds of artillery, but their presence proved that the Federals had already crossed the river. From there, Johnston wired Davis to report that the army had fallen back again. He tried to put the best face on it: "We kept near him to prevent his detaching to Virginia, as you directed; and have repulsed every attack he had made." Unlike his deliberate evacuation of Dalton and Resaca, this could not be disguised as a strategic maneuver. At Allatoona, Johnston also received a reply to his earlier telegram in which he had informed Davis of his withdrawal from Resaca. Davis acknowledged receipt of Johnston's wire and noted his "disappointment." Johnston replied: "I know that my dispatch must of necessity create the feeling you express." In his defense, he insisted that "I have earnestly sought an opportunity to strike the enemy." But he claimed that Sherman's careful advance, during which he fortified as soon as he stopped, plus his numerical superiority, made an assault "too hazardous." Besides, he noted lamely if accurately, "in making this retrograde march we have [not] lost much by straggling and desertion."[21]

That same day, Hood also wrote a letter to Davis—a private letter of introduction for Henry P. Brewster, a Texas lawyer who had attached himself to Hood's staff at Dalton and had become Hood's confidante and advocate. Brewster was now on his way to Richmond. Hood took the opportunity to suggest that Brewster could "give you [Davis] an account of the operations of this army." Although no record exists of what Brewster reported in Richmond, the general thrust of his remarks can be guessed by Brewster's subsequent public criticism of Johnston and his effusive praise of Hood. Brewster told all who would listen that Johnston had "no plan," that he was "afraid to risk a battle," and that despite Hood's repeated urgings to go on the offensive, Johnston overrode both Hood and Polk and insisted upon retreat. "Hood and Polk wanted to fight," Brewster asserted to an audience at General Chesnut's, but Johnston "resisted their council." Brewster claimed that Johnston "is afraid to trust them because they do not hate Jeff Davis enough. . . ." After listening to Brewster's report, Davis indicated that he believed Johnston would have to be removed. It is hard to imagine that Brewster disagreed.[22]

The men of the Army of Tennessee observed the Sabbath on May 22 in camp around Allatoona. While his army rested, Johnston searched his soul as he reviewed the campaign. "There never was a time when the comfort of your love was more necessary to me," he wrote to Lydia, "for I have never been so little satisfied with myself. . . . I have seen so much beautiful country given up. . . . You can not imagine how distressing it is and at the same time humiliating to see the apprehension of the people of a country abandoned to the enemy." Johnston was sure his enemy would try yet another flanking movement, but he was unsure which way Sherman would jump: eastward to outflank his right, or westward across Pumpkinvine Creek. He notified all his corps commanders to "be ready to move in any direction at a moment's notice." In fact, the army would remain near Allatoona for most of three days. The respite was salutary for army morale, and it brought hundreds of stragglers back into the ranks; but it also allowed Sherman to retain the initiative.[23]

When Sherman did move, it was to the west. Ten miles west of Cartersville, the three Federal armies crossed the Etowah and moved south, converging on the crossroads hamlet of Dallas, Georgia. The Army of Tennessee broke camp just after dawn on May 24 and marched south toward Dallas through a heavy spring rain. Hardee led, followed by Polk, with Hood in the rear. Johnston reported to Davis that "The enemy crossed the Etowah near Stilesborough," and that he was moving "to intercept him and oppose his further progress."[24]

In some respects, Johnston considered Sherman's move to the west fortuitous. He continued to hope that Sherman's penetration into Georgia would produce a strain on his supply system that could be exacerbated by the raids of rebel cavalry. Sherman's abandonment of the railroad meant that his supply lines would be even more vulnerable. If Johnston could inflict a defeat on Sherman here in the Georgia woods, fifteen miles from the railroad, and south of the Etowah River, Sherman's position would be precarious indeed.

The army marched all day on the 24th before resting, and the men were

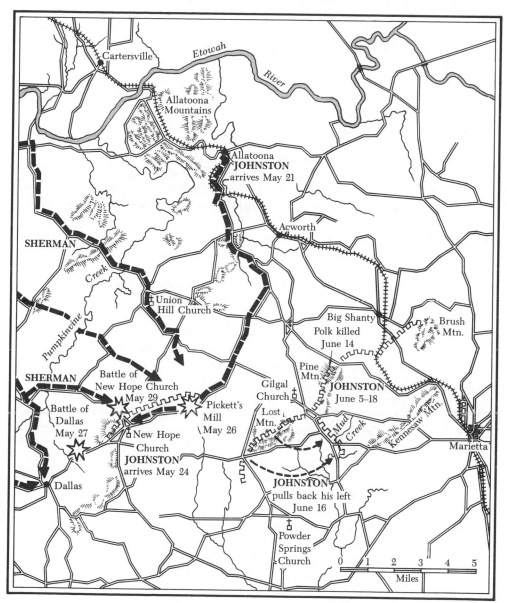

Fighting Around New Hope Church, May–June 1864

up again before dawn the next day striding along the dirt roads toward the southwest. That afternoon the men of Hood's corps were near a small country church which its parishioners had named New Hope when Wheeler's cavalry reported to Johnston that the enemy was very near—and in force. From a prisoner, the rebels learned that the Federals belonged to "Fighting Joe" Hooker's corps. Johnston sent the news to Hood, who immediately put his men into line of battle. The Confederates "hastily threw up log breastworks" and awaited the Yankee onslaught. The Federals opened with a few rounds of artillery as if attempting to flush the game, and at five o'clock they drove in the rebel skirmishers and launched what one Confederate officer called "the most determined and solid charge I ever knew them to make." The Federals thought they were pursuing skirmishers, and when they hit Hood's line of veterans, they reeled back in confusion. Re-formed and reinforced, they came on again—twenty thousand of them—concentrating on Alexander Stewart's division of less than a quarter that number. The fight raged all afternoon and through the twilight into pitch darkness. At dusk, the afternoon heat was broken by "a drenching rain," and thunder added to the din of battle.[25]

The Federals made five successive charges. Before each one they gave three cheers, which may have bolstered their courage but also let Stewart's men know when they were coming. The Confederates answered with the rebel yell. Twice, the Yankees drove to within fifty yards of the Confederate line before giving way. They tended to shoot high in the thick woods; since the Confederates were in a slight depression, the singing minie balls passed over their heads, snipping off branches in the trees. Despite the fierce fighting and the absence of strong fieldworks, the Confederates "were not driven back an inch." Johnston sent a courier to Stewart to ask if he needed reinforcements, but Stewart answered, "My own troops will hold the position." And they did, though when the bluecoats finally gave up the fight, many of the Confederates had their last round of charges in their rifles. From prisoners, and from assessing the carnage in front of their lines, Stewart estimated Federal losses at no less than 5,000, though Hooker later claimed he had lost only 1,665. One Confederate soldier wrote in his diary: "Such desperate fighting has never been witnessed in this army. Some of their dead were within 40 feet of our line. I never saw men lying so thick in all my life."[26]

Johnston spent the night at Hood's headquarters. As the rain continued to fall outside, they discussed the day's fight and the next day's outlook. Despite his disappointment at Cassville, Johnston continued to depend more on Hood for advice than on either of his other corps commanders, and he consulted with him now about the next day's fight. Hood suspected that Sherman would shift to the east in the morning and try to find a way around the rebel line. To counter this move, Johnston ordered Patrick Cleburne to move his crack division to the right flank near Pickett's Mill.[27]

At dawn on May 26, both lines were quiet. Only the sharp report of the occasional sharpshooter's rifle broke the wooded silence. But as Johnston and Hood had suspected, Sherman was on the move behind the lines. At 4:30 P.M. a solid line of blue infantry, several ranks deep, broke from the woods near Pickett's Mill and assailed Cleburne's waiting veterans. As at New Hope Church the day before, the blue ranks were shattered by rebel volleys. As before, the Federals brought up reinforcements and tried again. And as before, they fell apart under the withering fire of entrenched defenders. One officer recalled that the fighting "was marked by great daring on the part of the enemy, some of them getting up as close as thirty feet to our lines." By nightfall, when the Federals pulled back, they left nearly 1,500 men on the field. Cleburne had lost less than a third that number.[28]

Having twice repulsed Sherman's assaults, Johnston began thinking of a counterattack. If Sherman was reaching for the Confederate right, his own right might be vulnerable. Johnston directed Hardee to feel out the enemy in front of him, and Old Reliable sent William Bate's division forward. This Battle of Dallas was Pickett's Mill in reverse. Bate's men were cut down by volleys from Federal forces shooting from behind strong entrenchments. Collectively, these three wilderness battles showed clearly the folly of attempting to launch frontal assaults against troops that were well placed, even if they were not fully entrenched.

That night, as the men of both armies continued to dig in, Johnston again conferred with Hood. The Texan suggested an attack on the Federal left flank. Johnston accepted the idea at once, and together the two men sketched out a general plan. Hood would pull his men out of the battle line, requiring Hardee and Polk to stretch to the right to fill the void. Then Hood would march his corps eastward, behind Cleburne's division, to strike Sherman in flank and rear. As he rolled up the Union line, Polk and Hardee would join the fight.[29]

In the last hour before dawn on May 29, Johnston once again found himself in his headquarters anticipating the first sound of an attack by Hood. The men of Polk's and Hardee's corps waited with him, for the signal of Hood's attack was to be their own signal to go forward. But dawn arrived and no sound came. As the hours passed, it became clear that there was not going to be an attack. At midmorning a courier from Hood arrived at Johnston's headquarters. The Federals had prepared a new line of entrenchments behind their own left flank, Hood reported, and he insisted that an attack under such circumstances would be "inexpedient." Later Hood explained to Johnston that when he reached the designated jumping-off point for the attack, he discovered that it was not the Federal flank in front of him, but their well-fortified front, for they had pulled back during the night. Almost certainly, Hood's decision to cancel the attack was wise; but it was the second time in two weeks that Hood had been entrusted with the army's attack and had failed to deliver.[30]

Both armies spent the next few days improving their entrenchments. Meanwhile, the evidence increased that the Federals were moving eastward, returning to the line of the railroad. Sherman had apparently abandoned the idea of moving around Johnston to the west. Except for nearly continuous sharpshooting, the next two days were quiet along the front. Still, Johnston was sure that Sherman was up to something. At 10:00 P.M. on May 30, he ordered his staff to pack up and be ready to move; but Johnston still waited for Sherman to commit himself. Finally, on June 1, he concluded that Sherman was once again attempting a lateral movement, this time to the east, and he reported to Bragg: "We are making a corresponding movement to our right."[31]

The brief respite gave Johnston the opportunity to contemplate the events of the past several days. He found ample cause for satisfaction. His line had held firm against repeated and determined assaults, during which his forces had inflicted horrible casualties on the enemy. Mansfield Lovell estimated that Sherman had lost 13,000 men in the fighting around Dalton, another 5,800 at Resaca, and 8,000 to 10,000 in the battles around Dallas—a total of more than 25,000; in addition, Lovell estimated that the Federal army had lost another 10,000 to the sick list, and 10,000 more to straggling. Lovell estimated Sherman's total losses at some 45,000 men. "If these figures be true," he wrote, "his army must be greatly diminished." It was relatively easy for Johnston to convince himself that Lovell's estimates were accurate, and to conclude that despite his own disappointment in not having been able to offer battle, the campaign was actually working out quite well. His chief of staff, W. W. Mackall, wrote home that week to explain what was now the headquarters view of things: "We have to keep close up to the enemy, watch carefully every movement, and then try and take advantage of every mistake he [Sherman] makes; by so doing, we have thus far succeeded in making him pay three or four for one of ours out of a state of service by death or wounds; if we can keep this up, we win."[32]

In addition, Johnston concluded that the fight in the North Georgia countryside must have stretched the Federal supply system to the breaking point. A staff member brought Johnston a letter intercepted from Federal Brigadier General William B. Hazen in which Hazen admitted that the Federal troops "were suffering from scarcity of provisions." Johnston reported to Bragg that "Prisoners and the report of the citizens represent his [Sherman's] cavalry and transportation animals in a suffering condition." Johnston suspected that Sherman would be forced to fall back to the railroad, to fortify himself in the Allatoona Hills and await the reconstruction of the railroad in order to reestablish his supply line. The speculation among the staff was that Sherman "will not hazard [an] engagement for some time."[33]

Johnston was only partly right. Sherman's casualties in the fighting since Dalton had been heavy, but not as severe as Lovell calculated. The tendency of brigade and division commanders to exaggerate the losses they had inflicted on their oppenent led to inflated "body counts," so that whereas Johnston assumed that Sherman had suffered at least twenty thousand casualties, he had in fact lost only about half that number. At the same time, Johnston had suffered 5,500 battlefield casualties of his own, and another

3,000 were still missing after the confusion of successive withdrawals. More-over, Sherman could replace his losses, whereas Johnston could add only William Quarles's 2,500-man brigade from Mobile. It was a numbers game that Johnston could not win. Then, too, Sherman's supply situation was not as desperate as Johnston thought—or hoped. To be sure, the Yankees now had to get by on hardtack and coffee, but their rations were no worse, and in most cases considerably better, than those of their gray-clad counterparts. The only real advantage Johnston had gained over his opponent was that Sherman was growing increasingly frustrated by his inability to pin down his elusive foe.

The next day, June 4, was "the quietest day since near New Hope Church." That night, Johnston finally issued orders to move eastward to the high ground around Lost Mountain. The campaign was returning to the line of the railroad. Johnston's army had had the best of it in the wooded country-side of Georgia around Dallas; the battles of New Hope Church and Pick-ett's Mill were undisputed Confederate victories. But neither of them had been decisive, and for the second time in two weeks, though the shield had proved unbreakable, the sword had failed to strike.[34]

CHAPTER TWENTY

"We Have Not Cavalry Enough"

Johnston ordered his soldiers to evacuate their lines in the tangle of wilderness around New Hope Church on June 4. That night they marched eastward through a steady rain to new positions near Lost Mountain. "It was a disagreeable night," one officer noted in his diary. "Mud, mud everywhere, and the soldiers sink over their shoe tops at every step. It took seven hours to move six miles." More prosaically, a Georgia private wrote: "It rains so mutch I hasnt bin dri in 2 days and knights." Even after the tired soldiers fell into their new bivouacs, the rain continued to fall. All that week and throughout the weeks to come it became a constant presence. The roads and the rifle pits filled with the runoff, making the most routine activities a challenge. The mud permanently stained the men's uniforms, and even seasoned their food. Most simply gave up on the idea of ever being dry again. They went to sleep wet, and they woke up wet—but they kept their powder dry.[1]

As Johnston had suspected, Sherman withdrew his armies to the high ground around Acworth, a few miles south of Allatoona, and set his engineers to work rebuilding the railroad bridge over the Etowah. Since Acworth was ten miles north of New Hope Church, this was Sherman's first retrograde movement of the campaign, and since it also represented a return to the line of the Western & Atlantic Railroad, it was a tacit admission that his flanking maneuver to Dallas had been a failure.

On June 5, Johnston deployed his three corps to take advantage of the high ground offered by a series of low hills: Lost Mountain on the left (or western) end of the line; Pine Mountain in the center; and Brush Mountain on the right, covering the railroad. These hills rose from 300 to 500 feet above the forrested terrain, and provided good cover for the defenders, but they were so far apart that Johnston's line extended more than eight miles from end to end—as one soldier wrote, it was impossible for the troops at one end of the line to know what was going on at the other end.[2]

That day, too, Johnston reported the army's relocation to Bragg, explaining that his forces were now on a line "nearly parallel to the Chattahoochee." Bragg saw little in Johnston's report to inspire confidence. The Chattahoochee, after all, was the last natural barrier before Atlanta, and Bragg was becoming increasingly alarmed by Johnston's failure to drive Sherman from Georgia. On the day that Johnston began his move, Bragg wrote Davis that "The condition of affairs in Georgia is daily becoming more serious," fearing that if Sherman concentrated his forces on Johnston, "we may well apprehend disaster."[3]

There was no doubt that Sherman was building up his strength for another push. Confederate cavalry patrols reported that new regiments were arriving in Acworth with astonishing regularity; military bands in the Federal camp welcomed new arrivals so frequently, it seemed to some that a round-the-clock concert was under way. Johnston was convinced that Sherman would not launch a general offensive until his engineers had repaired the railroad bridge over the Etowah, but he was also concerned that Sherman might send a cavalry division around his flanks to seize Atlanta. To prevent such a move, Johnston ordered volunteer troops from the Georgia State militia to construct redoubts guarding the crossings of the Chattahoochee. To his detractors, such orders proved that Johnston was thinking too much about retreat and not enough about attack.[4]

It was true that Johnston had all but given up on the idea of executing a general attack against the Federal army. In the woods around New Hope Church he had seen further proof that infantry assaults against even temporary defenses were suicidal. And since neither army moved now without digging in almost at once, any general attack would require the troops to assail entrenchments. Having witnessed firsthand the importance of such fieldworks, the soldiers in both armies no longer carped at digging, and they often began entrenching even before the orders were issued. When either army halted, even for a night, trenches and redoubts appeared as if by magic; whole armies simply burrowed into the soggy Georgia red earth as soon as they stopped marching. A staff officer later recalled that breastworks "were thrown up immediately upon assuming position; and as the movements were generally executed at night, the earth works were always there in the morning." Although Johnston still hoped that he might find an opportunity to execute a successful flank attack or an assault against an isolated element of Sherman's force, the idea of a general offensive against the Federal main body he dismissed out of hand.[5]

Instead, he began to rely more and more on his corollary strategy of cutting Sherman's supply lines. If Sherman could not feed his men and his animals, his slow, siegelike advance would become impracticable, and he would be forced to choose between two undesirable alternatives: attacking Johnston's defenses, or withdrawing from Georgia to secure his own communications. After New Hope Church, Johnston began to see the severing of Sherman's supply lines as his only viable strategy.

Unfortunately, Wheeler's troopers could not be spared for this work, as they had to screen the army and provide intelligence about Sherman's movements. Wheeler was eager for an adventure behind the enemy's lines. He complained to Bragg, his mentor, that "I have begged General Johnston to allow me to go to the enemy's rear nearly every day," but that Johnston wouldn't let him go. Johnston needed Wheeler to conduct the more routine but unglamorous picket and patrol duties of the army. Johnston did order "Red" Jackson's small cavalry division to go northward, to "catch trains, cut telegraph wires, and destroy small bridges" between Dalton and Acworth. But Jackson's cavalry was so worn down by constant service that he could send only about seventy-five men to carry out these activities on which so much depended. Of necessity, therefore, Johnston sought to have cavalry forces from other commands directed to operate against Sherman's supply lines. In particular, he urged Stephen D. Lee in Mississippi to send a brigade of cavalry into Tennessee. Since Mississippi was outside Johnston's command authority, he had to persuade Lee to do it voluntarily, urging that "Your troops can do no other service so valuable to the country."[6]

Stephen Dill Lee had become responsible for all of Mississippi and Alabama when Polk joined Johnston's army at Resaca. Only thirty-one years old, this "other" Lee felt somewhat overwhelmed by his new responsibilities. He had even asked to be released from the burden of command, and when that was denied, he decided that he needed every trooper and every soldier that he had to defend his far-flung command. While sympathetic to Johnston's dilemma, he would not send forces from his own command to aid the Army of Tennessee unless ordered to do so, and such orders could come only from Bragg or Davis.

Another possible source of cavalry support was Nathan Bedford Forrest's force in northern Alabama. Forrest had proven his effectiveness as a cavalry commander from the first days of the war. His unique status as an independent commander was the result of a quarrel with Bragg which had led him to demand that he be released from Bragg's authority. Now Johnston requested Davis to order Forrest to operate on Sherman's supply lines. Bragg may have wondered why Johnston was eager for Forrest (an avowed Bragg enemy) to go raiding in Tennessee while he denied that opportunity to Wheeler (a

Bragg protégé). Johnston even encouraged his corps commanders to write directly to Davis; both Polk and Hardee (but not Hood) did so, asking Davis to order Forrest "to operate on the enemy's communications. . . ."[7]

To Davis and Bragg, Johnston's cries for help were only the latest chorus in a tune that had grown tedious. In their view of things, Johnston had spent the last month frittering away offensive opportunities, and he was now promoting this cavalry scheme largely because he was unwilling to take on Sherman himself. If cavalry raids were so important to his success, they wondered, why didn't he send his own cavalry to do the job? The president wrote to Robert E. Lee that "Unless General Johnston strikes before the enemy have brought up all the reinforcements reported to be moving, his chances will be greatly diminished for the success which seemed attainable before he retreated, and still seems to be practicable." In the end, Davis and Bragg declined to divert Confederate cavalry to Sherman's line of communications. Johnston would have to find some other way to stop him.[8]

Sherman renewed his advance the second week of June. As early as June 10, Bate's division on Pine Mountain was skirmishing with forward units of the enemy. The rain continued unabated, and the roads all but disappeared under standing pools of water. Concerned that prompt movement would be difficult, Johnston ordered all of the army's wagons except ordnance wagons south of the Chattahoochee to forestall another traffic jam like that which had accompanied the crossing of the Etowah. But he was not preparing for an early decampment. In spite of the rain, the mud, and the odds, Johnston was considering an attack.

As at Cassville and New Hope Church, Johnston planned to use Hood's corps as a mobile reserve to strike the enemy when and if Sherman left him an opening. He began by asking Polk and Hardee to estimate the minimum number of men they needed to defend their positions. Each replied that five thousand men per corps could hold their line against all but a determined attack. This suggested that a relatively small portion of the army could act defensively, while Hood, reinforced with elements from Polk's and Hardee's corps, carried out an offensive. Johnston therefore ordered Polk and Hardee to extend their lines to occupy the entrenchments held by Hood's corps, and he ordered Hood to pull his men out of line and mass them on the right.[9]

Johnston originally planned to execute this maneuver on June 12. At one o'clock that afternoon, he ordered Hood to move when the rain slackened. But the rain intensified, and at three-fifteen Johnston suspended the movement due to the "inclemency of the weather." Two days later, he was ready to try again. This time, Hood's movement was to commence "promptly at daylight" on June 14. That morning dawned dry and almost clear, with patches of blue sky showing through the clouds, though the roads were still mired in thick mud. While he waited for the roads to dry, Johnston agreed to accompany Hardee on a reconnaissance of William Bate's position on Pine Mountain.[10]

Bate's men had come under pressure from Federal units that had worked their way around the eastern flank of the hill; Hardee was concerned that if they were left in this salient, they might be cut off and forced to surrender. Johnston decided to ride up to Pine Mountain with Hardee and have a look. Because it was a chance to examine the ground in front of his own lines, Polk went with them. The three Confederate generals rode up to the crest of Pine Mountain around eleven o'clock in the morning.

Johnston strode over to a battery near the crest of the hill which offered a good view of the Federal lines and, stepping up onto the earthworks, turned his field glasses toward the enemy. A brief examination satisfied him that the position was indeed vulnerable, and he told Hardee to pull the unit back after nightfall. Just as he was stepping down from the battery, a single Federal cannon shot, apparently deliberately aimed, passed over his head and smashed into a tree just behind him. Johnston noted that a crowd of staff officers and curious soldiers had gathered, and he calculated that they had attracted the enemy's attention. He ordered the crowd to disperse and turned his field glasses back toward the enemy battery that had fired the shot. After a brief inspection, he stepped down again and started toward the reverse slope of the hill. Hardee headed in one direction and Polk and Johnston in the other. A second shot passed over their heads, and within less than a minute, a third. Johnston was just turning the shoulder of the hill when this third shot fell, and he looked over at Polk to satisfy himself that the shot had missed. But Polk was not there: the third shot had struck his left shoulder, passed through his torso, and exited his right shoulder before it struck a tree and exploded. The force of the blow propelled Polk's body to the top of the hill, where it lay, face upward, with what was left of his arms across his breast as if the bishop had been laid out for a funeral. Johnston rushed to his side, and Hardee, too, soon knelt by the lifeless body. Johnston reached out and laid his hand on Polk's forehead. "I would rather anything but this," he said tearfully.[11]

While Confederate artillerists unleashed a fury of counterbattery fire that lasted about half an hour, staff officers signalled for stretcher bearers, and Polk's body was carried down to the base of the hill. There it was placed in an ambulance, which carried it to Marietta. There was no attempt to disguise the tragedy from the troops; Johnston rode alongside the ambulance, and his grief was evident to the men as they passed. That afternoon, Johnston wrote two messages—one to Davis to inform him of the "calamity" of Polk's death; the other to the army: "In this distinguished leader we have lost the most courteous of gentlemen, the most gallant of soldiers. The Christian patriot soldier has neither lived nor died in vain. His example is before you; his mantle rests with you."[12]

Polk's death was more to be regretted for its impact on troop morale than for his military skills. "As a soldier," one general officer reflected, "he was more theoretical than practical." But the loss stunned the army. To some rebel soldiers it seemed particularly heinous that the Yankees had fired artillery shells for the express purpose of trying to kill high-ranking officers, and the fact that one of those deliberately aimed shells had actually killed an Episcopal bishop was incomprehensible unless one concluded that Yankees were completely unredeemable. That night, after dark, Bate's division withdrew from Pine Mountain, and before dawn Yankee soldiers occupied the trenches, where one of them found a note left behind for them by a rebel infantrymen: "You damned Yankee sons of bitches have killed our old Gen. Polk."[13]

Johnston appointed Major General William W. Loring, the senior division officer in the corps, as temporary commander. But the immediate impact of Polk's death was that it again postponed any offensive. Three times Hood's corps had been pulled out of line for an offensive, and by now Hood was desperate for an opportunity to attack. Both publicly and privately (mostly in secret letters to Davis and Seddon), Hood had promoted himself as the champion of offensive warfare; but despite opportunities at Cassville, at New Hope Church, and now at Brush Mountain, he had yet to demonstrate the validity of that claim.

At least there was some good news that night when dispatches arrived at Johnston's headquarters telling of a Confederate victory at the Battle of Tishemingo, or Brice's Crossroads, on June 10. Nathan Bedford Forrest had been headed for Sherman's supply lines in Tennessee with 4,800 troopers, when Grant and Sherman dispatched a column of 8,000 men under Major General Samuel D. Sturgis to head him off. The two forces met at Brice's Crossroads in northern Mississippi, and Forrest thoroughly routed his much stronger opponent, taking eighteen guns and one thousand six hundred prisoners. Johnston was elated. He telegraphed Bragg his unsolicited opinion that Forrest should now be given overall command of rebel cavalry in Tennessee and put in charge of coordinating attacks on Sherman's supply lines. In the enthusiasm of the moment, few appreciated that despite his one-sided victory, Forrest had failed to achieve his objective, and that Sherman's supply lines remained intact. Sturgis had been sent to distract Forrest, not defeat him, and in that at least he had been successful.

Meanwhile, skirmishing continued unabated along Johnston's extended front. Sherman was using the sheer weight of numbers to maintain constant pressure on Johnston's thin line, hoping to discover a weak spot. On June 16, he found one—at Gilgal Church on the Confederate left near Lost Mountain. There a Yankee battery occupied a small hill which could enfilade Cleburne's position, effectively turning the army's left once again. This forced Johnston to swing his left flank back like a door, and Cleburne's men took position behind the aptly named Mud Creek on a line running north-south and facing west. The new Confederate line resembled a capital L, with the long stem facing north and the short leg facing west. Johnston thought he could successfully defend this position from any direct attack, but he also knew that it was only a matter of time before Sherman tried yet another flanking maneuver and forced him to pull back. So he dispatched his engineers to lay out new lines on the slopes of Kennesaw Mountain.[14]

Big Kennesaw Mountain rears up imposingly out of the North Georgia countryside, its steep sides rising to a height of 700 feet, dwarfing the smaller hills
around it. At least one Union soldier decided that Providence had placed it
there solely for the purpose of blocking the path of an advancing army. Next
to it is Little Kennesaw Mountain, less dramatic at 400 feet, but nevertheless
daunting to an invader. After dinner on June 18, Johnston relocated his
headquarters to a small cottage, rather grandly named Fair Oaks, about a
mile north of Marietta, and that night the army moved into its new lines on
Kennesaw Mountain. Shortly afterward, the Federals moved up to occupy
the abandoned Confederate works. Johnston dispatched another of his regular reports to Bragg, notifying him of the move to Kennesaw. Once again, he
suggested that Bragg send cavalry forces to operate against Sherman's supply lines. "Since my last dispatch the enemy has, as usual, been approaching
by fortifying. I can find no mode of preventing this. I repeat the suggestion
that the cavalry in Alabama be put in the enemy's rear." To Bragg, this was
just more of the same: Johnston was retreating, refusing to offer battle, and
calling for someone else to save him.[15]

Johnston's new line on Kennesaw Mountain was at least as formidable a
position as any that he had occupied in North Georgia, including Rocky Face
Ridge. Presumably, Sherman would attempt to execute yet another flanking
maneuver. Wheeler's scouts reported that three Federal corps appeared to
be maneuvering to turn the rebel left while McPherson held the line in front.
But now the heavy rain proved to be a Confederate ally, for the roads remained mired in thick mud that made any flanking movement extremely
difficult. Instead, the Federals slogged up to the base of Kennesaw Mountain
and initiated an artillery barrage. The Confederates were awed by the Federal profligacy with their ammunition. "They shelled us very heavy," one
soldier recalled, "cutting down treetops on us. . . ." The Federal shells
mowed down the trees on Big and Little Kennesaw Mountains like a scythe
cut through wheat; soldiers began to joke that Kennesaw would soon have to
be renamed Bald Mountain. Some of the shells sailed completely over the
mountain and exploded near Johnston's headquarters, forcing him to relocate to a campsite off the Dallas Road.[16]

All day on June 20, and again on the 21st, enemy artillery shells poured
down on Kennesaw Mountain. Federal sharpshooters worked their way forward to the base of the hill and began sniping at the rebel infantry. It was
clear to Johnston that Sherman was up to his old game of pinning down his
army with constant pressure while trying to turn a flank. To protect his
threatened left, Johnston pulled Hood out of position on the extreme right
and sent him marching behind the front to the left flank, while Wheeler's
cavalry occupied Hood's abandoned entrenchments. If evidence were
needed that Wheeler's men could not be spared for a raid against Sherman's
supply lines, their having to occupy a section of the main defensive line was
eloquent testimony.[17]

Johnston had pulled Hood's corps out of line three times in the previous
four weeks with the idea of using it to spearhead an attack; this time his

purpose was merely to shift his strength from right to left. In all three earlier maneuvers, Hood had failed to come to grips with the enemy. Now he was perhaps too eager. Hood's men arrived at their assigned blocking position on the Powder Springs Road in the pre-dawn darkness of June 22. At once they began to dig in.

The new day dawned clear and cloudless for the first time in weeks; it may have occurred to Hood that it was good weather for an attack. Early that afternoon, Hood's skirmishers in front of the main line encountered two Federal regiments advancing gingerly. Hood decided that these units were the spearhead of a Federal assault, and he deployed his corps to repel them. When the two Federal regiments fell back, Hood sent his own men forward to "pursue." In effect, he launched an attack—and he did so without notifying Johnston.[18]

The two Federal regiments withdrew in some haste. Hood believed he was onto something: he ordered a general advance, thinking that he had at last found the enemy flank against which Johnston had three times ordered him to operate. But Hood had not conducted any reconnaissance and did not know what was in front of him. It was, in fact, Schofield's Army of the Ohio and Hooker's XXth Corps, and it was not their exposed flank but their entrenched front that lay across his line of advance. When his men encountered the Federal line and recoiled from the massed firepower, Hood ordered them to re-form and attack again. They were repulsed with heavy losses, but he rallied them and ordered them forward yet again, with the same result. Darkness finally ended what became known as the Battle of Kolb's Farm.

Hood claimed a victory. He reported that his men had driven the Federals back upon their reserve line and were on the verge of routing Hooker's whole corps when Federal reinforcements arrived. His men had captured a dozen field pieces and inflicted heavy losses on the enemy. Friendly southern newspapers, starved for some good news, reported that Hood's attack had brought the Confederates within grasp of final and complete victory. At Johnston's headquarters in the suburbs of Marietta, the assessment was more restrained. A staff officer noted in his diary that Hood's men "drove [the] enemy from a line of trenches, but [achieved] no important results." And to Richmond, Johnston reported that Hood "drove back the enemy, taking one entire line of breast-works," but that "The pursuit was stopped by exposure to fire of fixed batteries."[19]

In fact, Hood's men "drove" only the two advanced Federal regiments back onto the Federal main line, then his soldiers had to advance across an open field subject to the fire of Union artillery on their flank. The Confederates suffered over 1,000 casualties—Stevenson's division alone lost 870— while the Federals suffered losses of only 350. Hood had his moment of glory and reclaimed his reputation as an aggressive commander, but at a cost the Confederacy could ill afford.

The most charitable construction that could be placed on Hood's behavior at Kolb's Farm was that at least he had demonstrated that he was willing to do something. To Johnston's critics in Richmond, it seemed that Johnston was unwilling to do anything other than request reinforcements from other theatres. Of course, not everyone in Richmond distrusted Johnston's judgement. There was always Wigfall. On June 24, the Texas senator arrived at army headquarters in Marietta. He was on his way to Texas to touch base with his constituents, and he had left Charlotte and the girls with Lydia in Atlanta while he made a quick trip up to the front to learn from Johnston how things were going. He also brought news from Richmond. Wigfall warned his friend that rumors in the Confederate capital held that Davis was extremely disappointed with the lack of progress in the West, and that the president was considering removing Johnston from command.[20]

Such warnings probably had no impact on Johnston. Convinced that his strategy was correct, and that it was working, he would not change it simply because it was unpopular. Even if Davis had told him bluntly to attack or be dismissed, Johnston would have refused. A poor strategy did not become a good one simply because the president advocated it. Wigfall may also have mentioned that one of the names most frequently suggested as Johnston's successor was that of John Bell Hood. Up to this point Johnston had relied heavily on Hood for advice and support. Only a week earlier Hardee, perhaps jealous of Johnston's close relationship with Hood, had written his wife that "Hood . . . is helping the General to do the strategy, and from what I can see is doing most of it." Now, Johnston had to wonder if Hood could be relied upon. Looking back, he may have reflected on Hood's inconsistency during the campaign: his failure to attack at Cassville and New Hope Church, his impetuosity at Kolb's Farm. How much did Hood's ambition affect his actions in those incidents? How much did his loyalty to Davis affect his strategic advice to Johnston? Johnston's uncertainty about Hood's loyalty, and the news of Davis's lack of confidence, isolated him even further.[21]

Johnston explained his strategic plan to Wigfall in detail—more detail, in fact, than he had to Davis or Bragg. In particular, Johnston confided that he believed Sherman would be most vulnerable *after* he had crossed the Chattahoochee. A defeat inflicted on him with the Chattahoochee at his back would be decisive, whereas if Sherman proved victorious in such a battle, Johnston would have the Atlanta entrenchments to fall back on. The best moment to attack, Johnston suggested, would be when the Federal army tried to cross Peachtree Creek. Wigfall was impressed, and he left the conference convinced that Johnston was doing the right thing.[22]

Davis and Bragg were not so sure. Though Johnston was submitting regular and timely reports, they repeated the same familiar themes. First, he emphasized the difficulty of striking a blow against Sherman—partly because the Federals entrenched as they moved, and partly because the rains were so heavy that maneuvering off the roads was impossible, but mostly because of the Federal superiority of numbers. Second, he repeatedly emphasized the importance of sending cavalry raids to attack Sherman's lines of supply: "The enemy is gradually pressing us back," he wrote on June 16.

"To defeat his design it is necessary to break the railroad this side of Dalton. We have not cavalry enough. Can you not send such an expedition from East Tennessee or Mississippi?"[23]

On June 27, Johnston wrote Bragg a long letter recapitulating the campaign. Although at Dalton he had expressed hope that he could repulse Sherman's attacks and then launch a counterattack, he now advanced a different strategy. The events of the past month had convinced him that he and Sherman were engaging in a new kind of warfare:

> I have been unable so far to stop the enemy's progress by gradual approaches on account of his numerous army and the character of the country, which is favorable to his method. Our best mode of operating against it would be to use strong parties of cavalry to cut his railroad communications. Our own cavalry is so weak compared with that of the Federal army that I have been unable to do it. If you can employ cavalry in that way quickly great benefit must result from it—probably Sherman's speedy discomforture.[24]

"We have not cavalry enough." That was Johnston's plea and his excuse. Was it true? Davis and Bragg were skeptical. On June 10, Johnston had reported that there were 10,903 cavalry "effectives" and an "aggregate present" of 27,256 horsemen. Surely that was sufficient to detail some portion of it to attack Sherman's supply lines, especially if, as Johnston insisted, it was the key to the campaign. But the numbers were more than misleading, they were incorrect. Wheeler's cavalier attitude toward administration was partly responsible, for his habitual inclusion of all men—sick or well, with or without horses, present or absent—on his muster rolls made it appear that he had thousands more troopers than he did. Instead of the 17,568 cavalrymen that appeared on the June 10 report as belonging to his division, Wheeler could put only 2,419 men in the field. Foolishly, Johnston had forwarded those reports. Now his claim that his cavalry was inadequate provoked only skepticism. He would pay, and pay dearly, for the habit of distrust that had grown up between himself and the administration. Davis and Bragg discounted his explanations and accepted his June report at face value. They simply refused to believe that Johnston did not have sufficient cavalry to operate against Sherman if he were determined to do it. Bragg's response to Johnston's plea was direct: "We have no cavalry in East Tennessee, and that in Mississippi is fully occupied. . . ."[25]

Despairing now of help from other theatres, Johnston asked Wheeler to send raiding parties against Sherman's supply lines; but Wheeler could spare few troopers for the job. In the end, Sherman's communications were never seriously threatened. Throughout June and July, twenty-four trains a day left Nashville loaded with food and supplies that kept Sherman's army in the field. Before the trains reached Chattanooga, they crossed more than a dozen major bridges, the destruction of any one of which would have slowed the flow of supplies. But the bridges remained intact, and Sherman's soldiers remained well fed.[26]

If Bragg and Davis were frustrated with Johnston, so to was Sherman. The Federal commander had expected to trap Johnston at Resaca; he had hoped to do so again at Dallas; and again at Lost Mountain. He reported to Washington that "As fast as we gain one position the enemy has another all ready." Frustrated by Johnston's slipperiness, by his own inability to get around Johnston's flanks, and by the constant rain, which ruined the roads, he decided that the time had come to stop sparring and launch a full-scale attack on Johnston's entrenched troops. For Johnston, this was a stroke of luck.

Sherman's plan was to feint against the Confederate flanks, hoping to entice Johnston to send reinforcements there, then smash through the weakened center. It was a plan similar to the one he had helped to execute at Missionary Ridge against Bragg. But the troops on Kennesaw Mountain were far more confident and determined than those who had occupied Missionary Ridge, even though they were, in many cases, the same men. Whereas in 1863 they had distrusted Bragg, they were now supremely confident not only of their commander, but more importantly, of themselves.

June 27 dawned clear for the third day in a row, but the humidity remained and it was swelteringly hot. Soldiers sought shade under nearby trees or draped blankets over the cross posts in the trenches to create their own. "The heavens seemed made of brass, and the earth of iron," one soldier recalled. Loring, whose days in command of Polk's old corps were now numbered, was posted atop Big and Little Kennesaw Mountain; Hardee, "Old Reliable," held the center, running more than two miles southward from Pigeon Hill on Loring's left to what would soon become known as Cheatham's Hill; and Hood occupied the left near Kolb's Farm, where he had squandered a thousand Confederate casualties five days earlier.[27]

Soon after first light, the Federals opened a concentrated bombardment on Kennesaw Mountain with fifty artillery pieces. At 8:15 A.M. a mile south of Kennesaw Mountain, on a shoulder of Little Kennesaw known as Pigeon Hill, 5,500 Federals started forward. They brushed aside the rebel skirmishers and started up the slope. The Confederates opened up with artillery, musketry, and even rolled stones down on the Yankees who were scrambling up the steep slope. A few Federal units tried to hold the ground they had taken, but the rebels made it too hot for them. Within two hours they withdrew, leaving behind 850 casualties; the Confederates had lost perhaps 200.[28]

The main attack was yet to come. This time it was Major General George H. Thomas, the Rock of Chickamauga, who would direct the attack. Thomas's army, the Army of the Cumberland, was the largest of the three Federal armies, and arguably the toughest—it was Thomas's men who had held the line at Chickamauga and who had scaled Missionary Ridge. Their object now was a milewide piece of ground where the only geographic advantage for the defenders was a modest rise, barely perceptible at a distance. But because the ground was less imposing, it was here that Hardee

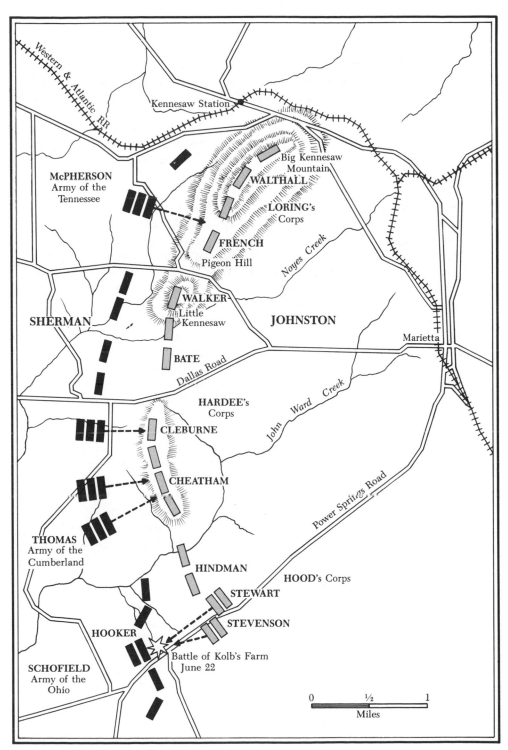

The Battle of Kennesaw Mountain, June 27, 1864

had placed his best troops, the divisions of Frank Cheatham and Pat Cleburne.

The Federal high command had decided that the best chance of breaking through Johnston's line was to attack with massed columns of troops—projectiles of humanity—rather than with the traditional broad front. Such a force, Sherman thought, could pierce through the thinly held rebel line, rendering Johnston's entire position untenable. Because it depended on speed and shock, Sherman ordered the men to remove the firing caps from their rifles to prevent them from stopping to fire, and to attack on the dead run with bayonets fixed.

At nine o'clock, the men of Cleburne's division heard two distinct cannon shots, almost certainly a signal of some kind. Moments later, eight thousand Yankees burst from the treeline across the shallow valley in front of them and swarmed to the attack. The rebel pickets were overrun at once, the Yankees barely stopping to notice. The massed columns with fixed bayonets glinting in the sunshine were an awesome sight. The blue-coated ranks jogged forward irresistibly; they were only forty yards from the Confederate line when it exploded with artillery and musketry fire that swathed the hill in smoke. Almost as one man, the front rank of Federals went down under the weight of this massed Confederate volley. Those in the second and third ranks who survived the volley instinctively deployed so that they could shoot back (most had disobeyed the orders to remove their firing caps), thus weakening the impact of their column formation. The planned assault by massed columns broke down almost at once. The attack dissolved into a melee; those in the rear pushed forward, those in the front died.

Finally, the Yankees began to fall back. The field was littered with their dead and wounded. Worse, the flash of muskets had set the woods afire and the hundreds, perhaps thousands, of Federal wounded were in danger of being cooked alive. Colonel W. H. Martin of the First Arkansas saw the danger. Tying a handkerchief to a ramrod as a flag of truce, he stepped up onto the rampart and called across to the Federals to come rescue their wounded. "We won't fire a gun till you get them away," he called. "Be quick!" Soldiers on both sides ran out into the open and helped drag the wounded from danger. Then they returned to their lines to continue the war.[29]

South of Cleburne's position. Cheatham's division occupied a salient that jutted out in front of the line to follow the curve of the modest ridgeline. Curiously, his engineers had laid out the division's lines at the very crest of the hill instead of on the forward slope. That error allowed the attacking Yankees to cling to a modest depression about thirty yards in front of the line, where they found some shelter from the fierce Confederate fire. But that was not enough to affect the outcome of the battle. The Federal soldiers attacked bravely, so bravely that at least one Confederate was amazed that they could take death so coolly—like wooden men, he said—but they failed to break the line. Indeed, they failed to reach it. Afterward, Confederates found Union bodies within fifteen paces of the line, but none closer. The men of Cheatham's and Cleburne's corps were spent—some vomited from dehydration and exhaustion, a few passed out from sunstroke—but they had held the line.[30]

Back in his headquarters, Johnston listened to the sound of the fight. On his extended front of more than five miles, he could best direct the action from the rear. But today, at least, no direction was necessary or even possible. Success depended on the steadiness of the men in the trenches, and the leadership of brigade and division commanders at the point of contact. If Johnston deserved any credit for the Confederate victory at Kennesaw Mountain, it was for the training he had instilled in his men at Dalton, and the confidence they had developed in themselves during the long retreat since May.

In the immediate aftermath of the battle, the scope of the Confederate victory on the slopes of Kennesaw Mountain was unclear. Johnston had to learn from prisoners that Sherman had intended his attack as a general assault on the army, not merely another feint. From field reports, he calculated that the Federals had lost between five and eight thousand men in their gallant but futile attempt to break his lines. Sherman, trying to put the best face on it, reported losses of only 2,500, though he later revised that figure upward to 3,000. Confederate losses were 552.[31]

Johnston wired the good news to Bragg: "The enemy advanced upon our whole line to-day. Their loss is supposed to be great; ours known to be small." But the authorities in Richmond had grown skeptical of Johnston's reports. Josiah Gorgas, chief of ordnance, noted in his diary: "No striking military events have occurred, if we except that Johnston telegraphs he repulsed a general attack of the enemy with 'supposed' heavy losses. There are no particulars and I have little confidence in the state of affairs in that quarter." Bragg passed the news on to Davis, but added that although "every available man" had been sent to Johnston, he continued to fall back. Bragg claimed that Johnston's numerical inferiority to Sherman was less than than that faced by Confederate forces elsewhere. Relying on the total "aggregate present and absent" carried on the army's muster rolls, Bragg told Davis that Johnston had some 137,931 men available, and a supporting force of another 7,000 to 10,000 militia at Atlanta. He concluded: "I see no way in which he can be reinforced. . . ." The tone of his letter suggested that what Bragg really meant was Johnston did not *deserve* to be reinforced.[32]

Johnston could not allow himself a period of celebration after the Battle of Kennesaw Mountain, for his strategic situation had not changed appreciably. Indeed, by demonstrating once again the futility of frontal assaults, it confirmed conclusions he had already reached about the wisdom of attacks on entrenched forces. Unless he could direct cavalry attacks on Sherman's supply lines, his strategy would collapse. Worse yet, even while the Federal infantry had been halted in its tracks, Federal cavalry units had worked their

way around the Confederate left, and some units were now closer to the
Chattahoochee River crossings than the rebels.

On July 1, Johnston received a visit from Senator Benjamin H. Hill of
Georgia, a friend and political associate of Davis who, as a Georgian, was
becoming increasingly alarmed by Johnston's continued withdrawals. Wigfall, Governor Brown, and others had urged Hill to write to Davis and support Johnston's plea for cavalry support. Hill determined to go to Richmond
personally. First, however, he would visit Johnston's army to be sure that he
had the latest facts.[33]

For the second time in two weeks, Johnston explained his strategic ideas to
a Confederate senator. Hill listened carefully. He congratulated Johnston on
the losses he had inflicted on Sherman so far, but that being the case, he
asked, wasn't the disparity between the two armies less now than before?
And if so, couldn't Johnston now consider an attack? Johnston admitted that
the two armies were indeed closer in numbers than at any time in the campaign, but he repeated that the Federals were always entrenched and that
he was unwilling to send his men against entrenched troops. The only way
out, he insisted, was to send Stephen D. Lee's cavalry to cut Sherman's
supply lines.

But if Lee's cavalry was withdrawn from Mississippi, it would uncover
Johnston's resource base; and even if such a raid were successful, it would
take time. How long, Hill asked, could Johnston hold Sherman north of the
Chattahoochee? Would it be long enough for cavalry forces to cut Sherman's
lines and for the impact to be felt? Johnston assured Hill that even if he had
to evacuate his lines on Kennesaw Mountain, he could hold Sherman north
of the Chattahoochee for some time—a month at least.[34]

Hood, who up to this point had remained silent, now spoke up to disagree.
If the Yankees broke through the Kennesaw Mountain line, he said, they
could push forward to the Chattahoochee quickly. With the new insight to
Hood provided him by Wigfall's recent visit, Johnston may have wondered
whether this was a genuine military estimate, or Hood the schemer impress-
ing a friend of Jefferson Davis with the bankruptcy of Johnston's ideas.[35]

Hill came away from the meeting unsatisfied. Unlike Wigfall, who was
predisposed to accept Johnston's explanations because they were so useful to
him in his private war with Davis, Hill was predisposed to reject them. He
agreed to carry Johnston's request for cavalry support to Richmond, but he
was convinced that Johnston would not fight for Atlanta, and that he should
therefore be replaced. Hill arrived in Richmond on July 10 and met with
Davis at length. When he told Davis that Johnston had asserted he could
hold the enemy north of the Chattahoochee for a month, Davis replied that
Federal forces were already across the river. It was the last straw for Hill,
who sent Johnston a brief wire: "You must do the work with your present
force. For God's sake do it."[36]

On July 2, reports from Wheeler's scouts and other sources suggested that
Sherman was disengaging from the Kennesaw Mountain line and beginning

a move for the Chattahoochee—"flanking as usual." That same afternoon, Johnston issued orders for the army to withdraw. Sherman supposed that Johnston's next move after abandoning Kennesaw Mountain would be to fall back over the Chattahoochee immediately, but Johnston had no such intention. With Wheeler covering the movement, the army filed into new lines near New Smyrna, six miles south of Kennesaw Mountain but still more than three miles north of the river. Although the position had none of the natural advantages of Kennesaw Mountain, Johnston's decision caught Sherman by surprise. He was so sure Johnston was headed for the river, and so eager to catch up with him, that when his advance units reported that Confederate troops were blocking the road, Sherman was skeptical. It is only rear guard skirmishers, he told them. Drive them off. Instead, the Yankees were themselves driven back with losses, and Sherman had to redeploy and reevaluate.[37]

Such minor victories were possible because the men in the Army of Tennessee retained their self-confidence. "There is one thing that we all know, or think so anyway," one wrote in his diary that day, "that is that we will whip the yankees whenever and wherever we fight. Our confidence in ourselves and Gen. Johnston is unshaken notwithstanding we have retreated eighty miles. The only fear of this army is that Grant will overwhelm Lee with superior numbers, never by skill. All the powers and hopes of the north are concentrated on these two armies, defeat them, and we have seen our darkest days." That same night, General French wrote in his diary: "It is wonderful how well our soldiers understand this falling back. Never before did an army constantly fight and fall back for seven weeks without demoralization. . . ."[38]

The line at New Smyrna held Sherman off for only a day or two. On July 4, the Yankees again tried a turning movement against the Confederate left. General Stewart, recently promoted by Davis to permanent command of Polk's corps, was nearly captured and had to escape "by hard riding." Johnston sent Cheatham's division to cut off the Yankee probe, but the Federals pulled back. Sherman wanted no part of an open field engagement when he could achieve the same results by entrenching and flanking. Two days later, with the Federals continuing to extend their lines, Johnston fell back once again, this time into a seemingly impregnable semicircular series of fortifications that backed up to the Chattahoochee River and covered the major crossings. The military term for such a structure was *tête-du-pont*, and it was the brainchild of Brigadier General Francis A. Shoup, who had suggested it to Johnston weeks before. Shoup's idea was to erect a fortification north of the river that was so strong a single corps could hold it indefinitely, leaving the other two corps free to operate against Sherman when he tried to cross the river. Shoup later concluded that Johnston failed to carry out his scheme because he did not fully understand it. But the real reason was that although Johnston understood it, so did Sherman.[39]

The Federal commander gingerly tested the strong Confederate position and backed off. Then he began to entrench. Thomas's Army of the Cumberland dug in around the *tête-du-pont*, while the Federal cavalry and the other two Federal armies explored alternate crossings up- and downriver. On the night of July 8, Schofield crossed the Chattahoochee a dozen miles upstream at Roswell and immediately entrenched. Each side now had a fortified foothold on the enemy's side of the river. According to Shoup's scheme, Johnston should now cross to the south (or east) bank of the Chattahoochee with two of his three corps and attack Schofield's entrenched army, leaving a single corps behind to defend the *tête-du-pont*. One problem with this plan was that the Confederate works were too extended to be defended effectively by a single corps. This was largely Johnston's fault. He had asked Shoup to extend his lines to cover as many fords across the river as possible. The second problem was that Johnston had little confidence that his other two corps could defeat Schofield's entrenched force. Nothing he had seen since Dalton made Johnston confident that he could carry Schofield's position quickly by a *coup de main*. The most likely response was in some respects the most dangerous: Schofield's entrenched position would hold off Johnston's attack long enough for other Federal forces to cross the river and come up in Johnston's rear.

Weighing all these factors, Johnston judged—rightly or wrongly—that an attack on Schofield's entrenched salient involved unacceptable and unnecessary risk. He did not think it was time yet for desperate measures. After all, he had told Wigfall (but not Davis) that Sherman would be most vulnerable *after* he crossed the Chattahoochee. Johnston therefore decided to evacuate the *tête-du-pont* and cross the Chattachoochee with his whole army, taking up a position a few miles south of the river. The orders were by now almost routine: the artillery would move out at dusk, the infantry would leave the trenches at 10:00 P.M., and the skirmishers would withdraw at one o'clock in the morning. The movement was achieved without incident. Another successful withdrawal, another retreat. But this time Johnston had, in effect, given up the last ditch. And once again he had done so without a fight. His move provoked alarm in Atlanta. The citizens started to pack up and move out; state authorities began to evacuate government property. That same day Senator Hill arrived in Richmond with Johnston's message that he could hold on north of the Chattahoochee for at least a month.[40]

Davis now wrote to Johnston to remind him that the rest of the Confederacy had been stripped of protection to afford him the largest force possible: "The announcement that your army has fallen back to the Chattahoochee renders me more apprehensive." We are, the president reported, "dependent on your success." Johnston felt obliged to reply. He asserted once again that "We have been forced back by the operations of a siege, which the enemy's extreme caution and greatly superior numbers have made me unable to prevent." But he returned to a familiar theme, asking Davis to order the cavalry in Mississippi and Alabama to attack the railroad south of Dalton, "thus compelling Sherman to withdraw." Once again Davis replied that if cavalry were necessary to break the railroad between Dalton and Atlanta,

Johnston should use his own. "If it be practicable for distant cavalry," he asserted, "it must be more so for that which is near."[41]

Johnston had been told—several times—that relying on cavalry forces from other theatres was a strategy that was unacceptable to the administration, and that he would have to do the job with the forces he had. Instead, he continued to insist that the government order cavalry from Mississippi and Alabama, and failed to offer an alternative. His critics were astonished and increasingly furious that Johnston would not take no for an answer and that he refused to devise a different strategy. But Johnston was convinced that there *was* no other strategy. To his mind, attacking Sherman's perpetually entrenched army was out of the question unless he could trap an isolated element, and he did not have sufficient cavalry of his own to break Sherman's supply lines. So he gave ground and called for help.

For Jefferson Davis, Johnston's retreat south of the Chattahoochee was the last straw. The Confederate president believed that he had practiced patience until it was no longer a virtue. In the highly charged political environment of wartime Richmond, the news of Johnston's repeated withdrawals sharpened the antagonism between champions and critics of the administration. Of course, Wigfall and his circle put all the blame on Davis's lack of support. Davis's defenders insisted that Johnston's long retreat through North Georgia was irrefutable evidence that the general simply lacked the will to fight. Meanwhile, the disaffection that he provoked and even encouraged was "eating into the very vitals of our distracted country." Davis might have been willing to tolerate Johnston's personal enmity as long as he was winning battles, but there was growing evidence that he was unwilling even to fight one. Johnston's excuses and explanations seemed more labored every day. All the while Bragg was at Davis's elbow insisting that Johnston's army contained nearly 150,000 men, that it was as well supplied as any army in the Confederacy, and that the men in the ranks were eager for a fight. From the front Hood reported that Johnston had had plenty of opportunities to strike Sherman a blow, and that he had allowed them all to slip away. Davis could see for himself that Johnston had become, in Mary Chestnut's words, "the core round which all restless halfhearted disappointed people concentrated." Johnston was a liability Davis could no longer afford.[42]

CHAPTER TWENTY-ONE

"You Are Hereby Relieved"

At nine o'clock in the evening of July 17, Johnston was in his headquarters at the Nelson House on the Marietta Road three miles north of Atlanta, discussing the Atlanta fortifications with Colonel Stephen Presstman, when a courier entered and handed him a telegram. It was from Samuel Cooper in Richmond, and had been copied out in longhand by the military telegraph operator at Atlanta:

> Lieutenant-General J. B. Hood has been commissioned to the temporary rank of general under the late law of Congress. I am directed by the Secretary of War to inform you that as you have failed to arrest the advance of the enemy to the vicinity of Atlanta, far in the interior of Georgia, and express no confidence that you can defeat or repel him, you are hereby relieved from command of the Army and Department of Tennessee which you will immediately turn over to General Hood.[1]

Johnston did not lose his famous temper. Perhaps the occasion was too serious for histrionics. Or perhaps he was not entirely surprised. Even though he did not know all of the events that took place behind the scenes in

the critical week before this message arrived, he could not have missed the
signals that Davis was running out of patience—Wigfall had told him as
much three weeks before. Convinced of Davis's hostility, Johnston may even
have expected such a telegram long before this. Indeed, the telegram, and
the decision that led to it, had a long gestation. Much of the background to
the decision took place offstage and involved actors who played roles that
Johnston did not appreciate until many months—and in some cases years—
later. It is a tangled and controversial drama; to untangle it requires changing scenes from Johnston's headquarters north of Atlanta to Davis's study in
Richmond.

Davis had considered relieving Johnston for some time—as early as May by
some accounts—but he had delayed, in part because he could think of no one
to replace him. "It is very easy to remove the General," he told his cabinet,
"but where will you find the man to fill the place?" Davis had rejected
P.G.T. Beauregard as a candidate back in December, and the mercurial
Creole was no more attractive to him now. James Longstreet had proved less
than fully successful during his brief stint in the West, and in any case he was
still recuperating from a wound received in the Battle of the Wilderness in
May. Edmund Kirby Smith was a possibility, but he was doubly disqualified:
first as a friend of Johnston's, and second as an enemy of Bragg's who, as
Davis's military adviser, was in a position to exercise a de facto veto power
over nominees for the job. Besides, Kirby Smith was commanding the trans-
Mississippi West and could not be spared. Of the three corps commanders
within the Army of Tennessee, William Hardee was the most senior and in
many ways the logical choice. But he had refused the assignment once already, and Hood had hinted in his secret letters that Hardee was pro-John-
ston, implying that his appointment would probably not lead to a change in
policy. Moreover, Hardee, like Kirby Smith, had played a major role in the
anti-Bragg cabal in 1863 and was therefore unacceptable to Bragg. Hood
was next in line, and he had two characteristics to recommend him: first, he
was undoubtedly a fighter—Hood had gone out of his way to make that very
clear in his many clandestine letters to Richmond; and second, he had played
no role in the infighting that had accompanied Bragg's ouster in 1863. Indeed, by writing complimentary letters to Bragg during the winter of 1863–
64, Hood had managed to become a kind of protégé. Alexander Stewart, the
third corps commander, was also a friend of Bragg's, but he had only recently replaced Loring and lacked the experience to command an army. So it
was Hood by default.[2]

Still, Davis hesitated to make the change unless there was no other way,
for he understood the negative impact that could result from changing commanders in the midst of a campaign. On the other hand, Atlanta was not just
another Dalton or Cassville. The heart of the cotton-belt South, the center of
its rail network, and host to many of its wartime industries, if Atlanta should
fall, with or without a fight, the southern Cause would suffer a near-mortal

blow. Davis had to ascertain whether Johnston intended to defend it. On July 9, he ordered Bragg to go to Atlanta to interview Johnston personally.

While Bragg travelled west on the patchwork southern railroad network, events unfolding in Richmond served to clarify Davis's mind. On July 10, Senator Hill arrived with Johnston's latest appeal for cavalry support; there was certainly nothing new in that. But Hill also put forward his opinion, based on a lengthy personal interview, that Johnston was not likely to fight for Atlanta and that he should be removed. The next day, Davis read a telegram from Johnston to Bragg in which Johnston, without explanation, recommended the immediate evacuation and redistribution of the Federal prisoners at Andersonville Prison. Davis took it to mean that he was contemplating yet another retreat; he answered on Bragg's behalf, firing back a telegram that guarding Andersonville was Johnston's responsibility, not Bragg's. That same day he wired Robert E. Lee: "Johnston has failed. It seems necessary to relieve him at once. Who should succeed him? What think you of Hood for the position?" Lee's reply was unenthusiastic: "It is a bad time to release the commander of an army situated as that of Tenne. We may lose Atlanta and the army too. Hood is a bold fighter. I am doubtful as to other qualities necessary." Later that evening, Lee wrote Davis a longer letter in which he suggested that "It would be better to concentrate all the Cavy. in Misspi. and Tenn. on Sherman's communications." Davis did not find Lee's response particularly helpful. He too was not entirely convinced of Hood's capacity for army command, but, unlike Lee, he was convinced that Johnston had to go. On July 13, Gorgas noted in his diary that "Everybody has at last come to the conclusion that Johnston has retreated far enough." Although when he dispatched Bragg to Atlanta, Davis had not yet made up his mind to remove Johnston, he was all but certain by the time Bragg arrived. Still, he would wait to read Bragg's report before he acted.[3]

Bragg, too, had made up his mind. Despite Johnston's stalwart support during Bragg's controversial tenure in command of the Army of Tennessee a year earlier, Bragg felt under no obligation. He believed that Johnston had neglected offensive opportunities throughout the winter and spring, and that the army deserved better. Perhaps he thought the army needed his own firm hand at the helm; he may also have envied the obvious affection that the troops had for Old Joe, something they never showed for Bragg. In any case, Bragg's actions after his arrival in Atlanta indicate that he had no intention of sending Davis an impartial report. Instead, he compiled an indictment.

Bragg arrived in Atlanta on July 13. He immediately telegraphed Davis that Johnston's army had evacuated the north bank of the Chattahoochee, and that "indications seem to favor an entire evacuation of this place," meaning Atlanta. That afternoon he sent another wire informing Davis that two Yankee corps had crossed to the south side of the river. "Our army is sadly depleted," he wrote. "I find but little encouraging."[4]

Back in Richmond, Bragg and Davis had been building what Johnston would have called "castles in the air." In their imaginations they saw the

Army of Tennessee as they wanted it to be: over a hundred thousand strong and eager for a fight if only its commander would unleash it. The reality was much grimmer, and compared to these fantasies, the army was indeed "sadly depleted." Its actual battlefield losses were not all that great—less than ten thousand—far less than the losses suffered by the Army of Northern Virginia during the same period. But rather than credit Johnston with having done well with limited resources, Bragg held him responsible for the difference between what he had imagined and what he saw.

Bragg's job was to discover Johnston's plans, but he failed to do it, and his failure was deliberate. Lieutenant Mackall noted in his journal that Bragg spent the entire day at Johnston's headquarters on July 13; Johnston estimated that he and Bragg had engaged in conversation for more than twelve hours; and Bragg himself said in a letter to Davis that he had spent "most of the day" with Johnston. Yet Bragg reported that Johnston never "afforded me a fair opportunity of giving my opinion." The truth was that Bragg never offered it, or, more accurately, he deliberately withheld it. Throughout these lengthy conversations, Bragg never hinted that Davis was reaching the end of his patience or that Johnston should consider a different strategy. He did not ask Johnston if he planned to hold Atlanta or evacuate it, or anything else about his plans. Bragg's excuse was that Johnston never brought it up. Since Johnston didn't ask for his opinions or advice, Bragg felt perfectly justified in withholding them. Bragg admitted as much to Davis: "He has not sought my advice, and it was not volunteered." What, then, did they talk about? To Johnston, Bragg asserted that his visit was largely a social call, a stopover en route to visit Stephen Lee's command in Mississippi, his purpose being to find out if either S. D. Lee or Kirby Smith could send reinforcements to Johnston's army. Naturally, Johnston told Bragg that reinforcements would be helpful indeed, and he emphasized again the importance of attacking Sherman's supply lines with cavalry drawn from Mississippi and Alabama. Bragg listened politely, with apparent interest, but he kept both his real purpose and his opinions to himself. Johnston later reported to Wigfall that Bragg "left me impressed with the belief that he was pleased with my operations & what he learned of the condition of the army."[5]

But Johnston was not so naive that he couldn't guess the purpose of Bragg's visit. His chief of staff noted in a letter to his wife, "Joe looks uneasy this morning. I am sorry to see him so fretted." For his part, Mackall guessed Bragg's mission at once. "I fancy it is the design of Mr. D. to take advantage of the discontent he has sensed in Richmond, and the temporary excitement in Ga. produced by our own near approach to Atlanta, to make a display of his distrust of Johnston & if he finds he can infuse it into the army, to relieve him." Mackall, however, did not think the army could be swayed. "I think he will signally fail."[6]

Bragg was back at Johnston's headquarters at nine o'clock the next morning. This time, Johnston had asked his corps commanders to be present. He invited Bragg to discuss the army's situation with any or all of them. Bragg replied that he would visit with them separately "as friends, but only in that way, as his visit was unofficial." True to his word, Bragg visited only his friends. Of all the army's general officers, Bragg visited two: Hood and Wheeler. There is no evidence that he talked to the other two corps commanders, Hardee and Stewart, nor apparently, did he consult with any of the division or brigade commanders, and he never visited the camps of the army itself. Bragg was not anxious to talk—or to listen—to Hardee, Cleburne, Cheatham, or any other of the men who had been his "enemies" during his tumultuous days in command. He was unlikely to credit their views in any case. Instead, he talked to his known allies—Hood and Wheeler—both of whom had written Bragg secret letters critical of Johnston throughout the campaign. They proved a sympathetic audience.[7]

Hood told Bragg that throughout the spring and summer he had repeatedly urged Johnston to attack, but that Johnston had insisted upon withdrawal. Wheeler confirmed Hood's version of events. Hood even took it upon himself to write Bragg a long letter emphasizing the points he had made in their conversation. Whether Bragg asked for such a letter, or Hood simply wanted to make sure he had made his point, is unclear, but it leaves no doubt about the character of their conversations. Hood's self-aggrandizing letter portrayed Johnston as both ineffective and weak-willed. He insisted that the army "had several chances to strike the enemy a decisive blow" during the recent campaign, but that in each case Johnston had "failed to take advantage of such opportunities. . . ." Knowing Bragg's (and Davis's) concern about the fate of Atlanta, Hood emphasized that "we should not, under any circumstances, allow the enemy to gain possession of Atlanta," and he indicated how this could be achieved: "we should attack. . . ." But Hood stepped over the line from unprofessional to outright subversive: "I have, general, so often urged that we should force the enemy to give us battle as to almost be regarded reckless by the officers high in rank in this army, since their views have been so directly opposite." Since Johnston and Hardee were the only officers in the army who were senior to Hood, there could be no doubt of his meaning. This remarkable document concludes with sycophancy: "I regard it as a great misfortune to our country that we failed to give battle to the enemy many miles north of our present position. Please say to the President that I shall continue to do my duty cheerfully and faithfully, and strive to do what I think is best for our country, as my constant prayer is for our success."[8]

Even Hood's sympathetic biographer admits that "No motive other than ambition can be ascribed to the writing of this letter." And the historian of the Army of Tennessee deduced that "At best, Hood was a chronic liar. . . ."[9] In the first place, any letter touching upon the army of which he was a part should have been routed through the commanding general. Even if Bragg had requested it, Hood was obliged to send a copy to Johnston not only by military courtesy but by law. In delivering it to Bragg behind his commander's back, Hood violated both decorum and regulations. Combined with the letters he had sent from Dalton to both Davis and Bragg, it formed a consistent pattern of aggressive self-interest.

Second, Hood deliberately exaggerated the respective roles that he and Johnston had played in the campaign. Hood asserted that Johnston had rejected any offensive out of hand. But at least three times from Dalton to the Chattahoochee, Johnston had ordered Hood to launch attacks—at Resaca, at Cassville, and at New Hope Church—and he had certainly considered it at Brush Mountain. Hood had attacked twice—once at Resaca and once without orders at Kolb's Farm. Twice Hood had found circumstances not propitious for an attack. Even if Hood's reasons for failing to attack at Cassville and at New Hope Church had been valid, there was no foundation for his assertion that Johnston had refused to consider the tactical offensive. Johnston might have defended himself from these charges; but since he never saw the letter, he was unaware of them, and so they went unanswered.

Armed with Hood's letter, Bragg wrote two reports to Davis from Atlanta. They are key documents in the controversy that followed. The first was a brief telegram, which travelled over the military telegraph that same day. It was relatively even-handed: "I have made General Johnston two visits, and been received courteously and kindly." Then Bragg made four points: (1) that Johnston did not ask for advice, nor did Bragg offer any; (2) that Johnston had no specific plan for saving Atlanta ("I cannot learn that he has any more plan for the future than he has in the past. He will await the enemy on a line some three miles from here, and the impression prevails that he is now more inclined to fight"); (3) that Sherman was advancing very cautiously and entrenching immediately; and (4) that the army's morale was still good. The report was brief, accurate, and clear. To be sure, Bragg revealed his own views by his choice of words. That Johnston was "now more inclined to fight" implied both past disinclination and continued reluctance. Still, the telegram was not an unfair summary of the situation.[10]

When Bragg sat down to compose his longer letter, he became not a reporter but an advocate—one who was willing to exaggerate and even lie to win his point. In this longer letter, Bragg offered a brief whose purpose was to convict Johnston and promote Hood. First, he emphasized that "As far as I can learn we do not propose any offensive operations. . . ." That was true enough, but Bragg went on to insist that given the army's desperate position, "There is but one remedy—offensive action." Admitting that the army's morale was "still good," he then deduced that it "would hail with delight an order of battle." Bragg also exaggerated the army's losses, accepting and reporting as fact Hood's estimate of "more than 20,000" while neglecting to mention that Johnston reported losses of "less than 10,000." Finally, Bragg reported Hood's exaggerated version of Johnston's conduct of the spring campaign: "During the whole campaign, from and including our position in front of Dalton, General Hood has been in favor of giving battle, and mentions to me numerous instances of opportunities lost. . . . The commanding general, from the best information I can gain, has ever been opposed to seeking battle." That "best information," of course, was Hood himself. Bragg never checked this interpretation with the other corps commanders, or with any of the division commanders. His only other source was Wheeler, his eager protégé, who of course confirmed Bragg's suggestions of Johnston's culpability. All these observations led inevitably to the conclusion that Johnston should be dismissed. Hardee, he claimed, "would produce no change in the policy" and lacked "the confidence of the army." Bragg concluded that "If any change is made Lieutenant-General Hood would give unlimited satisfaction, and my estimate of him, always high, has been raised by his conduct in this campaign."[11]

This indictment of Johnston and paean to Hood probably did not reach Richmond in time to be decisive, but it provides insight into Bragg's frame of mind. In any case, Davis, on July 16, wrote to Johnston directly. His purpose was to give Johnston one last chance to indicate that he had a specific plan to save Atlanta. "I wish to hear from you as to present situation, and your plans of operations so specifically as will enable me to anticipate events." In particular, was he going to hold Atlanta? Hood later wrote that "If General Johnston had, at that time, informed President Davis that he could see no reason why Atlanta should not be held 'forever,' he would have been retained in command." Hood was probably right. But neither Bragg nor Davis had suggested to Johnston that his answer here was particularly critical. Johnston responded innocently with a typically noncommittal reply that was sure to disappoint and anger the chief executive: "As the enemy double our number, we must be on the defensive. My plan of operations must, therefore, depend upon the enemy. It is mainly to watch for an opportunity to fight to advantage." But what about Atlanta? "We are trying to put Atlanta in condition to be held for a day or two by the Georgia militia, that army movements may be freer and wider." As at Vicksburg, Johnston wanted to hold the fortified city with reserve troops while the Army of Tennessee maneuvered in the field, seeking an opportunity to strike at an isolated element of the enemy army. But the phrase that jumped off the page to Davis's eye was "a day or two." Was that it? He would hold Atlanta for "a day or two"? Although Johnston did not suspect it, this wire was his death knell. Davis later explained that Johnston's reply "confirmed previous apprehensions," convincing him that a change of commanders was essential.[12]

At the morning cabinet meeting on July 17, Davis laid the case before his advisers. Secretary Benjamin insisted on Johnston's immediate dismissal. Even Seddon, disillusioned now by Johnston's continued withdrawals, agreed. Davis ensured that every member of the cabinet concurred before announcing his decision. That afternoon he ordered Cooper to dispatch the telegram that was handed to Johnston at nine o'clock the same night.

Davis's removal of Johnston from command was one of the most controversial decisions of the war. Even now it tends to polarize opinion: it was either a terrible mistake by the president, who failed to understand the wisdom of

Johnston's strategy, or it was fully justified by Johnston's continual with-drawals, his refusal to fight, and his unwillingness to commit himself to a defense of Atlanta. Historians and biographers have often attempted to prove that one man was right by showing that the other was wrong. Such efforts are unfruitful in that they can only be hypothetical. Johnston's strat-egy might have worked if Davis had provided complete support; Davis's strategy might have worked if Johnston had embraced it fully. More likely, neither strategy would have worked because of Sherman's skill and his nu-merical and matériel superiority.

At the time, Johnston's friends claimed that his dismissal was the product of Davis's "cold snaky hate," and Johnston's biographers have implied as much by noting that Davis "viewed everything Johnston did with a preju-diced critical eye." But Davis's distrust of Johnston was certainly not one-sided, and if his goal from the outset had been to give Johnston enough rope to hang himself, as some critics suggest, he need not have waited until Sher-man was on Atlanta's doorstep to act. The fact is that Davis had tolerated Johnston's continued retreats and ambiguous reports longer than he thought wise, and relieved him in the genuine conviction that Johnston could not be counted on to fight for Atlanta. On this issue, too, the two sides disagree. One view is that Johnston would have held Atlanta and thereby extended the life of the Confederacy; the other is that Johnston would have abandoned the city and continued his southward flight.[13]

Would Johnston have defended Atlanta? Both at the time and later, John-ston claimed that it was never his intention to give up Atlanta without a fight. A month after his dismissal, he wrote to Wigfall and to his brother Beverly that the charge, which appeared in several pro-administration newspapers, was a "falsehood." And a decade after the war, in his *Narrative*, he denied it again. The proof, he argued, was that he had ordered the city to be fortified, that he had arranged to have heavy guns brought from Mobile, and that his own family was living there. But such arguments are unconvincing. He had given up fortified positions and heavy guns before. And while it is true that Lydia was staying in Atlanta and looking out for the two Wigfall girls who were spending the summer, Johnston's own correspondence suggests that he was at least keeping an open mind about the city's fate. He wrote Wigfall as early as June 28, the day after the Battle of Kennesaw Mountain, to advise him against leaving his daughters in Atlanta for the summer. "The more I think of the matter, the more it seems to me that you expose your children to risk by leaving them in Atlanta while its fate is uncertain." Two weeks later, with the Federals across the Chattahoochee, Johnston wrote to Lydia sug-gesting she send off the Wigfall girls at once, "until the fate of the city was decided." She did so, sending them to Macon, and shortly afterward Louise Wigfall wrote her mother: "The plan is now, if Atlanta falls, for her [Lydia] to come immediately to Macon, and try to get a house. . . . If *au contraire* Atlanta should not fall, we will return to her. . . ." Such calculations would not have been necessary if Johnston intended to hold Atlanta "forever."[14]

Almost certainly Johnston did intend to fight a battle for Atlanta. The plan he had sketched out for Wigfall in June was similar to the one he suggested to Hood on the eve of his departure from the army: to strike at Sherman as his army crossed Peachtree Creek. If the attack was successful, it would place Sherman in a very difficult position with the Chattahoochee at his back; and if it failed, the Southern army could still fall back into the Atlanta defenses. But to say that Johnston would not have given up Atlanta *without a fight* is not to say that he would have defended it to the last man. Johnston had no intention of allowing the Army of Tennessee to be pinned inside the Atlanta fortifications to withstand a siege. It is clear from his advice to Pemberton the year before that he believed that no city, however valuable, was worth sacrificing an army. His enemies argued that this meant he would have evacuated Atlanta and fallen back again, and again—perhaps all the way to the Gulf of Mexico. But what Johnston had in mind was exactly what he had advised Pemberton to do at Vicksburg: turn the city into a fortified bastion defended by Home Guard and state militia troops, while the Army of Tennessee acted independently as a field force. And if the Home Guard troops failed to hold Atlanta? First of all, Johnston thought that unlikely, for Sherman would be unable to bring his full strength to bear against the city while the Army of Tennessee was free to operate in the countryside. Like Johnston, Sherman saw the enemy army, not Atlanta, as his primary objective. Even if Atlanta should fall, it was, after all, only a place, and places could be retaken later. If in his opinion the military situation had required the evacuation of Atlanta, Johnston would certainly have authorized it. Johnston's strategic logic was unassailable; but his assessment of the political realities was flawed. Atlanta was important not only because it was the hub of southern railroads and the center of much of the Confederacy's improvised wartime industry, but because it was a symbol of southern resistance. Its fall might not be a military disaster, but it would be a political disaster.

Johnston's defenders argued later that whatever course he chose, Johnston would almost certainly have held the city longer than Hood subsequently did. With national elections pending in the North, they claimed, a stalemate at Atlanta with the Confederate army still intact might have convinced the northern electorate that Lincoln's war policy was a failure. Such a perception would have boosted the Democratic campaign of George B. McClellan, whose election might have led to a negotiated settlement to the war. A decade later, Johnston himself suggested that he was aware of the possibilities in such a scenario. Sherman's failure to take Atlanta, Johnston wrote, "would have strengthened the peace party greatly; so much, perhaps, as to have enabled it to carry the presidential election, which would have brought the war to an immediate close." But this was hindsight. There is no evidence that Johnston was thinking in political terms in 1864, or that he even recognized the impact that holding Atlanta until November might have on the elections in the North.[15]

Davis was almost certainly correct in his suspicion that Johnston was willing to consider abandoning Atlanta. It is unlikely that Johnston would have pledged himself to an unqualified defense of the city even if Bragg had told him that doing so was a condition of his remaining in command. Johnston was convinced that the strategy he had been following was the correct one, and he defended it publicly for the rest of his life. True, he might have taken some pains to explain his plans to Davis in greater detail. But maybe it was too late for that, for the mutual distrust that existed between president and general made full and free communication impossible.

Even so, Johnston's removal at such a moment and under such circumstances was a truly desperate act, one that almost certainly worked to the detriment of the Confederate cause. The military situation in Georgia was serious but not yet irretrievable, and Davis's decision to remove Johnston in mid-campaign suggests a sense of panic. Davis was led to it not only by the military circumstances and his own distrust of Johnston, but also by the public and private actions of the advocates of each side. The president and his general might never have reached this crisis but for the roles played by Louis Wigfall, Braxton Bragg, and John Bell Hood.

Wigfall's political and public advocacy of Johnston's cause had become a blunt instrument that he used to bludgeon the administration. The Texas senator claimed that he was motivated by personal admiration for Johnston, yet the ultimate result of his actions was to destroy any vestige of confidence the president had left in Joseph E. Johnston as a field general. Bragg's behavior was equally divisive, even less honorable, and seems particularly churlish in view of the lengths to which Johnston had gone the year before to defend him from both public and official criticism. Even then, Bragg had resented Johnston's interference, and in the months since it is possible that he had grown jealous of Johnston's popularity in the army. Now, by championing Hood's promotion, Bragg could revenge himself on the army that had rejected him and on the man who had replaced him. Hood's role speaks for itself: from the moment he joined the army in February, his actions had betrayed a desperate ambition. His secret letters, from Dalton before the campaign and to Bragg during his visit in July, breathed an almost pathological need for acceptance and a sycophancy that is unbecoming at least.

Two hours after Johnston received the telegram dismissing him from command, Hood received one of his own informing him that he was promoted to general and elevated to command of the army. Now that he had what he had lobbied so hard to get, Hood adopted the public position that the appointment was a surprise, and not altogether welcome. He sent a note to Johnston that he was very much alarmed by the appointment, and to Cooper he wired that it was "dangerous to change commanders of this army at this particular time." The next morning, he joined with Hardee and Stewart to urge Johnston to delay accepting the orders until the fate of Atlanta was decided. But Johnston knew he could not refuse to abide by explicit orders from the president. If Davis rescinded the order, Johnston would agree to stay on; he could not ignore a direct command. At 9:00 A.M., Hood, Hardee, and Stewart sent a telegram to Davis asking him to suspend the order. Davis's clearcut reply arrived at 5:20 P.M.: "The order has been executed, and I cannot suspend it without making the case worse. . . ."[16]

That night, Johnston wrote out a general order turning over command of the army to Hood. It was his farewell to his soldiers: "I cannot leave this noble army without expressing my admiration of the high military qualities it has displayed. A long and arduous campaign has made conspicuous every soldierly virtue, endurance of toil, obedience to orders, brilliant courage. The enemy has never attacked but to be repulsed and severely punished. You soldiers have never argued but from your courage, and never counted your foes. No longer your leader, I will watch your career, and will rejoice in your victories." To Cooper, he wrote: "Your dispatch of yesterday received and obeyed." He could not resist a brief defense of his campaign: "I assert that Sherman's army is much stronger compared to that of Tennessee than Grant's compared with that of Northern Virginia. Yet the enemy has been compelled to advance much more slowly to the vicinity of Atlanta than to that of Richmond. . . ." He saved his best barb for last: "Confident language by a military commander is not usually regarded as evidence of competency."[17]

Johnston rode out of camp that same night. Hood thought he left too precipitately, and later claimed that Johnston "deserted" him in the midst of a crucial campaign. That accusation was mainly a product of postwar bitterness and disappointment. Before he left, Johnston had two conversations with Hood in which he explained his plans for an attack as the Federals crossed Peachtree Creek. Both Johnston and Hood knew how awkward his continued presence would be in the midst of a decisive battle for Atlanta. Johnston left quietly, without particular fanfare, though the news of his going had spread through the ranks and men came out to watch, some of them lining the road. The brigades of Finley and Walker gave him three cheers; a few broke ranks to run up to the general and shake his hand. More than one had tears in his eyes. Johnston, sitting erect in the saddle as always, probably raised his hat in return salute. If he was downcast, he did not show it. Halsey Wigfall came to say goodbye, and wrote his father: "No one could ever have told from his countenance or manner that anything unusual had occurred. Indeed he seemed in rather better spirits than usual though it must have been at the cost of much exertion." Howell Cobb, commanding the Georgia militia, saw him the next day and noted that Johnston "indulges in no spirit of complaint, speaks kindly of his successor and very hopefully of the prospect of holding Atlanta."[18]

The news of Johnston's dismissal sent a shock wave through the army. Word passed through the camps faster than Johnston's farewell message could circulate. Some were saddened, others angered; nearly all were worried. One officer on Stewart's staff recalled that "It was necessary to call together the brigade commanders and through them take steps to soothe and quiet the men, whose devotion to 'Old Joe,' as Gen. Johnston was universally called, made the danger of a mutiny imminent. I believe that a word from any Col. of good standing, would have induced the army to stack arms then and there unless their old Gen. was restored." Three years later, after the war, this officer added: "I am free to say I now regret that word was not spoken."[19]

That such worries were well founded is suggested by the conversation purportedly overheard by one soldier out on the picket line:

"Boys, we've fought the war for nothing. There is nothing for us in store now."

"What's the matter now?"

"General Joe Johnston is relieved, Generals Hardee and Kirby Smith resigned, and General Hood is appointed to take command of the Army of Tennessee."

"My God! Is that so?"

"It is certainly a fact."

"Then I'll never fire another gun. Any news or letters that you wish carried home? I've quit, and am going home. Please tender my resignation to Jeff Davis. . . ."

The five men on picket duty then threw down their guns, took off their cartridge boxes, emptied their pockets, and walked off. According to the witness, "it was the last we ever saw of them."[20]

Since there was no large-scale desertion in the days following the announcement of Johnston's dismissal, this scene was not typical, but there is no doubt that the men in the ranks were upset by the news. One soldier recorded in his diary that Johnston's dismissal "is regretted by the whole army as Gen. Johnson [sic] had won the respect and admiration of all, and especially the love of the men by his untiring efforts to save his men and feed them well." Another wrote: "The War Department perhaps knows best, but the troops are dissatisfied with the change, for Gen. Johnston was the idol of the army. . . ." A Georgia soldier wrote only: "They hav made ole J. Johnston quit us because he falls back. I am sorrow of it."[21]

Johnston spent the night of July 18 in Atlanta. Early the next morning, he took the train for Macon. Along with Lydia and the Wigfall girls, he moved into a large roomy house, three stories high, "with tall pillars reaching from the roof to the piazza" on the outskirts of Macon. It looked out over "a beautiful valley—beyond which rose a range of hills." He was, of course, a celebrity in the town, but an awkward one. Some were embarrassed for him, others eager to demonstrate their continued faith. That Sunday as he left church after the sermon, Mrs. Clement Clay, wife of a former U.S. senator from Alabama, "rushed up to him with hands outstretched, and rising on tip toe imprinted on his bronze cheek a warm kiss . . . in the face of the whole congregation." Louise Wigfall recalled that "The effect was magical. A low murmur went around among the people, tears sprang into many eyes, as they saw the blush mount to his brow. . . . Surrounded by a half laughing, half tearful crowd, the Old General made his way down the church steps and hurried homewards."[22]

That week, too, Johnston learned about Hood's fight for Atlanta. True to his promise, Hood wasted little time before attacking the Federal army. On July 20, he struck Thomas's Army of the Cumberland as it crossed Peachtree Creek. The attack was not well coordinated, and the Confederates failed to inflict a decisive defeat. Hood blamed the lack of success on the timidity of the men in the ranks who, he claimed, had forgotten how to fight under Johnston's command, though the casualties (more than five thousand), suggested that they fought hard. Then, only two days later, Hood struck again, east of the city, in what became known as the Battle of Atlanta. In another hard fight, the Federals were pushed back a mile or two and Major General McPherson was killed; but the Confederates lost an additional seven thousand men. Despite the long casualty lists, these battles failed to achieve the decisive results hoped for. Soon it became clear that the battles had cost more than the Confederacy could afford—Atlanta was more vulnerable than ever.

By now Johnston was beginning to learn something about the role that Bragg had played in his dismissal. A friend wrote to tell him that "The chief actor in all this foul drama . . . is your *Quondam* friend Braxton Bragg, he whose reputation you shielded, he for whom, I might add, you had alienated friends, if not made enemies." Bragg had made stops in Montgomery, Columbus, and Macon on his way back to Richmond; at each stop he had offered public and private statements that exaggerated the losses of the army, asserted Johnston had disregarded the wishes of the executive, and claimed Johnston had refused to accept orders to fight. Johnston was indignant, and he felt betrayed. Bragg had given him assurances of sympathy and understanding while all the time urging his dismissal in Richmond. "A man of honor," he wrote to Dabney Maury, "would have communicated with me as well as with Hood on the subject."[23]

Johnston's former chief of staff, W. W. Mackall, who retained his job under Hood, also came to believe that Bragg had behaved dishonorably. Two days after the Battle of Atlanta, Bragg was back in Atlanta to discuss strategy with Hood. The commanding general sent for Mackall to include him in the discussions, but when Mackall arrived and saw Bragg, he stiffened, and when Bragg extended his hand, Mackall refused to take it. Furious, Hood dismissed him on the spot. Thirty minutes later, Mackall was handed the orders relieving him.[24]

A week later, Hood fought his third battle for Atlanta. The results were more disappointing and more tragic than the first two. The movement of troops was again confused: instead of defending a crucial crossroads near Ezra Church west of the city, the Confederates ended up attacking entrenched Federals who had arrived there first. Another 5,000 men were lost, reducing Hood's effective force to about 35,000. By accepting the tactical offensive, Hood had so bled the army that he now had little choice but to fall back into defensive lines around the city. He called upon Richmond for reinforcements and sent Wheeler's cavalry in an attempt to break Sherman's supply lines. But it was too late. There were no reinforcements to be had, and Wheeler's men found the bridges so well guarded they were unable to inflict any significant damage on the railroad. For another month Atlanta awaited its fate.

In late July, Sherman dispatched 6,500 cavalry troopers under Major General George Stoneman with orders to cut the rail lines south of Atlanta. One column of this force closed in on Macon on July 27, and the city fathers offered Johnston command of the meager Home Guard troops. He declined the command but offered to provide military advice, which events made unnecessary when the Federals turned away from Macon to flee Wheeler's Confederate troopers who were in hot pursuit. Wheeler caught and defeated the Federal probe, ending the immediate threat.

Inexorably, however, Sherman worked his way around the city to the west, extending his flanks as always; on the last day of August, Hood decided he would have to try to drive off this latest probe or surrender the city. In the Battle of Jonesboro, Hood's attacking columns were again driven back. The next day, Hood evacuated Atlanta.

All that time, the Johnstons lived "quietly & comfortably" at their rented house in Macon. It was difficult for Johnston to sit idly while the news from the front was so terrible, especially in light of increasing evidence that Hood, as well as Bragg, had schemed behind his back. In August, Johnston wrote his brother Beverly that "there is no doubt . . . that Hood, while spending several hours a day in my quarters, was writing to Richmond to my injury." He concluded that Hood had "earned his promotion by misrepresenting me." Although Johnston withheld public criticism, he was anxious that his friends in Congress be apprised of the true story, and he wrote both Wigfall and Beverly, who was still living in Richmond, to ask them to guard his public reputation. He asked Beverly to share a copy of his official report with members of Congress who, he thought, had a right to see it, but he noted that since it was an "executive" document, Beverly "must be very careful in sharing it."[25]

Johnston's report found a ready audience in Richmond. Across the South, Hood's string of defeats made him the target of considerable public abuse. Just as Johnston had been the parlor-room villain in midsummer, by fall Hood had become the target of public vituperation. "Hood cannot be sufficiently abused," Mary Chesnut recorded in September. It would have been easy for Johnston to accept Hood's failures as his own vindication, yet publicly he avoided doing so. Lydia in particular was careful not to take any satisfaction in the bad news. Mrs. Chesnut noted that Lydia "is quiet and polite and carefully avoided awkward topics."[26]

But Johnston was feeling more stress than his dignified manner showed. In late August, he wrote Beverly, "I can't reconcile myself to inaction in this time of great events." And in September, he came down with a severe case of shingles—a virus often triggered by stress—that lasted several weeks. "Such a covering, let me tell you, is worse than none," he wrote to a friend. He was still laid up in late September when Jefferson Davis, alarmed by the fall of Atlanta, made a trip to Georgia to boost morale and encourage a spirit of resistance. In Macon, Davis spoke at the Baptist Church and defended himself from criticism that he had removed Johnston precipitously. "If I knew that a General did not possess the right qualities to command, would I not be wrong if he were not removed?" the president asked rhetorically. Although Atlanta had fallen anyway, Davis justified Johnston's removal by noting that he had put "a man in command who I knew would strike an honest and manly blow for the city, and many a Yankee's blood was made to nourish the soil before the prize was won." Disgusted, Johnston afterward sarcastically referred to Hood in his private correspondence as "the Striker of Manly Blows."[27]

In early October, Hood recrossed the Chattahoochee, placing what was left of his army in a position to threaten Sherman's rail connections with Chattanooga. Johnston thought the move foolish. "I fear our commanders trust too much to Sherman's ignorance," he wrote to a friend. Johnston believed that Hood's move uncovered the rest of the state and provided Sherman with an opportunity "to destroy our shops at Columbus, Macon, & Augusta & cut off Genl. Lee's supplies." As for Sherman's communications, "the sea furnishes him as good a base at Charleston, Savannah, Pensacola, or Mobile as he can find in Chattanooga." In other words, Johnston predicted that Sherman was likely to ignore his rail communications, destroy the cities of Georgia, and march to the sea to reestablish a base.[28]

Nevertheless, Hood took the Army of Tennessee northward, skirting the Federal garrison at Rome, and by mid-month he was at Dalton, where the campaign had begun nearly six months before. Sherman soon chased him from there, and Hood fled west into Alabama. This time Sherman did not follow him. Instead, he dispatched Thomas and Schofield, his two most trusted subordinates, to keep an eye on Hood, then took the main body of the Federal army back to Atlanta. Georgia lay open, unprotected, and Sherman had plans to take advantage of that.

The Johnstons' lease on the house in Macon expired on October 1. Because they could not afford to rent another, they accepted William Mackall's invitation to move in with his family in Vineville, a small town adjoining Macon. They lived in "a snug little house at the end of the village street." It was comfortable enough, but the wartime fare was sparse. The noon meal consisted of "cornbread and sorghum molasses," the same food the soldiers in the field were eating. In the evenings, the company gathered in the common room and entertained one another with "music, song and dancing." Louise Wigfall recalled that "Mrs. Johnston . . . was full of life and vivacity and even ready to further the gaiety of young people. . . ."[29]

One of those young people was Thomas Mackall, a cousin of General Mackall, who had also served on Johnston's staff. A shy and serious young man, Tom became the object of some flirtatious teasing by the young ladies, and he conspired with Lydia to gain revenge. He and Lydia let it be known that a fancy-dress party was going to be held, and made out false invitations. The excited girls set to work modifying their dresses so they could pass for party dresses, they worked hard all afternoon to Mackall's amusement. But Johnston thought the prank mean-spirited, and he talked to both his wife and young Captain Mackall, who agreed to call it off and confess.[30]

The war news remained gloomy. In mid-November, Sherman set fire to Atlanta and abandoned the city, plunging east on his march to the sea. At about the same time, Hood struck north into Tennessee, hoping—vainly as it proved—that he could draw Sherman out of Georgia in pursuit. On November 30, Hood fought another battle at Franklin, where he ordered a foolish frontal assault that left six thousand more Confederate soldiers and no fewer than twelve generals on the field as casualties. Six generals, including Pat Cleburne, were killed. Although it seemed impossible, the news got worse. Two weeks later, Hood's army was assailed outside Nashville by vastly superior Federal forces and virtually destroyed. Only scattered remnants—fewer than eighteen thousand men altogether—managed to make their way south through terrible weather into Alabama. For all practical purposes, the Army of Tennessee ceased to exist.

A week later Sherman reached the sea at Savannah.

PART FOUR

A PLACE IN

HISTORY

CHAPTER TWENTY-TWO

Commanding the Lost Cause

In the last winter of the war, the ragged southern armies fought on stubbornly despite growing evidence that the Cause was already lost. Hood's disastrous defeat at Nashville and the midwinter retreat that followed had all but destroyed the Army of Tennessee. The Stars and Bars still floated defiantly over Richmond, but it required an act of faith to believe that the men of Lee's starving and ill-equipped Army of Northern Virginia could break the siege of the vastly superior Federal army that held them pinned within their lines. Moreover, with the coming of spring, Grant would renew his relentless pressure on Lee's supply lines. Sherman's army, after its devastating march to the sea across Georgia, turned north and was moving through the Carolinas toward Lee's back door. Across the rest of what remained of the Confederate South, evidence of a collapsing economy was everywhere: inflation was out of control, the transportation system had broken down, and the government seemed paralyzed.

The Johnstons moved eastward from Vineville to Columbia, South Carolina. "We chose this place," Johnston wrote to Kirby Smith, "because she [Lydia] has a sister & I friends in the neighborhood." There, within their small circle of friends, blame for the collapse was laid at Davis's feet. Johnston's advocates across the South agreed. "The feeling against Mr. Davis is becoming very bitter," Mackall reported to Johnston from Vineville. One former defender of the president's told Mackall that Davis was so "utterly incapable of conducting the war" that he was "ready to have him removed by any means constitutional or revolutionary." Hood's star, too, had plummeted. Hood's reputation "went up like a skyrocket," one wag commented, and "came down like a stick." So bitter was the public feeling against Hood that a rumor that he had been killed set some of the citizens of Columbia to celebrating. But Hood soon showed up in Columbia, stopping there briefly on his way to Richmond where he would put the final touches on the official report of his disastrous campaign. Hood stayed with the Chesnuts in Columbia, and was uncharacteristically subdued and melancholy, staring moodily into the fire during conversations, unaware of what was being said.[1]

Johnston's star meanwhile was once again in the ascendant. Wigfall and his allies in the Confederate Congress claimed that Johnston's dismissal was the cause of the Confederacy's woes. Josiah Gorgas recorded in his diary on February 3 that "The country continues to cry out for the reappt. of Gen. Jos. Johnston to command the Army of Tenn. . . ." Mackall wrote to Johnston: "It is the settled conviction from one end of the land to the other that you alone can bring back the old soldiers to their colors or engage others to join." Indeed, he reported that "soldiers are inveigling the deserters to their colors by telling them that you have joined the Army of Tennessee. . . . It may be fanaticism with me, but I have never faltered in my faith that you would have to finish this war and be the savior of our independence so rashly jeopardized as nearly lost."[2]

This outcry from the public and the ranks of the military was genuine, but it was rooted in a sense of desperation; the country needed a savior. In Richmond, the public concern gave a stronger hand to those who sought to undermine the authority of Jefferson Davis. The political fight in the Confederate capital distilled into two camps. "We thought this was a struggle for independence," wrote the savvy Mary Chesnut in her diary, "now it seems it is only a fight between Joe Johnston and Jeff Davis." Although the Confederacy was on its last legs, neither side would give an inch. Because Davis delayed in publishing copies of Johnston's report on the North Georgia campaign, Wigfall and his allies called loudly for it to be printed immediately. Beverly Johnston, who had a copy of the report, leaked it to selected congressmen. Hearing a rumor that Davis planned to discredit the report, he wrote to his brother to urge him to come to Richmond and defend himself.[3]

Joe Johnston arrived the week before Christmas. The holiday season could not lift the gloom off the city, besieged by Grant's army and beset by economic woes. Johnston must have been struck by the metamorphosis. In 1861, when he had first come South to offer his services, Richmond was a large town, not yet a city but bustling with the electricity of youth and adventure. By 1862, it was nearly twice as large, though sobered by the casualties of the Seven Days Battles—more mature and less naive. Now the city itself seemed weary of the war, going about its business with a tired fatalism.

Johnston at once threw himself into the intramural battle with the government. As Beverly had suspected, Davis's endorsement to Johnston's report all but called him a liar: "The case as presented," Davis wrote, "is very different from the impression created by other communications contemporaneous with the events referred to." Johnston demanded to know the source of those "impressions." He asked Samuel Cooper for the names of those who had written to the administration, and the substance of their reports, so that he could respond. Cooper declined even to answer, but others in Richmond were more sympathetic. Both houses of Congress offered Johnston "a privileged seat" on the floor, where Wigfall and his allies displayed him like a trophy. They praised him effusively, though everyone present—except perhaps Johnston—fully understood that their praise was intended primarily to embarrass Davis.[4]

Johnston returned to Columbia unsatisfied. During the rest of the unhappy winter of 1864–65 he lived there quietly, about as far from the war as it was possible to get in what remained of the Confederacy. But the war was coming his way. Following his march to the sea, Sherman gathered his forces for a push north through the Carolinas toward Virginia, thus reducing the size of Lee's logistic base and threatening his back door. Though delayed by wet weather, Sherman's threatened advance put the residents of Columbia in a panic; those who could, left. Soon after the new year, Joe put Lydia on a train for Charlotte, North Carolina, although he remained behind to offer his services in the defense of Columbia. Lydia was loath to go. "I'll never forget his pale face & moist eyes," she wrote to Louise Wigfall. She blamed everything on Davis now, the man who had stripped her husband of his command and set the country on the path to ruin—"Never will I forgive the man that has crippled such a true soldier." From Charlotte, Lydia headed west to Lincolnton in western North Carolina. The whole journey took two days and two nights—a testiment to the dilapidated condition of the southern railway system—and it left Lydia perfectly heartsick. The countryside was stripped of everything, and in Lincolnton she found the townspeople without food or hope. "The sight of this town to-day is lamentable," she wrote to Charlotte Wigfall, "women hunting in every direction for shelter—and the people themselves beginning to move off for a safer place." Only a few weeks before, Mary Chesnut had commented on Lydia's "keen sense of fun"; this trip had broken her spirits. "Oh these terrible times of shipwreck—everything looks hopeless to me now," Lydia told Charlotte, "and then if we are to go down—we are so far apart that we can see nothing of each other, but the glimpse of a pale face as it sinks out of sight!"[5]

On January 14, 1865, Wigfall celebrated his own personal victory over Jeff Davis when the Confederate Senate voted 14–2 for a bill to endow Robert E. Lee—by name—with the powers of general-in-chief. At the same time the bill recommended "the assignment of General Joseph E. Johnston to the command of the Army of Tennessee." Four days later, the House passed the measure by a vote of 50 to 25. Although the bill "respectfully but earnestly" advised the president to make these appointments, it was an unmistakable vote of no confidence in Davis's direction of the war. Wigfall and his friends had succeeded in wresting control of the war away from the commander-in-chief. Johnston thought it unfortunate. From Lincolnton, where he joined Lydia in late January, Johnston wrote to Mackall that Congress had violated "an excellent rule—that of confining one's self to one's own business." It was not the job of Congress, he believed, to appoint generals. For better or worse, that was the president's responsibility.[6]

Davis was not about to give up without a fight. He appointed Lee to the newly created position of general-in-chief willingly, but refused to restore Johnston to command of the Army of Tennessee. For another month he held fast as the pressure grew. Fifteen senators petitioned Lee to make the appointment himself; knowing Davis's opposition, and believing that a continual change of commanders was unhealthy, Lee respectfully declined. Davis, meanwhile, wrote a memo of over four thousand words, reviewing Johnston's wartime career and chronicling his own disillusionment with Johnston's capacity for command: "At different times during the war, I have given to General Johnston three very important commands, and in each case experience has revealed . . . defects which unfit him for the conduct of a campaign." Davis painted a portrait of a man who failed at every assignment: from Harpers Ferry to Centreville, from Yorktown to Dalton, every position he had occupied was "untenable." In each case, Johnston had evacuated the site he was ordered to defend, and surrendered valuable supplies to the enemy. He had refused to undertake the offensive even when the government made every effort to support him. Johnston was "deficient in enterprise, tardy in movement, defective in preparation, and singularly neglectful of the duty of preserving our means of supply and transportation." In Georgia, not only did he fail to advance as the government ordered him to do, he began to retreat almost at once; and without fighting "any general engagement," he withdrew all the way to the outskirts of Atlanta. Davis concluded: "My opinion of General Johnston's unfitness for command has ripened slowly and against my inclinations into a conviction so settled that it would be impossible for me again to feel confidence in him as the commander of an army in the field."[7]

Davis prepared this memo with the intention of submitting it to Congress, but he never sent it. Despite his antipathy for Johnston, it was obvious by February that, if nothing else, Ole Joe's restoration to command would help boost sagging morale in the army. That same week, Lee suggested that Johnston should be reappointed to command. Just four days after writing his detailed critique of Johnston's unfitness for command, with feelings that can only be imagined, the president made the appointment. He probably should have destroyed his bitter memo at the same time. Instead, he sent a copy to a friend, which surfaced after the war to become the first salvo in a postwar

"Battle of the Books" that brought little credit to either side.[8]

Johnston for his part felt little satisfaction at the turn of events, and he had more than a few doubts about his assignment. His new command encompassed two military districts: the Department of Tennessee and Georgia, and the Department of South Carolina, Georgia, and Florida. (North Carolina was added to his command in early March 1865.) In effect, he would command everything east of the Mississippi except Lee's beleaguered army at Richmond. Lee's orders were direct: he was to "Concentrate all available forces and drive back Sherman." Johnston wondered if he were not being set up to become the scapegoat for the collapse of the Confederacy. The next day, on a walk, he ran into Mary Chesnut, who recorded in her diary that Johnston professed to be "very angry to be ordered to take command again." Apparently his anger was not a pose, for Lydia too confided that her husband was "in the very devil of a bad humor" convinced that "He was only put back to be the one to surrender."[9]

Johnston shared his suspicions with Wigfall. Davis had restored him to command, Johnston wrote, so that the opprobrium of surrender would fall on him. "You are mistaken," Wigfall replied from besieged Richmond. "It was out of confidence & kindness & a real desire to obtain the benefit of your ability in this crisis." Far more important was the information that "It was Lee, & not Davis," who had restored Johnston. "Lee I believe fully sustains you & is now I understand hated by Davis as much as you are." Wigfall claimed that Lee had become Johnston's champion in Richmond. "He does not hesitate to speak of your removal as unfortunate & having caused all our present difficulties. . . ." As for Jefferson Davis, Wigfall wrote that the president was "in high dudgeon & his wife is furious." He urged Johnston to take his new assignment seriously. "For God's sake, communicate with Lee fully & freely . . . & give him the full benefit of your judgement in this hour of peril."[10]

By the time Johnston received this information, weeks later, he was already deeply involved in his new assignment, trying to cobble together an army that might slow Sherman's advance. Wigfall's news that it was Lee who had restored him to command, and that his old classmate still had confidence in him, made all the difference in the world. Johnston had not met face to face with his former classmate since Seven Pines, and in the months and years since, he had grown jealous of him. After all, Lee had taken charge of Johnston's army after Seven Pines and had achieved great things with it. Perhaps Johnston secretly suspected that he could not have matched Lee's string of improbable triumphs even had he never been wounded. That fear—the suspicion that Lee really was his superior—may have been the root cause of Johnston's jealousy, and almost certainly contributed to his defensiveness. Johnston also suspected that Lee had willingly participated in all of Davis's strategic decisions since Seven Pines, including his own demotion after Vicksburg and his dismissal in front of Atlanta. Lee, Johnston believed, had become one of "them."[11]

Now he learned that it was not so, that Lee was an ally, and a great weight was lifted off his heart. "In youth and early manhood I loved and admired him more than any man in the world," he wrote back to Wigfall. "Since then we have had little intercourse and have become formal in our personal intercourse. . . . I have long thought that he had forgotten our early friendship." The evidence of Lee's confidence encouraged and inspired him. "Be assured," he added, "that Knight of old never fought under his King more loyally than I'll serve under Gen. Lee."[12]

When Johnston accepted his assignment in February, however, this news was still two weeks in the future, and his first instinct was to make sure that Lee harbored no unrealistic expectations. "It is too late to expect me to concentrate troops capable of driving back Sherman," he wrote to his old friend, now his commander. He repeated this view three days later after he arrived in Charlotte to take up his duties: "Your order . . . implies that you regard these forces as adequate to the object. . . . In my opinion these troops form an army too weak to cope with Sherman." Lee was fully aware of the severe limitations under which Johnston assumed his new duties; he could do no more than ask him to do his best. Lee warned that "nothing can be sent from here to your assistance"; he also noted "the vital importance of checking General Sherman." I will rely on you, Lee concluded, and we will both hope for the best.[13]

Johnston assumed command at Charlotte, North Carolina, on February 25. The backbone of his "army" was the force of seven or eight thousand men under Hardee that had been trying to slow Sherman's advance through South Carolina under Beauregard's general supervision. This force was now at Cheraw, South Carolina, less than a dozen miles from the North Carolina border. Another source of manpower was the five or six thousand men under Braxton Bragg whom Davis had sent to take charge of the defense of the port city of Wilmington, North Carolina. That city surrendered on the very day that Johnston received his orders; Bragg had since pulled back to Goldsboro, 100 miles north of Wilmington, and 150 miles northeast of Hardee's force at Cheraw. Finally, remnants of the Army of Tennessee were making their way east to join their former commander in his last-ditch defense of the Confederate heartland. By mid-March these would total four to five thousand, though they would arrive piecemeal, and Johnston could not be sure when or how many he could count on. If all these forces could be brought together, they would total some twenty thousand men, few enough to contend with Sherman's advancing hordes; but for now they were widely separated. Wade Hampton wrote that "It would scarcely have been possible to disperse a force more effectually. . . ."[14]

If there were few soldiers, there were plenty of generals. Mary Chesnut noted that the towns seemed to be "swarming with troopless generals." Not only was this a case of "too many cooks," but the cooks were not always disposed to cooperate with one another. Bragg found the prospect of serving

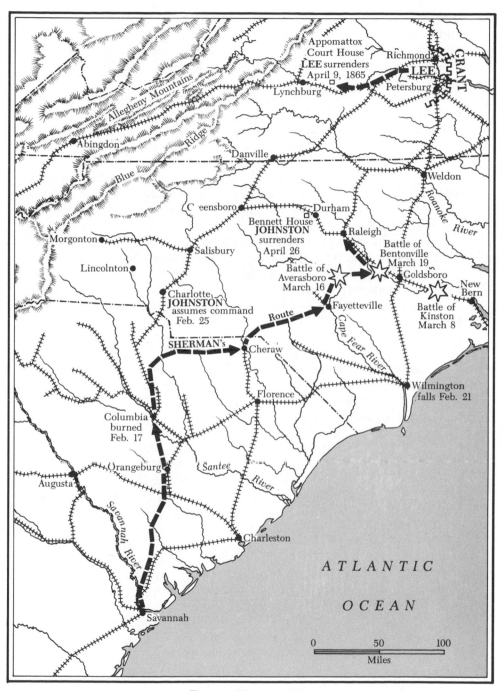

Eastern Theatre, 1865

under Johnston hugely awkward, and he begged Davis to relieve him from such an "embarrassing position." But Davis was no longer calling the shots, and Bragg remained. Ironically, Bragg's next move was to ask Johnston for reinforcements so that he could turn on his pursuers and attack them. Although he faced odds of at least twenty to one on his own front, Johnston decided it was worth a try.[15]

Some historians have found Johnston's agreement to reinforce Bragg curious at best, and have faulted him for fragmenting his forces even further, calling the decision "foolhardy." Why did he do it? First of all, Johnston saw that he was at the center of converging Federal columns, and appreciated that checking the advance of one of them would buy time for the soldiers coming to join him from the ruins of the Army of Tennessee. But Johnston may also have recalled Bragg's repeated refusals to send reinforcements to him at Dalton. By responding favorably now, Johnston could show that he was the bigger man.[16]

In a further irony, the only force near enough to reach Bragg in time was D. H. Hill's division at Smithfield, and Hill hated Bragg because of the way that officer had treated him after Chickamauga. Johnston nevertheless ordered Hill to march to Bragg's aid, adding: "I beg you to forget the past for this emergency." Hill obeyed the order, though he afterward protested to Johnston: "I hope that it may be possible & consistent with [the] intents of the service to give me another commander than Genl. Bragg. He has made me the scapegoat once & would do it again."[17]

In addition to smoothing over quarrels between his generals, Johnston had to find some way to feed and supply this patchwork army, for the supply system and railroads had virtually ceased to function. As always, Johnston's first concern was the welfare of the men. He requested permission to distribute four months pay immediately, including some of it in specie, and when he learned that the Confederate navy held a large supply of precious coffee, sugar, and spirits at Charlotte, he appealed to J. C. Breckinridge, the newest Secretary of War, for permission to seize it. Breckinridge replied that he could go ahead and take whatever supplies he could, but there was no money; the government was "almost universally paralyzed for want of means." He could only recommend that Johnston "make the best" of it. In essence that was Lee's advice, too. He wrote to suggest that Johnston endeavor to supply his army "by collecting subsistence through the country."[18]

The strategic picture was no brighter. At first Johnston wondered if it might not be possible to unite the scattered elements of his own forces with Lee's army at Richmond to attack Sherman and Grant in turn. After all, the one advantage the South still held was its interior position. Johnston wired Lee to ask if he could hold Richmond and Petersburg with half of his army and bring the other half to North Carolina "to crush Sherman." Afterward, Johnston suggested, "we might then turn on Grant." Lee made short work of such "castles in the air," replying that his hold on Richmond was so tenuous he could not spare any troops to join in an attack on Sherman. It was vital to protect the area around Raleigh because it was his only remaining source of supplies. If you have to give up Raleigh and fall back northward, Lee wrote, "both armies would certainly starve."[19]

Johnston never gave up on the idea of joint action with Lee's army, but he recognized the immediate need to bring together the disparate elements of Confederate forces scattered across North Carolina before Sherman's advancing forces picked them off one by one. Sherman had been advancing on a broad front, almost dismissive of Confederate abilities to stop him. On March 6, however, he learned that Johnston had been restored to command, and the news forced him to change his plans. "I knew then that my special antagonist, General Jos. Johnston was back, with part of his old army," he wrote later in his memoirs, "that he would not be misled by feints and false reports, and would somehow compel me to exercise more caution than I had hitherto done." Another Federal officer noted in his diary: "The important news is that Johnston has been restored to command. I do not imagine for a moment that this change of Rebel commanders will influence General Sherman in his purpose, yet it will alter the modus operandi, for Johnston cannot be treated with the contempt Sherman shows for Beauregard."[20]

Initially, Johnston ordered his scattered forces to concentrate at Fayetteville, halfway between Hardee's force at Cheraw and Bragg's at Goldsboro, and he moved his headquarters there on March 4. But as Sherman pushed rapidly north, Johnston soon saw that it was "too late" to make a stand at Fayetteville, and he instead directed a concentration at Raleigh, sixty miles further north. From Fayetteville, Johnston wrote to Lee that Sherman was still operating on an "extended front" and that he hoped for an opportunity to "to fight his divided troops." But he also noted, in a subsequent wire, that "I would not fight Sherman's *united* army unless your situation makes it necessary." Lee responded: "You must judge what the probabilities will be of arresting Sherman by battle. If there is a reasonable probability I would recommend it. A bold and unexpected attack might relieve us."[21]

It was Bragg, however, emboldened by the reinforcements sent him by Johnston, who launched the first counterattack. The Federal division of Major General Jacob D. Cox had been transferred from Tennessee to North Carolina by sea after the collapse of Hood's campaign. Its appearance at New Bern on the Carolina coast was what had prompted Bragg to request the reinforcements. Now, bolstered by D. H. Hill's men, Bragg turned to attack Cox at Kinston on March 8. The Confederates succeeded in driving Cox back, taking three artillery pieces and more than 1,000 prisoners while suffering only 134 casualties. Bragg even pursued briefly. He wanted to expand his modest success into a full-scale victory, but Cox entrenched and brought up reinforcements, so Bragg broke off contact and set out for Raleigh.[22]

Cox's presence created a dilemma for Johnston. Sherman, by then advanced as far as Fayetteville, might march directly for Raleigh, or he could turn east for a junction with Cox near Goldsboro. If Raleigh was Sherman's objective, Johnston would have to concentrate there, for Lee had informed him that holding Raleigh was essential to the survival of his own army at Richmond. But if Sherman moved toward Goldsboro, Johnston's best hope was to hit Cox with everything he had before Sherman could arrive. Uncertain which way Sherman would move, Johnston split the difference, ordering the army to concentrate at Smithfield, halfway between Raleigh and Goldsboro. From there he could advance to attack the flank of Sherman's force whichever way it moved. Fortuitously, the Federals were now advancing more slowly, for the rains and soggy ground forced them to corduroy the roads. If Cheatham's division, still en route from Mississippi, could arrive before the Federals did, it would help even the odds a bit.[23]

Three days later Hardee's small army, giving ground slowly as it backed northward from South Carolina, was driven from the crossroads near Averasboro at the crossing of the Cape Fear River. Hardee made a strong stand, holding off two full Federal corps for much of the day before falling back. Afterward, Wade Hampton's Confederate cavalry reported that Sherman's victorious columns had turned east toward Goldsboro. At once, Johnston issued orders for the army to move toward the small crossroads community of Bentonville. There he would launch the "bold and unexpected attack" that Lee suggested. He hoped to catch the overconfident Federals unawares, inflicting a painful defeat that would at least force them to advance more cautiously and thus buy the Confederacy more time.[24]

On three days in mid-March 1865, Joseph E. Johnston directed his last battle. It was a forlorn hope. With a patchwork force that was hugely outnumbered, officered by men who bore personal grievances against one another, the ranks filled by soldiers who were keenly aware that there was almost no hope of ultimate victory, Johnston nevertheless inflicted a severe check on Sherman's army. His battle plan was virtually identical to the one he had hoped to employ at Cassville but that had been stymied by Hood's cancellation of the attack: he would ambush Federal forces who believed they were in pursuit of a retreating army. This time Bragg's force would play the role assigned to Polk at Cassville: blocking the road and forcing the Federals to deploy. Then Hardee and Stewart would strike the enemy flank. The target of this ambush was the left wing of Sherman's army, composed of two corps—the XIVth and the XXth—commanded by Major General Henry W. Slocum. Serendipitously, the XIVth Corps was under the command of Federal Major General Jefferson C. Davis.

Johnston and most of the army reached the ambush site at Bentonville late in the day on March 18. Time was crucial now, for Johnston had underestimated how long it would take Hardee's corps to reach the battlefield, and Hardee's men were still five miles away when the army went into camp that night. Nevertheless, early the next morning, Johnston deployed his available forces behind a cavalry screen provided by Wade Hampton. Bragg's men deployed left and right of the road to Goldsboro, and Stewart's men—minus

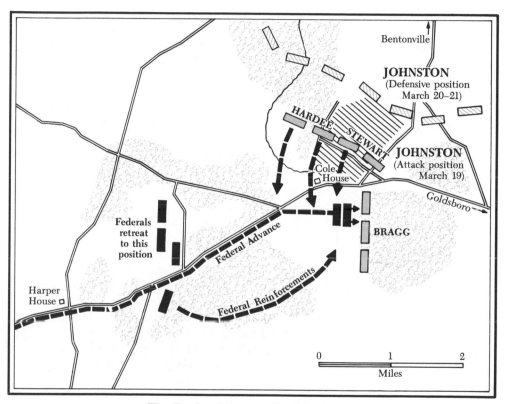

The Battle of Bentonville, March 19, 1865

Cheatham's division, which was still en route—took up a position on the right. Neither Hardee nor Cheatham had yet arrived when the advanced Federal skirmishers ran into Hampton's cavalry and slowly drove them back onto the main line.

Confident of another easy success, the Federals deployed to contest the road, and at about ten o'clock they struck Bragg's blocking force, particularly the division of Robert F. Hoke, entrenched behind a rail fence. Hoke had the only Confederate artillery on the field, and his guns now opened on the startled Federals. The Union commander fed more brigades into the fight. Soon the two sides were fully engaged. Even so, Slocum believed that the force in front of him "consisted only of cavalry with a few pieces of artillery." He informed Sherman that he needed no reinforcements, and ordered his lead brigades "to press the enemy closely." Within the hour, Slocum learned that it was infantry, and not merely cavalry in his path, and a prisoner told him that Johnston had assembled an army of forty thousand men. At once he went over to the defensive and called up his reserves.[25]

This was the moment Johnston had planned to launch his flanking attack. But two factors delayed him. The first was Hardee's late arrival; the second was Bragg's request for reinforcements. "Old Reliable" did not reach the field until well past noon, and by then Hoke's division was being severely pressed. Bragg pleaded for support, and Johnston detached McLaws's division from Hardee's arriving troops to bolster Hoke's line. This weakened the impact of Hardee's attack, but Johnston felt he could not deny Bragg's request. Even without McLaws, the rebels proved they could still hit. A few minutes before three, Johnston launched his flanking attack. It was the last grand charge of the war for the Confederacy, and it was sadly stirring: the rebels advanced in perfect alignment, their colors unfurled and their bayonets fixed. But the units had been so bled by four years of war that many brigades were no larger than regiments, and regiments were the size of companies. Regimental colors were closely bunched along the line because many regiments had no more than forty or fifty men. Still, it made a grand show. One witness from the Federal side thought "the onward sweep of the rebel lines was like the waves of the ocean, relentless." Hardee's troops drove over the Federal line and outflanked two Union brigades, which broke and fled. Many of the Federals threw away their rifles and ran "like a flock of sheep" according to one witness; the XIVth Corps was shattered. Seeing the backs of their enemies was a tonic to the rebel infantry who bounded after them. But the hours of delay now proved costly, for Slocum had had time to bring up his reserves, even dismounting the hated "foragers" and throwing them into the line. More importantly, the brigades of the XXth Corps began to arrive on the field. The engagement turned into a hotly contested fight at close range, the outcome hanging in the balance.[26]

Hardee halted his attack briefly to realign his units, then he advanced again; but much of the impetus from the original assault had dissipated. As his men crossed the Goldsboro Road, they struck fresh units of the XXth

Corps and recoiled. Now Hoke advanced from his blocking position to join the attack, and once again the Federals gave way. Bragg, however, recalled Hoke and ordered him to focus on a frontal assault against a Federal redoubt. On parts of the field, the fighting was hand-to-hand: men on opposing sides clubbed each other with their muskets because there was no time to reload. The rebels attacked no fewer then five times, but each time the patchwork Federal line held. The firing petered out with falling darkness, and the Confederates withdrew to their original line of departure.

That night Slocum brought up more reinforcements, and it became clear that nothing further could be accomplished on that particular battlefield. Still Johnston refused to withdraw. He changed position so that he could defend against the expected arrival of Slocum's reinforcements, but he stubbornly held his position for two more days. His official explanation was that he wanted to recover the Confederate wounded who were still on the battlefield, and also that he hoped Sherman might be lured into making a frontal assault. Perhaps, too, he was loath to withdraw lest his critics be provided with yet another example of his willingness to surrender territory. By the afternoon of March 20, the Federals had four corps on the field and they attacked the rebel line several times without success. At one point, a Federal division charged toward a weak point in the rebel line and Hardee sent a regiment to plug the hole. Only days before he had reluctantly given his own sixteen-year-old son permission to leave school and join a cavalry regiment. It was that regiment whose charge now blunted the Federal spearhead. The Federals withdrew, but Hardee's son fell, mortally wounded.

The next day, faithful to character, Sherman sent a corps around Johnston's flank to cut off his line of retreat. Johnston had no option but to withdraw, and that night he pulled the army back from Bentonville toward Raleigh. Although the men marched all night until daylight on the 22nd, their morale was high—they had proven that they could still whip the Yankees. D. H. Hill wrote to his wife that "Our men fought well and are in good spirits."[27]

Only in terms of its impact on morale can Bentonville be called a Confederate victory. Sherman held the ground afterward, and, as usual, the attacking army suffered most of the casualties. The Confederates lost a total of 2,606; Union losses were 1,646. But Sherman's men learned that the war was not yet over, and that the Confederate army was still dangerous. They would be more wary now. "Johnston is very careful of his men and will make the most of them," one Yankee officer wrote in his diary after Bentonville, "though it is [now only] a question of men, and who can endure the draught of blood the longest."[28]

Johnston was moderately pleased with what had been accomplished. If nothing else, the battle had proven that the men of the Army of Tennessee would still fight. By now Johnston was well aware that Hood had justified his own failures in command by asserting that the men in the ranks had lost the will to fight. Yet even now, after their defeat in Tennessee, the long retreat to Alabama, and the overland march to North Carolina, those men had assailed an army more than twice their number and sent it fleeing, at least temporarily.

Johnston wired Lee proudly: "Troops of Tennessee army have fully disproved slanders that have been published against them." Ominously, he also suggested to Lee that "it is no longer a question of whether you will leave present position; you have only to decide where to meet Sherman. I will be near him."[29]

That same week, Johnston finally saw a copy of Hood's official report on his tenure in command of the Army of Tennessee. Hood had completed a draft as early as January, and and Wigfall had summarized its contents in a letter to Johnston dated February 27, but not until April did Johnston actually see it. It was a curious document. The first third did not concern Hood's operations at all, but was a review of Johnston's management of the army and his conduct of the campaign from Dalton to Atlanta. Hood's purpose in including such a survey was to prove that Johnston had ruined the army before Hood ascended to the command. It is at least possible that Hood was encouraged to adopt this gambit by his friends in Richmond. In his room at the Spotswood Hotel, Hood read a copy of his report to Isham Harris, the Confederate governor of Tennessee, who had accompanied the army on much of its campaign. Harris suggested that Hood's criticism of Johnston had no place in a report that was ostensibly an account of his own tenure in command. Emotionally, Hood broke down and agreed, claiming that he knew it was wrong to do it, but that it was now too late, for the report had been seen and accepted by the administration. Harris concluded from that conversation that "Hood was a puppet in the hands of others who were sacrificing him to gain their own ends—and striking through him a blow at Genl. Johnston."[30]

Johnston could not have been surprised by Hood's attack. Weeks before, an article in the Atlanta *Daily Constitutionalist* had extolled Hood as "fully equal to Lee himself," and castigated Johnston. The author remained anonymous, but his initials were given as "G.W.S." and Johnston suspected that the author was Gustavus Woodson Smith, his former friend and comrade. The article was reprinted in the Richmond *Sentinel* on February 17, two days after Hood submitted his report; the similarity in phrasing and organization suggests that whoever wrote it had access to early drafts of Hood's report.[31]

In that report, Hood wrote that "Nearly all the men and resources of the West and South were placed at his [Johnston's] disposal." Indeed, "extraordinary efforts" had been made to ensure an "easy victory" if only Johnston had advanced. But instead, he commenced a retreat of seventy-four days, even though Sherman's army was "but little superior in numbers." Johnston abandoned one strong position after another, Hood maintained, fought no battles, and completely destroyed the morale of the men in the ranks—"the inevitable result of the strategy [he] adopted." Hood's report laid everything at Johnston's feet. The army behaved badly at Atlanta and during the Tennessee campaign because it had been ruined by Johnston's policy of constant retreat. Hardee, Cheatham, and others were castigated as well. Most unjustly of all, Hood blamed the men in the ranks who, he claimed, had forgotten how to fight.[32]

In marked contrast to the reluctance he had shown to disseminate copies of Johnston's report, Davis sent Hood's report to Congress at once with a recommendation that it be printed. Johnston was furious. In particular, he was angered by Hood's assertion that he had wanted to fight at Cassville but that Johnston had prevented him. He notified Hood by telegraph that same day that he intended to call him to answer before a court-martial. Hood acknowledged receipt of the telegram, informing Johnston that he would "be ready to meet any charges you may prefer."[33]

While Johnston and Hood exchanged terse telegrams, Lee contemplated how he might break Grant's hold on Petersburg and Richmond. The week after the Battle of Bentonville, he sent Major General Gordon to attack Fort Stedman, one of the Federal strongpoints in the encircling lines outside Petersburg. Despite some initial gains, the attack was repulsed, and Lee knew then that he had to consider an evacuation of Richmond. On April 1, a defeat at Five Forks exposed the army's southern flank and threatened the South Side Railroad; the next day, the Federals broke through the thin Confederate lines at Poplar Springs in a battle which took the life of A. P. Hill. That night Lee began to evacuate the city.

At Raleigh, Johnston had no idea that things were so grim in Virginia. On April 8, the day that Lee arrived at Appomattox, Johnston received a telegram from a friend assuring him: "All private accounts cheering and represent the army in good condition and spirits. . . ." But it was not so. With Lee's defeat, the Confederacy could not survive. Even Wigfall began to lose hope. As early as March he had asked Johnston, "Can the war be longer carried on? Do you regard the cause as now hopeless & does humanity now demand that we shall make the best terms we can?" Indeed, he was already looking ahead to an unhappy future. "In the event of a crash what do you suppose doing with yourself?" His own view was dark: "I have no future."[34]

The mood of the rest of the country is perhaps best captured by a vignette recorded by Mary Chesnut in her diary. On March 30, she watched a deserter being dragged off by the provost marshal to rejoin the army. His wife called out to him for all to hear: "You desert agin, quick as you kin—come back to your wife and children." Her voice rose as the distance grew. "Desert, Jake! Desert agin, Jake!"[35]

By the second week of April, Johnston knew that Lee had evacuated Richmond, but he did not know the details, and he nourished a secret hope that this meant Lee was bringing the Army of Northern Virginia to join his own forces in North Carolina. This was his frame of mind on April 11 when he boarded a train at midnight in response to a summons from Davis to meet with him in Greensboro. He travelled all night, arriving sometime after eight in the morning on April 12. As he stepped off the train, the town was full of rumors that Lee had surrendered three days earlier at Appomattox. Beauregard was there, too, and Johnston went to see him first. At about ten o'clock, both generals were both summoned to Davis's private car. In addition to the president, three cabinet members—Judah P. Benjamin (State), Stephen Mallory (Navy), and John H. Reagan (Postmaster)—were present.[36]

Johnston was prepared to present a status report on the condition of the army and its recent military operations. Instead, he found himself the object of a pep talk. Davis insisted that recent setbacks could be overcome by calling back to the colors all those who had deserted. Johnston had never heard a more unlikely proposition. He responded that "men who had left the army when our cause was not desperate . . . would scarcely, in the present desperate condition of affairs, enter the service upon mere invitation." But Davis cut him short and adjourned the meeting, announcing that they would reconvene after the arrival of acting Secretary of War Breckinridge, who was expected that night.[37]

Meanwhile, Johnston spoke with Beauregard and Navy Secretary Stephen Mallory. To Beauregard, he remarked that with the surrender of Lee's army, a continuation of the war would be "criminal." When Mallory pressed Johnston to suggest a specific course of action, Johnston stated: "We must stop fighting at once and secure peace upon the best terms we can obtain." Mallory agreed, and suggested that as commander of the only remaining Confederate army in the East, it was Johnston's duty to share those views with the president. "I will, if you please, state all this to the president," Mallory said, "but I think *you* had better do so at once, and explicitly." Johnston accepted the assignment. "You will not find me reticent," he promised.

Breckinridge arrived late in the afternoon, bringing with him confirmation of Lee's surrender at Appomattox, and at eight o'clock that night Davis reconvened the cabinet in the second-floor bedroom of a private home in Greensboro. The president began by making a few conversational remarks, then turned to Johnston.

"I have requested you and General Beauregard, General Johnston, to join us this evening, that we may have the benefit of your views. . . ." Davis volunteered his own opinion that the situation was "terrible" but "not fatal." "I think we can whip the enemy yet if our people will turn out."

There was a moment of awkward silence in the room as everyone awaited Johnston's response. But Johnston remained quiet. Davis had to prompt him: "We should like to have your views, General Johnston."

Then, in "his terse, concise, demonstrative way," Johnston began to speak. "My views, sir," he began, "are that our people are tired of the war, feel themselves whipped, and will not fight." He delivered this statement with conviction—almost "spitefully," Mallory thought—pausing for emphasis afterward. "Our country is overrun, its military resources greatly diminished, while the enemy's military power and resources were never greater and may be increased to any extent desired. . . . My men are daily deserting in large numbers and are stealing my artillery teams to aid their escapes to their homes. Since Lee's surrender they regard the war as at an end. If I march out of North Carolina her people will all leave my ranks. . . . My small force is melting away like snow before the sun, and I am hopeless of recruiting it." Davis did not look up while Johnston spoke, but sat quietly, "with his eyes fixed on a scrap of paper, which he was folding and refolding abstractly."

Even after Johnston finished, Davis's head stayed bowed. For several minutes there was absolute in silence in the small room as the president worried the piece of paper in his hands. Finally he broke the silence: "What do you say, General Beauregard?"

"I concur in all General Johnston has said."

Still Davis did not look up, as he continued to play with the paper in his hands. He asked the cabinet members their opinions. One by one they spoke for peace; only Benjamin, loyal to the end, suggested that they should continue to fight. "Well, General Johnston," Davis said at last, "what do you propose?" Davis claimed that the North would not treat with him since it did not recognize the Confederacy.

Johnston responded by noting that in past wars, the military commanders in the field had often initiated peace negotiations, and that perhaps Sherman would treat with him. He asked permission to send a note through the lines to Sherman. After a pause, Davis said, "Well, sir, you can adopt this course, though I confess I am not sanguine as to ultimate results."[38]

Immediately, paper and pens were produced, and Davis dictated the text of a letter that was taken down by Mallory and signed by Johnston. It proposed a meeting to arrange an armistice "to permit the civil authorities to enter into the needful arrangements to terminate the existing war." The letter was read aloud, and Davis approved the wording. Johnston signed it. Delivery was entrusted to Hampton's cavalry.[39]

Johnston returned to the army at Hillsboro that same night, where he announced Lee's surrender to the men in the ranks. Aware now that they constituted the only remaining Confederate army in the field east of the Mississippi, they wondered if they, too, would soon be surrendering. Quietly but steadily the number of deserters increased. Two days later Johnston received a reply from Sherman, who agreed to meet to discuss an armistice. Johnston thought the tone of the letter "conciliatory," and he hurried to Greensboro to show it to Davis, but Davis and his entourage had gone on to Charlotte. Johnston did not follow him there, but returned to his army, leaving it to Hampton to arrange a time and place for the meeting with Sherman. The site chosen was a house on the Raleigh Road near Durham Station, halfway between the picket lines of the two armies.[40]

On April 17, Johnston met Sherman face to face for the first time outside a rough-hewn wooden cabin owned by James Bennett and his wife Nancy.

The owners evacuated their home for the occasion, and the staff and escorts of the two generals sat outside in the shade of trees, or lounged against the rail fence. Once they were alone inside the house, Sherman drew a telegram from his pocket and passed it to Johnston. It contained the news that President Lincoln had been assassinated two days before. Johnston read it in silence, then looked up at Sherman. It was, he said, "the greatest possible calamity" that could befall the South, and he hoped that Sherman did not think this was the result of any southern plot. Sherman assured him he was positive the Confederate army had had nothing to do with it, but that he would not say the same of Jefferson Davis. Johnston declined to comment.[41]

For the business at hand, the two men sat together at a small wooden table set against an interior wall. Sherman offered Johnston the same terms that Grant had offered Lee at Appomattox: the men would surrender their arms and go home on parole. But Johnston asked if they could not "arrange the terms of a permanent peace." Sherman was willing to try, though he wondered aloud if Johnston had sufficient authority to arrange such a peace. Unquestionably, he did not. But Johnston's conviction that further hostilities would constitute "murder" led him to step beyond his authority and endeavor to "make one job of it." If Sherman would not accept his authority, Johnston noted that Secretary of War Breckinridge was expected that night, and he could speak for the government. Now Sherman feared that he might be overstepping his own authority, for he was not empowered to treat with representatives of the civil government. Johnston reminded him that Breckinridge was also a major general in the Confederate army, and could be included in their discussions in that capacity. As anxious for peace as Johnston, Sherman agreed.[42]

The two men met again the next day, April 18. This time Breckinridge was also present, and before they set to work, Sherman offered both Confederate generals a drink of bourbon. Breckinridge perked up noticeably at this announcement, and prepared himself by discarding his plug of tobacco and rinsing his mouth before tossing back his drink with evident satisfaction. The three men then wrestled with the issues—political, now, as well as military. Sherman had brought with him a memorandum to use as the basis of an agreement. It called for the dissolution of all southern armies, but also for the restoration and recognition of state governments. Deep in thought, Sherman stood up at one point and went to his saddlebag to retrieve his bottle of bourbon. Almost absent-mindedly he poured himself a drink and replaced the bottle in his bag. Johnston was unperturbed, but Breckinridge was outraged. He fell silent and afterward complained to Johnston that Sherman was no gentleman. "General Sherman is a hog. Yes, sir, a hog. Did you see him take that drink by himself?"[43]

Johnston rode away from the Bennett House on April 18 believing that he had signed the document that ended the war. But it was not to be. A few days later, Sherman sent him a bundle of northern newspapers filled with angry editorials about Lincoln's assassination, and a note in which he expressed concern that such a mood might wreck their agreement. He was right. Grant himself came to North Carolina to tell Sherman that the deal was off. Dutifully, Sherman wired Johnston that hostilities would resume in forty-eight hours, but he also invited him to meet again to discuss a surrender of his army without reference to political issues. Johnston sought instructions from Breckinridge, but they were not what he expected. Breckinridge urged him to "bring off the cavalry" even if he had to surrender the infantry. Armed with this telegram, Johnston met with his generals, who told him that there was no fight left in the men; more than four thousand had deserted in the past few days. Johnston wired Breckinridge: "We have to save the people, spare the blood of the army, and save the high civil functionaries. Your plan, I think, can only do the last. . . ." In short, Johnston was not willing to ask his soldiers to shed any more of their blood merely to keep Jeff Davis in office for a few more days. Later that same day he notified Breckinridge that he had written to Sherman proposing "military negotiations in regard to this army." On April 26, Johnston met with Sherman in the Bennett House for the third and last time. They confined themselves to military topics and Johnston formally surrendered his army. For the rest of his life, Davis would consider Johnston's decision to surrender his army when he was neither surrounded nor defeated an act of treachery.[44]

Through the last days of April, Johnston continued to issue orders and directives coordinating the various activities consequent upon the military convention. Then, on May 2, 1865, he said goodbye to the army for the last time in a general order:

COMRADES: In terminating our official relations I most earnestly exhort you to observe faithfully the terms of pacification agreed upon, and to discharge the obligations of good and peaceful citizens at your homes as well as you have performed the duties of thorough soldiers in the field. By such a course you will best secure the comfort of your families and kindred and restore tranquillity to your country. You will return to your homes with the admiration of our people, won by the courage and noble devotion you have displayed in this long war. I shall always remember with pride the loyal support and generous confidence you have given me. I now part with you with deep regret, and bid you farewell with feelings of cordial friendship and with earnest wishes that you may have hereafter all the prosperity and happiness to be found in the world.[45]

CHAPTER TWENTY-THREE

The Battle
of the Books

. . . bald, quiet Joe Johnston,
The little precise Scotch-dominie of a general,
Stubborn as flint, in advance not always so lucky,
In retreat more dangerous than a running wolf—

He could make men cheer him after six-weeks retreating.

He had to write his reminiscences, too,
And tell what he would have done if it had not been
For Davis and chance and a dozen turns of the wheel,
That was the thistle in him—the other strain—
But he was older then.

—STEPHEN VINCENT BENÉT,
John Brown's Body

Not all of Johnston's wars were over. For the rest of his life, he would fight a furious rear guard action in defense of his reputation. He became obsessed with setting the record straight, and he could think of no other way to do it than to discredit Jefferson Davis, his most prominent detractor and tormentor. Johnston's inability to resist this obsession was a personal tragedy, for his legalistic excuses amid the ruins of the Confederacy seemed petty, and his public assault on a man whom most of the South considered a martyr resulted only in tarnishing his own reputation. It brought him no satisfaction and embittered his remaining years. Shortly after his death in 1891, one of his lifelong friends wrote sadly to another, "If Genl. Johnston had never written any thing . . . how much better it would have been!"[1]

Johnston was only one of many former Confederates who took up the pen to justify their war record. Some historians have suggested that this derived from a collective need to revive a damaged self-image and to assuage personal honor. Johnston had an additional motive, for he believed that he had been wronged, and that if he failed to reply it would constitute a tacit admission of his own shortcomings. Johnston had never had his day in court to refute the charges levied against him by Pemberton in his report on the Vicksburg campaign; the end of the war had denied him the opportunity to confront Hood with a court-martial for the accusations in his report; and his treatment by Davis still rankled. His friends told him to let it go. But he couldn't.

For the first few years after the war, Johnston was preoccupied by the necessity to make a living, but the determination to exonerate himself was never far from his mind. He constructed elaborate justifications for his actions as army commander, and the very act of writing them down calcified them into dogma. Increasingly, Johnston came to view his dispute with Davis and his allies as a conflict between good and evil. In his mind, Davis's vindictiveness, Bragg's duplicity, and Hood's ambition made them villains, as if they were all characters in a morality play. Johnston of course was the noble victim, but he was not willing to accept the role of martyr, and in the postwar years he fought to reclaim his good name. Ironically, his assaults on Davis served mainly to reveal him as a disloyal subordinate; rather than salvaging his reputation, his war of words lost him many friends without routing his enemies. Arguably, this unworthy "Battle of the Books" was Johnston's greatest defeat.

During the first months of peace, the Johnstons remained in central North Carolina near Greensboro, where he had disbanded his army. He was impressed by the professionalism and restraint of the Federal occupation troops under the command of Major General Jacob Cox. "These men conducted themselves precisely as if they had been in the towns of Ohio Pennsylvania or Massachusetts," he wrote to a friend. Indeed, throughout the period of Reconstruction, Johnston objected less to military occupation than to what he considered the excesses of civilian Radicals, whose thirst for public office and public monies he found both disagreeable and tawdry. Military occupation, after all, was a fair and just result of defeat, and the four years of war had engendered mutual respect between the soldiers of both sides. Nor did he mourn the passing of slavery, for Johnston believed that even if the South had won, it could not have sustained the institution for long. Later, in 1884, he wrote that "At all events the South is in far better condition now than when slavery existed."[2]

Due to "the necessity of working for a living," Johnston's determination to write a public defense of his tenure of command had to wait. He had made his way for more than thirty-five years as a soldier, a profession that was now closed to him. At the age of fifty-eight, lacking property or other assets, branded a traitor by the government he had served for thirty years as a soldier, he had to find a job. What could he do? Lydia wrote to her husband's former chief of staff Ben Ewell, now restored to the presidency of William & Mary College, to ask if he knew of any prospects in Richmond. "Engineering he rather prides himself on, but would take anything that would keep the kettle boiling." For a few weeks Johnston hoped that he might be elected president of the Mobile & Ohio Railroad. As a West Point-trained engineer, who had also pioneered railroad construction in Texas in the 1850s, he had some claim to expertise. But he lost to the incumbent Milton Brown. "I have had another defeat," he wrote to Dick Ewell, Ben's brother. His search for work was made more urgent by Lydia's deteriorating health. Sadly, he told a friend that "Every change of weather from good to bad, makes a corresponding change in her condition."[3]

Johnston accepted employment briefly with the National Express & Transportation Company, but the firm had trouble securing financial backing in the post-Civil War South, so he took another position as president of the Alabama & Tennessee River Rail Road Company, a small local enterprise that ran a line from Selma, Alabama, to Blue Mountain, Georgia. He held this post from May 1866 to November 1867, during which time the road was reorganized into the Selma, Rome, & Dalton Railroad. It was not a job he enjoyed. "My business relations are uninteresting," he wrote a friend in May, "in fact a bore." Lydia was also unhappy. Neither was particularly disappointed when this company too failed for lack of sufficient capital. Johnston was again "thrown out of employment," as he put it.[4]

Finally he found "permanent" employment in the insurance business. He had retained the affection and loyalty of many of those who had served with him; recognizing the power of his name, a London-based insurance company invited him to become manager of its Southern Department, a combination figurehead and spokesman. In the fall of 1868, Johnston sailed for Europe and a visit to the home office. He returned to establish Joseph E. Johnston & Company, agent for the Liverpool and London and Globe Insurance Company, with business headquarters in Savannah. Johnston invited several other former Confederate officers to join the firm, whose names and reputations lent prestige to the enterprise. Within four years he presided over more than 120 agents in Georgia, Alabama, and Mississippi. He and Lydia often spent the Christmas holidays in Baltimore. Most of their summers were passed at Warm Springs, Virginia, for the sake of Lydia's health.[5]

The new financial security allowed Johnston to return to work on his memoirs. He wrote to his former corps and division commanders (except Hood) asking them to send him any papers they might have, or, failing that, their recollections. In a typical request, he told Thomas C. Hindman: "I should be glad to publish any thing to the honour of our gallant army, & to that of their adversaries too." In some cases he wrote out his own recollections of particular events, requesting that his correspondents confirm or correct them. To his closest friends, he frequently suggested what they should write. To Mackall he wrote, "Do you remember that Hood urged the abandoning of every position we held long before anybody else thought of it? If so, please state the fact with some fullness." When the response was not all he had hoped, he gave Mackall a little nudge: "I enclose a copy of your letter in relation to the Ga. campaign, and beg you to reconsider certain parts of it." He even quibbled over word choice: "Don't you think the word 'compelled' unnecessarily unfavorable?"[6]

Johnston was particularly anxious to gather evidence of Davis's responsibility for Confederate defeat. But Davis was an unfortunate target. After his capture by Federal authorities in May 1865, the former Confederate president had been taken to Fortress Monroe and kept there as a prisoner for most of two years, some of it shackled in leg irons. He proved to be a better martyr than he had a president. During his incarceration, all but his bitterest critics came to forgive and forget; even his jailers developed a grudging respect for his courage. By 1868, Reconstruction had turned punitive, and most southerners now believed it was essential to band together lest the South's spirit be broken. Davis's imprisonment, which he bore stoically and manfully, represented the South's suffering—in effect, he did pennance for his people.

With this in mind, Wade Hampton wrote to Johnston in 1870, primarily to ask for a letter of recommendation to the Viceroy of Egypt, who Hampton thought might employ him as an officer, but also to suggest that Johnston's determination to pursue his feud with Davis would threaten the unity of purpose necessary to survive. "I feel sure no good could come in any way by any publication by you raising an issue on the point. Any controversy between Mr. Davis & yourself would jar upon the feelings of thousands who are friendly to both of you & would tend to throw discredit on our cause." The publication of official reports from the field, and the memories of his own soldiers, would provide "ample justification of your conduct," but Hampton warned: "Do not allow yourself to be drawn into any personal altercation. . . ." It was good advice, yet Johnston ignored it, believing that if he let Davis's interpretation stand unchallenged, it would constitute tacit admission of all the criticism Davis had heaped on him during the war, and would be tantamount to refusing a challenge.[7]

Some of the first books to be published after the war took Johnston's side. Henry S. Foote and Edward A. Pollard, both of whom had loudly criticized Davis during the war, rushed into print immediately afterward with "histories" that were thinly disguised editorials. Both men found it useful to criticize Davis by praising Johnston. Foote attacked Davis's "unjust and illiberal treatment of the some of the most meritorious Confederate military commanders," and Pollard called Johnston "the greatest military man in the Confederacy." Johnston, Pollard argued, "saw more clearly than any single person each approaching shadow of the war, and prophesied, with calm courage, against the madness of the Administration at Richmond. . . ." In 1868, Frank Alfriend published the first biography of the Confederate president. Alfriend's book did not criticize Johnston—indeed, it barely mentioned him—but it praised Davis so extravagantly that Johnston found it irritating. Davis was himself contemplating a history of the Confederacy. He sat down to begin work on such a project as early as 1867, the year of his release from prison, but his examination of the papers so depressed him that he decided to put it off.[8]

Johnston's developing theme in his own memoirs was that the strength of the South had lain in its soldiers, and its great weakness in its political leadership. As he wrote to a friend years later, "It was from no want of courage, constancy, and zeal that the Southern people were overcome, but from their want of discretion in selecting a leader." So he focused less on the events of the war than on the specific criticisms aimed at him by Pemberton, Hood, and Davis. He expected that by publishing the original letters containing those criticisms, and responding carefully point by point, he could demonstrate both the wisdom of his own actions and the vindictive nature of his opponents. His task was complicated because the Official Records had not yet been compiled or published, and he had to gather copies of the original orders. After his nephew, John W. Johnston, was elected to the U.S. Senate from Virginia in 1870, Johnston asked him to use his influence to allow him access to the Confederate archives in Washington.[9]

Without apology or introduction, Johnston began his narrative *in medias res* with a brief account of the secession of Virginia and his own resignation from the Army of the United States. Pointedly, he noted that "No other officer of the United States Army of equal rank, that of brigadier-general, relinquished his position in it to join the Southern Confederacy."[10] Then, in a prose style that manages to be at once matter-of-fact and stuffy, he plods forward chronologically through discussions of his command at Harpers Ferry, Manassas, Seven Pines, and Mississippi, into the mountains of Georgia, and on to the surrender at Durham Station. Unlike the man—who provoked such loyalty in some and such bitterness in others—the book is lifeless. Johnston was not a gifted writer, and his heavy reliance on the official correspondence, a great deal of which he quoted in full, bogged down his account. The impersonal tone and legalistic arguments make it tedious. It is, in short, a poor read.

Johnston's purpose was evident early on. His first salvo concerned Davis's role—or rather, his lack of role—at the Battle of Manassas. Alfriend's 1868 biography had placed the Confederate president on the Bull Run battlefield, and credited the victory in part to the power of his presence. In a benign passage, Alfriend noted that Davis arrived on the battlefield "while the struggle was still in progress," and that "His presence upon the field was the inspiration of unbounded enthusiasm among the troops, to whom his name and bearing were the symbols of victory." It did not help that Alfriend had described the Confederate force as "Beauregard's army," or that Johnston's name was mentioned only in passing as having provided reinforcements. Irritated, Johnston went out of his way to emphasize that Davis did not arrive at Manassas until after the battle was over, and that he had had nothing whatsoever to do with the Confederate victory. In the same vein, Johnston defended himself from the accusation that he had failed to follow up the victory. Davis, he wrote, gave no orders "to make any aggressive movement," nor did he do anything else to encourage a pursuit.[11]

Johnston devoted most of one chapter to addressing the great injustice, as he saw it, of Davis's decision in the summer of 1861 to rank Cooper, Lee, and Albert Sidney Johnston ahead of him. Unforgiving more than ten years later,

Johnston insisted that "This action was altogether illegal, and contrary to all the laws to regulate the rank of the class of officers concerned." He then laboriously outlined the legislation that he believed sustained him, and concluded that from that moment forward, Davis was prejudiced against him. His continued insistence on this point would strike many as petty—a "tempest in a teapot," one reader called it—but Johnston's resentment burned as hot as ever.[12]

Johnston devoted considerable attention to the Battle of Seven Pines, claiming that "No action of the war has been so little understood as that of Seven Pines." Indeed, it was a confusing battle—confusing at the time to Johnston, and confusing since to those who have tried to understand it. But if he were confused on the morning of May 31, 1862, Johnston now found a clarity of vision that made it possible for him to be dogmatic. Seven Pines, he insisted, was a Confederate victory. Southern forces had inflicted disproportionate losses on the enemy, and Confederate forces were in position to complete their victory the next day. "The chances of success on that day were all in favor of the Confederates," he insisted. The obvious implication is that after Johnston was carried wounded from the field, his successors failed to follow up on the opportunity he had created. A few contemporaries agreed with him, notably D. H. Hill, whose men bore the brunt of the fight, but most felt that the southern army's impetus had run out by the time Johnston fell wounded near Fair Oaks. Gustavus Smith, who succeeded to command of the army after Johnston was wounded, read Johnston's account as a personal attack.[13]

Never had Johnston fashioned a more elaborate castle in the air than the one he used to explain the Vicksburg campaign. As in 1863, he insisted that the junction of the forces of Pemberton and Holmes would have created an army capable of defeating, even destroying, Grant's army. Grant, he noted, had about 45,000 men, Pemberton some 35,000, and Holmes, he insisted, no less than 55,000 men near Little Rock, who were idle and "opposed to no enemy." Even the most optimistic estimates of Holmes's strength credited him with little more than ten thousand. But Johnston maintained for the rest of his life that "Genl. Holmes of the Confederate army had 55,000 effective soldiers about Little Rock." In his postwar vision, Johnston insisted that by uniting these Confederate armies, "we should bring above seventy thousand men against forty-five thousand, and secure all the chances of victory, and even the destruction of the Federal army." That this never happened was the fault of but one person: the man who insisted that Holmes and Pemberton could not cooperate. More accurately, Johnston also made a point of the fact that it was Davis who had detached Stevenson's corps from Bragg's army, sending it to Mississippi on the eve of the Battle of Murfreesboro and thereby wasting yet another opportunity.[14]

Davis's culpability is evident, again, in Johnston's account of the campaign in North Georgia. Johnston noted that he had retreated no further in Georgia than Lee had in Virginia, that he had done so more slowly, and that he had suffered far fewer casualties in the process, thus preserving the army. He emphasized that Richmond repeatedly refused to send cavalry to cut Sherman's supply lines: "It can scarcely be doubted that five thousand cavalry directed by Forrest's sagacity, courage, and enterprise, against the Federal railroad communications . . . would have compelled General Sherman to the desperate resource of a decisive battle on our terms. . . ." He also insisted that he fully intended to defend Atlanta, and he denied the claim in Hood's report that the army had become demoralized under his leadership. "The allegation is disproved," he asserted, "by the record of the admirable conduct of those troops on every occasion on which that general [Hood] sent them to battle—and inevitable disaster."[15]

By 1873, the project was nearing completion. Then, just before he finished, Johnston learned of the so-called Unsent Message that Davis had drafted in February 1865 to explain to the Confederate Congress why he could not again appoint Johnston to command. Determined to answer the charges it contained, Johnston tracked down a copy of the memorandum and composed a final chapter devoted to a line-by-line rebuttal.[16]

Johnston's lengthy volume, blandly entitled *Narrative of Military Operations Directed During the Late War Between the States,* appeared in 1874. It was less "Narrative" than a brief against Jefferson Davis. It sold poorly, and the publisher failed to turn a profit. Part of the reason, Johnston told himself, was that the people who were most likely to buy it were those who were the most destitute—the southern veterans who had fought for him. Another reason, surely, was that southerners were not interested in acting as jurors in an argument between Davis and Johnston. Johnston's legal brief, tedious in its argument and unsatisfying in its tone, did not fit the public moment. By 1874, many of the southern states had been "redeemed," returned to home rule; what southerners wanted to remember about the war was their devotion and sacrifice, not their mistakes, whoever made them. They wanted to believe that their soldiers had been heroic, their generals cunning and bold, their government supportive and determined. The principal theme of southern literature on the war was that the South had been overwhelmed by superior numbers. Most were perfectly willing to believe that all of their leaders had been heroes. The book's poor reception was a disappointment to Johnston. Years later, when a prospective biographer wrote to ask him to bless his project, the old general warned him that the public was not interested and prophesied that "the publication would be a dead loss."[17]

Johnston's book not only failed financially, it failed in its purpose. He had hoped to present a clear and incontrovertible case for his conduct as a general during the war. Instead, his argumentative tone betrayed his continuing resentment and bitterness. Davis wrote his wife that "Johnston has more effectively than another could shown his selfishness and his malignity." Sadly, the book irritated not only his obvious targets—Davis, Bragg, and Hood—but also some of his own friends, including Beauregard and G. W. Smith, who felt that Johnston had slighted their roles in the war. Beauregard believed his role at Manassas was insufficiently praised, and G. W. Smith saw at once that Johnston's version of Seven Pines made him the scapegoat.[18]

But it was Hood who took up the gauntlet. Jilted after the war by Buck Preston, Hood had married the former Anna Maria Hennon and moved to New Orleans, where his wife presented him with a series of healthy children, including three sets of twins. Hood was so angered by Johnston's volume that he set to work almost at once to reply. His goal was not so much to justify his own conduct as to assail Johnston, for in his writing, as in life, Hood's best defense was a good offense. Hood quoted passages from Johnston's *Narrative*, then criticized each one, offering his own arguments and commentary. Almost as an afterthought, he added three introductory chapters about his military life before 1864 in order to present the volume as an autobiography.

In his official report, written during the war, Hood had insisted that Johnston had already ruined the Army of Tennessee before Hood ever rose to command it. Now he elaborated on that theme, arguing that Johnston's campaign had been nothing but a long series of errors of omission and commission. He asserted that the army at Dalton was larger than Johnston had claimed, that Johnston's losses during the campaign to the Chattahoochee were more than double what he had reported, that he had needlessly surrendered impregnable positions and ignored priceless opportunities to offer battle. Despite all Johnston's talk about an offensive, Hood asked rhetorically, what did he do when Sherman appeared at Dalton? He retreated. "What followed at Resaca? Retreat. New Hope Church? Retreat. Cassville? Retreat. Kennesaw Mountain? Retreat." Hood concluded: "Had General Johnston possessed the requisite spirit and boldness to seize the various chances for victory, which were offered to him, he never would have allowed General Sherman to push him back one hundred miles in sixty-six days, from one mountain stronghold to another, down into the very heart of the Confederacy."[19]

It was certainly easier for Hood to attack Johnston than to defend his own strategy. By this time, even most of Johnston's critics had come to accept that Hood's campaign into Tennessee had been a disaster of the first order. The virtual destruction of his army in the bitter winter of 1864–65 was eloquent testimony to that. Sherman, in his *Memoirs*, published one year after Johnston's in 1875, wrote that Hood's campaign into Tennessee "played into our hands perfectly." Partly because of that, commentators had begun to praise Johnston's maneuvers in North Georgia and to compare them with those of the Roman general Fabius Maximus, who avoided battle with Hannibal's Carthaginian army until the invaders were worn out. Johnston objected to being compared to Fabius, "who was a dictator." In his mind, it was Sherman who had avoided battle by refusing to assault his lines the way Grant had assailed Lee at Spotsylvania, Cold Harbor, and Petersburg. Hood saw no ground for comparison either. Fabius, he pointed out, stayed in his mountain fastness and refused to come down. Johnston had retreated from Rocky Face Ridge to the Valley of the Etowah, and therefore did not deserve the comparison. (This was a curious argument, for the implication is that Johnston should have stayed at Dalton and allowed Sherman the free run of Georgia.)[20]

Hood finished his book, entitled *Advance and Retreat*, in 1879. But that same year he and his wife both died suddenly of yellow fever. It was Beauregard who saw the book through publication. Although Beauregard had been angered by Johnston's *Narrative*, his principal motive was his hope that the book's royalties would provide some income for Hood's ten orphaned children. Under such circumstances, Johnston forebore from attacking the author publicly. Just as the end of the war had denied him a chance to refute the calumnies of Hood's official report, so now Hood's tragic death denied him the opportunity to respond to his memoirs.[21]

Besides, his real enemy was already at work writing a memoir of his own. Jefferson Davis had begun a history of the Confederacy in earnest in 1877; it was published in 1881 as *The Rise and Fall of the Confederate Government*. One can imagine the eagerness with which Johnston devoured the book, scanning the pages for evidence of yet another slight. He looked mostly in vain. Davis refused to join in the mud slinging; far more restrained than either Johnston or Hood, he offered a dry and tortuous dissertation on the legitimacy of secession and the rightness of the southern Cause. When he did refer to military operations, and specifically to Johnston, he was reserved and presidential. The most critical thing Davis had to say about Johnston was that during the Georgia campaign, "retreat followed retreat, during seventy-four days of anxious hope and bitter disappointment, until at last the Army of Tennessee fell back within the fortifications of Atlanta." But he did not criticize Johnston directly. "Whether we might have obtained more advantageous results by a vigorous and determined effort to attack," he wrote, "are questions upon which it would be for me now neither useful nor pleasant to enter." Davis had defeated Johnston once again, for his restraint belied the general's claim that Davis had been motivated throughout the war by personal animus. A comparison of the two memoirs, without recourse to other sources, would suggest that all of the animus was on Johnston's part.[22]

Johnston did not think Davis's work at all reserved. After reading it, he wrote a friend that "Money at compound interest doesn't increase half as fast as J.D.'s venom has been accumulating against me." Shortly after the publication of Davis's book, Johnston met a Mr. Frank A. Burr on a train from Savannah to Richmond, and they fell into conversation. Burr was a reporter for the Philadelphia *Press*, and he took the opportunity of their chance meeting to question Johnston about the last days of the war. Upon their arrival in Richmond, they rode together to the Exchange Hotel, and after dinner they continued to talk in the general's room. At some point, Burr asked Johnston what had happened to the Confederate gold reserves. Johnston replied that only $179,000 of the more than $2 million in gold was ever accounted for to him. When Burr asked him what had happened to the rest, Johnston replied archly, "That I am unable to say. Mr. Davis has never given any satisfactory account of it. . . ." Burr's story appeared on December 18, 1881, with the headline: "Confederate Gold Missing—General Johnston Calls Jefferson Davis to Account for Over $2,000,000 in Specie."[23]

The story caused an immediate sensation. Davis, of course, was outraged, and so too were most southerners. Johnston's friends at first denied that he had ever said such a thing; Johnston himself claimed that he was "beguiled" into making the statement. But he would not explicitly disavow his comment, and public opinion turned sharply against him. Contrasted to the moderate tone of Davis's memoir, Johnston's mean-spirited innuendo struck the public ear with particular harshness. Davis's friends recognized at once that Johnston's implied accusation had backfired. Benjamin Hill, the former Confederate senator from Georgia who had worked so hard to convince Davis to dismiss Johnston in 1864, now wrote Davis that he felt sorry for Johnston. "He has always had a respectable party of admirers in the South. He will have none now."[24]

Johnston's indiscretion rekindled Davis's anger. If he remained moderate in public, in private he burned with resentment. When William Nelson Pendleton invited him to speak at the dedication of a statute of Robert E. Lee on the campus of Washington and Lee College, Davis declined because he knew that Johnston was president of the Lee Memorial Association and would be present. He wrote to Custis Lee to express his regret that he could not attend, but justified his decision by noting the "gross misrepresentation" of Johnston's book, and "his vile slander in regard to Confederate treasure." He concluded: "I could not with due self-respect appear before a meeting over which he was to preside." Ironically, Johnston did not attend either, pleading ill health.[25]

Instead of learning a lesson from his indiscretion, Johnston decided that there was enough error in Davis's published memoir to require a public response. He accepted a proposal from Robert U. Johnson and C. C. Buel to write an article for *Century* magazine as a part of their "Battles and Leaders" series. Ostensibly the topic was the Battle of Manassas, but Johnston's purpose from the outset was to respond to Davis. He warned the editors that "I am very much afraid that my article will not be what you expect. It is so personal to myself. I am attempting to show that his [Davis's] notices of me—all disparaging—are prompted by dislike." Johnston began by dredging up his old complaint about Davis's ranking of generals in 1861. He insisted that he "incurred Mr. Davis's displeasure" by protesting against this action, and that from that point on, Davis was motivated in all his decisions by personal animus, until finally in 1864, "he degraded me to the utmost of his power." He would prove this, Johnston wrote, by quoting passages from *The Rise and Fall of the Confederate Government* and then demonstrating, point by point, the evidences of Davis's bitterness. Thus he adopted the format that Hood had used in his memoir. Many of Johnston's paragraphs begun with "Mr. Davis says," followed by a quoted passage, which is itself followed by a rebuttal.[26]

A number of Johnston's "corrections" are petty, and the cumulative effect is to make the author himself appear petty. In response to Davis's comment that he met with Johnston on a hilltop during the Battle of Manassas from which he espied in the distance a column of enemy soldiers, Johnston devoted a paragraph to proving that it was, in fact, a friendly column of Confederate troops—the point being that Davis was never really involved, even as a witness, in the battle. While he was at it, Johnston also took a shot at Beauregard: "An opinion seems to prevail with some persons that important plans of General Beauregard were executed by him. It is a mistake. . . . As fought, the battle was made by me. . . . I decided that the battle was to be there, and directed the measures necessary to maintain it."[27]

In the same article Johnston defended his conduct of the peninsular campaign in 1862, and in particular the Battle of Seven Pines. Once again, his focus was less on a clear explication of events than in pointing out the many passages from *The Rise and Fall of the Confederate Government* in which "Mr. Davis is mistaken." Johnston insisted yet again that Seven Pines was a Confederate victory. One way to demonstrate this was to cite McClellan's initial panicky overestimate of Federal casualties, and compare it to Longstreet's field report, which equally underestimated Confederate casualties. Thus Johnston wrote in his article that at Seven Pines the Confederates lost three thousand men to the Federals' seven thousand. In the weeks and months after the battle, however, both sides had modified those initial estimates. Confederate losses were subsequently established at an aggregate of 6,134, and Federal losses at 5,031. But Johnston would not accept these numbers. When the editors suggested that his casualty estimates were inaccurate, Johnston argued with them, and insisted that the numbers he cited remain in the article. "As editor, you can contradict it if you choose, in a footnote." This they did, though when the article was subsequently reprinted in the hardbound *Battles and Leaders*, the newer and more accurate numbers were included. Even then, Johnston tried to compensate by noting that the Confederates also captured "10 pieces of artillery, 6700 muskets and rifles in excellent condition, a garrison flag, and 4 regimental colors, medical, commissary, quartermaster and ordnance stores, tents and sutler's property."[28]

Johnston wrote out his article in pencil; he was distressed when the page proofs came back covered with proofreader's corrections, claiming, "Your magazine hieroglyphics are above my intelligence." And he was unhappy with the suggested changes, begging the editors "to protect me from this corrector." When they explained that the changes were necessary for the sake of grammar, Johnston was chastened and offered to return his fee.[29]

Johnston's article was only one of many solicited by the editors of *Century* magazine, who recognized that accounts of the war by the men who had fought it would appeal to their readers. Johnston's piece appeared in the May 1885 issue, along with one by George B. McClellan, as well as installments of new novels by William Dean Howells (*The Rise of Silas Lapham*) and Henry James (*The Bostonians*). Johnston's article read like a litany, and certainly his prose suffered in comparison to that of Howells or James. Still, the editors professed themselves pleased, and they asked him to write several more focusing on other aspects of the war, specifically Vicksburg and the campaign in North Georgia.

Johnston readily agreed, though at the same time he registered a strong protest against the map of the Battle of Seven Pines which the editors had included as part of his article. The map showed the Federal forces in a continuous line of defense from Seven Pines in the south to the middle of the Nine Mile Road. Johnston insisted they should be depicted as two separate groups, thus illustrating the likelihood of their defeat in detail if the battle had been resumed. It was important for him to be able to assert that his army had been within striking distance of a complete victory when he was carried from the field. In his article, Johnston had written that when the battle ended, "The Southern troops were united, and in a position to overwhelm either faction of the Northern army, while holding the other in check." Knowing that the editors planned to reprint the article in a hardbound series, Johnston wanted the map changed before it was reprinted. The editors offered to add explanatory labels showing that the map represented unit positions at the end of the battle rather than at the outset. But Johnston insisted that the map "wrongs me" because it showed the corps of Sumner and Heintzelman to be in close contact when he insisted that they were not. "I say that the positions of the troops at 5 or 6 o.c[lock] June 1st justify the claim at the conclusion of my article. . . ." The editors' map was "exceedingly inaccurate." He sent them one of his own, "the authority of which no American can question."[30]

Characteristically, no compromise was acceptable to Johnston. Eventually, the argument grew heated. Two months after his article appeared, Johnston met with Robert U. Johnson, in the ornate Victorian lobby of the Fifth Avenue Hotel in New York City, and he again pressed his case. Now seventy-eight years old, he could still lose his temper, and he did so on this occasion. The white-haired old general, flushed with anger, was seen to shout at a New York City editor half his age. As always after one of his tirades, Johnston was contrite the next day and wrote to apologize, saying, "I very unreasonably worked myself into a state of excitement . . . the recollection of my share of that conversation is disagreeable to me."[31]

Finally the editors grew tired of his petty quarreling, and charged him with intransigence, sharp language, and an "assumption of professional authority." Perhaps in the process they began to sympathize with Davis, who had also grown weary of Johnston's wrangling. They noted that all other sources, Union and Confederate, agreed with the map they had prepared; only Johnston objected. Johnston's response was that since they could not agree, perhaps the map should be dropped altogether. Reluctantly, they agreed. Johnston's article on Seven Pines was reprinted in *Battles and Leaders* without an accompanying map. But the editors had the last word. The map to which Johnston objected so vehemently appeared instead accompanying G. W. Smith's article on Seven Pines. Moreover, Smith pointed out that "General Johnston is greatly in error in reference to the positions of the contending forces on the morning of June 1st."[32]

Johnston's subsequent articles for *Century*, which also appeared in *Battles and Leaders of the Civil War*, all flowed in the same vein—defensive, confrontational, argumentative. In his piece on Vicksburg, Johnston once again insisted that Davis had allowed Theophilus Holmes and 55,000 men to remain idle at Little Rock while Mississippi was lost; he also claimed that Davis's transfer of forces from Bragg to Pemberton had "caused" the Battle of Murfreesboro. His piece on the campaign in Georgia was his best, with fewer picky references to Davis's memoir, though it added little to what he had already stated in his own *Narrative*. Johnston closed his series of articles by defending his conduct of the 1864 campaign: "Mr. Davis condemned me for not fighting. General Sherman's testimony and that of the Military Cemetery at Marietta refute the charge."[33]

It is an irony that although Johnston's comrades in arms—Beauregard, G. W. Smith, Hood, Bragg, and of course Davis—all felt aggrieved by his public writings, his former adversaries, especially Sherman and Grant, strongly sustained him. Johnston was hugely gratified by their praise. "In war," he wrote in his *Narrative*, "the testimony of an enemy is one's favor is certainly worth more than that of a friend, as he who receives a blow can better estimate the dexterity of the striker than any spectator." And for Johnston, as for so many southerners, the respect of the adversary who had bested him was essential to his honor. No doubt Johnston was pleased to read in Sherman's *Memoirs*, published only a year after his own, that his old foe not only accorded him respect as a dangerous and wily opponent, but criticized both Hood and Davis. Grant's *Memoirs*, published ten years later, in 1885, were even kinder. Here Johnston's decision not to try to break the siege of Vicksburg was sustained: "Johnston evidently took in the situation, and wisely, I think, abstained from making an assault on us because it would simply have inflicted losses on both sides without accomplishing any result." As for the campaign in Georgia, Grant noted: "For my own part, I think that Johnston's tactics were right. Anything that could have prolonged the war a year beyond the time that it finally did close, would probably have exhausted the North to such an extent that they might then have abandoned the contest and agreed to a settlement." Johnston could not have failed to appreciate the irony that twenty years after the war his staunchest allies were Grant and Sherman, whose words he waved like a banner in front of his new enemies—former comrades in arms.[34]

Johnston's series of articles moved his private feud with Davis into the public arena, permitting a tawdry public airing of a personal disagreement. The continued sniping at Davis was particularly damaging to his public reputation, for Davis's refusal to fight back cast Johnston as the bully. The personal tragedy of Johnston's participation in this Battle of the Books is that it did not enhance his reputation as a strategist or army commander, and did a great deal to make him appear petty and uncooperative—exactly the traits that Davis had found so intolerable. Johnston's behavior contrasted markedly with that of his old classmate, Robert E. Lee, who adopted a dignified silence about all questions concerning the war. Lee wrote no memoir, and even refused interviews on the subject. Because Lee accepted full public responsibility for all his actions, the public concluded that he was not responsible at all, and his quiet stoicism elevated him to southern sainthood after his death in 1870. By contrast, Johnston's continued insistence that he was not at fault led many to assume he was probably guilty.

CHAPTER TWENTY-FOUR

"Funeral and Resurrection"

O bsessed by his vendetta against Davis, Johnston nonetheless did not spend all his time exploring the past. He had a business to run, a wife to support, an extended family that began increasingly to rely on him, and a famous name that drew him, inevitably, into politics. Joe Johnston lived for more than a quarter of a century after the end of the Civil War, and he did not live in retirement. In addition to being a successful businessman, he was a congressman from Virginia, an advocate of national Democratic candidates, and finally, in his seventies, Commissioner of U.S. Railroads. One by one, his friends, his brothers, and his enemies passed away. In 1887, he lost his wife Lydia, who, at the age of sixty-five succumbed finally to the ill health borne most of her life. Joe Johnston spent much of the last years of his life attending funerals. But he never lost his passion for life or his compulsion to work—even in his eighties he worked eight hours a day every day that he was able to do so, for work, after all, was the business of life.

Throughout this period, Johnston was perforce concerned about matters of health. His own health was remarkably good, but Lydia suffered almost constantly from what doctors diagnosed as "neuralgia," which in the nineteenth century covered a wide variety of symptoms, including headaches, tiredness, and general malaise. Her doctors prescribed lengthy visits to spas for rest and mineral water. Every spring Lydia travelled to Warm Springs, Virginia, or White Sulphur Springs, West Virginia, to take the waters. Joe went with her as often as he could, though his business obligations frequently prevented it. She returned home again in September or October, exhausted from the trip and usually no better. To a much lesser extent, Johnston, too, felt the reminders of advancing age. He suffered from "acute rheumatism," especially in the winter months, and experienced occasional bouts of vertigo.[1]

Duty had always been his pole star, and he simply could not conceive of an idle life. Though not the oldest of the surviving Johnston brothers, he was the most prominent, and he accepted the obligations of *paterfamilias*. Peter, his oldest brother, suffered from both poor health and poverty, and his pride would not allow him to accept charity. Joe therefore entered into a conspiracy with his nephew John W. Johnston, the son and namesake of the oldest Johnston sibling who had died in 1837. Now a U.S. senator from Virginia, John wrote to his Uncle Joe that he had visited Peter and found him sick and alone in the house at Abingdon. Joe immediately offered to pay the cost of hiring a retainer; but he knew it had to be done carefully. "Can an arrangement be made by which his board and other expenses are paid by me without troubling him on the subject?" he asked his nephew. John found a "trusty man" to stay with Peter, and Joe paid his salary. They also arranged to have Peter employed by a local attorney, secretly compensating the "employer" for the amount of Peter's salary.[2]

In the fall of 1873, Beverly Johnston died. In spite of his occasionally irritating antics, he was Joe's favorite brother, and his death saddened Johnston greatly. "I have been feeling more and more daily how great is the loss of that true and loving brother," he wrote to his nephew. "I shall not remain on earth long enough to recover from this great sorrow." In settling Beverly's affairs, the family decided that it was probably reasonable now to sell the estate at Panecillo. The furniture was sold, the books placed in storage, and the clothes given to the poor; Joe and Lydia purchased the silver. Joe rented a room for Peter in a hotel that promised to provide meals. Other family matters involved him less urgently: he acknowledged the birth of distant cousins, the holiday greetings of others, and offered advice when it was asked. He warned one nephew against an army career on the grounds that the Army was no longer what it once was, and when John W. Johnston reported that he planned to name a son for him, Joe wrote to ask that he perform an "act of kindness," specifically not to allow his son to be called "Joe." The name "is not only unbecoming to a gentleman, but unfavorable to such a character. I have been struggling with the impediment for many years. . . ."[3]

National politics began to engross him seriously in the 1870s. Throughout most of the Reconstruction era he had been only mildly interested. In 1868, he was enthusiastic about the candidacy of Frank Blair for the Democratic nomination, but had no time to devote to it because of the need to find employment. In 1872, he reported to his nephew that "Greeley has my best wishes—being now the Democratic candidate." But again he did not partici- pate, and again he was disappointed by the results when Grant handily defeated Horace Greeley at the polls.[4]

Johnston finally turned to national politics in the presidential election year of 1876. In the spring of that year, he became concerned about the pending Hawaiian Reciprocity Treaty, which provided for the custom-free exchange of agricultural goods between the United States and the Kingdom of Hawaii. Johnston's neighbors along the Georgia coast feared that the flood of cheap Hawaiian sugar and rice would drive them out of business. Johnston wrote his nephew the senator to remind him that "our best people," meaning the planters, were all opposed. If the Congress wanted to remove all tariffs, that would be reasonable, for it would remove the burden on southerners of paying inflated prices for manufactured goods; but to keep high tariffs on manufactures and eliminate them on rice and sugar was unfair. He ended his letter with the plea: "I beg you to make some effort to defeat the treaty." Along with most southerners, John Johnston voted against the treaty, but it passed anyway.[5]

Johnston's concern over this issue was the first indication that he was emerging from the obsession with his military reputation. He agreed to stand as a delegate from Georgia for the Democratic Convention that summer in St. Louis, but he did not campaign and therefore claimed not to be disap- pointed when he didn't get it. Nevertheless, his failure to be selected led him to complain about the southern system of selecting delegates by which "a few Managers" made all the important decisions. As a Virginia aristocrat, used to thinking of public service as a patriotic duty, he looked with distaste on the whole caste of men who made politics a profession. "These manag- ers," he noted to a friend, "are not generally of the best class. . . . And, naturally, are not disposed to put forward their superiors."

He also found it discouraging that the rank and file seemed to have no particular interest in who the Democrats might nominate at St. Louis. They were apparently willing "to accept the selection of the Northern Demo- crats—their delegates attending the meeting for instruction only." He thought it was time that the South began to assert itself within the party so as not to be taken for granted, otherwise, a Democratic president would be "but a slight improvement" on the Republicans. Rumors from Washington suggested that the contest would be between Winfield Scott Hancock and Thomas A. Hendricks, but Johnston thought Samuel J. Tilden and Thomas F. Bayard were likely contenders. Cynically, he conjectured to T. T. Gantt, a friend and political associate from Baltimore, that perhaps these two men were too high-principled to be considered effective politicians.[6]

On this occasion at least, Johnston's cyncism proved unfounded, for Tilden was not only the favorite at St. Louis, he was virtually unchallenged. Most of the country had grown tired of the much-publicized abuses of the Grant administration. However excellent he may have been as an army commander, Grant had proved to be a poor president, far too trusting of the professional politicians and businessmen who brought their ideas to him, and his naïveté created opportunities for the kind of abuse that had sullied the Republican Party. Tilden, who had cleaned up the Tweed Ring while governor of New York, ran as the reform candidate. Johnston was pleased by the nomination, and hoped that Tilden's election in the fall would bring an end to the worst abuses of Reconstruction.

The Republicans nominated Rutherford B. Hayes, who in his letter of acceptance suggested that he was willing to bring an end to Reconstruction as it had been defined for a decade and a half. He pledged that he would ensure that the South enjoyed "the blessings of honest and capable local self government."[7] This promise implied the withdrawal of Federal troops and the presumed collapse of the Republican governments they sustained. Of course, it also marked the end of the Republican Party's commitment to full political and social equality for the freed slaves.

Early returns seemed to suggest that Johnston's hope for a Democratic victory was about to be fulfilled. Tilden carried his own state of New York, as well as New Jersey, Connecticut, Indiana, and all the states of the former Confederacy. But Republicans disputed the returns in three southern states—Louisiana, Florida, and South Carolina—which, if counted for Hayes, would give the Republican a one-vote victory margin.

Democrats were furious. The Republican maneuvers were, to their eyes, so obviously fraudulent that a resort to arms would not be unjustified. Republicans countered with the argument that if southern whites had not committed gross voting frauds in the first place, Hayes would have been elected easily. Amid all the charges and countercharges, Tilden himself was remarkably unruffled. Rather than assert his victory and lay claim to the White House, he withdrew to his study and resigned himself to defeat. Finally, a bi-partisan congressional committee hammered out a "compro mise," the core of which was that Hayes would be certified as president with the understanding that he would bring an end to the military occupation of the South.

Johnston was disgusted. He argued that Tilden should never have agreed to surrender an office to which the votes of the people entitled him. "If he had the heart of a dung-hill hen," Johnston wrote to Gantt, "he would have claimed the Presidency, and been inaugurated. . . . it is as certain as any matter of opinion, that if he had been resolute he would have been backed by the whole democrat party, against which Grant would not have attempted to use his little military force." Johnston believed the Republican victory was the result of nothing less than military intimidation. It was, he said, "the fright inspired by Grant's 700 infantry in Washington and 5 ironclads on the Potomac." It was inconceivable that the Democrats genuinely believed the compromise a fair one, and he could "ascribe their acceptance of it to no motive but fear."[8] When John W. Johnston wrote that he intended to support the Hayes administration as part of the compromise agreement, Joe suggested that the Democratic Party should instead make its support conditional on presidential cooperation with other Democratic initiatives. Johnston thought Hayes was dragging his feet in living up to the promises of his "Southern policy."[9]

Johnston's interest in politics led him, perhaps inevitably, to candidacy for national office. The Johnstons moved from Savannah to Richmond in the winter of 1876–77, and in 1878 a local Democratic committee approached him with the suggestion that he allow himself to be a candidate for the U.S. Congress from Virginia. Johnston was coy, suggesting that he did not wish to campaign, and would be a candidate only if it were presented to him as the wish of the people. That way, he could accept the role as a duty. Several took his reluctance seriously, and a few hoped that he would reject the nomination, leaving the field open for them. After all, he was now seventy years old. But Johnston demonstrated his seriousness by taking the initiative to have his disqualification for office as a former Confederate officially removed. When the nominating committee approached him to request that he accept the Democratic Party's nomination for Congress, he gravely acquiesced.[10]

His friends had assured him that he would not have to canvass, or campaign, that his name and reputation would be enough to ensure his election. That proved to be false, and he found it just a little demeaning to sell himself to an electorate composed of all classes. Lydia shared her husband's view that campaigning was not a fit activity for gentlemen. "It's shameful," she exclaimed to a group of his backers, "a man of his age and reputation going around to your cross roads like a common member of Congress." Yet she did not hesitate to cash some bonds to help finance the campaign once it became clear that he would have organized opposition.[11]

There were, in fact, six other candidates, all of whom, in Johnston's view, "resorted to the lowest tricks to defeat me." The most unprincipled were the Greenbackers, who promised the electorate that a cheap money policy would ease their financial woes. Johnston thought such claims dishonest. He could understand the willingness of the oppressed to seize upon the promise of cheap money as a panacea, but he could not forgive those who held out the promise of relief, knowing that it was false, solely for the purpose of getting themselves elected. "Many of these people are desperate enough to catch at the wild hopes the 'Greenbacker' leaders offer them," he wrote to Gantt. Seeing the race now as a contest between good and evil, he committed himself to a vigorous campaign against what he considered "the most unprincipled demagogues that have appeared in the Country."[12]

Johnston believed there was nothing wrong with the national economy that was not a product of simple mismanagement during Carpetbag governments. The "destruction of the capital of banks planters and merchants" had made physical reconstruction difficult, and the misrule of carpetbaggers had sapped the spirit of the most enterprising. Still, the South was not entirely blameless. "The great blunder of the planting class was the determination to be nothing less than planters," he admitted privately to Gantt. As a result, they borrowed heavily against their crops and now found themselves deeply in debt. Thus the Greenback Utopia appealed to the formerly wealthy as well as the working poor. "The most difficult political problem we have is to substitute a constitutional financial system for the war measures of the U.S. that made our present [paper] currency."[13]

Despite his initial reluctance, Johnston argued his case heatedly and passionately from the stump. His principal goal was to convince the voters that money which was cheap to them would be just as "cheap" to their creditors and unlikely to secure them any relief. It was "the thriftless," he insisted, who clung to the idea. In the second week of November, at the height of the campaign, he was confined to his house by "a slight accident." He was satisfied with his campaign, though he feared that he had been "remarkably unsuccessful" in discrediting the Greenbackers' arguments.[14]

Johnston was elected to Congress not by virtue of the arguments he presented against the Greenbakers, but because of his name and reputation. He passed his one term as a congressman quietly. He served as a member of the Committee on Military Affairs, in which capacity he visited West Point as a member of the congressional oversight delegation. He voted to exonerate Fitz John Porter from the accusations John Pope had made that Porter had failed to do his duty at Second Manassas. Perhaps he saw in Porter's case something akin to his own persecution by Davis, though the more compelling parallel is Longstreet's denigration of Huger at Seven Pines. Generally speaking, Johnston was an unremarkable congressman. He sat, appropriately enough, in "the extreme outer row" near the center aisle. He initiated no legislation, seldom spoke in floor debates, and voted the straight Democratic Party line.[15]

As his largely uneventful term neared its end, he determined not to run again. Politics interested him, but he found campaigning demeaning. "I have informed those who induced me to be a candidate two years ago, that I will not be so this year," he told Gantt in May. "I consented formerly, because assured that I would not have a canvass to make. But it was greatly required, and would be again. In my estimation the game is not worth such a canvass."[16]

He was disappointed, too, by the apathy of the voting public in the South. Men who had been willing to march barefoot, live without rations, and fight to the death for Virginia, now found it too much trouble to walk "a few hundred yards" to cast a vote for an election on which the continuation of constitutional government depended. Some of the apathy he attributed to the electoral system of voting: "This political machinery has made our political ruin—by bringing the people to the belief that the machine is to make the government—and not they." But he also attributed some to a general depression of public morals, which he believed were "decidedly lower" than they were before the war. Now, candidates could purchase nominations for $1,500, and the political machinery seemed to have all the influence and power. He harkened back nostalgically to the day when gentlemen of character simply "offered" their name for consideration, letting the people decide. The kind of public canvass now required was both expensive and demeaning, certainly no occupation for a gentleman, even one who cared about the future of the country. He despaired that if the Republicans won the national canvass that fall, "we shall see or feel no more of political liberty." The Democratic Party, he believed, represented a majority of Americans, but it lacked the organization, discipline, and unity to be successful. His ideas about civil service reform, he told Gantt, were pleasant thoughts—like "Castles in the Air"—but unlikely of fulfillment.[17]

Despite his pessimism, Johnston was convinced that the Democrats were about to capture the White House for the first time in a quarter century. Winfield Scott Hancock, one of the heroes of the Federal victory at Gettysburg, was the Democratic candidate, and Johnston thought that his name and bearing would carry enough northern votes to put him in the White House. He was not so naive as to believe that such an event would usher in perfection, but at least it would result in "the overthrow of the most corrupt party that has ever existed," and perhaps that would "lead to a reform of public morals. . . ."[18]

That summer he and Lydia took a lengthy holiday, travelling to New York and New England. They enjoyed the beaches of Narragansett Bay and admired "the neatness of the farms and villages" of New England; Johnston thought Pittsfield "the most beautiful little town in the world, in a little tract of country like the greenest parts of England." He attended a meeting of the Aztec Club, a society of veterans of the War with Mexico, riding out from Pittsfield with Robert Patterson, whose maneuvers around Harpers Ferry had so puzzled him in the summer of 1861.[19]

The Johnstons returned from vacation to learn that Hancock had been defeated by Republican James A. Garfield by a mere 28,000 votes. Then only months after his inauguration, Garfield was assassinated by a disgruntled officeseeker and succeeded by his vice president, a political hack named Chester Arthur. The only good to come of this disaster, from Johnston's perspective, was that it provided the impetus to push a Civil Service reform bill through Congress.

The Democratic Party finally wrested the White House away from the Republicans in 1884 when Grover Cleveland defeated James G. Blaine by a scant 29,000 votes. The inaugural parade reflected the theme of national unity. Robert E. Lee's son led a marching regiment of troops attired in Confederate gray whose band played "Dixie" while, close behind, a blue-coated regiment of black troops marched to the tune of "The Union Forever." Recognizing the party's debt to its southern constituents, Cleveland and his advisers were determined to appoint a few prominent southerners to government posts. Johnston was seriously considered for a cabinet post, even the job of Secretary of War, though he was a former Confederate general and was now seventy-six years old. Eventually Cleveland's advisers decided that the nation would not accept a rebel, however reconstructed, as War Secretary, and Johnston instead was appointed U.S. Railroad Commissioner.[20]

In that capacity, he worked for the Secretary of the Interior, Lucius Q. C. Lamar, a Georgian who had served briefly on Johnston's staff in 1861. Johnston's principal responsibility was to inspect the nation's railroads each summer and report on them to the Secretary each fall. He left on his initial tour in early June 1885, and returned in late August, covering roughly two hundred miles a day, with lengthy stops in Omaha and San Francisco.[21]

Although he suffered from his usual bouts of rheumatism, and could not read at night even with his glasses, his health was remarkably good for a man of his age. He walked with the same military gait, and managed to bear long hours in the office and even longer trips of inspection without complaint. He attributed his good health in part to a daily consumption of wine. When Gantt complained of lameness, he responded: "A free use of the liquid the Greeks happily called the Milk of old men would put an end to these attacks of lameness."[22]

But Lydia's health was poorer than ever. The taxing trips to spas and the elixirs of the doctors registered no improvement. During the winter of 1887 she grew weaker, and on February 22, 1887, at the age of sixty-five, she died. Johnston was devastated. A month later he wrote in reply to a condolence letter that he was still unable to imagine that he would "never again hear her sweet voice, the gay tones of which gave me happiness." For the rest of his life he could not bring himself to write or speak her name.[23]

He compensated by working even harder. In June, he set out on another inspection of western railroads. For a man of seventy-nine, he set a grueling itinerary: "I leave Washington tonight for St. Louis," he wrote his editor at *Century* magazine, "where I shall be until Tuesday morning. Shall be at Kansas City Wednesday and Thursday—shall be three days on the way to Denver, and remain there three—probably And then be on the way to Omaha two days and remain there three or four. . . . From Omaha I shall go to San Francisco—in some ten days." He was moved by the size and beauty of the country. "Much that is grand was to be seen in the mountains," he told a niece, "and a great deal that is beautiful in the country beyond." Of course it was more than a scenic tour. Although he had intended to stop in Abingdon on the way home, delays on the trip forced him to return directly to Washington to write his report. "The want of liberty that an office inflicts upon one is an equivalent to taking away half or more of one's life," he complained halfheartedly.[24]

Johnston's tenure in national office came to an abrupt end in 1888 with Cleveland's electoral defeat by Benjamin Harrison. Harrison won election in the Electoral College even though he received sixty thousand fewer popular votes. Johnston had barely returned from his annual transcontinental trip when he learned of the electoral upset. It caught him quite by surprise, and he considered it nothing less than a "National disaster." In his disappointment he blamed the defeat on the Republican practice of assembling Negroes at the polls to vote en masse, and on the foolishness of "many whites of the class of respectable mechanics" who were convinced to turn in Republican tickets. The result of this disaster, Johnston believed, would be monumental. "The consequences to the south of . . . Gettysburg were small compared with the effect of Negro supremacy which the republican party will inevitably establish in all the former slave states." But the Republican commitment to racial equality had ended with Hayes. Harrison's election did not usher in the era of Negro rule that Johnston feared. It did, however, cost Johnston his federal job, and in 1889 he retired to his home on Connecticut Avenue in Washington.[25]

He was not forgotten. Invited to attend a Confederate memorial ceremony in Atlanta, he travelled there in the spring and renewed acquaintances with many of the officers who had served under him in the Georgia campaign. The most emotional moment occurred during the parade through the city. He was assigned to share an open carriage with Edmund Kirby Smith, escorted by the Governor's cavalry. The parade had hardly begun when, according to the reporter from the Atlanta *Constitution*, a voice from the crowd shouted out: "That's Johnston! That's Joe Johnston!" Dozens of men, then hundreds, burst from the crowd and surrounded the carriage, stretching out their hands to their old commander. Someone unhitched the horses, the men took hold of the traces, and they pulled him the length of the parade route, cheering wildly. The evidence of their continued devotion nearly caused the old man to break down. Witnesses saw tears coursing down his weathered cheeks.[26]

The very next month, Johnston was in Richmond to help unveil a huge equestrian statue of Robert E. Lee. After Archer Anderson delivered the dedication speech, Johnston was invited to uncloak the statue. Gravely, he approached the rope, and after a dramatic pause, yanked it to release the draping. The crowd of more than one hundred thousand—some said it was twice that—roared in unison. By May 1890 the shame of defeat had been replaced by pride in a battle well fought. "I felt," wrote one witness in the crowd, "as tho I were assisting at a combined funeral and resurrection."[27]

Funerals were a regular part of Johnston's life now. In 1885, he had returned early from the West Coast to serve as a pallbearer at Grant's funeral. Later that year he performed the same task for his old friend, and wartime adversary, George McClellan. Both men had been considerably younger than he. Other notable names of his generation passed away almost daily. Jefferson Davis died unmourned by Johnston in 1889. In the winter of 1891, Johnston travelled to New York to act as an honorary pallbearer at Sherman's funeral. It took place on a cold and wet February afternoon. As Johnston stood graveside with his hat in his hands, another mourner leaned forward to urge him to put on his hat lest he get sick. Johnston declined. "If I were in his place and he were standing here in mine," the old general pronounced, "he would not put on his hat."[28]

Johnston did catch cold, and over the ensuing weeks it worsened. In March his congestion became an infection, and his breathing grew difficult. Robert McLane sat by his brother-in-law's bed each evening, listening to the old general's labored breathing until he fell asleep. On Saturday, 21 March, Johnston seemed weaker. McLane sent for the doctor, who discovered no marked change, and left McLane to resume the death watch. Johnston slept fitfully the rest of the evening. At ten o'clock McLane rose quietly to his feet, notified Russell, the general's black attendant, that he was leaving, and walked slowly home. He had barely got back and begun preparations for bed when Russell pounded at the door to tell him that the general was failing. McLane rushed to Connecticut Avenue, but Johnston's labored breathing had stopped. It was a few minutes past eleven o'clock.

The funeral was held the next day. "All day long," according to the Washington *Star*, there was "a stream of callers at the residence on Conn. Ave." William Rosecrans and John M. Schofield, each of whom had led armies against Johnston in the field, were among the first to call. After the funeral, the body was moved to Greenmount Cemetery in Baltimore, where Joe Johnston was interred next to his wife in the McLane family plot.[29]

Newspapers across the South and throughout much of the North paid tribute to his memory. They recalled his long service in many wars, and passed quickly over the controversy of his dispute with Jefferson Davis. It was the "knightly soldier and spotless gentleman" they remembered now. But the best tribute came from the men who had served in the ranks of his armies—those veterans who had felt confident that Old Joe would look out for them, that he would do whatever was necessary to ensure that they were well fed and well shod, and that he would never throw them into battle thoughtlessly. It was Sam Watkins, infantryman of the First Tennessee Regiment, who offered the most appropriate epitaph, one that Johnston himself would have appreciated:

Such a man was Joseph E. Johnston, and such his record. Farewell, old fellow! We privates loved you because you made us love ourselves.[30]

Epilogue

In 1959, when he was asked to write an introduction for the reprint of Joseph E. Johnston's *Narrative of Military Operations*, Frank E. Vandiver began with a question: "Was Joseph E. Johnston a genius or a marplot?" It is a question that divided Johnston's contemporaries in the nineteenth century and divides historians still. Most have chosen one side or the other. Either Johnston was an unappreciated genius whose vision was ignored by Jefferson Davis out of jealousy and narrow-mindedness, or he was an officious incompetent whose combativeness with the government and timorousness with the enemy made him more of a handicap than an asset. Compelling as Vandiver's question may be, it is perhaps not the right one to ask, for the answer, surely, is that Johnston was neither.

Few deny that Johnston had some remarkable qualities. He was personally brave—all agreed on that. Moreover, he inspired loyalty, even devotion, from his men. Mary Chesnut, who was no admirer, admitted Johnston's power "to attach men to him." It was, she said, "a gift of the gods." Then, too, he *looked* like a general. E. P. Alexander, who served throughout 1863–65 as Lee's chief of ordnance, wrote that "Johnston was more soldier in looks, carriage & manner than any of our other generals . . . ," and Colonel E.

J. Harvie wrote simply that Johnston "appeared to me the very god of war." Johnston had other, more tangible strengths. He could organize, march, feed, clothe, and fight an army. As a strategist, he understood clearly—more clearly than many of his more celebrated contemporaries—the importance of focusing on the defeat of the enemy army as opposed to the capture, or defense of strategic places.

These military virtues, however, are not necessarily evidence of "genius." And examples of Johnston's weaknesses are just as easy to enumerate. Some were simply the result of his being part of a generation that was fated to redefine the character of warfare. The very size of armies in 1862 complicated both logistics and movement, and the Civil War was the first to witness the widespread use of the minie ball and rifled musket, the telegraph, and the railroad. All army commanders had to adapt to these transformations. Those who had an opportunity to apprentice themselves to this new style of warfare at a lower rank during 1861–62 were the ones who mastered it most effectively in 1864–65—notably Sherman and Grant. Johnston did not have the luxury of such an apprenticeship. He had to learn on the job, and inevitably he made mistakes as he did so.

Another weakness, particularly evident in the first two years of the war, was Johnston's tendency to be inspecific, even casual, in articulating orders to his subordinates, assuming their ability to divine his intentions. This, too, was the product of an adjustment to modern warfare. The officer corps of the Old Army was a fraternity where vague spoken orders generally had been sufficient. No less a commander than Robert E. Lee was also accustomed to issuing vague orders. In Lee's relationship with Stonewall Jackson this proved a happy circumstance, for Stonewall seemed able to read Lee's mind and immediately understand what was wanted. For Johnston at Seven Pines it proved nearly fatal, for despite all that was said afterward, there is no doubt that Longstreet misunderstood completely the intentions of his commander.

Another flaw in the record is Johnston's inability to credit, or even to appreciate, the importance of political factors in strategic planning. The American Civil War was a watershed in United States history. It was, and remains, the only total war the nation has ever experienced. In such a war, the relationship between political goals and military strategy is crucial; but most generals, Johnston among them, were largely insensitive to the political repercussions of military events. For Johnston, this was evident in his repeated insistence that the Confederacy concentrate its forces against the enemy army in the field. In 1861 and again in 1862 he argued that western Virginia, Kentucky, and the Carolinas should be stripped of troops to reinforce the main Confederate army in Virginia. In 1863, he argued that Arkansas could be evacuated temporarily in order to defend Vicksburg. It would be difficult to fault Johnston's military analysis in either instance, but he completely discounted the political ramifications of such movements. Davis, who understood them all too well, turned him down. This was partly because as head of government Davis was responsible for all of the Confederacy and felt he could not strip any one section to protect another. In addition, Davis's commitment to defending the Confederacy everywhere—even when that seemed militarily absurd—stemmed from his conviction that the fate of the Confederacy was tied up with the institution of slavery. Areas surrendered to the enemy, even temporarily, were afterwards ruined for slavery. Johnston would not admit that such considerations should dictate strategy. If the military circumstances called for concentration, and he believed that they did, then in his view a refusal to do was simply foolish.

Johnston's retreat from Dalton to the Chattahoochee is another example of his insensitivity to political realities. However deft and skillful his withdrawal, however defensible as a military maneuver, it allowed critics to wonder if Johnston would not retire all the way to the Gulf of Mexico. Moreover, as Johnston retreated from North Georgia, the troops from Tennessee and Alabama had to turn their backs on their homes and leave their families to the mercy of the Yankees. Although the soldiers retained faith in "Ole Joe," they were saddened by the thought that their loved ones at home had to bear the burden of enemy occupation. Finally, Johnston's continual withdrawals surrendered large chunks of southern territory, including the productive industrial cities of Rome, Georgia, and Selma, Alabama. It would matter little that Johnston's strategy was militarily correct if the Confederacy lost its heartland. Johnston's retreat through North Georgia was tactically brilliant, but politically ruinous.

In the end, the most perplexing and yet the most important aspect of Johnston's generalship concerned his personal weaknesses—his hair-trigger temper, his touchiness on matters of rank and personal prerogative—characteristics that undermined his ability to work effectively with others, and that contributed to his one great and fatal error, his alliance with Louis T. Wigfall. Johnston was politically unsophisticated, but he was no fool. He could not have been ignorant of the consequences of his alliance with Davis's leading political critic, nor of the implications of his public support by Confederate senators who opposed Davis's conduct of the war. Whatever the merits of his claim that he was mistreated by Davis, the record shows clearly that Johnston allowed his bitterness and wounded pride to affect his relationship with the chief executive and commander-in-chief. The resulting lack of mutual trust, which doomed their working relationship, was certainly as much his fault as Davis's.

More than one historian has suggested that there is some similarity between the wartime careers of Johnston and his old friend, George B. McClellan. Like Johnston, McClellan was loved by his men, he was reluctant to advance when urged to do so, and he was eventually dismissed by the chief executive. But the similarity is only superficial, for Johnston lacked McClellan's monumental ego and political ambition. Johnston sought no higher calling than to do his duty as a soldier; he never wanted anything more than command in the field and a clear definition of his authority and responsibility. While both men protested that they faced vastly superior armies in the field, in Johnston's case such claims were at least accurate.

If Johnston made mistakes in judgment, he also grew in the job. By the time he began his controversial campaign in North Georgia in the spring of 1864, he had mastered most of the elements of modern war. But by then he had also squandered his goodwill in Richmond, and the Confederacy had squandered its life's blood at Shiloh, Chickamauga, and Missionary Ridge. Neither genius nor marplot, Joseph E. Johnston was an old-style southern soldier who fought in a new-style war to the best of his considerable ability, and who foolishly allowed himself to be dragged into a political struggle that ruined his credibility in Richmond and eventually made it impossible for him to be effective in the field.

If Johnston the soldier is so clearly visible these six score years later, Johnston the man remains elusive. He lived his life by rules that he and his generation understood. He was loyal to his friends, and he relied on their loyalty in return; he was unflaggingly polite in both word and deed, and he was impeccable in his dress and manners. But in other ways he seemed a bundle of contradictions: he was stuffy yet passionate, intelligent yet naive, quick to temper but just as quick to cool. Sensitive to matters of rank, he disliked being called "Joe," believing that it was no name for a gentleman. Yet his soldiers in Texas addressed him by first name; he leaped from horseback to wrestle a gun from a mud hole on the Peninsula; and he silently endured the public rubbing of his bald head at Dalton in front of a cheering mass of soldiers who called him "Ole Joe." He told his wife that he cared not for the admiration of the crowd, yet he labored during the last quarter of life to protect his public reputation. Part of the explanation for these apparent contradictions is that Johnston was a romantic—both in his simple and emotional patriotism, and in his particular brand of chivalry. His honor and his good name were of first importance, his duty was second, his ambition third. He was a Virginian, a soldier, and a patriot, and for him, at least, there was no conflict among the three.

Finally, for all his serious mein and noble bearing, Johnston was saved from stodginess by virtue of the fact that he could laugh at himself. He knew that he tended to be stuffy at times, and yet he liked best stories that poked fun at poseurs. One of his favorites concerned an officer who had just returned from an extended trip to Florida. This officer told several friends how he had personally captured an alligator more than twenty feet long. When a diminutive listener voiced some skepticism, the storyteller responded, "Surprised are you?" "O, no," the doubter replied, "I am a liar myself." That story, one of Johnston's aides wrote later, never failed to leave the general holding his sides with laughter.

Even more illuminating is the account of an event that took place in the 1880s, a few years before Lydia's death. The elderly couple were resting on the verandah of their cottage at Sweet Chalybeate Springs, where they went

regularly in the summer for the sake of Lydia's poor health. They were
chatting with Dabney Maury, who had come by for a visit, when they heard
a shriek. Johnston went to investigate and found a young girl confronted by a
turkey that was blocking her path. She stood there obstinately shrieking
while the turkey ignored her. Disgusted, the old general remarked, "Why
don't you run away?" Mischeviously, Dabney Maury remarked, "That is
fine advice to come from a great commander." "Well, sir," Johnston responded, "if she won't fight, the best she can do is run away, isn't it?"
Without missing a beat, Lydia replied, "That used to be your plan, I know,
sir." The white-haired old general fixed his wife with a bemused stare, then
burst out laughing.

Notes

ABBREVIATIONS USED IN NOTES

AHS   Atlanta Historical Society, Atlanta, Georgia
ASP, M.A. *American State Papers: Documents, Legislative and Executive of the Congress of the United States. Class V, Military Affairs Series*
B&L   Battles and Leaders of the Civil War
Carlisle   U.S. Army Military History Research Collection, Carlisle Barracks, Pennsylvania
CV   Confederate Veteran
CWTI   Civil War Times Illustrated
Duke   Special Collections Department, William R. Perkins Library, Duke University, Durham, North Carolina
HEH   Henry E. Huntington Library, San Marino, California
JEJ   Joseph E. Johnston
JSH   Journal of Southern History
LC   Library of Congress, Washington, D.C.
MHS   Maryland Historical Society Library, Baltimore, Maryland
MVHR   Mississippi Valley Historical Review
NA   National Archives, Washington, D.C.
NYPL   New York Public Library, New York
ODU   Old Dominion University, Norfolk, Virginia
O.R.   War of the Rebellion: Official Records of the Union and Confederate Armies in the War of the Rebellion

O.R.N.   War of the Rebellion: Official Records of the Union and Confederate
             Navies in the War of the Rebellion
PHS   Pennsylvania Historical Society, Philadelphia, Pennsylvania
Sewanee   Jesse Ball du Pont Library, University of the South, Sewanee, Tennessee
SHSP   Southern Historical Society Proceedings
UNC   Southern Historical Collection, Manuscripts Department, University of
             North Carolina, Chapel Hill
USMA   United States Military Academy, West Point, New York
W&M   Earl Gregg Swem Library, College of William & Mary, Williamsburg,
             Virginia
WRHS   Western Reserve Historical Society, Cleveland, Ohio

PART ONE
Chapter 1

1. Information about Johnston's youth is very sparse, and much of what does exist is unreliable. Johnston did not write about his childhood except for brief responses to the enquires of Bradley T. Johnson, his first biographer. Later in life, Johnston claimed to have been born in 1809, but the burden of evidence points to the earlier date. See Bradley T. Johnson, ed., *A Memoir of the Life and Public Service of Joseph E. Johnston* (Baltimore: R. H. Woodward & Co., 1891), and Robert M. Hughes, *General Johnston* (New York: D. Appleton and Co., 1897). For information on Peter Johnston, see Lewis P. Summers, *History of Southwest Virginia, 1746–1786, Washington County, 1777–1870* (Baltimore: Regional Publishing Co., 1971), 765, 767–9. The source for the name of the Johnston estate in Prince George, which is elsewhere given as Cherry Grove, is JEJ to Bradley Johnson, 30 Sept. 1887, Bradley Johnson Papers, Duke.

2. Walter H. Hendricks, "A History of Abingdon, Virginia," Washington County Historical Society pamphlet; JEJ to Louisa Johnston, 25 June 1825, JEJ Collection, box 1, folder 1, W&M.

3. Diary entry of 12 June 1862 from C. Vann Woodward, ed., *Mary Chesnut's Civil War* (New Haven, Conn.: Yale University Press, 1981), 382.

4. Early chapters of Johnson, ed., *A Memoir,* and Hughes, *General Johnston.*

5. The newspaper advertisement appeared in the *Political Prospect* and is reprinted in "William King, Abingdon Academy, and William King High School," a pamphlet distributed by the William King Arts Center in Abingdon, 3.

6. Peter Johnston to J. C. Calhoun, 19 June and 20 Dec. 1824, JEJ to Calhoun, 4 March 1825, all in USMA Cadet Application Papers, RG 404, series 165, reel no. 32, file #238. See also Hughes, *General Johnston,* 14.

7. Douglas S. Freeman, *R. E. Lee, A Biography* (New York: Charles Scribner's Sons, 1934–35), 1:48; Stephen E. Ambrose, *Duty, Honor, Country: A History of West Point* (Baltimore: Johns Hopkins University Press, 1966), 33.

8. James L. Morrison, Jr., *"The Best School in the World": West Point, the Pre-Civil War Years, 1833–1866* (Kent, Ohio: Kent State University Press, 1986); also Ambrose, *Duty, Honor, Country.*

9. USMA Post Orders, vol. 3 (1823–25); *General Regulations of the Army* (Washington, D.C.: Davis & Force, 1825), 382; Freeman, *R. E. Lee,* 1:50–2.

10. USMA Post Orders, vol. 3 (1823–25); Ambrose, *Duty, Honor, Country,* 74–5; Freeman, *R. E. Lee,* 1:53.

11. USMA Post Orders, vol. 5 (1827–32).

12. Hudson Strode, *Jefferson Davis, American Patriot, 1808–1861* (New York: Harcourt Brace and World, 1955), 40–1; USMA Post Orders, vol. 3 (1823–25); see also H.

M. Monroe and J. T. McIntosh, eds., *The Papers of Jefferson Davis* (Baton Rouge, La.: Louisiana State University Press, 1971), 1:30–1n, 43–4.

13. USMA, *Register of Cadet Delinquencies*, RG 404, series 101, 2:409.

14. Clement Eaton described Davis as a "rather worldly young man" in his biography *Jefferson Davis* (New York: The Free Press, 1977), 14. The nineteenth-century rumor that Davis and Johnston quarrelled over a girl is almost certainly false.

15. "Synopsis of the Course of Studies . . .," 22 June 1825, and "Report of the Committee on the General Condition of the Military Academy," 20 June 1826, both in *ASP*, M.A., 3:150, 375–80.

16. Ambrose, *Duty, Honor, Country*, 92; Hughes, *General Johnston*, 16. The books from Johnston's library are held at the Swem Library at William & Mary.

17. JEJ to Louisa Johnston, 30 June 1825, JEJ Collection, box 1, folder 1, W&M.

18. Ambrose, *Duty, Honor, Country*, 80.

19. USMA, *Register of Merit*, RG 404, series 198 (1826).

20. JEJ to Wigfall, 14 March 65, quoted in Louise (Wigfall) Wright, *A Southern Girl in '61: War-Time Memories of A Confederate Senator's Daughter* (New York: Doubleday & Page, 1905), 240. A friend of Johnston's later wrote that "he hates to be beaten even at a game of billiards." See W. W. Mackall to his family, 21 Feb. 1848, in W. W. Mackall, *A Son's Recollections of His Father* (New York: E. P. Dutton, 1930), 127.

21. Mason was significantly older than most of his peers, having been admitted to the Academy only a few months shy of age twenty-one. USMA, *Register of Merit* (1826).

22. Ambrose, *Duty, Honor, Country*, 123; USMA, Staff Records, vol. 1 (1818–35), 428; USMA Post Orders, vol. 5 (1827–32), 320.

23. USMA Post Orders, vol. 5 (1827–32), 130–3, 182–4; USMA, *Register of Merit* (1829).

24. Hughes, *General Johnston*, 16. My thanks are due to Dr. Russell J. VanCoevering for the diagnosis of *retinitis pigmentosa*.

25. JEJ to Louisa Johnston, 25 Jan. 1829, JEJ Collection, box 1, folder 1, W&M.

Chapter 2

1. Quoted in Robert V. Remini, *Andrew Jackson and the Course of American Freedom, 1822–1832* (New York: Harper & Row, 1981), 147.

2. JEJ to Louisa Johnston, 25 Jan. 1829, JEJ Collection, box 1, folder 1, W&M.

3. JEJ to Louisa Johnston, 18 Nov. 1831, JEJ Collection, box 1, folder 1, W&M; Robert Arthur, "Historical Sketch of the Coast Artillery School," *Journal of the United States Artillery* (July–August 1915), 44:23–4; *Encyclopedia of Historic Forts*, 815–18.

4. Johnston referred to slavery as a "curse" in JEJ to T. T. Gantt, 2 Feb. 1884, JEJ Collection, box 2, folder 4, W&M; his reference to "my friend Sam" is in JEJ to Beverly Johnston, 23 Sept. 1835, JEJ Collection, box 1, folder 1, W&M; Eustis's order is quoted in Arthur, "Coast Artillery School," 33.

5. Quoted in Arthur, "Coast Artillery School," 33.

6. Special Order No. 2, 17 Jan. 1825, printed in Arthur, "Coast Artillery School," 32.

7. Lee to Mackey, 18 Feb. 1833, quoted in Freeman, *R. E. Lee*, 1:115; JEJ to Louisa Johnston, 18 Nov. 1831, JEJ Collection, box 1, folder 1, W&M.

8. Frank E. Stevens, *The Black Hawk War* (Chicago: Frank E. Stevens, 1903); Francis Paul Prucha, *Sword of the Republic: The United States Army on the Frontier* (New York: Macmillan, 1968).

9. JEJ to Louisa Johnston, 18 Nov. 1831, JEJ Collection, box 1, folder 1, W&M.

10. *Niles Register* (11 Aug. 1832), 42:422–3.

11. Captain A. Walker to Captain R. A. Bristol, n.d. Quoted in Stevens, *Black Hawk War*, 244; *Niles Register* (11 Aug. 1832), 42:423.

12. Stevens, *Black Hawk War*, 244–5.

13. See Philip St. George Cooke, *Scenes and Adventures in the Army* (New York: Arno Press, 1973), 156–87; Prucha, *Sword of the Republic*, 174–5, 226–9; Robert Anderson, "Reminiscences of the Black Hawk War," *Wisconsin Historical Society* (1888), 10:172.

14. William T. Hagan, *The Sac and Fox Indians* (Norman, Okla.: University of Oklahoma Press, 1958), 195.

15. *Niles Register* (17 Nov. 1832), 43:180; Stevens, *Black Hawk War*, 253.

16. JEJ to Beverly Johnston, 19 Nov. 1832, JEJ Collection, box 1, folder 1, W&M.

17. Charles C. Johnston to John B. Floyd, 16 Dec. 1831, John B. Floyd Papers, box 1, folder 1, W&M; [Algernon Sidney Johnston], *Memoirs of a Nullifier, Written by Himself* (Columbia, S.C.: The Telegraph, 1832), 103.

18. JEJ to Beverly Johnston, 9 Jan. and 25 March 1834, JEJ Collection, box 1, folder 1, W&M.

19. JEJ to Beverly Johnston, 25 March 1834, JEJ Collection, box 1, folder 1, W&M.

20. The best account of the origins of the Second Seminole War is John K. Mahon, *History of the Second Seminole War, 1835–1842* (Gainesville, Fla.: University of Florida Press, 1967), 87–113. See also Virginia B. Peters, *The Florida Wars* (Hamden, Conn.: Archon Books, 1979), 105–10, and John T. Sprague, *The Origin, Progress, and Conclusion of the Florida War* (Gainesville, Fla.: University of Florida Press, 1964), 72–95.

21. JEJ to Beverly Johnston, 18 Feb. 1836, JEJ Collection, box 1, folder 1, W&M.

22. The description of Fort Drane is from Mahon, *History of the Second Seminole War*, 107.

23. Scott's official report on this campaign is Scott to Jones, 12 April 1836, *ASP*, M.A., 7:267–70. See also the summary of "Documentary Testimony," ibid., 7:161–2; Mahon, *History of the Second Seminole War*, 151–8; Charles W. Elliott, *Winfield Scott, The Soldier and the Man* (New York: Macmillan, 1937), 304–5.

24. Scott's official report implied that volunteers did not make good troops. See Scott to Jones, 30 April 1836, *ASP*, M.A., 7:277–9. His charge that Floridians were prone to panic was included in his Order No. 48, dated 17 May 1836, ibid., 294. A subsequent Court of Inquiry about this campaign led to extensive testimony by Scott and others regarding his conduct of the Florida war. The testimony is printed in *ASP*, M.A., 7:125–59.

25. The "miserable little steamer" was the *Essayons*—Elliott, *Winfield Scott*, 307. Johnston's presence in the party, along with Colonel Gadsden and Captain Canfield, is indicated in Scott's testimony before the Court of Inquiry. The party of officers was fired on from ambush during this exploration. See *ASP*, M.A., 7:161–2. See also M. M. Cohen, *Notices of Florida and the Campaigns* (Gainesville, Fla.: University of Florida Press, 1836, 1964), 216.

26. For the Scott-Jesup feud, see Elliot, *Winfield Scott*, 322–31. Johnston's presence at the Battle of Wahoo Swamp is indicated in Col. Pierce to Governor Call, 26 Nov. 1837, *Army and Navy Chronicle* (1837), 5:8.

27. JEJ to Beverly Johnston, 13 June 1837, JEJ Collection, box 1, folder 1, W&M; Morrison, "*The Best School in the World*," 15.

28. *Army and Navy Chronicle* (1837), 5:136.

29. Morrison, "*The Best School in the World*," 20; Ambrose, *Duty, Honor, Country*, 87–124; Letter to the Editor from "The Officer's Friend," *Army and Navy Chronicle* (1836), 3:138.

Chapter 3

1. Quoted by Bray Hammond, *Banks and Politics in America from the Revolution to the Civil War* (Princeton, N.J.: Princeton University Press, 1957), 454.

2. Ibid., 451–67.

3. JEJ to Beverly Johnston, 13 June 1837, JEJ Collection, box 1, folder 2, W&M.

4. Johnston wrote a memoir of this episode. In it he suggests that the renewal of the war in Florida was his primary motive for offering his services to the Secretary of War. The handwritten document is dated 13 July 1890 and is in the R. S. Ewell Papers, LC; George E. Buker, *Swamp Sailors: Riverine Warfare in the Everglades, 1835–1842* (Gainesville, Fla.: University of Florida Press, 1975), 60.

5. Kenneth W. Power, "Florida Slaves and Free Negroes in the Seminole War," *JSH* (April 1943); Buker, *Swamp Sailors*, 8–9; Mahon, *History of the Second Seminole War*, 128–31.

6. Jacob R. Motte, *Journey into Wilderness: An Army Surgeon's Account of Life in Camp and Field During the Creek and Seminole Wars, 1836–1838*, edited by James F. Sunderman (Gainesville, Fla.: University of Florida Press, 1953), 168.

7. Motte, *Journey into Wilderness*, 161, 168.

8. Ibid., 161.

9. Ibid., 173; Buker, *Swamp Sailors*, 60.

10. Johnston memoir dated 13 July 1890, R. S. Ewell Papers, LC; Johnson, ed., *A Memoir of the Life and Public Service of Joseph E. Johnston*, 10–11; Hughes, *General Johnston*, 20–1.

11. Johnston memoir dated 13 July 1890, R. S. Ewell Papers, LC.

12. Motte, *Journey into Wilderness*, 182–3; *Army and Navy Chronicle* (1838), 7:93–4; Powell's official report is also printed in the *Army and Navy Chronicle* (1838), 7:125.

13. One of the five "killed" turned out to be missing and was later found wandering in the Florida wilderness in a confused state. There was also an unproved rumor that Dr. Leitner was not killed in battle, but was captured and killed later. See Motte, *Journey into Wilderness*, 184–5.

14. Johnston memoir dated 13 July 1890, R. S. Ewell Papers LC; Powell to Dallas, 17 Jan. 1838, *Army and Navy Chronicle* (1838), 7:125.

15. A later version of Fort Dallas was built on the northern bank of the Miami. Although naval records do not indicate that any permanent structures were built during the time that Powell and Johnston occupied the site, a claim for damages by a local settler states that the Indians burned a blockhouse at the site a few months later. It is fair to assume that the topographical engineer in the expedition laid out and supervised the construction of that blockhouse. See Nathan D. Shappee, "Fort Dallas and the Naval Depot on Key Biscayne, 1836–1926," *Tequesta* (1961), 13–40.

16. *Army and Navy Chronicle* (1838), 7:268.

17. Buker, *Swamp Sailors*, 65–6; *Army and Navy Chronicle* (1837), 6:268–9.

18. The army officers, including Magruder and McLane, and presumably Johnston, left Key West on board the cutter *Madison* on 27 April 1838. See Howard to Dallas, 26 April 1838, enclosed in Dallas to Secretary of the Navy, 3 May 1838, *Captain's Letters*, RG 45, NA.

19. Mahon, *History of the Second Seminole War*, 307.

Chapter 4

1. JEJ to Beverly Johnston, 9 Jan. 1834, JEJ Collection, box 1, folder 1, W&M.

2. Washington County Courthouse Records, Chancery Order Book A, Angela Hart, ed., *The Historical Society of Washington County, Va., Bulletin*, series II, 27:16; JEJ to Louisa Johnston, 25 Jan. 1839, and JEJ to Beverly Johnston, 18 Feb.

1836, both in JEJ Collection, box 1, folders 1 and 2, W&M. Peter Johnston had married Anne Berard in 1828. John Warfield Johnston, Jr., later became a U.S. senator.

3. JEJ to Preston Johnston, 23 March 1839, 16 March and 12 July 1840; JEJ to Beverly Johnston, 11 March 1840; all in JEJ Collection, box 1, folder 2, W&M.

4. JEJ to Beverly Johnston, 13 or 19 Nov. 1832 [date unclear], and JEJ to Beverly Johnston, 13 June 1837, both in JEJ Collection, box 1, folders 1 and 2, W&M. Beverly never did marry. Indeed, of the eight Johnston brothers, only four ever married, and only two fathered children.

5. JEJ to Louisa Johnston, 18 Nov. 1831, JEJ Collection, box 1, folder 1, W&M.

6. JEJ to Preston Johnston, 16 March 1840, JEJ Collection, box 1, folder 2, W&M.

7. JEJ to Preston Johnston, 12 July 1840, JEJ Collection, box 1, folder 2, W&M.

8. Louis McLane, Jr., to his wife, 18 Aug. 1853, quoted in John A. Munroe, *Louis McLane: Federalist and Jacksonian* (Brunswick, N.J.: Rutgers University Press, 1973), 583. McLane's West Point difficulties are discussed at p. 334.

9. Ibid., p. 334.

10. JEJ to Preston Johnston, 19 Nov. 1840, JEJ Collection, box 1, folder 5, W&M.

11. Robert M. McLane, *Reminiscences, 1827–1897* (Wilmington, Del.: Scholarly Resources, 1972), 71.

12. Hughes, *General Johnston*, 22.

13. McLane, *Reminiscences*, 66.

14. Ibid., 74–5.

15. JEJ to Preston Johnston, 13 May 1841, 2 June 1841, 13 June 1841, and 16 Sept. 1841, all in JEJ Collection, box 1, folder 3, W&M; Account books of Evans, Owen & Co., 1841–43, JEJ Papers, JO 345, HEH Library.

16. JEJ to Preston Johnston, 13 May 1842, JEJ Collection, box 1, folder 3, W&M.

17. Munroe, *Louis McLane*, 488; JEJ to Preston Johnston, 30 May 1839, JEJ Collection, box 1, folder 2, W&M.

18. Warren W. Hassler, Jr., *With Shield and Sword* (Ames, Iowa: Iowa State University Press, 1982), 114–15; William A. Ganoe, *The History of the United States Army* (New York: D. Appleton and Co., 1924), 188–9; JEJ to Preston Johnston, 27 Nov. 1842, JEJ Collection, box 1, folder 3, W&M.

19. Lee to John Mackay, 3 Feb. 1846[?], quoted in Freeman, *R. E. Lee*, 1:411n.

20. JEJ to Preston Johnston, 4 April 1843, JEJ Collection, box 1, folder 3, W&M.

21. JEJ to Preston Johnston, 25 May 1843, JEJ Collection, box 1, folder 3, W&M.

22. Canfield to JEJ, 16 July 1845, JEJ Collection, box 1, folder 3, W&M.

23. John S. Wise, "Joseph E. Johnston," *The Circle* (May 1908), 288. See, for example, JEJ to Lydia Johnston, 27 Jan. 1862, McLane-Fisher Family Papers, MS. 2403, box 6, MHS.

24. JEJ to Lydia Johnston, 1 April 1865, McLane-Fisher Family Papers, MS. 2403, box 6, MHS.

Chapter 5

1. K. Jack Bauer, *The Mexican War, 1846–1848* (New York: Macmillan, 1974), 48, 67.

2. Ibid., 235, 202. To let Taylor down easy, Polk sent Johnston's friend and new brother-in-law Robert McLane, now a volunteer major, to inform Taylor in person that he was about to be superseded.

3. Marcy to Scott, 23 Nov. 1846, House Exec. Doc. 60, 30th Cong., 1st sess., 372.

4. Winfield Scott, *Memoirs of Lieut-General Scott* (New York: Sheldon & Co., 1864), 400–3.

5. Freeman, *R. E. Lee*, 1:221; William H. Parker, *Recollections of a Naval Officer* (New York: Charles Scribner's Sons, 1883), 92–3.

6. Dabney Maury, *Recollections of a Virginian* (New York: Charles Scribner's Sons, 1894), 32; Bauer, *The Mexican War*, 248.

7. Maury, *Recollections*, 34.

8. Alfred Hoyt Bill, *Rehearsal for Conflict: The War with Mexico, 1846–1848* (New York: Alfred A. Knopf, 1947), 13; R. W. Johannsen, *To the Halls of the Montezumas: The Mexican War in the American Imagination* (New York: Oxford University Press, 1985), 101; Scott to Juan Morales, 22 March 1847, Scott to Marcy, 23 March 1847, both in House Exec. Doc. 1, 30th Cong., 1st sess., 225–6, 224..

9. Maury, *Recollections*, 34–5; General Orders No. 80, 30 March 1847, House Exec. Doc. 1, 30th Cong., 1st sess., 240.

10. Raphael Semmes, *The Campaign of General Scott in the Valley of Mexico* (Cincinnati: Moore & Anderson, 1852), 60; Cadmus Wilcox, *History of the Mexican War* (Washington, D.C.: The Church News Publishing Co., 1892), 271.

11. Twiggs to Scott, 19 April 1847, House Exec. Doc. 1, 30th Cong., 1st sess., 277; P. G. T. Beauregard, *With Beauregard in Mexico: The Mexican War Reminiscences of P. G. T. Beauregard*, edited by T. Harry Williams (Baton Rouge, La.: Louisiana State University Press, 1956), 33.

12. Bill, *Rehearsal for Conflict*, 12.

13. Maury, *Recollections*, 39; Parker, *Recollections*, 113.

14. Maury, *Recollections*, 40, 41; E. Kirby Smith, *To Mexico with Scott: Letters of E. Kirby Smith to His Wife* (Cambridge, Mass.: Harvard University Press, 1917), 137.

15. Bauer, *The Mexican War*, 283; Scott to Marcy, 20 May 1847, and Scott to Trist, 29 May 1847, both in Sen. Exec. Doc. 52, 30th Cong., 1st sess., 159–68, 173.

16. Scott to Marcy, 4 June, House Exec. Doc. 60, 30th Cong., 1st sess., 993–4.

17. Wilcox, *History*, 305.

18. Ibid., 335; Bill, *Rehearsal for Conflict*, 264; Justin H. Smith, *The War with Mexico* (New York: Macmillan, 1919), 2:432; Bauer, *The Mexican War*, 273.

19. Bill, *Rehearsal for Conflict*, 265.

20. Smith, *To Mexico with Scott*, 192.

21. Bill, *Rehearsal for Conflict*, 272.

22. Beauregard, *With Beauregard in Mexico*, 52.

23. Bauer, *The Mexican War*, 293; Wilcox, *History*, 366.

24. Scott to Marcy, 19 Aug. 1847, House Exec. Doc. 1, 30th Cong., 1st sess., 303–6.

25. Wilcox, *History*, 369.

26. Scott to Marcy, 28 Aug. 1847, House Exec. Doc. 1, 30th Cong., 1st sess., 310.

27. Maury, *Recollections*, 41; Lee to Mrs. Totten, 22 Aug. 1847, quoted in Freeman, *R. E. Lee*, 1:260, 266; JEJ to Beverly Johnston, 25 Aug. 1847, JEJ Collection, box 1, folder 4, W&M.

28. JEJ to Eliza Johnston, 12 Jan. 1848, JEJ Collection, box 1, folder 4, W&M. Preston's position in the First Artillery was filled by another young lieutenant, Thomas J. Jackson, later known as "Stonewall."

29. Bill, *Rehearsal for Conflict*, 279.

30. Ibid., 289.

31. Roswell S. Ripley, *The War with Mexico* (New York: Harper & Brothers, 1849), 2:373.

32. Worth to Scott, 10 Sept. 1847, House Exec. Doc. 1, 30th Cong., 1st sess., 366.

33. Bill, *Rehearsal for Conflict*, 292–3.

34. Wilcox, *History*, 458.

35. Bill, *Rehearsal for Conflict*, 295; Wilcox, *History*, 458; Smith, *The War with Mexico*, 2:154; Bauer, *The Mexican War*, 316–17.

36. Beauregard, *With Beauregard in Mexico*, 79–80.

37. Ibid., 81.

38. Wilcox, *History*, 462; John R. Kenly, *Memoirs of a Maryland Volunteer* (Philadelphia: J. B. Lippincott & Co., 1873), 458–9; Smith, *The War with Mexico*, 2:157.

39. R. E. Lee to John Mackay, 2 Oct. 1847, R. E. Lee and G. W. C. Papers, Carlisle.

40. JEJ to Capt. Page (AAG), 12, 15, and 25 March 1848, all in Cadwalader Collection, PHS; W. W. Mackall to his wife, 21 Feb. 1848, in Mackall, *A Son's Recollections of His Father,* 126–7.

41. Quoted in Bauer, *The Mexican War,* 322.

42. JEJ to McClellan, 21 March 1856, McClellan Papers, B-3, LC.

43. Maury, *Recollections,* 41.

Chapter 6

1. JEJ to McClellan, 3 Dec. 1860, McClellan Papers, B-6, LC.

2. David Potter, *The Impending Crisis, 1848–1861* (New York: Harper & Row, 1976), 18–50.

3. William H. Goetzmann, *Army Exploration in the American West* (New Haven, Conn.: Yale University Press, 1959), 9, 209.

4. See W. F. Smith, "Report . . . on Routes from San Antonio to El Paso, 1850," Sen. Exec. Doc. No. 64, 31st Cong., 1st sess.; Goetzmann, *Army Exploration,* 228–31. See also JEJ to Abert, 1 June 1849, Records of the Topographical Bureau, RG 77, reel 37, NA.

5. JEJ to Brooke, 28 Dec. 1849, Sen. Exec. Doc. No. 64, 31st cong., 1st sess., 26–28; JEJ to Abert, 31 Dec. 1849, Records of the Topographical Bureau, RG 77, reel 37, NA.

6. JEJ to Abert, 11 Sept. 1850, Records of the Topographical Bureau, RG 77, reel 37, NA; JEJ to Abert, 16 April 1850, Sen. Exec. Doc. No. 64, 33rd Cong., 1st sess., 39–40.

7. JEJ to Abert, 1 Dec. 1851 and 29 Feb. 1852, both in Records of the Topographical Bureau, RG 77, reel 37, NA.

8. JEJ to McClellan, 2 Jan. 1857, McClellan Papers, B-3, LC; Goetzmann, *Army Exploration,* 261.

9. JEJ to Abert, 25, 26, 28 Nov., 23 Dec. 1853, 6 Jan., 27 Feb., 23 March, 14 April, 23 May, 3 June, 11 and 16 July, 25 Sept. 1854, all in Records of the Topographical Bureau, RG 77, reel 37, NA.

10. JEJ to Edward Johnston, 6 Jan. 1851, JEJ Collection, box 1, folder 3, W&M.

11. JEJ to Edward Johnston, 6 Jan. 1851, JEJ Collection, box 1, folder 1, W&M; JEJ to Brooke, 28 Dec. 1849, Sen. Exec. Doc. No. 64, 31st Cong., 1st sess., 28.

12. JEJ to Edward Johnston, 6 Jan. 1851, JEJ Collection, box 1, folder 3, W&M.

13. Johnston had applied for promotion and command a year earlier, in February 1854. See JEJ to Cadwalader, 11 Feb. 1854, and Cadwalader to Cooper, n.d., Cadwalader Papers, PHS. He renewed his application in a letter to Cooper dated 24 February 1855, JEJ Papers, Duke.

14. JEJ to Cadwalader, 7 March 1855, Cadwalader Papers, PHS.

15. JEJ to McClellan, 21 March and 13 April 1856, McClellan Papers, B-3, LC.

16. JEJ to McClellan, 30 March, 13 April, 21 March, and 30 March 1856, all in McClellan Papers, B-3, LC.

17. JEJ to McClellan, 2 Dec. 1855, McClellan Papers, B-3, LC.

18. JEJ to McClellan, 21 March 1856, McClellan Papers, B-3, LC.

19. JEJ to McClellan, 13 April 1856, McClellan Papers, B-3, LC.

20. JEJ to McClellan, 2 Dec. 1855, McClellan Papers, B-3, LC. Lydia occasionally wrote to McClellan as well, referring to her husband as "Col. Joe." Lydia Johnston to McClellan, 7 April 1857, McClellan Papers, B-4, LC.

21. JEJ to McClellan, 2 Jan. 1857, McClellan Papers, B-3, LC.

22. JEJ to McClellan, 13 April 1857, McClellan Papers, B-5, LC.

23. JEJ to McClellan, 2 Dec. 1855, McClellan Papers, B-3, LC.

24. Alice Nichols, *Bleeding Kansas* (New York: Oxford University Press, 1954), 23–57; Potter, *Impending Crisis,* 199–224.

25. Nichols, *Bleeding Kansas*, 49–56; Potter, *Impending Crisis*, 207–8.

26. JEJ to McClellan, 2 Dec. 1855, McClellan Papers, B-3, LC.

27. Samuel A. Johnson, *Battle Cry of Freedom* (Lawrence, Kans.: University of Kansas Press, 1954), 189; Potter, *Impending Crisis*, 207–8; Nichols, *Bleeding Kansas*, 49–56.

28. JEJ to McClellan, 10 Aug. 1856, McClellan Papers, A-8, LC. See Davis's report for 1856: Sen. Exec. Doc. No. 5, 34th Cong., 3rd sess., 49ff.

29. JEJ to McClellan, 25 Oct. and 18 Nov. 1856, both in McClellan Papers, A-8, LC; George H. Steuart to Captain George H. Steuart, 17 Aug. 1856, George Hume Steuart Papers, Duke.

30. JEJ to McClellan, 18 Nov. and 10 Aug. 1856, McClellan Papers, A-8, LC.

31. Nyle H. Miller, ed., "Surveying the Southern Boundary Line of Kansas," *Kansas Historical Quarterly* (February 1932), 1:106.

32. Eugene Bandel, *Frontier Life in the Army, 1854–1861* (Philadelphia: Porcupine Press, 1932, 1974), 123; JEJ to McClellan, 4 June 1857, McClellan Papers, B-4, LC.

33. Miller, "Surveying . . . Kansas," 113–15; George A. Root, ed., "Extracts from Diary of Captain Lambert Bowman Wolf," *Kansas Historical Quarterly* (May 1932), 1:195–210.

34. Bandel, *Frontier Life*, 126; JEJ Journal entry of 8 July 1857, printed in Miller, "Surveying . . . Kansas," 117–18.

35. JEJ to McClellan, 15 Sept. 1857, McClellan Papers, B-5, LC.

36. Bandel to his parents, 13 July 1857, Bandel, *Frontier Life*, 127; JEJ to McClellan, 15 Sept. 1857, McClellan Papers, B-5, LC.

37. Bandel to his parents, 30 May 1857, Bandel, *Frontier Life*, 123.

38. JEJ to McClellan, 15 Sept. 1857, McClellan Papers, B-5, LC.

39. Bandel Diary, 24 Sept. 1857, Bandel, *Frontier Life*, 195; Miller, "Surveying . . . Kansas," 131; JEJ Journal entry of 26 Sept.

40. Charles H. Brown, *Agents of Manifest Destiny* (Chapel Hill, N.C.: University of North Carolina Press, 1980); Edward S. Wallace, *Destiny and Glory* (New York: Coward-McCann, 1957); JEJ to McClellan, 6 Dec. 1857. McClellan Papers, B-4, LC.

41. Buchanan's Annual Message to Congress, 6 Dec. 1858, James A. Buchanan, *The Messages of President Buchanan* (New York, 1888), 52–97.

42. J. Fred Rippy, *The United States and Mexico* (New York: Alfred A. Knopf, 1926), chapter 12.

43. Buchanan's 1858 message in Buchanan, *Messages*, 73–5.

44. JEJ to McClellan, 9 March 1858 and 31 Jan. 1859, both in McClellan Papers, B-5, A-11, LC. The other members of the cabal may have been Gustavus Woodson Smith and Mansfield Lovell. See JEJ to Lovell, 3 July 60, Mansfield Lovell Papers, LC.

45. JEJ to McClellan, 29 April and 28 March 1859, McClellan Papers, A-11, LC.

46. JEJ to McClellan, 7 April 1859, McClellan Papers, A-11, LC.

47. JEJ to McClellan, 29 April 1859, McClellan Papers, A-11, LC.

48. JEJ to McClellan, 12 May 1859, McClellan Papers, A-11, LC; Rippy, *The United States and Mexico*, 225.

49. Juarez continued his war without American aid. By 1860 he had won the "War of the Reform" and assumed the presidency of a near-bankrupt government. A year later, with the United States embroiled in its own Civil War, French troops landed in Mexico on the pretext of collecting debts to establish a protectorate. Juarez retreated to El Paso del Norte (now Ciudad Juarez) to carry on another war of resistance that ended in 1867 with the execution of the French puppet Maxmilian. Juarez then served as Mexico's president until 1872. See Robert E. May, *The Southern Dream of a Caribbean Empire* (Athens, Ga.: University of Georgia Press, 1989), 160–2.

50. JEJ to McClellan, 12 May 1859, McClellan Papers, A-11, LC.

51. JEJ to McClellan, 3 Dec. 1860, McClellan Papers, B-6, LC.

Chapter 7

1. JEJ to Edward Johnston, 6 Jan. 1851, JEJ Collection, box 1, folder 3, W&M.

2. Lee to Anna Fitzhugh, 6 June 1860, quoted in Freeman, *R. E. Lee,* 1:410.

3. "Report on the Claim, April 15, 1858, of Lt. Colonel Johnston, 1st Cavalry, to the rank of Brevet Colonel," JEJ Collection, box 1, folder 3, W&M.

4. Ibid.

5. On January 18, 1856, Davis delivered his opinion that the case "had been decided by his predecessors and could not be opened." By that time Johnston had been posted to the First Cavalry.

6. "Report on the Claim . . . ," JEJ Collection, box 1, folder 3, W&M.

7. Floyd to Adjutant General, 6 March 1860, JEJ Collection, box 1, folder 3, W&M.

8. Alexander and Cooke to Davis, 15 March 1860, noted in L. L. Crist and M. S. Dix, eds., *The Papers of Jefferson Davis* (Baton Rouge, La.: Louisiana State University Press, 1989), 6:644–5; Lee to Custis Lee, 16 April 1860, quoted in Freeman, *R. E. Lee,* 1:411. Freeman incorrectly cites this letter as Lee's response to Johnston's promotion to Quartermaster General.

9. For the Johnston's attendance at McClellan's wedding, see Stephen Sears, *George B. McClellan, The Young Napoleon* (New York: Ticknor & Fields, 1988), 63. For Johnston's appointment as Quartermaster General, see Robert W. Hughes, *General Johnston* (New York: Appleton & Co., 1897), 33–25, and Gilbert E. Govan and James W. Livingood, *A Different Valor: The Story of General Joseph E. Johnston* (Indianapolis: Bobbs-Merrill, 1956), 25. Both of these biographies contain references to a presumed dispute between Davis and Floyd over confirmation of Johnston's appointment. There is no official record, however, of such a dispute.

10. Henry Adams is quoted in Margaret Leech, *Reveille in Washington* (New York: Harper and Bros., 1941), 5. JEJ to W. W. Mackall, 22 Sept. 1860, Mackall Papers, file #2, UNC; Lee to JEJ, 30 July 1860, JEJ Collection, box 1, folder 3, W&M.

11. "Report of the Quartermaster General," 12 Nov. 1860, Sen. Exec. Doc. No. 1, 36th Cong., 2nd sess., 234, 236. A month later, Floyd, who was having budgetary problems of his own, wrote to ask "whether the expenses in the military department of the Government could be reduced." Johnston could only repeat his suggestion that the Department close some of the western forts. See JEJ to Floyd, 18 Dec. 1860, *O.R.,* III, 1:18.

12. Bruce Catton, *The Coming Fury* (New York: Doubleday & Co., 1961), 428.

13. JEJ to McClellan, 3 Dec. 1860, McClellan Papers, B-6, LC.

14. Woodward, ed., *Mary Chesnut's Civil War* (diary entry of 25 Feb. 1865), 729; Mrs. Eugene McLean, "When the States Seceded," *Harper's Monthly* (February 1914), 128:440; Varina Davis, *Jefferson Davis: A Memoir by His Wife* (New York: The Belford Co., 1890; reprinted Baltimore: N&A Press, 1991), 1:261.

15. JEJ to T. T. Gantt, 23 June 1888, JEJ Collection, box 2, folder 5, W&M.

16. Floyd to JEJ, 24 Nov. 1860, and JEJ to Floyd, 1 Dec. 1860, both in *O.R.,* III, 1:7–8.

17. Joseph E. Johnston, *Narrative of Military Operations* (New York: D. Appleton, 1874; reprinted Bloomington, Ind.: Indiana University Press, 1959), 10; "Reminiscences of Washington in 1861," Simon Cameron Papers, LC; Allan Nevins, *The War for the Union: The Improvised War, 1861–1862* (New York: Charles Scribner's Sons, 1959), 108–9. In addition to the national crisis, there was bad news that winter that touched the Johnston's personally. Lydia's middle brother, George, who was pursuing a career in the army, was killed in New Mexico during a skirmish with the

Navajos. Lydia was devastated. "She has been more affected by it than I can tell you," Johnston wrote to McClellan, "was made seriously sick & is just now recovering. . . ." JEJ to McClellan, 3 Dec. 1860, McClellan Papers, B-6, LC.

18. Woodward, ed., *Mary Chesnut's Civil War* (diary entry of 2 Sept, 1861), 187.

19. Peter Johnston to JEJ, 10 March 1861, JEJ Collection, box 1, folder 4, W&M (italics in original); Richmond *Examiner* quoted in Henry T. Shanks, *The Secession Movement in Virginia* (New York: AMS Press, 1971), 158.

20. Quoted in Shanks, *The Secession Movement*, 162.

21. Peter Johnston to JEJ, 10 March 1861, JEJ Collection, box 1, folder 4, W&M; Richmond *Enquirer,* 5 march 1861 (italics in original).

22. Quoted in Shanks, *The Secession Movement*, 179, 263n; Peter Johnston to JEJ, 10 March 1861, JEJ Collection, box 1, folder 4, W&M (italics in original); L. P. Walker to JEJ, 15 March 1861, *O.R.*, IV, 1:165–6. Walker made the same offer to Lee on the same date.

23. Quoted in Shanks, *The Secession Movement*, 187.

24. "Reminiscences of Washington in 1861," Simon Cameron Papers, LC; Johnston, *Narrative*, 12.

25. Mrs. Eugene McLean, "When the States Seceded," 288.

26. Johnston, *Narrative*, 12; General Orders No. 3, 26 April 1861, *O.R.*, I, 2:783.

27. Johnston, *Narrative*, 13; Mrs. Eugene McLean, "When the States Seceded," 441.

28. Cooper to JEJ, 15 May 1861, *O.R.*, I, 2:844–5.

PART TWO
Chapter 8

1. Ezra Warner, *Generals in Gray* (Baton Rouge, La.: Louisiana State University Press, 1959), 279–80, 334–5.

2. Cooper to JEJ, 15 May 1861, *O.R.*, I, 2:844; JEJ, *Narrative*, 15.

3. Johnston, *Narrative*, 17.

4. JEJ Orders dated 24 May 1861, and Jackson to JEJ, 24 May 1861, both in *O.R.*, I, 2:871, 872; Johnston, *Narrative*, 14–15.

5. Warner, *Generals in Gray*, 134–5, 151–2, 296–7; James I. Robertson, Jr., *General A. P. Hill, The Story of a Confederate Warrior* (New York: Random House, 1987), 38; Emory M. Thomas, *Bold Dragoon, The Life of J. E. B. Stuart* (New York: Harper & Row, 1986), 73.

6. Johnston, *Narrative*, 16; JEJ to Garnett, 26 May 1861, *O.R.*, I, 2:880–1.

7. Johnston, *Narrative*, 16.

8. JEJ to Garnett, 28 May 1861, *O.R.*, I, 2:889.

9. L. P. Walker to Lee, 10 May 1861, *O.R.*, I, 2:827; JEJ, *Narrative*, 17; Lee to JEJ, 1 June 1861, *O.R.*, I, 2:897, 898.

10. JEJ to Lee, 6 June 1861, *O.R.*, I, 2:907–8.

11. Lee to JEJ, 7 June 1861, *O.R.*, I, 2:910.

12. JEJ to Lee, 12 June 1861, and Lee to JEJ, 21 June 1861, both in *O.R.*, I, 2:922, 945.

13. JEJ to Cooper, 17 June 1861, *O.R.*, I, 2:934; JEJ, *Narrative,* 22.

14. Edward Hungerford, *The Story of the Baltimore & Ohio Railroad, 1827–1927* (New York: G. P. Putnam's Sons, 1928), 2:8–9; JEJ, *Narrative*, 26. Johnston sent the First Maryland Regiment back to Harpers Ferry on the 18th with orders to salvage whatever they could, and burn the rest. Bradley Johnson, "Memoir of First Maryland Regiment", *SHSP* (1881), 9:351–2. Jeffrey Lash characterizes Johnston's actions in destroying the rolling stock of the B&O Railroad as an "egregious blunder" be-

cause it provoked an outcry from stockholders. But this was before the fully destructive nature of the war had become clear. See Jeffrey Lash, "Joseph E. Johnston and the Virginia Railways, 1861–62," *Civil War History* (1989), 35:11–12. See also Lash, *Destroyer of the Iron Horse: Joseph E. Johnston and Confederate Rail Transport* (Kent, Ohio: Kent State University Press, 1991), 7–40. Lash is unreasonably critical of Johnston's tendency to destroy rolling stock to prevent it from falling to the Yankees.

15. Johnston, *Narrative*, 23–24; JEJ to Cooper, 17 June 1861, *O.R.*, I, 2:934.

16. Cooper to JEJ, 13 June 1861, *O.R.*, I, 2:923–5.

17. JEJ to Cooper, 15 June 1861, and Cooper to JEJ, 18 June 1861, both in *O.R.*, I, 2:929–30, 934.

18. JEJ to Cooper, 24 June, 2 July, and 4 July 1861; Davis to JEJ, 13 July 1861; all in *O.R.*, I, 2:948–9, 969, 977.

19. Beauregard to Davis, and JEJ to Cooper, 9 July 1861, both in *O.R.*, I, 2:969.

20. A summary of this plan is included in James Chesnut to Beauregard, 16 July 1861. Beauregard's letter to JEJ is dated 13 July. Both are in Alfred Roman, *The Military Operations of General Beauregard* (New York: Harper & Bros., 1884), 1:85–6, 87. Johnston's forces numbered about eleven thousand by mid-July. See D. S. Freeman, *Lee's Lieutenants* (New York: Charles Scribner's Sons, 1934), 1:42–3.

21. JEJ to Cooper, 14 Oct. 1861, *O.R.*, I, 2:472.

22. Samuel D. Buck, *With the Old Confeds, Actual Experiences of a Captain of the Line* (Baltimore: H. E. Houck & Co., 1925), 22.

23. JEJ, *Narrative*, 21; JEJ to Cooper, 14 Oct. 1861, *O.R.*, I, 2:471, 473. See also JEJ to Cooper, 9 July 1861, *O.R.*, I, 2:969.

24. JEJ to Cooper, 14 Oct. 1861, *O.R.*, I, 2:473.

25. Cooper to JEJ, 17 July 1861, *O.R.*, I, 2:478. In his October 14 report on the campaign, Johnston wrote that the telegram ordered him to make the movement "after" sending his sick and wounded to Culpeper. Endorsing the report, Davis noted and objected to the addition of that word. Thirteen years later, Johnston responded to this rather pointless charge by claiming that "I did not profess to quote his own words, but to give their meaning, which was done correctly"—Johnston, *Narrative*, 34n. Davis's motive was almost surely due to the fact that by October, he and Johnston had already had their falling out. Johnston's response is in JEJ to Cooper, 18 July 1861, *O.R.*, I, 2:982. In his *Narrative*, Johnston noted that he did not sleep at all during the three nights preceding July 20—*Narrative*, 41.

Chapter 9

1. Johnston, *Narrative*, 34–5.

2. Ibid., 34.

3. Buck, *With the Old Confeds*, 23.

4. Johnston, *Narrative*, 36; Bradley T. Johnson, "Memoirs of First Maryland Regiment," *SHSP* (1881), 9:351. Johnston's artillery officer, Captain E. P. Alexander, was more impressed than his commanding officer. He called the march by Jackson's men "an excellent march under the circumstances." See Edward P. Alexander, *Military Memoirs of a Confederate* (New York: Charles Scribner's Sons, 1910), 19. Jeffrey Lash credits Beauregard with the foresight that ensured the two trains were waiting at Piedmont. See Lash, "Joseph E. Johnston and the Virginia Railways, 1861–62," *Civil War History* (1989), 35:11.

5. Johnston, *Narrative*, 38; William C. Davis, *Battle at Bull Run: A History of the First Major Campaign of the Civil War* (Garden City, N.Y.: Doubleday & Co., 1977), 138.

6. Johnston, *Narrative*, 37–8.

7. Davis to JEJ, 20 July 1861, *O.R.*, I, 2:985.

8. JEJ to Cooper, 14 Oct. 1861, *O.R.*, I, 2:473; Johnston, *Narrative*, 39.

9. Johnston, *Narrative*, 41.

10. Special Orders No.—, 20 July 1861, *O.R.*, I, 2:479–80; Johnston, "Responsibilities of the First Bull Run," *B&L*, 1:246.

11. Years later, Johnston noted that "want of promptness in the delivery of these orders frustrated this plan—perhaps fortunately." Johnston, *Narrative*, 42.

12. Memorandum of T. L. Preston to R. M. Hughes, 21 July 1891, Robert M. Hughes Collection, box 1, folder 2, W&M (Preston was Johnston's aide-de-camp at Manassas); Johnston, "Responsibilities of the First Bull Run," *B&L*, 1:246.

13. Johnston, *Narrative*, 46; Johnston, "Responsibilities of the First Bull Run," *B&L*, 1:247.

14. JEJ to Cooper, 14 Oct. 1861, *O.R.*, I, 2:475; Johnston, "Responsibilities of the First Bull Run," *B&L*, 1:247–8; Alexander, *Military Memoirs*, 32–4, and *Fighting for the Confederacy: The Personal Recollections of General Edward Porter Alexander*, edited by Gary W. Gallagher (Chapel Hill, N.C.: University of North Carolina Press, 1989), 53; T. L. Preston to R. M. Hughes, 21 July 1891, Robert M. Hughes Collection, box 1, folder 2, W&M.

15. The commander of the Fourth Alabama, Colonel J. B. Jones, was killed on Matthew's Hill; the regiment's lieutenant colonel and major both fell at Young's Branch. See J. A. Chapman, "The 4th Alabama Regiment," *CV* (1922), 30:197; Alexander, *Military Memoirs*, 36; T. L. Preston to R. M. Hughes, 21 July 1891, Robert M. Hughes Collection, box 1, folder 2, W&M.

16. T. L. Preston to R. M. Hughes, 21 July 1891, Robert M. Hughes Collection, box 1, folder 2, W&M.

17. JEJ to Cooper, 14 Oct. 1861, *O.R.*, I, 2:475.

18. Bradley T. Johnston, "Memoir of the First Maryland Regiment," *SHSP* (1881), 9:482; Diary of E. Kirby Smith quoted in " 'Blucher of the Day' at Manassas," *CV* (1899), 7:108.

19. R. H. Kim, *A Soldier's Recollections* (New York, 1911), 34–5; J. M. Howard, *Recollections of a Maryland Confederate Soldier* (Baltimore, 1914), 36–7.

20. Johnston, "Recollections of the First Bull Run," *B&L*, 1:249.

21. Ibid., 248.

22. E. P. Alexander was critical of Johnston's failure to oversee the pursuit personally. See Alexander, *Military Memoirs*, 41–3. Whiting's interference is noted in James Longstreet, *From Manassas to Appomattox: Memoirs of the Civil War in America* (Philadelphia: J. B. Lippincott Co., 1896), 52–3. The confusion over Squires's battery is in the memoir of Charles W. Squires, CWTI Collection, Carlisle.

23. Davis recalled that Johnston was "upon a hill which commanded a general view of the field" when he rode up. See Jefferson Davis, *The Rise and Fall of the Confederate Government* (New York: D. Appleton & Co., 1881), 1:350.

24. Johnston, *Narrative*, 64; Johnston, "Responsibilities of the First Bull Run," *B&L*, 1:245; Alexander, *Military Memoirs*, 49–50. Davis's telegram was dated 21 July 1861; see *O.R.*, I, 2:986.

25. Davis, *Bull Run*, 248; Johnston, "Responsibilities of the First Bull Run," *B&L*, 1:250.

26. Johnston, *Narrative*, 64.

27. Ibid., 54.

28. Johnston, "Responsibilities of the First Bull Run," *B&L*, 1:250, 252; A. C. Cummings to JEJ, 27 Dec. 70, JEJ Collection, box 1, folder 5, W&M; Johnston, *Narrative*, 56, 60–1.

Chapter 10

1. JEJ to Davis, 24 July and 3 Aug. 1861, both in JEJ Papers, Duke.

2. See, for example, JEJ to Davis, 10, 16, and 17 Aug. 1861, all in *O.R.*, I, 5:777, 789–90; Davis's response is Davis to JEJ, 5 Sept. 1861, *O.R.*, I, 5:829–30.

3. See, for example, George Deas to JEJ, 1 July 1861, JEJ Papers, box 1, HL; JEJ to Cooper, 29 July 1861, *O.R.*, I, 2:1007; Dabney Maury to Richard S. Ewell, 28 Aug. 1891, R. S. Ewell Papers, LC; JEJ to Cooper, 24 July 61, in Varina Davis, *Jefferson Davis*, 2:138–9.

4. John Cheves Haskell, *The Haskell Memoirs* edited by Gilbert E. Govan and James E. Livingood (New York: G. P. Putnam's Sons, 1960), 19; "An Act to Provide for the Establishment and Organization of the Army of the C.S.A." 6 March 1861, *O.R.*, I, 1:127–31.

5. Davis later offered several explanations for ranking Johnston fourth, the most prominent of which was that Johnston's brigadier generalcy in the Old Army was a staff appointment. But so was Cooper's. See Davis to James Lyons, 30 Aug. 1878, printed in Varina Davis, *Jefferson Davis*, 2:157–8.

6. Bertram Wyatt-Brown, *Southern Honor: Ethics and Behavior in the Old South* (New York: Oxford University Press, 1982), 45.

7. JEJ to Davis, 12 Sept. 1861, *O.R.*, IV, 1:605.

8. J. E. Johnston, "Responsibilities for the First Bull Run," *B&L*, 1:240. Even Johnston's friends thought he had overreacted and believed his letter was intemperate. See the Stephen Mallory Diary, 16 Sept. 1861, quoted by Joseph T. Durkin, *Confederate Navy Chief: Stephen R. Mallory* (Columbia, S.C.: University of South Carolina Press, 1987), 229n.

9. Davis to JEJ, 14 Sept. 1861, *O.R.*, I, 1:611; Stephen Mallory Dairy, 16 Sept. 1861, quoted in Durkin, *Confederate Navy Chief*, 229n.

10. JEJ to Benjamin, 26 Sept. 1861, *O.R.*, I, 5:881–2.

11. Johnston, *Narrative*, 77; R. G. H. Kean, *Inside the Confederate Government: The Diary of Robert Garlick Hill Kean* (New York: Oxford University Press, 1957), 7.

12. Memorandum by G. W. Smith, dated 1 Oct. 1861, *O.R.*, I, 5:885–6.

13. Ibid. See also Wigfall to Beauregard, 20 March 1864, and Beauregard to Wigfall, 30 March 1864, both in *O.R.*, I, 51(2):839–40, 843.

14. There are three accounts of this meeting—all three written some time after the fact, and all designed to justify a particular interpretation. The most contemporary is the memorandum written by G. W. Smith, which is dated October 1, and is included in the *Official Records* (I, 15:885–6), though it actually written the following January. Smith's purpose seems to have been his (and presumably Johnston's) desire to have a written record of the conversation, so that Davis could not subsequently accuse his generals of having declined to launch an offensive. Nevertheless, in his *The Rise and Fall of the Confederate Government* (1:449–50), Davis did exactly that. In his account of the meeting, Davis insisted that Johnston and Beauregard claimed they would need "twice as many" troops as they currently had, and that they declined to consider smaller forays into Yankee territory. Johnston's own account, included in his *Narrative* (75–76), largely agrees with Smith's.

15. Haskell, *The Haskell Memoirs*, 15–16.

16. Even Benjamin's sympathetic biographers admit that through the Secretary had "keen intelligence" and "tremendous industry," he also possessed an "unmilitary temperament" that brought him into conflict with the officers of the army. Robert D. Meade, *Judah P. Benjamin* (New York: Oxford University Press, 1943), 180; Eli N. Evans, *Judah P. Benjamin: The Jewish Confederate* (New York: The Free Press, 1988), 134–5.

17. Benjamin to JEJ, 13 Oct. 1861, *O.R.*, I, 5:896–7.

18. JEJ to Cooper, 2 Nov. 1861, *O.R.*, I, 5:934.

19. For the weather, see Kean, *Inside the Confederate Government*, 18; JEJ to Beauregard, 2 Nov. 1861, JEJ Papers, Duke.

20. Benjamin to JEJ, 7 Nov. 1861, JEJ to Whiting, 11 Nov. 1861, and JEJ to Benjamin, 13 Nov. 1861; all in *O.R.*, I, 5:941–2, 948–9, 951.

21. Buck, *With the Old Confeds*, 26; Benjamin to JEJ, 17 Nov. 1861, *O.R.*, I, 5:962.

22. Benjamin to JEJ, 7 Oct. 1861, and Davis to G. W. Smith, 10 Oct. 1861, both in *O.R.*, I, 5:892, 893–4.

23. JEJ to Beauregard, 30 Nov. 1861, JEJ Papers, Duke.

24. Benjamin to JEJ, 9 Dec. 1861, *O.R.*, I, 5:987; Johnston, *Narrative*, 84. In fact, McClellan was ill in December with typhoid fever.

25. JEJ to Benjamin, 13 Dec. 1861, and Benjamin to JEJ, 27 Dec. 1861, both in *O.R.*, I, 5:993–4, 1011–2.

26. JEJ to Benjamin, 1, 14, and 16 Jan. 1862, and Benjamin to JEJ, 5 Jan. 1862, both in *O.R.*, I, 5:1015–16, 1020–1, 1028, 1035. D. S. Freeman speculates that "Johnston's conduct on this episode perhaps was construed in Richmond as proof that he would eat humble pie when it was put before him by a stern cook. . . ." Freeman, *Lee's Lieutenants*, 1:120.

27. Benjamin's order is in *O.R.*, I, 5:1016. JEJ to Benjamin, 18 Jan. 1862, Benjamin to JEJ, 25 Jan. 1862, and Benjamin to JEJ, 3 Feb. 1862, all in *O.R.*, I, 5:1036–7, 1045, 1059.

28. JEJ to Benjamin, 1 Feb. 1862, *O.R.*, I, 5:1057–8.

29. JEJ to Davis, 1 March 1862, *O.R.*, I, 5:1086–7.

30. Davis to JEJ, 4 March 1862, *O.R.*, I, 5:1089. Of course, since Benjamin had signed a sheaf of blank furloughs in January, they were still being distributed in February and March. Steven Newton discusses this issue in some detail in his "Joseph E. Johnston and the Defense of Richmond," unpublished Ph.D. dissertation, William & Mary (1989), 59n.

31. Beauregard to Davis, 20 Oct. 1861, and Benjamin to Jackson, 30 Jan. 1862, both in *O.R.*, I, 5:920, 1053.

32. Jackson to Benjamin, 31 Jan. 1862, and JEJ to Jackson, 3 Feb. 1862, both in *O.R.*, I, 5:1053, 1059–60.

33. JEJ to Lydia Johnston, 13 Feb. 1862, McLane-Fisher Family Papers, MS. 2403, box 6, MHS.

34. Harrison A. Trexler, "The Davis Administration and the Richmond Press, 1861–1865," *JSH* (1950); Woodward, ed., *Mary Chesnut's Civil War* (diary entry of 13 Feb. 1862), 289.

35. Henry S. Foote, *War of the Rebellion, or Scylla and Charybdis* (New York: Harper & Bros., 1866), 356.

36. Johnston, *Narrative*, 108.

Chapter 11

1. William H. Russell, *My Diary North and South* (New York: Alfred A. Knopf, 1988), 310.

2. John B. Gordon, *Reminiscences of the Civil War* (New York: Charles Scribner's Sons, 1903), 52.

3. JEJ to G. W. Randolph, 28 April 1862, *O.R.*, I, 11(3), 470–1.

4. Benjamin to Beauregard, 17 Oct. 1861, *O.R.*, I, 5:904; Beauregard's Report on the Battle of Manassas is in *O.R.*, I, 2:484–504. Johnston wrote to Benjamin to complain about the reassignment of "this distinguished officer . . . especially at the present time." But his complaint was largely pro forma. See JEJ to Benjamin, 29 Jan. 1862, *O.R.*, I, 5:1051.

5. Warner, *Confederates in Gray*, 136–7, 192–3.

6. Lash, *Destroyer of the Iron Horse*, 27. Lash blames the delays on Johnston for crowding too much rolling stock on this one line.

7. Johnston, *Narrative*, 108. See also JEJ to Davis, 22 Nov. 61, *O.R.*, I, 51(2):1072–3.

8. In his *Narrative*, Johnston wrote that this meeting took place on the 20th. Steven Newton relies on the diary of Attorney General Thomas Bragg to date it on February 19. See Newton, "Joseph E. Johnston and the Defense of Richmond," 67n. See also Durkin, *Confederate Navy Chief*, 176.

9. Johnston, *Narrative*, 96. Davis does not mention this conference in *Rise and Fall*, but his correspondence indicates his surprise at Johnston's subsequent withdrawal.

10. JEJ to Davis, 23 Feb. and 13 March 1862, both in *O.R.*, I, 5:1079, 527. Johnston's assertion that it was the wife of a cabinet member who leaked the news of the planned withdrawal is in the rough draft of his *Narrative* (p. 18) in the R. M. Hughes Papers, ODU.

11. Davis to JEJ, 28 Feb. 1862, 10 and 15 March 1862, all in *O.R.*, I, 5:1083–5, 1096, 527; Davis, *Rise and Fall*, 1:464. Steven Newton has argued that the figure of 1 million pounds of meat is greatly exaggerated. Of the 2,706,733 pounds at the plant in February, 86.3 percent, he maintains, was evacuated. Another 200,000 pounds was distributed to local farmers, leaving only 169,819 pounds to be burned. See Newton, "Joseph E. Johnston and the Defense of Richmond," 144–5.

12. Cooper to Lee, 13 March 1862, *O.R.*, I, 5:1099.

13. McClellan to Stanton, 11 March 1862, *O.R.*, I, 5:742. Other elements of the rebel force in Virginia left even more precipitately. Joe Hooker reported from Budd's Ferry that "The rebels left everything behind." See Hooker to Williams, 14 March 1862, *O.R.*, I, 5:756.

14. Alexander, *Fighting for the Confederacy*, 73.

15. Lee to T. Holmes, 16 March 1862, *O.R.*, I, 5:1103.

16. Davis, *Rise and Fall*, 1:465; JEJ to Lee, 20 March 1862, and Davis to JEJ, 22 March 1862, in *O.R.*, I, 11(3):392 and 12(3):832. Johnston, *Narrative*, 108. A. P. Mason (Johnston's AAG) prepared the subsequent orders (Special Orders No. 83). In them G. W. Smith was assigned command of the Aquia District; Walker and Wilcox's brigades were detailed to go with Holmes. See *O.R.*, I, 11(3):392.

17. Huger to Lee, 24 March 1862, Charles Collins to J. A. Winston, 24 March 1862, and Magruder to Randolph, 25 March 1862, all in *O.R.*, I, 11(3):394, 395.

18. Lee to JEJ, 25 March 1862, and JEJ to Lee 27 March 1862, both in *O.R.*, I, 11(3):397, 405.

19. Johnston, *Narrative*, 110; both letters to Lee are dated 28 March 1862, and are in *O.R.*, I, 11(3):408, 408–9.

20. Lee to JEJ, 4 April 1862, *O.R.*, I, 11(3):420.

21. Johnston's orders are in *O.R.*, I, 12(3):846. They endowed him with authority to "direct the military and naval operations in these departments." But local commanders were still to make independent reports to Richmond. Johnston's concern about the weakness of the Confederate defenses near Yorktown was the subject of a letter that has not survived. Lee's reply, dated 21 April, simply said that he hoped Johnston would do his best to improve them. Lee to JEJ, 21 April 1862, *O.R.*, I, 11(3):452. See also Johnston, *Narrative*, 11–13.

22. Accounts of the 14 April meeting are in Freeman, *R. E. Lee*, 2:21–2; Johnston, *Narrative*, 112–116; Davis, *Rise and Fall*, 2:70–1. See also Johnston, "Manassas to Seven Pines," *B&L*, 2:203.

23. JEJ to Cooper, 19 May 1862, *O.R.*, I, 11(1):275.

24. John S. Wise, "Joseph E. Johnston," *The Circle* (May 1908), 287.

25. See General Orders No. 1, *O.R.*, I, 11(3):448.

26. The authority is Steven Newton, who counted letters that were alluded to in

other correspondence but never found. Nine of the letters were addressed to Lee and five to Secretary Randolph. See Newton, "Joseph E. Johnston and the Defense of Richmond," 313n.

27. JEJ to Lee, 22 April 1862, *O.R.*, I, 11(3):456.

28. JEJ to Lee, 24, 27, and 29 April 1862, Davis to JEJ, 1 May 1862, all in *O.R.*, I, 11(3): 461, 469; 485. JEJ's telegram to Davis is in JEJ to Lee, 1 May 62, Bragg Papers, WRHS.

29. JEJ to D. H. Hill, 1 May 1862, Lee to JEJ, 2 May 1862, both in *O.R.*, I, 11(3):486, 488, 492; JEJ to J. R. Tucker, 2 May 1862, JEJ Papers, JO 514, HEH Library.

30. Johnston's staff did issue a General Order on 2 May for the evacuation, but it did not specify which units were to use which roads. See *O.R.*, I, 11(3):489–90. See also JEJ to D. H. Hill, 1 May 1862, and Whiting to D. H. Hill, 1 May 1862, both in *O.R.*, I, 11(3):486, 488.

31. Hill to Sorrel, 11 Jan. 1863, *O.R.*, I, 11(1):606.

32. Alexander, *Fighting for the Confederacy*, 49.

33. Stuart to T. G. Rhett (Johnston's AAG), 10 May 1862, *O.R.*, I, 11(1):570; F. Y. Dabney, "General Johnston to the Rescue," *B&L*, 2:276.

34. Alexander, *Fighting for the Confederacy*, 81.

35. Longstreet to Rhett, 16 May 1862, *O.R.*, I, 11(1):565. See also Hill's report, Hill to Sorrel, 11 Jan. 1863, *O.R.*, I, 11(1):604. Johnston's General Order is in *O.R.*, I, 11(1):568–9. Confederate casualties totalled 1,700 against Federal losses of 2,200.

36. Hill to Sorrel, 11 Jan. 1863, *O.R.*, I, 11(1):605.

37. See JEJ to Lee, 7 May 1862, *O.R.*, I, 51(2):552–3, and JEJ to Lee, 8 and 9 May 1862, both in *O.R.*, I, 11(3):499, 503. See also JEJ to Ewell, 17 May 1862, *O.R.*, I, 12(3):896–7.

38. Hood's report of the Battle of Eltham's Landing is in *O.R.*, I, 11(1):630.

39. J.H.L., "Hood 'Feeling the Enemy,' " *B&L*, 2:276. In fact, the Union forces at White House Landing had no intention of being drawn away from the water's edge. General William B. Franklin, their commander, later wrote that "My instructions were to await orders after landing, and not to advance. . . ." *B&L*, 2:222n.

40. Alexander, *Fighting for the Confederacy*, 82.

41. Haskell, *The Haskell Memoirs*, 6.

42. G. W. Smith, "Seven Pines," *B&L*, 2:222; JEJ to Lee, 9 and 10 May 1862, both in *O.R.*, I, 11(3):502–3, 506.

43. Davis to JEJ, 11 May 1862, *O.R.*, I, 11(3):507–8; JEJ to Lydia Johnston, 12 May 1862, McLane-Fisher Family Papers, MS. 2403, box 6, MHS. Davis reiterated his theme of brigade reorganization in another letter written two weeks later. See Davis to JEJ, 26 May 1862, *O.R.*, I, 11(3):546–7.

44. See the organizational table of the army in *O.R.*, I, 11(3):530–3.

45. Davis, *Rise and Fall*, 2:101; Johnston, "Manassas to Seven Pines," *B&L*, 2:206.

46. JEJ to Lydia Johnston, 15 May 1862, McLane-Fisher Family Papers, MS. 2403, box 6, MHS.

47. Taylor (Lee's AAG) to Pemberton, 12 May 1862, and Lee to Henry T. Clark (governor of North Carolina), 13 May 1862, both in *O.R.*, I, 11(3):511, 512.

Chapter 12

1. Johnston, *Narrative*, 130.

2. Johnston, "Manassas to Seven Pines," *B&L*, 2:211; Clifford Dowdey, *The Seven Days: The Emergence of Lee* (Boston: Little, Brown, 1964), 81–3; JEJ to Wigfall, 12 Nov. 1863, Wigfall Family Papers, LC; Johnston, *Narrative*, 130–1.

3. Smith, "Seven Pines," *B&L*, 2:224; Johnston, *Narrative*, 131; JEJ to Wigfall, 12 Nov. 1863, Wigfall Family Papers, LC.

4. Smith, "Seven Pines," *B&L*, 2:224; Johnston, *Narrative*, 131. Clifford Dowdey claims that "no action in the war was planned with such slovenly thinking or prepared so carelessly"—*Seven Days*, 84.

5. JEJ to Wigfall, 12 Nov. 1863, Wigfall Family Papers, LC.

6. JEJ to Cooper, 24 June 1862, *O.R.*, I, 11(1):933.

7. Johnston may also have begun to lose confidence in Smith. He confessed to Senator Wigfall eighteen months later that Smith had "suggested so many difficulties & objected so strongly" to the plan for May 29 "that I thought it certain that his part must fail." JEJ to Wigfall, 12 Nov. 1863, Wigfall Family Papers, LC.

8. Five brigades out of an available thirteen actually fought at Seven Pines; four more fought at Fair Oaks later that afternoon. It is another comment on the lack of coordination that even these nine brigades did not assault the enemy simultaneously.

9. Alexander, *Military Memoirs*, 75.

10. JEJ to Smith, 30 May 1862 (9:15 P.M.), and Hill to Rains and Rodes, 31 May 1862 (4:45 A.M.), both in *O.R.*, I, 11(3):563, 563–4.

11. JEJ to Huger, 30 May 1862, *O.R.*, I, 11(1):938.

12. JEJ to Huger, 31 May 1862, *O.R.*, I, 11(1):938.

13. Johnston, *Narrative*, 133; Keyes to Williams (Union AAG), 13 June 1862, *O.R.*, I, 11(1):873; Drury L. Armistead, "The Battle in Which General Johnston Was Wounded," *SHSP* (1890), 18:185; Alexander, *Military Memoirs*, 75; Smith, "Seven Pines," *B&L*, 2:227.

14. Dowdey, *Seven Pines*, 107–8; G. W. Smith, *The Battle of Seven Pines* (New York: C. G. Crawford, 1891; reprinted Dayton, Ohio: Morningside Bookshop, 1974), 142.

15. A. P. Mason to Whiting, 31 May 1862, *O.R.*, I, 11(3):564.

16. Smith, "Seven Pines," *B&L*, 2:242; Dowdey, *Seven Pines*, 107. Lieutenant Washington's capture warned the Federals that something was afoot. Silas Casey reported that the event led him "to exercise increased vigilance." Casey to C. C. Suydam (Union AAG), June 1862, *O.R.*, I, 11(1):914.

17. Alexander, *Military Memoirs*, 78–9.

18. Ibid., 77; JEJ to Cooper, 24 June 1862, *O.R.*, I, 11(1):933–5.

19. Hill to Rodes, 31 May 1862 (6:30 A.M.), *O.R.*, I, 11(3):564. Longstreet says he ordered Hill forward. Hill merely reports that "the signal guns were fired" at one o'clock. While it would be characteristic of the pugnacious Hill to advance without orders, it would be equally uncharacteristic of the cautious Longstreet to order it. This suggests, therefore, that Hill acted without orders. See D. H. Hill to Longstreet, n.d., and Longstreet to T. G. Rhett (AAG), 10 June 1862, *O.R.*, I, 11(1):939–46.

20. Dowdey, *Seven Pines*, 114.

21. Report of Cadmus Wilcox, 12 June 1862, *O.R.*, I, 11(1):986–9; Dowdey, *Seven Pines*, 100–1.

22. Alexander, *Military Memoirs*, 85. Dowdey claims that the acoustics of the day were such that the musketry could be heard outside the house, but not inside—*Seven Pines*, 114.

23. Dowdey, *Seven Pines*, 112; Johnston, *Narrative*, 136; Freeman, *R. E. Lee*. 2:68–9.

24. Alexander, *Military Memoirs*, 92–3; Davis, *Rise and Fall*, 2:122.

25. Hood's brigade suffered only thirteen casualties in the day's battle.

26. Frobel to G. W. Smith, 1868, quoted in Smith, "Seven Days," *B&L*, 2:245.

27. Smith later reported that "Federal reinforcements . . . were likely to break through . . . and reach Longstreet's flank and rear." Presumably this would happen only if they had more luck than Hood in *finding* Longstreet's flank and rear. Smith, "Seven Pines," *B&L*, 2:247.

28. Armistead, "The Battle in Which . . .," *SHSP* (1890), 18:187.

29. Davis to Mrs. Davis, 2–3 June 1862, in Varina Davis, *Jefferson Davis*, 2:291–2; Armistead, "The Battle in Which . . .," *SHSP* (1890), 18:187–8.

30. Longstreet to Rhett, 10 June 1862, *O.R.*, I, 11(1):939.

31. Smith, "Seven Pines," *B&L*, 2:229; Alexander, *Military Memoirs*, 77. D. S. Freeman assesses the errors by both Huger and Longstreet in detail in *Lee's Lieutenants*, 1:254–60. He concludes, however, that for the original misunderstanding in orders "Johnston in large measure was responsible" (260).

32. JEJ to G. W. Smith, 28 June 1862, in Smith, *The Battle of Seven Pines*, 19–20. Johnston's contemporaries were perplexed by his defense of Longstreet. Hill wrote: "I cannot understand Longstreet's motive in coming over to the Williamsburg road, nor can I understand Johnston's motive in shielding him." Hill to G. W. Smith, 18 May 1885, in Smith, *The Battle of Seven Pines*, 151. Longstreet's biographers suggest that Johnston "could not resist Longstreet's magnificent self-assurance and physical largeness." H. J. Eckenrode and Bryan Conrad, *James Longstreet, Lee's War Horse* (Chapel Hill, N.C.: University of North Carolina Press, 1986), 55.

33. Dowdey, *Seven Pines*, 102; Johnston's letter to "My dear Gustavus" is dated June 28 and is printed in Smith, *The Battle of Seven Pines*, 19–20. The omitted sections of Smith's report are also printed in Smith's volume, 20–22; Johnston, *Narrative*, 133.

34. Huger's endorsement to Longstreet's report, 10 Aug. 1862, Huger to JEJ, 20 Sept. 1862, and Remarks accompanying letter of Randolph to JEJ, 2 Oct. 1862, all in *O.R.*, I, 11(1):942, 935.

35. JEJ to Randolph, 4 Oct. 1862, and Davis to Randolph, 28 Sept. 1862, both in *O.R.*, I, 11(1):938–9.

36. Smith, *The Battle of Seven Pines*, 172.

Chapter 13

1. A plaque is embedded in the sidewalk in front of the house where Johnston was first brought after the battle. Edward A. Pollard, *Lee and His Lieutenants* (New York: E. B. Treat, 1867), 374.

2. Longstreet to JEJ, 10 June 1862, Smith to Rhett (AAG), 23 June 1863, and JEJ to Cooper, 24 June 1863, all in *O.R.*, I, 11(1):939–41, 989–94, 935; JEJ to Smith, 28 June 1862, in Smith, *The Battle of Seven Pines*, 19–20; D. H. Hill to his wife, 10 June 1862, D. H. Hill Papers, Carlisle.

3. Lee to Lydia Johnston, 2 June 1862, quoted in Govan and Livingood, *A Different Valor*, 9; Charlotte Wigfall to Louise Wigfall, 25 June 1862, in Wright, *A Southern Girl in '61*, 80.

4. Russell, *My Diary*, 87.

5. Alvy L. King, *Louis T. Wigfall, Southern Fireeater* (Baton Rouge, La.: Louisiana State University Press, 1970), 4. The ensuing summary of Wigfall's career is drawn from King.

6. P. L. Faust, ed., *The Historical Times Illustrated Encyclopedia of the Civil War* (New York: Harper & Row, 1986), 845.

7. Thomas C. De Leon, *Belles, Beaux, and Brains of the 60s* (New York: G. W. Dillingham, 1907), 402.

8. Wright, *A Southern Girl in '61*, 90.

9. Louise Wigfall to Halsey Wigfall, 14 Nov. 1862, Wright, *A Southern Girl in '61*, 91–2.

10. Lydia to Charlotte Wigfall, 17 May 1863 and 2 Aug. 1863, both in Wigfall Family Papers, LC.

11. JEJ to Wigfall, 5 April 1864, Wigfall Family Papers, LC.

12. Gerry Van der Heuvel, *Crowns of Thorns and Glory, Mary Todd Lincoln and*

Carina Howell Davis: The Two First Ladies of the Civil War (New York: E. P. Dutton, 1988), 161. See also J. C. Haskell to "Ma," 21 Nov. 1862, Rachel Susan Cheves Papers, Duke. Mrs. Burton Harrison wrote that Lydia Johnston "had a little court of her own." Mrs. Burton Harrison, *Recollections Grave and Gay* (New York: Charles Scribner's Sons, 1911), 154.

13. Davies to McKeever, 14 Sept. 1862, Banks to McClellan, 15 Sept. 1862, Pleasanton to Parke, 10 Nov. 1862, all in *O.R.*, I, 19(2):123, 292, 299.

14. It was also in September that JEJ had to respond to Huger's plea for justice. See Huger to JEJ, 20 Sept. 1862, Randolph to JEJ, 2 Oct. 1862, JEJ to Randolph, 4 Oct. 1862, all in *O.R.*, I, 11(1):935–6, 937, 939.

15. Wright, *A Southern Girl in '61*, 90–1; JEJ to Elizabeth Holmes, 7 Nov. 62, George F. Holmes Papers, LC.

16. Thomas L. Connelly, *Army of the Heartland: The Army of Tennessee, 1861–1862* (Baton Rouge, La.: Louisiana State University Press, 1967), 221–42; Archer Jones, *Confederate Strategy from Shiloh to Vicksburg* (Baton Rouge, La.: Louisiana State University Press, 1961), 78–82, 224.

17. Bragg to JEJ, 11 Jan. 1863, *O.R.*, I, 20(2):492–3.

18. Johnston, *Narrative*, 148. See also JEJ to Wigfall, 15 Dec. 1862, Wigfall Family Papers, LC.

19. Johnston, *Narrative*, 149.

20. King, *Louis T. Wigfall*, 160–1.

21. Charlotte Wigfall to Louis Wigfall, and Louise Wigfall to Halsey Wigfall, both 5 Dec. 1862, in Wright, *A Southern Girl in '61*, 98. Johnston's staff included Lieutenant Wade Hampton, Jr. See General Orders No. 1, 4 Dec. 1862, *O.R.*, I, 17(2):782

22. Lydia to Charlotte Wigfall, 12 Dec. 1862, Wigfall Family Papers, LC. See also Varina Davis, *Jefferson Davis*, 2:413.

PART THREE
Chapter 14

1. JEJ to Wigfall, 4 Dec. 1862, in Wright, *A Southern Girl in '61*, 98–9.

2. Thomas L. Connelly, *Autumn of Glory: The Army of Tennessee, 1862–1865* (Baton Route, La.: Louisiana State University Press, 1971), 69–73; Grady McWhiney, *Braxton Bragg and Confederate Defeat* (New York: Columbia University Press, 1969).

3. Samuel Carter III, *The Final Fortress: The Campaign for Vicksburg, 1862–1863* (New York: St. Martin's Press, 1980), 82–3.

4. Richard M. McMurray discusses some of the problems of the western command in *Two Great Rebel Armies: An Essay in Confederate Military History* (Chapel Hill, N.C.: University of North Carolina Press, 1989), 56–69.

5. JEJ to Cooper, 4 Dec. 1862, *O.R.*, I, 17(2):781; JEJ to Cooper, 4 and 6 Dec. 1862, JEJ to Pemberton, 4 Dec. 1862, Pemberton to JEJ, 5 Dec 1862, all in *O.R.*, I, 20(2):436, 437, 440–1. At Johnston's suggestion, Wigfall wrote Seddon a strong letter in support of his views on December 8. See Wright, *A Southern Girl in '61*, 101–2.

6. Holmes to Cooper, 5 Dec. 1862, Davis to Holmes 6 and 11 Dec. 1862, all in *O.R.*, I, 17(2):783, 786, 793. Pemberton saw the handwriting on the wall, writing Johnston: "I have no hope of any assistance from General Holmes." Pemberton to JEJ, 5 Dec. 1862, *O.R.*, I, 17(2):784–5.

7. JEJ to Wigfall, 15 Dec. 1862, Wigfall Family Papers, LC.

8. Ibid. In fact, of course, Sherman would do precisely that at Kennesaw Mountain.

9. Lydia Johnston to Charlotte Wigfall, 12 Dec. 1862, Wigfall Family Papers, LC.

10. JEJ to Wigfall, 15 Dec. 1862, Wigfall Family Papers, LC.

11. Lydia Johnston to Charlotte Wigfall, 25 Dec. 1862 and 1 Jan. 1863, Wigfall Family Papers, LC.

12. JEJ to Bragg, 17 Dec. 1862, *O.R.*, I, 20(2):452.

13. JEJ to M. L. Smith, 19 Dec. 1862, and JEJ to Davis, 22 Dec. 1862, both in *O.R.*, I, 20(2):454, 459–60.

14. JEJ to Davis, 22 Dec. 1862, *O.R.*, I, 17(2):800.

15. Official returns for Confederate forces in Mississippi in January 1863 showed 18,015 in Vicksburg, plus 15,000 at Grenada, 10,000 at Port Hudson, and 3,600 at Jackson and Columbus—a total of 46,600. See *O.R.*, I, 17(2):833. JEJ to Pemberton, and Pemberton to JEJ, both dated 29 Dec. 1862, Pemberton to JEJ, 30 Dec. 1862, all in *O.R.*, I, 17(2):809–11.

16. JEJ to Bragg, 2 Jan. 1863, *O.R.*, I, 20(2):476–7.

17. JEJ to Van Dorn, 2 Jan. 1863, *O.R.*, I, 17(2):822; JEJ to Wigfall, 8 Jan. 1863, in Wright, *A Southern Girl in '61*, 108; JEJ to Davis, 6 Jan. 1863, *O.R.*, I, 20(2):487–8.

18. JEJ to Davis, 6 Jan. and 28 March 1863, *O.R.*, I, 17(2):822, and 23(2):727; JEJ to Wigfall, 8 and 26 Jan. 1863, in Wright, *A Southern Girl in '61*, 106–8; JEJ to Davis, 22 and 31 Dec. 1862, and 6 Jan. 1863, JEJ Collection, box 1, folder 4, W&M.

19. Bragg to JEJ, 11 Jan. 1863, *O.R.*, I, 20(2):492–3.

20. Davis to JEJ, 22 Jan. 1863, *O.R.*, I, 23(2):613–4. See also *O.R.*, I, 20(1):682–4, 699, 701–2.

21. JEJ to Davis, 3 and 12 Feb. 1863, *O.R.*, I, 23(2):624, 632; Bragg's staff comment is quoted in McWhiney, *Braxton Bragg*, 376; JEJ to Wigfall, 14 Feb. 1863, Wigfall Family Papers, LC.

22. Seddon to JEJ, 5 Feb. 1863, and JEJ to Davis, 12 Feb. 1863, both in *O.R.*, I, 23(2):626–7, 633. See also JEJ to Davis, 2 March 63, *O.R.*, I, 52(2):816–17.

23. Wigfall to JEJ, 27 Feb. 1863, JEJ Papers, JO 290, HEH Library.

24. JEJ to Wigfall, 4 March 1863, Wigfall Family Papers, LC; Polk to Davis, 30 March 1863, *O.R.*, I, 23(2):730.

25. Lydia Johnston to Charlotte Wigfall, 16 March 1863, Wigfall Family Papers, LC.

26. Davis to JEJ, 19 Feb. 1863, and Seddon to JEJ, 3 March 1863, both in *O.R.*, I, 23(2):640, 659.

27. JEJ to Wigfall, 27 Dec. 1863, Wigfall Family Papers, LC.

28. JEJ to Wigfall 26 Jan. 1863, in Wright, *A Southern Girl in '61*, 122; JEJ to Wigfall, 14 Feb. and 8 March 1863, Wigfall Family Papers, LC; R. Taylor to JEJ, 24 Jan. 1863, JEJ to J. G. Shorter, 8 Feb. 1863, and JEJ to Bragg, 24 Feb. 1863, all in *O.R.*, I, 15:958–9, 14:971, 23(2):646.

29. Lydia Johnston to Charlotte Wigfall, 16 March 1863, Wigfall Family Papers, LC.

30. JEJ to Wigfall, 8 March 1863, Wigfall Family Papers, LC; Kean, *Inside the Confederate Government* (diary entry of 12 April 1863), 50; Woodward, ed., *Mary Chesnut's Civil War* (diary entry of 2 June 1864), 613; JEJ to Wigfall, 14 Feb. 1863, Wigfall Family Papers, LC.

31. Wigfall to JEJ, 28 Feb. 1863, JEJ Papers, JO 291, HEH Library.

32. Seddon to JEJ, 9 March 1863, JEJ to Seddon, 12 March 1863, JEJ to Seddon, 19 March 1863, all in *O.R.*, I, 23(2):674, 684, 708.

33. Johnston urged Davis to allow the younger Johnston to include Mississippi in his tour to see for himself the unworkability of the command system. See JEJ to Davis, 31 March 63, JEJ Papers, Duke. Also W. P. Johnston to Davis, 15 April 1863, *O.R.*, I, 23(2):761.

34. JEJ to Davis, 10 April 1863, JEJ Papers, Duke. See also Connelly, *Autumn of Glory*, 85–92.

35. Seddon to JEJ, and JEJ to Seddon, both dated 9 May 1863, *O.R.*, I, 23(2):825–6.

Chapter 15

1. JEJ to Seddon, 13 and 16 May 1863, *O.R.*, I, 24(1):215–16.

2. Johnston, *Narrative*, 176; JEJ to Pemberton, 13 May 1863, quoted in several reports, see *O.R.*, I, 24(1):261, 325; Ulysses S. Grant, *Personal Memoirs of U. S. Grant* (New York: J. J. Little & Co., 1885), 1:499ff.

3. Pemberton to Cooper, 2 Aug. 1863, *O.R.*, I, 24(1):269.

4. Pemberton to Gardner, 8 May 1863, *O.R.*, I, 24(1):842.

5. Pemberton to JEJ, 14 May 1863, *O.R.*, I, 24(1):262.

6. Ulysses S. Grant, "The Vicksburg Campaign," *B&L*, 3:505–6.

7. Carter, *Final Fortress*, 192; Grant, *Memoirs*, 1:506.

8. JEJ to Pemberton, 14 May 1863, *O.R.*, I, 24(1):270.

9. JEJ to Pemberton, 15 May 1863, *O.R.*, I, 24(1):263.

10. Grant, "The Vicksburg Campaign," *B&L*, 3:507–8; Pemberton to JEJ, 17 May 1863, *O.R.*, I, 24(1):218.

11. JEJ to Pemberton, 17 May 1863, *O.R.*, I, 24(1):272.

12. Pemberton's report is dated 2 Aug. 1863 and is in *O.R.*, I, 24(1):249–95; Pemberton to JEJ, 18 May 1863, *O.R.*, I, 24(1):273.

13. Grant, "The Vicksburg Campaign," *B&L*, 3:513,

14. The message was dated May 19. It is quoted in JEJ to Cooper, 1 Nov. 1863, *O.R.*, I, 24(1):242.

15. JEJ to Gardner, 19 May 1863, *O.R.*, I, 26(2):9; J. E. Johnston, "Jefferson Davis and the Mississippi Campaign," *B&L*, 3:480; JEJ to Cooper, 25 May 1863, *O.R.*, I, 24(1):219–20.

16. Besides Loring's brigade, Johnston's reinforcements consisted of the brigades of Gist, Ector, McNair, and Maxey; see JEJ to Cooper, 1 Nov 63, *O.R.*, I, 24(1):242. Pemberton to JEJ, 25 May 1863, and Davis to JEJ, 24 May 1863, both in *O.R.*, I, 24(1):278, 193; Grant is quoted by Bruce Catton in *Grant Moves South* (Boston: Little, Brown, 1960), 460.

17. From the Joseph D. Alison diary entry of May 17, quoted in Carter, *Final Fortress*, 207.

18. Carter, *Final Fortress*, 232, 236, 237.

19. JEJ to Pemberton, 29 May 1863, *O.R.*, I, 24(1):279.

20. JEJ to Davis, 27 May, Davis to JEJ, 23, 24, and 28 May, Pemberton to JEJ, 25 May 1863, all in *O.R.*, I, 24(1):192–4, 278.

21. Davis to JEJ, 30 May 1863, and Seddon to JEJ, 8 June 1863, both in *O.R.*, I, 24(1):195, 226.

22. JEJ to Seddon, 12 June 1863, *O.R.*, I, 24(1):226.

23. JEJ to Davis, 16 June 1863, Davis to JEJ, 17 June 1863, JEJ to Davis, 20 June 1863, Davis to JEJ, 30 June 1863, and JEJ to Davis, 5 July 1863, all in *O.R.*, I, 24(1):196–8.

24. Davis to JEJ, 15 July 1863, and Seddon to JEJ, 5 June 1863, both in *O.R.*, I, 24(1):202–7, 224.

25. JEJ to Seddon, 15 June 1863, and Seddon to JEJ, 16 June 1863, both in *O.R.*, I, 24(1):227.

26. JEJ to Mackall, 7 June 63, Mackall Papers, file #2, UNC; Elgee to Taylor, 22 June 1863, *O.R.*, I, 26(2):74–5.

27. JEJ to Lydia Johnston, 25 June 1863, John Warfield Johnston Papers, Duke.

28. JEJ to Pemberton, 3 July 1863, and C. A. Dana to Stanton, 22 June 1863, both in *O.R.*, I, 24(1):281, 105–6. Samuel French, *Two Wars: An Autobiography* (Nashville, Tenn.: Confederate Veteran, 1901), 182.

29. JEJ to Seddon, 7 July 1863, JEJ to Davis, 9 July 1863, both in *O.R.*, I, 24(1):199–200; Richmond *Examiner*, 23 July 1863.

30. Richmond *Examiner*, 23 July 1863.

31. JEJ to Pemberton, 17 May 1863, *O.R.*, I, 24(1):272; JEJ to Davis, 2 Jan. 1863, *O.R.*, I, 17(2):823.

32. Davis to Lee, 31 May 1863, *O.R.*, I, 25(2):841–3; Davis, *Rise and Fall*, 2:404–5; Jeffrey N. Lash, "Joseph E. Johnston's Grenada Blunder," *Civil War History* (1987), 32:114–28, also Lash, *Destroyer of the Iron Horse*, 73–103; Josiah Gorgas, *The Civil War Diary of Josiah Gorgas*, edited by Frank Vandiver (University, Ala.: University of Alabama Press, 1947), 50.

33. See Pemberton's official report, Pemberton to Cooper, 2 Aug. 1863, *O.R.*, I, 24(1):269.

34. John C. Pemberton, *Pemberton, Defender of Vicksburg* (Chapel Hill, N.C.: University of North Carolina Press, 1942), 241.

Chapter 16

1. Gorgas, *Diary*, 55; Kean, *Inside the Confederate Government*, 70; Shelby Foote, *The Civil War, A Narrative* (New York: Random House, 1958–74), 2:642.

2. Special Orders No. 176, 25 July 1863, *O.R.*, I, 23(2):931; Kean, *Inside the Confederate Government* (diary entry of 26 July), 83. Connelly calls Hardee's transfer "one of the most serious misuses of talent in the West"—*Autumn of Glory*, 154.

3. Davis to JEJ, 15 July 1863, *O.R.*, I, 24(1):202–7.

4. JEJ to Wigfall, 12 Aug. 1863, Wigfall Family Papers, LC.

5. Lydia Johnston to Charlotte Wigfall, 2 Aug. 1863, Wigfall Family Papers, LC.

6. JEJ to Davis, 8 Aug. 1863, *O.R.*, I, 24(1):209–13; JEJ to W. W. Mackall, 18 Aug. 63, in Mackall, *A Son's Recollections*, 191.

7. Interestingly, Johnston passes over this period without a single reference in his *Narrative*. Of course this is partly because there were no significant military operations, but perhaps too he chose to pass over this painful period as if it had never happened—*Narrative*, 205–61. For the congressional resolutions, see *Journal of the Congress of the Confederate States of America, 1861–1865* (Washington, D.C.: Government Printing Office, 1905), 6:530, 575; 7:309, 463, 472.

8. Wigfall to JEJ, 8 June 1863, JEJ Papers, JO 293, HEH Library.

9. Pemberton to Cooper, 2 Aug. 1863, *O.R.*, I, 24(1):269.

10. Wigfall to JEJ, 11 Aug. 1863, JEJ Papers, JO 296, HEH Library; Richmond *Sentinal*, 9 July 1863.

11. Wigfall to JEJ, 9 and 11 Aug. 1863, both in JEJ Papers, JO 295, HEH Library. Wigfall's lobbying prompted Seddon to write a pointed letter to Pemberton asking why he had failed to obey Johnston's order to attack on May 13. "Will you explain more fully the motives for your deviation from the direct execution of the instructions . . . ?" Pemberton's reply was lame. He argued that a move on Clinton "would have been hazardous in the extreme" and would have jeopardized "my lines of communication and retreat." The most important argument, however, was that such a move would have made Vicksburg vulnerable, "the retention of which . . . I knew to be the great aim and object of the Government." Seddon to Pemberton, 1 Oct. 1863, and Pemberton to Seddon, 10 Nov. 1863, *O.R.*, I, 24(1):321, and 30(4):322–3.

12. Richmond *Examiner*, 25 July and 8 Aug. 1863; Wigfall to JEJ, 6 Oct. 1863, JEJ Papers, JO 297, HEH Library. See also Harrison A. Trexler, "The Davis Administration and the Richmond Press, 1861–1865," *JSH* (1950), 16:177–95.

13. Richmond *Sentinel*, 27 Aug. 1863.

14. D. W. Yandell to J. M. Johnson, 17 June 63, printed in Dunbar Rowland, ed., *Jefferson Davis, Constitutionalist: His Letters, Papers, and Speeches* (Jackson, Miss.: Mississippi Department of Archives & History, 1923), 4:2–13; JEJ to Davis, 8 Sept. 1863, *O.R.*, I, 30(4):625; JEJ to Davis, 9 Sept. 1863, JEJ Papers, Duke.

15. JEJ to W. W. Mackall, 18 Aug. 63, in Mackall, *A Son's Recollections*, 190;

Toombs to JEJ, 27 Aug. 1863, JEJ Collection, box 1, folder 4, W&M; JEJ to Cooper, 4 Sept. 1863, *O.R.*, I, 26(2):201–2; JEJ to Wigfall, 4 and 15 Sept. 1863, both in Wigfall Family Papers, LC; Wigfall to JEJ, 6 Oct. 1863, JEJ Papers, JO 297, HEH Library.

16. JEJ to Cooper, 1 Nov. 1863, *O.R.*, I, 24(1):248. Significantly, a copy of this letter is in the Wigfall Family Papers, LC. Pemberton saw a copy of the report in early December and rushed for pen and paper to file his own amended report. In it he argued once again that "The battle of Baker's Creek and the entire consequences of my movement resulted from General Johnston's order, and he is in part responsible for them. . . ." Pemberton to Seddon, 14 Dec. 1863, *O.R.*, I, 24(1):325–30.

17. Davis to JEJ, 7 Sept. 1863, *O.R.*, I, 30(4):618–19; JEJ to Wigfall, 15 Sept. 1863, and Wigfall to JEJ, 11 Aug. 1863, both in Wigfall Family Papers, LC; Woodward, ed., *Mary Chesnut's Civil War* (diary entry dated October 1963), 482–3.

18. See, for example, Richard M. McMurry's comparison of Lee's and Johnston's letters to Davis in *Two Great Rebel Armies*, 137–9.

19. Wigfall to JEJ, 15 June 1863 and 18 March 1863, JEJ Papers, JO 294 and JO 300, HEH Library.

20. Connelly, *Autumn of Glory*, 112–34.

21. Cooper to JEJ, 2 and 6 Aug. 1863, *O.R.*, I, 28(2):250, 259; Bragg to JEJ, JEJ to Cooper, and Cooper to JEJ, all dated 22 Aug. 1863, JEJ to Cooper and JEJ to Bragg, both dated 24 Aug. 1863, Bragg to JEJ, and JEJ to Cooper, both dated 6 Sept. 1863, all in *O.R.*, I, 30(4):529, 540–1, 607.

22. JEJ to Bragg, 5 Nov. 1863, *O.R.*, I, 31(3):639. Connelly criticizes Johnston for not sending his entire army to Bragg—see *Autumn of Glory*, 151.

23. Maury to JEJ, 24 Aug. 1863, and Semmes to JEJ, 22 Nov. 1863, both in *O.R.*, I, 26(2):178, 434–5.

24. JEJ to Maury, 22 Sept. 1863, and JEJ to Bragg, 23 Sept. 1863, both in *O.R.*, I, 30(4):687, 696; JEJ to Wigfall, 15 Sept. 1863, Wigfall Family Papers, LC.

25. S. D. Lee to JEJ, 1 Sept. 1863, JEJ to S. D. Lee, 2 Oct. 1863, and JEJ to Bragg, 29 Sept. 1863, all in *O.R.*, I, 30(4):576–8, 724, 713. See also Herman Hattaway, *General Stephen D. Lee* (Jackson, Miss.: University Press of Mississippi, 1976), 99–111.

26. S. D. Lee to B. S. Ewell, 10 Oct. 1863, B. S. Ewell to S. D. Lee, 16 Oct. 1863, and JEJ to Longstreet, 10 Oct. 1863, all in *O.R.*, I, 30(4):740–1, 755, 734.

27. Woodward, ed., *Mary Chesnut's Civil War*, (diary entry of October 1863), 482.

28. Cooper to Bragg, 4 Oct. 1863, *O.R.*, I, 30(4):727; Mackall to JEJ, 13 Oct. 1863, JEJ Papers, JO 238, HEH Library.

29. Connelly, *Autumn of Glory*, 245; Mackall to JEJ, 13 Oct. 1863, JEJ Papers, JO 238, HEH Library.

30. B. S. Ewell to Loring, 21 Oct. 1863, Davis to Polk, 23 Oct. 1863, both in *O.R.*, I, 30(4):574, 582.

31. Lydia Johnston to Charlotte Wigfall, n.d., JEJ to Wigfall, 12 Nov. and 15 Sept. 1863, all in Wigfall Family Papers, LC.

32. Bragg to JEJ, 27 Nov. 1863, *O.R.*, I, 30(1):681.

33. Hardee to Cooper, 30 Nov. 1863, Polk to Davis, 8 Dec. 1863, and Davis to Lee, 5 Dec. 1863, all in *O.R.*, I, 31(3):764–5, 796–7, 785; Mackall to JEJ, 9 Dec. 1863, JEJ Papers, JO 516, HEH Library.

34. Davis to JEJ, 16 Dec. 1863, *O.R.*, I, 31(3):835–6.

35. Wigfall to JEJ, 18 Dec. 1863, JEJ Papers, JO 298, HEH Library; JEJ to Wigfall, 27 Dec. 1863, and Lydia Johnston to Charlotte Wigfall, 18 Dec. 1863, both in Wigfall Family Papers, LC.

Chapter 17

1. Sam R. Watkins, *"Co. Aytch," Maury Grays, First Tennessee Regiment, or A Side Show of the Big Show* (Wilmington, N.C.: Broadfoot Publishing Co., 1987), 131.

2. J. C. Thompson to A. D. Stewart, 8 Dec. 1867, JEJ Collection, box 1, folder 5, p. 3, W&M.

3. Ibid.

4. Taken from Civil War Volunteer questionnaires, quoted in Fred A. Bailey, *Class and Tennessee's Confederate Generation* (Chapel Hill, N.C.: University of North Carolina Press, 1987), 91; Watkins, *"Co. Aytch,"* 132.

5. Nathaniel C. Hughes, Jr., *General William J. Hardee: Old Reliable* (Baton Rouge, La.: Louisiana State University Press, 1965); Warner, *Generals in Gray*, 124–5; Connelly, *Autumn of Glory*, 315.

6. Christopher Losson, *Tennessee's Forgotten Warriors: Frank Cheatham and His Confederate Division* (Knoxville, Tenn.: University of Tennessee Press, 1989); Warner, *Generals in Gray*, 47–8; Connelly, *Autumn of Glory*, 84–5, 251.

7. Irving A. Buck, *Cleburne and His Command* (Jackson, Tenn: McCowat-Mercer, 1959); Warner, *Generals in Gray*, 53–4; Connelly, *Autumn of Glory*, 318.

8. John P. Dyer, *"Fightin' " Joe Wheeler* (University, La.: Louisiana State University Press, 1941); Warner, *Generals in Gray*, 332–3; Connelly, *Autumn of Glory*, 317.

9. JEJ to Wigfall, 9 Jan. 1864, Wigfall Family Papers, LC.

10. Warner, *Generals in Gray*, 203–4.

11. JEJ to Davis, 2 and 15 Jan. 1864, JEJ to Cooper, 16 Jan. 1864, all in *O.R.*, I, 32(2):511, 560, 563–4. See also McMurry, *Two Great Rebel Armies*, 137–9.

12. E. J. Harvie, "Gen. Joseph E. Johnston." *CV* (1910), 18:522; this article is also printed in *SHSP* (1910), 38:340–7. See also Cooper to JEJ, 4 Feb. 1864, *O.R.*, I, 32(2):670.

13. Davis to L. B. Northrop, 24 April 79, Bragg Papers, WRHS.

14. J. C. Thompson to Stewart, 8 Dec 67, JEJ Collection, box 1, folder 5, W&M.

15. Hardee to J. C. Ives (aide-de-camp at Richmond), 24 Dec. 1863, *O.R.*, I, 31(3):860.

16. Davis to JEJ, 23 Dec. 1863, and Seddon to JEJ, 18 Dec. 1863, both in *O.R.*, I, 31(3):856–7, 842–3. For Johnston's reaction to the letters, see his *Narrative*, 269.

17. JEJ to Seddon, 28 Dec. 1863, *O.R.*, I, 31(3):873–4; JEJ to Davis, 2 Jan. 1864, *O.R.*, I, 32(2).510–11.

18. JEJ to Davis, 1 Feb. 1864, *O.R.*, I, 32(2):644–5. See also the report of W. N. Pendleton in *O.R.*, I, 32(3):687.

19. Brown to JEJ, 16 Jan. 1864, and JEJ to Brown, 25 Jan. 1864, both in *O.R.*, I, 32(2):564–5, 612; JEJ to Gorgas, 1 Feb. 1864, *O.R.*, I, 32(2):644; J. E. Johnston, "Opposing Sherman's Advance to Atlanta," *B&L*, 4:260. See also Lash, *Destroyer of the Iron Horse*, 122–3.

20. JEJ to Davis, 15 Jan. 1864, and JEJ to Davis, 1 Feb. 1864, both in *O.R.*, I, 32(2):559–60, 644–5.

21. JEJ to Wigfall, 27 Dec. 1864, Wigfall Family Papers, LC.

22. Brown to JEJ, 16 Jan. 1864, Northrop endorsement to JEJ to Davis, 1 Feb. 1864, and Lawton to JEJ, 21 Jan. 1864, all in *O.R.*, I, 32(2):564–5, 646–7, 591–2.

23. JEJ endorsement dated 10 Feb. 1864, *O.R.*, I, 32(2):661.

24. JEJ to Governor Brown, 25 Jan., and JEJ to Colonel William M. Browne, 8 Feb. 1864, both in *O.R.*, I, 32(2):612, 697–8; JEJ to Beverly Johnston, 15 Feb. 1864, JEJ Collection, box 1, folder 4, W&M.

25. General Order No. 5, dated 8 Jan. 1864, *O.R.*, I, 31(3):530–1; Tom Stokes to Mary Gay, 15 March 1864, in Mary A. H. Gay, *Life in Dixie During the War* (Atlanta, Ga.: Charles P. Byrd, 1897), 78.

26. JEJ to Wigfall, 9 Jan. 1864, Wigfall Family Papers, LC; Watkins, "Co. Aytch," 133.

27. Polk to JEJ, and JEJ to Polk, both dated 3 Feb. 1864, O.R., I, 32(2):662; other pertinent letters are on pp. 729–30. See also JEJ to Davis, 15 Feb. 1864, Samuel Richey Collection, Miami.

28. JEJ to Davis, 16 Feb. 1864, and JEJ to Hardee, 23 Feb. 1864, both in O.R., I, 32(2):751–2, 799; Davis to JEJ, 17 Feb. 1864, O.R., I, 52(2):621.

29. Watkins, "Co. Aytch," 145; JEJ to Davis, 25 and 27 Feb. 1864, and JEJ to Longstreet, 25 Feb. 1864, all in O.R., I, 32(1):476, 803; Johnston, Narrative, 284–5. After the war, the various participants engaged in a quarrel about whether this Federal thrust was a full-scale assault. Johnston's friends declared that it was; his detractors said it was not. Thomas, whose army it was, claimed that his purpose was to force Johnston to recall Hardee. The timing of the movements, however, suggests otherwise. Thomas's purpose was probably exactly what it seemed to Johnston at the time: a reconnaissance in force to determine the location and strength of Johnston's position, and to provide a distraction for Sherman's maneuver in Mississippi.

30. JEJ to Wigfall, 6 March 1864, Wigfall Family Papers, LC.

31. Watkins, "Co. Aytch," 135.

32. Army of Tennessee Official Returns, O.R., I, 32(3):602–3, 720, 768, 866.

33. JEJ to Davis, 2 Jan. 1864, O.R., I, 32(2):511; JEJ to Wigfall, 4 Jan. 1864, in Wright, A Southern Girl in '61, 168–9; JEJ to Wigfall, 9 Jan. 1864 and 3 Feb. 1864, both in Wigfall Family Papers, LC..

34. Cleburne's "Memorial" is printed in O.R., I, 52(2):586–92. See also Davis to Walker, 13 Jan. 1864, and JEJ to Seddon, 2 Feb. 1864, both in O.R., I, 52(2):596, 608–9.

35. General Order No. 20, dated 6 Feb. 1864, O.R., I, 32(2):683; JEJ to Wigfall, 6 March 1864, Wigfall Family Papers, LC. See also Cooper to JEJ, 2 April 1864, and J. S. Preston to JEJ, 6 April 1864, both in JEJ Papers, JO 318 and JO 251, HEH Library.

36. General Orders No. 23, dated 24 Feb. 1864, O.R., I, 32(2):799.

37. Bragg to JEJ, 4 and 7 March 1864, O.R., I, 32(3):584, 592.

38. Bragg to Cooper, 3 Oct. 1863, O.R., I, 30(4):726.

39. Bragg to JEJ, 12 March 1864, O.R., I, 32(3):614–15.

40. JEJ to Bragg, 16, 17, and 18 March 1864, and JEJ to Longstreet, 13 March 1864, all in O.R., I, 32(3):636–7, 649, 653–4, 618.

41. JEJ to Bragg, 18 March 1864, O.R., I, 32(3):653–4 (Davis's postscript is not in the version printed in the O.R., but is on the original letter, which is in the JEJ Papers, Duke); JEJ to Wigfall, 30 April 1864, Wigfall Family Papers, LC.

42. JEJ to Wigfall, 1 April 1864, Wigfall Family Papers, LC.

43. The comments are in Woodward, ed., Mary Chesnut's Civil War (diary entries of 31 Jan. and 8 Feb. 1864), 551, 559. See also Richard M. McMurry, John Bell Hood and the War for Southern Independence (Lexington, Ky.: University Press of Kentucky, 1982), 68–9, 89–92, and Connelly, Autumn of Glory, 321–2.

44. Woodward, ed., Mary Chesnut's Civil War (diary entry of 13 Feb. 64), 565; McMurry, John Bell Hood, 86–8. See also Thomas R. Hay, "The Davis-Hood-Johnston Controversy of 1864," MVHR (June 1924).

45. Hood to Davis, 7 March 1864, and Hood to Seddon, 10 Mar. 1864, both in O.R., I, 32(3):606–7; Hood to Bragg, 3 April 1864, Braxton Bragg Papers, WRHS.

46. Hood to Bragg, 13 April 1864, O.R., I, 32(3):781.

47. JEJ to Bragg, 12 March 1864, O.R., I, 32(3):613–14.

48. JEJ to Beverly Johnston, 19 Feb. 64, JEJ to Wigfall, 11 April 64, both in Wigfall Family Papers, LC; Wigfall to JEJ, 18 March 1864, JEJ Papers, JO 300, HEH Library.

49. Wigfall to JEJ, 19 March 1864, JEJ Papers, JO 301, HEH Library.

50. Pendleton to Cooper, 29 March 1864, and Cole to Maj. Gibbons (Chief Inspec-

tor, Transportation), 11 April 1864, both in *O.R.*, I, 32(3):684–6, 772–4. See also Pendleton to JEJ, 21 March 1864, ibid., 695–6.

51. JEJ to Ewell, 14 April 1864, *O.R.*, I, 32(3):781.

52. Ewell to JEJ, 29 April 1864, *O.R.*, I, 32(3):839–42.

53. Davis to JEJ, 15 Feb. 64, Samuel Richey Collection, Miami; Connelly, *Autumn of Glory*, 308–9.

54. Longstreet to R. E. Lee, and R. E. Lee to Davis, 2 and 3 Feb. 1864, JEJ to Bragg, 25 and 29 March 1864, all in *O.R.*, I, 32(3):653, 667, 674, 684; JEJ to Wigfall, 23 April 1864, Wigfall Family Papers, LC.

55. Mackall to Wheeler, 22 and 29 April 1864, *O.R.*, I, 32(3):810, 838; Thomas L. Deavenport Diary, quoted in McMurry, *John Bell Hood*, 100.

56. Halsey Wigfall to Charlotte Wigfall, 29 April 1864, in Wright, *A Southern Girl in '61*, 175.

Chapter 18

1. Johnston's defender is Russell Weigley, *The American War of War: A History of United States Military Strategy and Policy* (New York: Macmillan, 1973), 123; the critic is Richard M. McMurry, *John Bell Hood*, 94.

2. There is much disagreement about casualty figures, especially for Confederate armies. In 1864, Lee's army simply stopped keeping accurate records. Johnston reported his own losses during May and June at 9,972 killed and wounded, plus another 2,468 missing, captured, or deserted. These figures closely match those of Thomas L. Livermore in *Numbers and Losses in the Civil War in America, 1861–65* (Bloomington, Inc.: Indiana University Press, 1957), 119–20. After the war, Hood, who by then had reason to try to discredit Johnston, claimed that these numbers were too small by half, and insisted that the army suffered 25,000 casualties from all causes during Johnston's tenure. See the excellent discussion of this question in Connelly, *Autumn of Glory*, 388–90. The metaphor of a minuet is borrowed from Shelby Foote.

3. The pundit was Henry P. Brewster, a Texas lawyer holding forth in the drawing room of the Chesnuts. See Woodward, ed., *Mary Chesnut's Civil War* (diary entry of 4 June 1864), 616. Johnston, *Narrative*, 318.

4. Evidence of Davis's commitment to slavery is manifest in Varina Davis, *Jefferson Davis;* Johnston's own views about slavery are in JEJ to T. T. Gantt, 13 June 1876 and 3 Jan. and 2 Feb. 1881, all in JEJ Collection, box 2, folders 2 and 4, W&M. There are no prewar letters from Johnston to suggest these views, but during the war Lydia regularly expressed her opposition, telling Charlotte Wigfall that she would never own a slave. See also Richard M. McMurry, " 'The Enemy at Richmond': Joseph E. Johnston and the Confederate Government," *Civil War History* (March 1981), 27:25.

5. Grant to Sherman, 4 April 1864, *O.R.*, I, 32(3):246.

6. J. E. Johnston, "Opposing Sherman's Advance to Atlanta," *B&L*, 4:262; JEJ to Polk, 4 May 1864, *O.R.*, I, 38(4):660.

7. Connelly, *Autumn of Glory*, 330.

8. Mackall to Wheeler, 5, 6, and 7 May 64, all in *O.R.*, I, 38(4):664; Mackall Journal (A), 6 May 1864. This journal was kept by Lieutenant Thomas Bennett Mackall, a cousin of Johnston's chief of staff. The original journal is in the JEJ Collection, box 5, at the Swem Library at the College of William & Mary. It has an interesting history which has been chronicled by Richard M. McMurry in "The Mackall Journal and Its Antecedents," *Civil War History* (1974), 20:311–28. In referring to this source, I will use McMurry's system: an (A) will refer to the original journal, and (O) to the expanded version, written at a later time and published in the *Official Records*, I, 38(3):978–91. See also Johnston, *Narrative*, 303.

9. JEJ to Bragg, 2 May 1864, and circular from J. W. Ratchford (Hood's AAG), 4

May 1864, both in *O.R.*, I, 38(4):657, 663; Johnston, "Opposing Sherman's Advance to Atlanta," *B&L*, 4:263; Connelly, *Autumn of Glory*, 334–5; McMurry, *John Bell Hood*, 101; Mackall to Cantey, 5 May 1864, *O.R.*, I, 38(4):663. Cantey's men did not reach Resaca until the morning of May 9. See James Cooper Nisbit, *Four Years on the Firing Line* (Jackson, Miss.: McCowat-Mercer Press, 1963), 184.

10. W. P. C. Breckinridge, "The Opening of the Atlanta Campaign," *B&L*, 4:278. Johnston and Mackall also blamed Wheeler. When afterward Cleburne asked Mackall how Snake Creek Gap could have been left unguarded, Mackall answered that "it was the result of a flagrant disobedience of orders, by whom he did not say." Clearly, however, he had Wheeler in mind. Cleburne to Sellers (Hood's AAG), 16 Aug. 1864, *O.R.*, I, 38(3):721.

11. JEJ to Beverly Johnston, 7 May 1863, in Robert M. Hughes, ed., "Some War Letters of General Joseph E. Johnston," *Journal of the Military Service Institution of the United States* (1913), 319; JEJ to Bragg and Cooper to Polk, both dated 4 May 1864, *O.R.*, I, 38(4):659–60, 661. Bragg's displeasure is evident in Polk to Bragg, 22 May 1864, *O.R.*, I, 38(4):735.

12. Watkins, *"Co. Aytch,"* 145; J. Thompson to Stewart, 8 Dec. 1867, JEJ Collection, box 1, W&M; Cantey to Mackall, 8 May 1864, *O.R.*, I, 38(4):678.

13. JEJ to Polk, and Mackall to Cantey, both dated 7 May 1864, *O.R.*, I, 38(4):678, 675; Mackall Journal (A), 7 May 1864. Thomas Connelly concludes that Johnston's response to the threat of a flanking movement by McPherson was "somewhat apathetic," but he also attributes it to "the confused nature of scout reports"—*Autumn of Glory*, 335–6.

14. JEJ to Cooper, 20 Oct. 1864, and Cleburne to Sellers (Hood's AAG), 16 Aug. 1864, both in *O.R.*, I, 38(4):614, 720–1; Johnston, *Narrative*, 306.

15. Hood to Mackall, 8 May 1864 (2:40 P.M.), JEJ Papers, JO 315, HEH Library; C. Thompson to Stewart, 8 Dec. 1867, JEJ Collection, box 1, folder 5, W&M; JEJ to Cleburne and Mackall to Cantey, both dated 8 May 1864, *O.R.*, I, 38(4):679.

16. Cleburne to Sellers (Hood's AAG), 16 Aug. 1864, *O.R.*, I, 38(3):721; Hood to Mackall, 8 May 1864 (5:30 P.M.), JEJ Papers, JO 328, HEH Library; Mackall Journal (A), 8 May 1864.

17. Mackall Journal (A), 8–9 May 1864; Mackall to Wheeler, 9 May 1864 (7:30 A.M.), Mackall to Cleburne, 9 May 1864 (6:30 A.M.), and Mackall to Cantey, 9 May (no time noted), all in *O.R.*, I, 38(4):682, 681, 684.

18. Johnston, "Opposing Sherman's Advance to Atlanta," *B&L*, 4:266.

19. When he heard that McPherson was safely through Snake Creek Gap, Sherman is supposed to have exclaimed: "I've got Joe Johnston dead!" Sherman's criticism of McPherson is in W. T. Sherman, *Memoirs of William Tecumseh Sherman* (New York: D. Appleton & Co., 1875), 2:34.

20. Mackall Journal (A), 10 May 1864; Hood to Mackall, 10 May 1864 (11:45 A.M.), and Johnston's endorsement to same, JEJ to Cooper, 20 Oct. 1864, and Hardee to Wheeler, 10 May 1864, all in *O.R.*, I, 38(4):686, 614, 687. In the *Official Records*, Johnston urged Hood to use his discretion about the placement of the two divisions— Walker's and Cleburne's. But in his *Narrative*, Johnston says he "directed" Hood to leave the two divisions at Tilton, "one on each road"—*Narrative*, 308.

21. Mackall to Polk, 10 May 1864, *O.R.*, I, 38(4):689; Cantey to JEJ, Mackall to Polk, JEJ to Polk, and Mackall to Cleburne, all dated 11 May 1864 between 8:00 and 9:30 A.M.; Mackall to Cheatham, same date (11:30 A.M.), all in *O.R.*, I, 38(4):693–4. Johnston, *Narrative*, 308.

22. McMurry, *John Bell Hood*, 103.

23. JEJ to Polk and Polk to JEJ, both 12 May 1864, *O.R.*, I, 38(4):700–2; McMurry, *John Bell Hood*, 103; Mackall Journal (A), 12 May 1864.

24. J. S. Thrasher to JEJ, 11 May 1864, *O.R.*, I, 38(4):697.

25. Watkins, *"Co. Aytch,"* 148.

26. Johnston, "Opposing Sherman's Advance to Atlanta," *B&L*, 4:265; Mackall's sketch of the army's positions at Resaca is in the JEJ Papers, box 4, HL; Taylor, ed., *Reluctant Rebel*, 165.

27. Diary of Mumford H. Dixon, Perkins Library, Duke; Watkins, *"Co. Aytch,"* 148.

28. Philip Secrist, "Resaca: For Sherman a Moment of Truth," *Atlanta Historical Society Journal* (Spring 1978), 18–19; Watkins, *"Co. Aytch,"* 148.

29. H. D. Clayton to Maj. Hatcher, 29 May 1864, *O.R.*, I, 38(3):832; C. Thompson to Stewart, 8 Dec. 67, JEJ Collection, box 1, folder 5, W&M.

30. Mackall Journal (O), *O.R.*, I, 38(3):978–9.

31. Johnston, "Opposing Sherman's Advance to Atlanta," *B&L*, 4:265; Mackall Journal (O), *O.R.*, I, 38(3):978–80.

32. Mackall Journal (O), *O.R.*, I, 38(3):980–1. In his postwar *Narrative*, Johnston unnecessarily stressed the point that Hood had "exposed and abandoned" these guns. Stung, Hood responded in his own memoir that "they were four old iron pieces not worth the sacrifice of the life of even one man"—Johnston, *Narrative*, 313, 351; John Bell Hood, *Advance and Retreat: Personal Experiences in the Unites States & Confederate Armies* (Bloomington, Ind.: Indiana University Press, 1959), 96. For more about this disagreement, see chapter 23.

33. Walker to Mackall, 15 May 1864, *O.R.*, I, 38(4):714; Mackall Journal (O), *O.R.*, I, 38(3):981. Johnston attributed the delay in cancelling Stewart's orders to tardiness in Hood's headquarters. See Johnston, "Opposing Sherman's Advance to Atlanta," *B&L*, 4:266.

34. Mackall Journal (O), *O.R.*, I, 38(3):981; Nisbit, *Four Years on the Firing Line*, 187.

35. As always, Confederate losses are difficult to determine. These numbers are estimates from Richard M. McMurry, "Resaca: A Heap of Hard Fitin,'" *CWTI* (November 1970), 9:48. Sherman listed his own losses at 600 killed and 3,375 wounded. If both assessments are accurate, Sherman's losses were only slightly greater than Johnston's. Sherman, *Memoirs*, 2:36.

36. Davis to JEJ and JEJ to Davis, 15 May 1864, *O.R.*, I, 38(4):705, 712. Also Davis to Lee, 15 and 20 May 1864, *O.R.*, I, 51(2):933, 952.

Chapter 19

1. Polk to JEJ, 17 May 1864, JEJ to Davis, 16 May 1864, W. W. Porter to Wheeler, 16 May 1864, and Martin to Mackall, 16 May 1864, all in *O.R.*, I, 38(4):721, 716, 717.

2. Mackall Journal (O), *O.R.*, I, 38(3):982.

3. Polk to JEJ, 17 May 1864 (10:45 A.M.), *O.R.*, I, 38(4):721; Dixon Diary, 13 May 1864, Duke; Losson, *Tennessee's Forgotten Warriors*, 146–7.

4. Johnston, *Narrative*, 320. In the published (O) version of the Mackall Journal is the line: "[Hood] has been anxious to get from this place south of the Etowah" (*O.R.*, I, 38[3]:982). But the line does not appear in the original (A) version, and was added later after Johnston and Hood had engaged in their Battle of the Books (see chapter 23).

5. Mackall Journal (O), *O.R.*, I, 38(3):982.

6. Lydia Johnston to Polk, 16 May 1864, and Polk to Mrs. Polk, 21 May 1864, both quoted in Joseph H. Parks, *General Leonidas Polk, CSA, The Fighting Bishop* (Baton Rouge, La.: Louisiana State University Press, 1962), 377–8; Mackall to his wife, 18 May 1864, Mackall Papers, file #3, UNC.

7. Diary entry of 22 July 1864, quoted in Arnold Gates, ed., *The Rough Side of War: The Civil War Journal of Chesley Mosman* (Garden City, N.Y.: The Basin Publishing Co., 1987), 246.

8. Mackall Journal (A), 18 May 1864; Wheeler to JEJ, 18 May 1864 (11:50 A.M.), *O.R.*, I, 38(4):726.

9. Mackall Journal (O), *O.R.*, I, 38(3):983. The estimate of 45,000 casualties was only slightly exaggerated. Federal losses in the Virginia campaign through May 16 totalled 36,872, though that included nearly 11,000 missing. On the other hand, Confederate casualties in the East were also high.

10. Johnston, *Narrative*, 321.

11. General Order dated 19 May 1864, *O.R.*, I, 38(4):728.

12. The quotation and Johnston's request for a map are from the Mackall Journal (O) version, but neither contradicts the more sparce (A) version, which is the source for the sequence of events at headquarters. See *O.R.*, I, 38(3):983.

13. Memorandum of W. W. Mackall, dated 19 May 1864, *O.R.*, I, 38(3):622; Mackall Journal (A), 10 May 1864. Hood's version of the events is in Hood to Cooper, 15 Feb. 1865, *O.R.*, I, 38(3):635.

14. JEJ to Davis, 20 May 1864, *O.R.*, I, 38(4):728; Johnston, *Narrative*, 321; Richard M. McMurry, "Cassville," *CWTI* (December 1971), 8.

15. At the time, Johnston swallowed his disappointment; he and Hood continued to work well together on cordial terms. But years later, after the war, when he discovered that Hood had been writing secretly to Davis contrasting his own aggressiveness with Johnston's caution, he looked back on Hood's actions at Cassville as a deliberate attempt to undercut the campaign—see chapter 23. Connelly argues that "Both Hood and Johnston share the blame"—*Autumn of Glory*, 347–8.

16. Johnston, *Narrative*, 322; Thompson to Stewart, 8 Dec. 1867, JEJ Collection, box 1, folder 5, W&M.

17. McMurry, *John Bell Hood*, 108–9; McMurry, "Cassville," *CWTI*, 45.

18. Mackall Journal (O), *O.R.*, I, 38(3):984. In his memoirs, Hood claimed that what he really wanted was for the army to go over to the offensive, and that at this meeting he urged Johnston to attack; but no contemporary evidence supports his claim. French, who was present, wrote that "whilst I was there, [Hood] made no reference to being in a good position for acting on the aggressive and making an attack"—French, *Two Wars*, 198. Thomas Connelly has done a very thorough job of piecing together the evidence on this discussion. See *Autumn of Glory*, 350–1.

19. Mackall Journal (A), 20 May 1864; JEJ to Lydia Johnston, 21 May 1864, McLane-Fisher Family Papers, MS. 2403, box 6, MHS.

20. JEJ to Wheeler, 20 May 1864, *O.R.*, I, 38(4):729; Mackall Journal (A), 20 May 1864.

21. Mackall Journal (A), 21 May 1864; JEJ to Davis, 20 and 21 May 1864, *O.R.*, I, 38(4):728, 736.

22. Hood to Davis, 21 May 1864, quoted in Ellsworth Eliot, Jr., *West Point in the Confederacy* (New York: G. A. Baker & Co., 1941), 100–1; Brewster's criticism of Johnston was recorded by Mary Chesnut; see Woodward, ed., *Mary Chesnut's Civil War* (diary entries of 4 June, 25 July, and 14 Aug. 1864), 616, 624, 635.

23. JEJ to Lydia Johnston, 23 May 1864, McLane-Fisher Family Papers, MS. 2403, box 6, MHS; Mackall to corps commanders, 22 May 1864 (3:30 P.M.), *O.R.*, I, 38(4):735.

24. Mackall Journal (A), 24 May 1864; JEJ to Davis, 25 May 1864, *O.R.*, I, 38(4):742.

25. Thompson to Stewart, 8 Dec. 1867, JEJ Collection, box 1, folder 5, W&M; Hampton's Journal, 23 May 1864, *O.R.*, I, 38(3):704; H. D. Clayton to Maj. Hatcher, 29 May 1864, *O.R.*, I, 38(3):833.

26. Thompson to Stewart, 8 Dec. 1867, JEJ Collection, box 1, folder 5, W&M; Dixon Diary, 27 May 1864, Duke; H. D. Clayton to Maj. Hatcher, 29 May 1864, *O.R.*, I, 38(3):833; B. L. Ridley, "The Battle of New Hope Church," *CV* (1897), 5:459–60. Cleburne's losses were between five hundred and eight hundred.

27. Mackall Journal (A), 25 May 1864.

28. Ibid., 27 May 1864; McMurry, *John Bell Hood*, 111; Hampton's Journal, *O.R.*, I, 38(3):706.

29. Johnston, *Narrative*, 333; Hood, *Advance and Retreat*, 118–21.

30. Thomas Mackall wrote in his journal that night that the attack failed "on acct of their [the Federal's] line being drawn back too far"—Journal (A), 28 May 1864.

31. Ibid., 2 June 1864.

32. Lovell to JEJ, 31 May 1864, *O.R.*, I, 38(4):749; W. W. Mackall to his family, 29 May 1864, in Mackall, *A Son's Recollections*, 212.

33. JEJ to Bragg, 1 June 1864, *O.R.*, I, 38(4):752–3; Mackall Journal (A), 3 June 1864.

34. Mackall Journal (A), 4 June 1864.

Chapter 20

1. Samuel French, *Two Wars* (diary entry of 4 June 1864), 201; J. N. Wyatt to J. B. Cunningham, 10 Aug. 1864, *CV* (1897), 5:520; Benjamin Rountree, "Letters from a Confederate Soldier," *The Georgia Review* (1964), 18:287.

2. Mackall Journal (A), 5 June 1864; Dixon Diary, 17 June 1864, Duke.

3. JEJ to Bragg, 5 June 1864, Bragg to Davis, 4 June 1864, and Bragg to JEJ, 7 June 1864, all in *O.R.*, I, 38(4):759, 762.

4. JEJ to Governor Brown, 4 June 1864, and Mackall to G. W. Smith, 12 June 1864, both in *O.R.*, I, 38(4):758, 770–1.

5. Thompson to Stewart, 8 Dec. 1867, JEJ Collection, box 1, folder 5, W&M.

6. Wheeler's letters to Bragg are dated 5 June and 1 July 1864, Bragg Papers, WRHS; W. H. Jackson to JEJ, 14 June 1864, and JEJ to S. D. Lee, 11 June 1864, both in *O.R.*, I, 38(4):775–6, 769. Johnston wrote Lee an identical request on 14 June. See also Mackall Journal (A), 10 June 1864.

7. JEJ to Bragg, 13 June 1864 (7:00 P.M.) and Polk and Hardee to Davis, 13 June 1864, both in *O.R.*, I, 38(4):773, 774.

8. Wheeler to Bragg, 5 June 1863, Bragg Papers, WRHS; Davis to R. E. Lee, 9 June 1864, *O.R.*, I, 51(2):996.

9. JEJ to Polk and Polk to JEJ, both dated 13 June 1864, *O.R.*, I, 38(4):772–3.

10. Mackall to Polk, et al., 12 June 1864, and Mackall to JEJ, 13 June 1864 (8:00 P.M.), both in *O.R.*, I, 38(4):770, 773; Mackall Journal (A), 13 and 14 June 1864.

11. JEJ to Bishop Quintard, 9 Oct. 1885, Quintard Papers, Sewanee; Steven Davis, "The Death of Bishop Polk," *Blue and Gray Magazine* (June 1989), 6:11. According to some sources, it was not the crowd of staff officers that attracted Federal attention, but the sun glinting off Johnston's field glasses. "How saucy they are," Sherman is supposed to have remarked. "Make 'em take cover." In his *Memoirs*, Sherman wrote that he spotted the group of men on the crest and ordered General Howard to compel them to take cover, but that "at that distance we could not even tell that the group were officers. . . ." (53–4).

12. JEJ to Davis, 14 June 1864, and General Order No. 2, 14 June 1864, both in *O.R.*, I, 38(4):775.

13. French, *Two Wars* (diary entry of 14 July 1864), 202. The rebel note is quoted in Dennis Kelley, "Mountains to Pass, A River to Cross: The Battle of Kennesaw Mountain," *Blue and Gray Magazine* (June 1989), 6:12.

14. Dixon Diary, 17 June 1864, Duke.

15. JEJ to Bragg, 16 and 19 June 1864, *O.R.*, I, 38(4):777, 780.

16. Mackall Journal (A), 19 June 1864; Dixon Diary, 19 June 1864, Duke.

17. JEJ to Wheeler, 21 June 1864 (8:00 A.M.) and JEJ to Bragg, 21 June 1864, both in *O.R.*, I, 38(4):783, 784.

18. Richard McMurry, "The Affair at Kolb's Farm," *CWTI* (December 1968), 22.

19. Mackall Journal (A), 22 June 1864; JEJ to Bragg, 24 June 1864, *O.R.*, I, 38(4):788. See also Richard McMurry, *John Bell Hood*, 112–13.

20. Some sources date Wigfall's visit from June 28, but the Mackall Journal indicates that he arrived on the 24th.

21. Hardee to his wife, 20 June 1864, quoted in Connelly, *Autumn of Glory*, 366.

22. Mackall Journal (A), 24 June 1864; Wigfall to JEJ, undated, Wigfall Family Papers, LC.

23. JEJ to Bragg, 26 June 1864, *O.R.*, I, 38(4):792.

24. JEJ to Bragg, 27 June 1864, *O.R.*, I, 38(4):796. The difference between what he claimed to be his strategy in Dalton and what he advocated near Atlanta has led Johnston's critics to conclude either that he had no plan at all, or that he was deliberately misleading the government. A much simpler explanation is that he simply changed his mind as a result of his experiences during the campaign. Alas, it was difficult for Johnston to admit that he had made a mistake in the first place, so he tried to suggest that his strategy was consistent when it was not. See chapter 23.

25. Connelly, *Autumn of Glory*, 384; Bragg to JEJ, 27 June 1864, *O.R.*, I, 38(4):796. The army returns are in *O.R.*, I, 38(3):677.

26. Bragg did send Johnston one small regiment from Savannah, but the tone of all his correspondence suggests that he believed Johnston should rely on his own cavalry to do the job. Johnston made some efforts to send patrols from his own cavalry. See, for example, JEJ to Wheeler, 26 June 1864, *O.R.*, I, 38(4):792. Thomas Connelly discusses this issue at length in *Autumn of Glory*, 373–88.

27. Watkins, *"Co. Aytch,"* 156.

28. French, *Two Wars* (diary entry of 27 June 1864), 206.

29. Ibid., 211.

30. Watkins, *"Co. Aytch,"* 159.

31. French, *Two Wars*, 209; Mackall Journal (A), 27 June 1864. Johnston later charged that such modest estimates of Federal losses did a disservice to the bravery of the Union soldiers who made the charge. See Johnston, *Narrative*, 344.

32. JEJ to Bragg, 27 June 64, and Bragg to Davis, 29 June 1864, both in *O.R.*, I, 38(4):796, 805; Gorgas diary entry of 30 June 1864, *Diary*, 122.

33. For the best account of this meeting, see Hill to Seddon, 14 July 1864, *O.R.*, I, 52(2):704–7.

34. None of the principals kept a minute of the discussion, but after Hill reported to Davis in Richmond, Seddon sent Hill a letter of his recollections and asked him to confirm it. The notes taken by Seddon indicate that Johnston pledged to keep Sherman north of the river for "at least a month." Fourteen years later, Seddon claimed that Johnston had suggested he could hold them for nearer two months. See Seddon to Hill, 13 July 1864, *O.R.*, I, 52(2):695.

35. Hill to Seddon, 14 July 1864, *O.R.*, I, 52(2):706.

36. Davis to JEJ, 11 July 1864, and Hill to JEJ, 14 July 1864, both in *O.R.*, I, 38(5):875–6, 879. See also Connelly, *Autumn of Glory*, 407–10.

37. French, *Two Wars* (diary entry of 2 July 1864), 215; Mackall Journal (A), 2–3 July 1864.

38. Dixon Diary, 3 July 1864, Duke; French, *Two Wars* (diary entry of 3 July 1864), 215.

39. Thompson to Stewart, 8 Dec. 1867, JEJ Collection, box 1, folder 5, W&M; F. A. Shoup, "Dalton Campaign," *CV* (1895), 3:262–5.

40. Shoup, "Dalton Campaign," *CV* (1895), 3:262–5. French insisted that "The works of Gen. Shoup, with its stockades, did not give Johnston spare troops enough to prevent this movement of the enemy." See French, *Two Wars* (diary entry of 10 July 1864), 216. T. B. Roy (AAG) Confidential Memoranda, 9 July 1864, *O.R.*, I, 38(5):872–3; Mackall Journal (A), 10 July 1864.

41. Davis to JEJ, 7 July 1864, JEJ to Davis, 8 July 1864, and Davis to JEJ, 11 July 1864, all in *O.R.*, I, 38(5):867, 868–9, 875.

42. Woodward, ed., *Mary Chesnut's Civil War* (diary entries of 8 and 27 May 1864), 607, 609.

Chapter 21

1. Cooper to JEJ, 17 July 1864, *O.R.*, I, 38(5):885. The original is in JEJ Papers, HEH Library.

2. Quoted in Hudson Strode, *Jefferson Davis*, 3:73. See also Connelly, *Autumn of Glory*, 406, and McMurry, *John Bell Hood*, 122–3.

3. JEJ to Bragg, 11 July 1864, and Davis to JEJ, 12 July 1864, both in *O.R.*, I, 38(5):876, 877; Davis to Lee, 12 July 1864, *O.R.*, I, 52(2):692. Lee to Davis, 12 July 1864, in D. S. Freeman, ed., *Lee's Dispatches* (New York: G.P. Putnam's Sons, 1957), 282–4. Some historians have concluded that Lee temporized and gave Davis little guidance. But Lee seldom said no when he knew the president wanted him to say yes. For him, this was a very negative response. In editing *Lee's Dispatches*, Freeman noted that "the whole tone of the letter seems . . . to caution President Davis against a hasty change." See also Gorgas, *Diary*, 125.

4. Bragg to Davis, 13 July (both wires) 1864, *O.R.*, I, 38(5):878.

5. Mackall Journal (A), 13 July 1864; Bragg to Davis, 15 July 1864, *O.R.*, I, 38(5):881; JEJ to Wigfall 27 Aug. 1864, Wigfall Family Papers, LC.

6. Mackall to his wife, 13 July 1864, Mackall Papers, file #3, UNC.

7. Mackall Journal (A), 14 July 1864; Johnston, *Narrative*, 364.

8. Hood to Bragg, 14 July 1864, *O.R.*, I, 38(5):879–80.

9. McMurry, *John Bell Hood*, 118; Connelly, *Autumn of Glory*, 417.

10. Bragg to Davis, 15 July 1864, *O.R.*, I, 38(5):881.

11. Bragg to Davis, 15 July 1864, *O.R.*, I, 39(2):712–14. This letter probably did not reach Richmond in time to influence the cabinet discussion on July 17. It was hand-carried by Colonel H. W. Walter from Atlanta to Richmond. But the letter suggests the kind of advice that Bragg had offered Davis throughout the crisis, and is a representative protrayal of his views. See Connelly, *Autumn of Glory*, 420, 420n.

12. Davis to JEJ, 16 July 1864, and JEJ to Davis, same date, both in *O.R.*, I, 38(5):882–3; Hood, *Advance and Retreat*, 142.

13. The Richmond *Whig*, 22 July 1864, quoted in Connelly, *Autumn of Glory*, 405; Govan and Livingood, *A Different Valor*, 312–13.

14. JEJ to Wigfall, 27 Aug. and 28 June 1864, both in Wigfall Family Papers, LC; JEJ to Beverly Johnston, 28 Aug. 1864, R. M. Hughes, "Some War Letters," 321; Johnston, *Narrative*, 363; Louise Wigfall to Charlotte Wigfall, 11 July 1864, in Wright, *A Southern Girl in '61*, 178–9.

15. Johnston, *Narrative*, 363.

16. Hood to JEJ, 18 July 1864 (1:00 A.M.), Hood to Cooper, and Davis to Hood, both dated 18 July 1864, all in *O.R.*, I, 38(5):888–9.

17. General Order No. 4, 17 July 1864, and JEJ to Cooper, 18 July 1864, *O.R.*, I, 38(5):888.

18. Hood, *Advance and Retreat*, 162–3; Halsey Wigfall to Louis Wigfall, 31 July 1864, *A Southern Girl in '61*, 181–5. Cobb's remarks are quoted in Govan and Livingood, *A Different Valor*, 323.

19. Thompson to Stewart, 8 Dec. 1867, JEJ Collection, box 1, folder 5, W&M.

20. Watkins, *"Co. Aytch,"* 169.

21. Dixon Diary, 17 July 1864, Duke; J. N. Wyatt to J. B. Cunningham, 10 Aug. 1864, *CV* (1897), 5:521; Rountree, "Letters from a Confederate Soldier," 290.

22. Mackall Journal (A), 19 July 1864; Wright, *A Southern Girl in '61*, 185–6.

23. A. D. Banks to JEJ, 21 Aug. 1864, JEJ Papers, JO 5, HEH Library; JEJ to Wigfall, 27 Aug. 1864, Wigfall Family Papers, LC; JEJ to Dabney Maury, 1 Sept. 1864, printed in Michael Perman, ed., *Major Problems in the Civil War and Reconstruction* (Lexington, Mass: D. C. Heath & Co., 1991), 165.

24. Mackall Journal (A), 24 July 1864. Bragg reported to Davis that Mackall was dismissed because of his inefficient administration. See Bragg to Davis, 27 July 1864, *O.R.*, I, 52(2):712–14.

25. JEJ to Beverly Johnston, 28 Aug. and 8 Nov. 1864, both in Hughes, "Some War Letters," 321, 326; JEJ to Wigfall, 27 Aug. 1864, Wigfall Family Papers, LC; Wright, *A Southern Girl in '61*, 187.

26. Woodward, ed., *Mary Chesnut's Civil War* (diary entries of 27 Sept. and 25 Nov. 1864), 647, 673.

27. JEJ to Beverly Johnston, 28 Aug. 1864, in Hughes, "Some War Letters," 322; JEJ to Mansfield Lovell, 3 Oct. 1864, Mansfield Lovell Papers, LC; Rowland, *Jefferson Davis*, 4:341; Strode, *Jefferson Davis*, 3:93–5.

28. JEJ to Mansfield Lovell, 3 Oct. 1864, Mansfield Lovell Papers, LC. Johnston expressed the same view to his brother Beverly three days later: "If Sherman understands that either Charleston, Savannah, Pensacola, or Mobile is as good a point for him as Chattanooga, he will not regard Hood's move." JEJ to Beverly Johnston, 6 Oct. 1864, in Hughes, "Some War Letters," 324.

29. Wright, *A Southern Girl in '61*, 193–5.

30. Ibid., 194–200.

Chapter 22

1. JEJ to Kirby Smith, 30 Jan. 1865, Kirby Smith Papers, file #46, UNC; Mackall to JEJ, 16 Feb. 1865, JEJ Collection, box 1, folder 4, W&M; Woodward, ed., *Mary Chesnut's Civil War* (January entries), 704, 708.

2. Josiah Gorgas, *Diary*, 168; Mackall to JEJ, 16 Feb. 1865, JEJ Collection, box 1, folder 4, W&M. See also Michael Ballard, *A Long Shadow: Jefferson Davis and the Final Days of the Confederacy* (Jackson Miss.: University Press of Mississippi, 1986), 16.

3. Woodward, ed., *Mary Chesnut's Civil War* (diary entry of 27 Dec. 1864), 698.

4. Johnston's report is JEJ to Cooper, 20 Oct. 1864, *O.R.*, I, 38(3):612–21; Davis's endorsement is on p. 621. See also JEJ to Cooper, 21 Dec. 1864, in Johnston, *Narrative*, 464–5.

5. Lydia Johnston to Charlotte Wigfall, n.d., Lydia Johnston to Louise Wigfall, 19 Feb. 1865, both in Wigfall Family Papers, LC. Lydia's metaphor was a favorite of hers. See, for example, Lydia Johnston to Charlotte Wigfall, 2 Aug. 1863, ibid. Part of the letter to Louise is printed in Wright, *A Southern Girl in '61*, 228–9.

6. *Journal of the Confederate Congress* (Washington, D.C.: Government Printing Office, 1905), 4:453–4, 7:463; JEJ to Mackall, 26 Jan. 1865, Mackall Papers, file #4, UNC.

7. R. H. Walker, et al., to R. E. Lee, 4 Feb. 1865, in Wright, *A Southern Girl in '61*, 235–7. Davis's memo is dated 18 Feb. 1865 and is in *O.R.*, I, 47(2):1304–11.

8. The orders, Special Orders No. 3, are dated 22 Feb. 1865 and are in *O.R.*, I, 47(2):1248. Johnston devoted the last chapter of his *Narrative* to a line-by-line refutation of "The Unsent Memo." See chapter 23.

9. Special Orders No. 3, 22 Feb. 1865, and Lee to JEJ, same date, both in *O.R.*, I, 47(2):1248, 1247. Woodward, ed., *Mary Chesnut's Civil War* (diary entry of 23 Feb. 1865), 725, 729.

10. Wigfall to JEJ, 27 Feb. 1865, and 3 March 1865, JEJ Papers, JO 304 and JO 305, HEH Library.

11. Mrs. Benjamin Huger, who had reason to dislike Johnston after the way he had treated her husband following the Battle of Seven Pines, told Mary Chesnut: "Whenever General Lee could be found fault with, Johnston's joy was so exuberant he could not hide it." Woodward, ed., *Mary Chesnut's Civil War* (entry of 1 May 1865), 799.

12. JEJ to Wigfall, 14 March 1865, Wright, *A Southern Girl in '61*, 240.

13. JEJ to Lee, 22 and 25 Feb. 1865, and Lee to JEJ, 23 Feb. 1865, all in *O.R.*, I, 47(2):1247, 1271, 1256–7.

14. General Orders No. 1, 25 Feb. 1865, and Army Report dated 17 March 1865, both in *O.R.*, I, 47(2):1274, 1408; Wade Hampton, "The Battle of Bentonville," *B&L*, 4:701.

15. Lee to JEJ, 4 March 1865, and Bragg to Davis, 5 March 1865, both in *O.R.*, I, 47(2):1320, 1326.

16. One critic is Thomas Connelly in *Autumn of Glory*, 524.

17. JEJ to Hill, 7 March 1865, *O.R.*, I, 47(2):1338; Hill to JEJ, 15 March 1865, JEJ Collection, box 1, folder 4, W&M.

18. JEJ to Breckinridge, two letters dated 28 Feb. 1865, in *O.R.*, I, 47(2):1290; Lee to JEJ, 5 March 1865 (two letters), JEJ Papers, JO 381 and JO 382, HEH Library; Breckinridge to JEJ, 1 March 1865, *O.R.*, I, 47(2):1296–7. See also Johnston, *Narrative*, 375–6.

19. JEJ to Lee, 1 March 1865 (this letter appears twice in the *O.R.*, once in I, 47[1]:1051, and once in I, 47[2]:1297–8); Lee to JEJ, 11 March 1865, *O.R.*, I, 47(2):1372.

20. Sherman, *Memoirs*, 299; Thomas Osborn, *The Fiery Trail: A Union Officer's Account of Sherman's Last Campaigns*, edited by R. Harwell and P. N. Racine (Knoxville, Tenn.: University of Tennessee Press, 1986), 197.

21. Johnston, *Narrative*, 378; JEJ to Hardee, 6 and 7 March 1865, *O.R.*, I, 47(2):1333, 1337; JEJ to Lee, 8 and 12 March 1865, and Lee to JEJ, 11 March 1865, all in *O.R.*, I, 47(2):1347, 1372, 1380.

22. See Bragg to JEJ, 8 March 1865, *O.R.*, I, 47(1):1078.

23. JEJ to Lee 11 March 1865 and JEJ to Bragg, 11 and 13 March 1865, all in *O.R.*, I, 47(2):1372–3, 1375, 1388.

24. JEJ to Lee, 17 March 1865, *O.R.*, I, 47(2):1406; Johnston, *Narrative*, 384.

25. Slocum to Dayton (AAG), 30 March 1865, *O.R.*, I, 47(1):423.

26. J. C. Davis to Dechert (AAG), 28 March 1865, *O.R.*, I, 47(1):434–5. See John G. Barrett, *The Civil War in North Carolina* (Chapel Hill, N.C.: University of North Carolina Press, 1963), 333.

27. Johnston's official report on the battle is JEJ to Lee, 27 March 1865, *O.R.*, I, 47(1):1055–7; D. H. Hill to his wife, 23 March 1865, D. H. Hill Papers, Carlisle.

28. Osborn, *The Fiery Trail*, 200.

29. JEJ to Lee, 23 March 1865, *O.R.*, I, 47(2):1453–4.

30. Quoted in McMurry, *John Bell Hood*, 186.

31. A copy of Hood's report was printed in the Richmond *Sentinel* on 17 Feb. 1865. Hood's report is in *O.R.*, I, 38(3):628–36.

32. Hood to Cooper, 15 Feb. 1865, *O.R.*, I, 38(3):628–9. McMurry believes that the newspaper article by "G.W.S." may have been a rough draft of Hood's final report.

33. Wigfall to JEJ, 27 Feb. 1865, and Hood to JEJ, 4 April 1865, both in JEJ Papers, JO 304 and JO 129, HEH Library. The exchange of telegrams is printed in Hood, *Advance and Retreat*, 159.

34. Wood to JEJ, 8 April 1865, and Wigfall to JEJ, 4 March 1865, both in JEJ Papers, JO 308 and JO 306, HEH Library.

35. Woodward, ed., *Mary Chesnut's Civil War* (diary entry of 30 March 1865), 773.

36. Davis to JEJ, 11 April 1865, JEJ Papers, JO 369, HEH Library; *Narrative*, 396; JEJ to Beauregard, 26 Dec. 1867, JEJ Papers, JO 187, HEH Library.

37. JEJ to Beauregard, 26 Dec. 1867, JEJ Papers, JO 187, HEH Library; Johnston, *Narrative*, 397.

38. JEJ to Beauregard, 26 Dec. 1867, JEJ Papers, JO 187, HEH Library; Durkin, *Confederate Navy Chief* (diary entry of 15 April 1865), 340; Stephen R. Mallory, "Last Days of the Confederate Government," *McClure's* (December 1900), 240–2.

39. JEJ to Beauregard, 26 Dec. 1867, JEJ Papers, JO 187, HEH Library.

40. Breckinridge to Davis, 17 April 1865, JEJ Papers, JO 38, HEH Library.

41. Johnston, *Narrative*, 402; Sherman, *Memoris*, 347–50.

42. Foote, *The Civil War, A Narrative*, 3:990–1.

43. Ibid., 3:994–5.

44. Sherman to JEJ (two wires), JEJ to Breckinridge and Breckinridge to JEJ, all dated 24 April 1865, JEJ to Sherman 25 April 1865 (two wires), all in *O.R.*, I, 47(3):293–4, 835–6.

45. General Orders No. 22, 2 May 1865, *O.R.*, I, 47(1):1061.

Chapter 23

1. Dabney Maury to R. S. Ewell, 28 Aug. 1891, R. S. Ewell Papers, LC.

2. JEJ to Gantt, 13 June 1876, JEJ Collection, box 2, folder 2, W&M; JEJ to Gantt, 3 Jan. and 2 Feb. 1884, JEJ Collection, box 2, folder 4, W&M. Johnston's views on slavery constituted another point of disagreement with Davis, who saw the passing of slavery as one of the great tragedies of the war.

3. JEJ to Hindman, 21 Oct. 1867, JEJ Papers, AHS; Lydia Johnston to B. S. Ewell, 8 June 1865, quoted in Govan and Livingood, *A Different Valor*, 377–8; JEJ to R. S. Ewell, 16 May 1866, R. S. Ewell Papers, LC.

4. JEJ to Mackall, 26 Sept. 1865, Mackall Papers, file #4, UNC; Govan and Livingood, *A Different Valor*, 378; JEJ to R. S. Ewell, 16 May 1866, R. S. Ewell Papers, LC.

5. JEJ to the North American Insurance Company, 24 Aug. 1872, Society Collection, PHS; JEJ to Gantt, 2 Feb. 1884, JEJ Collection, box 2, folder 4, W&M.

6. JEJ to Hindman, 21 Oct. 1867, JEJ Papers, AHS; JEJ to Beauregard, 26 Dec. 1867, JEJ Papers, JO 187, HEH Library; JEJ to Mackall, 31 May 1867 and 20 July 1874, Mackall Papers, files #2 & #5, UNC.

7. Hampton to JEJ, 23 June 1870, JEJ Collection, box 1, folder 5, W&M.

8. Henry S. Foote, *War of the Rebellion*, 347; Edward A. Pollard, *The Lost Cause, A New Southern History of the War of the Confederates* (n.p., 1866), 440; Frank H. Alfriend, *The Life of Jefferson Davis* (Cincinnati and Chicago: Caxton Publishing House, 1868); Varina Davis, *Jefferson Davis*, 2:798–9.

9. JEJ to Gantt, 2 Feb. 1884, JEJ Collection, box 2, folder 4, W&M; JEJ to John W. Johnston, 20 Nov. 1872, John W. Johnston Papers, Duke.

10. Johnston, *Narrative*, 110.

11. Alfriend, *Jefferson Davis*, 305; Johnston, *Narrative*, 54, 64.

12. Johnston, *Narrative*, 71, 73; Richard Taylor, *Destruction and Reconstruction, Personal Experiences of the Late War* (originally published in 1877; reprinted New York, Longmans, 1955), 25.

13. Johnston, *Narrative*, 143, 145; Smith, *The Battle of Seven Pines*, 144–73.

14. Ibid., 148; JEJ to Gantt, 2 Feb. 1884, JEJ Collection, box 2, folder 4, W&M.

15. Johnston, *Narrative*, 362, 365.

16. Wigfall to JEJ, 22 April 1873, JEJ Papers, JO 307, HEH Library; Johnston, *Narrative*, 430–65.

17. JEJ to Bradley T. Johnson, 27 July 1887, Bradley T. Johnson Papers, Duke; JEJ to Ben Johnston, 17 Sept. 1887, JEJ Collection, box 2, folder 4, W&M.

18. Davis to Mrs. Davis, 26 April 1874, in Hudson Strode, ed., *Jefferson Davis: Private Letters, 1823–1889* (New York: Harcourt, Brace & World, 1966), 397.

19. John Bell Hood, *Advance and Retreat: Personal Experiences in the United States and Confederate Armies* (originally published 1880; reprinted Bloomington, Ind.: Indiana University Press, 1959), 144, 316.

20. William T. Sherman, *Memoirs of General William T. Sherman* (originally published 1875; reprinted New York: DaCapo Press, 1984), 2:167; JEJ to Robert Hunter, 8 Dec. 1875, JEJ Papers, Duke; Hood, *Advance and Retreat*, 313–16.

21. Richard N. Current, Foreword to 1959 edition of *Advance and Retreat,* viii–ix.

22. Davis, *The Rise and Fall of the Confederate Government,* 2:470, 471.

23. JEJ to Mackall, 26 June 1881, Mackall Papers, file #6, UNC; Hudson Strode, *Jefferson Davis, Tragic Hero* (New York: Harcourt Brace, 1964), 452–3.

24. Strode, *Jefferson Davis,* 465.

25. Gaines Foster, *Ghosts of the Confederacy: Defeat, the Lost Cause, and the Emergence of the New South* (New York: Oxford University Press, 1987), 88.

26. JEJ to R. U. Johnson, 22 Jan. 1885, Century Collection, NYPL; Joseph E. Johnston, "Manassas to Seven Pines," *Century* (May 1885), 30:99, 105–6. A revised version is printed as "Responsibilities of First Bull Run" in *B&L,* 1:250.

27. Johnston, "Manassas to Seven Pines," *Century,* 105–6.

28. JEJ to Buel, 12 March, 5 May, 30 May, and 2 July 1885, all in Century Collection, NYPL; Joseph E. Johnston, "Manassas to Seven Pines," *B&L,* 2:215. In his first draft of the field report on the Battle of Seven Pines, Longstreet listed 3,000 as "a rough estimate" of the casualties he had suffered. He corrected this estimate in later editions of his report, but Johnston never accepted any number other than 3,000. In the summer of 1877, he wrote to the editors of the *Southern Historical Society Proceedings* complaining that their copy of Longstreet's report was in error. The editors replied that they had printed the report "verbatim" as it appeared in Longstreet's letter book. See JEJ to Rev. J. W. Jones, 22 June 1877, *SHSP* (July–December 1877), 4:42.

29. JEJ to Buel, 17 and 20 Feb. 1885, Century Collection, NYPL.

30. Johnston, "Manassas to Seven Pines," *Century* (May 1885), 30:120. See also JEJ to Editor, *Century* magazine, 9, 11 and 14 May, 11, 17, and 30 June 1885, all in Century Collection, NYPL.

31. JEJ to R. U. Johnson, 11 Aug. and 12 Sept. 1885, Century Collection, NYPL.

32. Gustavus W. Smith, "Two Days of Battle at Seven Pines," *B&L,* 2:250.

33. Joseph E. Johnston, "Jefferson Davis and the Mississippi Campaign," *B&L,* 3:473, 475; Joseph E. Johnston, "Opposing Sherman's Advance to Atlanta," *Century* (August 1887), 34: 596; reprinted as "The Opening of the Atlanta Campaign," *B&L,* 4:277.

34. Johnston, *Narrative,* 461; Sherman, *Memoirs;* Grant, *Memoirs,* 1:549, 2:167.

Chapter 24

1. JEJ to John W. Johnston, 24 March 1873, and JEJ to Sally Lee, 9 March 1873, both in JEJ Collection, box 1, folder 5, W&M.

2. JEJ to John W. Johnston, 7 Nov. 1873, JEJ Collection, box 1, folder 5, W&M; JEJ to John W. Johnston, 8 Nov. 1873, John W. Johnston Papers, Duke.

3. JEJ to John W. Johnston, 3, 7, and 19 Nov. 1873, all in box 1, folder 5, W&M; JEJ to John W. Johnston, 20 Nov. 1873, John W. Johnston Papers, Duke.

4. JEJ to John W. Johnston, 26 July 1872, JEJ Collection, box 1, folder 5, W&M.

5. JEJ to John W. Johnston, 24 May 1876, JEJ Collection, box 2, folder 2, W&M.

6. JEJ to Gantt, 13 June 1876, JEJ Collection, box 2, folder 2, W&M.

7. Quoted in Eric Foner, *Reconstruction: America's Unfinished Revolution, 1863–1877* (New York: Harper & Row, 1988), 567.

8. JEJ to Gantt, 24 Sept. and 4 Nov. 1878, JEJ Collection, box 2, folder 2, W&M.

9. JEJ to John W. Johnston, 8 Oct. 1877, JEJ Collection, box 2, folder 2, W&M.

10. John S. Wise, "Joseph E. Johnston," *Circle* (May 1908), 288.

11. Johnson, ed., *A Memoir,* 249.

12. JEJ to Gantt, 24 Sept. 1878, JEJ Collection, box 2, folder 2, W&M.

13. Ibid.

14. JEJ to Gantt, 4 Nov. 1878, JEJ Collection, box 2, folder 2, W&M; JEJ to "My dear little namesake," 12 Nov. 1878, letter privately held by Joseph S. Johnston.

15. Washington *Post*, March 19, 1879; Govan & Livingood, *A Different Valor*, 390.

16. JEJ to Gantt, 14 May 1880, JEJ Collection, box 2, folder 3, W&M.

17. JEJ to Gantt, 14 May and 12 Sept. 1880, both in JEJ Collection, box 2, folder 3, W&M.

18. JEJ to Gantt, 25 Aug. 1880, JEJ Collection, box 2, folder 3, W&M.

19. JEJ to Gantt, 25 Aug. and 12 Sept. 1880, both in JEJ Collection, box 2, folder 3, W&M; JEJ to Robert Patterson, 5 Sept. 1880, Society Collection, PHS.

20. JEJ to John W. Johnston, 3 April 1883, John W. Johnston Papers, Duke.

21. JEJ to Buel, 4 July 1885, Century Collection, NYPL.

22. JEJ to O. H. Peck, 30 Nov. 1885, JEJ Papers, Duke; JEJ to Buel, 3 Dec. 1885 and 25 Jan. 1886, both in Century Collection, NYPL; JEJ to Gantt, 25 May 1887, Johnston Collection, box 2, folder 4, W&M.

23. JEJ to Sally Lee, 31 March 1887, JEJ Collection, box 2, folder 4, W&M.

24. JEJ to Buel, 5 April and 3 June 1887, both in Century Collection, NYPL; JEJ to Gantt, 25 May 1887, and JEJ to "My dear little niece," n.d., both in JEJ Collection, box 2, folders 4 and 5, W&M; JEJ to Elizabeth Hughes, 17 Sept. 1887, Robert W. Hughes Papers, box 1, folder 3, W&M.

25. JEJ to Gantt, 30 Nov. 1888, JEJ Collection, box 2, folder 5, W&M.

26. Atlanta *Constitution*, 25–27 April 1890; Govan and Livingood, *A Different Valor*, 396–7.

27. Foster, *Ghosts of the Confederacy*, 101–2.

28. Govan and Livingood, *A Different Valor*, 397.

29. Washington *Star*, 23 March 1891. See also Joseph E. Johnston Papers, Carlisle.

30. Watkins, *"Co. Aytch,"* 168.

Bibliography

I. MANUSCRIPT SOURCES

Crown Gardens & Archive, Dalton, Georgia
    Joseph E. Johnston Letters
Henry E. Huntington Library, San Marino, California
    Joseph E. Johnston Papers
Library of Congress, Washington, D.C.
    Simon Cameron Papers
    Richard Stoddert Ewell Papers
    George F. Hughes Papers
    Joseph E. Johnston Papers
    Mansfield Lovell Papers
    George B. McClellan Papers
    Leonidas Polk Papers
    Wigfall Family Papers
Maryland Historical Society Library, Baltimore, Maryland
    McLane-Fisher Family Papers
Miami University, Oxford, Ohio
    The Samuel Richey Collection of the Southern Confederacy
The New York Public Library, New York, New York
    Joseph E. Johnston Papers (Century Collection)

Miscellaneous Collection
Montague Collection
Pennsylvania Historical Society, Philadelphia, Pennsylvania
George Cadwalader Collection
Ferdinand J. Dreer Collection
Simon Gratz Collection
Society Collection
William R. Perkins Library, Duke University, Durham, North Carolina
Rachael Susan Cheves Papers
Mumford H. Dixon Diary
Bradley T. Johnson Papers
John Warfield Johnston Papers
Joseph E. Johnston Papers
George Hume Steuart Papers
Southern Historical Collection, Manuscripts Division, University of North
Carolina, Chapel Hill
Edward Porter Alexander Papers
William Whann Mackall Papers
William Nelson Pendleton Papers
Edmund Kirby Smith Papers
Earl Gregg Swem Library, College of William & Mary, Williamsburg, Virginia
John B. Floyd Papers
Robert Morton Hughes Collection
Robert William Hughes Papers
Joseph E. Johnston Collection
University of the South, Sewanee, Tennessee
Bishop Quintard Collection
Leonidas Polk Collection
U.S. Military Academy Library, West Point, New York
Cadet Papers
Post Orders
Register of Cadet Delinquencies
Register of Merit
Western Reserve Historical Society, Cleveland, Ohio
Braxton Bragg Papers

II. NEWSPAPERS

Abingdon *Democrat*
Atlanta *Constitution*
Richmond *Enquirer*
Richmond *Examiner*
Richmond *Sentinel*

III. OFFICIAL RECORDS AND PUBLISHED COLLECTIONS

Buchanan, James A. *The Messages of President Buchanan.* Edited by J. Buchanan
Henry. New York: J. B. Henry, 1888.
Confederate States Congress. *Journal of the Congress of the Confederate States of Amer-
ica, 1861–1865.* 7 vols. Washington, D.C.: Government Printing Office, 1905.
Culham, George W., Jr., ed. *Biographical Register of the Officers and Graduates of the
U.S. Military Academy.* Boston and New York: Houghton Mifflin & Co., 1891.

Davis, Jefferson. *The Papers of Jefferson Davis.* Edited by H. M. Monroe, Jr., and J. T. McIntosh. Baton Rouge, La.: Louisiana State University Press, 1971.

Davis, Jefferson. *The Papers of Jefferson Davis.* Edited by L. L. Crist and M. S. Dix. 6 vols. to date. Baton Rouge, La.: Louisiana State University Press, 1979–89.

Lee, Robert E. *Lee's Dispatches: Unpublished Letters of General Robert E. Lee, C.S.A. to Jefferson Davis and the War Department of the Confederate States of America, 1861–65.* Edited by Douglas S. Freeman. New York: G. P. Putnam's Sons, 1957.

Rowland, Dunbar, ed. *Jefferson Davis, Constitutionalist: His Letters, Papers, and Speeches.* 10 vols. Jackson, Miss.: Mississippi Department of Archives & History, 1923.

U.S. Army. *Cadet Application Papers.* Record Group 404, Series 165. National Archives, Washington, D.C.

U.S. Army. *General Regulations of the Army.* Washington, D.C.: Davis & Force, 1825.

U.S. Army. *Records of the Topographical Bureau.* Record Group 77. National Archives, Washington, D.C.

U.S. Army, *Report of the Quartermaster General,* 12 November 1860. Senate Exec. Doc. No. 1, part 13. 36th Congress, 2nd session, 233–6.

U.S. Congress. *American State Papers: Documents, Legislative and Executive of the Congress of the United States.* Class V, Military Affairs. 4 vols. Washington, D.C.: Gales & Seaton, 1832.

U.S. Congress. *Mexican War Correspondence.* House Executive Document No. 1. 30th Congress, 1st session (1847–48).

U.S. Congress. *Report of the Secretary of War* (1850). Senate Executive Document No. 64. 31st Congress, 1st session.

U.S. Congress. *Report of the Secretary of War* (1856). Senate Executive Document No. 5. 34th Congress, 3rd session.

U.S. Congress. *Report . . . on Routes from San Antonio to El Paso.* Senate Executive Document No. 64. 31st Congress, 1st session (1849–50).

U.S. Navy Department. "Letters Received by the Secretary of the Navy, from Captains [*Captain's Letters*], 1805–1861, 1866–1885." Record Group 45. National Archives, Washington, D.C.

War of the Rebellion. Official Records of the Union and Confederate Armies in the War of the Rebellion. 4 series, 128 volumes. Washington, D.C.: U.S. Government Printing Office, 1894–1922.

Official Records of the Union and Confederate Navies in the War of the Rebellion. Series I, 27 vols. Washington, D.C.: Government Printing Office, 1894–1922.

IV. PUBLISHED MEMOIRS

Alexander, E. P. *Fighting for the Confederacy: The Personal Recollections of General Edward Porter Alexander.* Edited by Gary W. Gallagher. Chapel Hill, N.C.: University of North Carolina Press, 1989.

———. *Military Memoirs of a Confederate: A Critical Narrative.* New York: Charles Scribner's Sons, 1910.

Anderson, Robert. "Reminiscences of the Black Hawk War." *Wisconsin Historical Collections* (1888), 10:167–76.

Bandel, Eugene. *Frontier Life in the Army, 1854–1861.* Translated by Olga Bandel and Richard Jente, edited by Ralph P. Bieber. Glendale, Calif.: Arthur H. Clark, 1932.

Beauregard, P. G. T. *With Beauregard in Mexico: The Mexican War Reminiscences of P. G. T. Beauregard.* Edited by T. Harry Williams. Baton Rouge, La.: Louisiana State University Press, 1956.

Buck, Samuel D. *With the Old Confeds: Actual Experiences of a Captain in the Line.* Baltimore: H. E. Houck & Co., 1925.

Cate, Wirt A. *Two Soldiers: The Campaign Diaries of Thomas J. Key, C.S.A., and Robert J. Campbell, U.S.A.* Chapel Hill, N.C.: University of North Carolina Press, 1938.

Chesnut, Mary. *Mary Chesnut's Civil War.* Edited by C. Vann Woodward. New Haven, Conn.: Yale University Press, 1981.

Church, Albert E. *Personal Reminiscences of the United States Military Academy.* West Point, N.Y.: U.S. Service Institute, 1878.

Cohen, M. M. *Notices of Florida and the Campaigns.* Gainesville, Fla.: University of Florida Press, 1964 (first published 1836).

Cooke, Philip St. George. *Scenes and Adventures in the Army, or Romance of Military Life.* New York: Arno Press, 1973 (first published 1857).

Curry, J. H. "A History of Company B, 40th Alabama Infantry." *Alabama Historical Quarterly* (1955), 17:159–222.

Davis, Jefferson. *The Rise and Fall of the Confederate Government.* 2 vols. New York: D. Appleton & Company, 1881.

Davis, Varina. *Jefferson Davis.* 2 vols. Baltimore: Nautical & Aviation Press, 1990 (first published 1890).

Foote, Henry S. *War of the Rebellion, or Scylla and Charybdis.* New York: Harper & Brothers, 1866.

French, Samuel G. *Two Wars: An Autobiography.* Nashville, Tenn.: Confederate Veteran, 1901.

Gay, Mary A. H. *Life in Dixie During the War.* Atlanta, Ga.: Charles P. Byrd, 1897.

Gorgas, Josiah. *The Civil War Diary of Josiah Gorgas.* Edited by Frank Vandiver. University, Ala.: University of Alabama Press, 1947.

Grant, Ulysses S. *Personal Memoirs of U. S. Grant.* New York: Da Capo Press, 1982 (first published 1885).

Harrison, Mrs. Burton. *Recollections Grave and Gay.* New York: Charles Scribner's Sons, 1911.

Haskell, John Cheves. *The Haskell Memoirs.* Edited by Gilbert E. Govan and James W. Livingood. New York: G. P. Putnam's Sons, 1960.

Hitchcock, Ethan Allen. *Fifty Years in Camp and Field.* New York: G. P. Putnam's Sons, 1909.

Hood, John Bell. *Advance and Retreat: Personal Experiences in the United States and Confederate States Armies.* Bloomington, Ind.: Indiana University Press, 1959 (first published 1880).

Hughes, Robert M. "Some Letters from the Papers of General Joseph E. Johnston." *William & Mary Quarterly* (October 1931), 319–24.

———. "Some War Letters of General Joseph E. Johnston." *Journal of the Military Service Institution of the United States* (1913), 50:318–28.

Johnson, Bradley T. "Memoir of First Maryland Regiment." *Southern Historical Society Proceedings* (1881), 9:344–53, 481–8; (1882), 10:46–56, 97–109, 145–53, 214–23.

[Johnston, Algernon Sidney]. *Memoirs of a Nullifier, Written by Himself.* Columbia, S.C.: The Telescope Office, 1832.

Johnston, Joseph E. *Narrative of Military Operations.* Bloomington, Ind.: Indiana University Press, 1959 (first published 1874).

———. "Surveying the Southern Boundary Line of Kansas: From the Private Journal of Col. Joseph E. Johnston." Edited by Nyle H. Miller. *Kansas Historical Society* (February 1932), 1:104–39.

Jones, J. B. *A Rebel War Clerk's Diary.* 2 vols. Philadelphia: J. B. Lippincott & Co., 1866.

Kean, Robert Garlick Hill. *Inside the Confederate Government: The Diary of Robert Garlick Hill Kean, Head of the Bureau of War.* New York: Oxford University Press, 1957.

Kenly, John R. *Memoirs of a Maryland Volunteer.* Philadelphia: J. B. Lippincott & Co., 1873.

Longstreet, James. *From Manassas to Appomattox: Memoirs of the Civil War in America.* Philadelphia: J. B. Lippincott & Co., 1896.

Mackall, William Whann. *A Son's Recollections of His Father.* New York: E. P. Dutton, 1930.

McLane, Robert M. *Reminiscences, 1827–1897.* Wilmington, Del.: Scholarly Resources, 1972 (first published 1903).

McLean, Mrs. Eugene. "A Northern Woman in the Confederacy." *Harper's Monthly* (January 1914), 128:440–51.

———. "When the States Seceded." *Harper's Monthly* (February 1914), 128:282–8.

Mallory, Stephen R. "Last Days of the Confederate Government." *McClure's Magazine* (January 1901), 16:239–48.

Maury, Dabney H. *Recollections of a Virginian in the Mexican, Indian, and Civil Wars.* New York: Charles Scribner's Sons, 1894.

Meade, George G. *The Life and Letters of George Gordon Meade.* 2 vols. New York: Charles Scribner's Sons, 1913.

Mosman, Chesley. *The Rough Side of War: The Civil War Journal of Chesley A. Mosman.* Edited by Arnold Gates. Garden City, N.Y.: The Basin Publishing Co., 1987.

Motte, Jacob R. *Journey into Wilderness: An Army Surgeon's Account of Life in Camp and Field During the Creek and Seminole Wars, 1836–1838.* Edited by James F. Sunderman. Gainesville, Fla.: University of Florida Press, 1953.

Nichols, George W. *The Story of the Great March from the Diary of a Staff Officer.* New York: Harper & Brothers, 1866.

Nisbit, James C. *Four Years on the Firing Line.* Edited by Bell I. Wiley. Jackson, Tenn.: McCowatt-Mercer Press, 1963.

Osborn, Thomas. *The Fiery Trail: A Union Officer's Account of Sherman's Last Campaigns.* Edited by Richard Harwell and Philip N. Racine. Knoxville, Tenn.: University of Tennessee Press, 1986.

Parker, William H. *Recollections of a Naval Officer.* Edited by Craig L. Symonds. Annapolis, Md.: Naval Institute Press, 1985 (first published 1883).

Patrick, Robert. *Reluctant Rebel: The Secret Diary of Robert Patrick, 1861–1865.* Edited by F. Jay Taylor. Baton Rouge, La.: Louisiana State University Press, 1959.

Pollard, Edward A. *Life of Jefferson Davis, with a Secret History of the Southern Confederacy.* n.p., 1869.

———. *The Lost Cause, A New Southern History of the War of the Confederates.* n.p., 1866.

Pryor, Mrs. Roger A. *Reminiscences of Peace and War.* New York: Macmillan, 1904.

Ridley, B. L. "Last Battles of the War." *Confederate Veteran* (1895), 3:25, 36–7, 70–1, 99, 134–5, 184–5.

Ripley, Roswell S. *War with Mexico.* New York: Harper & Brothers, 1849.

Root, George A., ed. "Extracts from Diary of Captain Lambert Bowman Wolf." *Kansas Historical Quarterly* (May 1932), 1:195–210.

Rountree, Benjamin. "Letters from a Confederate Soldier." *The Georgia Review* (1964), 18:267–97.

Russell, William Howard. *My Diary North and South.* Edited by Eugene H. Berwanger. New York: Alfred A. Knopf, 1988 (first published 1863).

Scott, Winfield. *Memoirs of Lieut.-General Scott.* New York: Sheldon & Company, 1864.

Semmes, Raphael. *The Campaign of General Scott in the Valley of Mexico.* Cincinnati: Moore & Anderson, 1852.

Sherman, William T. *Memoirs of General William T. Sherman.* New York: De Capo Press, 1984 (first published 1875).

Shoup, Francis A. "Dalton Campaign—Works at Chattahoochee—Interesting Story." *Confederate Veteran* (1895), 3:262–5.

Smith, E. Kirby. *To Mexico with Scott: Letters of E. Kirby Smith to His Wife.* Cambridge, Mass.: Harvard University Press, 1917.

Smith, Gustavus Woodson. *The Battle of Seven Pines.* Dayton, Ohio: Morningside Bookshop, 1974 (first published 1891).

Taylor, Richard. *Destruction and Reconstruction, Personal Experiences of the Late War.* New York: Longmans Green and Co., 1955 (first published 1879).

Watkins, Sam R. *"Co. Aytch," Maury Grays, First Tennessee Regiment, or A Side Show of the Big Show.* Wilmington, N.C.: Broadfoot Publishing Co., 1987 (first published 1882).

Wilcox, Cadmus. *History of the Mexican War.* Washington, D.C.: The Church News Publishing Company, 1892.

Wise, John S. "Joseph E. Johnston." *The Circle* (May 1908), 287–8.

Wright, Louise Wigfall. *A Southern Girl in '61: War-Time Memories of a Confederate Senator's Daughter.* New York: Doubleday & Page, 1905.

V. BOOKS AND ARTICLES

Alfriend, Frank H. *The Life of Jefferson Davis.* Cincinnati and Chicago: Caxton Publishing House, 1868.

Ambrose, Stephen E. *Duty, Honor, Country: A History of West Point.* Baltimore: Johns Hopkins University Press, 1966.

Arthur, Robert. "Historical Sketch of the Coast Artillery School." *Journal of the United States Artillery* (July–August, September–October 1915), 44:15–48, 164–203.

Bailey, Fred A. *Class and Tennessee's Confederate Generation.* Chapel Hill, N.C.: University of North Carolina Press, 1987.

Ballard, Michael B. *A Long Shadow: Jefferson Davis and the Final Days of the Confederacy.* Jackson, Miss.: University Press of Mississippi, 1986.

Barrett, John G. *The Civil War in North Carolina.* Chapel Hill, N.C.: University of North Carolina Press, 1963.

Bauer, K. Jack. *The Mexican War, 1846–1848.* New York: Macmillan Publishing Company, 1974.

Bearss, Edwin. *Decision in Mississippi: Mississippi's Important Role in the War Between the States.* Jackson, Miss.: Mississippi Commission on the War Between the States, 1962.

Beers, Henry P. "A History of the U.S. Topographical Engineers, 1813–1863." *Military Engineer* (1942), 287–91, 348–52.

Bender, Averam B. *The March of Empire: Frontier Defense in the Southwest, 1848–1860.* Lawrence, Kans.: University of Kansas Press, 1952.

Beringer, Richard E., Herman Hattaway, Archer, Jones, and William N. Still. *Why the South Lost the Civil War.* Athens, Ga.: University of Georgia Press, 1986.

Brown, Charles H. *Agents of Manifest Destiny: The Lives and Times of the Filibusters.* Chapel Hill, N.C.: University of North Carolina Press, 1980.

Buck, Irving A. *Cleburne and His Command.* Jackson, Tenn.: McCowatt-Mercer Press, 1959.

Buker, George E. *Swamp Sailors: Riverine Warfare in the Everglades, 1835–1842.* Gainesville, Fla.: University of Florida Press, 1975.

Carter, Samuel III. *The Final Fortress: The Campaign for Vicksburg, 1862–1863.* New York: St. Martin's Press, 1980.

Catton, Bruce. *Centennial History of the Civil War:* I. *The Coming Fury.* II. *Terrible Swift Sword.* III. *Never Call Retreat.* Garden City, N.Y.: Doubleday & Company, 1961–65.

————. *Grant Moves South*. Boston: Little, Brown, 1960.

Coffman, Edward M. *The Old Army: A Portrait of the American Army in Peacetime, 1784–1898*. New York: Oxford University Press, 1986.

Connelly, Thomas L. *Army of the Heartland: The Army of Tennessee, 1861–1862*. Baton Rouge, La.: Louisiana State University Press, 1967.

————. *Autumn of Glory: The Army of Tennessee, 1862–1865*. Baton Rouge, La.: Louisiana State University Press, 1971.

————. "Vicksburg: Strategic Point or Propaganda Device?" *Military Affairs* (1970), 34:49–53.

————, and Archer Jones. *The Politics of Command: Factions and Ideas in Confederate Strategy*. Baton Rouge, La.: Louisiana State University, 1973.

Daniel, Larry J. "Bruinsburg: Missed Opportunity or Postwar Rhetoric?" *Civil War History* (1986), 32:256–67.

Davis, William C. *Battle at Bull Run: A History of the First Major Campaign of the Civil War*. Garden City, N.Y.: Doubleday & Company, 1977.

De Leon, Thomas C. *Belles, Beaux, and Brains of the 60's*. New York: G. W. Dillingham, 1907.

Dowdey, Clifford. *The Seven Days, The Emergence of Lee*. Boston: Little, Brown, 1964.

Durkin, Joseph T. *Confederate Navy Chief: Stephen R. Mallory*. Columbia, S.C.: University of South Carolina Press, 1954.

Dyer, John P. *Fightin' Joe Wheeler*. University, La.: Louisiana State University Press, 1941; reprinted in 1961 as *From Shiloh to San Juan*.

Eaton, Clement. *Jefferson Davis*. New York: The Free Press, 1977.

Eckenrode, H. J., and Bryan Conrad. *James Longstreet: Lee's War Horse*. Chapel Hill, N.C.: University of North Carolina Press, 1936, 1986.

Eliot, Ellsworth, Jr. *West Point in the Confederacy*. New York: G. A. Baker & Co., 1941.

Elliott, Charles W. *Winfield Scott, The Soldier and the Man*. New York: Macmillan, 1937.

Evans, Eli N. *Judah P. Benjamin: The Jewish Confederate*. New York: The Free Press, 1988.

Foster, Gaines, M. *Ghosts of the Confederacy: Defeat, the Lost Cause, and the Emergence of the New South*. New York: Oxford University Press, 1987.

Freeman, Douglas S. *R. E. Lee, A Biography*. 4 vols. New York: Charles Scribner's Sons, 1934–35.

————. *Lee's Lieutenants*. 3 vols. New York: Charles Scribner's Sons, 1942–44.

Ganoe, William A. *The History of the United States Army*. New York: D. Appleton and Co., 1924.

Goetzmann, William H. *Army Exploration in the American West*. New Haven, Conn.: Yale University Press, 1959.

————. *Exploration and Empiore: The Explorer and the Scientist in the Winning of the American West*. New York: Alfred A. Knopf, 1966.

Govan, Gilbert, and James W. Livingood. *A Different Valor: The Story of General Joseph E. Johnston, C.S.A.* Indianapolis: The Bobbs-Merrill Company, 1956.

Hagan, William T. *The Sac and Fox Indians*. Norman, Okla.: University of Oklahoma Press, 1958.

Hammond, Bray. *Banks and Politics in America from the Revolution to the Civil War*. Princeton, N.J.: Princeton University Press, 1957.

Hassler, Warren W., Jr. *With Shield and Sword*. Ames, Iowa: Iowa State University Press, 1982.

Hattaway, Herman. *General Stephen D. Lee*. Jackson, Miss.: University Press of Mississippi, 1976.

Hay, Thomas R. "Confederate Leadership at Vicksburg." *Mississippi Valley Historical Review* (March 1925), 11:543–60.

————. "The Davis-Hood-Johnston Controversy of 1864." *Mississippi Valley Historical Review* (June 1925), 11:54–84.

Hughes, Nathaniel C., Jr. *General William J. Hardee: Old Reliable.* Baton Rouge: Louisiana State University Press, 1965.

————. *General Johnston.* New York: D. Appleton and Co., 1897.

Hungerford, Edward. *The Story of the Baltimore and Ohio Railroad.* 2 vols. New York: G. P Putnam's Sons, 1928.

James, Alfred P. "General Joseph Eggleston Johnston, Storm Center of the Confederate Army." *Mississippi Valley Historical Review* (December 1927), 14:342–59.

Johannsen, Robert W. *To the Halls of the Montezumas: The Mexican War in the American Imagination.* New York: Oxford University Press, 1985.

Johnson, Bradley T., ed. *A Memoir of the Life and Public Service of Joseph E. Johnston.* Baltimore: R. H. Woodward & Co., 1891.

Johnson, Samuel A. *The Battle Cry of Freedom: The New English Emigrant Aid Company in the Kansas Crusade.* Lawrence, Kans.: University of Kansas Press, 1954.

Jones, Archer. *Confederate Strategy from Shiloh to Vicksburg.* Baton Rouge, La.: Louisiana State University Press, 1961.

————. "The Vicksburg Campaign." *Journal of Mississippi History* (February 1962), 29:12–27.

King, Alvy L. *Louis T. Wigfall: Southern Fire-Eater.* Baton Rouge, La.: Louisiana State University Press, 1970.

————. "The Relationship Between Joseph E. Johnston and Jefferson Davis During the Civil War." Unpublished M.A. thesis, West Texas State College, El Paso, 1960.

Lash, Jeffrey N. *Destroyer of the Iron Horse: General Joseph E. Johnston and Confederate Rail Transport, 1861–1865.* Kent, Ohio: Kent State University Press, 1991.

————. "Joseph E. Johnston and the Virginia Railways, 1861–62." *Civil War History* (1989), 35:5–27.

————. "Joseph E. Johnston's Grenada Blunder." *Civil War History* (1987), 32:114–28.

Lane, Carl D. *American Paddle Steamboats.* New York: Coward-McCann, 1943.

Leech, Margaret. *Reveille in Washington.* New York: Harper & Bros., 1941.

Losson, Christopher. *Tennessee's Forgotten Warriors: Frank Cheatham and His Confederate Division.* Knoxville, Tenn.: University of Tennessee Press, 1989.

McMurry, Richard M. "The Affair at Kolb's Farm." *Civil War Times Illustrated* (December 1968), 20–27.

————. "The Atlanta Campaign: December 23, 1863 to July 18, 1864." Unpublished Ph.D. dissertation, Emory University, Atlanta, 1967.

————. "Cassville." *Civil War Times Illustrated* (December 1971), 4–9, 45–8.

————. "Confederate Morale in the Atlanta Campaign of 1864." *Georgia Historical Quarterly* (1970), 54:226–43.

————. " 'The Enemy at Richmond': Joseph E. Johnston and the Confederate Government." *Civil War History* (1981), 27:5–31.

————. " 'A Heap of Hard Fitin': The Battle of Resaca" *Civil War Times Illustrated* (November 1970), 4–12, 44–8.

————. "The Hell Hole: New Hope Church." *Civil War Times Illustrated* (February 1973), 32–43.

————. *John Bell Hood and the War for Southern Independence.* Lexington, Ky.: University Press of Kentucky, 1982.

————. "Kennesaw Mountain." *Civil War Times Illustrated* (January 1970), 19–34.

————. "The Mackall Journal and Its Antecedents." *Civil War History* (1974), 20:311–28.

————. *The Road Past Kennesaw: The Atlanta Campaign of 1864.* Washington, D.C.: National Park Service, 1972.

————. *Two Great Rebel Armies: An Essay in Confederate Military History*. Chapel Hill, N.C.: University of North Carolina Press, 1989.

McWhiney, Grady. *Braxton Bragg and Confederate Defeat*. Vol. I. *Field Command*. New York: Columbia University Press, 1969.

Mahon, John K. *History of the Second Seminole War, 1835–1842*. Gainesville, Fla.: University of Florida Press, 1967.

May, Robert E. *The Southern Dream of a Caribbean Empire*. Athens, Ga.: University of Georgia Press, 1989.

Meade, Robert D. *Judah P. Benjamin, Confederate Stateman*. New York: Oxford University Press, 1943.

Morrison, James L., Jr. *"The Best School in the World": West Point, the Pre-Civil War Years, 1833–1866*. Kent, Ohio: Kent State University Press, 1986.

Morrison, John H. *History of American Steam Navigation*. New York: Stephen Daye Press, 1958.

Munroe, John A. *Louis McLane: Federalist and Jacksonian*. New Brunswick, N.J.: Rutgers University Press, 1973.

Neely, Mark E., Jr., Harols Holzer, and Bagor S. Boritt. *The Confederate Image: Prints of the Lost Cause*. Chapel Hill, N.C.: University of North Carolina Press, 1987.

Nevins, Allan. *The War for the Union*. 8 vols. New York: Charles Scribner's Sons, 1959.

Newton, Steven. "Joseph E. Johnston and the Defense of Richmond." Unpublished Ph.D. dissertation, College of William & Mary, Williamsburg, Virginia, 1989.

Nichols, Alice. *Bleeding Kansas*. New York: Oxford University Press, 1954.

Parks, Joseph H. *General Leonidas Polk, C.S.A., The Fighting Bishop*. Baton Rouge, La.: Louisiana State University Press, 1962.

Pemberton, John C. *Pemberton, Defender of Vicksburg*. Chapel Hill, N.C.: University of North Carolina Press, 1942.

Peters, Virginia B. *The Florida Wars*. Hamden, Conn.: Archon Books, 1979.

Potter, David M. *The Impending Crisis, 1848–1861*. New York: Harper & Row, 1976.

Power, Kenneth W. "Negroes and the Seminole War, 1835–1842." *Journal of Southern History* (1964), 30:427–50.

Prucha, Francis Paul. *The Sword of the Republic: The United States Army on the Frontier*. New York: Macmillan, 1968.

Rippy, J. Fred. *The United States and Mexico*. New York: Alfred A. Knopf, 1926.

Roberts, Robert B. *Encyclopedia of Historic Forts: The Military, Pioneer, and Trading Posts of the United States*. New York: Macmillan, 1988.

Roman, Alfred. *The Military Operations of General Beauregard in the War Between the States, 1861 to 1865*. 2 vols. New York: Harper & Brothers, 1884.

Secrist, Phillip. "Resaca: For Sherman a Moment of Truth," *Atlanta Historical Journal* (Spring 1978), 22:8–41.

Shanks, Henry T. *The Secession Movement in Virginia, 1847–1861*. New York: AMS Press, 1971 (first published 1934).

Shappee, Nathan D. "Fort Dallas and the Naval Depot on Key Biscayne, 1836–1926." *Tequesta* (1961), 7:13–40.

Smith, Justin H. *The War with Mexico*. 2 vols. New York: Macmillan, 1919.

Sprague, John T. *The Origin, Progress, and Conclusion of the Florida War*. Gainesville, Fla.: University of Florida Press, 1964 (first published 1848).

Stevens, Frank E. *The Black Hawk War, Including a Review of Black Hawk's Life*. Chicago: Frank E. Stevens, 1903.

Strode, Hudson. *Jefferson Davis*. 3 vols. Vol. I, *American Patriot;* Vol. II, *Confederate President;* Vol. III, *Tragic Hero*. New York: Harcourt, Brace & World, 1955–64.

Thomas, Emory M. *Bold Dragoon, The Life of J. E. B. Stuart*. New York: Harper & Row, 1986.

Trexler, Harrison A. "The Davis Administration and the Richmond Press, 1861–1865." *Journal of Southern History* (1950), 16:177–95.

Van der Heuvel, Gerry. *Crowns of Thorns and Glory: Mary Todd Lincoln and Varina Howell Davis, The Two First Ladies of the Civil War*. New York: E. P. Dutton, 1988.

Wallace, Edward S. *Destiny and Glory*. New York: Coward-McCann, 1957.

———. "The United States Army in Mexico City." *Military Affairs* (1949), 13:158–66.

Weigley, Russell. *The American War of War: A History of United States Military Strategy and Policy*. New York: Macmillan, 1973.

Williams, T. Harry. *P. G. T. Beauregard, Napoleon in Gray*. Baton Rouge, La.: Louisiana State University Press, 1954.

Wooster, Ralph A. *The Secession Conventions of the South*. Princeton, N.J.: Princeton University Press, 1962.

Young, Otis E. *The West of Philip St. George Cooke, 1809–1895*. Glendale, Calif.: Arthur H. Clark Co., 1955.

Index

Page numbers in *italics* refer to maps and illustrations.